V.A. Gheorghiu P. Netter H.J. Eysenck
R. Rosenthal (Eds.)

Suggestion and Suggestibility

Theory and Research

In Collaboration with

K. Fiedler W.E. Edmonston, Jr. R.M. Lundy
P.W. Sheehan

Springer-Verlag Berlin Heidelberg NewYork
London Paris Tokyo HongKong

Professor Dr. phil. VLADIMIR A. GHEORGHIU
Justus-Liebig-Universität Gießen
Fachbereich Psychologie
Otto-Behaghel-Straße 10
D-6300 Gießen

Professor em. HANS J. EYSENCK
Institute of Psychiatry
University of London
Denmark Hill
London S.E.5, Great Britain

Professor Dr. med. Dr. phil. PETRA NETTER
Justus-Liebig-Universität Gießen
Fachbereich Psychologie
Otto-Behaghel-Straße 10
D-6300 Gießen

Professor ROBERT ROSENTHAL
Professor of Social Psychology
Harvard University
33 Kirkland Street, Cambridge
MA 02138, U.S.A.

ISBN-13: 978-3-642-73877-7 e-ISBN-13: 978-3-642-73875-3
DOI: 10.1007/978-3-642-73875-3

Softcover reprint of the hardcover 1st edition 1989

2126/3145-543210 Printed on acid-free paper

Foreword

This book contains the proceedings of the First International Symposium on Suggestion and Suggestibility, held at the University of Giessen in the Federal Republic of Germany, July 7-11 1987, upon the initiative of and organized by Dr. V.A. Gheorghiu and Dr. P. Netter. I regret that for personal reasons I was unable to accept his kind invitation to attend, for Dr. Gheorghiu and I are old friends. I am pleased, however, to have this opportunity to call attention to the significance of this volume. Most of the chapters were presented in approximately their present form at the symposium, though some have been extensively revised for publication.

It was a wise choice to divide the papers into four major sections. – I. Theoretical and Historical Perspectives, II. Assessment and Individual Differences of Suggestibility, III. Psychophysiological Aspects of Suggestibility, and IV. Social and Cognitive Aspects of Suggestive Processes – each with a summarizing commentary. In view of the variety and difficulty of the individual papers, it is a help to have the integration provided by these commentaries – on Part I by Sheehan (Chap. 7), on Part II by Lundy (Chap. 13), on Part III by Edmonston (Chap. 19), and on Part IV by Fiedler (Chap. 30). For those relatively new to this area of investigation it may be helpful first to read the appropriate commentary in order to understand the major issues and only then to turn to the detailed chapters to find out how these issues were indeed handled.

Suggestion has had a hoary history in psychology, starting long before Bernheim tied it closely to hypnosis. For example, Thomas Brown (1820/1960) proposed "laws of suggestion" as an alternative to "laws of association" on the grounds that in association one mental item "suggests" another. It is not surprising that conditioning (as a twentieth century alternative to association) enters into discussions of suggestion today. Brown's important contribution was to propose "secondary" laws of suggestion to supplement the "primary" laws (which dated back to Aristotle); e.g., similarity, contrast, and contiguity. Brown's secondary laws were what writers in this volume have called "moderating variables" added to the primary laws of suggestion. Brown influenced William James (1890), whose "laws" of habit, recency, vividness, and emotional congruity draw on Brown's secondary laws of suggestion. McDougall's (1908) concept of suggestion has to be understood in relation to two other social processes that he emphasized: imitation and sympathy. All of these earlier conceptions were based on common sense rather than on quantitative experimental studies, but this does not mean that we cannot learn from them. Gheorghiu outlines their history in his introductory chapter and Jahoda contributes a chapter on historical and cultural aspects (Chap. 20).

As experimental studies of hypnosis began in the first half of this century, the concept of suggestion became closely tied to hypnosis, as illustrated by book titles such as Hull's *Hypnosis and Suggestibility: An Experimental Approach* (1933), and Weitzenhoffer's *Hypnotism: An Objective Study in Suggestibility* (1953).

Soon some distinctions between types or categories of suggestion began to appear. Hull distinguished between postural sway, as usually produced by personal suggestion, and therefore representative of hypnosis, and suggestion of the Binet weight type, in which progressive changes in the weights can lead to the report that successive weights continue to increase after the physical changes are no longer there. This type Hull called "impersonal suggestion". Twelve years later Eysenck and Furneaux (1945), using the very examples selected by Hull (postural sway and Binet weights), made the identical distinction, but named the processes "primary" and "secondary" suggestibility. Their terms caught on and are prominent in this book.

The Eysenck/Furneaux distinctions are, however, the source of some confusion. The first confusion arises because they identified postural sway as the most characteristic tie between suggestion and hypnosis. In their original article, however, they found that a high weight was given to the heat hallucination, so that they made the claim that a combination of postural sway and heat illusion correlated strongly (.96) with susceptibility to hypnosis as measured by their scale. It is of no consequence that this correlation is probably too high; the important point is that they recognized, through the combination of postural sway and heat hallucination, that primary suggestibility, which for them had to do with hypnosis, had at least the *two* components of modified motor and sensory processes. It is not my purpose here to comment in any detail on the findings reported in the chapters which follow, but I mention some of these early issues merely to point out the value of the thorough review which the symposium, and now these published papers, provide. The components of hypnotic responsiveness have been given a great deal of attention in the years since the Eysenck and Furneaux studies appeared, and this is reflected in several chapters.

Until a few years ago the components of suggestion and suggestibility independent of hypnosis did not invite as much attention as hypnosis. A fine start had been made by Stukát (1958), however, and a little later Gheorghiu (1967) initiated his most thorough series of studies, continued through to the present with a number of associates. He deserves credit for proposing this symposium and for seeing that it actually took place.

In addition to the confusion caused by identifying hypnosis too strongly with postural sway, confusion arises through the identification of secondary suggestibility with what Hull called the "impersonal suggestions" of the Binet weight type when far more attention is paid to social suggestibility in its various forms of peer influence, as in the autokinetic sensation of movement of a spot of light in a dark room as influenced by a second observer, or in the form of the persuasiveness of communications, the role of the prestige of the communicator, the significance of leading questions, and the many facets of social influence that careful investigations have shown to be unrelated to hypnosis (e.g., Moore, 1964). Aspects of this are discussed in various chapters; the lack of relationship to hypnosis in the chapter by Evans (Chap. 10), the ties to social psychology in a number of chapters, but particularly those in Part IV. The components of suggestibility are surely not just two (or even three) in number. Several components can be found in hypnosis, several in sensory suggestibility, and several in social suggestibility. Gheorghiu's desire for a better taxonomy of suggestion is supported by the variety of approaches in the chapters of this book, but no agreement on revision of taxonomy emerged.

This book provides a fine airing of the current position in the confusing and multifaceted field of suggestion and suggestibility. There is nothing like it in the literature, and much good can come from it as the questions it raises continue to be answered more clearly.

ERNEST R. HILGARD

Stanford University
Stanford, California, USA

September 1, 1988

References

Brown, T. (1960). *Lectures on the philosophy of the human mind.* Memoir by D. Welsh (20th ed.). London: Tegg. (Original work published 1820)

Eysenck, H.J., & Furneaux, W.D. (1945). Primary and secondary suggestibility: An experimental and statistical study. *Journal of Experimental Psychology; 35,* 483-503.

Gheorghiu, V.A. (1967). Cu privire la conceptul de sugestie [On the concept of suggestion]. *Revista de Psihologie, 13,* 179-185.

Hull, C.L. (1933). *Hypnosis and suggestibility: An experimental approach.* New York: Appleton-Century.

James, W. (1890). *Principles of psychology* (Vols. 1-2). New York: Holt. (See also the authorized scholarly edition [Vols. 1-3]. Cambridge, MA: Harvard University Press, 1981).

McDougall, W. (1908). *An introduction to social psychology.* London: Methuen.

Moore, R.K. (1964). Susceptibility to hypnosis and susceptibility to social influence. *Journal of Abnormal and Social Psychology, 68,* 282-294.

Stukát, K.G. (1958). *Suggestibility: A factorial and experimental analysis.* Stockholm: Almqvist and Wiksell.

Weitzenhoffer, A.M. (1953). *Hypnotism: An objective study in suggestibility.* New York: Wiley.

Preface

The existence of the phenomena of suggestion and suggestibility has never been seriously disputed in psychology. If we exclude the field of hypnosis from consideration for the moment, research on suggestion has, however, not yet become an independent domain of psychology like, for example, the psychology of learning, imagination, or emotion. This is true in spite of the fact that useful theoretical and methodological approaches and concepts – in the beginning as well as in the subsequent development of psychological research – have never been lacking.

References to questions relating to the phenomenon of suggestion are missing in standard studies in cognitive, sociopsychological, or developmental psychology – with few exceptions. It is not difficult, however, to find instances in various domains of psychological research where processes that could also be discussed in connection with suggestion and suggestibility are analyzed using different terminology and frames of reference. Some of these include imitative behavior and social contagion, conformity and compliance, changes of attitude, phenomena of bias, processes of expectancy formation and attribution, and defense mechanisms.

There is great confusion regarding the terms "suggestion" and "suggestibility". Both concepts are mingled with related notions like obedience, persuasion, imitation, social influence, or hypnosis, or they are subsumed under the heading of "influence" without further distinctions. A "morphology" of the phenomena of suggestion in everyday life as applicable to medicine, education, psychotherapy, anthropology, marketing, political science, etc. is still missing. Too few useful devices to measure suggestibility in the waking state are yet available.

These difficulties are not only the result of inherent shortcomings in this field of research but have also undoubtedly been determined by the developmental course taken by the terminology, subject matter, and theories of psychology. In addition, not only has the area of suggestion been too often neglected by research, but it has also been systematically misused by pseudoscientists. As is generally known, a great many lay concepts about phenomena of suggestion and related subjects have become widely disseminated that have led to the rejection rather than the promotion of scientific efforts.

Recently, however, there has been a growing interest in the phenomena of suggestion. This can be attributed to the following developments elucidated in the reviews of the literature contained in the various chapters of this volume:

– In the course of discussions of integrative theoretical concepts, the points of contact with problems of suggestion become clearer. This is especially true for research on conscious and unconscious systems of control and monitoring, goal-directed behavior, the influence of expectancy, and self-fulfilling prophecies, as well as subjective or constructed reality, adherence to it, and its effects on the individual's behavior.

- Lately, cognitive psychologists have increasingly dealt with the influence of suggestion on processes of memory, perception, deception, and imagination.
- In recent years, suggestion has been used as a research tool in a wide variety of psychological investigations, in particular in psychophysiological studies on pain control, as well as in investigations on the central nervous system and the psychoneuroimmunologic system, cognition and emotion (e.g., mood and memory research), the influence of post-event information on memory distortion, and the placebo phenomenon. The latter, which is generally ascribed to the domain of suggestibility, is also extensively used as a means of investigating psychological, medical, and pharmacologic problems.
- Although the psychology of social influences is still rarely discussed in connection with processes of suggestion, a recent approach of social and cognitive psychology toward problems of suggestion may be noted. This applies to processes of expectation formation and attribution and to the influence of suggestive cues in processes of verbal and nonverbal communication.
- The most important progress is taking place in the area of applied psychology. Techniques of suggestion and relaxation are not only used more frequently in psychotherapeutic interventions but also with the aim of increasing performance, for example, in learning, in forensic psychology, or in sports.
- Undoubtedly, research on hypnosis, which has made great progress during the last three decades, offers important theoretical and methodological concepts and criteria for general research on suggestion and suggestibility. Yet, even researchers in this field have, with few exceptions, dealt insufficiently with phenomena of suggestion occurring independently of the hypnotic context. The relationship between hypnotizability and suggestibility has so far hardly been investigated.

The area of suggestion and suggestibility acts as the immediate background and challenge for integrative arguments. Various psychological or psychosomatic processes can in effect be influenced by diverse suggestive cues, often discrete and subtle. Depending on the specific situation and habitual factors, every person turns out to be susceptible to suggestive modes of influence, although the individual degree of susceptibility may vary. When describing rules of behavior, no field of application dealing with interpersonal relationships can seriously do without considering the mechanisms of suggestive factors.

In conceiving this volume, we were able to attract representatives of the major approaches of research in suggestion and suggestibility, who together present a multifaceted picture of the current evolution of this field. We have deliberately refrained from "streamlining" the contributions into a common format, in the interest of conveying the individual style of each author to the reader and revealing his or her personal way of attacking the problem. This of course occasionally results in partial overlap, for instance, with respect to historical aspects referred to in several chapters.

We gratefully acknowledge the help of the *Stiftung Volkswagenwerk* in sponsoring the first symposium on suggestibility, which brought the authors into personal contact for the exchange of ideas. Furthermore, we are very indebted to Springer-Verlag and its interest in this somewhat unconventional topic and, in particular, to Dr. Susan Kentner for her substantial editorial assistance and encouragement. We acknowledge with gratitude the contributions of Dr. Peter Kruse, who helped to proof-read several chapters and who gave his comments and advice, as well as Thomas Kettner, who typed, formatted, and laser-printed the manuscripts and helped to polish the English style and reference lists in several chapters.

University of Giessen
Giessen, Federal Republic of Germany
April 1989

V.A. GHEORGHIU
P. NETTER
H.J. EYSENCK
R. ROSENTHAL

Table of Contents

Foreword V

Preface IX

List of Contributors XVII

I. Theoretical and Historical Perspectives 1

1. The Development of Research on Suggestibility: Critical Considerations 3
V.A. Gheorghiu

2. Personality, Primary and Secondary Suggestibility, and Hypnosis 57
H.J. Eysenck

3. Conceptual Clarification of Hypnosis and Its Relationship to Suggestibility 69
W.E. Edmonston

4. The Internal Confirmation of Personal Constructs: Why Suggestions Are Not Accepted 79
R.M. Lundy

5. Some Suggestions About Suggestion and Hypnosis: A Radical Constructivist View 91
P. Kruse

6. The Difficulty in Explaining Suggestion: Some Conceivable Solutions 99
V.A. Gheorghiu

7. Commentary on "Theoretical and Historical Perspectives" . 113
P.W. Sheehan

II. Suggestibility: Assessment and Individual Differences . . . 121

8. Sensory Suggestibility: Measurement, Individual Differences, and Relation to Placebo and Drug Effects . . . 123
P. Netter

9. Theoretical and Empirical Aspects of Interrogative Suggestibility 135
G.H. GUDJONSSON

10. The Independence of Suggestibility, Placebo Response, and Hypnotizability 145
F.J. EVANS

11. Cognitive and Physiological Flexibility: Multiple Pathways to Hypnotic Responsiveness 155
H.J. CRAWFORD

12. Interpretational Sets, Hypnotic Responding, and the Modification of Hypnotizability 169
N.P. SPANOS

13. Measurement and Individual Differences of Suggestibility: Some Comments 177
R.M. LUNDY

III. Psychophysiological Aspects of Suggestibility 181

14. Cortical Event-Related Evoked Potential Correlates of Hypnotic Hallucination 183
D. SPIEGEL

15. Hypnotic Susceptibility and Cerebral Hemisphere Preponderance: Verbal-Imaginal Discrimination Task . . . 191
I. MÉSZÁROS, H.J. CRAWFORD, C. SZABÓ, A. NAGY-KOVÁCS and Z. RÉVÉSZ

16. 40-H_2 EEG and Hypnotizability During Mental Activity . . 205
F.S. MARUCCI, V. DE PASCALIS, M.P. PENNA and E. PESSA

17. Hypnotic Susceptibility, Alpha Waves and 40-H_2 EEG Rhythm, and Personality 221
V. DE PASCALIS

18. Perceptual Styles in Chromatic Binocular Rivalry, Hypnotic Susceptibility, and Cerebral Dominance 241
V. RUGGIERI, R. CAPOZZI and G. CLAVENZANI

19. Psychophysiological and Psychobiological Aspects of Suggestive Processes: A Commentary 249
W.E. EDMONSTON, JR.

IV. Social and Cognitive Aspects of Suggestive Processes . . . 253

20. Some Historical and Cultural Aspects of Suggestion 255
G. Jahoda

21. Suggestion as Social Biasing of Meaning Tests: A Heiderian Extension of the Miller, Galanter and Pribram Paradigm – Catalyzing McGuire's Theory of Attitude Change 263
E. Schwanenberg

22. Memory Modification and the Role of the Media 279
E. Loftus and M.R. Banaji

23. Response to Suggestions of Memory Distortion in Hypnosis: Sampling Cognitive and Social Factors 295
P.W. Sheehan

24. A Mediational Theory of Susceptibility to Social Influence . 305
W.J. McGuire

25. Suggestion and Credibility: Lie Detection Based on Content-Related Cues 323
K. Fiedler

26. Expectations, Confirmation Bias, and Suggestibility 337
H.W. Bierhoff and R. Klein

27. Indirect Suggestion as a Research Tool 347
H. Lachnit

28. Slight Manipulations with Great Effects: On the Suggestive Impact of Vocal Parameter Change 351
T. Gehm, J. Appel and D. Apsel

29. Suggestion, Self-Attribution, and Behavior 361
J. Haisch

30. The Manifold Facets of Social Influence: A Comment on the Social Psychological Contributions 371
K. Fiedler

Subject Index 375

List of Contributors

J. Appel
Justus-Liebig-Universität
Fachbereich Psychologie
Otto-Behaghel-Straße 10
6300 Gießen
Federal Republic of Germany

D. Apsel
Justus-Liebig-Universität
Fachbereich Psychologie
Otto-Behaghel-Straße 10
6300 Gießen
Federal Republic of Germany

M.R. Banaji
Department of Psychology
Yale University
New Haven, Connecticut 06520
U.S.A.

H.W. Bierhoff
Philipps-Universität Marburg
Fachbereich Psychologie
Gutenbergstraße 18
3550 Marburg
Federal Republic of Germany

R. Capozzi
Università degli Studi di Roma
Dipartimento di Psicologia
Via degli Apuli, 8
00185 Roma
Italy

G. Clavenzani
Università degli Studi di Roma
Dipartimento di Psicologia
Via degli Apuli, 8
00185 Roma
Italy

H. Crawford
Department of Psychology
Virginia Polytechnic Institute
and State University
Blacksburg, Virginia 24061
U.S.A.

V. De Pascalis
Università degli Studi di Roma
Dipartimento di Psicologia
Via degli Apuli, 8
00185 Roma
Italy

W.E. Edmonston jr.
Colgate University
Department of Psychology
Hamilton, New York 13346
U.S.A.

F.J. Evans
Pathfinders: Consultants
in Human Behavior
Box 298
Belle Mead, New Jersey 08502
U.S.A.

H.J. Eysenck
Institute of Psychiatry
Denmark Hill
London, SE5 8AF
Great Britain

K. Fiedler
Justus-Liebig-Universität
Fachbereich Psychologie
Otto-Behaghel-Straße 10
6300 Gießen
Federal Republic of Germany

T. GEHM
Justus-Liebig-Universität
Fachbereich Psychologie
Otto-Behaghel-Straße 10
6300 Gießen
Federal Republic of Germany

V.A. GHEORGHIU
Justus-Liebig-Universität
Fachbereich Psychologie
Otto-Behaghel-Straße 10
6300 Gießen
Federal Republic of Germany

G.H. GUDJONSSON
Institute of Psychiatry
University of London
De Crespigny Park
Denmark Hill
London SE5 8AF
Great Britain

J. HAISCH
Universität Ulm
Arbeitsgemeinschaft Allgemeinmedizin
Am Hochsträß 8
7900 Ulm/Donau
Federal Republic of Germany

G. JAHODA
Department of Psychology
University of Strathclyde
Turnbull Building
155 George Street
Glasgow G1 1RD
Great Britain

R. KLEIN
Philipps-Universität Marburg
Fachbereich Psychologie
Gutenbergstraße 18
3550 Marburg
Federal Republic of Germany

P. KRUSE
Fachbereich Psychologie
Universität Bremen
Bibliothekstraße MZH
2800 Bremen
Federal Republic of Germany

H. LACHNIT
Justus-Liebig-Universität
Fachbereich Psychologie
Otto-Behaghel-Straße 10
6300 Gießen
Federal Republic of Germany

E. LOFTUS
Department of Psychology
University of Washington
Seattle, Washington 98195
U.S.A.

R.M. LUNDY
Department of Psychology
Pennsylvania State University
417 Bruce v. Moore Building
University Park
Pennsylvania 16802
U.S.A.

F.S. MARUCCI
Università degli Studi di Roma
Dipartimento di Psicologia
Via degli Apuli, 8
00185 Roma
Italy

W.J. MCGUIRE
Department of Psychology
Yale University
2 Hillhouse Avenue
New Haven, Connecticut 06520
U.S.A.

I. Mészáros
Kossuth Lajos University
Institute of Psychology
4010 Debrecen 10
Pf. 28
Hungary

A. Nagy-Kovács
Institute of Psychology
Kossuth Lajos University
4010 Debrecen 10
Pf. 28
Hungary

P. Netter
Justus-Liebig-Universität
Fachbereich Psychologie
Otto-Behaghel-Straße 10
6300 Gießen
Federal Republic of Germany

M.P. Penna
Università degli Studi di Roma
Dipartimento di Psicologia
Via degli Apuli, 8
00185 Roma
Italy

E. Pessa
Università degli Studi di Roma
Dipartimento di Matemàtica
Piazza le Aldo Moro 5
00185 Roma
Italy

Z. Révész
Institute of Psychology
Kossuth Lajos University
4010 Debrecen 10
Pf. 28
Hungary

V. Ruggieri
Università degli Studi di Roma
Dipartimento di Psicologia
Via degli Apuli, 8
00185 Roma
Italy

E. Schwanenberg
Johann-Wolfgang-Goethe-Universität
Fachbereich Psychologie
Postfach 11 19 32
6000 Frankfurt/Main 11
Federal Republic of Germany

P.W. Sheehan
Department of Psychology
University of Queensland
St. Lucia, Queensland 4067
Australia

N.P. Spanos
Department of Psychology
Carleton University
Loeb Building
Ottawa K1S 5B6
Canada

D. Spiegel
Department of Psychiatry
Stanford University Medical Center
Stanford, California 94305
U.S.A.

C. Szabó
Institute of Psychology
Kossuth Lajos University
4010 Debrecen 10
Pf. 28
Hungary

I

Theoretical and Historical Perspectives

1. The Development of Research on Suggestibility: Critical Considerations

V.A. Gheorghiu

Three main trends of research on suggestion and suggestibility have prevailed over time: suggestion in connection with hypnosis, suggestion as a feature of personality, and suggestion as a psychosocial phenomenon. The purpose of this chapter is to discuss very selectively these lines of research. Selectivity is imperative not only because of the multitude of studies but also because there have already been frequent reports on them in recent years. This is particularly true of investigations of the effects of suggestion with respect to hypnotic phenomena or social influence. Consequently, those fields will be discussed here only as they relate to controversies of significance to the whole domain of suggestion. Fundamental aspects of suggestion and suggestibility are still relatively unexplored. This applies above all to suggestibility, which has been studied - independently of hypnosis and specific questions of social influence - for almost 100 years.

I shall try to take stock of the relevant research by paying particular attention to both complexities and inconsistencies. In the process, I shall endeavor not only to point out shortcomings and difficulties pertaining to this greatly underrepresented area of research but also to demonstrate that suggestion is a phenomenon whose ubiquity, persistence, and subtle influence are seriously underrated.

Suggestion and Hypnosis

The manifestation and nature of suggestion have been discussed in the literature primarily in connection with hypnotic events. Much of the concern for this topic came directly from research into hypnosis even when there was interest in the social implications of suggestion and the assessment of the so-called waking suggestibility (for a review, see Barber, 1969; Bernheim, 1888/1964; Hilgard, 1965; Hull, 1933; Shor, 1979; Sheehan & Perry, 1976; Weitzenhoffer, 1963). Suggestion, or other similar concepts, were not touched on at all in the early days of hypnotism. This can be explained by the then prevailing notion that physical influences (e.g., magnetism) played a role or by the lack of psychological methods of observation available to researchers at that time. The fact that Mesmer's and his students' therapeutic interventions contained innumerable suggestion cues is without question, however. Suggestion began to play a significant role when researchers started to consider hypnosis from a more psychological viewpoint, as in the early work of Bertrand (1823) and Braid (1846).

Suggestion first acquired an explicit status through the work of Bernheim (1888/1964), and a "doctrine of suggestion" was developed out of hypnosis by the Nancy School. Bernheim did not just merely consider suggestion to be a vehicle for the induction of hypnotic phenomena. He considered it to be a fundamental principle for the explanation of hypnosis itself. The characteristic feature of hypnosis, according to Bernheim, is increased suggestibility. Bernheim's suggestion theory has not prevailed in modern research on hypnotism. This may be due to the fact that the theory has a certain circularity, that discrepancies between theoretical explanations and fundamental facts are inherent to the suggestion doctrine, or that it claims to explain the multiplicity of hypnotic events by suggestion and suggestibility alone (see in this context Sheehan & Perry, 1976; Shor, 1979; Stukat, 1958). However, the influence of the Nancy School is still pervasive; as Shor (1979) wrote, "... even now ... the doctrine of suggestion remains deeply infused in modern thinking about hypnosis in many subtle and unanalyzed ways" (p. 28).

The link between suggestion and hypnosis is clear in modern research on hypnosis. All the phenomena ascribed to hypnosis are considered in close connection with the effects of direct or indirect suggestion. The available hypnotic susceptibility scales are based - with a few exceptions such as the Hypnotic Induction Profile of Spiegel (1978) - on suggestion items. The standardized hypnosis induction technique that precedes the use of these suggestion items also consists of suggestion communications. Whether people can be hypnotized, whether they find themselves in a hypnotic state, or whether the induced hypnosis is of superficial or deeply rooted nature is predominantly determined by referral to various test suggestions.

Experiments have tried to determine (a) whether relationships exist between the so-called waking suggestibility and hypnotic suggestibility (Eysenck & Furneaux, 1945; Hilgard, 1965; Stukat, 1958), (b) whether and to what extent a hypnotic induction procedure increases suggestibility (Barber, 1969; Hilgard & Tart, 1966; Weitzenhoffer & Sjoberg, 1961), and (c) whether the phenomena that are traditionally ascribed to hypnosis can be explained by the influence of suggestion alone (i.e., whether they can be elicited, as Bernheim assumed, independently of a hypnotic context).

Influential researchers into hypnotism attempt to understand the nature of hypnosis itself in conjunction with suggestion and suggestibility. Orne (1977), for example, defines hypnotism as the state in which suggestion can be used to give rise to distortions in perception and memory. Barber (1979) asserts that his alternative paradigm can be seen in contrast to the classical paradigm of hypnosis as suggested (hypnotic) behavior. Together with Spanos (1974), he considers hypnosis to be, in part, a process of involvement in suggestion-related imaginings. Tellegen (1978/1979) considers the ability to be hypnotized as the ability to respond to suggested events and states both imaginatively and enactively and in such a manner that they are experienced as real. Whatever "special processes" may occur in hypnosis, Kihlstrom (1986) notes, the result of the hypnotist's suggestion and the subjects' interpretation of those suggestions are shaped by the wider social context in which they are given (p. 478).

Methodological Problems

One can draw the following conclusions: The phenomena of suggestion and suggestibility are just as much evident nowadays in hypnosis research as they have ever been. This permanent juxtaposition of suggestion and hypnosis, however, has introduced some misleading ideas about the connection between them.

In spite of the constant references to the way in which suggestion affects hypnotic events, surprisingly little has been done to isolate the features that distinguish hypnotic from waking suggestion. Hartland's position of 1967 is just as valid today:

> Considering the importance of the part played by suggestion, both in the induction of hypnotic state, and in the application of hypnosis to clinical problems, I have always found it surprising that so little attention is paid to it as a subject well worth studying in its own right. It is perfectly true that, scattered throughout the various chapters of most books on hypnosis, you will come across numerous significant facts regarding suggestion, but so far, few attempts seem to have been made to correlate these into a comprehensive picture embracing the principles upon which it depends and which governs the effectiveness with which it is employed. (p. 211)

Several research approaches could be used to explain the relationship between suggestion and hypnotism. Three of them are detailed below.

Investigations Carried Out Independently of the Hypnotic Context

Researchers into hypnotism tend to subordinate questions relating to suggestion to questions relating to hypnosis. Along this line, suggestion is seen as a vehicle for the induction of hypnosis or for the production of hypnotic phenomena. Even hypnosis researchers such as Weitzenhoffer (1963, 1980) and Barber (1969, 1979), who have gone beyond the bounds of hypnosis itself and who have occasionally concerned themselves with the basic psychological aspects of suggestion and suggestibility, have ultimately come to deal with the problems associated with hypnosis.

The renewed debate about the relationship between suggestion/suggestibility and hypnosis now serves to show how important the critical analysis of general problems of suggestion and suggestibility really is. In contrast to the position of Bernheim (1888/1964), Hull (1933), and Weitzenhoffer (1963), which regards hypnosis as a (special) manifestation of suggestibility and which has often been criticized because of its circularity, it has been increasingly stressed in recent times that the nature of hypnotism cannot be limited to suggestion phenomena. In this connection, Hilgard (1987) mentions that "it may be noted that we no longer attribute everything about hypnosis to suggestion, despite its importance, for imagination and phantasy are equally important" (p. 252). Shor (1970) expresses himself in an even more categorical manner: "But suggestibility is just one of the many possible hypnotic phenomena. It is not an explanatory concept and not a dimension of hypnosis. As long as suggestibility is mistakenly taken as the universal defining characteristic of hypnosis - its common denominator, so to speak - these larger potentialities of hypnotic techniques cannot be seen with full clarity" (p. 97). Evans bases his final conclusions in Chap. 10 of this volume on a historical and empirical overview. In summary, the data appear so far to show that suggestibility and hypnosis are in part different processes (see Chap. 10, this volume). Edmonston (Chap. 3, this volume) fundamentally questions the relationship between hypnosis and suggestion: "Although suggestion may be a route for establishing the condition of hypnosis, we should agree that hypnosis is not suggestion and suggestion is not hypnosis, and that to study one is not necessarily to study the other."

These statements are related, of course, to the context out of which they were taken, and one is essentially faced with the basic problem that what is actually meant by suggestion and suggestibility remains for the most part unclear. We are uncertain, for instance, whether suggestion is a stimulation condition or a trigger for special forms of behavior, merely a context in which hypnosis can be produced, a method of deception and/or a placebo, a self-fulfilling prophecy, a dimension of personality, and so on. It seems clear that the researcher into hypnosis cannot dispense with the critical analysis of the general problems associated with suggestion as long as suggestion is closely connected with hypnosis. However, an investigation of suggestion/suggestibility that overlaps many lines of inquiry can help in understanding hypnosis and also facilitates the integration of hypnosis into the general body of literature on the confluence of cognitive, social, and other psychological factors.

Researchers into hypnosis are usually unconcerned with questions of suggestion and suggestibility that are not directly applicable to hypnotic phenomena. However, their contribution to the development of workable paradigms for matters relating to suggestion cannot be contested. One is reminded here of the relevance of Orne's (1959, 1962) concept of demand characteristics and Hilgard's (1977) neodissociation theory of multiple cognitive central systems as well as the contributions of Barber (1979), Coe and Sarbin (1977), Sarbin and Coe (1972), Sheehan (1980), and Spanos (1982). Through their work, we have learned much about the contextual complexity that is incorporated in suggestibility and about the goal-directed nature of subjects' responses.

Research on Hypnosis Limiting the Role of Suggestion

The opinion that hypnosis cannot be reduced to the effects of suggestion alone or that hypnosis has relatively little in common with suggestion/suggestibility can be seen as a challenge to the above accounts. This view stresses research into hypnotic phenomena without focusing on the influence of suggestion. Bowers (1983) and Hammer, Walker, and Diment (1978) emphasized that the association of hypnosis and suggestion has drawn attention away from the question of whether hypnosis has features or outcomes independent of suggestion.

A number of efforts were made in early studies to identify phenomena of hypnosis that occur without explicit suggestion. Attention was especially given to spontaneous amnesia, identified by the classical researchers as a typical feature of hypnosis. Since one seldom comes across spontaneous amnesia, at least under laboratory conditions (Cooper, 1979; Hilgard, 1969), this form of amnesia, as opposed to the suggested form, has increasingly been neglected. A comparable state of affairs applies to other manifestations ascribed to hypnosis which also apparently occur without being specifically influenced by suggestion, for example, the subsidence of the planning function (Hilgard, 1965). Spontaneous states of relaxation under hypnosis have been investigated in great detail. In particular, Edmonston (1981) tried to demonstrate that relaxation can occur together with the onset of hypnosis, independently of explicit suggestions.

There is special significance in the analysis of spontaneous manifestations under hypnosis. In recent times, for example, there have been reports of spontaneous hypnotic events evoked by using the techniques of the traditional healer (Azuma & Stevenson, 1988; Olivier, 1987).[1] There

---

[1] I have personally noted that, under conditions of active involvement in the hypnotic situation, subjects are not very interested in what happened during hypnosis after the hypnosis itself has been cancelled. Even though it may be the first hypnotic experience, one has the impression that we are dealing with a quality of experience that is taken for granted. This is not the case for other people who are less intensively involved in the situation. They tend to ask more readily about their behavior.

are also less striking outcomes of hypnosis, which indeed also occur without the direct influence of suggestion, but which can only be recorded indirectly. For example, in a study in which introspective reports were systematically analyzed, Hammer et al. (1978) found that a hypnotic induction procedure carried out with susceptible subjects caused a greatly increased incidence of primary process thinking in response to some sorts of verbal stimuli, even though no suggestions regarding this effect were given. Studies analyzing the experience of time during periods of hypnotic involvement also show evidence of nonsuggested effects. Bowers and Brenneman (1979), Bowers (1979), and St. Jean, MacLeod, Coe, and Howard (1982), for example, report that subjects retrospectively underestimate the hypnosis portion of the hypnotic susceptibility scale administered to them.

Any attempt to observe hypnosis independently of suggestion effects is not without its problems. With reference to spontaneous events, it must be repeatedly stressed that we are probably dealing with the influence of indirect suggestions. This influence was postulated especially in conjunction with the appearance of spontaneous posthypnotic amnesia (Barber, 1979; Cooper, 1979; Hull, 1933; Hilgard, 1965). Basically, a process that more or less pre-programs the disappearance of memory after removal of the hypnosis is suspected. In this regard, some mechanism can be posited that possibly plays a central role in the implementation of suggestive contents, but whose special features still have to be individually determined. The question to be asked is which intervening variables contribute to the self-fulfilling tendency that results in the expected behavior. Furthermore, we should test whether it is expectancy itself that triggers the so-called spontaneous hypnotic event.

Let us, for example, consider amnesia once more, but this time in greater detail. It has repeatedly been reported that nonexplicit suggested anmesia appears more often if subjects experience the hypnosis as a state of sleep and therefore believe that they cannot remember anything afterwards (Hilgard, 1969; Kline, 1966; Gheorghiu, 1973; Watkins, 1966). The subjects' opinion is that they have been dreaming, and they think that they have forgotten what has happened in the intervening period or that it is impossible for them to remember what has taken place during the hypnosis. The subjects, rationalizing their amnesic behavior, consolidate their point of view with these ad hoc arguments. Here, one can talk of a "general negation." Insofar as the test candidates negate having had intrahypnotic experiences, they furthermore tend to avoid the questions put to them by the investigator concerning the features of the hypnosis itself. Persistence on the part of the investigator meets with resistance that at the same time tends to become more entrenched.

The use of indirect procedures can easily produce changes in this behavior. Orne (1966), among others, has shown that posthypnotic amnesia can easily be removed if questions about what was experienced are asked by someone other than the person who induced the hypnosis. It can also be shown that subjects can remember the events well if they are asked to report about their dreams (Gheorghiu, 1973). When the subjects have been brought back to a nonhypnotic state, they must, as hypnotized persons, be adapted to "normal" conditions so that they can find their way back into their normal frame of reference. The transition from the hypnotic to the nonhypnotic situation can be seen as a type of fluctuation or separation between two differing contexts (Orne, 1966; van Parreren, 1966; Wellek, 1968). This is confirmed by the fact that subjects can remember their experiences after reinstatement of the hypnotic context. Difficulties in remembering that may otherwise arise are possibly reinforced by the speed of transition to the normal state. The sudden change can cause a retroactive inhibition of what has been experienced shortly before. The subject is dominated by the present and not by the past. It is precisely at this moment that the investigator asks questions about the hypnotic events, and the unusual character of the challenge converts it into an excessive demand. Foppa (1966) argues that even in daily life one is hardly able to describe the things one experiences in full detail when unexpectedly requested to reproduce them. Investigators who insist on answers to their questions perhaps inhibit reproduction.

In the assertion that posthypnotic amnesia is induced indirectly by the expectations of the subject, it is easy to conclude that these expectations were more or less present right from the beginning. It appears to me to be more meaningful to assume that the relevant expected behaviors crystallize in the process of hypnotic involvement. Puysegur's celebrated case of Victor (1809), in whom posthypnotic amnesia was observed, had no precedents. However, this subject experienced the hypnotic state as a deep sleep. Posthypnotic amnesia can occasionally occur with inexperienced naive subjects who are in hypnosis for the first time.

This phenomenon is especially manifest in people who believe that they cannot remember experiences which have taken place in the time between two hypnosis sessions (Gheorghiu, 1973). No amnesia would ordinarily be expected in the intervening period, consisting of an interval of 15-20 min in which the subject behaves in a normal way. A loss of memory probably occurs because of the separation induced by cancellation of the second hypnosis. This "interhypnotic amnesia" also shows that the loss of memory can be remedied during a new hypnosis session without any great difficulty.

These observations on posthypnotic amnesia bear upon the following considerations:

1. Hypnosis without suggestion ought to be conceived as hypnosis without *explicit* suggestion. We need to acknowledge the many subtle, indirect, or implicit cues that induce a certain sense of direction in the person addressed and that put the person's experiences and behaviors into a certain context.
2. A consideration of the effects of suggestion - explicit or implicit - is of little interest without taking into account the appropriate moderating variables. Although the deficiencies of Bernheim's suggestion theory have not led to the total abandonment of the role of suggestion in the hypnotic process, it has led to a refocussing of attention by many investigators on other inner processes of the subject that have been influential in the past (Sheehan & Perry, 1976, p. 41). In this context, the interest in the role of imaginational processes, expectation, belief, delusion, and dissociation should be mentioned. One can certainly think of many other processes that have preoccupied researchers since then, such as attention focussing, goal-directed responsiveness, motivation (including subtle contextual demand characteristics), absorption, role enactment, and interactions. The question arising here, however, is the extent to which the influence of varying suggestion cues is taken into account in all these process-oriented investigations. Already, Binet (1900) mentioned that suggestibility should be understood in a broader sense and that disposition of attitudes, expectations, and imagination must also be taken into account when suggestion/suggestibility is assessed. Field (1979) was also able to demonstrate the special influence of indirect suggestion on motivation and attitudes when hypnosis is induced. All these processes are related to a certain extent to hypnotic involvement. Both hypnotist and subject strive step by step to activate the ability that

makes involvement possible. This takes place (even in the case of self-hypnosis) with the help of explicit and implicit suggestions. They occur in a specific context and correspond to a defined purpose. Therefore, it is appropriate to talk of the goal-directed nature of hypnotic responsiveness (Spanos, 1982).

3. The assertion that hypnotic involvement is goal-directed is in no way in conflict with the fact that unforeseen experiences and behaviors are possible during the process of the involvement itself or through the resulting switching over of the organism (Schultz, 1932). Writers' efforts in the realization of their work can certainly be identified as being goal-directed, but the act of writing frequently creates spontaneous and unexpected ideas that seem to develop their own logic. A similar process applies to hypnotized people. The more they become involved in the assumed role and show the ability to identify with it, the greater the latitude for unpremeditated behaviors. This applies to both indirect and direct suggestions. When an age regression is suggested, for instance, only the "basic frames" are established, which are then filled out by the hypnotized person. The "person who has been taken back in time" remembers apparently forgotten languages, for example (As, 1962; Fromm, 1970). During suggestion of an age regression, three of my patients spontaneously started to speak a language that they had spoken as a child and that they could speak reasonably well even up to then, but which they seldom used. These were all languages which the hypnotist neither understood nor spoke. The behavior was not specifically suggested but occurred suddenly in the context of the suggested age regression (Gheorghiu, 1973).
   The tendency to show tolerance for logical incongruity ("trance logic," see Orne, 1959), which is regarded as an essential, though not uncontroversial feature of hypnosis (see Spanos, 1986), can also be classified as an unexpected effect of suggestion. For example, a certain hallucination may be suggested to subjects, but they mix freely their perceptions derived from reality with those stemming from their imagination.

No doubt other examples could be given of the occurrence of spontaneous, nonexplicitly suggested effects. The very nature of hypnosis as role-taking possibly results in the assessment of nonexplicit suggested behaviors, which in themselves are difficult or impossible to predict and which furthermore can only be simulated in certain limited cases. The essence of hypnosis lies in the subjective experience of the hypnotized person (see Orne, Dinges, & Orne, 1986).

Development of Research on Suggestion Independent of Hypnosis and Research on Hypnosis Independent of Suggestion (of the Explicit Type) Facilitates the Critical Analysis of Questions Raised About the Relationship Between Suggestion and Hypnosis. Methodological difficulties are evident in studies investigating these questions (Bowers, 1983; Hilgard, 1973; Hilgard & Tart, 1966; Weitzenhoffer & Sjoberg, 1961). For example, the comparison between waking and hypnotic situations poses methodological problems when the subjects are used as their own control group, particularly because of tendencies for subjects to modify their behavior under waking conditions when they know that a hypnotic session is to follow (Zamansky, Scharf, & Brightbill, 1964). This tendency can only occur if the subject knows that other subjects are being hypnotized (Hilgard & Tart, 1966). The latter authors additionally point out that failure to use subjects as their own controls greatly limits the possibility of finding differences that are theoretically important. They go on to say that in group comparisons the weight must be carried by those few subjects who make substantial gains between waking and hypnosis. An overall comparison between two groups that does not take account of the correlation between waking responsiveness and hypnotic responsiveness will understate the gains that take place for some subjects (p. 197).

Whenever the responsiveness to suggestion is compared between groups with and without hypnotic treatment, subjects are given different explanations. In the nonhypnotic situation, the subjects are told that they will be given tests of responsiveness to waking suggestion or that they will not be hypnotized (Hilgard & Tart, 1966; Weitzenhoffer & Sjoberg, 1961). In contrast, in the hypnotic situation it is clearly pointed out that they will be hypnotized and given a number of tests. It remains an open question whether the increased suggestibility values found in the hypnotic situation, as opposed to the waking situation, should be ascribed to the differing explanations or to the suggestive induction. Because of the lack of suitable procedures to record waking suggestibility, tests such as the body-sway test (see, for example, Hull, 1933) are used, or suggestion items are taken from hypnotic susceptibility scales that subjects can easily relate to the hypnosis tests. Hilgard and Tart (1966), who used ten items from the Stanford Hypnotic Susceptibility Scale (Form C), felt in all their comparison groups that they had to explain clearly to the subjects in the waking situation about the possibility of having a hypnotic experience.

Comparing waking with hypnotic situations has proved to be problematic because the response to suggestion may be at a high level already. A possible increase in responsiveness may no longer be recorded after induction of hypnosis because of the ceiling effect. Furthermore, it is very difficult to talk of a comparison between the waking state and hypnosis in subjects who respond very little to hypnotic procedures. Subjects in this category experience the hypnosis situation more or less as a normal situation. One can accordingly expect practically no changes at all in responsiveness to suggestion for these subjects.

One of the greatest difficulties lies in the two different functions of assessing responsiveness to suggestion: One aim is to determine the degree of hypnotizability in individuals, whereas the other is to show possible differences in responsiveness to suggestion dependently and independently of the hypnotic context. Hilgard and Tart (1966), who have analyzed the comparison made among waking, imagination, and hypnotic instructions are fully aware of this situation. They argue that "it would be desirable to develop some measure of the extent to which a person is actually hypnotized other than measures of his responsiveness to standard suggestion." They continue, "... that it is quite possible that in the deeper states of hypnosis that responsiveness to some suggestions will disappear without this meaning the weakening of the hypnosis" (p. 207). Every experienced hypnotist would probably agree.

The methodological problems associated with this area of research are important, and the following points require clarification: (a) To what extent can certain quantitative and qualitative effects of suggestion be ascribed to the influence of the hypnosis? (b) Is there a relationship between the so-called waking suggestibility and the ability to be hypnotized?

Among other factors, there is still a general lack of procedures enabling us adequately to assess waking suggestibility, hypnotic susceptibility (without explicit suggestion tests), and the phenomenological experience of hypnosis itself.

In order to emphasize that hypnosis has only limited connections with responsiveness to suggestion, it has been suggested by Bowers (1983) and Hilgard (1973) that indirect suggestion procedures have nothing in common with the ability to be hypnotized (Eysenck & Furneaux, 1945; Stukat, 1958); that forms of social suggestibility, described as conformity and gullibility, are not correlated with hypnotic-like behaviors (Moore, 1964); and that responses to placebo are distinguishable from hypnotic-like responsiveness (McGlashan, Evans, & Orne, 1969). In view of the importance of these arguments for the status of suggestion/suggestibility within the domain of hypnosis itself, and in view of the final conclusions about the characteristics of hypnosis, it appears appropriate to investigate this category of problems more systematically. New research strategies are needed in addition to replication studies, and tests of deception, for example, or other indirect (impersonal) suggestion procedures are still not utilized sufficiently for the assessment of suggestibility under hypnotic conditions. Even though it should be ultimately confirmed that the influence of such test procedures has much less effect than that arising from direct suggestion procedures (Gheorghiu & Holdevici, 1980), it will still be necessary to elucidate the mechanisms on which these differences are based.

Suggestibility Independent of Hypnotic Context

Experimental work on the influence of suggestibility independent of the hypnotic context was already performed in the last decade of the nineteenth century (Binet, 1900; Gilbert, 1894; Scripture, 1893; Seashore, 1895; Sidis, 1898). However, the contributions of these pioneers have not been given enough credit. As far as I know, Binet's outstanding book *La Suggestibilité* (1900), for example, has never been published in another language.

The majority of researchers at that time refrained, either implicitly or explicitly, from focussing on the topic of hypnosis. To assess the suggestibility of a person "without involving hypnosis or without other manipulations" as Binet says in his first sentence, is the main concern of his book. He takes the opportunity to list a series of reservations (e.g., that hypnosis cannot be successfully practiced with everyone without triggering spontaneous automatic responses). However, he does not avoid making references to behaviors related to hypnotic characteristics when analyzing processes of suggestion in the waking state.

It was not Binet's purpose - he was originally (Binet & Féré, 1888) closely involved with hypnotism - to negate the hypnotic phenomenon itself, as one can clearly conclude from the criticisms of Scripture and of his students, Gilbert and Seashore. Rather, Binet was irritated by the way in which they expressed themselves in relation to hypnotism and hypnotists "... qu'ils ont traités de jongleurs et de charlatanes ..." (1900, p. 63).

The development of investigations into "waking suggestibility" were undoubtedly strongly influenced by the disputes that took place at that time between the Salpêtrière school (Charcot) and the Nancy school (Bernheim). In contrast to Charcot's theory, which viewed hypnotic phenomena from a psychopathological point of view, Bernheim claimed that hypnosis and suggestion have a psychological character. Bernheim was personally less interested in waking suggestibility as such. He was more concerned with demonstrating that the effects of suggestion ascribed to hypnosis could also be triggered independently of the hypnotic induction procedure.

Binet, Seashore, and Sidis, on the other hand, were primarily concerned with proving that something like normal suggestibility actually exists and that it could be observed empirically. Bernheim's contribution in this matter was acknowledged by them: "Although the instances Prof.

Bernheim adduces do not certainly establish the fact of the universality of normal suggestibility, they are still interesting for us as they show the presence of normal suggestibility in some particular cases" (Sidis, 1898, p. 25).

Researchers investigating the relation of suggestibility to hypnotism also make criticisms directed toward the "mode" of influence. Even when one occasionally tries to influence somebody in a normal state, one does so, as Binet (1900) notes, " by using the same procedures as those of hypnotism, in other words, by using authoritative affirmations leading to automatic obedience on the part of the subject and by suspending his will and his critical sense" (p. 2). This direct, authoritative form of suggestion is in contrast to an indirect form of influence that relies, for example, on technical devices and procedures used in the production of illusions, with the aim of concealing the actual intention of suggestion and reducing the personal influence of the investigator.

Many aspects still of interest can be traced back to the central questions posed by Binet and his contemporaries:

1. Should suggestion be understood as a single component or as a multi-dimensional phenomenon?
2. Are there relationships between suggestibility and other personality characteristics or between suggestion and other psychological phenomena?
3. Is it possible to identify factors involved in the production of responses to suggestion?

The following discussion draws attention to representative lines of research relating to these questions. Reference is also made to the contributions that have appeared in the intervening period and that have critically analyzed the scientific work done by early investigations (Coffin, 1941; Evans, 1967; Hull, 1933; Stukat, 1958; Weitzenhoffer, 1953).

Is Suggestibility a Single-Component or a Multi-Dimensional Phenomenon?

Binet (1900) observed that unconscious motor reactions induced by means of suggestion actually take place independently of other forms of responsiveness to suggestion. In his book *La Suggestibilité*, Binet raised the fundamental question of whether the individual proves responsive to suggestion when subjected to differing types of suggestion tests. He notes the following:

> But since there is certainly not one unique and absolute aptitude for suggestion and since one is prone to suggestion from all possible directions and through every way in which one perceives and reasons, whether one is conscious of it or whether one wishes it, there are grounds for wondering whether a person's suggestibility, when verified by process a, becomes probable as a result of process b, c ... d, and so on (Binet, 1900, p. 389; my translation).

The problem of different forms of suggestibility has been experimentally investigated by many psychologists. Suggestion procedures have been used to influence (a) sensory processes or sensory and perceptive judgments (by using indirect techniques such as the apparent presentation of stimuli and model or prestige situations), (b) motor processes (especially by the repetition of persuasive direct instructions), and (c) memory processes (especially by using the technique of leading questions). The majority of authors found very weak or no relationships among the differing suggestion procedures (Aveling & Hargreaves, 1921; Estabrooks, 1929; Otis, 1924; Scott, 1910; Town, 1916). Eysenck and Furneaux (1945) found that two factors are generally inherent in the measurement of suggestibility: one factor loading on the direct motor procedure, or so-called ideomotor procedures (primary factor of suggestibility), and another factor (secondary factor of suggestibility) correlating with indirect sensory test procedures. The latter shows clearly reduced functional coherence in comparison with direct motor procedures.

No relationship has been found between the direct motor tests and the indirect sensory tests. Other authors have either not confirmed the results of Eysenck and Furneaux (Benton & Bandura, 1953) or could only partially confirm them (Stukat, 1958). Evans (1967) and Hammer, Evans, and Bartlett (1963) used a battery of test items to identify other factors of suggestibility (see Chaps. 2, 3, and 10 in this volume for a detailed account of this line of research). Even the so-called interrogative suggestibility, which is based on the leading question technique, does not correlate with other dimensions of suggestibility (Gheorghiu, Grimm, & Hodapp, 1978; Gudjonsson, 1987b; Young, Bentall, Slade, & Dewey, 1987).

Another interesting problem is the relationship between the placebo effect and responsiveness to other categories of suggestion. However, this relationship has been measured primarily in connection with hypnotic susceptibility. Test procedures to determine waking suggestibility have very seldom been used. Evans concludes that the placebo response is directly related to neither the domain of suggestibility nor hypnotizability (see Chap. 10, this volume). Netter (1977, 1980, 1984, 1986), who has also investigated the relationship between the placebo effect and suggestibility, does not agree with the generality of this conclusion. She points out (Chap. 8, this volume) that little has been published concerning this relationship in the years following the much-quoted work of Evans (1967). A study conducted by Classen, Feingold, and Netter (1983) showed that a relationship between the placebo response and suggestibility can be identified if placebo response and suggestibility are measured on the same sensory channel.

The only clear conclusion that can be made from the many and varied investigations is that a single factor of suggestibility does not exist (Eysenck, 1947). In spite of certain trends, the number of different test procedures hardly enables one to draw up a generally acceptable, empirically founded classification.

Correlates of Suggestibility

In addition to the question of the uniformity of suggestiblity, another issue that has often been raised is whether responsiveness to suggestion is related to other features of personality such as neuroticism, psychosis, age, or sex.

Mental Health, Intelligence, Age, and Sex Variables

One topic of investigation relates to whether ill people are more suggestible than healthy people. Eysenck (1947), Furneaux (1952), and Ingham (1954) found that neurotic people respond more to the body-sway test (primary suggestibility) than do normal people. In contrast, Stukat (1958) found that neurotics are significantly more suggestible in most secondary suggestibility tests, whereas no reliable differences were found with respect to direct suggestibility tests (motor tests like the body-sway test). Responsiveness to suggestion was most pronounced in tests where the suggestions are characterized by personal influence. Stukat did not exclude the influence of lack of confidence and situational factors nor of traits like anxiety, uncertainty, and feelings of inferiority.

Barber (1964) concludes in his critical review of research findings regarding suggestibility and personality that, with the exception of Eysenck's study, both neurotics and non-neurotics have not differed significantly with respect to suggestibility or hypnotizability. Gudjonsson (1983) recently contradicted this conclusion. He was able to establish that "interrogative suggestibility" correlates significantly with neuroticism (see also Chap. 9, this volume). Contrary to the traditional opinion that hysterics are highly suggestible, Eysenck (1943) found no difference in any of the eight tests of suggestibility used to compare hysterical subjects (conversion hysterics) with other nonhysterical neurotics. Stukat's (1958) findings are similar. Young et al. (1987) have recently measured responsiveness to the Barber Suggestibility Scale and to the Gudjonsson Scale of Interrogative Suggestibility in a group of healthy subjects and a group of psychotics; they found no significant differences between the groups. Stukat (1958) already demonstrated that the differences between schizoids and nonschizoids are in any case slight and do not indicate any definite association between suggestibility and the schizoid state. He drew attention, however, to the difficulties involved in making this type of comparison (e.g., that increased suggestibility can be due to the fact that the patient is tested in a hospital). Stukat found consistent differences in suggestibility only between oligophrenics and subjects of normal intelligence. Wegener (1961) was able to achieve high suggestibility scores only with tests based mainly on prestige factors.

The relationship between suggestibility and degree of intelligence has been repeatedly investigated. No relation could be shown using direct motor tests of suggestibility (Berreman & Hilgard, 1936; Duke, 1967; Eysenck, 1947). Even oligophrenics were no more suggestible in these tests than were people with normal intelligence (Wegener, 1961). Feingold (1982) found a negative correlation between intelligence and suggestibility in a sample of male subjects. Summarizing older research in this area, Coffin (1941) inferred that there is little relationship between suggestibility and intelligence. Even Eysenck (1947) was reserved on this point. He found lower suggestibility in test subjects at both extremes of intelligence than in test subjects who scored in the middle IQ ranges. He concluded that any relationship between intelligence and suggestibility can be ignored.

Dimensions of suggestibility have been repeatedly examined for a wide assortment of personality questionnaires and tests (anxiety, extraversion, neuroticism, etc.). Up to the present, no noteworthy relationship has been found between responsiveness to indirect sensory suggestibility tests and the scales and subscales of various personality inventories (Feingold, 1982; Gasiorowska, Kowalik, Migaszewska, Martin, & Paryzek, 1976; Gheorghiu et al., 1978; see also Chap. 8, this volume). Only occasionally has a relationship been established between sensory tests and the susceptibility to social influence. Abraham (1962), for example, used the results obtained from two sensory tests and a persuasibility test (opinion change tests) to make the rather daring generalization that suggestibility (in the older sense of response to sensory cues like heat or odor) is clearly related to persuasibility (susceptibility to propaganda or verbal persuasive communications, p. 183). Low but significant correlations were obtained by Duke

(1967) between direct motor (primary) suggestibility tests and a questionnaire measuring selected life experience (Eysenck, 1960; Eysenck, Granger, & Brengelmann, 1957). Ingham (1954, 1955) does not differentiate between extroverts and introverts concerning "primary suggestibility" (for a review see Eysenck, 1960).

The picture is somewhat different in the area of interrogative suggestibility. Gudjonsson and Lister (1984) found a strong negative correlation between self-esteem and suggestibility. Gudjonsson (1987b) also found that interrogative suggestibility is related to external locus of control and to anxiety - with state anxiety being more highly correlated with suggestibility than is trait anxiety. (Gudjonsson gives a detailed analysis of interrogative suggestibility in relation to other dimensions of personality in Chap. 9, this volume.) Bottenberg and Wehner (1972) were able to find a relationship between interrogative suggestibility and anxiety in a sample of 12- to 13-year-old girls.

There are also conflicting results as far as sex differences are concerned. Females have been found to be more suggestible (Hull, 1933; Seashore, 1895; Stukat, 1958), to be less suggestible (Aveling & Hargreaves, 1921; Eysenck, 1947; Otis, 1924), and to be just as suggestible compared to males (Feingold, 1982; Gheorghiu & Reyher, 1982; Gheorghiu, Netter, & Tichi, 1988). As Brown (1916) and Eysenck (1947) point out, a discussion of sex differences with respect to suggestibility inevitably raises the question of the sex of the experimenter. Only a few investigations have given consideration to this issue (see also Chap. 8, this volume).

The majority of authors are in full agreement that responsiveness to suggestion decreases with age (see Coffin, 1941 for older sources). Recent investigations (Chemnitz, Feingold, & Gheorghiu, 1981; Feingold, 1982; Stokvis & Pflanz, 1961; Stukat, 1958) confirm earlier findings.

Investigations that have more closely examined the influence of suggestion on thought processes have shown, however, that even the relation between age and suggestibility is not without complications. There is a review on this topic in an excellent book on children's eyewitness memory (Ceci, Toglia, & Ross, 1987). Some of the papers in this volume (Ceci, Ross, & Toglia; Goodman, Aman, & Hirschman; King & Yuille; Lindsay & Johnson; Sayvitz; Zaragoza) deal mainly with the question of whether children are more susceptible to suggestion than adults. With the exception of Zaragoza's investigations, these authors report evidence for a decrease in suggestibility with age; however, generally the effect is small. In one paper in that volume, Lindsay and Johnson refer to other studies of developmental changes in susceptibility and draw attention to the fact that there is relatively little rigorous empirical evidence on this point. Some studies (e.g., Cohen & Harnick, 1980; Dale, Loftus, & Rathbun, 1978; Murray, 1983) have found that suggestibility decreases with age, whereas others (e.g., Duncan, Whitney, & Kunen, 1982; Marin, Holmes, Guth, & Kovac, 1979) have found no systematic change.

Whether or not children are more susceptible to suggestion than are adults depends upon the interaction of age with other factors, such as attention, comprehension, and interest (Lindsay & Johnson, 1987; Loftus & Davies, 1984). The same holds true for other variables mentioned above.

Suggestibility, Conditioning, and Satiation

The possibility of a relationship between suggestibility and conditioning was mentioned by Pavlov (1927/1953). Hull (1933) identified the possible relationship with special reference to motor suggestibility (for a review of this topic see Evans, 1967; Eysenck, Chap. 2, this volume; Stukat, 1958; Weitzenhoffer, 1953). Lohr and Souheaver (1981) have critically analyzed investigations of conditioning and motor suggestibility. They conclude that methodological and empirical differences render ambiguous previous research on classical conditioning interpretations. In their own study, they extended the procedures for language (higher-order classical) conditioning of evaluative word meaning to investigate the nature and function of suggestibility. They predicted that, given differential representation of evaluative word meaning, highly suggestible individuals would show greater classical conditioning of word meaning than would people low in suggestibility. However, even with the methodological improvements of their study, the results provided no support for the hypothesis that suggestibility is based on higher-order classically conditioned language processes, as assumed by Pavlov (1927/1953) and Das (1964). In another study, Lohr and Souheaver (1982) investigated in greater detail the question of whether connections exist between suggestibility and locus of control. They found no relationship between suggestibility and internal or external control and concluded that suggestibility is not based on a common instrumental conditioning mechanism. Apparently mechanisms other than conditioning principles are responsible for the development or functioning of suggestibility. Ellson (1941) demonstrated that responsiveness to sensory conditioning is a conditioned suggestibility process by showing that an auditory response could be obtained to light, the basic paradigm being to associate a tone with a visual stimulus (60 to 80 trials). Subjects conditioned to the light stimulus reported that they had auditory sensations (hallucinations) even in the absence of the auditory stimulus. These results have recently been replicated by Davies and Charlton (1985) and Warburton, Wesnes, Edwards, and Larrad (1985) (for a review, see Davies, 1987).

The studies concerning suggestibility and satiation (lapse of meaning following word repetition) are closely connected with investigations into suggestibility and conditioning. Das (1966, 1968) proposed that suggestibility is analogous to a state of selective cortical inhibition. In the body-sway test, just as in hypnosis, a few verbal suggestions are repeated over and over again; these words may be integrated as a conditioned response. If the state of selective inhibition is attained through the comprehension of the meaning of the words used in the suggestion, it seems reasonable - in Das's opinion - that those who satiate quickly would show poor suggestibility. Das (1966, 1968) found that semantic satiation is negatively related to waking suggestibility as measured by the body-sway test and by verbal conditioning. He sees this as a confirmation of his theoretical assumption. It is possible to ask whether poor suggestibility and quick satiation can be associated with the lack of attentive concentration. The negative correlation between suggestibility and verbal satiation found by Das might also be examined as to whether it has something to do with "sensation seeking." The sensation seeker is seen, according to Zuckerman, Bone, Neary, Mangelsdorff, and Brustman (1972), as a person who needs varied, novel, and complex sensations and experiences to maintain an optimal level of arousal. "When stimuli and experience become repetitive it is assumed that the sensation seeker will become bored and non-responsive more quickly than most other persons" (p. 308).

Suggestibility and Imagination

Early researchers realized that responsiveness to suggestion has elements in common with imaginative ability and that certain manifest forms of suggestibility are based on processes of imagination (Binet, 1900; Seashore, 1895). In particular, researchers' interest in the field of ideomotor reactions stimulated a critical analysis of the role of imaginative processes (Arnold, 1946; Eysenck, 1947; see also Chap. 2, this volume; Hilgard, 1977; Hull, 1933; Sheehan, 1979; Stukat, 1958; Weitzenhoffer, 1963).

Two main procedures were used in the investigations. In one, the existence of relationships between the magnitude of motor reaction and the reported vividness of imagery was analyzed. In a well-known study using Hull's technique of the body-sway test, Arnold (1946) asked the subjects to imagine falling forward. She found a correlation between the degree of body sway and the report of vividness. In accord with the principle of ideomotor action, she concluded that the degree of suggested postural sway is a function of the vividness of imagery. Richardson (1969) reported similar results.

The second type of procedure sought to establish whether motor reactions, which are traditionally triggered by direct suggestion, could also be evoked by inviting the subject to imagine. Berreman and Hilgard (1936) found that when investigations were carried out by using the body-sway test, imagined falling resulted in responses highly correlated with those occurring when the subject spoke suggestions aloud to himself or received permissive suggestions from the experimenter. A single order ("Imagine that you are falling forward") had the same effect (Eysenck & Furneaux, 1945, p. 500). Stukat (1958) obtained a similar result in a sample of children.

Comparable investigations have been made in the sensory field. Hammer et al. (1963) examined three variations of the heat-illusion test. In the first two variations, different methods were used to simulate an objective heat stimulus. In the third variation, the apparatus was clearly disconnected from the power supply, and the subjects were asked to imagine that the bar they grasped became warm. Positive relationships were found among all three variations. Gheorghiu, Netter, and Tichi (1987) have applied the 12 items of a sensory suggestibility scale (SSS) under stimulation conditions and implemented an "imagination variable" (details of the SSS can be found in Chap. 8, this volume). Their study resulted in a number of findings: (a) Subjects who are highly sensitive to suggestion (subjects who often respond to a faked stimulus) react more frequently to the imagination conditions than do subjects who are not so susceptible to suggestion; (b) the score of the imagination condition is significantly higher than the score of the fake variants; and (c) a positive and significant relationship exists between both variants irrespective of order of presentation. According to Gheorghiu et al. (1978), however, no significant relationship could be found between the SSS and imagination tendencies measured by questionnaires (Sheehan's questionnaire of mental imagery, 1967; Gordon's test of imagery control, 1949). The relationship between the SSS and CIS (the Creative Imagination Scale; Wilson & Barber, 1978) was also found to be nonsignificant (Gheorghiu & Gerendy, 1980).

The relationship between suggestibility and imagination has received special attention in the context of hypnosis research, where suggestibility is defined as hypnotic suggestibility (Arnold, 1946; Barber, 1979; Coe, 1984; Coe, St. Jean, & Burger, 1980; Crawford, 1981; Gur & Reyher,

1976; Hilgard, 1970; Sheehan, 1979). These investigations contained important information for the analysis of the relationship between imagination and waking suggestibility. However, the investigations are also not free of problems. A reasonable method for measuring suggestibility and imaginative ability has to be found. The role of the demand characteristics of the experimental situation is quite considerable. The difficulty of finding appropriate items for imagination questionnaires are well known. Furthermore, the questionnaires are used at the end of an investigation, which is tedious enough in itself, so that the subject's powers of concentration are often greatly reduced (Gheorghiu et al., 1978). Imagination conditions, which are used in both motor and sensory procedures, are very similar to the suggestion conditions. Normally, heterosuggestive influences are involved in every request to indulge in imaginary thoughts: The test subject is usually encouraged to imagine himself clearly as being in the suggested situation (i.e., thinking with the suggestions and imagining the suggested effects; Barber, 1979, and Coe, St. Jean, and Burger, 1980, used the term "imagination suggestion" for this kind of instruction). Even in autosuggestion, there is no clear division between suggestive influences and the process of imagination. In the direct suggestion procedure, suggestions given to the test subject in anticipation of certain behaviors intermingle with the suggestive request to activate the powers of imagination. This interrelationship is especially apparent in the Wilson and Barber Creative Imaginative Scale (1978).

In studies where the various test procedures have been carried out directly in succession, as in the above-mentioned imagination and suggestibility conditions, additional biasing tendencies have to be confronted. Sheehan (1979) has also drawn attention to the importance of the wording of the item. Arnold's instructions to subjects, Sheehan noted, may have had implicit effects, since she used the word "imagine" rather than the word "image," and subjects may have simply "thought hard" about swaying (p. 395). Such considerations do not cast fundamental doubt on the experimentally demonstrated relationship between suggestion and imagination, but they raise important questions about the meaning or validity of the reported results.

Factors Influencing Suggestibility

In the preceding remarks, frequent reference was made to various factors that influence suggestible modes of behavior. After all, every empirical investigation of suggestibility is always at the same time an investigation of the conditions under which responsiveness to suggestion can be evoked.

The number of influencing factors is large. The roles of the following factors have mainly been examined: (a) constructs of personality, such as disposition to delusion, imagination, involvement, or conformity; (b) habitual and/or current states, such as motivation, attention, disposition, or expectation; and (c) the influence of situational components, such as prestige factors, unstructured stimulus situations, group pressure, the influence of different verbal and nonverbal techniques of suggestion, or the effect of models, drugs, or placebos.

I have already reported on some of the above-mentioned factors of influence and will turn to others in the following sections of this paper.

Next, I would like to draw attention briefly to influential tendencies, which will also be subsequently referred to in the discussion of theoretical approaches. At issue is the influence of suggestion under conditions of uncertainty. Best known are the classic experiments of Sherif (1935), who by means of the autokinetic phenomenon was able to establish that the lack of structure of a stimulus situation creates extremely favorable conditions for directed influence: Magnitude and direction of the apparent movement can be clearly influenced by verbal suggestion. Influence on the autokinetic phenomenon can be demonstrated repeatedly even if the contents of suggestion are transmitted nonverbally (see for review Levy, 1972; Royce, Carran, Aftanas, Lehman, & Blumenthal, 1966).

In other studies, the degree of structure of the stimulus situation varied (Coffin, 1941; Luchins, 1945; Thrasher, 1954). For example, in his investigation of the relationship of suggestibility to the stimulus structure, Coffin (1941) used three tonal attributes representing gradations of a stimulus structure: pitch, volume, and orthosonarity (a fictional attribute created especially for the experiment). Results showed that suggestion was most effective with the fictitious tonal attribute (i.e., with the stimulus situation that is characterized by the highest degree of ambiguity).

In a series of experiments initiated by Binet (1900), the objective was not so much to utilize absence of structure in the stimulus world, but rather by means of suggestive manipulation to attempt to create a state of uncertainty that would impede the use of adequate control mechanisms. This is achieved, for example, with the aid of the technique of leading questions. A special feature of this suggestive manipulation, familiar from interrogations of witnesses, is based on the use of so-called disjunctive questions. The subject is confronted with two alternative answers, both of which are wrong. The purpose of this artificial conflict situation is to make the subject decide in favor of one alternative. (Did the bicycle lean against the wall or against the tree beside it? In fact, there was no bicycle at all. See in this context Binet, 1900; Bottenberg & Wehner, 1971; Gudjonsson, 1984, 1987a; Stern, 1903; Zimmermann, 1982.) Binet's (1900) study is also the origin of procedures that aim at increasing responsiveness to suggestion through intensifying the subjects' uncertainty. For instance, the experimenter repeatedly calls into question the entirely correct judgments of the subjects or makes statements that increasingly run counter to the objective situation. This procedure, called contradictory suggestion, was intensively used in Stukat's (1958) experiments among others.

The principle of producing uncertainty by creating conflict situations is often used not only for research purposes, but also in practice (e.g., with the technique of confusion and with Erickson's paradoxical intervention; Rossi, 1976). Whatever the particular techniques or the characteristics of actual, everyday situations that engender a climate of uncertainty (lack of structure, ambiguity, rapid change, extreme complexity, inconsistency, surprise, etc.), this is one of the most important preconditions for influence by suggestion. Binet (1900) emphasizes that suggestibility concerning a particular point is in inverse relation to the person's degree of certainty on this point. The fainter or more ambiguous a stimulus, the more easily it can be given a new interpretation. This is one of the few findings that have remained undisputed in research on suggestion.

Suggestibility has frequently been investigated with respect to effects on sociopsychological factors, such as conformity and group pressure, persuasion, and persuability. In the innumerable studies on this area of research, the concept was mostly recognized in connection with specific problems of social influence (influence through suggestion is not always explicitly referred to, however). (See for review and their respective contributions: Asch, 1952; Coffin, 1941; Hofstätter, 1957; McGuire, 1985; Moscovici, 1985; Schmerl, 1972; Schmidt, 1971; Schmidt, Schmerl, & Steffens, 1971; Sherif & Sherif, 1969; Stukat, 1958; and Chaps. 21 and 24 by McGuire and Schwanenberg, this volume.)

Critical Comments

The variety to be found in procedures used to measure suggestibility is quite impressive, but no less impressive is the creativity of the ideas on which they are based. The results obtained - which sometimes strongly contradict each other - are in contrast to this, however. We know far too little about the phenomenology of suggestibility and even less about its psychological mechanisms (cf. Bottenberg & Wehner, 1971; Duke, 1964; Evans, 1967; Eysenck, 1947, 1960; Gheorghiu, 1972, 1982; Weitzenhoffer, 1963). A critical analysis of the available literature and the various studies I have undertaken in this area have led me to the following conclusions.

Inadequacies of Test Procedures

Very few standardized test batteries are available for the measurement of suggestibility - even in the motor area in which the influence of suggestion has been tested most frequently. Although several of the best-known suggestion tests have been used for years (e.g., the body-sway test, the heat-illusion test, or the pendulum test), there are still no generally accepted and established rules for the implementation of these procedures. The same procedure is frequently applied under different conditions, different explanations are given to the test subject, and differences also exist concerning the embedding of tests in other procedures, reinforcement from existing objective stimuli, the way in which the sequence of test items is understood, and the time available for test completion. Owing to these discrepancies, research results cannot usually be fruitfully compared. When confronted with contradictory results obtained by using the same or similar procedures applied to comparable test samples (see, e.g., Benton & Bandura, 1953 and Stukat, 1958), we are hardly in a position to find a plausible explanation for the serious differences in results. One strongly suspects that the unsatisfactory development of this field of research can be explained in part by the deficiencies resulting from the procedures implemented.

Differentiation Between Direct and Indirect Suggestion

Direct and indirect procedures of suggestion have been discussed at various points in this chapter. This distinction plays a significant role even today in the assessment of suggestibility (see Field, 1979; Frichton & Roth, 1985; Gheorghiu, Meiu, Onofrei, & Timofte, 1966; Lynn, Neufeld, Matyi, Weekes, Dudley, & Weiss, 1987; McConkey, 1984; Stone & Lundy, 1985; Stukat, 1958). The ambiguities surrounding these different modes of suggestion result in permanent confusion. The explicit differentiation made between direct and indirect suggestion can be traced back to Sidis (1898). Direct suggestion is, according to him, typified by the plainness or directness with which it is given (e.g., "without any circumlocution, without any evasions", p. 18/19). Indirect suggestion is seen by Sidis rather as a negation of direct suggestion; "... instead of openly telling the subject what he should do, the experimenter produces some object or makes a movement, a gesture which in silent fashion tells the subject what to do" (p. 19).

Subsequently, a "factual" differentiation was brought more and more into prominence. Binet (1900) took great care to distinguish between procedures that could be applied to hypnosis and were based on the "moral influence" of the investigator and procedures that were suited to waking suggestibility and accordingly tried to minimize this "moral influence" as far as possible. The division into direct and indirect procedures, which are also frequently designated as personal and nonpersonal (or prestige and nonprestige) procedures, was adopted later by many suggestion researchers (see Aveling & Hargreaves, 1921; Hull, 1933). This division takes on a special importance in the classification of "primary" or "secondary" suggestibility (Eysenck & Furneaux, 1945).

The classification of suggestibility has become so firmly entrenched that relevant suggestion tests are identified as primary, direct motor tests or as secondary, indirect sensory tests, often without giving any additional explanation at all. Classifications are too sweeping and do not give justice to the special features of the procedures that have been employed.

In the investigation of Eysenck and Furneaux (1945), one finds that all the *motor procedures* (e.g., the body-sway test, the Chevreul pendulum) have a *direct character* and all the *sensory procedures* (e.g. the ink blot test, the heat-illusion test), have an *indirect character.* Primary suggestibility is thus connected to *motor activities* and to the *direct* suggestion mode. Secondary suggestibility, on the other hand, has become associated with *sensory activities* and with the *indirect* suggestion mode. This one-sided connection - namely the direct suggestion mode with motor processes and the indirect suggestion mode with sensory processes - can in no way be justified in terms of content. The association is only a historical one. When one adopts this procedural method, the *modus* - the way in which the influence of suggestion actually exerts an effect - loses its autonomy in relation to the field of operation. Both *motor* and *sensory* processes can indeed be influenced by *direct* and *indirect* suggestions. We know this from our everyday experience, and it has also been established in several experimental studies (Hammer et al., 1963; Gheorghiu et al., 1966; Gheorghiu, 1971; Mordey & Bryan, 1965; Stukat, 1958).

Under the influence of Erickson's suggestive techniques (see Rossi, 1976), indirect suggestion has been defined in recent times as a permissive mode of influencing and direct suggestion as an authoritative one (Stone & Lundy, 1985). However, this too is problematic because a direct influence can also be achieved in a permissive, nonauthoritative way. Sidis (1898) drew attention to this fact: "The essential future of the direct suggestion however is not so much the authoritativeness for in many cases it may be totally absent, and a courteous, bland way of expressions may be used" (p. 19).

Several aspects must be taken into account with respect to the differences and similarities of the direct and indirect suggestion procedures:

1. Both categories are primarily based on the mode of the suggestion. In other words, they are based on "how" a suggestion procedure is implemented, rather than "what" is suggested. On the other hand, if one connects the mode of the suggestion with the very nature of the suggestion itself, the indirect aspect comes into prominence, because each suggestion - as a

specific mode of influencing - affects the experiences and behavior of the individual in a mediated way. Young (1931), in a subtle article on suggestion as indirection, quite rightly pointed out that suggestion is a "method of indirect appeal to the person to be influenced" (p. 89).

2. The essential difference between *direct* and *indirect* suggestion procedures can be described as follows: The intention of the influencing is overt in the first category, whereas, in the second category, this intention remains concealed.
3. Depending on whether the intention is to reveal or not reveal the real goal of the experiment, certain explanations are given to the subject, and different verbal or nonverbal vehicles of suggestion are employed. In many experimental studies, there is no information about the given explanations or about special implications of the vehicles used. This makes the assessment of the results attained far more difficult (see Evans, 1967).
4. The difference between the extent of the direct and the indirect suggestion procedures may only be relative. One can speak of a predominance of one of the two modes of suggestion, depending on the concrete tasks in the test and the context in which the tests are carried out. It therefore seems appropriate to think of a continuum between the *direct* and the *indirect* mode. *Direct extremes* might arise when it is clearly pointed out that it is an objective of the experiment to find out how one is influenced by suggestion using an unequivocally direct suggestion procedure. *Indirect extremes* would then be the guaranteed outcome of a nearly perfect congruence between the concealed objective and the plausible indirect suggestion procedure that has been used.
5. It seems more reasonable to talk of *indirect-direct* or *direct-indirect* suggestion procedures. In investigations of responsiveness to leading questions (Binet, 1900; Bottenberg & Wehner, 1971; Gudjonsson, 1984; Stern, 1903; Zimmermann, 1982), it becomes evident - if not from the instruction itself then from the context of the procedure - that at least a few questions are designed to dupe the subject. The procedure is therefore *direct*, because it is based in a specific way on manipulation by using suggestive questioning procedures, but it is also *indirect*, in that the test subject cannot know which concrete questions are used to suggest the answer. The same principle is applied in the recording of sensory suggestibility (the *indirect-direct* variants of the sensory suggestibility scale are discussed below). A *direct-indirect* mode can also be seen in the motor procedures, for example, which indeed primarily retain their direct character but which are also based on an indirect vehicle of suggestion (e.g., in the form of pseudoexplanations, Weitzenhoffer, 1957).

Insufficient Consideration of Contextual Influences

Up to now in this discussion, I have focussed on the position of the investigator rather than on that of the subject. In recent times, researchers into hypnotism have frequently issued criticisms that subjects are treated as a type of machine in a suggestion experiment and are thought to react more or less blindly to the suggestions put to them. Special emphasis is placed in this respect to the meaning of the concrete context of the experiment (Coe & Sarbin, 1977; Sheehan & McConkey, 1982; Spanos, 1982). Yet, it is precisely here that problems arise in the assessment of waking suggestibility, and it is necessary to take into account the possibility that critical subjects can ask themselves questions about the rather strange test tasks. When this occurs, subjects are concerned with finding out what is actually being investigated. It therefore appears appropriate to approach the experimental situation as a type of problem-solving situation (Sheehan & McConkey, 1982).

Let us now take a closer look at two differing test tasks that are quite common when observing waking suggestibility: (a) the elicitation of deceptive perceptions by using what is called the "indirect" suggestion procedure and (b) the initiating or modification of motor reaction by using the so-called "direct" suggestion procedure.

In the first task, the aim is to verify the extent to which the subjects can be influenced to believe that they are perceiving something in the absence of an adequate stimulus. Here, we are concerned with perceptions in conditions where the occurrence of a stimulus or the cancellation of an already existing stimulus is simulated. The actual purpose of the experiment is kept secret (either by giving details of another objective or by describing a more neutral area of investigation, such as the formation of perceptive judgments or the investigation of perceptual thresholds). The form of influencing basically corresponds to the context of analogy (see Chap. 6, this volume). Apparently normally functioning stimulus generators are used as the vehicle for the intended reactions. The concrete modes of influencing are very different in this context: (a) The functioning of the stimulus generators is shown; (b) objective stimuli are given at the beginning and sometimes at the end of the experiment; (c) additional verbal and nonverbal suggestions are given during the experiment; (d) influence of intermodality is induced; and (e) attempts at deception are embedded in traditional tests of perception.

Beginning with the early literature (Seashore, 1895), many variations have been elaborated concerning the contents, forms, and modes of suggestion. However, two important aspects of these attempts to influence perception have not been developed adequately. The main indicator of responsiveness to sensory deception is the subject's report of a stimulus that is clearly, vaguely, or not at all experienced. Depending on the context, the demand characteristics of the experimental situation can decisively influence the behavior of the subject. Studies have established that, when the subject's interest in the objective of the investigation is implicitly stimulated, the values measured turn out to be much higher than otherwise (Gheorghiu, Holdevici, & Horghidan, 1979).

Closely related to problems of compliance, the credibility of the test subject is typically questioned in this type of experiment. In the process of deception, as Irle (1979) points out, we are always concerned with a minimization of the veridicality of the situation and with a maximization of the subjective certainty of judgments. The objective of a deception experiment is therefore to maximize the subjective certainty of the subject. Most studies conducted in the field of sensory suggestibility show a lack of plausibility when the subject is not deceived.

The danger that subjects will discover the exact objective of the experiment is far from minimal (Gheorghiu, Netter, & Tichi, 1989). What is called an indirect-direct variant has been developed for these types of experiments because of such considerations. This variant is indirect in that stimuli are never presented to the subject and direct in that subjects are cautioned that a stimulus might not actually be presented. The specific instruction given to the subject concerning whether the announced stimulus is to be presented or not depends on a "program" that the subject blindly chooses from an assessment of "program cards."

In addition to achieving greater plausibility of the experimental conditions, this *indirect-direct* procedure serves the purpose of enabling the experimenter to be perceived as being not at all responsible for what is presented to the subject. Thus, favorable responses aimed at pleasing the experimenter and prestige suggestion are relatively reduced (Feingold, 1982; Gheorghiu, 1976; Gheorghiu & Reyher, 1982; see also Chap. 8, this volume).

Let us now turn to procedures used to influence motor behavior. The aim of these direct suggestibility tests is to induce (involuntary) reactions. By means of a suggestion, an attempt is made (a) to initiate a movement, (b) to modify a movement, or (c) to block a movement. Studies that have been carried out have primarily been concerned with the initiation of movements (Duke, 1964; Eysenck & Furneaux, 1945; Stukat, 1958). The contents of the suggestion are given in a verbal form that essentially defines the so-called "indication or cues context." Various persuasive or authoritative modes of manipulation can be implemented to induce the tendency to make unconscious movements. The experimenter repeatedly and clearly draws attention to a specific type of behavior during the experiment, and, in this way, subjects are forced to concentrate only on the experimenter's words and to let themselves be led by these words (Hull, 1933; Eysenck & Furneaux, 1945; Stukat, 1958). The emphasis with which the words are spoken reduces the subject's ability to reflect upon the situation. The monotonous tone of voice preferred in this experiment is closely analogous to the hypnosis procedure.

There are, however, special problems associated with this suggestibility experiment. One of the principal difficulties lies in the attempt to find an adequate justification for the experiment. Although under hypnotic conditions the persuasive influencing of motor behavior can be explained in terms of the context itself, special explanation is necessary for this approach under waking conditions, since the generally given request to "react without intention" is in a way a logical contradiction in itself. (We have repeatedly heard this from our subjects; Gheorghiu, Hoeme, & Pieper, 1988.) In most studies using direct persuasive suggestion to influence motor behaviors, no precise details of the experimental objectives given to the subjects are described. We are thus unable to conclude either from the investigation or from the context whether and what explanations have been given to the subject. Differing expectations can be associated with differences in suggestion cues, instructions given to relax, or requests given to indulge in imaginative thoughts. These differences can result in either an increased tendency to comply or, contrariwise, enhanced self-control.

It is also not easy to answer the question of the significance of these direct procedures. The main assumption is that we are dealing with "involuntary" reactions in terms of ideomotor processes (Arnold, 1946; Eysenck, 1947; Hull, 1933; Weitzenhoffer, 1953). The ideomotor approach is used as an explanatory concept or as a descriptive term in need of its own explanation (Stukat, 1958). In view of the fact that with motor suggestion procedures we are dealing with intended movements on the one hand and with persuasive methods on the other, we must ask whether this type of experiment is not really a recording of compliance (the tendency to acquiesce to and comply with the suggestion, in the terminology of Barber, 1979). The extent to which verbal suggestions are given during the experiment and their persuasive character dominates significantly influences the measured values (Gheorghiu et al., 1988; Gheorghiu & Walter, 1989). The degree to which reactions can be identified as "involuntary" remains a moot point, with the main difficulty residing in the fact that the motor behavior triggered cannot be clearly classified by the subject as a spontaneous or unintended reaction (Pöll, 1951).

Recently, several researchers have pointed out in the literature on hypnosis that the report of nonvolition also depends on subtle context cues (Lynn, Nash, Rhue, Frauman, & Sweeney, 1984;

Spanos, 1982). We have found in studies dealing with the influence of direct and indirect suggestion procedures on motor behavior that the nonintentional character of the reactions can be recorded indirectly (e.g., by using baseline values), which can then be demonstrated to be spontaneously influenced by the context of the experiment (Gheorghiu & Walter, 1989).

The Overconcern with Procedures Instead of Constructs

Up to now, the assessment of suggestibility as a feature of personality has been discussed mainly in reference to Eysenck's classification (in this context, see Chaps. 2, 3, and 10, as well as the foreword by Hilgard in this volume). The so-called *primary* and *secondary* types of suggestibility certainly draw attention to a relevant difference, which can be shown via the way in which various types of suggestion procedures take effect. It was initially attempted to impose a certain order in the large amount of facts that have accumulated by using isolated and heterogenous suggestion tests. It is known that Eysenck's classification attempt (which is best exemplified by Stukat's study of 1958) has stimulated new methodical and theoretical considerations. However, it has simultaneously created the conditions for its own criticism (see Benton & Bandura, 1953; Evans, 1967; Gheorghiu et al., 1966; Hedberg, 1974; Hilgard, 1965; Mordey & Bryan, 1965; Stukat, 1958). The fact that the so-called secondary suggestibility, and consequently also the classification itself, has often been called into question (Duke, 1964; Evans, 1967; Hilgard, 1965) has made some general reconsiderations necessary.

1. The development of many suggestion tests has in a way taken on a momentum of its own. Even today such tests determine, to a certain extent, the way in which questions are formulated in the study of suggestibility. The researchers emphasized the interpretation of correlations and factors obtained from applying the test procedures; too little weight was placed on the development or adaptation of suggestion procedures to reflect the basic formulation of questions about the assumed dimensions of suggestibility.
2. Still valid up to the present is the observation made by Guilford (1961) in support of Littell's work (1946) that it is not possible to find a single dimension acting as a common factor of the suggestibility tests (p. 48). Analyzing the variety of studies devoted to clarifying the concept of suggestibility, Netter (1980) arrived at the conclusion that the construct of suggestibility is still extremely ambiguous and perhaps should not even be termed a construct.
3. One of the greatest contributions to the development of suggestion procedures was undoubtedly made by Binet (1900), who was primarily interested in studying individual differences in suggestibility. However, Binet developed his tests of suggestion by starting from a basic problem that has been more or less ignored ever since (in contrast to his tests). He followed up the question of the relation between responsiveness to suggestion and (a) obedience to moral influence emanating from another person, (b) imitation that combines with the moral influence of suggestion in certain cases and remains an isolated phenomenon at other times, (c) susceptibility to a preconceived idea, *l'idée directrice*, which abrogates the faculty of criticism, (d) expectative attention, which can influence imaginative capacity, and (e) subconscious phenomena that occur for example during a state of distraction. Binet assumed that an individual might be provided with certain dispositions that make it possible for suggestible modes of behavior to be activated. This idea is somewhat more clearly expressed in his considerations of the "errors of imagination," where he supposes dispositions to originate in autosuggestive expectations. He had great hopes for a systematic

investigation of those dispositions and was surprised at the fact that nobody had hit upon the idea until then.

4. One should return to the views expressed by Binet because they consider typical everyday phenomena of suggestibility; they encourage integrative research tying together imagination, imitation, expectancy, etc; and they indicate that suggestibility can probably only be understood in connection with other constructs relating to influenceability (Allport, 1961, 1968; Stokvis & Pflanz, 1961).

Considering the fact that susceptibility to suggestive demand situations refers to the most dissimilar psychic processes and that it is created by complex cognitive, affective, and socio-psychological moderator variables, it seems rather utopian to trace features of personality that can be exclusively related to a tendency toward suggestibility. Instead, it seems more realistic to start from complex fields of attributes and to trace so-called nodes (in the sense of Dörner, 1983) within them that are more likely related to a tendency toward suggestibility.

This heuristic approach has proved relatively effective, as can be seen from research efforts on integrative personality constructs incorporating aspects of suggestibility. It is pertinent here to refer to investigations of the tendency towards involvement, evoked with the aid of absorption procedures (Tellegen & Atkinson, 1974), imagination, relaxation (Wilson & Barber, 1978), or imaginative involvement (Hilgard, 1970). [Hypnotic involvement can also be subsumed under the above-mentioned line of research. Without doubt, it is in this area that the most experience has been gained (see for review, Sheehan & McConkey, 1982). Irrespective of the designation used for the concept of hypnosis/hypnotizability - whether organismic switching (Schultz, 1932) or involvement (Sarbin & Coe, 1972), goal-directed fantasy (Spanos, 1971; Spanos, Rivers, & Ross, 1977), or imaginative involvement (Hilgard, 1970) - most authors obviously agree that we are dealing with a disposition whose manifestations and features are primarily evoked by influence through suggestion.] Another type of study involves the tendency toward deception, brought about independently from hypnosis, for example, by means of procedures testing interindividual susceptibility to memory distortion (Bottenberg & Wehner, 1971, 1972; Gudjonsson, 1983, 1984, 1987b; see also Chap. 9, this volume; Irving, 1987; Smith & Gudjonsson, 1986; Zimmermann, 1982) or to sensory distortion (De Pascalis & Caddia, 1985; Feingold, 1982; Gheorghiu, Hodapp, & Ludwig, 1975; Gheorghiu & Reyher, 1982; Gheorghiu et al., 1989; Miller, 1980; Stukat, 1958; see also Chap. 8, this volume). Finally, a third type of research examines the tendency towards compliance such as in the classic investigations of persuasibility (Janis & Field, 1959; McGuire, 1968) or in the studies dealing with persuasive or authoritative influence on sensory-motor behavior (Duke, 1967; Evans, 1967; Eysenck & Furneaux, 1945; Gheorghiu & Walter, 1989; Hull, 1933; Stukat, 1958).

Lack of Studies on Specific Effects of Suggestion

The historical development of research on suggestion shows from the beginning a strong emphasis on the differential-psychological aspects rather than on the effects of suggestion. Therefore, more knowledge has been gathered about interindividual differences than about the phenomenon underlying the differences (Evans, 1967; Gheorghiu, 1966). Influence by suggestion always affects cognitive and psychosomatic domains.

Traditionally, influence by suggestion is especially studied in connection with sensory, motor, or memory processes. On the one hand, researchers, especially those dealing with suggestibility in the sensory field, are rarely knowledgeable about specific research problems relating to perception. On the other hand, experts on perception very often ignore the influence of suggestion in this domain: For instance, psychologists dealing with perception seldom consider the effects of suggestion in their studies but instead try to avoid the very problems that researchers concerned with suggestibility tackle. For example, they are interested in objective procedures to measure sensory thresholds and make every effort to eliminate subjective factors like deception due to anticipation. These, however, are the very aspects that constitute an important part of research on suggestibility. Cooperation in this sector alone would be fruitful for both sets of interests. The question put by Binet (1900) on whether sensory thresholds and suggestibility are related still remains unanswered. Many phenomena of perception and/or imagination have indeed been associated with suggestion from time to time (see among others Engel, 1976; Hariu, 1970; Kleeberger, 1983; Kruse & Hoffmann, 1986; Zielberg, 1983; Zubek, 1969), but their complex interrelations have never been systematically examined (e.g., the relation between suggestion/suggestibility and synesthesia, sensory intermodality, reversal figures, afterimages, perceptive sets, social perception).

The potential for mutual fertilization of research on suggestibility and on perception arising from studies investigating their interrelations can be derived from a study of the autokinetic effect, which has already been reported. In a study on expectation and autokinesis, Leibowitz, Shupert, Post, and Dichgans (1983) were able to show that, even for experienced psychophysical observers, suggestion and expectation play a major role in the direction of reported autokinetic illusion, whereas unbiased results in studies of autokinetic illusion can only be obtained from subjects who have no expectations regarding this phenomenon. Thus, psychologists dealing with perception can use suggestion as a research tool to comprehend the role of both important moderator variables such as expectation and anticipation and suggestive processes by specifically influencing a phenomenon of deception (the autokinetic effect). Autokinesis is an important but difficult problem (Royce et al., 1966), and - as with other phenomena of deception that have been made the object of influence by suggestion - the cooperation among researchers from the fields of suggestion and perception is the most promising solution.

The subject of deception, neglected for a long time, has in recent years become a matter of growing interest in psychology. Most of the investigations are based on the pioneer research conducted by Binet and Féré (1888), Binet (1900), Ellson (1941), James (1896), Koffka (1935), Külpe (1902), Perky (1910), Seashore (1895), and Sully (1903/1982). In the last decade, several concepts have been developed with respect to a number of areas, including reality decision and control (Johnson & Raye, 1981; Kruse, 1989; Segal, 1971), the relation between imagery and perception (Davies, 1987; Finke, 1985; Segal, 1971), phenomena of self-deception (Sackeim & Gur, 1978, 1985), and deception as a research tool in social psychology (Irle, 1979; Moscovici, 1976, 1981b). I regard these interests in research on deception as a favorable prerequisite for exploring the relevance of deception to sensory and other kinds of suggestibility and imagination; thereby a broader basis for the psychology of deception can be established.

Despite the efforts of such researchers as Easton and Shor (1976), Hilgard (1977), Hull (1933), and Weitzenhoffer (1953, 1980) to analyze the problem of influence on motor processes in a more general frame (e.g., in connection with ideomotor or conditioning mechanisms) there are far too few points of contact. To my knowledge, kinesiologists are hardly interested in the problem of suggestive influence on motor processes. This holds true even when they tackle questions that are usually discussed in connection with effects of suggestion. In relevant studies on theoretical and methodological problems of ideomotor processes, for example, there is no reference whatsoever to the mechanisms of suggestion (Greenwald, 1970; Prinz, 1987).

A much better state of affairs seems to prevail in the area of research on memory. Problems of memory distortion as a result of, for example, suggested amnesia, leading questions, or infiltration of post-event information have been studied from a more general perspective of memory psychology (Bowers & Hilgard, 1988; Coe, Basden, Basden, Fikes, Gargano, & Webb, 1988; Geiselman, McKinnon, Fishman, Jaenick, Larner, Schoenberg, & Swartz, 1983; Lindsay & Johnson, 1987; Loftus, 1975, 1979; Loftus & Loftus, 1980; see also in this context Chaps. 22 and 23, this volume). This is also the case for the intention to modify memory performance through procedures of suggestion, imagination, and relaxation (Bower, 1981; Fiedler & Stroehm, 1986; Geiselman, Fisher, McKinnon, & Holland, 1985).

What has been emphasized above with respect to perceptive or motor processes holds equally true for all other psychological or psychophysiologic processes. The specific mechanisms of suggestion should be identified and investigated systematically and adequately.

Suggestion/Suggestibility: The Stepchild of Psychology

Suggestion and suggestibility were among the initial topics of psychological research (see also Chap. 24, this volume), and interest in these phenomena continues. However, apart from the area of hypnosis, research into suggestion has still not managed to establish itself as an independent branch of psychology like the psychology of learning, cognition, imagination, or attribution.

Relatively few books come to terms explicitly with problems of suggestion or suggestibility (Barber, 1969; Baudouin, 1921; Bechterew, 1899; Binet, 1900; Gheorghiu & Ciofu, 1982; Lerède, 1981; Lozanov, 1979; Poll, 1951; Sidis, 1898; Stokvis & Pflanz, 1961; Stukat, 1958; Weitzenhoffer, 1953). With very few exceptions, no references are made to this topic in standard works on social psychology, personality, perception, or the psychology of emotions and motivation. The term "suggestion" (independently of hypnosis) does not even appear in some dictionaries of psychology (Gregory, 1987). In fact, suggestion research itself shows an erratic development. Most authors who have been actively involved in this line of research, like Binet, Seashore, Eysenck, or Stukat, have unfortunately concentrated on the truly fundamental questions only for a relatively short period of time. In contrast, hypnosis has remained for decades the dominant area of investigation for many researchers (e.g., Barber, Bernheim, Forell, Fromm, Hilgard, Orne, and Shor, to name but a few of the better known authors).

There are without doubt several closely related reasons for the lack of interest shown in questions of suggestion/suggestibility. The following discussion addresses this issue and draws special attention to the complexity and difficulties of the topic, the tendency to underrate its importance, the scanty theoretical integration of current research, and the insufficient analysis of the psychological basis of suggestion/suggestibility.

Problems Inherent to the Field

Difficulties in this area of research were identified at quite an early date (see in this connection Binet, 1900; Seashore, 1895). However, their extent and complexity have apparently not been adequately taken into consideration. After all, we are concerned with "influences on influencing processes." For example, the effect caused by the investigator himself is not just a simple situational factor, but rather a variable that acquires a particular value within suggestion phenomena themselves. We are talking here about a special type of influence that is exerted by the person who acts as the propagator of ideas related to suggestion. Previous experience can also function as an independent suggestion factor (Hull, 1933; Weitzenhoffer, 1963).

The procedures used in the assessment of suggestibility have to be examined for their own dependence on external influencing factors. Researchers have known for a long time about the sensitivity of suggestibility tests to situational factors (Binet, 1900; Guilford, 1961; Krech & Crutchfield, 1948; Seashore, 1895; Stukat, 1958). Referring to the influence of sensory processes, Seashore (1895) writes: "A seemingly insignificant word, thing or circumstance may determine what the observer shall perceive or not" (p. 63). The strong dependence of suggestibility on situational factors led Krech and Crutchfield (1948) to conclude that one should rather talk of suggestibility "as a trait of the situation rather than that of the person" (p. 337). Guilford (1961) was less astonished by the way in which test procedures could be influenced by a specific test situation. He writes that, in view of the subtle cues used in suggestibility tests to reduce different individual reactions, the influence of situation has to be taken for granted (p. 418). Contrary to most other psychological measurement procedures, a suggestibility test attempts to orient the subject toward a specific reaction. We must be prepared for several different types of reaction independently of whether the subject is explicitly/implicitly, or directly/indirectly oriented towards a specific type of behavior. Among these: The expected effect does not occur; there is a reaction similar to the intended reaction; there is a reaction in the opposite direction (instead of falling backward as suggested during the body-sway test, the subject sways forward); there is a reaction of instability (the test subject sways backward and forward, though still within the terms of the body-sway test). The absence of an expected reaction thus cannot simply be interpreted as a lack of responsiveness to the test procedure. The paradoxical reaction - if investigated at all - is defined as "negative suggestibility" (see Stokvis & Pflanz, 1961).

Fiedler draws attention to another complex aspect (see Chap. 30, this volume). He stresses the temporal-pragmatic conditions of suggestive influence as a central organizer. If we take into account three relevant constituents of the test situation (namely, presentation of stimulus information, the suggestion, and the subsequent test or response measure), we can speak of the following configurations. The suggestion situation can (a) reside between the "stimulus information" and the "response measure" (as happens with the leading question technique), (b) be simultaneous with the "response measure" (as happens in test situations where a specific result is suggestively reinterpreted), (c) be simultaneous with the "stimulus information" (in the case of direct motor suggestibility tests), and (d) precede the stimulus information (as is the case when inducing a special expectancy). Interestingly enough, Binet envisaged all of these types of suggestion situations. Taken together, they highlight the variability to be found in the methods of suggestion that one also finds in everyday life and in the workplace.

One additional category should be taken into consideration, namely, a situation in which the suggestion comes after the "response measure" (this is indeed always the case if experiences and behaviors are reinterpreted through suggestive influences). Depending on the test task, the components of the test situation mentioned can remain in force for a variable period lasting seconds or even days.

Suggestion does not always refer to well-structured messages used to attain specific objectives. Rather, we are normally dealing with suggestive cues that are a sort of concomitant of other demand situations or cognitive processes (relating to perception, imagination, emotion, decision, and attribution). Cues can consist of very different influences whose various features can work together to create complex patterns. The often covert way in which these cues operate is the subject of many contributions in this volume.

The scope and complexity of research on suggestion and the resulting difficulties inherent in it become most evident when one considers the various contexts in which phenomena of suggestion are investigated. Suggestion/suggestibility can represent (a) factors influencing cognitive, affective, and conative processes; (b) features of personality; (c) a research tool to study psychological and psychophysiological occurrences; and (d) applied techniques.

Attitudes Toward Suggestion

One of the most facinating topics in psychology is suggestibility, writes Guilford (1961), especially because this term is associated with a certain mysteriousness and mysticism (p. 417). It is however very possibly this mysteriousness which sometimes leads researchers to avoid this topic. There is probably also the desire not to have to deal with phenomena that are considered trivial because of their routine occurrence and ubiquity. Furthermore, influence by suggestion is viewed negatively as a means of manipulation (Le Bon, 1896; Rubinstein, 1984; Sloterdijk, 1983).

There are many nonscientific theories of suggestion and related phenomena, which have led to a rejection rather than to an encouragement of scientific efforts in this area. Jacobson (1929) always insisted that suggestion was not involved in the use of his technique of progressive relaxation. This point of view was subsequently corrected - but not by Jacobson himself - since each relaxation procedure is caused by explicit or implicit suggestion and is reinforced by it (Schultz, 1932; Stokvis & Wiesenhutter, 1963). Read (1944/1963), who became known for his relaxation procedure in obstetrics, also pointed out at first that his technique had nothing to do with suggestion. Both examples strongly suggest an effort to prevent the discrediting of relaxation techniques through their association with "irrational components."

Ignorance of the basic underlying principles of suggestion (Stokvis & Pflanz, 1961) is largely responsible for the negative assessment of the phenomenon that has prevailed for so long among researchers in the field and prevented them from realizing that suggestive components are part of every therapeutic process. In other fields of research as well, like the psychology of advertising, the terms "suggestion" and "suggestibility" are seldom used.

Stokvis and Pflanz (1961) mentioned that the topic of suggestion gives rise to a certain feeling of unease. In the literature on suggestion, one often finds a pessimistic view of man in connection with suggestibility. Being suggestible is equated with being immature and indecisive. Furthermore, suggestion itself is perceived as illegitimate or underhanded, a process which degrades people as it affects them. The therapeutic use of suggestion is sometimes seen as a type of cheating or at least as an inferior form of therapy, a substitute or solution born of necessity. Stokvis and Pflanz (1961) see suggestion as something that has no counterpart in medical therapy (p. 187), a position also argued by Kretschmer (1963).

At the same time, however, there is no lack of simplistic generalizations or overexpectations. "Not sociability, nor rationality but suggestibility is what characterizes the average specimen of humanity, man is a suggestible animal," wrote Sidis in 1898 (p. 17). He believed, like both Baudouin (1921) and Ross (1908), that he had discovered the main laws of suggestible behavior. Coué's praise of autosuggestive techniques (1976) also reveals a tendency towards uncritical overestimation of the therapeutic possibilities of these methods (for details see Meichenbaum, 1977; Stokvis & Wiesenhütter, 1963).

Insufficient Integration of Current Research

Research into suggestion shows a lack of integrative efforts in its development. The insufficient contacts between hypnosis and suggestion research have already been mentioned. There is also a clear gap between experimental and theoretical studies of suggestion and suggestibility. The latter deal with general psychological, sociological and philosophical aspects of suggestion and its applications (see, e.g., Baudouin, 1923; Haeberlin, 1927; Lerède, 1980; Pöll, 1951; Stovkis & Pflanz, 1961). Empirical results, however, remain unmentioned in most of these studies, but the reverse is also true. This, among other things, results in suggestion procedures that have been already developed for some time sometimes being discovered anew. The well-known body-sway test, which has been ascribed to Hull, was actually used much earlier (see in this connection Baudouin, 1923; Schneck, 1972; Weitzenhoffer, 1972). A lack of knowledge of foreign languages may have contributed to the fact that Binet's studies on the leading question technique and its associated problems is given only incidental mention in modern works on the so-called interrogative suggestibility (Bottenberg & Wehner, 1971; Ceci et al., 1987; Gudjonsson, 1984; Zimmermann, 1982). Binet devoted 100 pages of his book to a detailed analysis of the procedure and referred to its complex psychological aspects. It is also not well known that Binet's book made an important integrative contribution. He took great care to relate everyday experience with psychological, pedagogical, and clinical observations and experimental discoveries to phenomena of suggestion/suggestibility. (Binet always hints at results and observations made by contemporary psychologists, teachers, doctors, writers, artists, and especially magicians, in whom he took a special interest in order to obtain a glimpse of how techniques of suggestion worked.)

One encounters inadequate integration of the results of suggestion research itself. Various types of psychological explanations have been proposed for the various dimensions of suggestibility identified. The issue of finding a common ground is a central one, but it is neglected in these works. In attempting to throw light on the psychological basis of the hypnotic dimensions of suggestibility, one runs the risk of not giving due attention to the common ground of suggestibility as well as making artificial divisions. For example, Stukat (1958) assumes that the mental manifestations ascribed to the primary and secondary factors of suggestibility are based on different mechanisms. In this connection, he analyzes a whole series of theories in which his critical analysis is based almost exclusively on one of the two factors. When he talks about conditioning, he does so only in terms of discussing the nature of primary suggestibility. On the other hand, his explanation of the meaning of "expectation," "attitude," or "tendency to agree" is related only to secondary suggestibility. Thus, an artificial split is made. It is often mentioned that conditioning plays an important role, especially in "secondary" suggestibility tests (Ellson, 1941; Evans, 1967; Leuba, 1940; Mowrer, 1960; recently, Davies & Charlton, 1985 and Warburton et al., 1985). More incidentally, Stukat himself mentions that the conditioning principle is valid not only for motor but also for sensory reactions and for suggestion-induced hallucinations (p. 178). Eysenck (1947) ascribes the explanatory principles of attitude and aptitude, which are of general importance, entirely to "primary" suggestibility.

In addition to the lines of research discussed so far that are directly concerned with phenomena of suggestion, other questions exist that are also closely connected with suggestion but refer to these same objectives and findings in other contexts. This applies, for example, to placebo studies, which are frequently conducted and interpreted from a medical or pharmacological point of view. A comprehensive and highly informative book on therapy, research, and mechanisms relating to the placebo effect (White, Tursky, & Schwartz, 1985) refers to correlates of suggestion effects only in three of 30 contributions. Studies on the placebo effect which analyze aspects of suggestion are often the exception (Evans, 1974, 1985; Feingold, 1982; Netter, 1977, 1980, 1984, 1986; Klebelsberg, 1974; Shapiro, 1964; Stokvis & Pflanz, 1961; Wickramasekera, 1985).

Last but not least, the inconsistent usage of special terms also reveals a lack of coordination in research efforts and indeed has even worked to bring about this development (see also Chap. 6 in this volume). It is quite easy to establish that related or even identical facts are referred to by different terms. Mowrer (1960) noted in a study that one of his subjects reacted when the objective stimulus (electrical stimulation) was no longer present. (One day there was a power failure, quite by chance. The experimenter was able to observe this, but the subject, who had been given the task of operating a cut-off switch as soon as he felt the electrical shock, was not.) Mowrer mentioned that behaviors of this type were usually reported under the heading "suggestion," but that he would like to classify them as "temporally" conditioned sensation of shock, or a sort of periodic "hallucination." He went on to say: "By a word, another image, or some other stimulus, the individual is *reminded* of the object and reacts somewhat *as if* it were actually present. In other words, a part of the total experience produced by the object itself is here being aroused as a learned, conditioned response; and this response we call an image - and the process of its arousal *imagination*" (p. 166). Others prefer the term "hallucination" (Davies, 1987; Ellson, 1941; Leuba, 1940; Warburton et al., 1985) or the terms "suggestion" or "suggestibility" (Eysenck, 1947; Gheorghiu et al., 1975; Stukat, 1958) in this context. Thus, experimentally obtained results are discussed using different terms in different contexts. This particularly applies, as already mentioned, to the terms "influenceability," "persuasibility," "gullibility," "compliancy," and "imitation," which are often equated with the term "suggestibility".

Many Theoretical Concepts Explaining Few Phenomena

There is no lack of explanations put forth to account for phenomena related to suggestion, nor is there any lack of discussion of other basic concepts (for review, see especially Allport, 1968; Lerède, 1980; Stukat, 1958). In order to understand current developments in the field, it is essential to draw attention to these attempts.

Let us start with the notion of suggestion as a stimulus situation with a certain demand character. This idea is indeed contained in the "suggestion doctrine" of Bernheim (1884), as well as in Binet's (1900) consideration of suggestion as a "guiding idea." According to Titchner (1916; see also Allport, 1968, p. 36), suggestion is "any stimulus, external or internal, accompanied or unaccompanied by consciousness, which touches off a determining tendency." According to Young (1931), suggestion resides "in the attempt" (p. 89). He also points out that suggestion can also be discussed independently of the suggestee. Whether it is ultimately accepted or rejected, writes Young, a theory that cannot accomodate suggestion as such cannot be a comprehensive theory (p. 71). He is one of the few writers to draw attention to the potential character of the suggestion situation and to assert that suggestion and suggestibility are separate and distinct, both as concepts and as facts. His explanations do not however sufficiently clarify these differences or point out the peculiarities of suggestion in relation to other influencing situations.

That the experts could not agree upon a general conceptualization of the stimulating function of suggestion can be readily understood. It was Freud, among others (1940/1963), who spoke of the necessity of formulating an adequate definition of suggestion, since, as he noted, the use of the term was continuing to spread, taking on an increasingly imprecise meaning that could eventually be used to describe any kind of influence (p. 97). He welcomed McDougall's efforts to fix by convention the usage of the term "suggestion." McDougall's conceptualization (1908) led to the currently prevailing opinion that the effects of suggestion are to be found in the realm of the nonrational or the irrational (Allport, 1961; Kretschmer, 1952; Stovkis & Pflanz, 1961; Young, 1931). What is meant here is that the influence of suggestion causes people to react without critical reflection. Aside from this very general point of view, it can be seen that this position has stood the test of time, since it outlines the areas in which typical manifestations of suggested behavior and experience arise. The direction taken by psychological research in the tradition of Binet, Seashore, and Sidis furthermore facilitates the investigation of the nonreflective behavior via suggestion. The facts of everyday life forced McDougall to admit that attitudes of belief or action induced by suggestion need not be opposed to reason and that their influence can be enhanced through argumentation. He did not change his basic concept, however (see in this connection Chap. 6, this volume).

Authors who have investigated phenomena of suggestion/suggestibility in depth usually favor a single explanatory concept. One such concept is *monoideism*, which is based on the notion that suggestion is the vehicle of an idea that becomes dominant under certain conditions and tends therefore to prevail over other competing ideas. This concept was explicitly formulated by Braid (1846). Similar to the earlier work of Faria (1819), he observed that, when hypnosis is induced, attention is concentrated, which favors the accomplishment of a dominant idea. Braid ascribed the occurrence of other special behaviors to the effects of a dominant idea (the extended trance state of the fakirs, the presumed effects of magnets, etc.). *Monoideism* is certainly described in the very loose formulation of Bernheim (1910) that suggestion is the act by which an idea is aroused in the brain and accepted by it (p. 24). Binet proceeds in a more differentiated way, with his concept of the guiding idea (*idée directrice*) - a specific form of suggestion/suggestibility that manifests itself for instance in diverse suggestion tests (progressive lines, weights, or leading question procedures). Even the ideomotor construct (from James, 1890), which is seen as an explanatory principle for motor suggestibility, postulates the effect of a dominant idea (see for details Eysenck, 1947; Hilgard, 1977; Hull, 1933; Weitzenhoffer, 1963).

Monoideism is no longer set forth in the form it originally took. However, it is contained, in one way or other, in specific constructs designated to be moderating variables for suggestive processes: These include expectancies, concentrated or selective attention, set (*Einstellung*, or *ustanovka* according to the Russian term, Baudouin, 1923; Binet, 1900; Bzhalava, 1967; Coffin, 1941; Eysenck, 1947; Leibowitz et al., 1983; Seashore, 1895; Sherif, 1935; Usnadze, 1939), stimulation with predominant meaning (Pavlov, 1924/1953), "necessary" prejudices (Faguet, 1911), demand characteristics, determining tendency, and goal-directed behavior (Barber, 1979; Gheorghiu, 1982; Orne, 1962; Spanos, 1986; Titchener, 1916; Weitzenhoffer, 1963; Young, 1931). The concept of the self-fulfilling prophecy should also be mentioned in this context. This has become established in psychology in particular through the provocative work of Rosenthal and his colleagues (Jussim, 1986; Rosenthal, 1966, 1974; Rosenthal & Rubin, 1978; Watzlawick, 1981). As far as I know, only a few studies clearly relate the concept of the self-fulfilling prophecy to the effects of suggestive processes (see Smale, 1977).[2] One can quite easily imagine that there is a self-fulfilling mechanism in all processes of suggestibility that is either implicitly or explicitly based on expectancy processes. The question is to what extent the situation that is seen as plausible (whether true or not) has an inherent tendency to realize itself automatically. The phenomenal spectrum of events of this type is huge and ranges from situations in which, for instance, a student becomes more talented because of being treated as talented (Rosenthal & Jacobson, 1968) to more fundamental somatic changes, such as those occurring in false pregnancy (Pavlov, 1927/1953). One must indeed admit that the problems related to this construct could offer a considerable opening for research into suggestive processes.

In order to explain how suggestion arises and functions, an associative mechanism was assumed. The Scottish psychologist Brown (1820) employed the term "suggestion" as a synonym for "association" (see Allport, 1968, p. 35). Asch (1952) reminds us of Freud's clear statement that association constitutes the basis for the phenomena of suggestion. In the translation of Bernheim's work on suggestion, the term "suggestion" means the mutual arousal of psychological states in accordance with the laws of association (Asch, p. 402). The studies viewing conditioning as the basic principle of suggestive behavior also must certainly be categorized under the tradition of associative models of thinking. I have already referred to several of these studies in Chap. 6 in this volume (for a more complete review, see Edmonston, 1967; Evans, 1967; Eysenck, 1947; Hull, 1933; Platonov, 1959; Weitzenhoffer, 1963).

Quite often, one encounters Pavlov's idea that suggestion is the simplest form of conditioned reflex, although the context in which he set forth this notion is seldom mentioned. In connection

---

2 Rosenthal had planned to contribute to the symposium on which this volume is based. Unfortunately, he was not able to give his lecture titled "Suggestion as Self-fulfilling Prophecy" for reasons of health.

with the effect of hypnotic suggestion, Pavlov (1927/1953) talks about the function of the word, which he considers to be a conditioned reflex, like all other conditioned reflexes observable in animals. He goes on to say that the word is a much more comprehensive stimulus, which is connected in the cortex with all the other external and internal stimuli in the life of an individual. Words can signal everything to people; they can replace everything; and they can give rise to all the actions and reactions of the organism caused by these stimuli. In this context, Pavlov then expresses the opinion that suggestion is the simplest form of conditioned reflex in man (p. 341). It seems to me that we are dealing here with a looser, nonprogrammatic characterization of suggestion more reminiscent of a metaphorical formula than an attempt at definition. This view is borne out by the fact that Pavlov seems to stress other characteristics of suggestion in another context (Pavlov, 1924/1953, p. 446).

Let us reconsider Pavlov's statement concerning the word as a comprehensive stimulus that can replace all other conditioned stimuli or that can induce any reaction conditioned by these stimuli. Experiments have repeatedly shown that it is possible to create hallucinations via suggestion by using the procedure of associative learning-conditioning (for more details, see Davies, 1987; Psonik, 1952; Warburton et al., 1985). The general relevance of Pavlov's point of view resides in particular in its relation to the idea of substitution or replacement by verbal suggestion; thus, it is grounded in the "as if" condition of the suggestion itself. As a physiologist, Pavlov was concerned with finding an explanation for the well-known fact that verbal suggestion can be used to exert an influence on various types of somatic functions (Bechterew, 1899; Klumbies, 1977; Platonov, 1959). In this connection, he stresses the role of the word as "the signal of the signal." However, for Pavlov, perceptions, ideas, emotions, and the like can also function as suggestive stimuli (1924/1953, p. 446). This is a point of view that deserves much more attention in the literature.

Pavlov's conception (1927) of suggestion as a typical conditioned reflex was rejected in principle by certain authors. For Asch (1952), it is nothing more than an extension of earlier, simple explanations based on association (p. 402). For Stovkis and Pflanz (1961), the hypothesis of the conditioned reflex, as applied to procedures of suggestion, represents an extreme view of man as "homo reagens." Certainly, this is a criticism of explanations based on physiological reductionism. Stukat (1958) found that there is a specific relationship between "primary" suggestibility and the ability to be easily conditioned. He assumed that a conditioning mechanism is to some degree involved in primary suggestibility, but he also conceded that a conditioned response model allows for only a partial explanation of these phenomena. Such factors as the subject's attitude and the interaction between the subject and the examiner are too complex to be embraced in a conditioning theory (p. 239). Thus, while theories of conditioning continue to stimulate research into suggestibility (see also Chaps. 2 and 27, this volume), a critical analysis of conditioning and suggestibility taking into account recent theoretical concepts and empirical results is nonetheless needed (see in this connection Lohr & Souheaver, 1981, 1982, quoted above).

Another theory also predominantly concerned with the mechanism of hypnosis views the influence of (hypnotic) suggestion as an expression of a subconscious state, dissociated or disaggregated from normal consciousness. This dissociative theory, which has since become a well-known concept, was prevalent in the nineteenth and early twentieth centuries. It has been resurrected again in recent years, especially by Hilgard (1977). This notion of dissociation - Hilgard calls it neodissociation - postulates a hierarchy of control systems operating at any one time in a given individual and considers that hypnosis modifies the hierarchical arrangement of these controls so that they become dissociated from others. In this modified theory, dissociated control systems must not be totally independent of one another. There may be indirect links between dissociated control structures that pass through other structures with which communication has been preserved (see also Kihlstrom, 1984). The neodissociation theory was originally used in particular to account for hypnotic analgesia. It has been extended step by step to include not only a whole series of other hypnotic phemonena but also other, nonhypnotic phenomena such as multiple personality, hysteria, and various categories of everyday experiences (divided attention, the recovery of unavailable memories, pain, distress, and so on). As far as I know, the neodissociation theory has not yet been used to elucidate suggestion effects occurring independently of a hypnotic context. It is however reasonable to assume that this line of thought will represent an important impetus for research in the immediate future. Of special, though controversial, value is its ability to stimulate the researcher interested in suggestion into starting from an extensive control and monitoring system that permits information processing and behavior management to proceed without conscious representation. The question can in principle be formulated as follows: To what extent are at least certain suggestion effects based on substitution processes that are - though unnoticed - controlled via cognitive subsystems (see Bowers, 1984; Hilgard, 1977). This point of view is in agreement with the assumption that the suggestion mechanism has a general coping function (Gheorghiu, 1982; Stokvis & Pflanz, 1961).

Other theoretical positions are concerned with assumptions about more special forms of suggestibility. I shall only mention approaches that have had a comparatively large influence or that are of special value for research into suggestibility. For McDougall (1908, 1935), responsiveness to suggestion is more or less equivalent to the individual's tendency toward submissiveness. The subject of the suggestion is motivated into believing or obeying without having any reasonable grounds for his or her belief or obedience. Submissiveness, as already mentioned in another context, could be one of the dimensions of suggestive behavior, although this still remains to be proved. The persistence of this tendency as the most important characteristic of suggestibility is one reason for the negative image of suggestion/suggestibility that has resulted. Freud often discussed the topic of suggestion beyond its relation to hypnosis, to which he devoted himself particularly. Freud's interest in questions of suggestion is demonstrated by his disappointment that an explanation had not yet been proposed "on the nature of suggestion, in other words of the conditions under which influences can arise without sufficient logical justification" (Freud, 1940/1963, p. 97). In his sociopsychological analyses, he relates suggestion to identification. Freud searched for a fundamental explanation for mass psychological phenomena, which, in his opinion, had been interpreted too superficially and rudimentarily by Tarde, Le Bon, and McDougall. Freud saw the cause of alienating social phenomena primarily in the internal motivational structure of the individual. In terms of his transference theory, he referred to libido mechanisms, which cause individuals in a mass situation to identify themselves with the leader as the object of love. Or, as Freud put it, the power of Eros keeps the masses together. Individuals abandon their individuality in the mass and open themselves to suggestion by others to do things because they experience the need to agree with rather than oppose others (Freud, 1940/1963, p. 100). Freud explains the subordination tendencies that can lead to inappropriate behaviors almost exclusively on the basis of affective processes. Some modern sociologists and psychologists base their analyses of propaganda and mass psychology partially on Freud's concept of suggestion and hypnosis (among others, Adorno, 1972; Moscovici, 1981a). However, Freud's attempt to explain suggestion, which admittedly draws attention to a central emotional factor (McDougall's principle of primary affective induction appears to be too ill defined for him) is too generalized. He overlooks the value of other suggestive functions, such as the mutual influencing of individuals in the group, the complex way in which prestige factors work, and the influence of verbal stimulus situations already investigated by his predecessors Sighele (1891), Tarde (1903), Le Bon (1896), and McDougall (1908). A detailed and competent analysis of both old and new psychoanalytic positions in relation to the topics of suggestion and suggestibility is contained in the work of Stovkis and Pflanz (1961) (see also Lèrède, 1980).

To explain the effects of suggestion on perception, Sherif (1935) used a cognitive model that has become known as the "frame of reference." His main assumption is that in an unstructured situation characterized for example by a high degree of ambiguity, there is no simple "perception of chaos." Sherif showed that organization still takes place, and internal functions like attitudes, set, drive, emotional states play a dominant role in the organization or grouping process (p. 49). Under these conditions, the probability that the suggestions given allow the individual to perceive stable structures increases. On the other hand, the readiness to respond to situations governed by *structured* circumstances is relatively small (see also Coffin, 1941; Luchins, 1945; Newcomb, 1950). This conclusion was limited by Asch's findings (1956). He concluded that even clearly structured stimulus situations could be reinterpreted by group pressure. In this view, suggestibility is to be understood as a process of interpretation or reinterpretation as long as the influence of suggestion is involved in the formation and/or the changing of judgments concerned with "simple" perceptions or complex attribution processes and belief systems (see also Allport, 1968, and Asch, 1952, on cognitive restructuring).

Sherif's (1935) concept of "frame references" provides us with the first integrative model of influencing cognitive structures, which has since acquired an ever increasing importance in cognitive and social psychology (Bandura, 1978, 1986; Hilgard, 1977; Kelly, 1955; Kihlstrom, 1984; Lewin, 1946; Meichenbaum, 1977; Miller, Galanter, & Pribram, 1960; Neisser, 1976; Piaget, 1937; Sarbin & Coe, 1972).

Sherif's approach seems to me to be especially important since it considers suggestibility phenomena from a wide cognitive and social psychology point of view. In this way, he takes into account both the system character of psychology and the anchoring of people in their changing environment. At the same time, he focusses on conditions that lack objective structure in some aspects and that give rise to the individual's uncertainty and increased suggestibility. Sherif stressed that under these conditions one can be strongly influenced by a series of stimulus situations, including words, actions, or other communications of individuals, groups, and mass media (Sherif & Sherif, 1969, p. 71). I have talked about Sherif's influence on suggestibility research at another point in this chapter.

What final conclusions can we make with regard to this theoretical discussion? We could indeed agree with Allport (1968) that most, if not all, of the views concerning suggestion/suggestibility contain some truth (p. 39). Significant aspects have been stressed such as the permanence of suggestion situations and the multiplicity of inter- and intraindividual influences. The relevance of important intervening variables such as concentrated attention, expectancy, anticipation, set, motivation, and bias factors were identified at a relatively early date. Emphasis was placed according to prevailing psychological developments in the analysis of processes of suggestion, and the main protagonists such as Freud, Pavlov, and McDougall have worked directly on the topic of suggestion. There is benefit, however, in analyzing the statements made by the classical suggestion researchers in more detail in order to appreciate the comprehensive and subtle ways in which they expressed themselves with respect to suggestion phenomena in spite of, or indeed because of, their basic conceptions.

In the foregoing, I have tried to present a critical discussion of a number of major theoretical approaches. There are however a few general aspects of these theories that I would like to mention very briefly:

1. Not only verbal stimuli function effectively in relation to suggestive content. When reading most discussions of suggestion/suggestibility, one has the impression that suggestion exerts an influence exclusively through the "power of the word." Mood states are not taken into account often enough. This also holds true for behavior patterns whose suggestive content is transmitted by nonverbal components. Additionally, suggestion mechanisms are generally elucidated in terms of cognitive structures (Asch, 1952; Sherif, 1935; Sherif & Sherif, 1969), but affective components are insufficiently taken into account (see also the criticism of Stukat, 1958).
2. The role that suggestion/suggestibility plays as an adaptation or coping mechanism has not been adequately explored. Furthermore, it is surprising that "defense mechanisms," which are connected to a substitution process and which come into prominence (for example) in tendencies to rationalize, have not been discussed from the perspective of a "suggestion doctrine" (but see Gheorghiu, 1982). An explicit statement of the coping function of suggestion can be found in Stokvis and Pflanz (1961). These authors state that the essential feature of suggestibility is the tendency to balance out existing deficiencies. They do not use the term "deficiency" as an evaluation but use it rather in a phenomenological sense to denote a certain condition that contains a tendency to overcome in itself (p. 45). Their statements unfortunately do not allow us to determine in what way the deficiency that has to be compensated for through suggestion differs from other situations of deficiency, which in themselves are to be overcome via other biological, psychological, or social mechanisms. A theory on the coping mechanism of suggestion must reflect, for example, the conditions under which substitution processes affected by suggestion play a role in (a) the exclusion of contradictory alternative solutions or the facilitation of reasonable solutions, (b) the activation of usable psychological or psychosomatic dispositions that are insufficiently trained or not trained at all under consciously controllable conditions, (c) the acceptance of behaviors that facilitate the necessary readiness to react, and (d) the individual's endeavor to gain more stability through flexible framing and reframing of cognitive/emotional processes, even under conditions of uncertainty. It is clear that an account of the coping function of suggestive processes must also consider the fact that the influence of suggestion can have a negative effect under certain conditions.
3. Neither the conceptual analysis nor the discussions of the nature of suggestion and suggestibility that appear in the literature offer sufficient starting points for assessing the individuality and importance of problems associated with suggestion within other systems of influencing. What Hilgard (1973) undertook in relation to hypnosis is missing in the entire field of suggestion and suggestibility: to define the scope of this domain of research more closely. I have tried to draw attention to these problems, which show the difficulties of endeavors of this type, in Chap. 6 of this book.

Prospects

There are undeniable deficiencies and difficulties inherent to an analysis of suggestion that can in part be traced to the deficiencies and problems inherent to psychology. To overcome them, various complementary strategies could be implemented.

Phenomenological Approach

There are very few approaches to a general morphology of human behavior and experience (Dörner, 1983). Such a system would surely be necessary in order to describe the phenomena of suggestion evident in everyday life, in the fields of medicine, psychology, ethnology, sociology, political science, education, jurisprudence, and economics, or in the interaction of therapists and their patients, teachers and their pupils, artists and their audiences, sellers and buyers, etc.

Certainly, there are many observations as well as inductive descriptions and categorizations of suggestive situations and techniques, which have been recorded for all of these various areas over time. They have however been scientifically investigated only to a partial degree. Packard's (1957) analyses of hidden manipulative procedures in the world of advertising or Frank's (1974) book on persuasion and healing are relevant examples.

Only through specific and systematic observations, however, will theory and practice be able to profit. Thus, it is true that modern psychotherapy owes much to Erickson, especially for his contribution to the development of subtle procedures of suggestion. However, only the efforts of a number of psychologists and physicians, who took an interest in his abilities and could directly follow his psychotherapeutic interventions, made it possible to transform Erikson's procedures, which he himself had not analyzed in great depth, into a common property of both scientific theory and practical applications (Haley, 1973; Rossi, 1976). In order to arrive at general principles of both theory and application that go beyond the mere description of observations, useful criteria of classification are necessary. The criteria available so far are by no means adequate.

Need for Integrative Theories

Progress without the implementation of comprehensive theoretical formulations is nearly impossible. The problems posed by suggestion challenge discussion of general theoretical aspects. As has been mentioned, suggestion is related to different mental and psychophysiological processes. From the variety of integrative approaches which could make possible an intensive discussion of problems concerning the psychological bases of suggestion and suggestibility, I want to describe a few briefly.

One fundamental quality of behavior and experience, which has been neglected in psychology, is directedness of personality. Directedness, which is an essential feature of the individual and can be proved empirically to be a determinant, does not at all refer to a metaphysical teleology or a meaningful interpretation of life (Roth, 1969, p. 33). In concretely analyzing the goal-directed character of behavior, proponents of this notion particularly emphasize the significance of motivational factors (Leontjew, 1975; Lewin, 1946; Rubinstein, 1984). If one considers directedness to be a principal characteristic of suggestion, it seems imperative to choose this general concept of the directedness of personality as a basis for studying the psychology of phenomena of suggestion. There is a close connection between this notion and theories dealing with the psychological and psychophysiological mechanisms of set, expectation, or anticipation (Anokhine, 1975; Bruner & Postman, 1951; Kelly, 1955; Lomov, 1988; Stadler & Wehner, 1985; Usnadze, 1939).

Another, more general frame of reference deals with heuristic concerns in the investigation of unconscious, and therefore unobserved, cognitive processes. Approaches along this line examine, among other things, decision processes under conditions of uncertainty (Tversky & Kahneman, 1974), confirmation bias and self-fulfilling processes (Fiedler, 1983; Frank, 1961; Jussim, 1986; Rosenthal, 1968), and the monitoring function of reality information, for example in distortions of perception or memory (Bowers, 1984; Hilgard, 1977; Johnson & Raye, 1981). This line of research goes along with the recently growing interest in problems of unconscious phenomena, an area that was either taboo or regarded as being exclusively the domain of psychoanalysis (see in particular Bassine, 1973; Bowers, 1984; Chertok, 1984; Hilgard, 1977; Kihlstrom & Cantor, 1984; Meichenbaum & Gilmore, 1984, as well as the volumes on the psychology and psychophysiology of unconscious phenomena edited by them; Bowers & Meichenbaum, 1984; Prangishvili, Sherozia, & Bassin, 1978). The characteristic effect of suggestion works unnoticed, and certainly an investigation of its underlying mechanisms also calls for a theoretical discussion of information processing under conditions that are not (consciously) monitored.

Whatever the effect of suggestion is in detail - whether it refers to cases of self-fulfilling prophecy, to an unconscious adoption of other people's opinions, or to an experience of perception lacking a corresponding stimulus - those affected create their own reality in the process. They believe that they have definitely perceived something and that they themselves have formed the opinions they utter, etc. The psychology of self-created realities and systems of belief and interpretation is becoming increasingly important in psychological research dealing with the formation of cognitive structures (v. Foerster, 1981; v. Glasersfeld, 1987; Kelly, 1955; Kruse & Stadler, 1987; Maturana & Varela, 1979; Piaget, 1937; Watzlawick, 1976). It is almost self-evident that suggestion and suggestibility have to be conceptualized from a constructivist view. Two articles in this volume investigate this orientation: Lundy tries to discuss suggestibility from the point of view of Kelly's (1955) personal construct psychology, and Kruse analyzes suggestion and hypnosis on the basis of Maturana's self-organization theory of cognition.

There can be no profound discussion of the coping function of suggestion without referring to theories that deal fundamentally with questions of coping mechanisms or, in a more general manner, with the psychological and psychophysiological homeostasis of individuals. This, however, implies at the same time that theoretical considerations capable of determining the status of suggestive differentiations within the complex cognitive structures of the "system man" acquire a more prominent place. This is where, for example, debates about systems of self-organization (Bandura, 1986; Kruse, 1989; Maturana & Varela, 1979) as well as those about the self-as-unitary or self-as-fragmentary structure (Epstein, 1973; Kihlstrom, 1984; Neisser, 1988) belong. Also of importance, the theoretical positions concerning adaptation, coping, mastery, and defense (all concepts with overlapping claims according to White, 1974) have to be investigated in this context (Haan, 1977; Lazarus & Falkman, 1984). Useful approaches for understanding the coping function of suggestive processes can be derived, for example, from Lazarus' (1979) concept of defense mechanisms. He considers defense mechanisms, and self-deception in general, to be ways of coping with stress and emphasizes especially the role of denial tendencies and illusion as false or optimistic beliefs about reality. This view, which surely applies only to particular suggestive situations, is important insofar as it makes clear that self-deception - and therefore suggestion - is not always beneficial.

In connection with the coping function of self-deception, the approach of attribution psychology must also be mentioned. This perspective deals with cognitive processes of causal explanation and motivational attribution that can decisively influence one's own behavior. Heckhausen (1980) states that, regardless of whether it is unprofessional, incomplete, or wrong, the attribution of the acting person must always be taken into account if behavior is to be explained scientifically. What counts is only the subjective truth of the acting person. The way he or she forms opinions and uses or processes information is the central topic of attribution theory and related research (p. 443).

Here, Heckhausen implicitly touches upon a central problem of suggestibility. On the one hand, the act of attribution can be considered a typical process of substitution because it is possible through such cognitions to eliminate unconsciously competing alternatives. The contents of attribution thus tend to become independent and dictate the rules of behavior. On the other hand, this way of thinking reveals an aspect that researchers studying suggestion have tried to stress from time to time. After all, it is the relevance that the subject attaches to the self-created reality that is important and not the significance ascribed to it from outside the individual's inner world. The individual is generally forced to fix points of reference in the many uncertain situations of his/her environment (the choice may be correct for that person, but not necessarily for someone else). As Sherif and Sherif (1969) emphasize, one additional mechanism to obtain the stability needed under these conditions is the individual's susceptibility to hetero- and autosuggestion.

These are some of the framework conditions toward which research on suggestion is increasingly directing attention, or at least ought to focus on. This is difficult because all of the approaches mentioned have controversial aspects. It is the only way, however, to liberate the domain of suggestion/suggestibility from its present isolation. Furthermore, this is the way to convince psychologists from the different areas of research that the problem of suggestion - as a result of its comprehensive nature - always concerns aspects of their own research fields as well.

Progress is possible on this basis with respect to (a) the conceptualization of suggestion/suggestibility and related phenomena; (b) the description of both characteristic suggestion situations and the conditions that favor or impair phenomena of suggestibility; (c) the identification of suggestive aspects - hidden in processes of attribution, decision, coping etc. - which are usually not taken into consideration; (d) the further development of adequate procedures designed to use suggestion either as a research tool or for practical purposes; and (e) research on relevant substitution processes caused by suggestion and their underlying mechanisms.

Substitution as the Essence of Suggestibility

In this final section, I would like to emphasize the last point mentioned above because in my opinion it concerns a central problem of suggestion and suggestibility. In order to facilitate compliance with the demand given, the influence of suggestion operates on the basis of a substitution process in which the conscious monitoring authority is bypassed. If people affected are aware of their behavior at all, they experience it *as if* they had no alternative solution at their disposal in the given situation or *as if* this behavior were appropriate to the circumstances.

Of course, this process is much more complex than can be outlined here. (For instance, it is true that the person affected is subject to influencing, yet through the effect of intervening variables the process of influencing may operate in a direction that differs from the one actually suggested. In addition, the person may judge his/her reaction quite critically in retrospect, and so on.) The point in question, however, is the principle of substitution and the extent of its generality.

It is not the purpose of this excursion about the development of research on suggestion to probe deeply into the characteristics of substitution processes and the as-if situations connected with them. With regard to the significance, which, as I am constantly claiming, must be attached to them, it seems necessary to point out at least the general framework of conditions that can contribute to a systematization of substitution processes caused by suggestion.

A principal, more philosophical aspect that must be taken into consideration is the fact that a tendency towards substituting is rooted in the contradictory nature of man itself. Contradictions, for example, can be seen between the inner reality of a person and the world said to be objectively on the outside, but they can only be subjectively experienced. Kelly (1955) spoke of the tendency of man to "view the world through the filter of his own constructs." That is, the world is seen between the two poles of possibility and attainability, between fiction and reality (the contents of wishes and ideas are turned into facts or characteristics of one's ideas are lent to aspects of reality, if they are not simply "thought away"), between the variety of possible alternatives and the urgent necessity of accepting only one of them. Strictly speaking, these contradictory tendencies should be permanently borne in mind when trying to elucidate the fundamental psychological principles of substitution processes.

I have already discussed in detail the psychological framework of conditions forming the basis of the phenomena of suggestion. Therefore, the following list is confined to some typical syndromes that make possible or facilitate the occurrence or assertion of substitutive tendencies:

(a) Individuals have to face the demands, including suggestion, of their inner and outer worlds. It is therefore impossible *not* to react (not complying with a demand or behaving in a different manner are also ways of reacting). (b) Actually, individuals have at their disposal only limited possibilities for monitoring and controlling the situations with which they are confronted, and frequently they do not even make use of those available. This leads, among other things, to an autonomy of cognitive contents that can become dissociated from the mind affected. (c) Individuals must be concerned about economy. One often cannot afford a confrontation with the pros and cons; one tries to simplify things by putting them in concrete terms, reducing them to a common denominator, labelling them, or categorizing them according to interpretative frameworks and stereotypes, etc. (d) In order to be able to react more quickly, more adequately, and without being surprised by events, individuals use biases; they thereby manifest compliance and show the influence of self-fulfilling processes. (e) In some respects, everybody lives under the pressure of "the here and now" (i.e., under the dictates of stimuli, objectives, and activities). However, this increased receptivity to situational necessities, corresponding to whatever motives have become predominant, frequently "blinds" people owing to a concomitant increase in selectiveness. (f) The individual is capable of replacing facts to a certain extent with the power of words (and other symbols), of thought, and of imagination. (Pavlov, 1927/1953, pointed out that words could make people become alienated from reality, p. 543-4.) (g) No matter what kind of relationships a person has with others nor his/her position within an interpersonal hierarchy, the individual is in a sense always dependent on other people and groups. People are hardly aware of this; even less do they realize that this influence enables them to avoid competing solutions. To a still higher degree, however, individuals are dependent on their own personality traits as well as interests, attitudes, and belief systems, which - according to the situation - induce them more or less strongly to react to suggestive stimuli. (h) In adopting a role as a member of the social world in which one moves, everyone learns to play the game of pretending (every person constantly deceives himself). Simulation is one of the characteristic features of human behavior (Biberi, 1945; Ciofu, 1974; Goffman, 1959; Ralea, 1964). (i) To a certain extent, all individuals show a tendency to let themselves be guided by pseudological or psycho-"logical" conclusions, fallacies, etc. Everyone is influenced by fallatious reasoning such as the *ignoratio elenchi* sophism (i.e., the error of referring for example to an authority and replacing the necessary rational argumentation with examples), conclusions of the *pars pro toto* or the *post hoc, ergo propter hoc* type, or the tendency to follow the logic of a situation - once initiated - to the end because of a tendency to persist.

Essential psychological aspects pertaining to opportunities of substitution through suggestion appear most plainly in a systematic analysis of the various suggestion techniques: techniques involving distraction, reframing, paradoxical intervention, persuasion, leading questions, group pressure, etc. (for details see Benesch, 1981; Dilts, Grinder, Bandler, Bandler, & De Lozier, 1980; Hull, 1929; Kretschmer, 1963; Weitzenhoffer, 1957). In addition, the characteristics of substitution processes can be identified more clearly when we choose for examination typical contexts in which suggestive contents are transmitted (in this connection, see the author's other contributions on the contexts of analogy, cues, model, involvement, and challenge, Chap. 6).

As previously mentioned, these are very general approaches that usefully draw attention to the field of substitution phenomena. Thus, it becomes obvious that we are not dealing with isolated events, but with a series of psychological phenomena, some of which, under various names, have been the object of psychological research for a very long time. Perhaps the only new aspect is the point of view from which such phenomena should be studied. In any case, an efficient investigation of this subject is only possible through comprehensive research efforts requiring intra- and interdisciplinary cooperation.

Acknowledgments. This research work has been supported by the Deutsche Forschungsgemeinschaft (DFG) (Az: Ne 216/5-1). Above all, my thanks are due to Dr. Peter Kruse, who suggested very useful alterations to the original German paper, to Ina Gilchrist, who translated the text into English, and to Dr. Peter Sheehan, who provided critical comments on the last English version.

References

Abraham, H.H.L. (1962). The suggestible personality: A psychological investigation of susceptibility to persuasion. *Acta Psychologica, 20*, 167-184.

Adorno, T. (1972). Freudian theory and the pattern of fascist propaganda. In T. Adorno, *Gesammelte Schriften* (Vol. 8, pp. 408-433). Frankfurt: Suhrkamp.

Allport, G.W. (1961). *Pattern and growth in personality*. New York: Holt, Rinehart, & Winston.

Allport, G.W. (1968). The historical background of modern social psychology. In G. Lindzey & E. Aronson (Eds.), *The handbook of social psychology* (2nd ed., Vol. 1, pp. 1-80). Menlo Park, CA: Addison-Wesley.

Anokhine, P. (1975). *Biologie et neurophysiologie du réflexe conditionné*. Moscow: Editions Mir.

Arnold, M.B. (1946). On the mechanism of suggestion and hypnosis. *Journal of Abnormal and Social Psychology, 41*, 107-128.

As, A. (1962). The recover of forgotten language knowledge through age regression: A case report. *American Journal of Clinical Hypnosis, 5*, 24-29.

Asch, S.E. (1952). *Social Psychology*. Englewood Cliffs: Prentice Hall.

Asch, S.E. (1956). Studies of independence and conformity: A minority of one against a unanimous majority. *Psychological Monographs, 70*(9, Whole No. 416), 1-12.

Aveling, F., & Hargreaves, H.L. (1921). Suggestibility with and without prestige in children. *British Journal of Psychology, 12*, 53-75.

Azuma, N., & Stevenson, I. (1988). "Psychic surgery" in the Philippines as a form of group hypnosis. *American Journal of Clinical Hypnosis, 31*(1), 61-67.

Bandura, A. (1978). The self-system in reciprocal determinism. *American Psychologist, 33*, 344-358.

Bandura, A. (1986). *Social foundations of thought and action: A social cognitive theory*. Englewood Cliffs: Prentice-Hall.

Barber, T.X. (1964). Hypnotizability, suggestibility, and personality: A critical review of research findings. *Psychological Reports, 14*, 299-320.

Barber, T.X. (1969). *Hypnosis: A scientific approach*. New York: Van Nostrand Reinhold.

Barber, T.X. (1979). Suggested ("hypnotic") behavior: The trance paradigm versus an alternative paradigm. In E. Fromm & R.E. Shor (Eds.), *Hypnosis: Developments in research and new perspectives* (2nd ed., pp. 217-271). New York: Aldine.

Barber, T.X. (1984). Changing "unchangeable" bodily processes by (hypnotic) suggestions: A new look at hypnosis, cognitions, imagining, and the mind-body problem. In A.A. Sheikh (Ed.), *Imagination and healing* (pp. 69-127). Farmingdale, NY: Baywood.

Bassine, P. (1973). *Le problème de l'inconscient*. Moscow: Editions Mir.

Baudouin, C. (1921). *Psychologie der Suggestion und Autosuggestion*. Dresden: Sibyllenverlag.

Bechterew, W. v. (1899). *Suggestion und ihre soziale Bedeutung*. Leipzig: Georgi.

Benesch, H. (1981). *Wörterbuch zur klinischen Psychologie* (Vol. 2). München: Deutscher Taschenbuch Verlag.

Benton, A.L., & Bandura, A. (1953). "Primary" and "secondary" suggestibility. *Journal of Abnormal and Social Psychology, 48*, 336-340.

Bernheim, H. (1888). *Hypnosis and suggestion in psychotherapy*. (repr. New York: University Books, 1964).

Bernheim, H. (1910). *Hypnotisme et suggestion*. Paris: Doin & Fils.

Berreman, J., & Hilgard, E.R. (1936). The effects of personal heterosuggestion and two forms of autosuggestion upon postural movement. *Journal of Social Psychology, 7*, 289-300.

Bertrand, A. (1823). *Traité du somnambulisme*. Paris: Dentu.

Biberi, I. (1945). *Individualitate si destin* (Vol. 2). Bucharest: Editura Fundatilor.

Binet, A. (1900). *La suggestibilité*. Paris: Schleicher Frères.

Binet, A., & Féré, C. (1888). *Animal magnetism* (Trans.). New York: Appleton. (Original work published 1886)

Bottenberg, E.H., & Wehner, E.G. (1971). Suggestibilität I: Konstruktion und empirische Überprüfung des Würzburger Suggestibilitäts-Tests (WST). *Praxis der Kinderpsychologie und Kinderpsychiatrie, 20*, 161-165.

Bottenberg, E.H., & Wehner, E.G. (1972). Suggestibilität II: Einige persönlichkeits- und leistungsdiagnostische Korrelate des Würzburger Suggestibilitäts-Tests (WST). *Praxis der Kinderpsychologie und Kinderpsychiatrie, 21*, 282-289.

Bower, G.H. (1981). Mood and memory. *American Psychologist, 36*, 129-148.

Bowers, K.S. (1979). Time distortion and hypnotic ability: Underestimating the duration of hypnosis. *Journal of Abnormal Psychology, 88*, 435-439.

Bowers, K.S. (1983). *Hypnosis for the seriously curious*. New York: Norton. (Original work published 1976)

Bowers, K.S. (1984). On being unconsciously influenced and informed. In K.S. Bowers & D. Meichenbaum (Eds.), *The unconscious reconsidered*. New York: Wiley.

Bowers, K.S., & Brenneman, H.A. (1979). Hypnosis and the perception of time. *International Journal of Clinical and Experimental Hypnosis, 27*, 29-41.

Bowers, K.S., & Hilgard, E.R. (1988). Some complexities in understanding memory. In H.M. Pettinati (Ed.), *Hypnosis and Memory* (pp. 3-18). New York: Guilford.

Bowers, K.S., & Meichenbaum, D.W. (Eds.). (1984). *The unconscious reconsidered*. New York: Wiley.

Braid, J. (1846). *The power of the mind over the body*. London: John Churchill.

Brown, T. (1820). *Lectures on the philosophy of the human mind*. Edinburgh: Ballantyne.

Brown, W. (1916). Individual and sex differences in suggestibility. *University of California Publications in Psychology, 2*, 291-430.

Bruner, J.S., & Postman, L. (1951). An approach to social perception. In W. Dennis & R. Lippitt (Eds.), *Current trends in social psychology* (pp. 71-118). Pittsburgh: University of Pittsburgh.

Bzhalava, I.T. (1967). Set as a mechanism of suggestion. *Voprosy Psyhology, 2*, 102-108.

Ceci, S.J., Ross, D.F., & Toglia, M.P. (1987). Age differences in suggestibility: Narrowing the uncertainties. In S.J. Ceci, M.P. Toglia, & D.F. Ross (Eds.), *Children's eyewitness memory* (pp. 79-91). New York: Springer.

Ceci, S.J., Toglia, M.P., & Ross, D.F. (Eds.). (1987). *Children's eyewitness memory*. New York: Springer.

Chemnitz, G., Feingold, E., & Gheorghiu, V.A. (1981). Beeinflussung kognitiver Prozesse von Schülern verschiedenen Alters und Geschlechts durch ihre Mitschüler. *Psychologie in Erziehung und Unterricht, 28*, 7-12.

Chertok, L. (1984). Suggestio rediviva. In L. Chertok (Ed.), *Résurgence de l'hypnose* (pp. 11-38). Paris: Desclée de Brouwer.

Ciofu, I. (1974). *Comportamentul simulat: Cercetari psihofiziologice experimentale*. Bucharest: Editura Academiei.

Classen, W., Feingold, E., & Netter, P. (1983). Influence of sensory suggestibility on treatment outcome in headache patients. *Neuropsychobiology, 10*, 44-47.

Coe, W.C. (1980). Expectations, hypnosis, and suggestion in behavior change. In: F.H. Kanfer & A.P. Goldstein (Eds.), *Helping people change* (2nd ed., pp. 423-469). New York: Pergamon.

Coe, W.C., Basden, B.H., Basden, D., Fikes, T., Gargano, G.J., & Webb, M. (1988). *Directed forgetting and posthypnotic amnesia: Information processing and social context*. Abstracts, 24th International Congress of Psychology, Sydney.

Coe, W.C., & Sarbin, T.R. (1977). Hypnosis from the standpoint of a contextualist. *Annals of the New York Academy of Sciences, 296*, 2-13.

Coe, W.C., St. Jean, R.L., & Burger, J.M. (1980). Hypnosis and the enhancement of visual imagery. *International Journal of Clinical and Experimental Hypnosis, 28*, 225-243.

Coffin, T.E. (1941). Some conditions of suggestion and suggestibility: A study of certain attitudinal and situational factors influencing the process of suggestion. *Psychological Monographs, 4*, 53.

Cohen, R.L., & Harnick, M.A. (1980). The susceptibility of child witnesses to suggestion. *Law and Human Behavior, 4*, 201-210.

Cooper, L.M. (1979). Hypnotic amnesia. In E. Fromm & R.E. Shor (Eds.), *Hypnosis: Research and developments* (pp. 305-350). New York: Aldine.

Coué, E. (1976). *Oeuvres complètes*. Paris: Astra.

Crawford, H.J. (1981). Hypnotic susceptibility as related to Gestalt closure task. *Journal of Personality and Social Psychology, 40*, 376-383.

Dale, P.S., Loftus, E.F., & Rathbun, L. (1978). The influence of the form of the question on the eyewitness testimony of preschool children. *Journal of Psycholinguistic Research, 7*, 269-277.

Das, J.P. (1964). Hypnosis, verbal satiation, vigilance, and personality factors: A correlational study. *Journal of Abnormal and Social Psychology, 68*, 72-78.

Das, J.P. (1966). Relation between semantic satiation and verbal conditioning. *British Journal of Psychology, 57*, 87-91.

Das, J.P. (1968). Body-sway suggestibility and semantic satiation. *British Journal of Psychology, 59*, 17-21.

Davies, P. (1987). Conditioning and perception. In G. Davey (Ed.), *Cognitive processes and Pavlovian conditioning in humans* (pp. 183-210). Chichester: Wiley.

Davies, P., & Charlton, E. (1985). *Conditioned auditory hallucinations*. Paper presented at the 1st scientific meeting of the Psychobiological Section of the British Psychological Society.

De Pascalis, V., & Caddia, F. (1985). Effect of suggestion on perception: Replication of Gheorghiu and Reyher's study. *Perceptual and Motor Skills, 61*, 123-130.

Dilts, R., Grinder, J., Bandler, R., Bandler, L.C., & De Lozier, J. (1980). *Neuro-linguistic programming* (Vol. 1). Cupertino: Meta.

Dörner, D. (1983). Empirische Psychologie und Alltagsrelevanz. In G. Jüttemann (Ed.), *Psychologie in der Veränderung* (pp. 13-29). Weinheim: Beltz.

Duke, J.D. (1964). Intercorrelational status of suggestibility tests and hypnotizability. *Psychological Record, 14*, 71-80.

Duke, J.D. (1967). Primary suggestibility, life experiences, and aptitude measures. *Perceptual and Motor Skills, 25*, 73-78.

Duncan, E.M., Whitney, P., & Kunen, S. (1982). Integration of visual and verbal information in children's memories. *Child Development, 53*, 1215-1223.

Easton, R.D., & Shor, R.E. (1976). An experimental analysis of the Chevreul pendulum illusion. *Journal of General Psychology, 95*, 111-125.

Edmonston, W.E., Jr. (1967). Stimulus-response theory of hypnosis. In J.E. Gordon (Ed.), *Handbook of clinical and experimental hypnosis* (pp. 345-387). New York: MacMillan.

Edmonston, W.E., Jr. (1981). *Hypnosis and relaxation. Modern verification of an old equation.* New York: Wiley.

Ellson, D.G. (1941). Hallucinations produced by sensory conditioning. *Journal of Experimental Psychology, 28*, 1-20.

Engel, R.R. (1976). Note on effects of suggestion on perception of small changes in temperature. *Perceptual and Motor Skills, 42*, 1130.

Epstein, S. (1973). The self-concept revisited, or a theory of a theory. *American Psychologist, 28*, 404-416.

Estabrooks, G.H. (1929). Experimental studies in suggestion. *Journal of Genetic Psychology, 36*, 120-139.

Evans, F.J. (1967). Suggestibility in the normal waking state. *Psychological Bulletin, 67*(2), 114-129.

Evans, F.J. (1985). Expectancy, therapeutic instructions, and the placebo response. In L. White, B. Tursky, & G.E. Schwartz (Eds.), *Placebo: Theory, research, and mechanisms* (pp. 215-228). New York: Guilford.

Eysenck, H.J. (1943). Suggestibility and hysteria. *Journal of Neurology and Psychiatry, 36*, 349-354.

Eysenck, H.J. (1947). *Dimensions of personality*. London: Routledge & Kegan Paul.

Eysenck, H.J. (1960). *The structure of human personality*. London: Methuen.

Eysenck, H.J., & Furneaux, W.D. (1945). Primary and secondary suggestibility: An experimental and statistical study. *Journal of Experimental Psychology, 35*, 485-503.

Eysenck, H.J., Granger, G.W., & Brengelmann, J.C. (1957). *Perceptual processes and mental illness*. London: Chapman & Hall.

Faguet, E. (1911). *Les préjugés necessaires*. Paris: Societé Francaise d'Imprimerie et de Librairie.

Faria, J.C.A. de (1819). De la cause du sommeil lucide on l'étude de la nature de l'homme. Paris: Henri Jouve.

Feingold, E. (1982). *Untersuchungen zur sensorischen Suggestibilität sowie zum Zusammenhang zwischen sensorischer Suggestibilität und der Placebo-Ansprechbarkeit im Schmerzbereich*. Dissertation rer. nat. Mainz: Johannes-Gutenberg-University.

Fiedler, K. (1983). Beruhen Bestätigungsfehler nur auf einem Bestätigungsfehler? Eine Replik auf Gadenne. *Psychologische Beiträge, 25*, 280-286.

Fiedler, K., & Stroehm, W. (1986). What kind of mood influences what kind of memory: The role of arousal and information structure. *Memory & Cognition, 14*, 181-188.

Field, P.B. (1979). Humanistic aspects of hypnotic communication. In E. Fromm & R.E. Shor (Eds.), *Hypnosis: Developments in research and new perspectives* (pp. 605-618). New York: Aldine.

Finke, R.A. (1985). Theories relating mental imagery to perception. *Psychological Bulletin, 98*(2), 236-259.

Foerster, H. v. (1981). *Observing systems*. Seaside, CA: Niederzisten Intersystems.

Foppa, K. (1966). *Lernen, Gedächtnis, Verhalten: Ergebnisse und Probleme der Lernpsychologie*. Köln: Kiepenheuer & Witsch.

Frank, G. (1961). *Persuasion and healing: A comparative study of psychotherapy*. Baltimore: John Hopkins University.

Freud, S. (1963). Massenpsychologie und Ich-Analyse. In *Gesammelte Werke* (Vol. 13). Frankfurt/M.: Fischer. (Original work published 1940)

Frichton, J.R., & Roth, P. (1985). The effects of direct and indirect hypnotic suggestions for analgesia in high and low susceptible subjects. *American Journal of Clinical Hypnosis, 27*, 226-231.

Fromm, E. (1970). Age regression with unexpected reappearance of a repressed childhood language. *Journal of Clinical and Experimental Hypnosis, 18*, 79-88.

Furneaux, W.D. (1952). Primary suggestibility and hypnotic susceptibility in a group situation. *Journal of General Psychology, 46*, 87-91.

Gasiorowska, T., Kowalik, Z., Migaszewska, J., Martin, T., & Paryzek, L. (1976). Proba ustalenia osobowsciowych wyznacznikow podatnosci na sugestie. *Przeglad Psychologiczny, 19*, 479-489.

Geiselman, R.E., Fischer, R.P., McKinnon, D.P., & Holland, H.C. (1985). Eyewitness memory enhancement in the police interview: Cognitive retrieval mnemonics versus hypnosis. *Journal of Applied Psychology, 70*, 401-412.

Geiselman, R.E., McKinnon, D.P., Fishman, D.L., Jaenick, C., Larner, B.R., Schoenberg, S., & Swartz, S. (1983). Mechanisms of hypnotic and nonhypnotic forgetting. *Journal of Experimental Psychology: Learning, Memory, and Cognition, 9*, 626-635.

Gheorghiu, V.A. (1966). Probleme metodologice ale cercetarii sugestiei si sugestibilitatii. *Revista de Psihologie, 12*, 377-383.

Gheorghiu, V.A. (1971). Direkte und indirekte Suggestion. In A. Katzenstein (Ed.), *Hypnose: Aktuelle Probleme in Theorie, Experiment und Klinik* (pp. 143-157). Jena: Fischer.

Gheorghiu, V.A. (1972). On suggestion and suggestibility. *Scientia, 107*, 811-860.

Gheorghiu, V.A. (1973). *Hypnose und Gedächtnis*. München: Goldmann.

Gheorghiu, V.A. (1976). An attempt to control for compliance behavior in the measurement of sensory suggestibility [Summary]. *International Journal of Clinical and Experimental Hypnosis, 24*(3), 362.

Gheorghiu, V.A. (1982). Aspecte psihologice ale sugestiei si sugestibilitatii. In V.A. Gheorghiu & I. Ciofu, *Sugestie si sugestibilitate: Aspecte psihologice si psihofiziologice* (pp. 11-148). Bucharest: Editura Academiei.

Gheorghiu, V.A., & Ciofu, I. (1982). *Sugestie si sugestibilitate: Aspecte psihologice si psihofiziologice*. Bucharest: Editura Academiei.

Gheorghiu, V.A., & Gerendy, I. (1980). *Corelate ale scalei de sugestibilitate seuzoriala*. Unpublished manuscript, Institute of Pedagogical and Psychological Research, Bucharest.

Gheorghiu, V.A., Grimm, M., & Hodapp, V. (1978). Standardisierung einer Skala zur Erfassung der sensorischen Suggestibilität (indirekte Variante) an Schülern der Sekundarstufe II. *Diagnostica, 14*, 350-361.

Gheorghiu, V.A., Hodapp, V., & Ludwig, C. (1975). Attempt to construct a scale for the measurement of the effect of suggestions on perception. *Educational and Psychological Measurement, 35*, 341-352.

Gheorghiu, V.A., Hoeme, A., & Pieper, W. (1988). Beeinflussung motorischer Prozesse durch objektive, vorgetäuschte (suggerierte) und imaginierte Druckreize. *Experimentelle und Klinische Hypnose, 4*, 27-50.

Gheorghiu, V.A., & Holdevici, I. (1980). Attempt to test suggestibility by "direct", "indirect", and "indirect-direct" approaches following hypnotic induction. *Revue Roumaine des Sciences Sociales, Serie de Psychologie, 24*, 161-173.

Gheorghiu, V.A., Holdevici, I., & Horghidan, V. (1979). Variation of compliance tendency by testing suggestibility dependent of the experimental context. *Revue Roumaine des Sciences Sociales, Serie de Psychologie, 23*, 63-70.

Gheorghiu, V.A., Meiu, G., Onofrei, A., & Timofte, G. (1966). Experimental investigation on suggestibility: Effects of direct and indirect suggestions. *Revue Roumaine des Sciences Sociales, Serie de Psychologie, 10*, 163-174.

Gheorghiu, V.A., Netter, P., & Tichi, H.J. (in press). A test of sensory suggestibility, its dependence on experimental context, and its relation to other tests of deception. In K. McConkey & H. Bennet (Eds.), *Proceedings of the 24th International Congress of Psychology, 3.*

Gheorghiu, V.A., Netter, P., & Tichi, H.J. (1987). Untersuchungen zur sensorischen Suggestibilität. In P. Netter, V.A. Gheorghiu, A. Höme, & H.J. Tichi, *Einflußfaktoren der Suggestibilität* (DFG Report No. Ne 216/5-1). Giessen: Justus-Liebig-University.

Gheorghiu, V.A., & Reyher, J. (1982). The effect of different types of influence on an "indirect-direct" form of a scale of sensory suggestibility. *American Journal of Clinical Hypnosis, 24*(3), 191-199.

Gheorghiu, V.A., & Walter, B. (1989). The effect of suggestion and countersuggestion on motor processes. *Personality and Individual Differences, 10*, 239-246.

Gilbert, J.A. (1894). Researches on the mental and physical development of school children. *Studies from the Yale Psychological Laboratory, 2*, 40-100.

Glasersfeld, E. v. (1987). *Wissen, Sprache und Wirklichkeit: Arbeiten zum radikalen Konstruktivismus*. Braunschweig: Vieweg.

Goffman, E. (1959). *The presentation of self in everyday life*. New York: Doubleday.

Goodman, G.S., Aman, C., & Hirschman, J. (1987). Child sexual and physical abuse: Children's testimony. In S.J. Ceci, M.P. Toglia & F. Ross (Eds.), *Children's eyewitness memory* (pp. 1-23). New York: Springer.

Gordon, R. (1949). An investigation into some of the factors that favour the formation of stereotyped images. *British Journal of Psychology, 39*, 156-167.

Greenwald, A.G. (1970). Sensory feedback mechanisms in performance control: With special reference to the ideo-motor mechanism. *Psychological Review, 77*, 73-99.

Gregory, R.L. (Ed.). (1987). *The Oxford companion to the mind*. Oxford: Oxford University.

Gudjonsson, G.H. (1983). Suggestibility, intelligence, memory recall and personality: An experimental study. *British Journal of Psychiatry, 142*, 35-37.

Gudjonsson, G.H. (1984). A new scale of interrogative suggestibility. *Personality and Individual Differences, 5*, 303-314.

Gudjonsson, G.H. (1987a) A parallel form of the Gudjonsson Suggestibility Scale. *British Journal of Clinical Psychology, 26*, 215-221.

Gudjonsson, G.H. (1987b). Historical background to suggestibility: How interrogative suggestibility differs from other types of suggestibility. *Personality and Individual Differences, 3*, 347-355.

Gudjonsson, G.H., & Lister, S. (1984). Interrogative suggestibility and its relationship with self-esteem and control. *Journal of the Forensic Science Society, 24*, 99-110.

Guilford, J.P. (1961). *Persönlichkeit* (Trans.). Weinheim: Beltz.

Gur, R.C., & Reyher, J. (1976). Enhancement of creativity via free-imagery and hypnosis. *American Journal of Clinical Hypnosis, 18*, 237-249.

Haan, N. (1977). *Coping and defending: Processes of self-environment organization*. New York: Academic.

Haeberlin, P. (1927). *Die Suggestion*. Basel: Kober.

Haley, J. (1973). *Uncommon therapy: The psychiatric techniques of Milton Erickson*. New York: Norton.

Hammer, A.G., Evans, F.J., & Bartlett, M. (1963). Factors in hypnosis and suggestion. *Journal of Abnormal and Social Psychology, 67,* 15-23.

Hammer, A.G., Walker, W.L., & Diment, A.D. (1978). A nonsuggested effect of trance induction. In F.H. Frankel & H.S. Zamansky (Eds.), *Hypnosis, at its bicentennial.* New York: Plenum.

Hariu, I. (1970). Some considerations on the productive conditions of hallucinations by suggestion. *Tohoku Psychologica, 1-2,* 1-13.

Hartland, J. (1967). The general principles of suggestion. *American Journal of Clinical Hypnosis, 9*(3), 211-219.

Heckhausen, H. (1980). *Motivation und Handeln.* Berlin: Springer.

Hedberg, A.G. (1974). The effect of certain examiner and subject characteristics on responsiveness to suggestion. *International Journal of Clinical and Experimental Hypnosis, 22,* 354-364.

Hilgard, E.R. (1965). *Hypnotic susceptibility.* New York: Harcourt, Brace, & World.

Hilgard, E.R. (1969). *Experimental psychology and hypnosis.* Berlin: Springer.

Hilgard, E.R. (1973). The domain of hypnosis, with some comments on alternative paradigms. *American Psychologist, 28,* 972-982.

Hilgard, E.R. (1977). *Divided consciousness: Multiple controls in human thought and action.* New York: Wiley.

Hilgard, E.R. (1987). Research advances in hypnosis: Issues and methods. *International Journal of Clinical and Experimental Hypnosis, 35,* 248-264.

Hilgard, E.R., & Tart, C.T. (1966). Responsiveness to suggestions following waking and imagination instructions and following induction of hypnosis. *Journal of Abnormal Psychology, 71,* 196-208.

Hilgard, J.R. (1970). *Personality and hypnosis: A study of imaginative involvement.* Chicago: University of Chicago.

Hofstätter, P.R. (1957). *Gruppendynamik: Kritik der Massenpsychologie.* Hamburg: Rowohlt.

Hull, C.L. (1929). Quantitative methods of investigating waking suggestion. *Journal of Abnormal Social Psychology,* 153-169.

Hull, C.L. (1933). *Hypnosis and suggestibility: An experimental approach.* New York: Appleton-Century-Crofts.

Ingham, J.G. (1954). Body-sway suggestibility and neurosis. *Journal of Mental Science, 100,* 432-441.

Ingham, J.G. (1955). Psychoneurosis and suggestibility. *Journal of Abnormal and Social Psychology, 51,* 600-603.

Irle, M. (1979). Das Instrument der "Täuschung" in der Verhaltens- und sozialwissenschaftlichen Forschung. *Zeitschrift für Sozialpsychologie, 10,* 305-330.

Irving, B. (1987). Interrogative suggestibility: A question of parsimony. *Social Behaviour, 2,* 19-29.

Jacobson, E. (1929). *Progressive relaxation.* Chicago, IL: University of Chicago.

James, W. (1896). *The principles of psychology.* New York: Holt.

Janis, I.L., & Field, P.B. (1959). A behavioral assessment of persuasibility: Consistency of individual differences. In C.I. Hovland & I.L. Janis (Eds.), *Personality and persuasibility* (Vol. 2, pp. 29-54). New Haven, CT: Yale University.

Johnson, M.K., & Raye, C.L. (1981). Reality monitoring. *Psychological Review, 88,* 67-85.

Jussim, L. (1986). Self-fulfilling prophecies: A theoretical and integrative review. *Psychological Review, 93,* 429-445.

Kelly, G.A. (1955). *The psychology of personal constructs.* New York: Norton.

Kihlstrom, J.F. (1984). Conscious, subconscious, unconscious: A cognitive perspective. In K.S. Bowers & D. Meichenbaum (Eds.), *The unconscious reconsidered* (pp. 149-211). New York: Wiley.

Kihlstrom, J.F. (1986). Strong inferences about hypnosis. *Behavioral and Brain Sciences, 9,* 474-475.

Kihlstrom, J.F., & Cantor, N. (1984). Mental representations of the self. In L. Berkovitz (Ed.), *Advances in experimental social psychology* (Vol. 17, pp. 1-47). New York: Academic.

King, M.A., & Yuille, J.C. (1987). Suggestibility and the child witness. In S.J. Ceci, M.P. Toglia, & F. Ross (Eds.), *Children's eyewitness memory* (pp. 24-35). New York: Springer.

Klebelsberg, D. (1974). Zur Psychologie des Placebo-Effekts. *Psychologische Beiträge, 16,* 168-187.

Kleeberger, L. (1983). *Sensorische Suggestibilität und Wahrnehmungsfaktoren.* Dissertation med. Mainz: Johannes-Gutenberg-University.

Kline, M.V. (1966). Hypnotic amnesia in psychotherapy. *International Journal of Clinical and Experimental Hypnosis, 14*, 112-120.

Klumbies, G. (1977). *Psychotherapie in der Inneren und Allgemeinmedizin*. Leipzig: Hirzel.

Koffka, K. (1935). *Principles of Gestalt psychology*. New York: Harcourt.

Krech, D., & Crutchfield, R.S. (1948). *Theory and problems of social psychology*. New York: McGraw-Hill.

Kretschmer, E. (1963). *Medizinische Psychologie*. Stuttgart: Thieme.

Kruse, P. (1989). Stabilität - Instabilität - Multistabilität: Selbstorganisation und Selbstreferentialität in kognitiven Systemen. *Delfin, 6*, 35-73.

Kruse, P., & Hoffmann, F. (1986). Multistabilität als Methode zur Untersuchung von Suggestion und Suggestibilität [Summary]. In M. Amelang (Ed.), *Bericht über den 35. Kongreß der Deutschen Gesellschaft für Psychologie in Heidelberg 1986* (Vol. 2, p. 105). Göttingen: Hogrefe.

Kruse, P., & Stadler, M. (1987). Radikaler Konstruktivismus - Psychologische Überlegungen zu einem philosophischen Zweifel. In M. Amelang (Ed.), *Bericht über den 35. Kongreß der Deutschen Gesellschaft für Psychologie in Heidelberg 1986* (Vol. 2, pp. 199-210). Göttingen: Hogrefe.

Külpe, O. (1902). Ueber die Objektivirung und Subjectivirung von Sinneseindrucken. *Philosophische Studien, 19*, 508-556.

Lazarus, R.S. (1979, June). *The cost and benefits of denial*. Paper presented at the conference "The effectiveness and cost of denial", University of Haifa, Israel.

Lazarus, R.S., & Folkman, S. (1984). *Stress, appraisal and coping*. New York: Springer.

LeBon, G. (1896). *The crowd: A study of the popular mind*. London: Fisher Unwinn.

Leibowitz, H.W., Shupert, C.L., Post, R.B., & Dichigans, J. (1983). Expectation and autokinesis. *Perception and Psychophysics, 34*(2), 131-134.

Leontjew, A.N. (1975). *Tätigkeit, Bewußtsein, Persönlichkeit*. Berlin: Volk und Wissen.

Lerède, J. (1980). *Qu'est-ce que la suggestologie?* Toulouse: Privat editeur.

Leuba, C. (1940). Images as conditioned sensations. *Journal of Experimental Psychology, 26*, 345-351.

Levy, J. (1972). Autokinetic illusion: A systematic review of theories, measures, and independent variables. *Psychological Bulletin, 78*, 457-474.

Lewin, K. (1946). Behavior and development as a function of the total situation. In L. Carmichael (Ed.), *Manual of child psychology*. New York: Wiley.

Lindsay, D.S., & Johnson, M.K. (1987). Reality monitoring and suggestibility: Children's ability to discriminate among memories from different sources. In S.J. Ceci, M.P. Toglia, & F. Ross (Eds.), *Children's eyewitness memory* (pp. 92-121). Berlin Heidelberg New York: Springer.

Littel, S. (1946). The role of suggestibility in susceptibility to the size-weight illusion and the phenomenon of autokinetic streaming. *Denison University Bulletin, Journal Sci Lab, 39*, 156-170.

Loftus, E.F. (1975). Leading questions and the eyewitness report. *Cognitive Psychology, 7*, 560-572.

Loftus, E.F. (1979). *Eyewitness testimony*. Cambridge, MA: Harvard University.

Loftus, E.F., & Davies, G.M. (1984). Distortions in the memory of children. *Journal of Social Issues, 40*, 51-67.

Loftus, E.F., & Loftus, G. (1980). On the permanence of stored information in the human brain. *American Psychologist, 35*, 409-420.

Lohr, J.M., & Souheaver, G.T. (1981). Primary waking suggestibility and classical conditioning of world meaning. *Psychological Reports, 48*, 119-126.

Lohr, J.M., & Souheaver, G.T. (1982). Relationship between suggestibility and locus of control of reinforcement. *Psychological Reports, 50*, 10.

Lomov, B.F. (1988). *On the problem of determinism in psychology*. Abstracts of the 24th International Congress of Psychology, Sydney.

Lozanov, G. (1979). *Suggestology and outlines of suggestopedia*. New York: Gordon and Breach.

Luchins, A.S. (1945). Social influences on perception of complex drawings. *Journal of Social Psychology, 21*, 257-273.

Lynn, S.J., Nash, M.R., Rhue, J.W., Frauman, D.C., & Sweeney, C.A. (1984). Nonvolition, expectancies, and hypnotic rapport. *Journal of Abnormal Psychology, 93*, 295-303.

Lynn, S.J., Neufeld, V., Matyi, C.L., Weekes, J., Dudley, K., & Weiss, F. (1987). Direct versus indirect suggestions. *Hypnos, 14*, 113-120.

Marin, B.V., Holmes, D.L., Guth, M., & Kovac, P. (1979). The potential of children as eyewitnesses. *Law and Human Behavior, 3*, 295-305.

Maturana, H.R., & Varela, F.J. (1979). *Autopoiesis and cognition.* Boston: Reidel.

McConkey, K. (1984). The impact of an indirect suggestion. *International Journal of Clinical and Experimental Hypnosis, 32*, 307-314.

McDougall, W. (1908). *Introduction to social psychology.* London: Methuen.

McDougall, W. (1935). *The energies of men: A study of the fundamental of dynamic psychology* (3rd ed.). London: Methuen.

McGlashan, T.H., Evans, F.J., & Orne, M.T. (1969). The nature of hypnotic analgesia and placebo response to experimental pain. *Psychosomatic Medicine, 31*, 227-246.

McGuire, W.J. (1968). Personality and susceptibility to social influence. In E.F. Borgatta & W.W. Lambert (Eds.), *Handbook of personality theory and research* (pp. 1130-1187). Chicago: Rand-McNally.

McGuire, W.J. (1985). Attitudes and attitude change. In G. Lindzey & E. Aronson (Eds.), *Handbook of social psychology* (3rd ed., Vol. 2, pp. 233-346). New York: Random House.

Meichenbaum, D.W. (1977). *Cognitive-behavioral modification.* New York: Plenum.

Meichenbaum, D.W., & Gilmore, J.B. (1984). The nature of unconscious processes: A cognitive behavioral perspective. In K.S. Bowers & D.W. Meichenbaum (Eds.), *The unconscious reconsidered* (pp. 273-298). New York: Wiley.

Miller, G.A., Galanter, E., & Pribram, K.H. (1960). *Plans and the structure of behavior.* New York: Holt, Rinehart, & Winston.

Miller, R.J. (1980). The Harvard group scale of hypnotic susceptibility as a predictor of nonhypnotic suggestibility. *International Journal of Clinical and Experimental Hypnosis, 28*, 46-52.

Moore, R.K. (1964). Susceptibility to hypnosis and susceptibility to social influence. *Journal of Abnormal and Social Psychology, 68*, 282-294.

Mordey, T., & Bryan, J.H. (1965). Suggestibility and its distribution. *American Journal of Clinical Hypnosis, 7*, 226-228.

Moscovici, S. (1976). *Social influence and social change.* London: Academic.

Moscovici, S. (1981a). *L'âge des foules.* Paris: Fayard.

Moscovici, S. (1981b). Bewußte und unbewußte Einflüsse in der Kommunikation. *Zeitschrift für Sozialpsychologie, 12*, 93-103.

Moscovici, S. (1985). Social influence and conformity. In G. Lindzey & E. Aronson (Eds.), *Handbook of social psychology* (3rd ed., Vol. 2, pp. 347-412). New York: Random House.

Mowrer, O.H. (1960). *Theory and the symbolic process.* New York: Wiley.

Murray, S. (1983). *The effect of postevent information on children's memory for an illustrated story.* Unpublished manuscript, Aberdeen University, Scotland.

Neisser, U. (1976). *Cognition and reality: Principles and implications of cognitive psychology.* San Francisco: Freeman.

Neisser, U. (1988). *The self: An ecological analysis.* Abstracts of the 24th International Congress of Psychology, Sydney.

Netter, P. (1977). Der Placebo-Effekt. *Münchener Medizinische Wochenschrift, 119*, 203-208.

Netter, P. (1980). Suggestibilität und Medikamentenwirkung. *Medizinische Psychologie, 6*, 195-213.

Netter, P. (1984). Psychologische Faktoren bei der Wirksamkeitsprüfung von Arzneimitteln. In *Arzneimittel in der modernen Gesellschaft* (pp. 171-215). Köln: Heymanns.

Netter, P. (1986). Systematik der am Placeboeffekt beteiligten Faktoren und Beispiele für ihre statistischen Wirkungen und Wechselwirkungen. In H. Hippius (Ed.), *Das Placebo-Problem* (pp. 61-75). Stuttgart: Fischer.

Newcomb, T.M. (1950). *Social psychology*. New York: Dryden.
Olivier, L. (1987). The use of hypnosis as a therapeutic technique by traditional African healers. *Hypnos, 14*, 174-182.
Orne, M.T. (1959). The nature of hypnosis: Artifact and essence. *Journal of Abnormal and Social Psychology, 58*, 277-299.
Orne, M.T. (1962). On the social psychology of the psychological experiment: With particular reference to demand characteristics and their implications. *American Psychologist, 17*, 776-783.
Orne, M.T. (1966). On the mechanisms of posthypnotic amnesia. *International Journal of Clinical and Experimental Hypnosis, 14*, 121-134.
Orne, M.T. (1977). The construct of hypnosis: Implications of the definition for research and practice. *Annals of the New York Academy of Sciences, 296*, 14-33.
Orne, M.T., Dinges, D.F., & Orne, E.C. (1986). Hypnotic experience: A cognitive social-psychological reality. *Behavioral and Brain Sciences, 9*, 477-478.
Otis, M.A. (1924). A study of suggestibility of children. *Archives of Psychology, 11*(70).
Packard, V. (1957). *The hidden persuaders*. New York: McKay.
Pavlov, I.P. (1953). *Sämtliche Werke*. Berlin: Akademie. (Original work published 1924-1927)
Perky, C.W. (1910). An experimental study of imagination. *American Journal of Psychology, 21*, 422-452.
Piaget, J. (1937). *La construction du réel chez l'enfant*. Neuchâtel: Delachaux et Niestlé.
Platonov, K.I. (1959). *The word as a physiological and therapeutic factor*. Moscow: Foreign Languages.
Pöll, W. (1951). *Die Suggestion: Wesen und Grundformen*. München: Kösel.
Prangishvili, A.S., Sherozia, A.E., & Bassin, F.V. (Eds.). (1978). *The unconscious: Nature, functions, methods of study* (Vols. 1-3). Tbilisi: Publishing House.
Prinz, W. (1987). Ideo-motor action. In H. Heuer & A.F. Sanders (Eds.), *Perspectives on perception and action* (pp. 47-76). Hillsdale: Erlbaum.
Psonik, A.T. (1952). *Kora golovnoyo mosga i rezeptoria functia organizma*. Moscow: Sovietskaia Nauka.
Puysegur, A.M.J., Ch. de (1809). *Memoires pour servir à l'histoire et à l'établissement du magnetisme animal* (2nd ed.). Paris: Cellat.
Ralea, M. (1964). Schita unui sistem de psychologie. *Revista de Psihologie, 10*, 273-280.
Read, G.D. (1963). *Mutterwerden ohne Schmerz* (Trans., 12th ed.). Hamburg: Hoffmann & Campe. (Original work published 1944)
Richardson, A. (1969). *Mental imagery*. New York: Springer.
Rosenthal, R. (1966). *Experimenter effects in behavioral research*. New York: Appleton-Century Crofts.
Rosenthal, R. (1974). *On the social psychology of the self-fulfilling prophecy: Further evidence for Pigmalion effects and their mediating mechanisms*. New York: MSS Modular.
Rosenthal, R., & Jacobson, L. (1968). *Pygmalion in the classroom: Teacher expectation and student intellectual development*. New York: Holt, Rinehart, & Winston.
Rosenthal, R., & Rubin, D.P. (1978). Interpersonal expectancy effects: The first 345 studies. *Behavioral and Brain Sciences, 3*, 377-415.
Ross, E.A. (1908). *Social psychology*. New York: MacMillan.
Rossi, E.L. (1976). *Hypnotic realities: The induction of clinical hypnosis and forms of indirect suggestion*. New York: Irvington.
Roth, E. (1969). *Persönlichkeits-Psychologie*. Stuttgart: Kohlhammer.
Royce, J.R., Carran, A.B., Aftanas, M., Lehman, R.B., & Blumenthal, A. (1966). The autokinetic phenomenon: A critical review. *Psychological Bulletin, 65*, 243-260.
Rubinstein, S.L. (1984). *Grundlagen der allgemeinen Psychologie* (10th ed.). Berlin: Volk und Wissen.
Sackeim, H.A., & Gur, R.C. (1978). Self-deception, self-confrontation and consciousness. In G.E. Schwartz & D. Shapiro (Eds.), *Consciousness and self regulation: Advances in research and theory* (Vol. 2). New York: Plenum.

Sackeim, H.A., & Gur, R.C. (1985). Voice recognition and the ontological status of self-deception. *Journal of Personality and Social Psychology, 48*, 1365-1368.

Saywitz, K.J. (1987). Children's testimony: Age related patterns of memory errors. In S.J. Ceci, M.P. Toglia, & D.F. Ross (Eds.), *Children's eyewitness memory* (pp. 24-35). New York: Springer.

Sarbin, T.R., & Coe, W.C. (1972). *Hypnosis: A social psychological analysis of influence communication.* New York: Holt, Rinehart and Winston.

Schmerl, C. (1972). Experimente zur Prestige-Beeinflußbarkeit III: Beeinflußbarkeit durch positives und negatives Prestige. *Archiv für Psychologie, 124*, 523-581.

Schmidt, H.D. (1971). Experimente zur Prestige-Beeinflußbarkeit I: Co-judge-Suggestibilität und Persönlichkeit. *Archiv für Psychologie, 123*, 49-64.

Schmidt, H.D., Schmerl, C., & Steffens, K.H. (1971). Experimente zur Prestige-Beeinflußbarkeit II: Dimensionen der Prestige-Beeinflußbarkeit. *Archiv für Psychologie, 123*, 97-119.

Schneck, J.M. (1972). A historical comment on Clark Hull: His postural sway test for suggestibility, and earlier descriptions of the maneuver. *International Journal of Clinical and Experimental Hypnosis, 20*, 25-30.

Schultz, J.H. (1932). *Das autogene Training.* Stuttgart: Thieme.

Scott, W.D. (1910). Personal differences in suggestibility. *Psychological Review, 17*, 147-154.

Scripture, E.W. (1893). Tests on school children. *Educational Review, 5*, 52-61.

Seashore, C.E. (1895). Measurement of illusions and hallucinations in normal life. *Studies from the Yale Psychological Laboratory, 2*, 1-67.

Segal, S.J. (1971). Processing of the stimulus in imagery and perception. In S.J. Segal (Ed.), *Imagery: Current cognitive approaches.* New York: Academic.

Shapiro, A.K. (1964). Factors contibuting to the placebo effect. *American Journal of Psychotherapy, 18*, 73-87.

Sheehan, P.W. (1980). Factors influencing rapport in hypnosis. *Journal of Abnormal Psychology, 89*, 263-281.

Sheehan, P.W. (1967). A shortened form of Betts' questionnaire upon mental imagery. *Journal of Clinical Psychology, 23*, 386-389.

Sheehan, P.W. (1979). Hypnosis and the processes of imagination. In E. Fromm & R.E. Shor (Eds.), *Hypnosis: Developments in research and new perspectives* (pp. 381-414). New York: Aldine.

Sheehan, P.W., & McConkey, K.M. (1982). *Hypnosis and experience: The exploration of phenomena and process.* Hillsdale, NJ: Erlbaum.

Sheehan, P.W., & Perry, C.W. (1976). *Methodologies of hypnosis: A critical appraisal of contemporary paradigms of hypnosis.* Hillsdale, NJ: Erlbaum.

Sherif, M. (1935). A study of some social factors in perception. *Archives of Psychology, 187*, 60.

Sherif, M., & Sherif, C.W. (1969). *Social psychology.* New York: Harper & Row.

Shor, R.E. (1970). The three-factor theory of hypnosis as applied to the book-reading fantasy and to the concept of suggestion. *International Journal of Clinical and Experimental Hypnosis, 18*, 89-98.

Shor, R.E. (1979). The fundamental problem in hypnosis research as viewed from historic perspectives. In E. Fromm & R.E. Shor (Eds.), *Hypnosis: Developments in research and new perspectives* (pp. 15-44). New York: Aldine.

Sidis, B. (1898). *The psychology of suggestion.* New York: Appleton.

Sighele, S. (1891). *La foule criminelle.* Paris: Baillière.

Sloterdijk, P. (1983). *Kritik der zynischen Vernunft* (Vols. 1-2). Frankfurt: Suhrkamp.

Smale, G.G. (1977). *Prophecy, behaviour and change: An examination of self-fulfilling prophecies in helping relationships.* London: Routledge & Kegan Paul.

Smith, K., & Gudjonsson, G.H. (1986). Investigation of the responses of "fakers" and "non-fakers" on the Gudjonsson Suggestibility Scale (GSS). *Medicine, Science and the Law, 26*, 66-71.

Spanos, N.P. (1971). Goal-directed fantasy and the performance of hypnotic test suggestions. *Psychiatry, 34*, 86-96.

Spanos, N.P. (1982). Hypnotic behavior: A cognitive, social-psychological perspective. *Research Communications in Psychology, Psychiatry, and Behavior, 7*, 199-213.

Spanos, N.P. (1986). Hypnotic behavior: A social-psychological interpretation of amnesia, analgesia, and "trance logic." *Behavioral and Brain Sciences, 9*, 449-502.
Spanos, N.P., & Barber, T.X. (1974). Toward a convergence in hypnosis research. *American Psychologist, 29*, 500-511.
Spanos, N.P., Rivers, S.M., & Ross, S. (1977). Experienced involuntariness and response to hypnotic suggestions. *Annals of the New York Academy of Sciences, 296*, 208-221.
Spiegel, H. (1978). *Manual for the hypnotic induction profile*. New York: Basic.
Stadler, M., & Wehner, T. (1985). Anticipation as a basic principle in goal directed action. In M. Frese & J. Sabini (Eds.), *Goal directed behavior: The concept of action in psychology* (pp. 67-79). Hillsdale: Erlbaum.
St Jean, R., MacLeod, C., Coe, W.C., & Howard, M.L. (1982). Amnesia and hypnotic time estimation. *International Journal of Clinical and Experimental Hypnosis, 30*, 127-137.
Stern, W.L. (1903). Aussagestudium. In: *Beiträge zur Psychologie der Aussage* (pp. 46-78). Leipzig: Barth.
Stokvis, B., & Pflanz, M. (1961). *Suggestion*. Stuttgart: Hippokrates.
Stokvis, B., & Wiesenhütter, E. (1963). *Der Mensch in der Entspannung*. Stuttgart: Hippokrates.
Stone, J.A., & Lundy, R.M. (1985). Behavioral compliance with direct and indirect body movement suggestions. *Journal of Abnormal Psychology, 94*, 256-263.
Stukat, K.G. (1958). *Suggestibility: A factorial and experimental analysis*. Stockholm: Almqvist & Wiksell.
Sully, J. (1982). *Illusions: A psychological study*. New York: Da Capo. (Original work published 1903)
Tarde, G. (1903). *The laws of imitation*. New York: Holt.
Tellegen, A. (1978/79). On measures and conceptions of hypnosis. *American Journal of Clinical Hypnosis, 21*, 2-3.
Tellegen, A., & Atkinson, G. (1974). Openness to absorbing and self-altering experiences ("absorption"), a trait related to hypnotic susceptibility. *Journal of Abnormal Psychology, 83*, 268-277.
Thrasher, J.D. (1954). Interpersonal relations and graduations of stimulus structure in judgment variation. *Sociometry, 17*, 228-241.
Titchner, E.B. (1916). *A textbook of psychology*. New York: MacMillan.
Town, C.H. (1916). An experimental study of the suggestibility of twelve- and fifteen-year old boys. *Psychol Clin, 10*, 1-12.
Tversky, A., & Kahneman, D. (1974). Judgment under uncertainty: Heuristic and biases. *Science, 185*, 1124-1131.
Uznadze, D.N. (1939). Untersuchungen zur Psychologie der Einstellung. *Acta Psychologica, 4*, 323-333.
Van Parreren, C.F. (1966). *Lernprozess und Lernerfolg*. Braunschweig: Westermann.
Warburton, D.M., Wesnes, K., Edwards, J., & Larrad, D. (1985). Scopolamine and the sensory conditioning of hallucination. *Neuropsychobiology, 14*, 198-202.
Watkins, J.G. (1966). Symposium on posthypnotic amnesia: Discussion. *International Journal of Clinical and Experimental Hypnosis, 14*, 139-149.
Watzlawick, P. (1976). *How real is real?* New York: Random House.
Watzlawick, P. (1981). Selbsterfüllende Prophezeiungen. In P. Watzlawick (Ed.), *Die erfundene Wirklichkeit*. München: Piper.
Wegener, H. (1961). Über die Beziehungen zwischen Intelligenzgrad und Suggestibilität. *Psychologische Beiträge, 6*, 303-320.
Weitzenhoffer, A.M. (1953). *Hypnotism: An objective study in suggestibility*. New York: Wiley. (Original work published 1953)
Weitzenhoffer, A.M. (1957). *General techniques of hypnotism*. New York: Grune & Stratton.
Weitzenhoffer, A.M. (1972). The postural sway test: A historical note. *International Journal of Clinical and Experimental Hypnosis, 20*, 17-24.
Weitzenhoffer, A.M. (1980). Hypnotic susceptibility revisited. *American Journal of Clinical Hypnosis, 2*, 130-146.
Weitzenhoffer, A.M., & Sjoberg, B.M. (1961). Suggestibility with and without "induction of hypnosis". *Journal of Nervous and Mental Disease, 132*, 205-220.
Wellek, A. (1968). Kritisches zur "kritischen" Hypnose-Forschung. *Archiv für die Gesamte Psychologie, 120*, 301-306.

White, R.W. (1974). Strategies of adaptation: An attempt at systematic description. In G.V. Coelho, D.A. Hamburg, & J.E. Adams (Eds.), *Coping and adaptation*. New York: Basic.

White, L., Tursky, B., & Schwartz, G.E. (Eds.). (1985). *Placebo: Theory, research and mechanisms*. New York: Guilford.

Wickramasekera, I. (1985). A conditioned response model of the placebo effect: Predictions from the model. In L. White, B. Tursky, & G.E. Schwartz (Eds.), *Placebo: Theory, research and mechanisms* (pp. 255-287). New York: Guilford.

Wilson, S.C., & Barber, T.X. (1978). The creative imagination scale as a measure of hypnotic responsiveness: Application to experimental and clinical hypnosis. *American Journal Of Clinical Hypnosis, 20*, 235-249.

Young, H.F., Bentall, R.P., Slade, P.D., & Dewey, B.A. (1987). The role of brief instructions and suggestibility in the elicitation of auditory and visual hallucinations in normal and psychiatric subjects. *Journal of Nervous and Mental Disease, 175*, 41-48.

Young, P.C. (1931). Suggestion as indirection. *Journal of Abnormal and Social Psychology, 26*, 69-90.

Zamansky, H.S., Scharf, B., & Brightbill, R. (1964). The effect of expectancy for hypnosis on prehypnotic performance. *Journal of Personality, 32*, 236-248.

Zaragoza, M.S. (1987). Memory, suggestibility, and eyewitness testimony in children and adults. In S.J. Ceci, M.P. Toglia, & D.F. Ross (Eds.), *Children's eyewitness memory* (pp. 53-78). New York: Springer.

Zielberg, R. (1983). *Sensorische Suggestibilität: Kognitive Steuermechanismen der Wahrnehmung und Indikatoren des Erregungsniveaus*. Dissertation med. Mainz: Johannes-Gutenberg-University.

Zimmermann, W. (1982). Probleme und Ergebnisse der weiteren Standardisierung des Suggestibilitätstests für 12- bis 16-jährige Schüler. *Kriminalistik und Forensische Wissenschaften, 46*, 47-76.

Zubek, J. (1969). *Sensory deprivation*. New York:

Zuckerman, M., Bone, R.N., Neary, R., Mangelsdorff, D., & Brustman, D. (1972). What is a sensation seeker? Personality trait and experience correlates of the sensation seeking scales. *Journal of Consulting and Clinical Psychology, 39*, 308-321.

2. Personality, Primary and Secondary Suggestibility, and Hypnosis

H.J. EYSENCK

Suggestibility is an important trait of personality, from the points of view of both theory and of practice. It covers a far wider field than is normally considered. One important area in which suggestibility plays a part is of course that of reactions to placebos. As Beecher (1959) has pointed out, "of the average pain relief produced by a large dose of morphine in treating severe pain, nearly half must be attributed to a placebo" (p. 65). Similarly, practically the whole effect of psychotherapy appears to be simply a "placebo reaction" (Prioleau, Murdock & Brody, 1983; Smith, Glass & Miller, 1980). Thus for instance Smith et al. find the average effect size for psychodynamic therapy to be 0.69 and for placebo treatment 0.56; the figure for Adlerian therapy is 0.62, and for client-centered therapy 0.62. Much of general medicine, and even more of psychiatry, apparently has effects which owe more to suggestion than to anything else!

In addition to psychiatrists and medical doctors, politicians, advertisers, and witch doctors, seducers and business men probably owe a great deal to the power of suggestion. There can thus be little doubt about its social importance.

Some of the effects of suggestion stress credulity. Thus Bruno Bloch (1927), the famous "wart doctor" of Zürich, used an impressive "wart-killing machine", with flashing lights, a noisy motor and "powerful X-rays". Patients placed their affected body parts in the machine, and when told that the warts were dead these were painted with a brightly coloured harmless dye. Patients were then told that the warts must not be washed or touched until they had disappeared. In 30 % of his cases, Dr.Bloch reported a complete disappearance of all warts after one treatment - a very much higher rate of success than that occasionally reported for spontaneous cures. Similarly, claims are made that female breasts can be enlarged. R.D. Willard (1977) performed a controlled study of 32 women between the ages of 19 and 54. Women were treated for 12 weeks, given suggestions of deep relaxation and told to imagine warming of the breasts, and to feel them pulsating. Nearly 85 % of the women were reported as having some breast enlargement, with 46 % requiring a larger bra size. Measurement revealed an average increase in breast size of 1 1/3 in. in circumference, over 1 in. horizontally, and 2/3 in. vertically. These findings are consistent with those of four other published reports of breast enlargement elicited by suggestion. (Haniotes, 1977; LeCron, 1969; Staib & Logan, 1977; Williams, 1974).

Again, allergic reactions of the skin can be provoked by suggestion alone. Two Japanese researchers (Ikemi & Nakagawa, 1962) performed a series of experiments on 13 high-school boys who were known to be highly allergic to a certain plant. Five of the boys were given an hypnotic induction with repeated suggestions of relaxation and drowsiness. The other eight were not given a formal hypnotic induction, but were merely given strong suggestions. With their eyes closed, all the boys were then told that they were being touched on the arm with the leaves of a "poison ivy-type" plant. In fact, they were being touched by the leaves of a harmless plant, yet all 13 boys demonstrated some degree of dermatitis, including itching, redness, papules, swelling, and blisters, in response to their belief that they were being touched by the poisonous leaves.

In the next stage of the experiment, the experimenters reversed the procedure, telling each boy that he was being touched by the leaves of a harmless plant when, in fact, he was being stroked on the arm with the poison ivy-type leaves. In this situation, when led to believe that the leaves were harmless, 11 of the 13 did not react to the poisonous leaves with their usual skin eruption.

These and many more examples of the powerful effects of suggestion and hypnosis have been well documented (e.g. Barber, 1984). Amputation of limbs under hypnosis, with the suggestion that no pain was being felt, has been reliably reported many times, and had it not been for the discovery of anaesthetics, hypnosis would undoubtedly have become much more popular in medical circles. These facts raise serious theoretical questions, and also suggest many practical applications of suggestion and hypnosis.

The experimental study of suggestibility has run into many problems, some of which may be worthy of mention.

The first, and possibly the most obdurate, is the fact that there is no unitary concept of suggestibility which can be supported by empirical study. It is easily assumed that because we have a single word to cover a variety of experiences of different types there must therefore be some unity among these, but this is not so. "Gullibility", "simplemindedness", "submissiveness" and many other similar terms are partly synonymous with aspects of what is popularly conceived of as "suggestibility", but these aspects may be quite separate and not in fact form part of a general concept. There is ample evidence to suggest that this is indeed so, and the early work of Eysenck (1943) and Eysenck and Furneaux (1945) demonstrated clearly the existence of at least two independent types of suggestibility, called "primary" and "secondary" respectively. Primary suggestibility was of the ideo-motor type, exemplified by the Body-Sway test; it correlated closely with hypnotizability, and with neuroticism. Secondary suggestibility was of the Binet type involving indirection; it correlated negatively with intelligence, and not at all with hypnotizability. The existence of a "tertiary" type of suggestibility was also adumbrated. Since then the existence of these and other types of suggestibility, including "interrogative suggestibility", has been verified in many studies, and the evidence is discussed in other papers in this book. The major point to remember is that there is no such thing as "suggestibility" covering all these different aspects of personality; there are, instead, different and independent suggestibilities which ought really to receive distinct names. Here we will be concerned mainly with primary or ideo-motor suggestibility, because that is the only type that is related closely to hypnosis.

A second problem that is not discussed frequently in the literature relates to the objectivity of measurement. It is usually assumed that the results of a test like the Body-Sway test can be measured on some scale or other. Here, the experimenter repeatedly says to the subject, who is standing upright, with his eyes closed, and whose movements are forwards and backwards: "You are falling, you're falling forward, you're falling forward now, you're falling, you're falling forward now....". While the actual measurement is objective, i.e., the amount of sway forward and backward, there is a good deal of subjectivity about the general arrangement. In one of our studies we had two experimenters, both female; one was rather tall with a loud and imperious voice; the other was small, mousy, and very uncertain and soft in her utterances. With subjects randomly assigned to these two, there was an almost 100 % difference in amount of body-sway in the means of the subjects receiving suggestion from these two experimenters! As might have been expected, the large, loud-voiced experimenter obtained far more body-sway than the small, mousy one.

The problem indicated here is not peculiar to the measurement of suggestibility. We encountered a very similar one in measuring persistence, in particular physical persistence, i.e., the length of time during which an individual was willing to pull a dynamometer at two thirds of maximum pull. The subjects were soldiers, and again we had two female testers. One was an elderly spinster, not very attractive; the other a rather buxom young woman, very pretty. Again there was an almost 100 % difference in the length of time during which subjects of these two women respectively were willing to endure the pain of the persistence experiment, with the soldiers doing their best to impress the pretty one, and not caring at all about the unattractive one.

To return to the measurement of suggestibility, we made an effort to make this more objective by recording the instructions, and this undoubtedly succeeded in reducing some of the subjectivity in the experiment. However, it was noticed that if by chance the subject was swaying slightly forward when the record said: "... you're falling forward *now*", the subject tended to become more suggestible, while if he was swaying backward when the record said: "... you're falling forward *now*" he became less suggestible. In other words, feeling that he was moving in line with the suggestion increased his receptivity, while felt movements in a direction opposite to that indicated by the suggestion had the opposite effect. Thus, chance effects of this kind may affect the objectivity of measurement.

This leads us to the third matter which requires discussion in connection with the measurement of suggestibility, and equally with the measurement of all psychological variables. This may be considered under the concepts of *attitude* and *aptitude*. We assume that people have different aptitudes, probably determined to some degree by genetic causes, and in part by antecedent life experiences, which determine to what extent suggestion can be effective, or hypnotic phenomena be produced. However, in addition to this aptitude we must consider also the attitude of the person to the general testing situation. If the subject is hostile, does not wish to cooperate, disregards instructions etc., he is very difficult to hypnotize, and his reactions to suggestions are much less positive than if he is in a friendly, cooperative mood, with a positive attitude towards the experimenter and the test in general. Gregory Kimble once stated that the results on an experiment on Pavlovian conditioning with humans were determined to the extent of 80 % before the subject ever entered the experimental laboratory! In other words, attitudes determine very largely what the subject's reactions will be, and these attitudes are formed by the behaviour of the experimenter, the general environment of the department and laboratory, what the subject knows about the department, about people who work there, about psychology in general, etc. What is true of Pavlovian conditioning is probably true of many other psychological experiments as well.

Eysenck & Rees (1945) carried out an investigation designed to look at this particular problem. Neurotic patients were used as the experimental subjects, screened by the Body-Sway test to form contrasting groups of high and low susceptibility to hypnosis. Subjects were tested in the normal state, and then in a narcotic state induced by the injection of sodium amytal (similar results were also obtained by using inhalation of nitrous oxide in place of the injected drug). We thought that these drugs would alter the subject's attitude and decrease his ability for conscious resistance to suggestion. In order to test subjects in the drugged condition, their reactions to suggestion were tested by a task they could perform easily in a totally relaxed condition, i.e., the press-release test. In this test, the subject lies on the couch holding a soft rubber bulb in his hand. The experimenter suggests that the subject is squeezing the bulb tighter and tighter, and the actual pressure on the bulb is recorded on a pneumatically controlled recording device.

It was found that in response to suggestion the pressure on the bulb was increased by narcosis for the group which was originally of high suggestibility when screened, but that narcosis did not alter significantly the response of those originally of low suggestibility. The subjects had been instructed to try to resist the effects of the suggestion and to keep their hand pressure constant. We therefore reasoned that the drug was *decreasing* conscious control in both groups, so that what as manifest in the drugged state was the differential degree of *aptitude* between the two groups. The group with high aptitude showed a greatly increased response, but the other group having little natural aptitude, showed little change in response, even when conscious control was decreased by the drug, i.e., when their attitudes were manipulated.

The importance of attitudes in psychological experiments is of course related to the point raised previously, i.e., the influence of specific experimenters, environmental influences, etc. These do not affect aptitude, but they do determine attitude to a very large extent. Many "failures to replicate" in psychological experiments are probably due to failure to control the factors that alter or change attitudes.

One wellknown example in the literature concerns the correlation between Pavlonian conditioning (eye-blink conditioning) and personality (Eysenck, 1981). Eysenck had postulated, and found, that conditioning of the blink response was correlated with introversion, but not with neuroticism; Spence (see Eysenck, 1981) conversely, had postulated and found that eye-blink conditioning was correlated with neuroticism, but not with introversion. Several replications merely confirmed each of the protagonists in his views, and failed to explain the opposite results of the other group of experimenters. Kimble (see Eysenck, 1981) finally solved the puzzle by observing closely the work of the Spence group, and found that their methodology was one which failed to relax the subjects, induced a state of high anxiety in them, and generally capitalized on differences in emotional reactivity. By contrast, the Eysenck group, very much like most experimenters in this field, reassured subjects, tried to ensure a state of relaxation, and attempted to induce a complete absence of fear and anxiety, thus reducing individual differences in neuroticism in so far as they affected the experiment. (For detail, see Eysenck, 1981).

Under the conditions in Spence's laboratory, therefore, the very strong arousal of fear and anxiety would be postulated to swamp any differences in arousal between extraverts and introverts. Hence in his laboratory, neuroticism was highly correlated with "conditioning ability". In the Eysenck type of the experiment, however, neuroticism played no part because instructions and the general arrangement of the experiment reduced differences in emotional reaction to such an extent that they did not interfere with the arousal differences between extraverts and introverts.

Typically, descriptions of experimental arrangements implying the elicitation of differing attitudes are not included in the accounts of experiments. In the case of the Spence-Eysenck debate, for instance, nothing in the published articles could have suggested the solution reached by Kimble by personal inspection of the methodologies used (Eysenck, 1981). It is difficult to discover these influences, or to describe them adequately, but investigators should be aware of their importance, and watch for them.

In the measurement of suggestibility, very much as in the measurement of intelligence and other psychological variables, it is important to discriminate, in any particular test, a portion which is related to the general trait itself, and a proportion which is specific to the test in question. Consider Figure 1, which shows the relationship between different degrees of neuroticism, ranging from normal subjects to highly neurotic subjects, both male and female, as related to degrees of suggestibility as measured by means of the Body-Sway test. For both sexes there is a marked increase in suggestibility with increase in neuroticism, with the normal subjects in each case having the lowest score. This relationship may be due to the differences in attitudes of

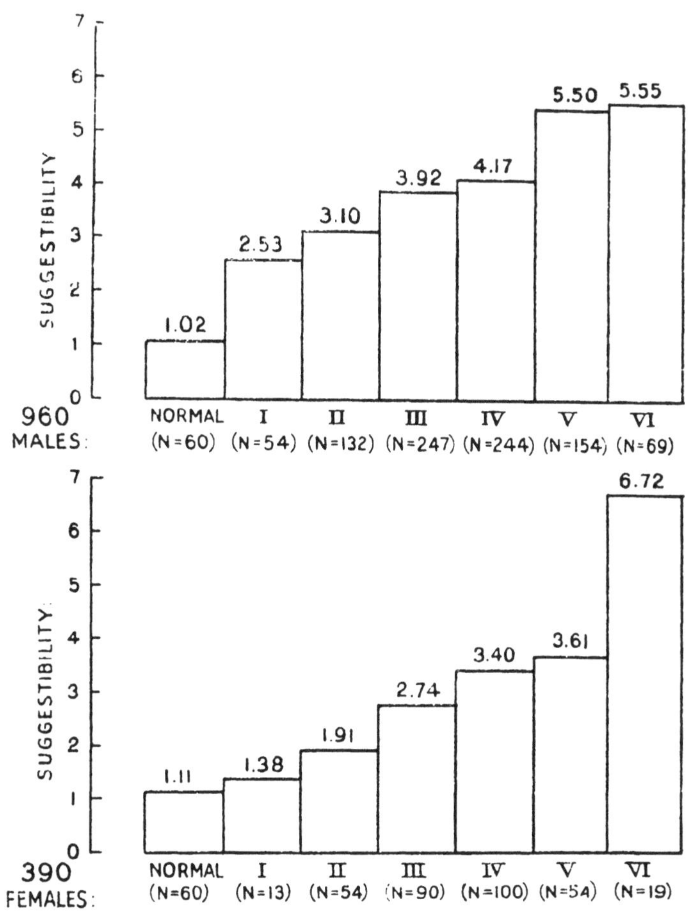

Figure 1. Average suggestibility (Body-Sway test) of normals and neurotics, showing increase of suggestibility with increase in degree of neuroticism. (Eysenck, 1947)

neurotics and normals, and the lack of ability of the neurotic subjects to follow the instruction that they should *resist* the suggestion. Or else it might be due to different aptitudes, although this is unlikely in view of results obtained by other investigators who did not give the instruction to resist suggestion. But what is of particular relevance here is the fact that static ataxia itself (the tendency of people to sway when standing straight up, with their feet together and their eyes closed) was significantly stronger in neurotics than in normals (Eysenck, 1947). Now for the test of body-sway suggestibility, static ataxia is a component of that variance which is *specific* to this test; it will play no part, for instance, in the press-release test used by Eysenck and Rees (1945) or in other measures of ideo-motor action. In trying to correlate primary suggestibility with any other variable, such as neuroticism, or hypnotizability, or whatever, it would be advisable to use a battery of tests, so that the general aspects of each individual test relevant to the trait combine, and the specificity of the elements are eliminated. This is an important recommendation which should be followed in all measures of traits or abilities.

If there is an aptitude involved in primary suggestibility, as seems certain, and if this aptitude is to some degree determined by genetic factors, then one would expect some correlation with personality. Such correlations as have been reported between primary suggestibility and the major dimensions of personality, namely extraversion and neuroticism, have not been very positive (e.g., Furneaux, 1961). Accepting the absence of direct relationships, Furneaux advocated the use of "zone analysis", i.e. the simultaneous taking into account of both dimensions of personality.

Furneaux put forward the following hypothesis, which is illustrated in Figure 2. On the basis of the Yerkes-Dodson law, he argued that a *curvilinear* relationship between Drive and Performance on the body-sway test would be expected. Following the theories of Hull and Spence, he regarded neuroticism (N) as a direct measure of drive, but he argued also that we must bear in mind the differing motivations which are produced in extraverts and introverts by identical stimuli (Eysenck, 1967). As Furneaux points out: "it is entirely consistent with the known characteristic of the extravert to assert that he has a strong and continued set to attend to stimuli associated with the activities of other people, and that the situations which lead him to enter states of high drive are predominantly interpersonal in character" (Furneaux, 1961, p. 197). This combination of high N and production of strong drive in extraverts through the interpersonal relations involved in tests of suggestibility would put the neurotic extravert beyond the optimal level of drive, and thus make him little suggestible. Similarly, the stable introvert, being low in drive and not motivated highly by interpersonal stimuli, would be below the optimal level of drive. Stable extraverts and neurotic introverts would according to the same argument be expected to demonstrate intermediate drive, and consequently, high body-sway. These results have indeed been found empirically by Furneaux (1961), and the relations discovered in his original paper have been dpulicated since in an unpublished study by Lindahl (1964). Furneaux & Gibson (1961) also have observed similar results in a procedure of hypnotic testing. Hilgard & Bentler (1963) failed to reproduce these results, but their work has been criticized by Furneaux (1963).

Work on this hypothesis was more recently taken up by Curran and Gibson (1974) and Gibson and Corcoran (1975). In presenting their data, they made use of a suggestion by Eysenck (1966) that the results of "zone analysis" might best be illustrated in terms of *polar coordinates*, rather than Cartesian coordinates, which are used almost universally. Figure 3 illustrates the difference

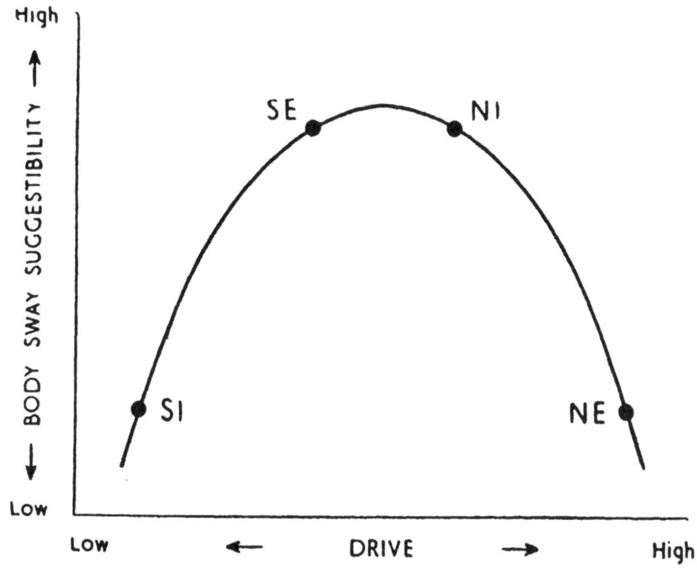

Figure 2. Relation between drive and body-sway suggestibility according to Furneaux (1961; 1963).
SE, stable extraverts; *SI*, stable introverts; *NI*, neurotic introverts; *NE*, neurotic extraverts

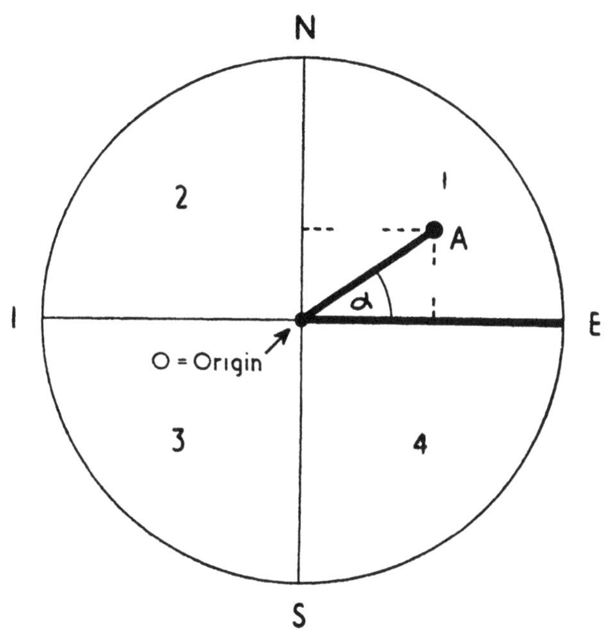

Figure 3. Difference between definitions of position of Subject A in two-dimensional factor space according to variously Cartesian and Polar Coordinates (Eysenck, 1966).
N-S, neuroticism-stability axis; *E-I*, extraversion-introversion axis; for explanation of *angle alpha* and *vector O-A*, see text

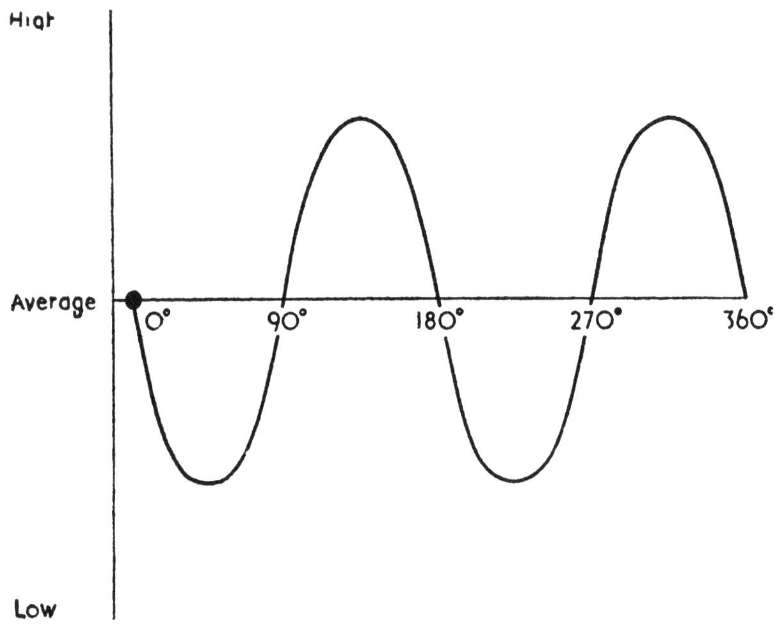

Figure 4. Application of the principle of polar coordinates to theory shown in Figure 2 (Eysenck, 1966)

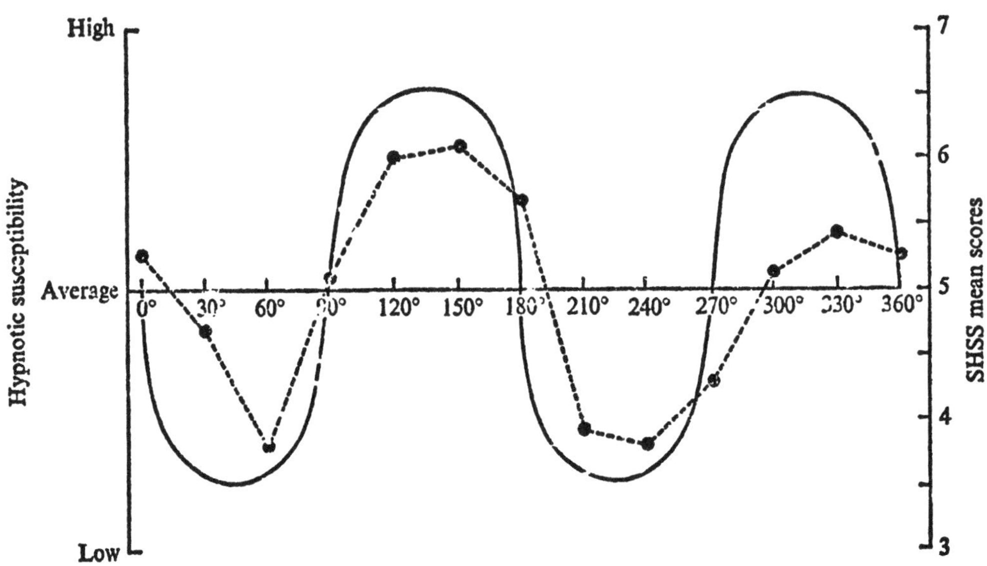

Figure 5. Polar coordinates; hypnotizability scores related to theoretical curve shown in Figure 4 (Gibson & Corcoran, 1975)

between these two methods, which are of course mathematically inter-convertible. The position of subject A is normally shown in the two-dimensional space generated by the two variables of personality, the one of neuroticism and stability (N-S) and the other of extraversion and introversion (E-I), this in terms of the projections of his position on the two coordinates, as shown by the broken lines. This subject would be in the first zone, represented here as quadrant 1. Using polar coordinates we should characterize his position by the angle alpha within the first quadrant and the radius vector of the line O-A. Given such a system, we could plot results such as those reported by Furneaux as in Figure 4, where the ordinate shows degree of suggestibility and the abscissa the angle alpha from 0° to 360°. The regular wave-form of the suggestibility scores clearly indicates the relationship obtained in a manner which would easily be duplicated by Cartesian analysis.

Figure 5 shows the results of the two experiments carried out by Gibson and his colleagues. The broken lines show the actual empirical results, whereas the full lines indicate the theoretical prediction. It will be seen that there is close agreement between prediction and experimental results, and it is clear that we do find considerable support for Furneaux's hypothesis. The actual correlation between personality and body-sway suggestibility is 0.39 which, when corrected for attenuation, rises to about 0.50. This is by no means a negligible relationship, which suggests that personality does to some degree determine primary suggestibility in the manner suggested by Furneaux.

In the past, that study of suggestibility and hypnosis has usually been a rather specialized field, having little relation to traditional theories in general psychology. Furneaux's appeal to the concept of arousal in explaining the existence of individual differences is an exception. Is it possible to suggest other relationships that might be of value ? An obvious relationship that has been studied amply in experimental psychology is the direct outcome of the old theory of "ideo-motor action", i.e., the idea that motor activity is initiated by and directly consequential upon the idea or image of such an action. Jacobson (1929) originated a whole series of studies in which subjects were asked to imagine motor movements, such as sweeping the floor, where measurements were being made of the excitation of the motor neurons involved in the particular muscular activity that was imagined. What was found was an almost one-to-one correspondence between the two. In other words, when a person imagined that he was sweeping the floor, rhythmic innervations of the arm muscles that would be involved in such movements were observed. Thus the fundamental idea of ideo-motor action has found considerable experimental support. The idea or image of movement is accompanied invariably by muscular innervation of a kind which would lead to the movement imagined if the innervation were stronger than that actually observed.

It is sometimes objected by behaviourists of the more narrow type that imagery is not a behaviour in the strict sense, and hence should not form part of any theoretical structure. This is not a reasonable objection. Concepts are admissible where the antecedent and consequent events can be specified in behavioural terms, and this is true in the case of imagery (Eysenck, 1982). The experimenter can tell a male subject to imagine a sexually explicit scene (stimulus), and observe and measure the resulting penile erection (response). It has been shown several times that when subjects practiced in their imagination throwing darts, or other physical skills, this "practice" improves their performance as much as does actucal physical practice. Thus, there is a great deal of objective evidence for the psychological meaningfulness of "imagery", and hence there is no reason for refusing to use the concept in our explanation of ideo-motor action.

However, even with a tenable hypothesis regarding differences of personality, and some experimentally verified data concerning ideo-motor action, there has been little effort to produce a theory of primary suggestibility and hypnosis which would explain the phenomena observed, and then link them with traditional psychological concepts. It cannot be the purpose of this introductory chapter to advance such a theory, but it would seem that the only likely candidate is one involving Pavlovian conditioning. There are many phenomena comprising conditioning, particularly interoceptive conditioning (Bykov, 1957). Those conditioning phenomena described by Bykov that concern the internal organs bear a striking similarity to some of the more inexplicable results of hypnotic suggestion.

The link between conditioning and primary suggestibility is of course Pavlov's "second signalling system", i.e., the use of words as conditioned stimuli and conditioned responses. Pavlov explicitly acknowledged this important extension in the case of humans of the general laws of conditioning, that are applicable to animals, and from the early days of Platonov (1959) to Staats (1964; 1968), this line of research has been pursued with some vigour, although unfortunately it has not extended to the investigation of verbal conditioning as basic to the phenomena of primary suggestibility. It is suggested that a combination of theories involving conditioning through Pavlov's second signalling system, ideo-motor activity instigated by mental images, and differences of personality along the lines suggested by Furneaux constitute the beginnings of a system of interpretation of hypnotic phenomena, and of primary suggestibility; this combination might be capable of extension and improvement, and ultimately lead us to a proper theoretical understanding of these odd, unusual, and at present inexplicable phenomena.

References

Barber, T.X. (1984). Changing "unchangeable" bodily processes by (hypnotic) suggestions: A new look at hypnosis, cognitions, imagining, and the mind-body problem. In A.A. Sheikh, *Imagination and Healing* (pp. 69-127). Farmingdale, NY: Baywood.

Beecher, H.K. (1959). *Measurement of Subjective Responses*. New York: Oxford University.

Bloch, B. (1927). Über die Heilung der Warzen durch Suggestion. *Klinische Wochenschrift*, *6*, 2271-2275, 2320-2325.

Bykov, K.M. (1957). *The cerebral cortex and the internal organs.* New York: Chemical Publishing.

Curran, J.D., & Gibson, H.B. (1974). Critique of the Stanford Hypnotic Susceptibility Scale: British usage and factorial structure. *Perceptual and Motor Skills*, *39*, 695-704.

Eysenck, H.J. (1943). Suggestibility and hypnosis. *Journal of Neurology and Psychiatry*, *6*, 22-31.

Eysenck, H.J. (1947). *Dimensions of Personality*. London: Routledge & Kegan Paul.

Eysenck, H.J. (1966). Personality and experimental psychology. *Bulletin of The British Psychological Society*, *19*, 1-28.

Eysenck, H.J. (1967). *The biological basis of personality.* Springfield, IL: C.C. Thomas.

Eysenck, H.J. (Ed.) (1981). *A Model for Personality.* New York Berlin Heidelberg Tokyo: Springer.

Eysenck, H.J. (1982). Whose is this image and superscription ? *Journal of Mental Imagery*, *6* (2), 30-32.

Eysenck, H.J. & Furneaux, W.D. (1945). Primary and secondary suggestibility: an experimental and statistical study. *Journal of Experimental Psychology*, *35*, 485-503.

Eysenck, H.J. & Rees, W.L. (1945). States of heightened suggestibility: narcosis. *Journal of Mental Science*, *91*, 301-310.

Furneaux, W.D. (1961). Neuroticism, extraversion, drive and suggestibility. *International Journal of Clinical and Experimental Hypnosis, 9*, 195-214.

Furneaux, W.D. (1963). Neuroticism, extraversion and suggestibility: a comment. *International Journal of Clinical and Experimental Hypnosis, 11,* 201-208.

Furneaux, W.D., & Gibson, H.B. (1961). The Maudsley Personality Inventory as a predictor of susceptibility to hypnosis. *International Journal of Clinical and Experimental Hypnosis, 9,* 167-177.

Gibson, H.B., & Corcoran, M.E. (1975). Personality and differential susceptibility to hypnosis: further replication and sex differences. *British Journal of Psychology, 66,* 513-520.

Haniotes, C.J. (1977). Hypnosis and breast enlargement - a pilot study. *Journal of the International Society of Professional Hypnosis, 6,* 8-12.

Hilgard, E.R., & Bentler, P.M. (1963). Predicting hypnotizability from the Maudsley Personality Inventory. *British Journal of Psychology, 54*, 63-69.

Ikemi, Y. & Nakagawa, S. (1962). A psychosomatic study of Contagious Dermatitis. *Kyushu Journal of Medical Science, 13,* 335-352.

Jacobson, E. (1929). *Progressive Relaxation.* Chicago: University of Chicago.

LeCron, L.M. (1969). Breast development through hypnotic suggestions. *Journal of the American Society of Psychosomatic Dentistry and Medicine, 16,* 58-61.

Platonov, K. (1959). *The Word as a Physiological and Therapeutic Factor.* Moscow: Foreign Languages Publishing House.

Prioleau, L., Murdock, M., & Brody, N. (1983). An analysis of psychotherapy vs. placebo studies. *Behavioural & Brain Sciences, 6,* 275-285.

Smith, M.L., Glass, G.V., & Miller, T.I. (1980). *The Benefits of Psychotherapy.* Baltimore: Johns Hopkins University.

Staats, A.W. (Ed.) (1964). *Human Learning.* London: Holt, Rinehart & Winston.

Staats, A.W. (1968). *Learning, Language and Cognition.* London: Holt, Rinehart & Winston.

Staib, A.R. & Logan D.R. (1977). Hypnotic stimulation of breast growth. *American Journal of Clinical Hypnosis, 19,* 201-208.

Willard, R.D: (1977). Breast enlargement through visual imagery and hypnosis. *American Journal of Clinical Hypnosis, 19,* 195-200.

Williams, E. (1974). Stimulated breast growth by hypnosis. *Journal of Sex Research, 10*, 316-326.

3. Conceptual Clarification of Hypnosis and Its Relationship to Suggestibility

W.E. EDMONSTON

"I had several times heard those effects of mine, which one wished to deny, attributed in a vague manner to imagination, but it was new for me to hear acknowledged effects, such as I had just produced for them, attributed to imagination" (Mesmer, 1781, p. 142). The speaker was Franz Anton Mesmer; the time, the late 1770s; the occasion, Mesmer's reply to his rebuff by the French Royal Academy of Sciences, then headed by Jean-Baptiste Le Roy.

But, as we know, Mesmer's rebuffs did not end there, for in 1784 the commission appointed by the French government reached a similar conclusion, that "the ... effects observed in patients under public treatment are due ... to the excitement of the imagination ..." (Hull, 1933, p. 8). Why was it so important to Mesmer that his work not be seen as "due to the power of imagination"? It was obvious to all who observed that the imaginations of his patients were affected. What was his point? It was simply this, that the observed effects were initiated, not by internal forces within the subject, but by a powerful, external life-force which he imparted to the patient. He fancied himself far more of a physicist than a physician. If imagination played a role, it was through the condition and influence of animal magnetism. It was not imagination alone, but the germination of imaginative forces in the context of the fertile soil of magnetism.

For what is imagination but the internal representation of sense perceptions past, present, or future? It is the central nervous system's template of sensory sensation, that is not present at the time of the imagination, of internal images, *sans* their appropriate external stimuli. Imagination, then, is the result of deception, either from within, as in a self-initiated fantasy, or from without, as in suggestions from outside the self. In either, an illusion is created, one that distorts stimuli already present or one that creates the effects of stimuli not present.

We are faced then with several questions. First and foremost is: Where does suggestion have its effect? As we will see, the solution to that question will lead us to consider the relationship between suggestion and hypnosis. To understand this relationship, we will need to explore briefly both the fundamental basis of hypnosis and the behavioral and subjective characteristics of hypnosis. Finally, I will suggest ways in which the behavorial and subjective markers of hypnosis and its fundamental basis - relaxation - interact to account for its relationship to suggestibility.

But first the primary question: Where then does suggestion have its effect? Certainly it is not on the senses themselves, for so far as the peripheral nervous system is concerned the stimuli are either there or not; the messages moving centrally continue regardless of suggestions for increased sensation, decreased sensation or distortion of sensation. It is in the central nervous system that suggestion has its major influence.

William Jàmes noted that suggestion is a directive which informs the senses to distort or change the interpretation of the sensed stimuli (James, 1981). Suggestion, therefore, misleads the senses, but the illusion thus created is "... not a fallacy of the senses proper, but rather of the intellect, which interprets wrongly what the senses give" (James, 1984, p. 278). And, these illusions created by suggestion are but fragile facsimiles of the real world, for once the real source or nature of the stimulation is known or appreciated the illusion is gone, the suggestion impotent.

Suggestion, then, is the central distortion of incoming sensory impulses, and what has been noted briefly above are two types of suggestion - autosuggestion and heterosuggestion. The former, of course, is imposed on the individual by him- or herself and the latter imposed from without, usually by another individual, i.e., there is a social interaction. One of the best-known proponents of autosuggestion in this century was Emile Coué (1923), whose ritualistic phrase "Day by day, in every way, I am getting better and better" embodied the major principle of his New Nancy School. Coué believed strongly that therapeutic effectiveness came not from the practitioner, but from the patient, through autosuggestion. These autosuggestive therapeutics operated out of the patient's awareness - a notion we encounter today in the works of Spanos (1986) and other social psychologists who are investigating *anesis* (what is usually called hypnosis). The heavy reliance on "out of awareness," "unconscious" terminology bears a striking resemblance to the principles taught in the 1950s and 1960s by Milton Erickson and his followers. Many of the Ericksonian techniques are little more than a modern restatement of Coué's New Nancy School, which, in turn, owed a heavy debt to the earlier methods of Lièbault (Edmonston, 1986a).

Although most suggestions are stated verbally, some can be nonverbal, as with gestures, nods of the head, inflections of voice, and so forth. Through the years of investigation of suggestive phenomena, an elaborate scheme of classification of suggestion has been developed, which Weitzenhoffer (1953) has summarized. Although Hull (1933) made prestige suggestion - the effectiveness of which depends upon the difference in social, political, academic or other status between the individual receiving the suggestion and the issuer of the suggestion - central to his definition of hypnosis as "a state of relatively heightened susceptibility to prestige suggestion" (p. 391), few others have embraced the concept. Eysenck (1947), for example, spoke of a "tertiary suggestibility" which was related to the prestige of the suggester, but Weitzenhoffer (1953, p. 25) objected to the classification because it did not "... give a unique characterization of suggestions." Eysenck and Furneaux's work (1945) empirically supported two types of suggestion: primary and secondary, the former highly correlated with hypnotizability and consisting of ideo-motor type tasks, and the latter consisting of indirect suggestions - suggestions in which the exact nature of the desired result is not explicit - which *do not correlate with hypnotizability*.

Thus we come to a most important dichotomy of suggestion classification: direct and indirect. This classification refers to the format of the individual suggestion. In direct suggestion, the result or response to the suggestion is stated clearly. A command, for example, has been proposed as an extreme type of direct suggestion. However, as should be apparent from the definition above of suggestion, a direct suggestion requires a distorted interpretation of sensory input; such is not necessarily the case with a command. Conversely, indirect suggestion does not make explicit the response expected, but leaves the result of suggestion to the subject or patient.

What makes this dichotomy of direct and indirect suggestion of particular interest is its relationship to hypnosis and hypnotizability. Eysenck and Furneaux (1945) showed that there was little or no correlation between the results of their secondary suggestion tests (Ink Blots, Odor, Weights) and hypnotizability. They characterized these secondary suggestions as "of the indirection kind." There is a difference between the kind of suggestion that is more or less successful during hypnosis and the kind given effectually without hypnosis. Exactly what this difference is is not readily apparent however (Stone & Lundy, 1985), for it was originally thought that "The suggestibility of waking persons follows an opposite law to that of hypnotic subjects. Suggestions must be *veiled* in the former case to be effective; in the latter case, the more direct and open they are the better" (James, 1983, p. 326).

Thus wrote William James in his introduction to Boris Sidis's book of 1898 titled *The Psychology of Suggestion.* Sidis was a Russian-born student and friend of William James, having studies with James at Harvard from 1892 to 1897, when he received his doctorate. His book came directly to grips with the differentiation of ordinary - Sidis called it "normal" - suggestion and suggestion taking place in the condition of hypnosis - which he termed "abnormal" suggestion. Sidis felt that it is "Not sociality, not rationality, but suggestibility (that) characterizes the average specimen of humanity, for *man is a suggestible animal*" (Sidis, 1898, p. 17).

That this suggestibility should take two major forms was testable, and he proceeded, through a series of experimental studies, to attempt to demonstrate the veridicality of James's statement. Using letters, numbers, and small squares he instructed subjects to recall or select a letter, number or square after the subjects had viewed a series of like objects. The experimental stimuli were arranged in ways that either directly or indirectly suggested which of the group should be selected. From these tests he proposed the following conditions of "normal" suggestibility: (a) Fixation of attention, (b) Distraction of attention, (c) Monotony, (d) Limitation of voluntary movements, (e) Limitation of the field of consciousness, (f) Inhibition, and (g) Immediate execution.

Unfortunately, Sidis did not administer the same tasks to his subjects while they were hypnotized, but instead developed a list of the conditions of "abnormal" suggestibility, of which hypnosis is the primary example, from the writings of Bernheim, Lièbault, Forel, and others. The list is identical with that for "normal" suggestibility with two exceptions: distraction of attention and immediate execution are not conditions underlying "abnormal" suggestibility. (A comparison of the two lists appears in Table 1). Sidis (1898) defined hypnosis both physiologically and psychologically. In the former, he anticipated Pavlov: "hypnosis is an inhibition of the inhibitory

Table 1. Conditions of "normal" and "abnormal" suggestibility

"Normal" Suggestibility	"Abnormal" Suggestibility
1. Fixation of attention	1. Fixation of attention
2. Monotony	2. Monotony
3. Limitation of voluntary movements	3. Limitation of voluntary movements
4. Limitation of the field of consciousness	4. Limitation of the field of consciousness
5. Inhibition	5. Inhibition
6. Distraction of attention	
7. Immediate execution	

Note. From Sidis (1898).

centres ...; a disaggregation of the superior from the inferior centres" (pp. 69-70). In the latter he anticipated Janet, and also Hilgard: "Dissociation is the secret of hypnosis" (p. 71). Finally, Sidis made a distinction to which I shall return later. He noted that if hypnosis is incomplete, then it is accompanied with more or less memory retention for the events which occured between induction and the termination of the condition. If, however, amnesia ocurs, the hypnosis was complete. "Amnesia is the boundary that separates (the two)" (p. 71).

How valid, then, is the James-Sidis proposal that there are two types of suggestion and suggestibility, that which occurs normally and that which occurs in hypnosis; or, in Eysenck's classification, secondary and primary? As early as 1967, Evans reviewed the literature on suggestibility in the normal waking state and concluded that: "... the old classification by Eysenck and Furneaux of 'primary' and 'secondary' suggestibility cannot be justified ... from (either) the original data presented to support it, (or) from subsequent research" (p. 127). He, in fact, suggested three types of suggestibility: Primary (passive motor responses), challenge (responses to direct "you cannot" commands), and imagery (responses to suggestions of sensory distortion).

However, recent studies have presented mixed results concerning the original classifications by James and Sidis. Stukat (1958) confirmed Eysenck's primary suggestibility, but left secondary and tertiary without firm confirmation. Duke (1964), reviewing 50 years of studies attempting to correlate tests of suggestibility and hypnotizability, found a functional independence of primary and secondary measures, the former correlating with hypnosis at 0.59. Moore (1964) also showed a general independence of hypnosis from other measures of suggestibility, with the possible exception of a test of influencibility involving "false peer group feedback" as the method of suggestion. Bodily sway, arm rigidity, hands moving together and amnesia - all tests of primary suggestibility in Eysenck's classification - were correlated highly with the total Stanford Hypnotic Susceptibility Scale. (The correlation with the amnesia sub-test was 0.85, a point to be kept in mind.) Wallace, Garrett, and Anstadt (1974), conversely, found a relationship between scores on the Harvard Group Scale of Hypnotic Susceptibility (Shor & Orne, 1962) and some measures (latency and number of changes) of the autokinetic effect. More recently, Miller (1980) showed that scores on a Suggested Syllables test paralleled those on the harvard Scale, but the author drew back from suggesting that suggestibility was an unidimensional trait. Most recently, Stone and Lundy (1985) confirmed that the two types of suggestion - direct and indirect - are differentially effective, depending upon the condition of the subject. However, these authors found, William James to the contrary, that indirect suggestions of the type described by Erickson had their greatest effect during hypnosis, rather than during a non-hypnotic period.

But while the exact nature of the relationship between direct and indirect suggestion and hypnosis remains unclear, it is readily apparent that "hypnosis" and "suggestion" are not synonymous terms. This was essentially Mesmer's point - animal magnetism and imagination (suggestion) were not the same. There is little doubt that imagination or suggestion can function more freely during the condition that Mesmer called *animal magnetism*, Braid (1855) re-named *hypnosis* and which more recently I have termed *anesis* (Edmonston, 1981). The monumental work of Hull and his students clearly demonstrated that during hypnosis there was a *quantitative* increase in response to suggestion. For Hull, the linch-pin of hypnosis was hypersuggestibility. "The only thing which seems to characterize hypnosis as such and which gives any justification for the practice of calling it a 'state' is its generalized hypersuggestibility. The difference between the hypnotic state and the normal is, therefore, a quantitative rather than a qualitative one" (Hull, 1933, p. 391).

Not only did Hull quote the visionaries of the past, such as Braid, Bramwell, Binet, Forel, and Wingfield, to justify this perception of hypnosis, but he did something few before him had dared; namely, he and his students developed experimental, laboratory evaluations of the nature of changes in suggestibility that occur during hypnosis. Hull and Huse (1930), Williams (1930), Caster and Baker (1932), and others all showed that responses to the Body-Sway test - that premier test of primary suggestibility - were significantly faster during hypnosis. Even the decay-rates of this hypersuggestibility (Krueger, 1931) suggested hypnosis as a condition different from the usual background upon which suggestions are imposed.

Although suggestion may be a route for establishing the condition of hypnosis, we should agree that hypnosis is not suggestion and suggestion is not hypnosis, and that to study one is not necessarily to study the other. "... It must be remembered that what *needs* explanation here is the fact that in a certain condition of the subject suggestions operate as they do *at no other time*" (James, 1981, p. 1201). I have already indicated that suggestion is the central distortion of incoming sensory impulses. What condition, then, maximizes, facilitates the hyper-response to suggestion that we see in hypnosis? What condition of the human organism is described by monotony, a limitation of voluntary movements, a limitation of the field of consciousness (the Freudians may call it a withdrawal of the ego), and inhibition?

"Inhibition" here is the key word. It is the keystone of Pavlov's notions on sleep, and hence his ideas on hypnosis as irradiated cortical inhibition, as well as the condition most often, historically, associated with hypnosis. I have outlined the history of this symbiosis elsewhere in great detail (Edmonston, 1981), and have opined that the fundamental basis of hypnosis is relaxation. But, as I pointed out in the book *Hypnosis and Relaxation* (Edmonston, 1981), the equation of hypnosis and relaxation does not rest upon historical precedent alone. It rests firmly upon both the experimental and the clinical literature as well. Both affirm that when subjects or patients are presented with non-hypnotically identified instructions to relax, the resulting changes in response do not differ from those elicited by the more traditional hypnotic induction techniques. The more recent literature on clinical applications of relaxation and the physiology of relaxation attests to this point.

The relief of pain, of course, has been a favorite objective of those practitioners applying relaxation to human miseries. As with the hypnosis studies of pain, the cold pressor test has been one of the laboratory models of relaxation studies. Mills and Farrow (1981), for example, found that the process of relaxation in Transcendental Meditation reduced significantly the incidence of verbal reports of distress from cold pressor. Holmes, Hekmat, and Mozingo (1983) also reported reduced subjective pain in the same situation (cold pressor); the same has been demonstrated in a test of ischemic pain. Cogan and Kluthe (1981) found 20 minutes of Lazarus's relaxation training superior to patterned breathing of finger-tapping distraction for raising the threshold of pain, while Wadden and de la Torre (1980) found that relaxation, in combination with medical treatment, resulted in significantly greater reductions in systolic and diastolic blood pressure (BP) than those resulting from medical treatment alone.

Most of the non-therapeutic work has centered on the physiology of relaxation. Christoph, Luborsky, Kron, and Fishman (1978) found reduced respiration and heart rates as a consequence of relaxation, but no change in BP levels. Conversely, Agras, Southam, and Taylor (1983) showed a stable decrease in diastolic BP after 15 months of relaxation practice. At least one study (Pollack and Zeiner, 1979) yielded no significant differences in heart rate, respiration rate, finger pulse, and skin conductance among groups under conditions of experimental relaxation, uninstructed relaxation, and sitting quietly. Puente (1981), too, found that neither transcendental meditation (short or long term) nor Benson's relaxation response were superior for reducing tonic arousal as measured by respiration rate, heart rate, EMG, EEG, and skin conductance, although individual measures (e.g. respiration rate, heart rate) did reflect the effects of relaxation. Skin conductance, however, was studied also by West (1979), who found that subjects who had been meditating regularly for 6 months had significantly lower skin conductance and numbers of spontaneous changes in conductance. When one considers the differences in methodologies among these studies, there remains a common thread of trophotropic physiology exemplified by reduced heart rate, skin conductance levels and spontaneous changes, and, most importantly, respiration rate. This latter response has been the most consistent index of relaxation reported in the studies of physiological responses in relaxation.

A number of investigators have been looking into the biochemical changes accompanying relaxation. Since a tonic or phasic biochemical response can either reflect the present state of the organism or indicate a compensatory effort of the endocrine or metabolic system elicited to counteract large deviations from homeostatic balance, such biochemical changes may be better observed through a stress probe. For example, Hoffman et al. (1982) recently reported an increase in norepinephrine plasma levels with 30 days' practice (twice for 20 min.) of Transcendental Meditation (TM) in response to orthostatic and isometric muscular stress. The significantly higher increase of plasma norepinephrine in the TM group (compared to a control group) was interpreted as a higher effort of the sympathetic system required to counteract orthostatic stress and to perform isometric muscular work following the elicitation of the relaxation response.

The parasympathetic mode of the autonomic system in deep relaxation as described before for the cardiovascular system in many studies may be found reflected on the biochemical level by an increase in the translucency of saliva and in a decrease in levels of saliva protein as observed by Morse et al. (1982) during relaxation. Kralik, Ho, Mathew, and Claghorn (1983) also found that 4 weeks of relaxation therapy changed not only the cognitive perception of chronically anxious subjects, but platelet monoamine oxidase (MAO) as well.

Somewhat earlier, Jevning, Prikle, and Wilson (1977) measured 13 neutral and acidic amino acids in the plasma of 28 young adults during Transcendental Meditation. The concentrations of plasma amino acids were all stable except of phenylalanine, which showed a significant increase during the actual 20-minute period of Transcendental Meditation in well-practiced (3-5 years) individuals. In fact, the new practice of Transcendental Meditation for periods of only 3-4 months yielded an increase in the phenylalanine concentration. Why plasma phenylalanine? One explanation offered by the authors is that phenylalanine, apart from being required for protein synthesis, is the precursor of tyrosine which is hydroxylated to norepinephrine. Reduced turnover of norepinephrine in the brain during relaxation, then, would result in higher levels of the precursor, phenylalanine, left circulating in the peripheral blood, indicating a reduced state of activity in the brain.

Preliminary EEG data from my laboratory project suggest just that - a deactivation pattern, rather than a specific activation in the right hemisphere, as others have proposed (e.g., Morgan, MacDonald, & Hilgard, 1974). In addition, the relationship of phenylalanine to various stages of sleep makes such an hypothesis even more possible and would weigh heavily in favor of a modernization of Pavlov's contention that hypnosis (relaxation, *anesis*) is marked by cortical inhibition. Could it be, then, that the fundamental nature of hypnosis-relaxation-accounts for the differences between Sidis's "normal" and "abnormal" suggestibility?

Unfortunately, the literature does not help us specifically, because the hypersuggestibility potential of non-hypnotically defined relaxation techniques has yet to be evaluated. What I have demonstrated is that the fundamental basis of what we persist in calling hypnosis is relaxation. The literature on the clinical, the physiological, the behavioral and the subjective aspects of hypnosis all attest to that conclusion.

Before this century, two phenomena were associated with hypnosis, "nonvoluntariness" and spontaneous amnesia. (Remember that Sidis concluded that the presence or absence of amnesia - spontaneous, not suggested - drew the line between complete and incomplete hypnosis.) The Stanford Scales and their many, many offspring do not take these historical bases of traditional description of hypnosis sufficiently into account (Weitzenhoffer, 1980). This lack on the part of these scales is critical to investigations into hypnosis because the Stanford Scales are the usual criteria by which subjects are chosen for experimental study. As a consequence, modern investigators of hypnosis run the risk of being less concerned with hypnosis as it has come to us historically and more concerned with socially facilitated suggestibility. We would do well to remember that the observational powers of our colleagues from the past were no less astute than our own.

Regarding amnesia, it was Braid (1855) who pointed out that there are two types of amnesia that accompany hypnosis, one accessible by rehypnotizing the subject, the other absolute and irretrievable. Both occur *spontaneously*. But we no longer report spontaneous amnesias in our studies. Almost all the present studies of amnesic phenomena involve the exploration of *suggested* amnesia, not spontaneous amnesia. Reversible, nonsuggested amnesias are rarely reported and nonreversible amnesias are nonexistent in the experimental literature (appearing only rarely in the clinical literature, and then usually during discussions of somnambulism or plenary trance). Today we study the phenomena of "social suggestibility", not hypnosis as Braid conceived the term. Little wonder that we apply social or dissociational explanations to the results of our investigations! We are ignoring the fundamental behavioral markers of hypnosis - nonvoluntariness and spontaneous amnesia - and studying social suggestion instead.

I have already proposed that suggestion and hypnosis are not synonymous terms, hypnosis being a condition - of relaxation, we now know - in which suggestibility is enhanced. Thus, in this century we have added a third phenomenon characteristic of hypnosis, namely hypersuggestibility. And unless we are willing in our future investigations to make (a) assessments of the changes between pre- and post-induction suggestibility *and* (b) post-hypnotic assessments of the degree of perceived subjective nonvoluntariness and extent of spontaneous amnesia occurring, we may not be measuring anything akin to traditional hypnosis, but rather a social interaction that we call suggestion and suggestibility. Spontaneous amnesia, as seen in hypnosis, is not a phenomenon that is concomitant with suggestion and suggestibility.

Finally, let us consider these three indicators (nonvoluntariness, amnesia, and hypersuggestibility) in the context of relaxation. Relaxation enhances the subjective experience of nonvoluntariness through the incompatibility of the experiences of voluntariness and relaxation. Voluntariness is perceived as an active, self-directed process, whereas relaxation is perceived as, and is, inactive and passive. Hypnosis (relaxation) tempers the experience of voluntary control and action.

It is similar with the phenomenon of amnesia, because recall is an active process, while true hypnosis (relaxation) and its attendant phenomena are passive. Passivity and active recall are incompatible, and, in the case of spontaneous hypnotic amnesia (not suggested amnesia), "absolutely incompatible with the active recall of what has occurred during the hypnotic condition" (Edmonston, 1986b, p. 471).

Hypersuggestibility, too, is enhanced by the relaxation inherent in hypnosis. Remember that suggestion misleads the senses through a disruption of central interpreting mechanisms. If Pavlov's theorizing and the studies noted above are correct, the cortical inhibition attendant to hypnosis will do just that. The disinhibition of the lower centers enhances the potential for sensory misinterpretation through the verbal suggestions reaching the "rapport zones," to use the Pavlovian concept. Alertness - specifically cortical alertness - enhances and sharpens the senses, concentrates the organism on anticipated action, tips the sympathetic/parasympathetic balance to the former, and elicits the ergotropic response. By and large, activity reduces the effectiveness of suggestion, whereas the vegetative, trophotropic response - relaxation, hypnosis, *anesis* - lays the groundwork for enhancing the effectiveness of suggestion.

What I have attempted to demonstrate, then, is: first, suggestion and hypnosis are not the same thing, but rather that the former (suggestion) is enhanced by the latter (hypnosis); second, that relaxation is the fundamental basis of hypnosis, which, thirdly, can account for both the behavioral and subjective markers of hypnosis and the relationship between suggestion and hypnosis.

Those of us working within the field of hypnosis must return to basics and study, not the social psychology of suggestibility or the dissociated self, but the historically defined condition of hypnosis and its *spontaneous*, unsuggested phenomena. We need to know that hypnosis has, in fact, occured before we discuss differences between "normal" suggestibility and "abnormal" suggestibility. We certainly need to know, that relaxation *is* the basic condition that leads to hypersuggestibility. We need to know the central nervous system mechanisms that lead to hypersuggestibility, spontaneous amnesias, the subjective experience of nonvoluntariness, and the misinterpretation of sensory input that we call suggestion.

References

Agras, W.S., Southam, M.A., & Taylor, C.B. (1983). Longterm persistence of relaxation-induced blood pressure lowering during the working day. *Journal of Consulting & Clinical Psychology, 51*, 792-794.

Braid, J. (1855/1970). *The physiology of fascination and the critics criticised.* In M.M. Tinterow (Ed.), *Foundations of hypnosis from Mesmer to Freud* (pp. 365-389). Springfield, IL: Charles C Thomas. (Original published Manchester, Eng.: Grant; 1855).

Caster, J.E., & Baker, C.S., Jr. (1932). Comparative suggestibility in the trance and waking states - A further study. *Journal of General Psychology, 7*, 287-301.

Christoph, P., Luborsky, L., Kron, R., & Fishman, H. (1978). Blood pressure, heart rate and respiratory responses to a single session of relaxation: A partial replication. *Journal of Psychosomatic Research, 22*, 493-501.

Cogan, R., & Kluthe, K.B. (1981). The role of learning in pain reduction associated with relaxation and patterned breathing. *Journal of Psychosomatic Research, 25*, 535-539.

Coué, E. (1923). *My method, including American impressions.* Garden City, NY: Doubleday.

Duke, J.D. (1964). Intercorrelational status of suggestibility tests and hypnotizability. *Psychological Record, 14*, 71-80.

Edmonston, W.E., Jr. (1981). *Hypnosis and relaxation: Modern verification of an old equation.* New York: John Wiley & Sons.

Edmonston, W.E., Jr. (1986a). *The induction of hypnosis.* New York: John Wiley & Sons.

Edmonston, W.E., Jr. (1986b). Hypnosis and social suggestibility. *Behavioral & Brain Sciences, 93*, 470-471.

Evans, F.J. (1967). Suggestibility in the normal waking state. *Psychological Bulletin, 67*, 114-129.

Eysenck, H.J. (1947). *Dimensions of personality.* London: Routledge & Kegan Paul.

Eysenck, H.J., & Furneaux, W.D. (1945). Primary and secondary suggestibility: An experimental and statistical study. *Journal of Experimental Psychology, 35*, 485-503.

Hoffman, J.W., Benson, H., Arns, P.A., Stainbrook, G.L., Landsberg, L., Young, J.B., & Gill, A. (1982). Reduced sympathetic nervous system responsivity associated with the relaxation response. *Science, 215*, 190-192.

Holmes, J.D., Hekmat, H., & Mozingo, B.S. (1983). Cognitive and behavioral regulation of pain: The facilitative effects of analgesia suggestions. *Psychological Record, 33*, 151-159.

Hull, C.L. (1933). *Hypnosis and suggestibility: An experimental approach.* New York: Appleton-Century-Crofts.

Hull, C.L., & Huse, B. (1930). Comparative suggestibility in the trance and waking states. *American Journal of Psychology, 52*, 279-286.

James, W. (1981). *The principles of psychology. Vol. II.* Cambridge, MA: Harvard University (Original work published 1890).

James, W. (1983). *Essays in psychology.* Cambridge, MA: Harvard University.

James, W. (1984). *Psychology: Briefer course.* Cambridge, MA: Harvard University. (Original Work published 1892).

Jevning, R., Pirkle, H.C., & Wilson, A.F. (1977). Behavioral alternation of plasma phenylalanine concentration. *Psychology & Behavior, 19*, 611-614.

Kralik, P.M., Ho, B.T., Mathew, R.J., & Claghorn, J.L. (1983). Kinetic evaluation of platelet monoamine oxidase following relaxation in chronic anxiety. *Acta Psychiatrica Scandinavica, 67*, 315-318.

Krueger, R.G. (1931). Variation in hypersuggestibility preceding, during and following the hypnotic trance. *Journal of Abnormal & Social Psychology, 26*, 131-140.

Mesmer, F.A. (1781). *Précis historique des faits relatifs au magnetisme animal jusqu'en avril 1781.* London: F.A. Mesmer.

Miller, R.J. (1980). The Harvard group scale of hypnotic susceptibility as a predictor of nonhypnotic suggestibility. *International Journal of Clinical & Experimental Hypnosis, 28*, 46-52.

Mills, W.W., & Farrow, J.T. (1981). The Transcendental Meditation technique and acute experimental pain. *Psychosomatic Medicine, 43*, 157-164.

Moore, R.K. (1964). Susceptibility to hypnosis and susceptibility to social influence. *Journal of Abnormal & Social Psychology, 68*, 282-294.

Morgan, A.H., MacDonald, H., & Hilgard, E.R. (1974). EEG alpha: Lateral asymmetry related to task and hypnotizability. *Psychophysiology, 11*, 275-282.

Morse, D.R., Schacterle, G.R., Furst, M.L., Goldberg, J., Greenspan, B., Swiecinski, D., & Susek, J. (1982). The effect of stress and meditation on salivary protein and bacteria: A review and pilot study. *Journal of Human Stress, 8*, 31-39.

Pollack, M.H., & Zeiner, A.R. (1979). Physiological correlates of an experimental relaxation procedure with comparisons to uninstructed relaxation and sitting. *Biological Psychology Bulletin, 5,* 161-170.

Puente, A.E. (1981). Psychophysiological investigations on Transcendental Meditation. *Biofeedback & Self-Regulation, 6,* 327-342.

Shor, R.E., & Orne, E.C. (1962). *Harvard group scale of hypnotic susceptibility: Form A.* Palo Alto, CA: Consulting Psychologists.

Sidis, B. (1898). *The psychology of suggestion.* New York: D. Appleton & Co.

Spanos, N.P. (1986). Hypnotic behavior: A social-psychological interpretation of amnesia, analgesia, and "trance logic." *Behavioral and Brain Sciences, 9 (3),* 449-502.

Stone, J.A., & Lundy, R.M. (1985). Behavioral compliance with direct and indirect body movement suggestions. *Journal of Abnormal Psychology, 94,* 256-263.

Stukát, K.G. (1958). *Suggestibility*: A factorial and experimental analysis. Stockholm: Almqvist & Wiksell.

Wadden, T.A., & de la Torre, C.S. (1980). Relaxation therapy as an adjunct treatment for essential hypertension. *Journal of Family Practice, 11.* 901-908.

Wallace, B., Garrett, J.B., & Anstadt, S.P. (1974). Hypnotic susceptibility, suggestion and reports of autokinetic movement. *American Journal of Psychology, 87,* 117-123.

Weitzenhoffer, A.M. (1953). *Hypnotism: An objective study in suggestibility.* New York: John Wiley & Sons.

Weitzenhoffer, A.M. (1980). Hypnotic susceptibility revisited. *American Journal of Clinical Hypnosis, 22(3),* 130-146.

West, M.A. (1979). Physiological effects of meditation: A longitudinal study. *British Journal of Social & Clinical Psychology, 18,* 219-226.

Williams, G.W. (1930). Suggestibility in the normal and hypnotic states. *Archives of Psychology,* No. 122.

4. The Internal Confirmation of Personal Constructs: Why Suggestions Are Not Accepted

R.M. LUNDY

Some suggestions are accepted, some are not. An interesting chore for social scientists and, clearly, the focus of this book is to explore the processes implied in the statement above. We might explore by asking what the suggestible person is like, by asking what the successful suggestion is like, by asking what kinds of suggestions are successful, and by asking in what kinds of settings or interactions suggestions are successful.

At times in our exploration it may be helpful to spend some effort integrating the various explorations, to try to bring the accounts of suggestible behavior under one construct or one set of constructs.

Three examples of such integrating efforts have come from the field of hypnosis: Hilgard's conception of an altered state of consciousness; Shor's three-factor theory; and Sarbin and Coe's role theory. Both Hilgard (1965) and Shor (1970) have stated that increased suggestibility occurs in the hypnotic state and have accounted for this increase through the subject's turning over certain attentional and executive functions to the hypnotist. For Sarbin and Coe (1972) the increased suggestibility found in hypnosis is the result of social and situational determinants and the role the subject assumes in the hypnotic situation.

The present paper will attempt to account for suggestibility by bringing the phenomena of suggestion into a theory of normal cognitive functioning and by viewing the social and situational elements of suggestibility from the perspective of that cognitive functioning.

The concept of internal confirmation of personal constructs is based on assumptions found in the personality theory developed by Kelly (1955). Two of these assumptions are: (a) a fruitful approach to understanding human behavior can be made by studying an individual's personal constructs; and (b) these constructs are the individual's characteristic way of ordering - constructing - his or her world. Personal constructs are the ideas or notions that make a difference in our behavior, that, in a sense, make us what we are. Internal confirmation of personal constructs is an addition to Kelly's theory, an hypothesized concept to help account for the consistency in human behavior and to account, in this particular case, for the behavior of the recipient in suggestibility situations.

Personal constructs may or may not be verbalized or readily verbalizable. Because Kelly's system is viewed as cognitive and logical, personal constructs themselves are often mistakenly thought to be entirely conscious and logical. It is true, as Kelly would say, that we should start our attempts to understand what a person is like by asking that person, and it is also true that the important constructs identified by Kelly's repertory test are verbalized by the subject of the test.

However, an example of a troublesome construct in a psychotherapy client was "I am superior to everyone else." Although this client's behavior was better understood by invoking this construct, the client would have had trouble verbalizing it, even to himself.

Many things we verbalize may not be personal constructs. I may say, "The sun will not rise tomorrow." It is possible that I am saying this, and, for that matter, that the sun will not rise. Yet this statement is not one of my personal constructs, and I do not behave in accordance with it. Kelly's theory, like other cognitive theories, is concerned with how people think and act not just with how they talk.

Now, a word about suggestion and suggestibility. Social scientists have studied attitude change, information processing, and social influence. In these areas of study and in such a seemingly diverse topic as hypnosis, we can find the singular paradigm of this conference: We present information, in some form, to a person, in some setting or condition, and we note any change in that person as a result of the information.

In Kelly's terms the change in the person is a change in that person's personal construct system: A new construct may be added; one of the constructs, which are bipolar, may be reversed; and the system itself may be changed. (The reader can find these changes elaborated in Kelly [1955]; for our purposes, we will deal simply with the changes as they relate to suggestions.)

Let us start with a statement, more or less theoretical, about this change process. An already existing construct changes when an event occurs that is relevant for that particular construct, yet the construct cannot adequately abstract the aspect of the event pertinent to the construct without itself being changed.

An example of this process might be the following: I have a personal construct that, in its verbalized form, sounds like this, "ballpoint pens write well." An event occurs that has relevance for this construct - I notice on my desk two ballpoint pens, neither of which writes very well at all. At this point a number of my personal constructs have been called into play to construe this event; writing instruments are found on my desk, pens are writing instruments, pens are solid objects, etc. There may be many more constructs needed in order for me to handle the event; but so far the constructs have been adequate. Two elements in the event - the ballpointedness of the pens and the poor writing quality of them - call in a construct ("Ballpoint pens write well") that cannot satisfactorily construe the event. In this case, since my perception of the event and the relevant construct occur *at the same time* and since the construct is not validated by the event, the construct must change to accommodate the event. My resulting construct may be: "Ballpoint pens write poorly." I have accepted a suggestion.

So far our theory states that construct change occurs when relevant yet nonvalidating events occur at the same time as the appropriate personal construct. Now we must specify the conditions under which no change takes place even though a relevant and nonvalidating event occurs.

When no change in the construct takes place it is because the construct is at the moment being validated, either by other confirming events in the environment, or by a postulated process which we will call internal confirmation. This latter process refers to a reaffirming of personal constructs in order for them to maintain their essential nature. This process is usually accompanied by a thought or verbalization. Thus, my saying "Ballpoint pens write well" would represent an internal confirmation of that construct at that moment.

If my construct is being internally confirmed at the moment I come upon the presence and condition of my two faulty pens, then that construct will not be changed.

The event itself remains, however, just as does the construct. Consequently, I must do something about this troublesome event. The two poor writing instruments might become elements in a new construct about writing instruments on my desk, a construct which (for me) has nothing to do with the construct about ballpoint pens. The event may be perceived by me in a strikingly different fashion from that perceived by another observer. I may see only one pen, or I may not see ballpoint pens but pencils or some other objects.

When the contrary event is the verbal presentation of some opposing notion, we do not require such elaborate defensive maneuvers. Such presentations become wrong or forgotten or discounted in some way. Our immediate concern, however, is not primarily with the processes of handling incompatible events but with the process of retention or change of the personal construct.

The principal proposition is that constructs are changed when information contrary to the construct enters awareness at a time when the construct is needed to construe the event but is not being confirmed. The information enters awareness at a time when the normal internal confirmation process has been interfered with, when the internal confirmation has been distracted from its normal process.

Is this the only way of changing ? There may be different approaches to the suggestion process, to the analysis of social influence, of attitude change, and of hypnosis, my own field; but, as I shall argue, these approaches may all be subsumed by our general statement. All of the techniques of changing constructs are means of distracting the process of internal confirmation of the individual's pertinent construct while presenting contrary material.

But don't people sometimes weigh evidence and then change beliefs ? Isn't there first a conflict between the pertinent construct and the contrary evidence and don't people then resolve this conflict by careful consideration of each side ? From introspection it certainly seems as though we have these conflicts and that we resolve them. And we undoubtedly do occasionally change under the weight of contrary evidence. The point of the present argument is that the weight of evidence is important in effecting change to the extent, and only to the extent, that it distracts or inhibits, internal confirmation. Thus, "evidence" becomes a means of changing beliefs, by inhibiting internal confirmation, through the same process and in the same sense that prestige of the communicator or role playing in the recipient may influence change.

Evidence may not change beliefs, of course. I may hear and believe that ballpoint pen factories are poorly operated or that my university stopped purchasing ballpoint pens because they were so poor. If these statements do not call up my construct, "Ballpoint pens write well," then the construct is unchanged, even though these statements of evidence, which may be damaging to the construct, are statements I believe. In other words, if it is possible to construe the evidence without the pertinent construct, then that construct will not be called up and will not need to be internally confirmed.

If the information about pen factories or university purchases calls up my construct about the quality of ballpoint pens and if the information also distracts me from confirming my construct, then I will find myself believing that ballpoint pens write poorly.

What happens to the old belief if it is not internally confirmed at the moment of hearing a contrary idea ? Does it cease to exist, or does it remain, hidden away somewhere ?

To examine this question I must state another assumption about the beliefs that people have. This assumption is that every belief implicitly contains its opposite. This means that in order to believe that something writes well, I must also have the notion that something can write poorly. The construct in its entirety is "writes well - writes poorly," and a belief refers to one end of the dichotomy.

Kelly (1955), in describing the dichotomous nature of personal constructs, is more detailed; for the purposes of this presentation, we can assume that the full statement of any belief is dichotomous and that change in belief is always to the other end of the construct. The two bad pens on my desk are perceived by means of my construct, "ballpoint pens write well (but not poorly)." If I confirm that ballpoints write well while perceiving the two pens, then the belief remains; if not, then I believe that ballpoint pens write poorly. That ballpoint pens write well is not "gone" with this change in my beliefs; rather, the construct has been reversed.

To understand why some constructs are not readily changed, and thus why the internal confirmation process cannot easily be distracted, we need to know the opposite pole of the expressed construct and the position of the construct in the person's personal construct system.

Consider the belief that Native Americans are socially inferior to whites. We may find that for one person the belief statement is part of the construct, "socially inferior-socially superior." For another person it may be part of the construct, "socially inferior-socially equal." We might expect, then, that the second person would be more easily persuaded that Native Americans are not socially inferior.

We might be quite wrong about this second person. In his construct system we may find the "socially inferior-socially equal" construct rigidly subsumed under a "white-nonwhite" construct. And subsumed under this construct we find all of the valued qualities of mankind as far as the person is concerned. Whites are rigidly all good human qualities, nonwhites are all bad human qualities. Therefore for this person to move a Native American, a nonwhite, into the socially equal end of the construct is tantamount to shaking up the whole system dealing with human qualities.

For another person a white-nonwhite construct may float loosely and unobtrusively somewhere off in the system, only minimally connected to the basic human qualities constructs.

Those of you familiar with Kelly's theory know that I'm taking some liberties, but the point is that some beliefs, or ideas, or personal constructs are more central and thus more likely to be internally confirmed, or more precisely, to be more resistant to distraction from the internal confirmation process.

Useful explanations of behavior, such as I would hope this account of suggestion to be, should offer explanations of the findings, or data, of the behavior under review. They should also make interesting predictions that can be subjected to experimental study. In the second half of this paper I will try to do both of these things. First, let us examine some of the major conclusions from the social influence and suggestion literature.

Enhancing Characteristics of the Source

Common sense, as well as experimental evidence, tells us that an enhanced communicator influences more effectively than an unenhanced one. Trustworthiness (Eagly, Wood, & Chaiken, 1978; Hovland, Janis, & Kelley, 1953), attractiveness (Janis & Hoffman, 1971; McGuire, 1969), prestige (Haiman, 1949), and expertise (Johnson & Izzett, 1969; Miller & Hewgill, 1966) have all been shown to increase the effectiveness of communications by enhancing the source.

The present theoretical explanation of this enhancing effect is that the enhancing qualities draw the recipient's attention away from internal confirmation of the pertinent personal constructs. The effect of the enhancement on the recipient is to distract from the internal confirmation process.

Communication Tactics

Distraction of internal confirmation has also taken place when successful tactics of persuasion have been used. Tactics, however, must be examined carefully; for, as the evidence has shown, a particular tactic can easily backfire and affect the enhancing qualities of the source.

The most familiar tactic is repetition of the message, the advertising business' most dependable device. Research has also lent its support for this tactic (Wilson & Miller, 1968), though much of the effect of repetition may be its power in learning new material (Hilgard & Bower, 1975).

It may be good to stop here to remember that our theory deals with changing constructs. New information or facts are added to one's store of knowledge by the regular laws of learning and memory. Thus, if I hear over and over that Brand X is a new light beer, I am more apt to learn and remember that fact.

If I have the construct, "New light beers are drinks to try," then I'm off to buy Brand X. If my construct is, "All light beers are to be shunned," then the commercial must do something to distract me from internal confirmation.

The interaction effect between the tactic and the source is also noticed when the tactic is an increased number of supporting arguments and the source is either an expert or an attractive person (Norman, 1976). The expert's influence was increased when the number of arguments was increased, presumably because the increased number confirmed the expert's status, while the attractive person's influence was the same regardless of the number. The influence effect, from our theoretical position, comes from the distracting qualities of the expert and the attractive person.

Another tactic that has been studied, although with less consistent findings than those from message repetition studies, is the use of emotion arousing content material or background.

Positive emotions such as those aroused by good food and drink (Janis, Kaye, & Kirschner, 1965) and by background music (Galizio & Hendrick, 1972) increase receptivity of the target person. They may do this by increasing the potency of the source or by directly distracting the internal confirmation process.

Messages that arouse fear are generally thought to be effective (Leventhal, Watts, & Pagano, 1967; Rochon, 1977), and the distracting quality of fear arousal is easily understood. If the fear is too intense, however, the recipient may not be influenced, especially when no instructions have been given about ways to avoid the fearful event (Janis & Feshbach, 1953). This defensiveness, as it has been called, may be the result of the arousal and internal confirmation of a central construct which might be verbalized, "Safety is within, danger is outside." The outside in this case includes the sounds and sights of the communication.

A defensive construct such as this is able to keep the recipient from being influenced, because its internal confirmation is so important that the original target construct is no longer needed to construe the event.

If the target construct of the persuasion message is "I drive fast," I will need that construct to understand the persuasive message about driving slow. If the message also distracts the internal confirmation by its effective or frightening qualities, then my construct will change. If, however, a defensive construct is called up by an extremely fearful message, then I no longer need "I drive fast" to construe the message; in my fear the only construct which I need is "Safety is within, danger is outside." And since the fast driving concept is no longer called up, it is not changed.

That face-to-face tactics of persuasion are more effective (Katz & Lazarsfeld, 1955) is accounted for in the present theory by the increased potential for distraction of internal confirmation in the face-to-face situation. Also, when subjects are distracted directly by another task, they are more likely to be persuaded by a communication (Festinger & Maccoby, 1964).

Characteristics of the Recipient

Whether or not there is a general suggestibility personality trait is somewhat open to question, but the prevailing conclusion is that a general trait has not been found (Hovland & Janis, 1959). The specific characteristics that have received the most study are intelligence and self-esteem.

these personal constructs, the opposite poles of the constructs, and the superordinate constructs under which the construct to be changed falls.

Suppose we want to change a person's belief that two plus two is four. From this theory's point of view, this persuasion attempt is doomed to failure, because there is something about beliefs of this kind that make them more subject to internal confirmation. Mathematical "truths" and a few other ideas or beliefs are rarely questioned by individuals in a particular culture. Most likely there are also some beliefs that are peculiar to an individual in their resistance to change.

When one asks why we cannot believe that two plus two equals anything other than four, most people would point out that, based on some long-standing, functional, and obvious assumptions regarding our common number system, we must believe it. That is, it follows logically and necessarily that the only way not to believe it is not to assume certain prior and essential things about numbers.

We could also understand the firmness of our belief by saying that it has been overlearned, that two plus two has always equalled four and that this fact has always been positively reinforced. There has never been any really effective negative instance.

The present theory, however, would focus on the immediate reaction to two plus two equals five. We feel at the moment, "It cannot be." My guess is that this simple mathematical statement is subsumed under a superordinate construct shared by almost all people that sounds something like, "This I know to be true;" The opposite pole of this superordinate construct is not "It could be false" but, rather, "I know nothing," or perhaps, "I am not me."

We must remember that we are talking about personal constructs. The "opposite" poles do not need to be logical opposites. The notion that two plus two is unchangeable is due to its being subsumed under a superordinate construct, the opposite of which has tragic consequences. It is very difficult, outside of psychosis, to accept "I know nothing" or "I do not exist."

Our search for the reason why some constructs are not easily distracted will lead us to study superordinate beliefs and the importance of the opposite poles of the beliefs' constructs. All of us know some people (those who disagree with us) who have many beliefs subsumed under one construct. It is hard to change their minds.

This theoretical position would also foster research interest in the timing of suggestions and of distracting efforts. The present theory would predict that the timing is critical. If the distracting aspects are not in effect during the time of the persuasion suggestion, then internal confirmation will result and no change will occur.

Since the present theory of suggestibility focuses attention on inhibiting thought processes, the techniques of hypnosis, which appear to inhibit temporarily the subject's ability to think, perceive, or act, should be fruitful areas of research.

As we know, the histories of hypnosis and of suggestibility have been intertwined. At times the study of hypnosis and of suggestion have been one and the same. Currently, as we also know, many hypnotists believe that the measure of hypnosis is more than just the measure of the acceptance of suggestion. The subjective experience of the hypnotized subject during an hypnotically induced suggestion is thought by many of us to be the critical measure of hypnosis.

But, as a hypnotist, I can attest to the astounding behaviors that some subjects will exhibit if these behaviors are suggested to them while they are hypnotized. Several theories, including the three above, have been advanced to explain this behavior; the present theory offers another explanation, namely, that the subject's response to the procedure of hypnosis or the subject's "state" as some are willing to call it, is one in which internal confirmation has been effectively negated.

It is interesting to observe that hypnosis has not been used in social persuasion studies or in studies of attitude change. Except for some clinical techniques directed, for instance, at changing a client's self-confidence level, the suggestions given to hypnotized subjects are almost always of a temporary nature. We hypnotists in the laboratory are careful, for ethical reasons, to make sure that the subject knows that the suggestion is just for the moment and that the original construct should be internally confirmed when the hypnotically induced suggestion is "taken away."

If we accept the present theory's emphasis on distraction, as in distracting the subject from internal confirmation, research that attempts to account for hypnotic phenomena may turn toward the hypnotized subject's capacity to be distracted and toward the best techniques to achieve that distraction. When I suggest to subjects that their arms are light and can float in the air, I marvel (being a one on the Stanford Scale) at the ability of these subjects to engage in such vivid imaginings about balloons attached to their arm, that their arms actually rise in the air.

From the present theory's position, I would also marvel at the subject's capacity to be distracted from the fact that their arm muscles are pulling the arm up. Not only are personal constructs about arm movements distracted from their internal confirmation during hypnotic suggestions but also perceptions and sensations of the cause of that movement.

Although reviews (Adams, 1957; McConnell, Cutler, & McNeil, 1958) long ago put to rest any fears that studies of subliminal stimulation would require a wholesale revision in our thinking about learning and perception, the present theory would suggest that changes in ideas and opinions may indeed be produced by presenting contrary notions such that the recipient is not sufficiently aware of what is going on to internally confirm the pertinent constructs. Although new information would undoubtedly be more effectively presented in a clear and supraliminal way, contrary material may have a better change under subliminal conditions.

Finally, in considering ways in which internal confirmation may be inhibited, we may be led to psychological or physical stress, to emotional excitement, or to surprise as variables affecting suggestion and suggestibility. Some of these techniques may lead us to study the practice of demagoguery; but we should certainly not be surprised to find there fertile hypotheses for experimental test.

References

Adams, J.K. (1957). Laboratory studies of behavior without awareness. *Psychological Bulletin, 54,* 383-405.

Bannister, D., & Mair, J. (1968). *The evaluation of personal constructs.* London: Academic Press.

Cox, D.F., & Bauer, R.A. (1964). Self-confidence and persuasibility in women. *Public Opinion Quarterly, 28,* 453-466.

Eagly, A.H., & Warren, R. (1976). Intelligence, comprehension, and opinion change. *Journal of Personality, 44,* 226-242.

Eagly, A.H., Wood, W., & Chaiken, S. (1978). Causal inferences about communicators and their effect on opinion change. *Journal of Personality and Social Psychology, 36,* 424-435.

Festinger, L., & Maccoby, N. (1964). On resistance to persuasive communications. *Journal of Abnormal and Social Psychology, 68,* 359-366.

Galizio, M., & Hendrick, C. (1972). Effect of musical accompaniment on attitude: The guitar as a prop for persuasion. *Journal of Applied Social Psychology, 2,* 350-359.

Gelfand, D.M. (1962). The influence of self-esteem on the rate of verbal conditioning and social matching behavior. *Journal of Abnormal and Social Psychology, 65,* 259-265.

Haiman, F.S. (1949). An experimental study of the effects of ethos in public speaking. *Speech Monographs, 16,* 190-202.

Hilgard, E.R. (1965). *Hypnotic susceptibility.* New York: Harcourt, Brace & World.

Hilgard, E.R., & Bower, G.H. (1975). *Theories of learning* (4th ed.). Englewood Cliffs, NJ: Prentice-Hall.

Hovland, C.I., & Janis, I.L. (1959). *Personality and persuasibility.* New Haven: Yale University.

Hovland, C., Janis, I., & Kelley, H. (1953). *Communication and persuasion.* New Haven: Yale University.

Janis, I.L., & Feshbach, S. (1953). Effects of fear-arousing communications. *Journal of Abnormal and Social Psychology, 48,* 78-92.

Janis, I.L., & Hoffman, D. (1971). Facilitating effects of daily contact between partners who make decisions to cut down on smoking. *Journal of Personality and Social Psychology, 17,* 25-35.

Janis, I.L., Kaye, D., & Kirschner, P. (1965). Facilitating effects of "eating while reading" on responsiveness to persuasive communications. *Journal of Personality and Social Psychology, 1,* 181-186.

Janis, I.L., & King, B.T. (1954). The influence of role playing on opinion change. *Journal of Abnormal and Social Psychology, 49,* 211-218.

Johnson, H.H., & Izzett, R.R. (1969). Relationship between authoritarianism and attitude change as a function of source credibility and type of communication. *Journal of Personality and Social Psychology, 13,* 317-321.

Katz, E., & Lazarsfeld, P.F. (1955). *Personal influence.* Glencoe, IL: Free Press.

Kelly, G.A. (1955). *The psychology of personal constructs.* New York: Norton.

Leventhal, H., Watts, J.C., & Pagano, F. (1967). Effects of fear and instructions on how to cope with danger. *Journal of Personality and Social Psychology, 3,* 367-372.

Lundy, R.M., & Berkowitz, L. (1957). Cognitive complexity and assimilative projection in attitude change. *Journal of Abnormal and Social Psychology, 55,* 34-37.

McConnell, J.V., Cutler, R.L., & McNeil, E.B. (1958). Subliminal stimulation: An overview. *American Psychologist, 13,* 229-242.

McGuire, W.J. (1968). Personality and susceptibility to social influence. In E.F. Borgatta & W.W. Lambert (Eds.), *Handbook of personality theory and research.* Chicago: Rand McNally.

McGuire, W.J. (1969). The nature of attitudes and attitude change. In G. Lindzey & E. Aronson (Eds.), *Handbook of social psychology* (Vol. 3, 2nd ed.). Reading, MA: Addison-Wesley.

Miller, G.R., & Hewgill, M.A. (1966). Some recent research on fear-arousing message appeals. *Speech Monographs, 33,* 377-391.

Norman, R. (1976). When what is said is important: A comparison of expert and attractive sources. *Journal of Experimental Social Psychology, 12,* 294-300.

Rochon, J. (1977). *An evaluation of the seat belt education campaign.* Ottawa, Canada: Department of Transport.

Sarbin, T.R., & Coe, W.C. (1972). *Hypnosis: A social psychological analysis of influence communication.* New York: Holt, Rinehart and Winston.

Shor, R.E. (1970). The three-factor theory of hypnosis as applied to the book-reading fantasy and to the concept of suggestion. *International Journal of Clinical and Experimental Hypnosis, 18,* 89-98.

Wilson, W., & Miller, H. (1968). Repetition, order of presentation, and timing of arguments and measures as determinants of opinion change. *Journal of Personality and Social Psychology, 9,* 184-188.

5. Some Suggestions About Suggestion and Hypnosis: A Radical Constructivist View

P. Kruse

A Few Inconvenient Phenomena

The ratio between the amount of systematically studied phenomena and their commonly accepted theoretical integration is one main characteristic of the developmental stage of a scientific discipline. The younger a discipline, the more unexplained phenomena exist in its sphere. With respect to this - and not only this - criterion, psychology is surely still a young science. But there are some psychological phenomena which are far too old and well known to accept the developmental stage of psychology as the only valid explanation for their insufficient theoretical integration. One example which may trouble an untroubled belief in scientific progress is the domain of suggestion and hypnosis.

The fact that suggestive influences are present in any form of communication is a matter of everyday experience, and the knowledge that a special behavioral potentiality exists in human beings which can be distinguished from normal states - called trance or hypnosis - is as old as human culture itself. Therefore, these phenomena have been chosen as an object of investigation since the early days of psychology. On the one hand, however, the interest in this topic is still open to great variation and until now has not - apart from its practical relevance, e.g., in psychotherapy - been generally accepted as scientifically serious, while on the other hand, there is considerable agreement only about the effects but considerable disagreement concerning theoretical explanations (e.g., Evans, 1767; Kihlstrom, 1985). Gheorghiu (1980) called suggestion one of the Cinderellas of psychology, and hypnosis may be pictured in such a metaphoric sense as a kind of glamor girl. Both the valuation of being seemingly unimportant and of being merely spectacular show the emotional difficulties scientific psychology tends to have with this domain. Where do these difficulties come from, and what consequences can be drawn for the preoccupation with suggestion and hypnosis?

In the tradition of Western philosophy, the process of cognition has been understood for the most part as a process of representation and informational input. The characteristics of an independently existing ontological reality are discovered via perception and action. The organization, stability, and richness of the *phenomenal* world is thought to be a direct result of the organization, stability, and richness of an *external* world. The axiomatic acceptance of this epistemological position in everyday life and largely also in science led von Glasersfeld (1981) to compare it with a religious belief system and to speak of a "metaphysical" realism. For any form of individual and social practice this belief seems to be a necessary assumption, and in the view of the evident success of that practice any doubt in the veridicality of cognition is easily discredited as intellectual sophistry (see von Glasersfeld, 1985). Scepticism is only tolerated as a standpoint one may take in one's study and forget about in the living room.

There are some psychological phenomena which clearly contradict the assumption that cognition is a mere representational process and which, on the basis of the described epistemological background, simply have to be treated as curious slips of the cognitive system. One of these is, for example, the phenomenon of multistable perception. The fact that in some cases a stable stimulus condition (like the well-known Necker cube) produces different continuously alternating percepts is at once attractive and hard to accept. The German Gestalt psychologist Wolfgang Metzger noted in this context: "Fortunately for the sake for peace of mind multistable patterns are so rare in nature" (Metzger, 1975, p. 53; translated by the author). The ambiguity of figure and ground, of perspective, of meaning, etc. demonstrates that the experienced stability of perception is not a trivial result of the stability of an external world but has to be regarded as an autonomous creation of order in the visual system (see Kruse, 1988).

Relative to the question of where the difficulties come from that scientific psychology tends to have with the domain of suggestion and hypnosis, one possible answer may be that these phenomena contradict the "metaphysical" realism in just the same way as perceptual multistability. For instance, positive and negative hallucinations and analgesia, without the reassuring explanation of drug effects, are also at once attractive and hard to accept and demonstrate provocatively the functional autonomy of cognition. In short - problems in psychology are sometimes psychological problems.

For the investigation of "curious" phenomena, like multistability or suggestion and hypnosis, and perhaps for the understanding of cognition in general, it will be necessary and fruitful to convey what Lang (1970) called a "Kantian change" in psychology; that is to say, understanding the phenomenal world no longer as a more or less direct representation of an ontological reality but as basically constructed by the cognitive system itself. It is the central intention of this contribution to outline general features of such a position and to consider the possible implications it may have for a theoretical integration of suggestion and hypnosis and for the investigation of these phenomena.

An Uncommon Theory of Cognition

Understanding cognition as a process of self-organization is not a new idea in psychology. Already in 1925, Köhler insisted that the creation of order in perception is best described as the reaching of a stationary equilibrium which unfolds spontaneously out of the inner dynamics of the visual system. It is by no means far-fetched to understand the total history of Gestalt psychology as a continuous attempt to demonstrate the autonomy of cognition (Kruse, Roth & Stadler, 1987; Stadler & Kruse, 1986, 1988). But only recently the dramatic development of concepts of self-organization in physics, chemistry, and biology (Eigen & Schuster, 1979; Haken, 1978; Prigogine, 1980) has initiated the formulation of an explicitly constructivistic theory of the functioning of cognitive systems (Maturana, 1982; von Foerster, 1985; von Glasersfeld, 1987).

An article entitled *Biology of Cognition*, which was published in 1970 by the neurophysiologist Humberto Maturana, is usually taken to be the most influential starting point of this theory. In Maturana's concept, the structure of a biological organism is the product of a process of self-organization, and the organism's only purpose of living is to maintain this structure. Any activity of the organism has to be understood as a part of this - as Maturana called it - *autopoietic* functioning. Cognition is nothing but a process of relating different innerorganismic events in order to guarantee structural maintenance (Maturana & Varela, 1980). Concerning this maintenance, the organism itself cannot judge these relations - e.g., relations between inner-organismic events one may call sensory and motor - as true or false but only as possible or impossible.

To illustrate this point, imagine the situation of a submarine approaching an unknown shore. For an observer the changes in course of the submarine will look like the result of a representation of or knowledge about existing shallow places but for the crew of the submarine it simply cannot be more than a matching between data indicated by the displays of different instruments. As long as they do not leave the submarine, none of the crew can judge the matching and therefore the course actually driven as true. They can only claim that the course was possible - naturally provided that they were able to avoid running shore (cf. Maturana and Varela, 1987).

The fact that an organism survives does not imply that it is capable of representing its environment but only demonstrates that its cognitions are not absurd enough to destroy its autopoiesis, or - as von Glasersfeld (1980) put it - that the relations the organism has established between different inner-organismic events are *viable.* In this view, being "adapted" means no more and no less than that an organism has found one possible way of dealing with the constraints set by its present environment.

In Maturana's definition, cognition exists in amebae as well as in higher mammals. But the more evolved the nervous system of an animal is, the more complex and the more indirect are the relations between different inner-organismic events. In the most complex nervous system known - in the human brain - cognition, therefore, has to be described as a process of relating relations of relations of relations, etc. Neurophysiologically the conditions in the brain are far more complicated than the submarine metaphor indicates. The maximal information the brain can receive from its environment is an endless concert of meaningless, quantitatively varying excitations (von Foerster, 1981). Whether an excitation is triggered by an external or by an internal event, whether it is visual or acoustic, whether it symbolizes something dangerous or something attractive, every association of meaning is a product of the brain itself. These associations can be the result of an evolutionary process, such as the determination of sensory modality which follows a strict localization principle or a matter of ontological or actual genetical self-organization (Roth, 1980, 1985, 1986).

The brain is part of an autopoietic system called "organism" which maintains its structure by a continuous exchange of energy and substance with its medium, and the brain may be put into fluctuation by external events, but the creation of meaning can be nothing but a result of its own autonomous activity. To sum up - in Maturana's sense the brain is an *open* system concerning its exchange of energy and substance and has to be regarded as functionally *closed* or *self-referential* concerning the creation of meaning. The ontological reality is postulated to be a limitation of the self-organization process, but there is no way of knowing anything about it.

A First Attempt of Application

During recent years some approaches have been established which try to extend the outlined concept to the spheres of other scientific disciplines. Referring to the epistemological background, these approaches are subsumed under the collective term of "radical constructivism" (Schmidt, 1987). An attempt will now be made to evaluate whether or not a radical constructivist view is able to enhance the theoretical understanding of suggestion and hypnosis and to initiate promising investigations in this domain. As a first step of this evaluation, some of the known phenomena are surveyed and exemplary possible empirical questions are deduced.

The Problem of Reality Criteria

As already mentioned, in the view of radical constructivism every case of an apparent inconsistency between subjectively and intersubjectively experienced reality, for example, is no longer easily discredited as a slip of the cognitive system of the person in minority. On this basis the fact that it is possible to induce positive and negative hallucinations by means of suggestive influences has to be treated as a self-evident consequence of the constructive character of the cognitive system. As proposed by Shepard - who said that he likes "caricature perception as externally guided hallucination, and dreaming and hallucination as internally simulated perception" (Shepard, 1984, p. 436) - the theoretical differences between perception and hallucination fade away. Instead the following questions arise:
- How does the cognitive system normally distinguish between perceptual phenomena, dreams, and hallucinations if this distinction cannot be regarded as the trivial consequence of the representational quality of perception?
- And, if there are some inner-systemic mechanisms responsible for this discriminative ability, what happens to them during suggestion and hypnosis?

The fundamental problem inherent in the first question was already formulated in the *Principles of Psychology* by William James, published in 1896. James wrote: "Everyone knows the difference between imagining a thing and believing in its existence, between supposing a proposition and acquiescing in its truth. In case of acquiescence or belief, the object is not only apprehended by the mind, but is held to have reality. Belief is thus the mental state or function of cognizing reality" (p. 283). And James also deduced the question, "Under what circumstances do we think things real?" (p. 287).

Although the question is probably of critical interest for the understanding of cognition, there is nearly no systematic research done on this topic. Innumerable investigations deal with the functional equivalence of imagination and perception or with the evident differences between them, but very few try to clarify why we can normally distinguish imagery from "real" stimuli and why sometimes we cannot.

The fascinating experiments Perky (1910) conducted taking up a study of Külpe (1902) are one of these rare exceptions. Perky found that if persons are asked to describe their own mental images of common objects while dim projections of the objects are presented before them, they report only an "imagery" not a "perceptual" experience. Another example - even closer to the question of interest - is an experiment by Metzger (1935). In his experiment a white skeletal cube was positioned in front of a white plane and illuminated by a bright spotlight. The resulting bold outlines of the cube's shadow were always perceived as the real object and the white skeletal cube as the shadow.

Obviously one criterion our cognitive system uses to determine the reality of a percept is its intensity. The more an object stands out against its background, the more "real" it seems to be. In the measurement of suggestibility, the reality criterion of intensity plays an important but usually not explicitly mentioned role. To give rise to suggestive effects in perception, often situations are used in which stimuli are presented, or said to be presented, near the perceptual threshold. The phenomenal production of nonexisting stimuli and the phenomenal suppression of existing stimuli are supported by suspending the criterion of intensity (e.g., Gheorghiu, Hodapp, & Ludwig, 1975).

One further important empirical contribution to the problem of "reality testing" or "reality decision" (cf. Segal, 1971) can be found in the work of Michotte (1948, 1957) and Phemister (1951). They were able to demonstrate that the apparent reality of a percept is attributed like a value on a continuous scale and not as a simple "either-or" decision.

Beside these exceptions there has been - as far as we know - nearly no systematic research done on this topic up to now. But the number of possible reality criteria which are of importance in the discrimination between perception and imagination can easily be extended by utilizing the knowledge of perceptual psychology as a basis of speculation (Segal, 1971; Stadler & Kruse, 1986; Kruse & Stadler, 1987).

Everything which is perceived as a coherent figure is experienced as being more "real" than the unstressed background. An already relieved object is thought to be rel when it is invariant, e.g., in the sense of constancy of size or of phenomenal persistence, when it is perceptible by different sensory modalities, when its qualities are manifold, when it appears to be concise, when its existence seems to be plausible, when it is attractive, when it is part of a "cause-effect" relationship, when its qualities or behavior can be anticipated, when its existence is intersubjectively confirmed, etc.

If one has a hallucination, that is, if one is the only one who thinks a certain thing real, the hallucination has to meet these criteria or the criteria have to be suspended in the cognitive system of the hallucinating person. Both happen during the process of suggestion and hypnotic induction. The possibility of intersubjective confirmation is clearly impaired by bringing a person into rapport. If two persons are in rapport, intersubjective confirmation and suggestive content are identical. In addition, on the one hand, the richness of perception is reduced by narrowing a person's attention, e.g., via fixation, and, on the other hand, the vividness of imagination is intensified by suggestive incorporation of different sensory modalities, etc. In this sense, induction techniques may be understood as an attempt to create situations in which the experienced difference between imagination and perception tends to be diminished.

But the circumvention, reduction, elimination, or masking of the possibility for discrimination, which is said to be typical for hypnosis and suggestion (e.g., Gheorghiu, 1972), is not limited to the experienced difference between imagination and perception. In just the same way, the readiness to believe in the truth of remembrance or intellectual knowledge seems to be significantly enhanced.

Concerning the criteria the cognitive system uses to determine the reality content of a remembrance, Johnson and Raye (1981) recently performed a number of interesting experiments. They investigated the process people use in deciding whether remembered information seems to be derived from external sources or seems to be generated by internal processes such as reasoning, imagination, and thought. The authors introduced the term "reality monitoring" for this. They found that during this reality monitoring the decision whether a memory is produced by an external or by an internal source follows similar rules as postulated for the discrimination between imagination, dreams, and hallucinations. Memories seem to be externally generated when they have many spatial and temporal contextual attributes, when they have many sensory attributes, and when they are semantically detailed. In this view the hypnotic phenomenon of hypermnesia may be understood as an inner-systemic artifact. The vividness of imagination during hypnosis may induce a disturbance in reality monitoring and this may possibly enable a person to accept his or her own construction as a "real" remembrance.

The last category of reality criteria which may be of interest in the context of suggestion and hypnosis and which will be mentioned here is the category of criteria used by the cognitive system to determine the truth of intellectual knowledge. Some possible criteria were collected by an der Heiden (1985). In his opinion, intellectual knowledge seems to be true when it is logically consistent; when it is coherent, that is, when it is supported by already accepted knowledge; when it is simple in the sense of conciseness; and when deduced predictions can be confirmed.

In the literature concerning suggestion and hypnosis it is often mentioned that the effect of a suggestion is influenced by its plausibility, by its logical consistency, and, therefore, by its ability to induce belief (for empirical substantiation see, e.g., Gheorghiu & Sander, 1973). In some of our own experiments we were also able to demonstrate that a suggestion is more compelling the more plausible it seems to be and the more it is confirmed by predictions which prove to be true (Kruse & Hoffman, 1987). Using predictions which are easily confirmed is often an element of hypnotic induction techniques (see, e.g., the fixation or the color contrast method).

It is evident to anyone who knows anything about suggestion and hypnosis that all the reality criteria mentioned up to now concerning perception, remembrance, and knowledge play a significant role in this domain. Therefore, it is of critical interest for the understanding and the practical application of suggestion and hypnosis to know more about these criteria, about the way they normally operate, about their interactions, and about the way they may be suspended (see Hilgard, 1977). To investigate this, an integrative effort of researchers engaged in perceptual and cognitive psychology and of researchers working with suggestion and hypnosis is required. For instance, personality differences in the functioning of reality criteria in normal situations may be a good indicator for a person's suggestibility, and suggestion and hypnosis may serve as a useful instrument for understanding the cognitive construction of reality.

Concluding Evaluation

In a radical constructivist view the effects of suggestion and hypnosis are by no means curious slips or the result of any spectacular ability of the cognitive system but a necessary consequence of its functional autonomy. Understanding cognition as a process of a *self-referential* construction of meaning produces entirely different questions from a representational concept. As demonstrated by the example of reality criteria, these questions are able to open new fields of research. Therefore, an investigation of the domain of suggestion and hypnosis against the background of radical constructivism can be evaluated without reserve as a promising task of further empirical work and theoretical discussion.

Acknowledgement. The author wishes to express his appreciation to Vladimir Gheorghiu, Uwe an der Heiden, Gerhard Roth, and Michael Stadler for stimulating discussions.

References

An der Heiden, U. (1985). Kognitive Selbstreferenz. In G. Pasternack (Ed.), *Schriftenreihe des Zentrums Philosophische Grundlagen der Wissenschaft: Vol. 1. Erklären, Begründen, Verstehen.* Bremen: Universität Bremen.

Eigen, M., & Schuster, P. (1979). *The hypercycle.* Berlin Heidelberg New York: Springer.

Evans, F.J. (1967). Suggestibility in the normal waking state. *Psychological Bulletin, 67,* 114-129.

Gheorghiu, V.A. (1972). On suggestion and suggestibility. *Scientia, 107,* 840-860.

Gheorghiu, V.A. (1980). One of the "Cinderellas" of psychology and medicine: The suggestion. *Svensk Tidskrift för Hypnos, 5,* 13-17.

Gheorghiu, V.A., Hodapp, V., & Ludwig, C.M. (1975). Attempt to construct a scale for the measurement of the effect of suggestion on perception. *Educational and Psychological Measurement, 35,* 341-352.

Gheorghiu, V.A., & Sander, D. (1973). Untersuchungen zur Änderung der Suggestibilität unter bestimmten Einstellungen. *Bericht über den 27. Kongreß der Deutschen Gesellschaft für Psychologie in Kiel 1970,* pp. 420-427.

Haken, H. (1978). *Synergetics: An introduction.* Berlin Heidelberg New York: Springer.

Hilgard, E.R. (1977). *Divided consciousness: Multiple controls in human thought and action.* New York: Wiley.

James, W. (1896). *The principles of psychology (Vol. 2).* New York: Holt.

Johnson, M.K., & Raye, C.L. (1981). Reality monitoring. *Psychological Review, 88,* 67-85.

Kihlstrom, J.F. (1985). Hypnosis. *Annual Review of Psychology, 36,* 385-418.

Köhler, W. (1925). Gestaltprobleme und Anfänge einer Gestalttheorie. *Jahresberichte für die gesamte Physiologie and experimentelle Pharmakologie für das Jahr 1922, 3,* 512-539. (Reprint in *Gestalt Theory 3,* 178-205).

Kruse, P. (1988). Stabilität, Instabilität, Multistabilität: Selbstorganisation und Selbstreferentialität in kognitiven Systemen. *Delfin, 11,* 35-57.

Kruse, P., & Hoffmann, F. (1987). Multistabilität als Methode zur Untersuchung von Suggestion und Suggestibilität. *Bericht über den 35. Kongreß der Deutschen Gesellschaft für Psychologie in Heidelberg 1986, 1,* 105.

Kruse, P., Roth, G., & Stadler, M. (1987). Ordnungsbildung und psychophysische Feldtheorie. *Gestalt Theory, 9,* 150-167.

Kruse, P., & Stadler, M. (1987). Radikaler Konstruktivismus - Psychologische Überlegungen zu einem philosophischen Zweifel. *Bericht über den 35. Kongreß der Deutschen Gesellschaft für Psychologie in Heidelberg 1986, 2,* 199-210.

Külpe, O. (1902). Ueber die Objektivierung und Subjektivierung von Sinneseindrücken. *Philosophische Studien, 19,* 508-556.

Lang, A. (1970). Über den Primat der subjektiven Wahrnehmungsdimension, dargestellt am Beispiel der Zeitdimension. *Schweizerische Zeitschrift für Psychologie, 29,* 45-51.

Machovec, F.J. (1979). The cult of Asclipios. *The American Journal of Clinical Hypnosis, 22,* 85-90.

Maturana, H.R. (1970). *Biology of cognition (Report BCL 9.0).* Urbana III: University of Illinois, Biological Computer Laboratory.

Maturana, H.R. (1982). *Erkennen: Die Organisation und Verkörperung von Wirklichkeit.* Braunschweig: Vieweg.

Maturana, H.R., & Varela, F.J. (1980). *Autopoiesis and cognition.* Dodrecht: Reidel.

Maturana, H.R., & Varela, F.J. (1987). *Der Baum der Erkenntnis.* Bern: Scherz.

Metzger, W. (1935). Tiefenerscheinungen in optischen Bewegungsfeldern. *Psychologische Forschung, 20,* 195-260.

Metzger, W. (1975). *Gesetze des Sehens.* Frankfurt: Kramer.

Michotte, A. (1948). L'énigme psychologique de la perspective dans le dessin linéaire. *Bulletin de l'Académie royale de Belgique, 5,* 268-288.

Michotte, A. (1957). Les variations de réalité apparente de la troisième dimension dans les perceptions visuelles. *Archivio di Psychologia, Neurologia e Psichatrica, 18,* 203-213.

Perky, C.W. (1910). An experimental study of imagination. *American Journal of Psychology, 21,* 422-452.

Phemister, M.R. (1951). An experimental contribution to the problem of apparent reality. *The Quarterly Journal of Experimental Psychology, 3,* 1-18.

Prigogine, I. (1980). *From being to becoming: Time and complexity in the physical sciences.* San Francisco: Freeman.

Roth, G. (1980). Cognition as a self-organizing system. In F. Benseler, P.M. Hejl, & W.K. Köck (Eds.), *Autopoiesis, communication, and society.* Frankfurt: Campus.

Roth, G. (1985). Die Selbstreferentialität des Gehirns und die Prinzipien der Gestaltwahrnehmung. *Gestalt Theory, 7,* 228-244.

Roth, G. (1986). Selbstorganisation und Selbstreferentialität als Prinzipien der Organisation von Lebewesen. In H.J. Sandkühler & H.H. Holz (Eds.), *Beiträge zu Philosophie und Wissenschaften: Vol. 12. Dialektik.* Köln: Pahl Rugenstein.

Schmidt, S.J. (Ed.), (1987). *Der Diskurs des Radikalen Konstruktivismus.* Frankfurt: Suhrkamp.

Segal, S.J. (1971). Processing of the stimulus in imagery and perception. In S.J. Segal (Ed.), *Imagery: Current cognitive approaches.* New York: Academic.

Shepard, R.N. (1984). Ecological constraints on internal representation: Resonant kinematics of perceiving, imagining, thinking, and dreaming. *Psychological Review, 4,* 417-447.

Stadler, M., & Kruse, P. (1986). Gestalttheorie und Theorie der Selbstorganisation. *Gestalt Theory, 8,* 75-88.

Stadler, M., & Kruse, P. (1988). Theory of Gestalt and self-organization. In E. Rosseel (Ed.), *Self-steering and cognition in complex systems.* New York: Gordon and Breach.

von Foerster, H. (1981). *Observing Systems.* Niederzissen: Innersystems Publications.

von Foerster, H. (1985). *Sicht und Einsicht.* Braunschweig: Vieweg.

von Glasersfeld, E. (1980). The concept of adaptation and viability in a radical constructivist theory of knowledge. In I. Sigel, R. Golinkoff, & D. Brodzinski (Eds.), *New Directions in Piagetian theory and their application to education.* Hillsdale: Erlbaum.

von Glasersfeld, E. (1981). Einführung in den radikalen Konstruktivismus. In P. Watzlawick (Ed.), *Die erfundene Wirklichkeit.* München: Piper.

von Glasersfeld, E. (1985). Reconstructing the concept of knowledge. *Archives de Psychologie, 53,* 19-101.

von Glasersfeld, E. (1987). *Wissen, Sprache und Wirklichkeit.* Braunschweig: Vieweg.

6. The Difficulty in Explaining Suggestion: Some Conceivable Solutions

V.A. Gheorghiu

When research on suggestion first began, the serious endeavor of most authors was to propose definitions, e.g. Baudouin (1924), Bernheim (1891; 1911), Janet (1919), and McDougall (1908), to name only a few of the well-known scientists (for reviews, see Allport, 1985; Chertok, 1984; Larède, 1980; Stokvis & Pflanz, 1961; Stukat, 1958).

The development of empirical goals in research led to the rapid decline of efforts to conceptualize the phenomenon. This was even true for Binet (1900), who realized that suggestion (suggestibility) is a multi-faceted phenomenon. As far as I know, he never committed himself to a definition. Even in contemporary research on suggestion phenomena, for example in the well-known works of Eysenck (1947), Eysenck and Furneaux (1945), and Stukat (1958), attempts to conceptualize suggestion and suggestibility are nonexistent. Both Eysenck and Stukat primarily attempt to explain the factors of so-called primary and secondary suggestibility. Considering the general aspects of suggestion and suggestibility, they maintain, in accordance with Binet's proposition, that the phenomenon in question is not a unitary one. Certainly, this statement is important for the entire research on suggestion, and, contrary to Eysenck's endeavors to classify suggestibility, it has never been seriously questioned. Consequently, we only learn what suggestion and suggestibility do *not* mean.

None of the definitions prevail today. Older interpretations, such as those given by Bernheim, Janet, and McDougall, are quoted in order to call attention to a particular development in research on suggestion and hypnosis, or to point out an especially influential tradition. Taking Bernheim's explications into account, it has become customary in the past few years to speak of a so-called classical suggestion effect, thus stressing the involuntary character of suggestible reactions (Weitzenhoffer, 1980).

The task of defining suggestion and suggestibility came to be more frequently undertaken by the publishers of various psychological, medical, and philosophical dictionaries. Confrontation with manifold viewpoints that are repeatedly expressed in connection with suggestion promotes confusion. One has to agree with Larède (1980), who notes that the definitions found in dictionaries, including the specialized ones, give the general impression "that when it comes to suggestion, one is dealing with an extremely complex phenomenon on which many different and often contradictory opinions exist. There seems to be no consensus except unanimity in many definitions accentuating the interruption of the concerned subject's capacity for critical disposition" (p. 26). The *Dictionary of Psychology* edited by the French psychologist Pièron (1963), is one of the few which expressly points out the vague and undefined character of the term "suggestion".

In some respects, it would be less difficult to determine the exact meaning of certain terms if they did not have such a long and complicated history of usage. Most likely it would be easier to develop a completely new terminology for suggestion, suggestibility, and other related terms. But even if the traditional terms could eventually be replaced successfully by new ones, the discussion of the existing concepts, contradictory as they may be, proves to be unavoidable. On the one hand, it helps us to "rediscover" useful aspects. On the other hand, trying to avoid confrontation with these concepts would seem utopian. Pseudoscientific interpretations, regularly flourishing in this field, will always catch up with us in the end.

Nowadays, discussion is turning more and more to techniques of suggestion and the possibilities for their practical application in clinical work, forensic psychology, education, and sports. There is much talk on the influence of suggestion in advertising and politics, suggestion and suggestibility in a hypnotic or normal waking state, suggestion and the placebo effect, suggestion as a research method, suggestion as an explanation for various processes of substitution, suggestion as self-fulfilling prophecy, and so on.

This list is long enough to point out the need for gaining more detailed knowledge of those attributes associated with the term. According to Bunge (1967), the scientific definition should, amongst other things, promote "logical hygiene" in order to reduce ambiguity and vagueness to a tolerable degree.

My main concern in the following is to point out those obstacles which make it so difficult to determine the general and specific components of suggestion. My statements will be based on some of my earlier publications (Gheorghiu, 1967; 1972; 1982; 1987).

Suggestion as a Demand (Incentive) Situation: The Principle of Alternative Solutions

Defining concepts has always been a difficult task. In the case of suggestion, there is the additional problem that useful criteria are lacking through which we can arrive at an agreed-upon basic definition, one which can be related meaningfully to other terminology. Suggestion is largely defined as an influential process, a communication process, or simply as a stimulus. Constructs of this kind turn out to be much too vague and ambiguous to provide an acceptable frame of reference.

Owing to the fact that suggestion can be considered as a multifaceted phenomenon, one will probably always have to operate within a loose frame of reference, provided that it conveys the essential idea of an incentive nature (*"Aufforderungscharakter"*), or valence as conceptualized by Lewin (1926), or demand characteristics as Orne (1962) calls it, which is inherent in every kind of suggestion. Whether directly or indirectly, authoritatively or persuasively, implicitly or explicitly, overtly or discretely, deliberately or unintentionally, the subject's behavior or experience will always be guided in a certain direction. It is this quality which is revealed in colloquial speech: suggestion in the sense of proposal, impulse, hint, allusion, recommendation, etc. For the most part, both Titchner (1916) and Weitzenhoffer (1963) regard suggestion(s) as stimuli with *determining tendencies*.

Underlining the demand or the inciting nature of suggestion expresses more clearly that we are dealing with a *potential trigger situation*. One can comply with a demand but must not necessarily do so. This means that, in the case of the suggestion situation, alternative reactions are also possible which are parallel to the intended reactions. A person to whom it has been suggested that he/she cannot separate his/her clasped hands disposes, theoretically at least, of the alternative not to act according to this demand. Should this alternative of *reacting differently* not be guaranteed because of a forced limitation on a person's freedom of action, i.e., limitations set by fixed behavioral patterns or external constraints, then we are no longer talking about a suggestion situation.

Still, this does not exclude the possibility that suggestive influences do play a part in the forming of stereotypic behavior. Such a type of behavior can provide favorable conditions for further suggestible reactions (for example, as in the case of firmly established superstitions or prejudices). Probably this also applies to the establishment of conditioned responses, and it seems to me that in this sense Pavlov (1927) may be understood when he calls suggestion the most elementary form of a typical conditioned response. The conditioned connection gradually coming into existence *suggests* step by step, so to speak, the formation of a reflex reaction. However, as soon as we are dealing with a fixed reactive behavior, we can no longer call it a suggestion situation, since under normal conditions it leaves no room for alternative responses. Still, suggestion effects can undoubtedly occur on the basis of conditioned responses or learning processes in general.

Suggestion has a paradoxical character: On the one hand it is *not coercive*, which means it does not evoke the intended reaction in an automatic manner. On the other hand, the reaction can readily *become compulsive* as a result of the suggestibility process initiated. This can be seen in people, for example, who unconsciously let their behavior be guided by the prediction of a fortune-teller and thus help a self-fulfilling prophecy become reality. Much the same applies to people who autosuggestively talk themselves into thoughts of suicide and then more or less compulsively surrender to them. As is well known, not all persons who are exposed to such a demand situation actually succumb to its influence but instead are able to find means of evasion (Gheorghiu, 1987).

The influential process initiated by suggestion, if it is indeed effective, preconceives a confrontation with the rival alternatives. Everyday experiences verify this fact quite well: "Let us take," Allport (1985) writes in this context, "the case of a man who buys a suit of clothes under the persuasion of a silver-tongued salesman. The seller points out its virtues in terms of fashion, flattering fit, and comfort. Bombarded by the arguments the customer yields to persuasion; but he has not given due weight to equally relevant considerations that might have blocked the purchase-expense, specific wardrobe needs, and personal preference. Even though the salesman may have introduced more determining tendencies than the buyer initially possessed yet, functionally speaking, the salesman has reduced the effective determinants. The buyer's purchase is therefore partly, if not altogether, the result of suggestion" (p. 19).

If a suggestion does prevail, then the person concerned does not realize - at least not while responding - that at the same time other possible reactions have been eliminated. This can best be illustrated in the case of leading questions. It is characteristic of this type of question that the answers are provided at the same time, often not even allowing the actual questions to take form. Suggestions always offer answers or solutions, so to speak, even when they create (suggest) the problem in the first place. They implicate proffered solutions as the only valid ones. Finally, the suggestions can be considered effective when they are able to eliminate rival alternatives whilst being unnoticed. The directedness which is put into effect in the suggestive situation turns into an unambiguous directedness within the subject's own cognitive reality.

Undoubtedly, the difficulty consists in not always being able to determine whether possibilities of evasion do actually prevail in the respective concrete demand situation (or whether internal or external compulsory factors such as limited comprehension, pathological circumstances or obligatory situations do not allow for alternative solutions). In trying to find criteria by which to classify suggestion, one would have to resign oneself to these epistemic limitations.

According to general psychological interpretations, as expressed by Lewin (1926; 1946), the terms "demand," "incentive," or "valence character" ("*Aufforderungscharakter*") point out possible connections between suggestion and motivation. The formation of a suggestive situation and its feasible effects has often been related to motivational factors (Allport, 1961; Krech & Crutchfield, 1948; McDougall, 1908; Stokvis & Pflanz, 1961; Stukat, 1958). The instigative nature of suggestion cannot be dissociated from the reciprocal effect between situation and need, motive and inclination, etc. These are either evoked by the suggestive situation, or they give the particular situation its incentive or provocative character.

Suggestion and the Nonrational: The Aspect of Substitution (To Put Under - Subgerere)

Another difficulty consists in distinguishing those qualities which characterize the uniqueness of the effect of suggestion. In dealing with this problem, most authors mention extinction, reduction, or evasion of the rational components of personality, thinking, and judgement. They indicate uncritical, involitional, and unconscious behavior and experience (Allport, 1959; McDougall, 1908; Stokvis & Pflanz, 1961; Young, 1931).

Considerations such as these undoubtedly refer to relevant aspects of suggestion, but they are not sufficient for delineating the specific characteristics. Certainly, there exists a range of non-rational, uncontrolled, and unconscious behavior patterns that cannot credibly be associated with the term "suggestion," especially because of their compulsive character (like an automatized behavior), which leaves no room for alternative solutions.

"Rationality" itself is a very controversial term. The nonrational is moreover often interpreted as irrationality, or the emotional factor is simply viewed as the negation of the rational. For many years, the concept of Stokvis and Pflanz (1961) has prevailed in German-speaking countries, according to which the elusion of rational personality factors affected by suggestion can be understood as the "emotional influencing of the physical-mental whole on the basis of an interpersonal, fundamental fulfillment of the emotional resonance effect" (p. 6).

Rational mechanisms are not the basis of suggestion processes, but they definitely can be one reason for their influence. McDougall (1935) already points out that plausible argumentation and manifest reasoning can potentiate the forces of suggestion. It is a matter of everyday experience that the human being more often believes that he/she has acted according to rational views, whereas actually he/she has succumbed to a suggestive influence.

There is yet another aspect to be considered here. By emphasizing the nonrationality of a suggestible action, it is easy to come to the conclusion that the absence of a response to suggestion coincides with the participation of rationality. Allport (1959) notes, for example, that as a result of suggestion, an individual accepts a mode of behavior or a view without the processes of thought and judgment *which properly should be present*, and play a part. Here one could insinuate that, if rational functions were involved, the person would not respond. That may or may not be the case. Imagine a patient who, by suggestion, is led to believe that the pain he/she feels is decreasing more and more and will finally disappear. Should he/she not respond to this analgesic suggestion, it does not necessarily mean that the respective person's attitude was especially critical. The same applies particularly to indirect methods which simulate a stimulation, for example, when dispensing a placebo or attempting to bring about sensations of heat by simulating the presentation of an objective stimulus (heat illusion). In instances of plausible simulation, neither the responder nor the "nonresponder" knows that they have been confronted with a suggestive demand situation. Das (1955) found that requests to develop critical attitudes do indeed greatly diminish the effects of suggestion but do not abolish them completely. We were able to prove that revealing the nature of indirect suggestion tests based on simulation methods does not prevent the suggestible subjects from responding in accordance with the suggestion when the experiments are repeated (Gheorghiu & Sander, 1973). The insight that a behavior is absurd does not always lead to discontinuation of the behavior. (The individual, for example, can become a victim of his own plausibly conceived pretense.)

The problem of finding the specific features of suggestion still persists. To refer to original connotations seems helpful in this context. "Suggestion" is derived from the Latin *subgero* or *subgerere* and means "to slide something underneath." As a matter of fact, it is within the *process of "putting under"* where *one of the decisive features of the suggestion effect* can be found. Whichever elements are upheld by the categories of suggestion or whichever methods of manipulation are employed or spontaneously arise, the effects of suggestion always appear to correspond to a replacement or substitution, equivalent to an *"as if"* situation. Similarities are considered identical, illusions as genuine, mere assumptions become proven statements, assertions and statements that have been merely indicated or left open to discussion gain authenticity. A model situation is experienced as if one could not avoid reproducing it, or, in compliance with a repeated persuasive allusion, is perceived as if it had an obligatory character. In the most general sense, "to put under" here means the tendency to respond in accordance with the proffered solution *as if* alternative solutions were nonexistent in the given suggestion situation. It must be emphasized, however, that the term "to put or place under" - which in everyday language has a rather negative connotation - is not used here in the sense of appraisal or estimation. Merely because the subject has not made use of the evasion possibilities principally available in the suggestion situation, it cannot be inferred that the occurrent substitution would not be of use to him or that the insinuated content must necessarily be false.

Especially Weitzenhoffer (1963) stresses the *"as if"* character of suggestion. He writes: "The subject reacts to the suggestion *as if* it were some other stimulus. Or, again, the suggestion acts as an *inadequate stimulus* for the particular observed response. Effectively then, a suggestion is a stimulus that, in combination with a general present objective stimulus situation, becomes equivalent to, or acts as a *surrogate* for, another non-present objective stimulus situation" (p. 272).

Suggestion and Suggestibility

One of the greatest difficulties in explaining suggestion is the fact that reference to the category of suggestibility cannot be eliminated. In a very general sense, suggestibility can be understood as those mechanisms considered responsible for the formation of suggestive directedness and its transformation into suggestible responses. If one defines suggestion as the potential trigger of responses, then one is always alluding to the intermediate processes.

But even the demand nature of a suggestion situation cannot be adequately defined without taking the subject into account. The suggestion stimulus in itself is not yet *self-evident, credible, surprising, infectious,* etc. The *prestige* of the suggestor by itself can sometimes evoke suggestible responses more strongly than the spoken word. But there is no prestige until the subject attributes it to the suggestor. Lewin (1946) views the demand characteristics - and the environment factor in general - as variables which are principally not independent of the person. Here it is not possible to discuss the complex questions of suggestibility processes. (Some observations concerning this subject can be found in the first chapter of this volume.) However, reference to a central mechanism seems essential. This must be assumed theoretically in order to be able to determine the peculiarities of suggestible behavior. As already mentioned, there is little sense in looking for this peculiarity in nonrational processes. The reference to control and monitory functions seems to be more crucial. An understanding of suggestion is directly associated with an understanding of those mechanisms which enable the control systems to distinguish between true and false, real and unreal, plausible and unplausible. Suggestion effects - as products of substitutive processes - always concur with an impairment of the subject's conscious control. The growing interest of researchers in suggestion concerning the mechanisms of control and monitoring processes seems entirely justified (in particular see Hilgard, 1977; Bowers, 1982; Lindsay & Johnson, 1987).

The close link between suggestion and suggestibility, however, does not preclude the differentiation of these two categories. They are therefore suitable for emphasizing the difference between *virtual* and *real*. According to McDougall (1908), whose definition still has great influence today, suggestion is *"a process of communication resulting in the acceptance with conviction of the communicated proposition in the absence of logically adequate grounds for its acceptance"* (p. 100). More attention is drawn to the process than to that which could cause suggestion. Consequently, it is too easy to come to the conclusion that, once present, suggestion inevitably results in behavior corresponding to the suggested message. If a subject does not respond to a suggestive demand - for example, if he opens his eyes although he has been given the suggestion that he cannot do so at the moment - it still cannot necessarily be concluded that he has been offered no suggestion at all. It is not the suggestion which has been dropped but rather the intended response. This generally applies to demands which allow for alternative solutions. "I shall not be provoked," we say in ordinary usage. However, this does not preclude provocation as such.

In converting the theoretical and practical question into the empirical, not only does the problem arise concerning the characteristics the receiver must possess in order to respond in compliance to a suggestive demand. There is also the relevant problem of which peculiarities of the stimulus situation make the susceptibility of the subject *more likely* (i.e., the degree of ambiguity of the stimulus situation, the embedding of the suggestion procedures in lifelike contexts, the use of persuasive, model-like or technical vehicles, etc.).

Based on the considerations mentioned above, I propose the following definition: *Suggestion is a demand situation which, founded on a substitutional or replacement ("to put under") process, can induce (conscious) uncontrolled responses. In the given situation, though, the subject must theoretically (potentially) also dispose of the alternative of being able to react in a different way.* Naturally, this is an extreme simplification. I take the risk to present it here in order to outline at least some of the major contours of the phenomenon in question.

Content, Form, and Mode of Suggestion

Adequate criteria for understanding the various facets of the suggestion phenomena from everyday life, in practical application and in research, are still for the most part lacking. This can be at least partly explained by the insufficient clarification of terminology. Instead of ascribing the term "suggestion" to a more general generic term, a subdivision into several classification categories is preferred: autosuggestion versus heterosuggestion, verbal versus nonverbal suggestion, personal versus impersonal suggestion, prestige versus nonprestige or neutral suggestion (Weitzenhoffer, 1963). These categories only permit insignificant conclusions about the common denomination of suggestion and its components which they promise to reveal. Here, as in the case of the general terms "suggestion" and "suggestibility", we are dealing largely with concepts treated as if they were self-explanatory.

Suggestions are primarily considered to be mere statements which are applied directly for the purpose of influencing a person: induction of a hypnotic situation, provocation of delusions as manifested in the placebo effect, or manipulation of opinions, attitudes, and decisions through advertising, propaganda, etc. Those statements which are concealed within leading questions can also be classified under this category. Largely under the influence of experimental and clinical work (last but not least in the field of hypnosis), the erroneous opinion has emerged that suggestion in any case requires a verbal form. Furthermore, the idea prevails that a demand situation can only be considered a suggestion situation, if the suggestion is applied intentionally. Unintended suggestions are seldom taken into consideration (Stokvis & Pflanz, 1961). A logical inconsequentiality has begun to spread. Deception of expectations, induced under laboratory conditions, is considered a phenomenon of suggestibility, whereas illusional perceptions which occur spontaneously on a similar basis in everyday situations are not. But even directly applied suggestion methods, which are very similar to those carried out under experimental conditions but are seldom used outside the laboratory, are barely discussed in connection with suggestion effects (i.e., various methods of distraction and deception used by mothers to quiet their children, methods used by magicians, etc.).

With the help of a many-faceted input/output model, McGuire (1985) analyzed complex processes of communication causing changes in attitude. The model consists mainly of five input variables taken from the classical analyses of communication (source, message, channel, receiver, target) and of 12 output variables. Although McGuire also included suggestion in his analysis and the model proved adequate for his approach, I do not believe that it would be suitable for our purpose here, because McGuire starts from a scheme conceptualizing the structure of social influence. Our aim, however, is the matter of providing a framework of conditions which should first make it possible to determine the circumstances which are circumscribed by the term "suggestion." To crystallize the characteristics of suggestion, it seems appropriate to include categories allowing for sufficient generalizations. In order to take the versatility and complexity of suggestion phenomena into account, one should make use of the categories *content*, *form*, and *mode*.

The Content of Suggestion

The *content* refers to the message contained in the suggestive directedness. This can be explained by pointing out effects which can be caused by suggestion. In the extreme and general sense one could, in this respect, speak of psychic events which are (a) evoked or annulled, (b) accentuated or diminished, or (c) conserved or distorted. In order to stress the specific character of suggestion effects as opposed to the effects of other demand situations - which indeed can also be characterized by these general categories -, the important point now is to examine which specific substitutional processes are involved in the three categories. We should consider, for instance, the substitutions which lead to the activation of latent dispositions or to the uncontrolled acceptance of instructions and decisions, as well as those substitutions which are exhibited in various delusive phenomena or paradoxical behavior.

In addition to the above-mentioned criteria, the contents of the suggestion can be determined with regard to their pragmatic relevance. The question is to what extent the induced effects possess a more positive, a more negative, or a neutral character for the subject. Influences of suggestion not only are omnipresent, they are also complex and contradictory. They can initiate and consolidate healing processes but also induce destructive effects which can even lead to self-destruction (so-called Thanatos suggestions), and so on.

The Form of Suggestion

With respect to the *content*, the problem of the *form* carrying the content and bringing it to account arises. Categories of form may be classified according to several aspects.

A first differentiation would refer to the various sources of the demand situation. In this respect, forms of suggestion pointing to primarily "intraindividual," "interindividual," or "extraindividual" aspects would have to be distinguished. In connection with the first categories, the distinction commonly made is between self-suggestion and heterosuggestion (in which case both categories can be understood more in the sense of verbally structured suggestion forms). So far, there is no special name for "extraindividual" situations that can function as suggestion situations in the physical and social environment.

One further view which should be discussed in more detail here concerns the reference to typical contexts in which the suggestive directedness originates or is formed. These contexts are: *contexts of analogy*, of *cues*, of *model situation*, of *involvement*, and of *challenge situation*.

Contexts of Analogy. A multitude of substitution processes originates on the basis of the similarity between illusion and reality. Accordingly, homologous phenomena are called identical, and partial aspects are identified with the whole. Examples, models, or metaphors are equated with factual circumstances or cognitions which themselves serve as helpful instruments for exploring the former. From the everyday lie all the way up to complicated simulation procedures, one endeavors to form the substitute in analogy to the genuine so that the subject succumbs to a mix-up. The number of substitutions which are brought about or implied by contexts of analogy is probably much larger than generally assumed. Suggestion phenomena such as manifested in *déjà vu* phenomena or in false generalizations as produced by the "*halo effect*" could, among others, be included here.

Context of Cues. In the course of a lifetime, man is permanently being instructed, advised, counseled, commanded. He/she receives indications and instructions in regard to a multitude of occurrences: tasks and their completion, rules of behavior to follow, the probable course of events, ways in which to judge oneself, other persons or situations, decisions in favor of or against certain solutions, etc. From this, favorable provisions for the initiation and accomplishment of substitutional processes affected by suggestion can result. Attention is selectively directed toward certain contents, and the instructions given occasionally develop into main ideas and dominant notions. Possible alternative solutions are more likely to be overlooked. This can especially be expected when the indicative stimuli are presented under conditions in which ambiguity or interpersonal dependencies prevail, in which the subject must act under time pressure or has only insufficient information at his disposal, etc.

Model Context. As a rule, suggestion effects of model situations refer to imitative tendencies (under the influence of a co-judge, for example). However, many model situations can be found in everyday life and under laboratory conditions that invite participation, have a contagious effect, or, in a broader sense, induce imitative tendencies (i.e., behavior models in street traffic, while shopping, or generally in estimating situations; presentation and demonstration models; models in the form of norm and value systems which are founded on a majority or which are supported by a striking minority or one person acting with certainty; and, last but not least, model situations which are firmly established in the subjective world or the behavior pattern of the subject himself). But one should also account for spontaneous deviations (including paradoxical reactions) from the model situations with demand characteristics. After all, they also originate under the influence of these forms of stimulation. Imitations and suggestion are difficult to separate clearly (Allport, 1985). The same is true of differences between conformity and suggestion (Allport, 1961; Gheorghiu, 1972; Stukat, 1958). The matter at hand is simply to point out contexts which lead to the limitation of freedom of choice and which stir up substitutions. Essentially, the possibility of responding differently is not taken away from the subject. He believes that he has made his own decision or formed his own personal opinion, whereas he has actually been largely influenced by a model.

Involvement Context. This refers to aspects of experience and behavior which develop while carrying out actions or participating in events. At work or play; while reading, listening, and watching; while arguing, debating, or confessing; while carrying on a monologue or dialogue; while concentrating or relaxing, and so on: In all of these contexts, one allows oneself to be carried away and projected into the circumstances or just allows oneself to become involved. Normally, involvement contexts are discussed in connection with influences of suggestion in situations that are induced directly with the help of suggestion and imagination techniques (i.e., hypnosis and relaxation conditions, mental training). Again, it was hypnosis researchers who directed attention to the relationships between hypnotic involvement and other involvement contexts (Hilgard, 1965; Sarbin & Coe, 1972; Shor, 1970). One can assume, though, that every participation that lays claim to the inner world of the individual produces favorable conditions for the forming of suggestive directedness. In the process of involvement, cognitive and/or emotional associations can predominate. Contents of moods, notions, and ideas tend to become independent and develop their own logic, which is within limits only accessible to the conscious control mechanisms. Consequently, the manifestation of inertia can be promoted, and it often proves difficult to make involvement fluctuate or to switch over to other contexts of experience and behavior. Engaging in a certain action can, if involvement becomes too strong, lead to the limitation or even loss of self-control (as shown in Milgram's obedience experiments (1974) or the Stanford prison study of Haney et al., 1973). These developments are, to a great extent, dependent on (a) the circumstances that induced or helped promote involvement (i.e., mere participation, factors of contagion, or being caught unawares in some situations); (b) the motives that incite and substantiate projection (only superficial participation or passionate involvement, as when being in love, a state which, as Freud pointed out (1940/1963) is related to hypnosis and suggestion); and (c) factors of habit or the novelty of the situation. It can be added that being present, taking part or projecting oneself into the given situation often takes place within the framework of certain role distributions which, for their part, are embedded in conventions and rituals that themselves exert independent influences of suggestion (i.e., in therapeutic situations, participation in experimental situations, or mass demonstrations).

Challenge Context. Man, as a self-regulative system, is constantly called upon to protect, defend or promote his biological, psychological, and social interests. He strives to overcome the obstacles that stand in the way of his self-realization and consequently hinder his needs for identity and social acceptance. Accordingly, he holds his own in the multitude of intraindividual, interindividual, and extraindividual situations that challenge him to act: in accordance with the behavior of others or in opposition to their actions and opinions, self-indulgently or with self-sacrifice; cautiously or spontaneously. In order to reach this goal, for which various levels of reduction of complexities (Luhmann 1984) are unavoidable, he makes use not only of rational mechanisms but also of nonrational, unconscious mechanisms, such as protective, self-deceptive, avoidance, relief, or compensational strategies (e.g., for the purpose of dissonance reduction). These coping mechanisms are closely related to substitutional processes that involuntarily help the individual to decide in favor of a certain alternative, to postpone or avoid decisions, to make explanations or interpretations, to develop or alter personal constructs and frames of reference.

The contexts cited above - there are possibly more to be found - can only serve as a rough system of reference. They serve to direct attention to the potential vehicles of suggestion.

Finally, while searching for typical forms of suggestion, one should presuppose that during the formation of suggestion contents certain internal and external components become prominent: these involve mainly *symbolic components* (of the verbal and nonverbal kind), *affective components* (in form of mood or state of arousal), *behavioral components* (specific responses in or outside a group situation), and so on.

The Mode of Suggestion

The *mode* refers primarily to the concrete means by which suggestive contents are conveyed within the suggestion forms. Although it is not especially emphasized, it appears that in particular the aspect of mode is taken into consideration when dividing suggestion into sub-units. Some of the features of suggestion refer more to *how* than to *what* is being conveyed (direct versus indirect, personal versus impersonal, prestige versus nonprestige suggestion). Further, other terms which are often mentioned in close connection with the concept of suggestion and suggestibility, such as persuasion, aim more at the mode of conveyance than at the content of the message to be conveyed. Suggestion is generally considered as a kind of manipulation or, in other words, a special mode of inducing influence.

That an aspect of mode must be taken into account can no doubt be derived from the fact that the same suggestive content can be transmitted by various ways and means. The suggestive contents are conveyed directly or indirectly; verbal or nonverbal reinforcers are employed; their credibility is dependent on the share of sensorial intermodality or the interference of persuasive or model procedures. This function of the modus becomes most apparent when the object is to develop suggestion techniques that can be applied as methods for research and practical purposes. In this case, a multitude of procedures that convey suggestive contents according to the specific contexts can be controlled as independent variables. Whether the suggestive directedness actually comes into play can depend, to a great degree, on the significance gained by the suggestion *mode* in the concrete suggestion situation.

When looking at the mode from a very general viewpoint, the significance of a major category can be ascribed to it because all kinds of demand situations - in relation to what their actual effect is - can be called modes: modes of influence on behavior and experience. But this general *mode* again is characterized by certain *contents*, *forms* and, of course, by various *modes* (which refer more to the concrete aspects of the conveyance of demand contents).

It does seem necessary to keep this very general meaning of mode in mind for the very reason that, in doing so, essential aspects take a definite form that would otherwise be overlooked by a more narrow view. A more general aspect of the demand situation - as a mode of influence - refers, for example, to whether it follows spontaneously or is deliberately produced. Furthermore, it is of interest whether the occurrence of the demand mode is gentle or shocklike, whether its effects take hold immediately or later, whether it exerts a momentary or long-lasting influence, whether it affects the peripheral or central mechanisms of the individual, etc.

The concepts *content*, *form* and *mode* are by no means strictly separated categories but a means of orientation. They have a close reciprocal relationship to each other, and one category can change into another. Still, it appears to be appropriate to use the classification as an organizing principle. On the basis of these concepts, the differences and similarities between suggestion and other demand categories can be more adequately described, for example those which leave no margin for alternative solutions, those which develop controllable directedness, those which provoke reflective processes, or those whose effects are not concomitant with substitutional processes.

The attempt to emphasize the universality of the suggestion situation leads to an extension of the limits that research tacitly has set for the field of suggestion. The scaffolding set up for construction is more extensive than the house being built under it. *Content*, *form*, and *mode* are as artificial as other categories of order. They are just conceived as a framework of conditions to make it possible to describe and classify various suggestion situations in everyday life, research and practice. The main concern here is to gather the factors and to proceed according to the principle "from the general to the specific" (Dörner, 1983). To do justice to this task is certainly a difficult and tedious undertaking that requires constant revision of the conceptual framework originally postulated.

In the network of suggestible phenomena, one can also discover "nodal points" such as "self-fulfilling prophecy," "a tendency to imagine things" (in the sense of delusions), "activation of latent dispositions," "involvement/absorbance," "paradoxical behaviors," "group pressure," etc., some of which were already mentioned above in a different connection. With their transgressive character, these can contribute to the comprehension of more general connections. As part of his heuristic reflections on psychological research, Dörner (1983) also discusses this category of variables. He is correct in emphasizing that as long as these transgressive variables have a direct, "everyday-psychological" significance, one can start from "everyday psychology" when establishing interpretive models. While still keeping everyday psychology in mind, at the same time one surpasses its restrictions by the process of successive differentiation (p. 26).

The difficulties in developing definitions of suggestion cannot just be attributed to shortcomings in suggestion research. They also result from the general problem of psychological research which actually offers us very few integrative approaches. Miller, Galanter and Pribram (1960) note in their well-known book *Plans and Structure of Behavior* that "the trouble is not that we lack a good theory of hypnosis, but that we lack a good theory of will" (p. 104).

To paraphrase that statement, one could say that what is lacking is not a theory of suggestion. Rather, what is missing are integrative theories of the formation of subjective reality with functional autonomy and of involuntary structuring and restructuring of cognitive reference systems; consistent theories of anticipatory function, directedness, and decision processes, as well as theories of self-control mechanisms, which are also essential points in the problem of suggestion.

Should a shift in paradigms in psychological research move suggestion phenomena from a marginal area into the central position where, in my view, they belong, owing to their special function within the influential processes, it can then be expected that this field of research will also contribute to the development of integrative theories. An outstanding example of this is that of modern research in hypnosis, of which the methodological and theoretical approaches have increasingly become the common property of psychological research.

Acknowledgements. The author expresses his thanks to R. Bender, N. File, T. Gehm, P. Kruse, P. Netter, H. Ophoff, E. Schwanenberg, P. Sheehan, and G. Vollmer for their critical comments on the first draft of this text and to M. Heinl-Hutchinson for the translation.

References

Allport, G.W. (1985). The historical background of social psychology (Vol. 1). In G. Lindzey & E. Aronson (Eds.), *The handbook of social psychology* (3rd ed.). New York: Random.

Allport, G.W. (1959). *Persönlichkeit: Entwicklung, Struktur und Erfassung* (2nd ed.). Meisenheim/Glan: Hain.

Allport, G.W. (1961). *Pattern and growth in personality*. New York: Holt, Rinehart, & Winston.

Baudouin, C. (1924). *Qu'est-ce que la suggestion?* Neuchâtel: Delachaux & Niestlé.

Bernheim, H. (1891). *De la suggestion et de ses applications à la thérapeutique*. Paris: Doin.

Bernheim, H. (1911). *Hypnotisme et suggestion*. Paris: Doin & Fils.

Binet, A. (1900). *La suggestibilité*. Paris: Schleicher.

Bowers, K. (1982). *Suggestion and control*. Invited address, Meeting of the American Psychological Association, Washington, D.C.

Bunge, M. (1967). *Scientific research* (Vol. 1). Berlin Heidelberg New York: Springer.

Chertok, L. (1984). Suggestio rediviva. In L. Chertok (Ed.), *Résurgence de l'hypnose*. Paris: Desclée de Brouwer.

Das, J.P. (1955). Understanding versus suggestion in the judgment of literary passages. *Journal of Abnormal and Social Psychology, 51*, 624-628.

Dörner, D. (1983). Empirische Psychologie und Alltagsrelevanz. In G. Jüttemann (Ed.), *Psychologie in der Veränderung*. Weinheim: Beltz.

Eysenck, H.J. (1947). *Dimensions of personality*. London: Routledge & Kegan Paul.

Eysenck, H.J., & Furneaux, H.D. (1945). Primary and secondary suggestibility: An experimental and statistical study. *Journal of Experimental Psychology, 35*, 485-503.

Freud, S. (1963). Massenpsychologie und Ich-Analyse. In Gesammelte Werke (Vol. 13, pp. 122-128). Frankfurt/Main: Fischer. (Original edition published 1940).

Gheorghiu, V.A. (1967). Cu privire la conceptul de sugestie [On the concept of suggestion]. *Revista de psihologie, 13/2*, 179-185.

Gheorghiu, V.A. (1972). On suggestion and suggestibility. *Scientia, 107*, 811-860.

Gheorghiu, V.A., & Sander, D. (1973). Untersuchungen zur Änderung der Suggestibilität unter bestimmten Einstellungen. In G. Reinert (Ed.), *Bericht über den 27. Kongreß der Deutschen Gesellschaft für Psychologie*. Göttingen: Hogrefe.

Gheorghiu, V.A. (1987). *Sugestia*. Warszawa: Wiedza Powszechna.

Gheorghiu, V.A., & Ciofu, I. (1982). *Sugesie si sugestibilitate: Aspecte psihologice si psihofiziologice*. Bucharest: Editura Akademiei.

Haney, C., Banks, C., & Zimbardo, P. (1973). Interpersonal dynamics in a simulated prison. *International Journal of Criminology and Penology, 1*, 69-77.

Hilgard, E.R. (1965). *Hypnotic susceptibility*. New York: Harcourt, Brace & World.

Hilgard, E.R. (1977). *Divided consciousness: Multiple controls in human thought and action*. New York: Wiley.

Janet, P. (1919). *Les médications psychologiques*. Paris: Alcan.

Krech, D., & Crutchfield, R.S. (1948). *Theory and problems of social psychology*. New York: McGraw-Hill.

Larède, J. (1980). *Qu'est-ce que la suggestologie?* Toulouse: Privat.

Lewin, K. (1926). Vorsatz, Wille und Bedürfnis, mit Vorbemerkungen über die psychischen Kräfte und Energien und die Struktur der Seele. *Psychologische Forschung, 7*, 294-385.

Lewin, K. (1946). Behavior and development as a function of the total situation. In L. Carmichael (Ed.), *Manual of child psychology*. New York: Wiley.
Lindsay, D.S., & Johnson, M.K. (1987). Reality monitoring and suggestibility: Children's ability to discriminate among memories from different sources. In S.J. Ceci, M.P. Toglia, & D.F. Ross (Eds.), *Children's eyewitness memory* (pp. 92-121). Berlin Heidelberg New York: Springer.
Luhmann, N. (1984). *Soziale Systeme: Grundriß einer allgemeinen Theorie*. Frankfurt/Main: Suhrkamp.
McDougall, W. (1908). *An introduction to social psychology*. London: Methuen.
McDougall, W. (1935). *The energies of men: A study of the fundamental of dynamic psychology* (3rd ed.). London: Methuen.
McGuire, W.J. (1985). Attitudes and attitude change (Vol. 2). In G. Lindzey & E. Aronson (Eds.), *The handbook of social psychology* (3rd ed.). New York: Random.
Milgram, S. (1974). *Obedience to authority*. New York: Harper & Row.
Miller, G.A., Galanter, E., & Pribam, K.H. (1960). *Plans and the structure of behavior*. New York: Holt, Rinehart, & Winston.
Orne, M.T. (1962). On the social psychology of the psychological experiment: With particular reference to demand characteristics and their implications. *American Psychologist, 17*, 776-783.
Pavlov, I.P. (1927). *Conditioned reflexes*. London: Oxford University Press.
Pièron, H. (1963). *Vocabulaire de la psychologie*. Paris: Presses Universitaires de France.
Sarbin, T.R., & Coe, C.W. (1972). *Hypnosis: A social psychological analysis of influence communication*. New York: Holt, Rinehart, & Winston.
Shor, R.E. (1970). The three-factor theory of hypnosis as applied to the book-reading fantasy and to the concept of suggestion. *International Journal of Clinical and Experimental Hypnosis, 18*, 89-98.
Stokvis, B., & Pflanz, M. (1961). *Suggestion*. Stuttgart: Hippokrates.
Stukat, K.G. (1958). *Suggestibility: A factorial and experimental analysis*. Stockholm: Almqvist & Wiksell.
Titchner, E.B. (1916). *A textbook of psychology*. New York: MacMillan.
Weitzenhoffer, A.M. (1963). *Hypnotism: An objective study in suggestibility* (2nd ed.). New York: Wiley.
Weitzenhoffer, A.M. (1980). Hypnotic susceptibility revisited. *American Journal of Clinical Hypnosis, 22*, 130-144.
Young, P.C. (1931). Suggestion as indirection. *Journal of Abnormal and Social Psychology, 26*, 69-90.

7. Commentary on „Theoretical and Historical Perspectives“

P.W. Sheehan

Since the beginning of the century, research on susceptibility to social influence has focused on common themes, and these still occupy the attention of the five authors in this opening section. Such themes include: (a) the generality of individual response to different suggestions; (b) the definition and assessment of the effects of suggestion on behavior; (c) the reasons why individuals vary in their responsiveness to suggestion (the issue of mechanism); and (d) definition of the most appropriate frame of reference for conceptualizing the influence of suggestion (phenomenal or real).

H.J. Eysenck: Personality, Primary and Secondary Suggestibility, and Hypnosis. Prof. Eysenck is the pioneer of much of the debate that occurred in this symposium. His work in 1943 and (with Furneaux) in 1945 presented us with data that drove home sharply the lesson that there are independent types of suggestibility. He offered us, for example, the important distinction between "primary" and "secondary" suggestibility and hinted at another type that was labeled by him (with Furneaux) "tertiary suggestibility." Primary suggestibility was indexed in terms of ideomotor tests, and measures of it correlate with hypnotizability. Secondary suggestibility consists of indirect suggestions where the precise nature of the desired end or result is not made explicit, and this type of suggestibility does not correlate with hypnotizability. The third form of suggestibility (tertiary) brings into the scheme of things an interpersonal quality that is defined in terms of the prestige of the suggester; it is this kind of suggestibility that bears an intuitive resemblance to what has been termed in the literature as "interrogative suggestibility." Eysenck's emphasis on taxonomy, and the experimental analysis of suggestibility, concerns us all. He talks of the oddities of "fact," but the evidence to hand seems no more unusual than the variety of ways in which suggestion itself may be categorized.

This summary of Eysenck's historical contribution is not meant at all to convey that his thinking in the field is uncontentious. Strong argument exists in the literature, for example, about the validity of the distinction he has drawn between primary and secondary suggestibility (see Evans, 1967). Secondary suggestibility has also been reported by Gudjonsson (this volume) as a more elusive entity than primary suggestibility; and Gheorghiu, also, has drawn attention (Chap. 6, this volume) to the need to unconfound the various components of suggestion. Interestingly, Eysenck pursues the relationship between drive level and suggestibility and I see this as not unrelated to Gheorghiu's notions of the incentive value of suggestion.

It is not the aim of this commentary to resolve these issues. Rather, it seems more appropriate to signal the importance of Eysenck's work in the overall debate. In this respect, his work has sharpened discussion in the literature about types of suggestibility, it has been a major stimulus for new classifications of suggestibility and it has lifted our consciousness about the need to develop and apply specific measurement techniques in the pursuit of a proper understanding of suggestion and how it operates. Eysenck's emphasis on measurement has been especially important. We have also seen Gheorghiu and Reyher (1982) develop an "indirect-direct" method for administering a scale of sensory items, and considerable attention has been placed in the literature on the relevance and validity of *the Gudjonsson suggestibility scale* (Gudjonsson, 1984) which may be considered an "indirect" test of suggestibility. The validity of Gudjonsson's test draws to some extent on the methods established by Eysenck in his work, in particular the practice of devising adequate assessment techniques.

It is important to acknowledge that Eysenck has applied a strong measurement emphasis to the task of analyzing the differentiation between attitude and aptitude, and he has contributed to the field distinctive methodologies such as "zone analysis." But like others among us, he has not answered the major theoretical questions that face the field. I am still, for example, uncertain of the meaning of "suggestibility," how drive is related to suggestibility, or of the value of conditioning theory as a route to our locating the right mechanism for understanding suggestion phenomena. None of us has answered these questions. However, we owe much to Eysenck in the search for answers. It is largely because of his work that there is now a consensus among us that suggestibility is *not* a generalizable phenomenon.

V. Gheorghiu: The Difficulty of Explaining and Defining Suggestion. Prof. Gheorghiu's paper on the difficulty of explaining and defining suggestion offers us an intriguing look at the complexity of the concept of suggestion itself. It is fitting for a paper such as this to be in the opening section of this volume, because it addresses centrally a theme that preoccupies everybody working in the field. It is a difficult, but not impossible, task to sort out and clarify this complexity. Working from the premise that the phenomena of suggestion and suggestibility are multifaceted, Gheorghiu's paper exposes us to a range of concepts that appear to be related. Following the arguments he offers us in his paper, we need to know which concept is best to choose when, and under what conditions, and the range of concepts for choice is extensive. The range incorporates the concepts of influence, imitation, conformity, susceptibility, suggestibility; one might add persuasibility, hypnotizability and perhaps gullibility, and also "interrogative suggestibility."

Importantly, Gheorghiu's paper highlights a number of important conceptual features of the process of suggestion. I want to focus on just two: his notion of the "incentive" nature of every suggestion, and the provocative link he draws between suggestion and lack of rationality. Both notions are theoretically significant.

Let me consider "incentive value" first. Gheorghiu intends the notion of "incentive value" to highlight the *motivational* features of suggestion. His discussion reminds me of a key characteristic of our discipline - themes and concepts reassert themselves through time. Mueller (1979), some time ago, drew our attention to the recycling of ideas in his *Annual Review of Psychology* survey of the discipline. So too, did the historian Robert Watson (1967) when he argued for the validity of the notion that prescriptions of science reoccur in new guises to make us rethink. More recently still, Ekehammer (1974) taught us how history had been talking about interactionism as a theory of personality well before modern theorizing rediscovered it. In what Gheorghiu has stated, I am reminded particularly of Allport's (1937) definition of trait as a "determining tendency to respond"; and Allport talked in this way, *before* Weitzenhoffer (1953) talked similarly with respect to suggestion. Allport's early emphasis on the quality traits possess to guide and direct our behavior in a motivated fashion was an important conceptual contribution that the current literature on suggestion has tended to forget. Gheorghiu's notion of "incentive value" resurrects the point.

It seems useful to take this concept a little further and expand the debate. If we regard suggestibility as a trait (in terms of guiding or directing behavior), one may ask what the impact of situations is on the motivated property of suggestibility. Situations clearly modify or alter the impact of suggestibility and shape the influence of suggestion. Thus, one may ask legitimately what influence situations will exert on this determining tendency to respond, on the motivating properties of suggestion.

Let me turn now to the link with rationality, the second feature of Gheorghiu's paper that I wish to single out for discussion. Gheorghiu's paper correctly, I believe, argues that suggestion should not simply be viewed as a lack of rationality. There are too many instances available to our experience and reported in studies in the published literature where suggestion operates in conjunction with signs of thoughtful, planful responding. The notion of hypnosis as a strategic enactment, argued by Spanos (1986) and Wagstaff (1981), for example, is based on this assumption. The field of hypnosis simply has to recognize that the deeply hypnotized person is problem solving in relation to the suggestions that are received. Gheorghiu's arguments allow us to assert that suggestion can induce reactions that more or less evade control and surveillance. We urgently need, as he says, theories to guide us on how the processes of control and surveillance operate, and to isolate the mechanisms which underly them. The question of what degree of surveillance holds in response to suggestion is critical to our understanding of many of the phenomena of suggestion, and to the meaning of hypnosis, in particular.

Let me try and expand on the fact that surveillance is not entirely extinguished in suggestion and look briefly again at the issue of the motivated properties of suggested behavior. In doing this, I would like to appeal to the relevance of social factors in Gheorghiu's analysis - a dimension not touched upon greatly in his paper here, but discussed by him elsewhere (Gheorghiu, 1982). For example, someone else is often the agent of motivated direction, and interactions between that person and a subject will structure the degree of surveillance that exists. Situations and interpersonal features of them, in particular, shape and mold the operation of suggestion and its influence, and they moderate the degree of control and surveillance that can be shown. I am, in a sense, here entering into the "situation" side of the *trait x situation* equation of Interactionism. Expanding Gheorghiu's thoughts in this way may be helpful in the enormously demanding task of accurately and comprehensively categorizing suggestion.

P. Kruse: Some Suggestions about Suggestion and Hypnosis: A Radical Constructivist View. Dr. Kruse's paper questions whether hypnosis has come of age "scientifically" - whether its reputation depends on the spectacular. His point is well taken, but I think his concern is much less a problem now than it used to be. I would suggest hypnosis is no longer a glamor girl, but rather something of a maturing person maintaining perhaps a little too much of the old seductive charm. The reason his concern is not so relevant at this point in time is that the knowledge base of hypnosis has of late been integrated much more into the mainstream of psychology. That integration, in a sense, is the main preoccupation of Kruse's paper. His goal is a commendable one, and one that is taken up by many of the other papers in this volume (see Lundy for example).

In proposing such integration, Kruse argues that hypnosis is best viewed as part of a process of construction associated with the cognitive system. This parallels a constructive view of perception, rather than a direct representational account. The view is attractive, and Kruse's paper pushes us to look at the ways subjects construct cognitions in response to suggestions. He alerts us to the importance of perhaps talking less about altered states of consciousness in hypnosis than about "alternate" modes of consciousness - a much more "active" notion. His view borrows from European psychology by looking to the influence of Kohler and the neurophysiological work of Maturana, and the important thinking of von Glaserfeld.

In pursuing his radical constructivist account, Kruse focuses on the problem of defining reality criteria. He proposes the view that the gap between private and, what I will call "consensual" reality, is *not* a slip in the cognitive system; rather, it is a meaningful expression of cognitive construction at work. Interestingly his paper looks at the "discriminability" of perception and hallucination, and of perception and fantasy. This reminds me of Binet and Fere's (1988) classic statement that in every image there is the germ of an hallucination, and I would want to extend Kruse's notion of discriminability to cover non-perceptual processes as well. There is for me a very fine line, at times, between so-called different modes of consciousness. In this respect, the relevant point of Perky's work (1910) is well taken; here, perception and imagery were entirely confused by subjects in the reports they gave about their experience. Clearly, cognitive processes labeled by us very differently are often hard to separate in the subjective reports that people offer, and this is a major problem for research to address.

Kruse's choice of variable on where *to go in on* the cognitive system is "intensity" and I want to discuss this choice more closely.

Kruse's paper lists relevant criteria for us to consider. They are overall phenomenologically or experientially oriented except for his last criterion that the existence of the object is "intersubjectively confirmed." Despite this last criterion - which attempts, I believe, to take us some distance toward an external standard - I see a problem in how well the constructivist account is able to distinguish "subjective conviction" (induced by the conditions of test) and reality which does not parallel, or accord with private conviction. Perhaps I am returning here to highlight the plea of Ericsson and Simon (1980) for guidelines to be drawn up so that we can know how far we can actually trust phenomenal (verbal) reports. It seems to me that Kruse seeks "objectivity" in part, but mostly the criteria he offers us and the importance he places on "intensity" emphasize the phenomenal world at the expense of the real one.

Despite this point - and I admit it is heavily philosophical - there are many consequences of Kruse's constructivist account with which all would agree. For example, induction is appropriately viewed as a situation where the experienced difference between imagination and perception diminishes. Interestingly, this "faculty of discrimination" (and I like the phrase) seems to relate directly to Gheorghiu's discussion of the link between hypnosis and rationality. Both Kruse and Gheorghiu agree that discrimination between suggested experience and perception may exist, though Kruse appears to admit to the possibility that the faculty of discrimination may not just be reduced, but, rather, eliminated or extinguished. Again, I would echo the theme (with which both would agree) that we must vigorously research the extent to which discriminability shifts. To me, this is one of the key theoretical issues in the whole field of suggestion. Johnson and Raye (1981) began to take us down the path toward addressing it with their concept of "reality monitoring," but we have not yet traveled along that route very far.

With Kruse, I think that we need to know the way reality criteria normally operate, the way they interact, and when and how they are suspended. And we have much still to learn, as Kruse says, about these problems as they occur in normal, waking subjects.

R.M. Lundy: The Internal Confirmation of Personal Constructs: Why Suggestions Are Not Accepted. Dr. Lundy's paper, like that of Kruse, embraces the goal of integration. In particular, Lundy attempts to broaden the scope of discussion by attempting to explain the phenomena of suggestion and suggestibility within the framework of the conceptual scheme established by George Kelly (1955). In particular, Lundy's paper highlights the importance of the notion of "internal confirmation." He posits this process as a necessary mediation factor in the creation of suggestion effects. The concept refers to "the hypothesized action of personal constructs to account for the behavior of the recipient in suggestibility situations," and there are many implications of such a view that are relevant to our understanding of effects in the broad social psychological literature. It can be predicted from this viewpoint, for example, that conditions emphasizing attention - as it is focused upon persuasion material and away from internal confirmation - will be most influential in producing attitude change. And as Lundy reports, Festinger and Maccoby (1964) have demonstrated that subjects distracted by a second task are more likely to be persuaded.

The major advantage of Lundy's extension of Kelly's personal construct model is that it places prime importance on the need to understand subject's personal conceptions of events, as they are suggested. It is clear that the person delivering suggestion can often have a mistaken conception of how suggestion fits (or does not fit) with the personal constructions of the recipient. Application of The Experiential Analysis Technique (Sheehan & McConkey, 1982), for example, has yielded ample evidence to demonstrate the point that subjects' private interpretations of suggestions are frequently out of phase with the interpretations of the person who is delivering a suggestion communication. Our explanation of suggestion effects has little chance of being correct unless we have an accurate conception of what people's understandings really are.

This emphasis on private understanding focuses on the essential property of a phenomenological approach to the explanation of suggestion. Kelly's model, like that of Kruse in this volume, requires that we focus upon the subjective experience of the person who receives suggestion. Where Kelly differs from a number of other theorists (e.g., Shor, 1979) who have taken a similar approach, however, is that he (like Sheehan and McConkey, 1982) focuses on the subject as a knowing, but thinking being. As Sechrest (1977) states, personal constructs are for Kelly "an individual's conclusions or interpretations or deductions about life. Kelly's psychology of personal constructs relates then to (our) cognition or private logic" (p. 205). It is the anticipation, the active cognizing and constructions that are important to Kelly, not reality.

Pursuing this emphasis a little further, it is important to recognize that Lundy chooses to derive a theory from Kelly which emphasizes, as others have done in this volume, the absence of a lack of rationality in response to suggestion. In this sense, we return again to the point made by Gheorghiu that some degree of surveillance is operating in suggestion response; the point reminds us also of Kruse's observations concerning the operation of the suggestible subject's "faculty of discrimination." Where Kruse emphasizes, however, that subjects construct cognitions in response to suggestions and appeals primarily to the processes of perception, Lundy's theory (as derived from Kelly), focuses upon the adoption, evaluation, and discarding of personal constructs and emphasizes, for the most part, change and the social psychological factors (such as a person's repertoire of roles) that affect it. With these differences in emphasis, there are, of course, varying implications for assessment. Kruse would appear to prefer methods that detect experienced differences between imagination, hallucination, and perception, while Kelly's model primarily implicates the diagnosis of personal constructs such as provided by Kelly's own method of Role Construct Repertory Test.

Before embracing a general model for the explanation of suggestion effects, such as the one Lundy proposes, it is as well to recognize that there are phenomena of suggestion that appear to be difficult to assimilate to a framework based on personal constructs, and further research is clearly needed. Such, for example, is the experience of duality in hypnosis where the highly suggestible, hypnotized subject reports on nonsuggested (real) affairs and suggested affairs as occurring in experience, at one and the same time. According to Kelly's model, change in belief is always to the other end of the construct, and personal constructs are essentially dichotomous in nature. The fluidity of the experience of duality, however, implies more of a floating set of constructs merging together and apart, both frequently and contemporaneously. However, it is the self-determining quality of Kelly's model that is its real conceptual strength, and Lundy's extension of Kelly's theorizing is an inventive and highly useful one that future research would do well to pursue.

W.E. Edmonston: Conceptual Clarification of Hypnosis and Its Relationship to Suggestibility. Dr. Edmonston's paper, like Gheorghiu's paper, aims to clarify conceptually the operation of suggestion, especially as it relates to hypnosis. Importantly, his paper argues that hypnosis and suggestion should not be equated - a conclusion that would meet with the agreement of all five authors to this section. The paper provides us with a detailed review of issues in the field and conceptually takes a stand on definition in pursuit of the task of clarification. It does so, like the papers of Gheorghiu and Kruse, by appealing to the history of ideas and observations on suggestion. We must surely all accept Edmonston's point that the observational powers of our colleagues are likely to have been as astute as our own, and too many workers in the field seem to have lost touch with the awareness of how hypnosis has come to us historically. In fact, all of the papers in this section teach us the lesson that we should not at any cost lose touch with our past.

Edmonston sees suggestion as the central distortion of incoming sensory impulses. In locating the mechanism of response to suggestion centrally, I am interested in what might be Kruse's reaction when he chooses to locate his mechanism centrally also. A constructivist account of response to suggestion, however, is not necessarily an inherently distorting one. Distortion is not a relevant issue to Kruse's model. Further, I am intrigued by Edmonston's argument that suggestion misleads through a "disruption" of central interpreting mechanisms. How much, for instance is this process of disruption akin to the cessation of rationality that Gheorghiu, Kruse, and Lundy all address?

There are a number of conclusions on the evidence that Edmonston offers us with which, again, all five authors would probably agree. One is that suggestion and hypnosis are not the same. Another is that suggestion is enhanced by hypnosis. Edmonston's major conclusion is that hypnosis is a relaxation response. It is this last conclusion which offers us the most controversial stance. By his position, Edmonston calls for a move away from social interactional analysis and he urges us to look at hypnosis viewed as a "condition of relaxation." The question for me is not so much how much relaxation accompanies nonvoluntary responding (it frequently does), but how essential relaxation is as a component of hypnosis. Finally, hypnosis for me - I think for Gheorghiu, Kruse, and Lundy, as well - is not entirely a passive phenomenon. Call it a lack of irrationality (as Gheorghiu does), or the presence of some surveillance (as Kruse does), or the active evaluation of personal constructions (as Kelley would), passivity does not seem to be as necessary a feature of hypnosis as Edmonston's paper implies. The properties of relaxation are also hard to reconcile with evidence such as that provided by Bányai and Hilgard (1976) which shows that hypnosis can be induced under quite altering conditions. However, the importance of relaxation has been underestimated, as the history of hypnosis makes clear, and Edmonston's paper raises theoretically significant questions that demand to be answered. Theorizing in the field would unquestionably advance if we knew the conditions that maximize hypersuggestibility in relation to nonhypnotic relaxation techniques.

Edmonston's paper also raises a wide variety of theoretical possibilities which, if addressed, would inevitably order the way we classify suggestion. Reading his paper and those that have preceded it makes it evident that such ordering is essential. He has introduced us to an enormous range of potentially relevant dimensions. There is primary, secondary, (and possibly tertiary suggestibility), and direct and indirect suggestion, and we have normal and abnormal suggestibility as well. To provoke a little, I might explicitly ask how "abnormal" suggestibility is in hypnosis. If Edmonston's theorizing on relaxation is correct, it is not likely to be very abnormal at all, and if we emphasize a social interactional analysis of the issues, we might come to the same conclusion. Our major challenge, then, probably resides in the problem of defining the limits of "normality."

Concluding Comments

There are a number of key recurring themes in this series of papers that can be summarized. One is the multidimensional nature of the concept of suggestibility. All would agree with this conclusion, and each author would agree that hypnosis and suggestibility are not the same. The second set of recurring themes that seems to have the consensus of the authors is that there is a general lack of dependence of theory on data, and we need to categorize the various components of suggestibility with care and precision. The challenge of arriving at an adequate taxonomy still looms large. Each author has also drawn attention to the relevance of past observations; the lessons to be learned from history must not be forgotten. In particular, the series of papers singles out the relevance of rationality, surveillance, or critical judgement. A major problem for all, also, is the association of phenomena with normalcy, and in one way or another special concern is expressed about links involving the processes of perception, and normal sociopsychological sources of influence. Finally, the series as a whole highlights very pointedly the philosophically difficult problem of distinguishing the extent to which we should adopt a model that is observer-oriented or externally oriented versus one that is experiential or phenomenological in outlook.

Clearly, this series of papers challenges our deep, underlying assumptions about the nature of the discipline of psychology and how we view the relationship between body and mind. Also the fact that a gap exists between the theoretical academic concepts we adopt and their applicability to the real world further extends the level of the debate. The various notions of suggestibility that we have canvassed here tell us just how complex one limited domain of personality is, but also how relevant it might be to look broadly across apparently different domains of inquiry in a searching and analytical way.

References

Allport, G.W. (1937). *Personality: a psychological interpretation.* New York: Holt.

Bányai, E.I., & Hilgard, E.R. (1976). A comparison of active-alert hypnotic induction with traditional relaxation induction. *Journal of Abnormal Psychology, 85,* 218-224.

Binet, A., & Fere, C. (1888). *Animal magnetism* (Trans.). New York: Appleton. (Original work published 1886)

Ekehammer, B. (1974). Interactionism in modern personality from a historical perspective. *Psychological Bulletin, 81,* 1026-1048.

Ericsson, K.A., & Simon, H.A. (1980). Verbal reports as data. *Psychological Review, 87,* 215-251.

Evans, F.J. (1967). Suggestibility in the normal waking state. *Psychological Bulletin, 67,* 114-129.

Festinger, L., & Maccoby, N. (1964). On resistance to persuasive communications. *Journal of Abnormal and Social Psychology, 68,* 359-366.

Gheorghiu, V.A. (1982). *Suggestion and suggestibility: Psychological and psychophysiological aspects.* Bucuresti, Edit. Academiei.

Gheorghiu, V.A., & Reyher, J. (1982). The effect of different types of influence on an "indirect-direct" form of a scale of sensory suggestibility. *American Journal of Clinical Hypnosis, 24,* 191-200.

Gudjonsson, G.H. (1984). A new scale of interrogative suggestibility. *Personality and Individual Differences, 5,* 303-314.

Johnson, M.K., & Raye, C.L. (1981). Reality monitoring. *Psychological Review, 88,* 67-85.

Kelley, G.A. (1955). *The psychology of personal constructs.* New York: Norton.

Mueller, C.G. (1979). Some origins of psychology as science. *Annual Review of Psychology, 30,* 9-30.

Perky, C.W. (1910). An experimental study of imagination. *American Journal of Psychology, 21,* 422-452.

Sechrest, L. (1977). Personal constructs theory. In R.J. Corsini (Ed.), *Current personality theories.* Itasca, IL: Peacock.

Sheehan, P.W., & McConkey, K.M. (1982). *Hypnosis and experience: The exploration of phenomena and process.* Hillsdale, NJ: Erlbaum.

Shor, R.E. (1979). A phenomenological method for the measurement of variables important to an understanding of the nature of hypnosis. In E. Fromm & R.E. Shor (Eds.), *Hypnosis: Developments in research and new perspectives.* Hawthorne, NY: Aldine.

Spanos, N.T. (1986). Hypnosis and the modification of hypnotic susceptibility: A social psychological perspective. In P. Naish (Ed.), *What is hypnosis? Current theories and research* (pp. 85-120). Milton Keynes, UK: Open University.

Wagstaff, G.F. (1981). *Hypnosis, compliance and belief.* New York: St. Martin's.

Watson, R.I. (1967). Psychology: A prescriptive science. *American Psychologist, 32,* 435-443.

Weitzenhoffer, A.M.C. (1953). *Hypnotism: an objective study of suggestibility.* New York: Wiley.

II

Suggestibility: Assessment and Individual Differences

8. Sensory Suggestibility: Measurement, Individual Differences, and Relation to Placebo and Drug Effects

P. NETTER

The present chapter is concerned with sensory suggestibility (SS), its measurement, its relation to other variables like psychological traits, states, and perceptual or autonomic functions, and its relations to the effects of placebos and drugs, relations which might help to elucidate the generality of the concept and possible underlying biological principles.

Measurement of Sensory Suggestibility

As has been outlined in the discussion on theoretical constructs of suggestibility in the first section of this book, the concept needs *precise definitions* and *instruments of measurement* so as to specify with which type and subcategory of suggestibility the researcher is concerned. For many decades, suggestibility was measured by an arbitrary selection of methods developed in the area of motor or sensory suggestibility mixed with procedures used for induction or tests of hypnosis. The systematic analysis of dimensions according to which suggestibility may be defined in a pluri-dimensional space was achieved by Gheorghiu's systematic approach to this problem, an approach which resulted in the development of his instrument for measurement of sensory suggestibility (Gheorghiu, Hodapp, & Thieding, 1972; Gheorghiu, Hodapp, & Ludwig, 1975; Gheorghiu, Grimm, & Hodapp, 1978; Gheorghiu & Feingold, 1981; Gheorghiu & Reyher, 1982). (The same categories of mode, content, and form of stimulus presentation, however, are also valid for scales of motor suggestibility which are being constructed by him.)

In Gheorghiu's scale, sensory stimuli are suggested to the individual according to the following principles:

1. The stimuli by themselves produce the kind and direction of suggestion the experimenter wishes to induce in the subject.
2. Induction or modification of stimuli to be perceived by the subjects is achieved by technical instruments.
3. Social manipulation of expectations and the suggestive process is achieved by instructions.

The dimensions according to which suggestion of sensory stimuli are manipulated are:

1. Appearance/disappearance
2. Intensity (increase/decrease)
3. Location (unilateral/bilateral)
4. Type of sensory organ (visual, auditory, tactile)

Suggestions may be brought about by (a) instruction or manipulation of technical devices; (b) preceding presentation of one or a series of objective stimuli; or by (c) coupling a stimulus with a second one in the manner of classic conditioning.

Gheorghiu's scale utilizes the following modalities developed for visual, auditory, and tactile stimuli:

1. Simulation of increasing intensity of a stimulus by manipulation of a device (visual example: subject has to announce when the light of a bulb becomes brighter while experimenter operates a switch).
2. Simulation of decreasing intensity by the preceding presentation of a series of objective stimuli of decreasing intensity (visual example: black cardboard discs with central color points of decreasing size and brightness, on the last of which the point is missing completely, are exposed to the subject).
3. Simulation of simultaneous bilateral stimulus presentation (auditory example: two stopwatches, only one of which is started, are brought close to the subject's ears).
4. Simulation of a stimulus by instruction and demonstration of a stimulus-eliciting device (auditory example: subject has to announce when a silent stopwatch, brought closer and closer to the subject's ears, starts ticking).
5. Simulation of a stimulus previously coupled to a second stimulus (visual/auditory example: an increasing sound of a motor seemingly causes increasing brightness of a bulb, that is, however, switched off for the test presentation).

The instruction for this procedure is based on what Gheorghiu calls the "indirect-direct" form (Gheorghiu & Kiel, 1976; Gheorghiu & Reyher, 1982). This instruction is indirect in that stimuli are never presented to the participants and direct in that the subjects are cautioned that a stimulus might not actually be presented. The subject is instructed that the stimulus may or may not be presented according to a "program" that the subject himself blindly chooses from an assortment of "program cards," thus suggesting random assignment of the subject to the experimental condition that determines how many stimuli are objectively presented or not presented in the test.

In this manner, the experimenter is perceived largely as not responsible for what is presented to the subject. Thus, favourable responses intended to please the experimenter and "prestige" suggestions are to a great degree eliminated.

Factor analysis of the items yielded a final version of 5 visual, 4 auditory and 3 tactile items to be presented to both left and right sensory organs and hands respectively. Items are added up to a single score of maximally 24 points. Scores obtained with several "generations" of the instrument in different populations of all ages and levels of intelligence invariably yielded a skewed distribution with a median of 4 (Gheorghiu & Kiel, 1976), or 5 (Feingold, 1982; Zielberg, 1983), and a mode usually 1 point below the median. The reliability ranged between $r = 0.75$ and $r = 0.83$ (Gheorghiu et al., 1972; 1975; 1978; Gheorghiu & Kiel, 1976; Feingold, 1982) when tested by repeated measurements, on different instruments (the old mechanical devices were replaced by electronic ones) (Feingold, 1982), or with different instructions (Gheorghiu, 1982).

Individual Differences in Sensory Suggestibility as Related to Personality Variables and Psychological Functions

Although SS proved to be fairly reliable across time, across experimental instruments, and even across instructions, suggesting that SS has a trait-like stability, endeavours to relate the construct to *personality measures* obtained by questionnaires (anxiety, extraversion, neuroticism), as well as to intelligence, perceptual style, or autonomic reactivity did not yield reliably reproducible results (for review, see Netter, 1980; Feingold, 1982; Zielberg, 1983; Kleeberger, 1983).

Therefore, the question to be asked is not so much which trait is related to SS, but under what circumstances is a certain personality trait or state related to suggestibility and with what type of relationship (linear or curvilinear) are we confronted?

One of the few variables which seem to be fairly reproducibly related to SS is *age*; children of younger age are more susceptible than adolescents (Chemnitz, Feingold, & Gheorghiu, 1981; Feingold, 1982), as shown on Figure 1. The figure demonstrates concomitantly that the presence of a blind cojudge to whom the stimuli were actually presented increases response frequency in the subject tested (Gheorghiu & Feingold, 1981).

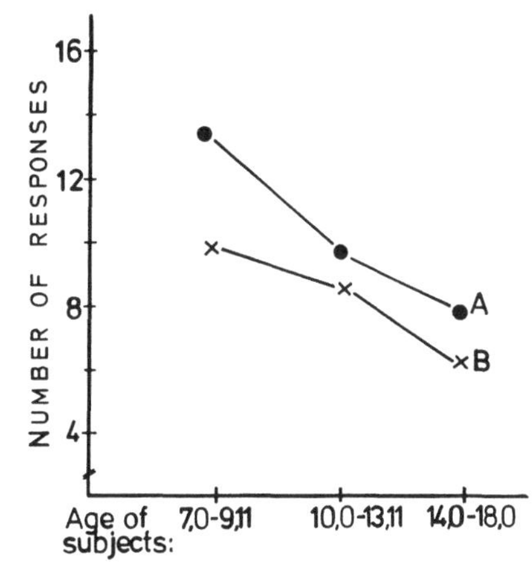

Figure 1. Average number of responses according to age of subjects and presence of cojudge (*A*, absent; *B*, present) (Feingold, 1982)

Sex of subjects shows interactions with sex of experimenter: subjects tested by experimenters of the same sex achieve higher scores than those tested by somebody of the opposite sex, as shown in table 1 (Gheorghiu & Kiel, 1976).

A negative relationship between SS and *intelligence* seems to emerge in males for total IQ (r = -0.38; $P < 0.01$) and for the subtests on similarities (r = -0.39; $P < 0.01$) and arithmetic (r = -0.41; $P < 0.01$), whereas respective correlations for females approximate zero; n = 50 for both male and female samples (Feingold, 1982).

Table 1. Means of suggestibility scores according to sex of subjects and sex of experimenter (Gheorghiu & Kiel, 1976)

Sex of experimenter	Sex of subjects	
	male	female
male	6.65	4.70
female	5.75	7.55

Certain variables of state also are differentially associated with SS. For males there is a positive correlation (r = 0.34; P < 0.05) between feeling activated and SS, while for females there is a tendency towards a negative correlation (r = -0.20; P = 0.10; Feingold, 1982). Also, activation showed an inverted u-shaped relationship to SS scores in a psychophysiological experiment performed by Neuhäuser, Schauren, Feingold, Chemnitz, Cordes, and Netter (1980). Subjects with an intermediate SS score (3-6 points) feel most activated, whereas subjects with high ($\geq$ 7 points) and low ($\leq$ 2 points) suggestibility had difficulty staying attentive and motivated for performance at their initial levels during the experiment (Neuhäuser et al., 1980; Figure 2). A similar relation was obtained for state anxiety when orthogonal polynomials were computed for suggestibility as the independent and state anxiety as the dependent variable (Zielberg, 1983).

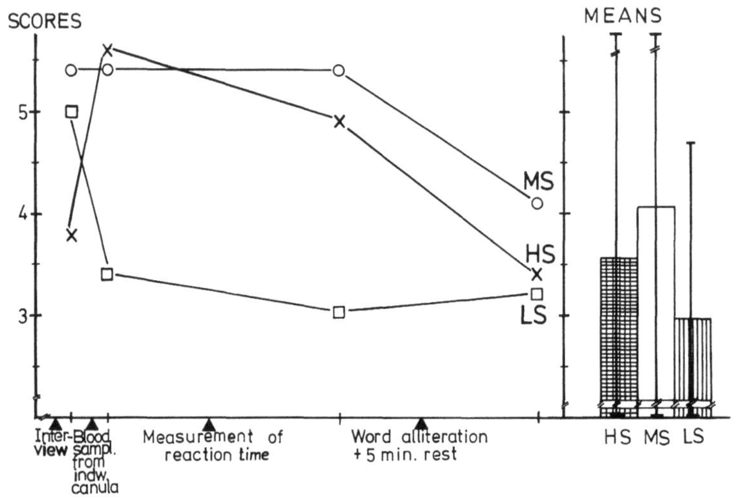

Figure 2. Scores on activation scale of adjective check list in 16 subjects of high suggestibility (*HS*), 25 of medium suggestibility (*MS*), and 16 of low suggestibility (*LS*) in 4 experimental periods.
Columns on the right, means across measurements; difference between group means: P < 5 % (Neuhäuser et al., 1980)

Curvilinear relations are additionally observed between SS and variables of *the autonomic nervous system*. Subjects of intermediate suggestibility have lower blood pressures and heart rates than have subjects of either high or low suggestibility (Figures 3 and 4). The subjects in this latter

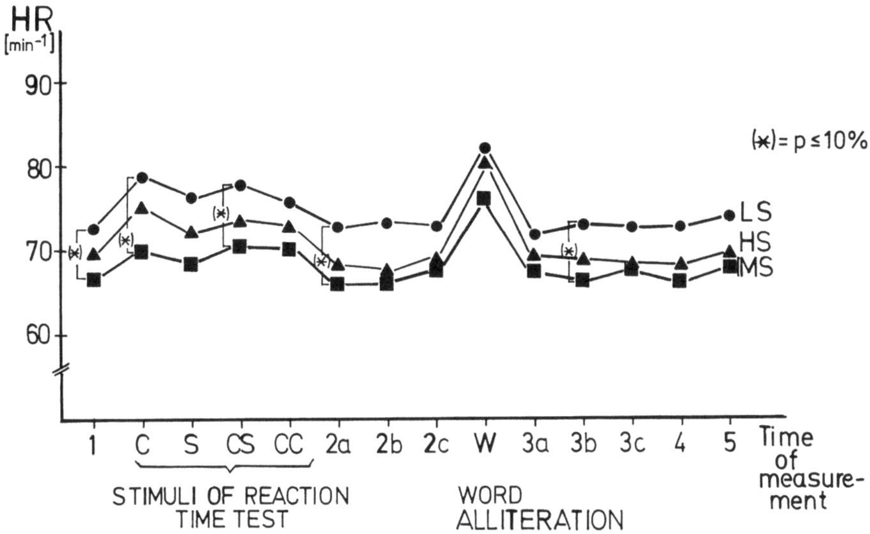

Figure 3. Means of the average heart rates in 16 subjects of high (*HS*), 25 of medium (*MS*), and 16 of low suggestibility (*LS*) (Neuhäuser et al., 1980).
(*) $P \leq 10$ %

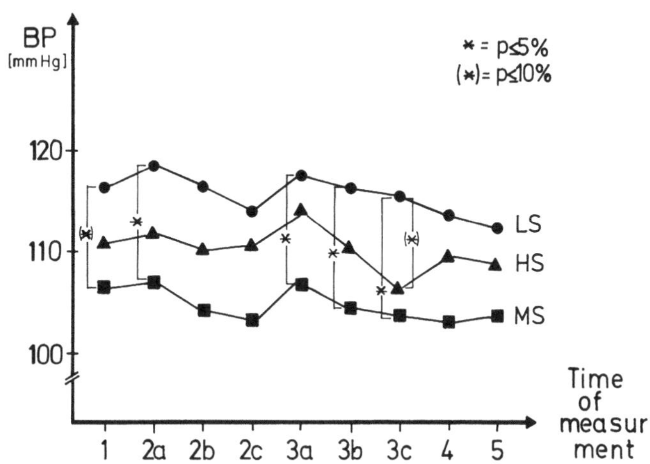

Figure 4. Mean systolic blood pressures in 16 subjects of high (*HS*), 25 of medium (*MS*), and 16 of low suggestibility (*LS*) (Neuhäuser et al., 1980).
* $P \leq 5$ %; (*) $P \leq 10$ %

group, who had the highest blood pressure and heart rates, seemed to exhibit a very tense, critical, and highly motivated attitude to the experiment, which prevented the subjects from being deceived by the suggestibility test or the experimenter (Neuhäuser et al., 1980).

Variables most likely to be related to sensory suggestibility are those in the *perceptual field*, such as sensory deception, judgement of size, flexibility of closure, speed of perception, the Stroop phenomenon, and field dependence (Kleeberger, 1983). Investigations in this area also revealed nonlinear relationships to scores on SS indicating that subjects both very low and very high in suggestibility may produce low responses in these tests of perception, whereas subjects with an intermediate score of suggestibility would achieve the highest scores in tests of perception. A summary of these findings, some of which revealed additional sex differences, is given in Table 2.

Relationships Between Sensory Suggestibility and Response to Analgesics and Placebos

Of those factors which were thought to be most likely related to suggestibility, one was reactivity to drugs, especially if there is little or no pharmacological effect. Evans (1967) was the first to review what had been claimed and published on reactivity to placebos and suggestibility. Since his widely acknowledged work came to the conclusion that there is no relationship between the two concepts (as outlined again by Evans, this volume) little with respect to this relationship was published and investigated in the following years.

The investigation by Classen, Feingold, and Netter (1983), however, differed in several ways from previous studies, as outlined by Feingold (1982). First, the modalities by which suggestibility was measured were identical with the modalities by which the effects of drugs were assessed. In the case of analgesics and their respective placebos, this is the modality of pain sensation. Therefore, it is logical to compare analgesic effects of placebos not to motor suggestibility but to sensory suggestibility which, with Gheorghiu's scale, is produced by instruments that are analogous to the suggestive elements that are inherent in tablets.

Furthermore, the study by Classen et al. (1983) used patients with pathological pain (headaches), and the assessment of sensory suggestibility was introduced as a device for testing general sensitivity to stimuli, implying a relationship between the patients' SS and their sensitivity to pain. The tests included also the assessment of electrically induced pain by a technique based on signal detection theory (SDT). Relationships between sensory suggestibility and responses to analgesics and to placebos were assessed by subjective ratings of headaches and scores of objective discrimination of painful stimuli in patients of high and low SS tested in a cross-over design of 5 weeks' duration in which two groups of 15 patients each were treated either according to the schedule OPDPP or ODPDD (where O = no treatment, P = placebos and D = 3 g of metamizole daily 3 times per day, with each treatment of 1 week's duration). The results yielded the following conclusions:

1. Responses to a placebo given for experimentally induced pain (which is less responsive to analgesics than are other kinds of pains) were not related to suggestibility.

Table 2. Relationships between measures of perception and sensory suggestibility

	Type of relationships			
Variable or measure	Males	Females	Total group	*P*
1. Stroop phenemenon				.025
2. Phi phenomenon (frequency for optimal impression of movement				.05
3. Critical flicker fusion and frequency (CFF)				.05
4. Estimation of size: level of subjective point of equivalence (inverted relation to estimated size, equals sensitivity for contrast)				.05 / .01
5. Müller-Lyer deception				.05
6. Reversible pictures (inflection rate)				.05
7. Speed and flexibility of closure (subscales 10, 11, 12 of the Horn Intelligence Test LPS)				.05
8. Perceptual speed according to Thurstone (number of errors in subtests "identical numbers" and "figure cancellation")				.01 / .025
9. Group Embedded Figures (number of correct responses)				.05

Note. The shape indicated is based on figures in which the abscissa is conceived as score of sensory suggestibility. Different curves for males and females are drawn only in case of significant sex differences (Data from Zielberg, 1983, and Kleeberger, 1983).

2. In pathological pain there was a positive relationship between suggestibility and decrease of headaches after treatment with drugs, as well as after treatment with placebos, over a period of 4 weeks, with no statistically significant difference between the effects of the two treatments. This applied only when patients were asked to rate the intensities of the headaches, not if they were asked directly whether the drug were effective. Drug efficacy was rated equally low in subjects of low and of high suggestibility.
3. An additional interesting finding concerned the patients' ratings on the competence and friendliness of their physician. Patients of high suggestibility rated their physician more favourably at the beginning of the study and less favourably after 4 weeks of treatment, whereas the subjects of low suggestibility showed the opposite trend. The combination of decreasing sympathy for the physician, disbelief in efficacy of the drug, and decreasing ratings of headache intensity (which however remained constant for the last 2 weeks of treatment) in patients of high suggestibility (Classen et al., 1983) was interpreted as the highly suggestible patient's attempt to force the physician to continue his endeavor to treat him, and as a tendency to attribute therapeutic success more to the physician than to the drug, and to become annoyed by stagnation of therapeutic success.
4. Since headaches were assessed about 1 h after each of the 3 daily drug applications for 5 weeks, a sufficient number of pain ratings following either placebo or analgesic (declared as analgesic in every case) was obtained for evaluating the data according to SDT. One of the measures derived is called "discriminative ability" (d'). This measure in this design indicates the subject's ability to discriminate between the analgesic and the placebo by ratings of the intensities of his headaches following drug intake (for details see Classen & Netter, 1985). This measure was related negatively to sensory suggestibility, a finding which implies that highly suggestible subjects are less capable of distinguishing (by their ratings of pain intensities) whether they are treated by a true drug or a placebo.

Sensory Suggestibility and Susceptibility to Effects of Nicotine

Experiments testing the effects of nicotine on the central nervous system by means of vigilance tasks in humans have revealed a biphasic action of nicotine (stimulating effects in small doses and reduction of arousal with larger doses) (Warburton & Wesnes, 1978; 1981). The individual point of shift from increase to decrease of arousal, however, varies from subject to subject, as would be expected from the inverted u-shaped curve relating performance and arousal on which Eysenck located introverts and extraverts smoking sham or real cigarettes (Eysenck & O'Connor, 1979). If subjects are arranged on a continuum of increasing susceptibility to nicotine, subjects of higher susceptibility will need lower dosages for equal increment or decrement of performance than will subjects of low susceptibility. Thus, values obtained with a constant dosage plotted into the coordinates of susceptibility and performance will form inverted u-shaped curves, with higher dosages having their peak at the lower end of the continuum of susceptibility, as shown in Figure 5.

The reason for combining the effect of nicotine with sensory suggestibility was that the anticholinergic drug scopolamine induces effects that are opposite to those of low doses of nicotine (i.e., scopolamine decreases vigilance, broadens instead of narrows attention, and increases divergent instead of convergent thinking (Warburton & Wesnes, 1981). Describing

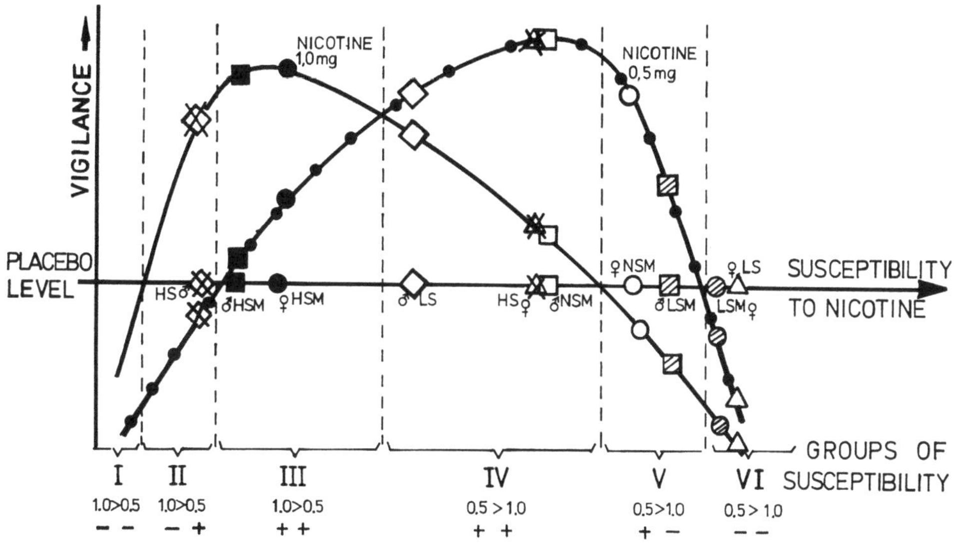

Figure 5. The hypothetical continuum of susceptibility to nicotine and means of differences between changes induced by nicotine and placebo in critical flicker fusion (CFF) in groups defined according to sex and smoking habit (n = 10 each) and in groups defined according to sex and sensory suggestibility (SS) (n = 15 each). I-VI, groups on continuum defined by relation of performance to dosages of 1.0 mg and 0.5 mg nicotine. ■, ●, heavy smokers (*HSM*); ▨, ◍, light smokers (*LSM*); □, ○, non-smokers (*NSM*); *squares*, male subjects; *circles*, female subjects; ⊠, ⩤, subjects of high suggestibility; ◇, △, subjects of low suggestibility; *diamonds*, male subjects; *triangles*, female subjects

these effects, the authors used, as an indicator of broadened attention, a device of sensory deception in which subjects treated with scopolamine tended to "respond" to acoustic stimuli, previously coupled to light stimuli, before they had been presented. Since this procedure has some elements in common with one of the subtests of the scale of sensory suggestibility, the hypothesis was raised that those subjects habitually high in sensory suggestibility would be in a state of cortical underarousal similar to that of subjects treated with scopolamine and would therefore be more resistant to the stimulating effects of nicotine.

After 3 days of training for obtaining optimal levels of exercise in the performance tasks, 60 subjects (30 males and 30 females divided into 3 subgroups according to smoking habits) were tested in a double-blind repeated measures design with 3 dosages of orally administered nicotine (0 mg = placebo, 0.5 mg, and 1.0 mg) in randomized sequence at intervals of 1 week. Subjects were divided into those with high and those with low SS according to the Gheorghiu scale and tested by several measures of vigilance including critical flicker fusion and frequency (CFF).

An indicator for susceptibility to nicotine was obtained by the relation between changes in the CFF obtained with the two doses of nicotine plotted as difference scores from respective placebo values. Six groups of susceptibility (I-VI) thereby resulted, as indicated in Figure 5. Means of CFF were computed for each of the subgroups as defined by sex and smoking habit (n = 10 each), as well as for subgroups as defined by sex and high versus low suggestibility (n = 15 each).

It could be shown that susceptibility to nicotine as thus defined was lower in males than in females, lower in heavy smokers than in light and non-smokers and lower in subjects of high sensory suggestibility than in those of low sensory suggestibility. This means that subjects of high sensory suggestibility will show their shift from stimulating to sedative effects of nicotine at a higher dose level.

This observation is taken as evidence that a state of mind that is defined by high sensory suggestibility is similar to the state that follows treatment by the anticholinergic drug scopolamine, an antagonist of nicotine. Those changes in vigilance following the administration of scopolamine that were observed by Warburton and Wesnes (1981) were similar to those found in our subjects of high suggestibility.

Perhaps even more noteworthy is the demonstration that drugs, here nicotine, may serve as tools of research in elucidating the nature of sensory suggestibility.

References

Chemnitz, G., Feingold, E., & Gheorghiu, V.A. (1981). Beeinflussung kognitiver Prozesse von Schülern verschiedenen Alters und Geschlechts durch ihre Mitschüler. *Psychologie, Erziehung und Unterricht, 28*, 7-12.

Classen, W., Feingold, E., & Netter, P. (1983). Influence of sensory suggestibility on treatment outcome in headache patients. *Neuropsychobiology, 15*, 44-47.

Classen, W., & Netter, P. (1985). Signalentdeckungstheoretische Analyse subjektiver Schmerzbeurteilungen unter medikamentösen Reizbedingungen. *Archiv für Psychologie, 137*, 29-37.

Evans, F.J. (1967). Suggestibility in the normal waking state. *Psychological Bulletin, 62*, 114-129.

Eysenck, H.J., & O'Connor, J. (1979). Smoking, arousal, and personality. In A. Rémond & C. Izard (Eds.), *Electrophysiological effect of nicotine* (pp. 147-157). Amsterdam: Elsevier.

Feingold, E. (1982). *Untersuchungen zur sensorischen Suggestibilität sowie zum Zusammenhang zwischen sensorischer Suggestibilität und der Placeboansprechbarkeit im Schmerzbereich*. Dissertation rer. nat. Mainz: Johannes-Gutenberg-University.

Gheorghiu, V.A. (1982). Testing stability of suggested behavior by means of a "forcing" system. In A. Kossakowski & K. Ubuchowski (Eds.), *Progress in the psychology of personality* (pp. 159-166). Berlin: VEB Deutscher Verlag der Wissenschaften.

Gheorghiu, V.A., & Feingold, E. (1981). The effect of a "cojudge" influence on sensory suggestibility. *Revue Roumaine des Sciences Sociales (Série de Psychologie), 25*, 159-167.

Gheorghiu, V.A., Grimm, H.J., & Hodapp, V. (1978). Standardisierung einer Skala zur Erfassung der sensorischen Suggestibilität (indirekte Variante) an Schülern der Sekundarstufe II. *Diagnostica, 14*, 350-361.

Gheorghiu, V.A., Hodapp, V., & Ludwig, C.M. (1975). Attempt to construct a scale for the measurement of the effect of suggestion on perception. *Educational Psychology Measurement, 35*, 341-352.

Gheorghiu, V.A., Hodapp, V., & Thieding, S. (1972). Untersuchungen zur taktilen, auditiven und visuellen Suggestibilität. *Archiv für Psychologie, 124*, 303-320.

Gheorghiu, V.A., & Kiel, M. (1976). Indirekte und indirekt-direkte Form einer sensorischen Suggestibilitätsskala. *Revue Roumaine des Sciences Sociales (Série de Psychologie), 20*, 29-46.

Gheorghiu, V.A., & Reyher, J. (1982). The effect of different types of influence on an indirect-direct form of a scale of sensory suggestibility. *American Journal of Clinical Hypnosis, 24*, 191-199.

Kleeberger, L. (1983). *Sensorische Suggestibilität und Wahrnehmungsfaktoren*. Dissertation med. Gießen: Justus-Liebig-University.

Netter, P. (1980). Suggestibilität und Medikamentenwirkung. *Medizinische Psychologie, 6*, 195-213.

Netter, P., Neuser, W., Homm, B., & Höbel, P. (1982). Sensory suggestibility as a modifying factor of the central nervous action of nicotine. (Abstract, p. 519). 13th *Collegium Internationale Neuro-Psychopharmacologicum* Congress, Jerusalem.

Netter, P., Neuser, W., & Hoffmann, J. (1983). Susceptibility to nicotine as related to smoking habits and personality factors. (Abstract). London: International Society for the Study of Individual Differences.

Neuhäuser, S., Schauren, M., Feingold, E., Chemnitz, G., Cordes, U., & Netter, P. (1980). Relations between sensory suggestibility and sympathetic nervous activity. (Abstract, Vol. 1, p. 312). 22nd International Congress of Psychology, Leipzig.

Shapiro, A.V. (1964). Placebogenics and iatroplacebogenics. *Medical Times, 92*, 1037-1043.

Warburton, D.M., & Wesnes, K. (1978). Individual differences in smoking and attentional performance. In E. Thornton (Ed.), *Smoking behavior*. (pp. 19-43). Edinburgh: Livingstone.

Warburton, D.M., & Wesnes, K. (1981). Cholinergic mechanisms and attentional dysfunction. In C. Perris, G. Struwe, & B. Jansson (Eds.), *Biological Psychiatry* (pp. 778-781). Amsterdam: Elsevier-North Holland.

Zielberg, R. (1983). *Sensorische Suggestibilität: Kognitive Steuermechanismen der Wahrnehmung und Indikatoren des Erregungsniveaus*. Dissertation med. Mainz: Johannes-Gutenberg-University.

9. Theoretical and Empirical Aspects of Interrogative Suggestibility

G.H. Gudjonsson

Introduction

This paper is in four parts. First, "interrogative suggestibility" is defined and its essential components are described. This is followed by a description of the ways in which interrogative suggestibility differs from suggestibility of other types. The author then presents a theoretical model of interrogative suggestibility, which he developed in cooperation with Noel Clark, his colleague in psychology. Finally, data on the testing aspects of the theoretical model are presented.

The author's interest in interrogative suggestibility began in 1980 when he took up a forensic post at the University of London. He was commonly asked to prepare court reports for defence and prosecution counsel. Some of the cases involved assessing the reliability of evidence in two different circumstances: in cases where (a) mentally handicapped victims were going to be called to give evidence; and (b) where defendants had retracted confessions made to the police during interviewing. Cases of the former type generally were referred by the prosecution, and the latter by defence counsel. It became clear to the author, whilst acting as an expert witness for either side, that the courts were commonly interested in the individual's level of suggestibility. The author had been unable to find any objective tests for measuring that phenomenon of suggestibility which would be relevant to police interviewing. A number of tests had been developed to measure "hypnotic" suggestibility, but these seemed to be of little relevance within the context of a police interrogation. He therefore decided to devise and develop a clinical instrument which could measure objectively, reliably, and experimentally, the behavioural characteristics of "interrogative suggestibility".

After developing such an instrument and validating it, the author began to work on a theoretical model which could help to further our understanding of "interrogative suggestibility". His current work is concerned with testing various parameters of the theoretical model.

Definition of Interrogative Suggestibility

Gudjonsson and Clark (1986) define interrogative suggestibility as "the extent to which, within a closed social interaction, people come to accept messages communicated during formal questioning, as the result of which their subsequent behavioural response is affected". This definition indicates that interrogative suggestibility has five interrelated components: (a) it generally occurs within a closed social interaction; (b) it involves a questioning procedure; (c) there is a suggestive stimulus which generally takes the form of a "leading question"; (d) it indicates a certain acceptance of the suggestive stimulus; and (e) it involves a behavioural response which indicates to the interviewer that the subject has accepted the suggestive stimulus.

How Interrogative Suggestibility Differs from Suggestibility of Other Types

Interrogative suggestibility as defined above bears little resemblance to the suggestibility of traditional definitions, whether classified into "primary" and "secondary" phenomena (Eysenck, 1947) or into "primary", "challenge", and "imagery" (Evans, 1967). However, the aspect of some sort of "uncritical" acceptance of a stimulus appears to be common to them all. The most distinguishing features of interrogative suggestibility are (Gudjonsson, 1986):

1. It involves a questioning procedure within a closed social interaction. The interviewing normally takes place in a closed room, the participants sit close to one another, interruptions are avoided, and the interviewing officer is in control of the interview and questions asked.
2. The questions are mainly concerned with past experiences and events, recollections, and remembered states of knowledge. This makes it quite different from suggestibility of those types that are concerned with the motor and sensory experiences of the immediate situation.
3. Interrogative suggestibility contains a strong component of uncertainty which is related to the cognitive processing capacity of the individual.
4. An important feature of the interrogative suggestibility is that it commonly involves a highly stressful situation with important consequences for the witness, victim, or suspect.

Schooler and Loftus (1986) highlight two different approaches to the study of interrogative suggestibility. These are referred to as the "experimental approach" and the "individual differences" approach. The former examines differences in the conditions under which leading questions are likely to influence the verbal account of witnesses. The individual differences approach examines the factors that are thought to determine why individuals respond differently to suggestions within an interrogative context (Gudjonsson & Clark, 1986).

Schooler and Loftus argue that the main advantage of the experimental approach is that it focuses on a central cognitive mechanism, "discrepancy detection", which has been found to mediate interrogative suggestibility. I have argued elsewhere (Gudjonsson, 1987a), that a major limitation of the experimental approach has been its reliance on college students as subjects whose intelligence and memory tend to be in the upper range. As the relationship between cognitive variables and suggestibility is subject to significant "range effect" (Gudjonsson, 1986), a proper understanding of the relevant cognitive variables can be achieved only by conducting studies utilising subjects who vary widely in their abilities. This has been one of the major advantages of the individual differences approach which has dealt much more with heterogeneous samples.

A Theoretical Model

The theoretical work of Gudjonsson and Clark (1986) provides a social-psychological model of interrogative suggestibility. That is, interrogative suggestibility is construed as arising through the existence of a particular relationship between the person, the environment, and significant others within that environment. The model was developed to be applicable to police interrogation

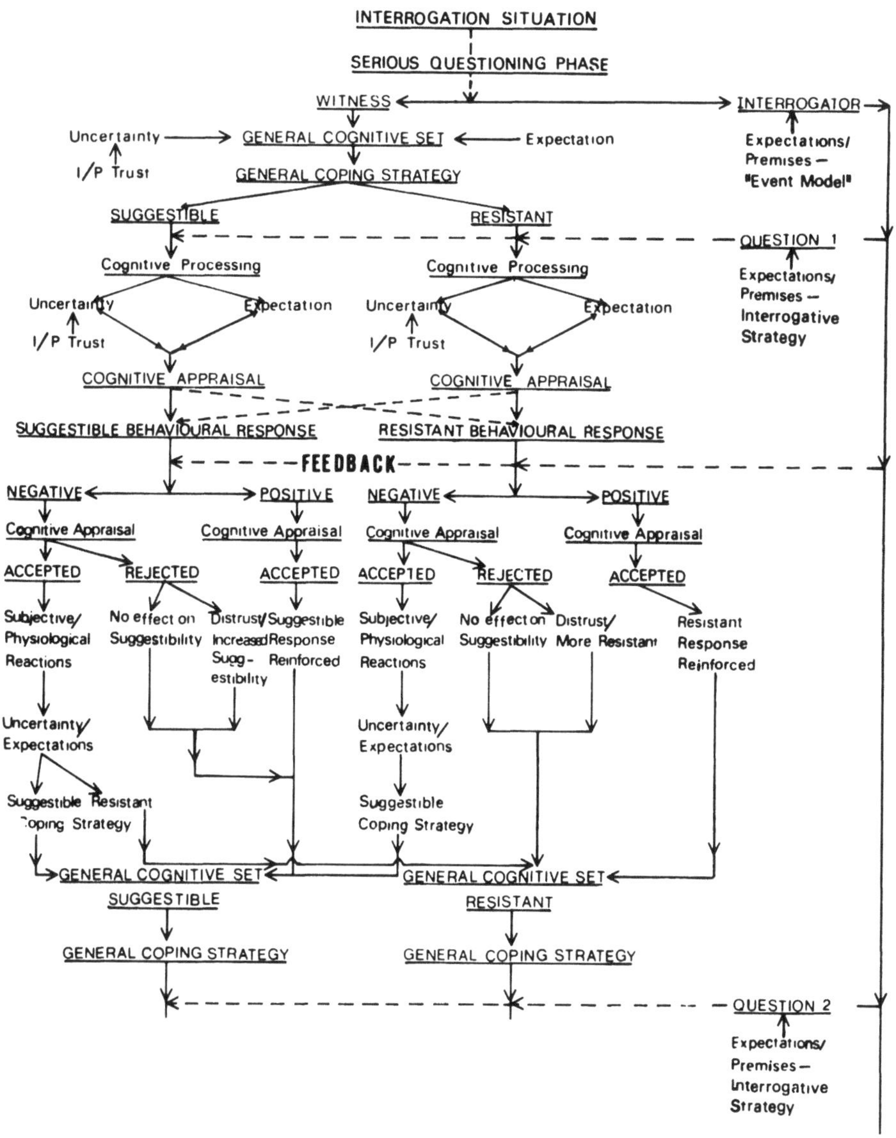

Figure 1. A theoretical model of interrogative suggestibility. (From G.H. Gudjonsson and N. Clarke, 1986)

situations. It integrates the "leading questions" and "negative feedback" aspects of suggestibility described by Gudjonsson (1984a) and provides a framework for understanding and researching the process and outcome of interrogations.

The model, which is graphically presented in Figure 1, states that interrogative suggestibility is dependent upon the copying strategies that subjects can generate and implement when dealing with the "uncertainty" and "expectations" within the interrogative situation. The model begins by defining the social situation and participants involved. The "general cognitive set" of the witness is then defined, and this set leads the witness to adopt a "general coping strategy" towards the interrogative situation which can facilitate either a *suggestible* or a *resistant* repertoire of general responses. The interviewer then poses a question which undergoes cognitive processing that employs one or more strategies of general coping. The processing involves *uncertainty* and *interpersonal trust* on the one hand and an *expectation* on the other. These three components are conceptualised as the essential prerequisites for the process of suggestibility.

Uncertainty means that the witness does not know definitely or surely the right answer to a question. When witnesses are asked a leading question, they may know for certain what the true answer is, but on occasion the perceived true answer may not agree with the expectations conveyed by the interviewer. When this happens, witnesses will give their true answers as they see them unless the expectations and premises contained in the question create doubts in their minds. Some witnesses may agree with a leading question, knowing that it is wrong, because they wish to please the interviewer or are reluctant to disagree openly. Such witnesses are being *compliant* rather than *suggestible.* The witness can be described as suggestible only if he or she privately accepts the suggestion or at least believes it to be plausible. This is inherent in the definition of interrogative suggestibility given earlier in this paper.

Interpersonal trust, a second prerequisite for yielding to suggestion, means that the person believes that the interviewer's intentions are genuine and that there is no trickery involved. People who are suspicious of the interviewer will be reluctant to yield to suggestions offered, even under conditions of increased uncertainty.

For a response to suggestion to occur, uncertainty must be present. In addition, leading questions must be sufficiently subtle so that they are perceived as being plausible, believable and without trickery; otherwise, they are likely to be rejected. A link exists between uncertainty and interpersonal trust in that the latter may depend on the extent to which people believe that they are being tricked. The clearer the person's memory of events, the more readily he or she is likely to detect an attempt to mislead.

Expectation of success is an important prerequisite for a response to suggestion to occur. This is because uncertainty and interpersonal trust alone are insufficient to make people yield to a leading question. After all, if people are uncertain about the correct answer to a particular question, they can declare that uncertainty by giving a reply of "don't know" or "not sure". Many people do not declare their uncertainty because they are made to believe that: (a) they must provide an answer; (b) they should know the answer to the question asked; and (c) they are expected to know the answer and to be capable of giving it.

In view of the above discussion, it is clear that most people are susceptible to suggestion provided the necessary conditions of uncertainty, interpersonal trust, and heightened expectation are present. To what extent the person yields to suggestion is a function of his or her cognitive appraisal of the situation and of the coping strategies adopted. A strategy of coping that is not amenable to suggestion involves being able to look objectively and critically at the situation and not commit oneself to an answer unless one is absolutely sure of the facts. A coping strategy that is amenable to suggestion involves an unrealistic appraisal of the situation and the reluctance to admit the fallibility of one's memory when uncertain.

An important aspect of the theoretical model that has not been discussed so far is "feedback". This is conceptualised as a signal intended to strengthen or modify subsequent responses of the witness, that is communicated by an interrogator to a witness, after he or she has responded to a question or a series of questions. The feedback may be positive (i.e., reinforcing the previous response) or negative (i.e., tending to modify an unwanted answer). The work that the author has carried out with his colleagues at the Institute of Psychiatry has highlighted the potentially dramatic effects associated with negative feedback. Although some witnesses become less suggestible after negative feedback, the general effect of negative feedback is to increase susceptibility to suggestions. The specific effects of positive and negative feedback in relation to previous answers given by witnesses are discussed in detail by Gudjonsson and Clark (1986).

Implications of the Theory

The theoretical model above describes *how* and *when* people are likely to give false and distorted testimony during questioning. The various components of the theory can be tested empirically. The main predictions that the theory generates are as follows:

1. The model's components of *uncertainty*, *trust* and *expectation* are open to environmental manipulations. These components can be manipulated within an experimental context so as to test specific hypotheses.
2. People with a suspicious cognitive set (e.g., those who do not trust the interviewer and are generally suspicious of the police) are less suggestible than those who enter the police interview with a trusting cognitive set.
3. The type of coping strategies people are able to use during interviewing are significantly related to their susceptibility to suggestion. The choice of strategy adopted depends upon the person's appraisal of the interview and upon the perceived options of coping and their expected consequences. The theoretical model views these coping strategies as dynamic entities which may be modified as the person re-appraises his or her position throughout the interrogation.
4. People with poor memory and/or who are of limited intelligence are generally more suggestible than those of superior cognitive abilities. But, as the relationship between cognitive variables and suggestibility is affected seriously by range effects (Gudjonsson, 1988a), the author has argued elsewhere (Gudjonsson, 1988b), that intelligence and memory facilitate suggestibility only when they are below a certain level. Once people have reached that critical level of cognitive capacity, other mediating variables (e.g., coping strategies, assertiveness, self-esteem, anxiety) become much more pronounced.

5. People who lack assertiveness, have strong fear of negative evaluation, and possess low self-esteem, are particularly susceptible to suggestions offered during police interviewing.

Testing Aspects of the Model

Attempts to test the various aspects of the theoretical model presented have utilised the Gudjonsson Suggestibility Scale, which has two parallel forms (Form 1, Gudjonsson, 1984a; Form 2, Gudjonsson, 1987b). The correlation between the two scales is very high even after a long test-retest interval (Gudjonsson, 1987c). This correlation shows that interrogative suggestibility is a highly stable behavioural characteristic when people are tested on two separate occasions under similar circumstances.

The two Gudjonsson Suggestibility Scales (GSS1 and GSS2) were developed as research and clinical tools to assess an individual's response to "leading questions" and "negative feedback" instructions when being asked to report a factual event from memory. For this reason, unlike most other tests of suggestibility, the two GSS forms are particularly applicable to legally significant situations, such as the questioning of witnesses and the interrogation of suspects by police. The first form (GSS1) employs a narrative paragraph describing a fictitious event, which is read to the subject. The parallel form (GSS2), with a different fictitious event, was developed mainly so that test-retest reliability of suggestibility could be examined. The problem with re-administering the GSS after an interval was that people appeared to have residual memory of the first administration at the second testing, even after several weeks. The parallel form overcame this problem. The GSS2 differs from the GSS1 in three respects: (a) the content making up the narrative paragraph is different and it does not like the GSS1 use a forensic narrative content; (b) the interrogative questions used are different from those of the GSS1; (c) the narrative content of the GSS2 was so constructed as to make it easily usable in most English-speaking countries. The basic instructions, administration, and scoring are the same for the two scales. After the person has given free immediate and delayed recall (the delay amounting to 50 min.) to the GSS1 or GSS2 story, he or she is asked 20 specific questions, 15 of which are subtly misleading. After answering the 20 questions, the person is told that he or she has made a number of errors (even if no errors have been made), and it is therefore necessary to ask all the questions once more. The person is instructed to try to be more accurate than before. Any change in the person's answers from the previous trial is noted and is scored as "shift". The extent to which people give in to the leading questions is scored as a "yield". "Yield" and "shift" are added together and give total suggestibility rating. Factor analysis of the GSS1 scores (Gudjonsson, 1984a) has shown the "yield" and "shift" scores to be independent of each other, and shown also that to some extent they correlate with different personality variables. For example, "shift" is clearly much more related than "yield" is to anxiety processes (Gudjonsson, 1988b).

The early work on the original GSS was concerned with validating the scale, and resulted in the development of the theoretical model presented in this paper. More recent work has focused on testing aspects of the theoretical model. Table 1 gives an indication of the cognitive, personality, and behavioural variables that have been found to correlate significantly with the suggestibility scores on the GSS1. The sizes of the correlations are not given in the Table, as they vary little

Table 1. Variables found to relate to suggestibility as measured by the Gudjonsson Suggestibility Scale (GSS1)

Variables	Correlation with GSS1
Cognitive	
I.Q.	Negative
Verbal memory	Negative
Personality	
Self-concept ("potency")	Negative
External locus of control	Positive
Fear of negative evaluation	Positive
Assertiveness	Negative
Arrow-Dot ego functioning	Negative
Social desirability	Positive
Anxiety	Positive
Facilitative coping strategies	Negative
Behavioural	
Denials during police interviewing	Negative
Accuracy of information during police interviewing	Negative
Number of previous convictions	Negative

from one study to another. What is given is the direction (i.e., positive or negative) of the correlations for the different variables.

Suggestibility has been shown in a number of studies to correlate negatively with intelligence and memory. The only studies that have failed to find a significant relationship have employed samples with a very restricted range of I.Q. (Gudjonsson, 1988a). Two studies (Gudjonsson & Lister, 1984; Singh & Gudjonsson, 1984) have found a strong negative correlation between self-esteem, as measured by the "potency" factor of the semantic differential technique, and suggestibility. That is, the higher the subjects' "potency" scores, the less suggestible they tended to be. The evaluative dimension (e.g., good-bad, kind-cruel) did not correlate with suggestibility. This indicates that it is the perception of being strong and forceful which helps people resist suggestions during interviewing. Whether they perceive themselves as being good or bad appears irrelevant. Related to this is the finding that suggestibility is related to external locus of control (Gudjonsson & Lister, 1984), "poor ego functioning" as measured by the Arrow-Dot Test (Gudjonsson, 1984b), low assertiveness and fear of negative evaluation (Gudjonsson, 1988b), and social desirability (Gudjonsson, 1983).

Anxiety has a rather specific relationship with suggestibility. The two most important findings are that *state* anxiety is more highly correlated with suggestibility than is *trait* anxiety and that GSS "shift" correlates more strongly with state anxiety than does "yield" (Gudjonsson, 1988b). These findings are consistent with the theoretical model presented earlier in this paper.

The theoretical model predicts that the coping strategies that subjects can generate and implement during interrogation are very important with respect to their responses to suggestions and negative feedback. In a recent study (Gudjonsson, 1988b), the author found that subjects who utilised "avoidance coping" (i.e., they avoided confrontation with the stressor) during the administration of the GSS1 were significantly more suggestible than subjects who had used "facilitative cognitive-behavioural" methods (e.g., being able to analyze the situation critically and objectively).

Various behavioural measures have been correlated with suggestibility. In one study, Gudjonsson and Singh (1984a) found a significant correlation between suggestibility and teachers' ratings of behavioural suggestibility. In another study, Gudjonsson and Singh (1984b) found a negative correlation between "shift" suggestibility and number of previous convictions among delinquent adolescents. One explanation for this finding is that adolescents who have had an extensive experience with procedures of interrogation learn to resist interpersonal pressure exerted by persons of authority. Similarly, recidivists may be characteristically more prone to resist interpersonal pressure than are less habitual offenders.

Tully and Cahill (1984) examined factors related to subsequent accuracy of information obtained from mentally handicapped and normal subjects during interviewing by police. One week before the police interview, all the subjects had been given a number of psychometric tests, including the GSS1, and were presented afterwards with a stage scenario which formed the basis for the subsequent interview. Suggestibility correlated highly negatively with the accuracy of information obtained during the interviewing. This supports the predictive validity of the GSS within the context of police interviewing.

Another study which supports the predictive validity of the GSS with regard to police interviewing is that by Gudjonsson (1984c). In this study, a comparison was made between the suggestibility scores of alleged "false confessors" (those who had retracted confession statements) and "deniers" (those who made no admissions in spite of forensic evidence against them) in criminal trials. The "deniers" were found to be significantly less suggestible than the "false confessors". The suggestibility scores were found to be more discriminative than I.Q. scores.

Conclusions

This brief paper gives up-to-date information about the author's work on the theoretical and empirical aspects of interrogative suggestibility. Much work remains to be done with respect to the testing of the theoretical model. This is currently being undertaken at the Institute of Psychiatry. Of particular interest is the possible relationship between suggestibility and compliance within a context of interrogation. The author is at present validating a compliance questionnaire relevant to police interrogation and looking in detail at the importance of suggestibility and compliance cases of retracted confessions (Gudjonsson & MacKeith, 1988).

References

Evans, F.J. (1967). Suggestibility in the normal waking state. *Psychological Bulletin, 67,* 114-129.

Eysenck, H.J. (1947). *Dimensions of personality.* London: Routledge & Kegan Paul.

Gudjonsson, G.H. (1983). Suggestibility, intelligence, memory recall and personality: an experimental study. *British Journal of Psychiatry, 142,* 35-37.

Gudjonsson, G.H. (1984a). A new scale of interrogative suggestibility. *Personality and Individual Differences, 5,* 303-314.

Gudjonsson, G.H. (1984b). Interrogative suggestibility and perceptual motor performance. *Perceptual and Motor Skills, 58,* 671-672.

Gudjonsson, G.H. (1984c). Interrogative suggestibility: comparison between "false confession" and "deniers" in criminal trials. *Medicine, Science and the Law, 24,* 56-60.

Gudjonsson, G.H. (1986). Historical background to suggestibility: how interrogative suggestibility differs from other types of suggestibility. *Personality and Individual Differences, 8,* 347-355.

Gudjonsson, G.H. (1987a). The relationship between memory and suggestibility. *Social Behaviour, 2,* 29-33.

Gudjonsson, G.H. (1987b) A parallel form of the Gudjonsson Suggestibility Scale. *British Journal of Clinical Psychology, 26,* 215-221.

Gudjonsson, G.H. (1988a). The relationship of intelligence and memory to interrogative suggestibility: the importance of range effects. *British Journal of Clinical Psychology, 27,* 185-187.

Gudjonsson, G.H. (1988b). Interrogative suggestibility: its relationship with assertiveness, social-evaluative anxiety, state anxiety and method of coping. *British Journal of Clinical Psychology, 27,* 159-166.

Gudjonsson, G.H., & Clark, N. (1986). Suggestibility in police interrogation: a social psychological model. *Social Behaviour, 1,* 83-104.

Gudjonsson, G.H., & Lister, S. (1984). Interrogative suggestibility and its relationship with self-esteem and control. *Journal of the Forensic Science Society, 24,* 99-110.

Gudjonsson, G.H., & MacKeith, J.A.C. (1988). Retracted confessions: legal, psychological, and psychiatric aspects. *Medicine, Science, and the Law, 28,* 187-194.

Gudjonsson, G.H., & Singh, K.K. (1984a). Interrogative suggestibility and delinquent boys: an empirical validation study. *Personality and Individual Differences, 5,* 425-430.

Gudjonsson, G.H., & Singh, K.K. (1984b). Criminal conviction and its relationship with interrogative suggestibility. *Journal of Adolescence, 7,* 29-34.

Singh, K.K., & Gudjonsson, G.H. (1984). Interrogative suggestibility, delayed memory and self-concept. *Personality and Individual Differences, 5,* 203-209.

Schooler, J.W., & Loftus, E.F. (1986). Individual differences and experimentation: complementary approaches to interrogative suggestibility. *Social Behaviour, 2,* 105-112.

Tully, B., & Cahill, D. (1984). Police interviewing of mentally handicapped persons: an experimental study. London: The Police Foundation.

10. The Independence of Suggestibility, Placebo Response, and Hypnotizability

F.J. Evans

Introduction

Suggestibility has been an important concept in the history of psychology and psychiatry. In addition to being equated with gullibility and persuasibility (Abraham, 1962), the concept of suggestibility has been central to the historical development of hypnosis (Weitzenhoffer, 1953), has been used to explain the placebo response in psychopharmacology (Trouton, 1957), and has been employed as a measure of personality characteristics, particularly neuroticism (Cattell, 1957; Eysenck, 1947). This review evaluates contemporary attempts to classify different types of suggestibility, and the relationship between suggestibility, hypnotizability, and the placebo response.

Classification of Suggestibility

Eysenck (1943; 1947), Furneaux (1946; 1952), and Eysenck and Furneaux (1945) presented empirical evidence demonstrating that there is no general, unitary trait of suggestibility. Two factors, or possibly more, were necessary to account for the intercorrelations among tests traditionally regarded as measures of suggestibility. The main factor, *primary suggestibility*, involved the subject's responding to direct (verbal) suggestions of occurrence of specified bodily or muscular movements without his/her active volitional participation. The Body-Sway and Chevreul Pendulum tests are familiar examples. The second factor, *secondary suggestibility*, is a more elusive entity involving "indirection" and "gullibility." Eysenck (1947) has described it as "the experience on the part of the subject of a sensation or perception consequent upon the direct or implied suggestion by the experimenter that such an experience will take place, in the absence of any objective basis for the sensation of perception" (p. 167). The Ink Blot, Progressive Lines, and Odor tests are typical examples.

Without empirical support, Eysenck (1947) also referred to tertiary suggestibility, apparently involving attitude change consequent upon persuasive communications originating from a prestige figure.

Contemporary Evidence

The classification presented by Eysenck and Furneaux (1945) has been widely accepted. Subsequent attempts to corroborate the original factorial studies of Eysenck (1943) and Eysenck and Furneaux (1945) have, however, produced equivocal results. Grimes (1948) found no evidence of a secondary suggestibility factor among 16 tests of suggestibility administered in group settings to 233 orphan boys varying in age from 8 to 15 years. The tests were mainly of the indirection, gullibility, or prestige types.

Benton and Bandura (1953) objected to generalizing from the neurotic army population used in the studies by Eysenck (1943) and Eysenck and Furneaux (1945). They administered tests of suggestibility to 50 undergraduates. The intercorrelations were mostly insignificant, and no evidence of either factor was found. Unfortunately, the sample was highly selected both in intelligence and in suggestibility. Similar criticism can be made of studies by Duke (1964) who administered nine suggestibility tests to veterans.

Factor analytic studies from three separate correlation matrices were reported to Stukat (1958). Sixteen variables were administered to 67 elementary school children, averaging 8.6 years of age; 24 variables were administered to 187 11-year-old school children; and 24 variables were given to 90 adults in their early twenties. A factor identified as primary suggestibility was isolated in all three factorial solutions. Secondary suggestibility, as described by Eysenck and Furneaux (1945), was not confirmed. Several small factors were found, usually defined by very few variables with low factor loadings.

Administering 15 suggestibility tests to 63 undergraduates, Hammer et al. (1963) reported two orthogonal factors from a factor analysis of the tetrachoric intercorrelations. One factor was identified as primary suggestibility, but there were no grounds for identifying the second factor with Eysenck's concept of secondary suggestibility. Three variations of the Heat Illusion test, together with a rating of the vividness of imagery in a suggested hallucinatory situation, defined the second factor. It was tentatively interpreted as an "imagery" factor. Some tests which were similar to secondary suggestibility tests in the classification of Eysenck and Furneaux (1945) did not load significantly on the imagery factor.

Subsequently, two parallel batteries of tests, similar to those usually administered during hypnosis, were given in the waking state to 50 undergraduates (Evans, 1967a). Tests similar to "secondary suggestibility" measures were not well represented. Of the five factors matched across the two sessions, three were identified as "primary suggestibility," "challenge suggestibility," and "imagery." The latter factor involved measures similar to the Heat Illusion.

Suggestibility

There has been a failure to replicate in exact detail the procedures employed by Eysenck (1943) and Eysenck and Furneaux (1945) in all these studies. The classification originally presented by Eysenck (1943) was based upon an examination of the intercorrelations among eight suggestibility tests, including two linearly and experimentally dependent methods of scoring both the Progressive Weights and Progressive Lines tests. Recognizing the limitations of this investigation, Eysenck and Furneaux (1945) replicated the study, administering suggestibility tests to 60 hospitalized soldiers.

A factor analysis was conducted on the intercorrelations among the tests. On the assumption that there were two factors in the correlation matrix of 12 tests, Eysenck and Furneaux (1945) subdivided the correlation matrix into two parts and extracted a general factor from each part. They argued that the correlations between tests in the first part of the table, primary suggestibility tests, with those in the second part, secondary suggestibility tests, were zero (apart from sampling errors). The validity of this assumption was not tested. The procedure rejected half of the intercorrelations among the 12 tests on the assumption that they were zero. However, some of the correlations ignored were higher than some of the "within" group correlations, particularly within the six "secondary suggestibility" tests. A reanalysis of the Eysenck and Furneaux data appeared justified (Evans, 1967a). A rotated centroid simple-structure solution conducted on the correlation matrix presented by Eysenck and Furneaux (1945) yielded at least three factors.

The primary suggestibility factor is clearly demarcated, but none of the remaining factors can be identified as "secondary suggestibility" as defined by Eysenck and Furneaux (1945).

Items loading on the second factor were administered in the imperative mood, almost as a command. The subject was "*told* (italics added) that they (12 boxes) all differed in weight" (Eysenck & Furneaux, 1945, p. 487). "The patient *would* (italics added) shake and open a box on coming out of hypnosis" (p. 488). However, tests with insignificant loadings were apparently administered passively. "The patient *was shown* (italics added) how the element became hot" (p. 487) for the Heat Illusion. The factor appears to involve a mixture of command and authority blended with prestige. It is possible that variations in the approach of the experimenter, from a passive coaxing tone to an authoritarian demand, may produce responses of differing factorial complexity. De Rivera (1959) found that body sway suggestions given in a calm descriptive manner were significantly more effective than when given in a more forceful manner. Our own early studies showed that subjects perceived simulated differences between a passive seductive male experimenter and a cold domineering female experimenter, even though these differences produced no differences in scores on primary suggestibility measures.

The third factor raises the perplexing problem of the role of the Heat Illusion test in classifying suggestibility phenomena. In earlier studies it has usually had loadings on both primary and secondary suggestibility factors. Our reanalysis indicates it probably forms the basis of a separate factor. The factor may be similar to the imagery factor reported by Hammer et (1963), and by many others subsequently in factorial studies of hypnosis scales, but this interpretation is not presented confidently because of the lack of items in the Eysenck and Furneaux (1945) data similar to those used by Hammer at el. (1963). There may be imagery components in the Picture Report, Ink Blot, and Odor tests used by Eysenck and Furneaux, but the latter test has an insignificant loading on the present factor.

Hypnosis and Suggestibility: Factor Analytic Studies

During my graduate research in the late 1950s, the theory that hypnosis was a form of suggestibility was fairly universally accepted, even though it was recognized that there was circularity in a definition in which one term is being explained by another undefined term. We were initially uneasy about the alleged close link between hypnosis and suggestibility, particularly as the latter was being measured in the context of the still influential research of Hull (1933) and Eysenck (1947) involving motor versus indirection paradigms. The existing tests and scales did not seem to reflect the full range of psychodynamic and dissociative experiences that occurred during hypnosis. The statement that waking suggestibility and hypnotic suggestibility were correlated had no more significance than the observation that a redheaded person in the normal waking state would still be redheaded if he/she became hypnotized! This led us to conduct factor analytic studies (Evans, 1965; Hammer et al., 1963) of a battery including tests of suggestion and traditional hypnotic phenomena and, as Hilgard (1965) and his colleagues were simultaneously doing, to explore the relationships between these suggestions when given with and without a standardized hypnotic induction procedure. It became clear that a general factor of hypnotizability of suggestibility could *not* account for the common variance among these measures of the domain of hypnosis (Hilgard, 1973). Three separate dimensions could be isolated in both waking and hypnotized performances involving passive responses and challenged responses and imagery. A fourth dimension involved a cluster of items, including posthypnotic suggestion, amnesia, and age regression. We labelled the fourth factor "dissociation."

At about the same time as these early factor-analytic studies were being conducted at the University of Sydney, the *Stanford Hypnotic Susceptibility Scales* (SHSS) were being developed by Weitzenhoffer and Hilgard (1959; 1962). Following tradition, it was assumed that suggestions of the type generally considered to lie within the domain of hypnosis defined a relatively unidimensional trait, loosely related to the classical concept of suggestibility, specifically primary suggestibility. Indeed, the hypnotizability scales, and measures of primary suggestibility, both have retest reliabilities in the high 0.90 range. However, even though it was assumed that all of the items in these hypnotizability scales were highly intercorrelated, it was noticed that there were more low and insignificant correlations on the item-correlation matrices than could be comfortably accepted. Indeed, the postural sway item of SHSS:A and B produced insignificant correlations with most of the other suggestions normally associated with deep hypnosis.

By now there have been several factor-analytic studies of several hypnosis scales (from the research laboratories of Hilgard, 1965; Sarbin & Coe, 1972; Sheehan & McConkey 1982; Peters, Dhanens, Lundy, & Landy, 1974; and others). Each of these studies reported that a single general factor does not seem to be sufficient to account for the intercorrelations between the scales's test suggestions. There is substantial agreement that the main factor contains those items that are traditionally related to primary suggestibility or simple motor suggestions (perhaps picking up some covariance from the challenge suggestion items). There is less agreement as to how the remaining factors should be interpreted. There are those who claim they are statistical artifacts of item difficulty, though this interpretation can probably be disconfirmed. While I will not present the data here, most of these studies can be made to produce orthogonal simple structure solutions yielding three to four factors that can be interpreted as dissociation, imagery, primary or motor suggestibility, and a factor splitting off the challenge from the motor suggestions in some cases.

These analyses confirm the validity of the primary or motor suggestibility dimension. Several studies have certainly shown that scores on these suggestibility measures do increase during hypnosis (particularly for those scoring in the middle ranges of the hypnotizability distribution). However, the data are clear that this is not the only or even the most important component of hypnotically induced behavior. A brief digression clarifying the distinction between primary suggestibility and hypnotizability will be made by reviewing some studies involving suggestibility and sleep.

Responding to Suggestions During Sleep

Several years ago we (Cobb, Evans, Gustafson, O'Connell, Orne, & Shor, 1965; Evans, 1977a; Evans, Gustafson, O'Connell, Orne, & Shor, 1969; Perry, Evans, O'Connell, Orne, & Orne, 1978) were able to show that during sleep we could administer suggestions of the kind "whenever I say the word 'itch' your nose will feel itchy until you scratch it," without arousing many of our subjects. Only those suggestions for which there were no EEG signs of arousal during stimulation were retained, indicating that the subjects remained asleep during the stimulation. The mere repetition of the cue word "itch" was sometimes sufficient to elicit the response aimed for, e.g. "nose scratching." These responses occurred almost exclusively in the REM sleep state. The response could be obtained when the suggestion was tested by giving the cue word in the same REM state, or when it was tested in a later REM period (without repeating the suggestion), 24 hours, or even 6 months, later - in spite of intervening unbreachable waking amnesia for the sleep-administered suggestion itself.

The ability to produce meaningful behavioral responses while asleep was significantly correlated with hypnotizability in three of the four studies we completed. The rate of successful response during sleep was particularly correlated with the *dissociative* rather than the *motor* and *imagery* clusters of hypnotically induced behavior (Evans et al., 1969).

Less hypnotizable subjects did not respond as much because they tended to wake up every time we tried to administer the test cue words and suggestions. The data implied that some subjects (who are also more hypnotizable) can process significant information even while maintaining control over their own sleep process. Other less hypnotizable subjects must momentarily awaken in order to process novel events occurring in their environment.

The fact that some hypnotizable subjects were able to control cognitive processes during sleep was more striking because of the related finding that these same subjects fall asleep much faster at night than unresponsive subjects, in terms of both laboratory EEG criteria and their own self-reported sleep patterns. Thus, a subgroup of subjects was isolated in whom three characteristics were noteworthy: (a) dissociative control of behavioral response during sleep; (b) ability to fall asleep quickly; (c) hypnotizability. It is especially noteworthy, however, that the cognitive control that was observed in our sleeping and hypnotizable subjects was control that did not imply volition. The control here (as in much of cognition) is outside the domain of awareness and is not related to suggestibility (Evans, 1987).

In summary, so far, the data appear to show that suggestibility and hypnosis are in part different processes. I will now examine the relationship between the placebo response and these two variables.

Suggestibility and Placebo

There has been a recurrent theme in clinical literature that the placebo reaction, responsiveness to an inert substance as if it were an active pharmacological agent, is a form of suggestibility (Evans, 1985). Trouton (1957) predicted that it would correlate with secondary, rather than primary, suggestibility.

Grimes (1948) measured the effect on a motor-cancelling task of a placebo pill alleged to prevent fatigue and improve performance. Reaction to the placebo in 223 orphan boys decreased to insignificance as age increased from 8 to 16 years. Correlations with 15 suggestibility measures covering a wide range of typical suggestibility tests were insignificant, with the exception of the Otis (1924) Nonprestige test (r = 0.40). One significant correlation in 15 measures should be attributed to chance. A significant correlation of 0.36 was found with a score based on seven tests involving prestige influences from the experimenter. However, the placebo score was not partialled out of this correlation, and as it did not correlate with the remaining six tests in the battery, this is hardly evidence of a significant association.

A study measuring the placebo response more adequately was conducted by Thorn (1962). Thorn defined placebo reaction in terms of the difference between the number of symptoms on a subjective checklist questionnaire for 4 consecutive days before and after ingesting a placebo tablet. Unequivocal demonstration of placebo reactors and nonreactors was reported. Thorn administered four tests of suggestibility selected to include either two measures each of primary and secondary suggestibility, or, alternatively, single measures of the four factors extracted in the Evan's reanalysis (1967a) of the Eysenck and Furneaux (1945) data reported above. The correlation between Body Sway and Arm Bending was 0.60, but this was the only significant correlation between the suggestibility measures, confirming the present reinterpretation of Eysenck and Furneaux data. The correlations between the four measures of suggestibility and responsiveness to placebo were insignificant.

These two investigations were conducted in an experimental context. Several other studies reporting correlations between suggestibility and placebo responsiveness in clinical settings have produced equivocal results.

Whitman (1961) reported a significant correlation between Body Sway and rated clinical improvement under placebo conditions, but reported an insignificant correlation between the Progressive Lines test and placebo improvement, with 30 schizophrenic patients. Gliedman, Nash, Imber, Stone, and Frank (1958) found no correlation between Body Sway and placebo with outpatients. The correlations between suggestibility and placebo in these two reports were only incidental findings to the respective main studies.

Duke (1962) used, as a measure of placebo effect, answers to two questions given to 91 hospitalized veterans asked about a regularly administered placebo sleeping pill, including (a) whether it helped them to go to sleep and (b) the difference in time reported between the length of time they claimed it took them to go to sleep without taking and after taking the pill. It is perhaps not surprising that measures of such dubious reliability and untestable validity should produce largely insignificant correlations (0.01-0.28) with Duke's nine measures of suggestibility.

Only three correlations, "improvement" with the Progressive Lines and Color Report tests, and "help" with the Picture Report test, were significant at the .05 level.

Steinbrook, Jones, and Ainslie (1965) measured placebo response as the decrease in the number of symptoms shown each week over 4 weeks of placebo therapy. They reported a high correlation (r = .67) between a primary suggestibility test and the decrease in symptoms during the first week of therapy. The correlation between the test and the continued decrease in symptoms after the first week was insignificant. This result is equivocal because it is impossible to determine whether suggestibility is correlated with the initial frequency of presenting symptoms, and hence is spuriously correlated with the immediate decrease in symptoms. In other words, no correlation was reported between suggestibility and the number of symptoms initially reported.

Imber, Frank, Gliedman, Nash, and Stone (1956) demonstrated that body sway suggestibility is greater in those patients who remain in psychotherapy than it is in those who drop out. The more suggestible the person, it seems, the more likely he/she is to respond to psychotherapy.

The equivocal relationship between suggestibility and the placebo response in clinical settings is in sharp contrast to the positive relationship between hypnotizability and treatment outcome, even when hypnosis is not involved in the treatment (Evans, 1987). In two randomly selected samples of psychiatric inpatients (n = 57, n = 55) hypnotizability predicted short-term outcome significantly (though the postural sway item did not). Somewhat paradoxically, hypnotizable patients were more likely to be rehospitalized by the end of the 2-year follow-up period.

Placebo, Suggestibility, and Hypnosis

Historically, many investigators have equated "placebo" and "suggestion" without specifying precisely what they mean by either term. In general, however, the few available clinical and experimental studies have found no consistently significant relationship between placebo response and a variety of measures of suggestibility (reviewed by Evans, 1967b; 1974; 1985). In addition, the placebo response is uncorrelated with susceptibility to hypnosis. However, even in subjects who are incapable of experiencing deep hypnosis, the context of hypnosis itself may (like any other powerful therapeutic intervention) produce a placebo effect. The placebo effect of the hypnotic situation is an expectational effect, which must be distinguished from whatever specific effects hypnosis itself may produce in deeply hypnotizable individuals.

This conclusion was supported (Evans, 1977b; 1981; 1985; McGlashan, Evans, & Orne, 1969; Orne, 1974) by administering an ischemic muscle pain task during three sessions: (a) during highly motivated baseline conditions; (b) following the induction of hypnotic analgesia; (c) after ingestion of a placebo capsule (presented to the subjects as an experimental pain-killing drug), serving as a control procedure against which to evaluate the effects of hypnosis. In the placebo session, the experimenter believed subjects were randomly given placebo or Darvon compound in double-blind fashion. Half of the 24 subjects were selected from the top 5 % of the hypnotic responsivity distribution and half from the bottom 5 % of the range of hypnotic ability. A simple but compelling deception procedure was used to legitimize an experimenter expectancy of a "glove" analgesia, using a hypnotic relaxation induction geared to each subject's prior minimal hypnotic experiences. This was tested by administering a brief electric shock to the fingers. These unhypnotizable subjects experienced the analgesia because the experimenter surreptitiously turned down the shock intensity from the pre-analgesic test level. The logic of this study was to maximize the placebo response, as is done in the clinic, rather than to control or eliminate it, as is done in traditional studies.

The improvement shown by these extremely hypnotizable and unhypnotizable subjects in tolerating excruciating ischemic muscle pain under suggestions of hypnotically induced analgesia and, subsequently, after ingesting a placebo was compared. Three aspects of the results should be noted:

1. There was a dramatic increase in pain tolerance for deeply hypnotizable subjects during hypnotically induced analgesia. This was presumably an effect directly attributable to the dissociative aspects of the hypnotic condition when it occurred in highly responsive "hypnotic virtuoso" subjects.
2. The much smaller but significant placebo-induced pain reduction was equal in magnitude for both highly hypnotizable and unhypnotizable subjects. Thus, there was no correlation between response to placebo and hypnotic responsivity.
3. Of most theoretical importance, the hypnotically induced analgesia suggestions significantly reduced pain even for unhypnotizable subjects who did not have the ability to enter hypnosis. This can be labeled as a "placebo component" of the hypnotic situation. Indeed, for these hypnotically unsusceptible subjects, the pain relief produced by the placebo component of the hypnotic context and that produced by the placebo component of ingesting a pill were about equal and highly correlated (.76, n = 12). The expectation that hypnosis can be helpful in reducing pain produced significant reductions in pain similar to the expectations derived from taking a pain-killing pill, particularly in those individuals who otherwise have no special hypnotic skills. It should be noted that the primary suggestibility measures were not correlated with the placebo response.

Summary and Conclusion

This historical and empirical review examined the data supporting a distinction between the phenomena of suggestibility, placebo, and hypnosis. Earlier factor-analytic evidence separated suggestibility phenomena into at least two different processes, often labelled "primary" and "secondary" suggestibility. Both of these dimensions account for some of the variance in hypnotizability scales, although the direct relationship between the suggestibility and hypnosis scale dimensions has not yet been carefully documented. In addition, a strong dimension accounting for much of the individual differences in hypnotizability includes a dissociative process that does not seem to relate directly to the waking suggestibility dimensions. The placebo response is directly related to neither the domain of suggestibility nor the domain of hypnosis hypnotizability. The placebo response is more directly related to expectancy variables, especially those that are related to the kinds of expectations that are central to the doctor/patient relationship and belief systems.

References

Abraham, H.L. (1962). The suggestible personality: A psychological investigation of susceptibility to persuasion. *Acta Psychologica, 20*, 167-184.

Benton, A.L., & Bandura, A. (1953). "Primary" and "secondary" suggestibility. *Journal of Abnormal and Social Psychology, 48*, 336-340.

Cattell, R.B. (1957). *Personality and motivation structure and measurement.* London: Harrap.

Cobb, J.C., Evans, F.J., Gustafson, L.A., O'Connell, D.N., Orne, M.T., & Shor, R.E. (1965). Specific motor response during sleep administered meaningful suggestion: An exploratory study. *Perceptual and Motor Skills, 20*, 629-636.

De Rivera, J. (1959). *The postural sway test and its correlations.* Report No. 3. Research project MR005.13-3001, United States Naval Aviation Medical Center, Pensacola, FL.

Duke, J.D. (1964). Intercorrelational status of suggestibility tests and hypnotizability, *Psychological Record, 14*, 71-80.

Evans, F.J. (1965). *The structure of hypnosis: a factor analytic investigation.* Unpublished doctoral dissertation, University of Sydney, Sydney, Australia.

Evans, F.J. (1967a). Suggestibility in the normal waking state. *Psychological Bulletin, 67*, 114-129.

Evans, F.J. (1967b). Placebo response: Relationship to suggestibility and hypnotizability. *Proceedings of the 77th Annual Convention of the American Psychological Association, 4*, 28-29.

Evans, F.J. (1974). The placebo response in pain reduction. In J.J. Bonica (Ed.), *Advances in neurology: Vol. 4. Pain* (pp. 289-296). New York: Raven.

Evans, F.J. (1977a). Hypnosis and sleep: The control of altered states of awareness. In W.E. Edmonston (Ed.), *Conceptual and investigative approaches to hypnosis and hypnotic phenomena. Annals of the New York Academy of Science, 296*, 162-175.

Evans, F.J. (1977b). The placebo control of pain: A paradigm for investigating non-specific factors in psychotherapy. In J.D. Brady, J. Mendels, W.R. Reyer, & M.T. Orne (Eds.), *The future of psychiatry* (pp. 129-136). New York: Spectrum.

Evans, F.J. (1981). The placebo response in pain control. *Psychopharmacological Bulletin, 17*, 72-76.

Evans, F.J. (1985). Expectancy, therapeutic instructions and the placebo response. In L. White, B. Tursky, & G.E. Schwartz (Eds.), *Placebo: theory, research, and mechanisms* (pp. 215-228). New York: Guilford.

Evans, F.J. (1987). *The hypnotizable patient.* Invited paper presented at the 4th European congress of Hypnosis and Psychosomatic Medicine, Oxford, England.

Evans, F.J., Gustafson, L.A., O'Connell, D.N., Orne, M.T., & Shor, R.E. (1969). Sleep induced behavioral response: Relationship to susceptibility to hypnosis and laboratory sleep patterns. *Journal of Nervous and Mental disease, 148*, 467-476.

Eysenck, H.J. (1943). Suggestibility and hysteria. *Journal of Neurology and Psychiatry, 6*, 22-31.

Eysenck, H.J. (1947). *Dimensions of personality.* London: Routledge & Kegan Paul.

Eysenck, H.J., & Furneaux, W.D. (1945). Primary and secondary suggestibility: An experimental and statistical study. *Journal of Experimental Psychology, 35*, 485-503.

Furneaux, W.D. (1946). The prediction of susceptibility to hypnosis. *Journal of Personality, 14*, 281-294.

Furneuax, W.D. (1952). Hypnotic susceptibility as a function of waking suggestibility. In L. LeCron (Ed.), *Experimental hypnosis* (pp. 115-136). New York: Macmillan.

Gliedman, L.H., Nash, E.H., Imber, S.D., Stone, A.R., & Frank, L.D. (1958). Reduction of symptoms by pharmacologically inert substances and by short-term psychotherapy. *Archives of Neurology and Psychiatry, 79*, 345-351.

Grimes, F.V. (1948). An experimental analysis of the nature of suggestibility and of its relation to other psychological factors. *Studies in Psychology and Psychiatry at the Catholic University of America, 7*(4).

Hammer, A.G., Evans, F.J., & Bartlett, M. (1963). Factors in hypnosis and suggestion. *Journal of Abnormal and Social Psychology, 67,* 15-23.

Hilgard, E.R. (1965). *Hypnotic susceptibility*. New York: Harcourt, Brace & World.

Hilgard, E.R. (1973). The domain of hypnosis with some comments on alternative paradigms. *American Psychologist, 28,* 972-982.

Hull, C.L. (1933). *Hypnosis and suggestibility: An experimental approach.* New York: Appleton-Century-Crofts.

Imber, S.D., Frank, J.D., Gliedman, L.H., Nash, E.H., & Stone, A.R. (1956). Suggestibility, social class, and the acceptance of psychotherapy. *Journal of Clinical Psychology, 12,* 341-344.

McGlashan, T.H., Evans, F.J., & Orne, M.T. (1969). The nature of hypnotic analgesia and placebo response to experimental pain. *Psychosomatic Medicine, 31,* 227-246.

Orne, M.T. (1974). Pain suppression by hypnosis and related phenomena. In J.J. Bonica (Ed.), *Pain.* New York: Raven.

Otis, M.A. (1974). A study of suggestibility in children. *Archives of Psychology, 1* (70).

Perry, C.W., Evans, F.J., O'Connell, D.N., Orne, E.C., & Orne, M.T. (1978). Behavioral response to verbal stimuli administered and tested during REM sleep: A further investigation. *Waking and Sleeping, 2,* 35-42.

Perry, C., Gelfand, R., & Marcovitch, P. (1979). The relevance of hypnotic susceptibility in the clinical context. *Journal of Abnormal Psychology. 88,* 592-603.

Peters, J.E., Dhanens, T.P., Lundy, R.M., & Landy, F.S. (1974). A factor analytic investigation of the Harvard Group Scale of Hypnotic Susceptibility, Form A. *International Journal of Clinical and Experimental Hypnosis, 22,* 377-387.

Sarbin, T.R., & Coe, W.E. (1972). *Hypnosis: A social psychological analysis of influence communication.* New York: Holt, Rinehart & Winston.

Sheehan, P.W., & McConkey, D. (1982). *Hypnosis and Experience.* Hillsdale, N.J.: Erlbaum.

Steinbrook, R.M., Jones, M.B., & Ainslie, J.D. (1965). Suggestibility and the placebo response. *Journal of Nervous and Mental Disease, 140,* 87-91.

Stukat, K.G. (1958). *Suggestibility: A factorial and experimental analysis.* Stockholm: Almqvist & Wiksell.

Thorn, W.A.F. The placebo reactor (1962). *Australasian Journal of Pharmacy, 43,* 1035-1037.

Trouton, D.S. Placebos and their psychological effects (1957). *Journal of Mental Science, 103,* 344-354.

Weitzenhoffer, A.M. (1953). *Hypnotism: An objective study in suggestibility* . New York: Wiley.

Weitzenhoffer, A.M., & Hilgard, E.R. (1959). *Stanford Hypnotic Susceptibility Scale, Forms A and B.* Palo Alto, CA: Consulting Psychologists.

Weitzenhoffer, A.M., & Hilgard, E.R. (1962). *Stanford Hypnotic Susceptibility Scale, Form C.* Palo Alto, CA: Consulting Psychologists.

Whitman, J.R. (1961). Suggestibility in schizophrenia. *Journal of Clinical Psychology, 17,* 203-205.

11. Cognitive and Physiological Flexibility: Multiple Pathways to Hypnotic Responsiveness

H.J. Crawford

The newly expanding field of cognitive psychophysiology will find the field of hypnosis research to be a rich gold mine for the investigation of interactions between cognitive and physiological functioning in alternate states of awareness, as moderated by individual differences in an important and enduring trait, namely hypnotic responsiveness. Up until recently, most hypnosis researchers examined separately the personality and cognitive correlates of hypnotic responsiveness, changes in cognitive processing during hypnosis, and possible physiological correlates of hypnosis. This paper will present a series of studies in which we have investigated, separately and together, possible individual differences in both cognitive and physiological flexibility. Based upon prior research, it is our belief that individuals who are highly responsive to hypnosis show greater cognitive flexibility and possibly greater physiological flexibility.

Cognitive flexibility is the degree to which an individual has and uses one of several available types of information processing strategies or styles during different tasks (Battig, 1979), as well as different states of awareness. A series of studies (e.g., Crawford, 1982; Crawford & Allen, 1983) support our hypothesis that high hynotizables can shift into alternate states of awareness more easily than low hypnotizables, and they demonstrate greater ease in shifting cognitive strategies such as from reality-boundedness to nonreality-boundedness and from analytic, detail-oriented to nonanalytic, holistic, and imaginal strategies. "Physiological flexibility" we define as the degree to which an individual shows different patterns of cerebral activation when performing different types of tasks or when applying different types of strategies to the same tasks. Recent research (e.g., Karlin, Goldstein, Cohen, & Morgan, 1980; MacLeod-Morgan & Lack, 1982; Mészáros & Bányai, 1985) has shown that high hypnotizables have greater hemispheric specificity when performing tasks during waking; that is, they show greater shifts in activation between the two hemispheres when performing analytic and nonanalytic tasks. Also, high, but not low hypnotizables, seem to show shifts in hemispheric activation, as seen in the EEG (e.g., Bányai, Mészáros, & Csokay, 1985; Chen, Dworkin, & Bloomquist, 1981; Karlin, Cohen, & Goldstein, 1981; MacLeod-Morgan, 1979, 1982; Mészáros, Bányai, & Greguss, 1985, 1986) and electrodermal responses (EDR) (e.g., Gruzelier, 1987; Gruzelier, Brown, Perry, Rhonder, & Thomas, 1984), when they enter into a hypnotic state. The greater shifts in EEG and EDR activation patterns found among hypnotically responsive individuals may reflect an underlying greater capacity in both cognitive and physiological flexibility.

While main treatment effects may or may not be significant, the evaluation of interactions with certain individual differences in personality and/or cognitive characteristics, either temporary or ongoing, can shed light on important differential treatment effects and enrich our theories. Through a combination of experimental and correlational methods, Cronbach (1975) and others (e.g., Tellegen, 1981) have shown the importance of studying trait (or aptitude) by treatment interactions. Using the hypnotic state in comparison to waking as moderated by hypnotic responsiveness level, we have been studying how differences in hypnotic responsiveness moderate memory, attention, problem solving, affect, and other cognitive processes, as well as differences in accompanying neurophysiological changes. We have been guided by Hilgard's (1977) theoretical model of multiple control systems, asking why some individuals can shift more easily from one control system to another, or from one state of awareness to another. In addition, we have been exploring whether there are cognitive and physiological changes which accompany these phenomenological shifts.

High hypnotizables can shift more easily into a hypnotic state where they are more responsive to suggestions and more likely to be non-reality bound. This characteristic of easily shifting states of awarenesses is not limited to the hypnotic state. Evans (1977) reported that highs fall asleep more rapidly at night and report more incidences of taking naps during the day. Hypnotically responsive individuals are better able to give up their generalized reality orientation (Shor, 1959) in a number of situations outside of hypnosis. They report more deeply involving, nonhypnotic imaginative activities and experiences on questionnaires and in interviews. In our laboratory, for instance, we have found that hypnotic responsiveness loads positively on a happy, vivid, and positive day-dreaming style in both adults (Crawford, 1982) and children aged 8-12 (Allen, 1985).

Clinicians, such as the Spiegels (Spiegel & Spiegel, 1978), argue that the skill to shift from reality to fantasy states can be so flexible that a certain subgroup has difficulty controlling these shifts. For this group, the shifts, rather than being something positive, are negative. Individuals who have dissociated behaviors such as multiple personality and phobias are found often to be higher in hypnotic responsiveness than the normal population is (e.g., Frankel, 1976).

Following up on clinical findings that phobics are often higher in hypnotizability than the general population (e.g., Frankel & Orne, 1976; Foenander, Burrows, Gerschman & de L. Horne, 1980), Crawford, Brown, and Heyman (1987) have found that in a large sample of normal, introductory psychology college students, those with intense fears, as reported on the Wolpe-Lang Fear Survey Schedule are higher in hypnotic responsiveness than the normal population. Those with multiple fears were even higher. Those reporting high fears also scored higher on the Tellegen Absorption Scale and the Vividness of Visual Imagery Questionnaire. These findings suggest that certain individuals self-suggest, perhaps out of awareness, their fears which may eventually develop into full-blown phobias. The fears are self-absorbing and vivid, and thus over time become overwhelming and quite real to them. When something is quite vivid and realistic in one's memory, it is thought more often to be true and factual, whether it is or not.

In a number of studies we and others have found that there is a curvilinear relationship between vividness of visual imagery and hypnotic responsiveness. In general, highs report high imagery vividness when asked to imagine things, but lows may be either low or high. Bowers' (1978) work on effortlessness may provide better understanding of this relationship. While the relationship has yet to be systematically studied, it may be effortless, not effortful, imagery that is related to hypnotizability.

Several studies have demonstrated enhanced imaginal processing of information in some hypnotically responsive individuals, particularly when the information to be remembered is literal or untransformed representations. This enhanced processing may be accompanied by reports of shifts in cognitive processing modes from a more verbal, detail-oriented style during waking to a more imaginal, holistic style during hypnosis. Using a timed spatial memory for an abstract forms task, we found that those subjects (usually highs) who reported shifting strategies in this manner showed enhanced performance during hypnosis (Crawford, Nomura, & Slater, 1983). Another study (Crawford & Allen, 1983) reported that hypnotically responsive individuals showed enhanced performance during hypnosis on a successive visual memory discrimination task that required detecting differences between two picture pairs. In these experiments subjects were asked to look at one picture for 10 s, close their eyes for 5-20 s dependent upon the study, and open them to look at another picture which was identical to the first except that something was changed in it, such as something added or deleted, moved, etc. We found that lows and highs performed similarly during waking. During hypnosis the lows performed similarly to waking, while the highs showed significant enhancements in performance. We asked subjects how they went about doing this task and were able to divide their reports into being either predominantly detail or predominantly holistically oriented. Consistently, the lows reported detail-oriented strategies in both states, while the highs reported a significant shift toward more imaginal and holistic-oriented strategies during hypnosis. This has been replicated by Karlin (personal communication, 1986) and his students at Rutgers University, using stories instead of pictures.

Following up on work by Wallace and his associates (Walker, Garrett, & Wallace, 1976; Wallace, 1978), Crawford, Wallace, Nomura, and Slater (1986) present further evidence that a very small percentage of high hypnotizables can produce eidetic-like visual memory for complex Julesz stereograms. None of the low hypnotizables demonstrated such memory skills. In all the studies but one, this eidetic-like memory occurred only in hypnosis; in our last experiment, a high produced the visual memory during waking. Taken together, these findings suggest that cognitive strategy may be extremely important.

We have yet to investigate the effect of cognitive strategy training on the performance of tasks that typically have differentiated low from high hypnotizables. Wallace (1986) at Cleveland State University has shown that lows, once they have been directed and retrained in their strategies, can perform like highs on tasks involving searching for letters or hidden objects in pictures, although there is no evidence for an accompanying enhancement in hypnotic responsiveness. Thus, our studies may, in part, be tapping differences in well established, but possibly trainable, preferences in cognitive processing, rather than enduring trait differences.

Attentional processing is another cognitive process that reflects individual differences in cognitive flexibility. It is commonly assumed that some individuals are better than others at controlling their attention, either by focusing or dividing it. Some of us can concentrate easily in a noisy room, while others cannot. With the Tellegen Absorption Scale, a number of studies (e.g., Tellegen & Atkinson, 1974) show a moderate correlation between hypnotic responsiveness and absorption, suggesting that highs can become totally involved and absorbed in nonhypnotic experiences, as they can also in hypnosis. In a recent study (Crawford, Brown, & Moon, 1987) of attentional correlates, we examined a series of tasks simultaneously that have been separately assessed in the literature: Tellegen Absorption Scale, the random number generation task of Graham and Evans (1977), Karlin's (1979) dichotic listening task, and two visual illusions in which high reporting of illusory effects correlates with hypnotic responsiveness (e.g., Wallace, Knight, & Garrett, 1976). In addition, because of our dissatisfaction with the complexity of the Absorption Scale and its limited assessment of certain kinds of attentional processing, we included a newly developed (Crawford & Grumbles, 1987) self-report questionnaire (Differential Attentional Processes Inventory, DAPI) which, when factor-analyzed, assesses four major factors: (l) moderate focused sustained attention; (2) extreme focused sustained attention;

(3) dual attention (two cognitive tasks); and (4) dual attention (one cognitive task; one motoric task). Factor analysis verified three factors in the attentional correlate study: (1) sustained attention in an impoverished environment (Necker Cube and autokinetic movement illusions); (2) extremely focused and absorptive sustained attention (Tellegen Absorption Scale and DAPI's extreme, focused attention scale); and (3) moderately sustained attention (Karlin's dichotic selective attention task and the DAPI moderately sustained attention/dual attention for two cognitive activities subscales.) Of the lows and highs, 73 % were significantly discriminated by tasks representing factors 1 and 2, both of which appear to involve extremely focused attention without interference from distraction. Multiple regression analysis showed these same variables played important roles in predicting hypnotic responsiveness. These research findings suggest that there is an important difference between the ability to moderately attend to tasks while not being bothered by the surrounding environment, although still cognizant of it, and the ability to attend intensely to tasks so that certain aspects of the environment are almost completely out of awareness and the absorptive involvement in the task or thought at hand is quite strong. It is only the latter that consistently correlates with hypnotic responsiveness level.

With regard to attentional changes during hypnosis, little research has addressed changes that may occur during hypnosis. Some researchers have reported enhanced vigilance performance during hypnosis, while others have not. For instance, we (Crawford & Brown, 1987a) found no significant changes in performance on the Stroop Color-Word Test or the autokinetic movement illusion task. Spiegel and his colleagues (Spiegel, Cutcomb, Ren, & Pribram, 1985) found changes in certain parts of the visual evoked potential (N2 and P3) when high subjects experienced obstructive hallucinations to visual stimulation, supporting earlier work by Mészáros and his colleagues who found changes in somatosensory evoked potentials following suggested hypnotic analgesia (e.g., Mészáros, Bányai, & Greguss, 1982). These findings suggest that high hypnotizables have greater flexibility in directing attention toward or away from a given perceptual channel.

Our most recent endeavor in our investigation of cognitive and physiological flexibility has centered around emotional intensity (Crawford & Brown, 1987b). Affect intensity, which has been shown to be unrelated to frequency of affective experiences, refers to stable individual differences in intensity of response to a given level of emotion-provoking stimulation (Diener, Larsen, Levine, & Emmons, 1985). If high hypnotizables report more absorbing experiences, we thought that they might also report greater involvement in, or intensity of, their emotional states. We administered a series of questionnaires, including one on affect intensity developed by Larsen and Diener (1987), to a large group of subjects who had been administered both the Harvard Group Scale of Hypnotic Susceptibility and the Stanford Hypnotic Susceptibility Scale, Form C, in such a manner that they did not know the questionnaires and hypnotic scales were related. As expected, high hypnotizables reported experiencing their emotions more intensely than did low hypnotizables. In therapy, hypnosis is often viewed as a state which can amplify emotional responses. To explore this, Crawford, Kitner-Triolo, Clarke, and Brown (1988) examined EEG correlates of sad and happy emotional states in waking and hypnosis as moderated by hypnotic responsiveness level. The self-reports of intensity of experience indicate that the highs reported more intense involvement in the produced emotions than the lows, regardless of condition. During the happy mood there was a substantial shift towards greater right hemisphere EEG activation in hypnosis for the high hypnotizables. During the sad mood it was the lows, not the highs, who showed substantial shifts towards greater right hemisphere EEG activation during hypnosis. This research is continuing in our laboratory.

Thus far our research has emphasized cognitive flexibility, but now we will turn to physiological flexibility. I need not review in detail the exciting, although conflicting, results from EEG laboratories around the world. Both MacLeod-Morgan (MacLeod-Morgan, 1979; MacLeod-Morgan & Lack, 1982) and Karlin (Karlin et al., 1980) have reported that high hypnotizables make greater task-specific shifts in EEG alpha cerebral activation than lows do when given tasks known to activate the left and right hemispheres differentially. Some studies (e.g., Chen et al., 1981; MacLeod-Morgan, 1982) have reported significant EEG activation shifts from the left to right hemisphere to occur while high, but not low, hypnotizables enter into hypnosis, although other studies (e.g., Sabourin, Cutcomb, & Pribram, 1987) have not found such laterality shifts. Here I would like to review two studies in which we have been involved that have addressed changes in physiological functioning in hypnosis and waking as moderated by hypnotic responsiveness: one dealing with cerebral blood flow, the other with EEG.

With Ruben and Racquel Gur and Brett Skolnick, at the Graduate Hospital, University of Pennsylvania, Deborah Benson and I examined the effect of hypnosis on regional cerebral blood flow, as measured by the 133-xenon inhalation method, as moderated by hypnotic responsiveness level (Crawford, Gur, Skolnick, Gur, & Benson, 1986; Crawford, Skolnick, Benson, Gur, & Gur, 1985). The subjects were stringently screened on three measures of hypnotic responsiveness (Harvard Group Scale of Hypnotic Susceptibility; Stanford Hypnotic Susceptibility Scale, Form C; Revised Stanford Profile Scale of Hypnotic Susceptibility, Form 1) as well as for strong right handedness, low anxiety, no depression, and a lack of medical and psychiatric disorders. Such screening resulted in five very high hypnotizables and six very low hypnotizables, all men. The highs had demonstrated the ability to turn off all cognitive awareness of pain, both cold pressor and ischemic pain.

Two sessions were conducted on separate days with the order of waking and hypnosis counterbalanced across subjects. Within each session, three measurements of regional cerebral blood flow (rCBF) were made in each of three conditions: rest, ischemic pain, and ischemic pain with analgesia suggestions. We shall examine only the measurements during rest in waking and hypnosis.

Measurements were made in a quiet, dimly lit room by a nuclear medicine technician. Subjects had their eyes closed as they lay in a supine position during each condition. For each measurement, the subject inhaled trace amounts of xenon-133 mixed with air for 1 min. Clearance of the isotope from the brain was monitored for 14 min by 32 sodium iodide crystal detectors, placed anteriorly to posteriorly over 16 homologous regions of each hemisphere. Each detector measures flow in a cylinder of tissue that includes primarily cortex and to a diminished extent deeper structures. The dependent measure which we will examine today is the initial slope measure of gray matter flow, which is the initial slope at time 0 of the mathematically equivalent instaneous bolus injection.

Unlike EEG studies, there were no significant differences between the overall blood flow of the left and right hemispheres during rest, although there were regional differences within the hemispheres. This is a common finding in rCBF studies of the resting state. There were no main effects for waking vs. hypnosis or for high vs. low hypnotic level. Most interesting to us today is a significant interaction between the waking and hypnosis sessions and hypnotic level ($P < .04$), as is shown in Figure 1. During waking the low and high hypnotizables had quite similar overall mean blood flows. Following a hypnotic induction, the lows remained the same while the high hypnotizables showed a dramatic increase in cerebral blood flow. Control measurements of CO_2 assured us that these differences were not due to differences in breathing rates.

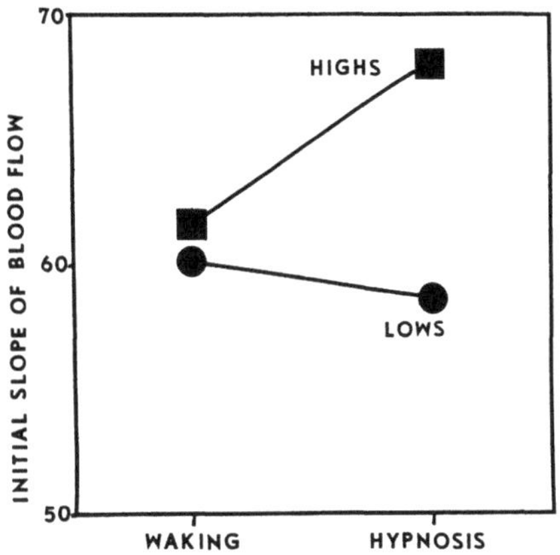

Figure 1. Overall cerebral blood flow differences in waking and hypnosis as moderated by hypnotic level

We examined four major regions of the brain, combining probes from both hemispheres for each region: anterior, parietal, temporal, and temporal-posterior. The occipital area was not measured by the configuration of probes we used. There was a very consistent hyperfrontal increase in blood flow (15 %-16 % greater than the overall mean), which has been consistently shown in other studies of rest. We examined the mean percentage of change in blood flow for each region during hypnosis in comparison to waking. Across all four regions the high hypnotizables demonstrated enhanced cerebral blood flow, ranging from 13 % to 28 %. The greatest enhancement was in the temporal region. By contrast, the lows showed very marginal and nonsignificant changes.

We think this interaction between hypnotic level and waking/hypnosis is evidence for the high hypnotizables showing greater physiological, as well as cognitive, flexibility than the lows. No matter what was presented to the lows, even ischemic pain, their overall rCBF was about the same. By contrast, the highs showed great rCBF enhancements during hypnosis (rest, ischemic pain with and without suggestions of analgesia), suggesting that they were involved in a cognitive task that took effort and attentional allocations which differed from waking.

The second study that demonstrates the importance of examining the moderating effects of a personality/cognitive trait on physiological functioning while performing various cognitive tasks was conducted with Professor Mészáros and his colleague Csaba Szabo in Debrecen, Hungary, as a cooperative study sponsored by United States and Hungarian Academies of Sciences. We did a study of underlying EEG changes which accompany hypnosis not only in terms of left vs. right hemispheric brain activation, but also in terms of anterior vs. posterior activation changes, as moderated by hypnotic level, partially because Pribram (1987) has argued the importance of looking at anterior vs. posterior regions as well as the typical left vs. right differences in cognitive processing. Our findings suggest possible hemispheric differences in the anterior and posterior regions, which may be another physiological concomitant of the important cognitive/personality trait of hypnotic responsiveness.

Nine low and eight high hypnotizables participated in one session in which, in counterbalanced conditions of waking and hypnosis, they did a series of tasks. I shall only address the rest baseline after either an hypnotic induction or listening to a magazine article about King Arthur, and two other tasks that were following this baseline: imagining a walk in the lovely Hungarian countryside or doing subtraction problems with eyes closed at all times. Mészáros, Crawford, Szabo, Nagy-Kovács, and Révész (this volume) discuss EEG and behavioral response changes that accompanied a visual discrimination task that was administered to these and additional subjects.

EEG recording sites were bipolar with grounding to the ear lobes. We examined two anterior sites (F3 and C3, F4 and C4) and two posterior sites (P3 and 01, P4 and 02). The brain wave activity signals were passed through bioamplifiers in a Medicor polygraph and then digitally stored on a hard disk in a personal computer, using the Computerscope ISC-16 system (R.C. Electronics, Santa Barbara) for the conversion of data from analogue to digital through a 16-bit analogue to digital board. Sampling was 500 points per second at 16 bits. Thirty-two seconds of data were stored in each measurement period.

The stored EEG data were edited to eliminate gross artifacts. Using R.C. Electronic's Computerscope-PHY spectrum analysis program, we analyzed two segments of data, each 14.32 s in length, and then averaged them, for each of the four channels from .07 to 35 Hz, applying data demeaning and the hanning window to normalize the spectrum analysis. Within this hertz range, we examined the integrated amplitude of specific frequency (Hz) bands (4.0-5.9, 6.0-7.9, 8.0-10.4, 10.5-12.9, 13.0-19.9, 20.0-26.9, 27.0-33.9).

Whenever we found differences between low and high hypnotizables, it was in the direction of highs having substantially more power, that is greater integrated amplitude, than lows. There were no differences in the low and high theta bands across the three tasks. Differences in integrated amplitude power between lows and highs during one or more of the tasks in the alpha and beta ranges are presented in Table 1. When we examined the individual sites, usually the left anterior, left posterior, and right posterior sites showed the significant difference. Only one significant difference was found in the right anterior site. The findings in Table 1 represent either a physiological trait difference or something due to the experimental setting, such as the highs being more relaxed. Since the differences are both in beta and alpha, we cannot argue for relaxation alone. We may be dealing with differences in cognitive arousal, effort, or attention.

There are some interesting significant interactions between hypnotic level and condition that also are consistent in their directions (Figure 2). In low theta and high theta, as well as low alpha - either across all sites or in the right posterior site - we find that highs go up in power during

Table 1. Integrated Amplitude Power: Sites at which highs produced significantly more power than low hypnotizables[a]

Hertz level	Baseline rest	Walking	Mathematics
Low alpha	Right posterior		
High alpha	Overall		
	Left anterior		
	Left posterior		
	Right posterior	Right posterior	Right posterior
Low beta	Overall	Overall	Overall[b]
	Left anterior	Left anterior	
	Left posterior	Left posterior	Left posterior[b]
	Right posterior	Right posterior	Right posterior[b]
Mid beta	Overall	Overall	Overall
	Left anterior	Left anterior[b]	Left anterior
			Right anterior
	Left posterior	Left posterior	
	Right posterior	Right posterior	
High beta		Right posterior	

[a] $P < .05$
[b] $P < .10$

hypnosis while lows stay about the same. We do not find the opposite in beta bands, as one might anticipate. In fact, contrary to a common assumption presented in the literature, alpha and beta correlated positively and very strongly at most sites and in both conditions.

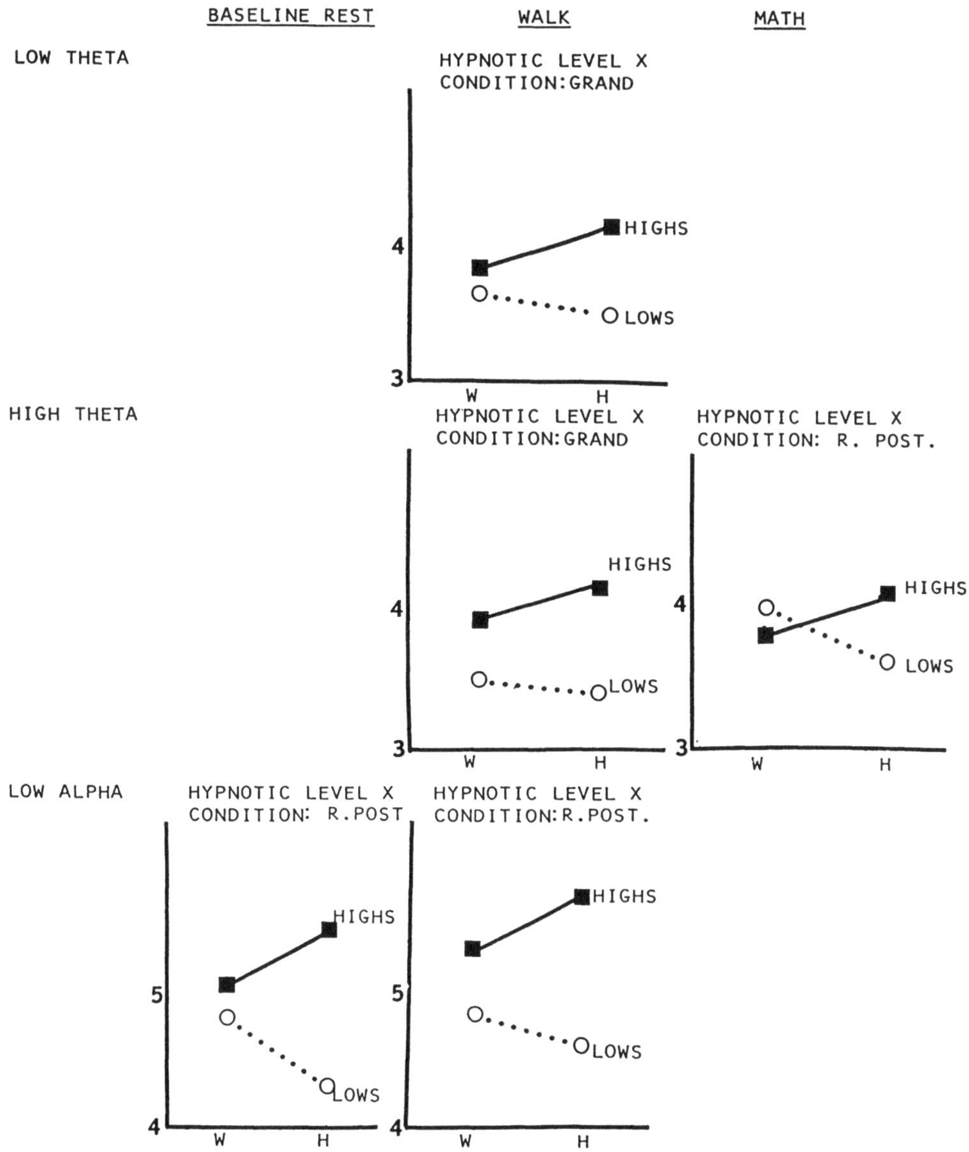

Figure 2. Integrated amplitude power: significant interactions found between highs and lows at certain sites in waking and hypnosis conditions

We then examined hemispheric laterality ratios: [(left - right) / (left + right)] x 100, where a positive number means left hemisphere dominant and a negative number means right hemisphere dominant. We did not find the expected shifts to right hemisphere dominance during hypnosis in the highs. Rather, we found a very interesting interaction between hypnotic level and site in the low and high alpha bands (Figure 3). We see consistently in the three tasks that the highs are more right hemisphere dominant in the posterior region and more left hemisphere dominant in the anterior region, while the low hypnotizables show the opposite pattern. "Why?" we have been asking ourselves, without a good answer yet. It is surprisingly consistent across subjects. What is the possible cause of such asymmetries? An examination of the literature suggests that the left frontal cortex is possibly related to global attentional processes, whereas the right deals with more localized attentional processes. The right parietal region is more associated with visuospatial and imaginal processing of information. Could it be then that these EEG asymmetries are reflecting differences in attentional or strategy differences found in low and high hypnotizables? Certainly we and others have been suggesting that low and high hypnotizables have differential preferences for certain cognitive and attentional strategies. The next step is to examine asymmetries of the frontal and posterior regions as associated with holistic and detail-oriented attentional strategies during the performance of cognitive tasks.

These studies point to further research which will examine more precisely differences between sites of the brain. I would recommend monopolar recording reference to a nonactive site rather than bipolar recording since that which is the same between the two active leads is cancelled out. We shall now need to look at anterior vs. posterior, as well as right vs. left hemispheric

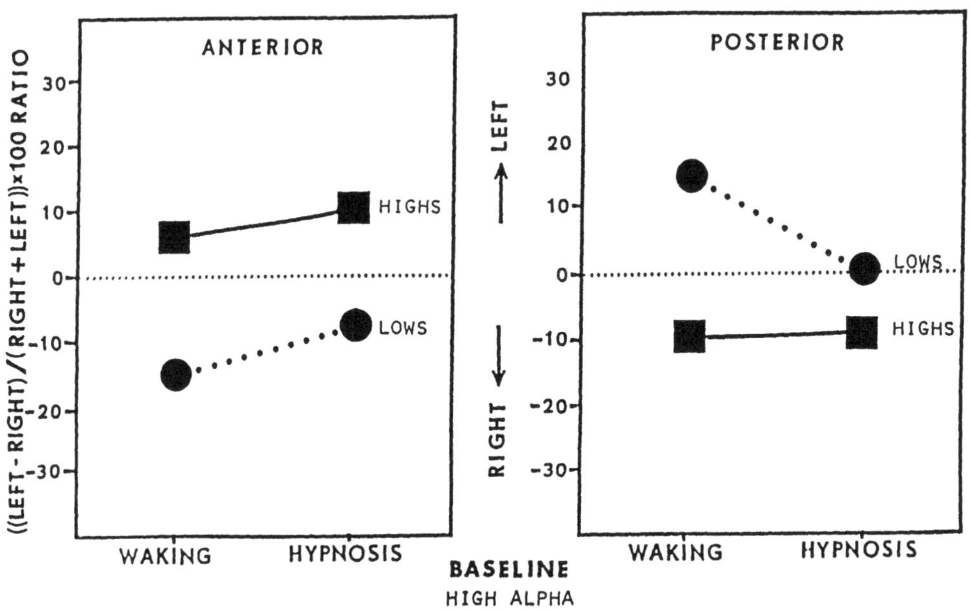

Figure 3. Hemispheric laterality ratio differences between low and high hypnotizables in high alpha range during baseline rest

differences. Additionally, we need to start examining EEG correlates while subjects perform various attentional tasks in waking and hypnosis to determine whether or not there are differences in the EEG patterns of low and high hypnotizables. Rather than considering hypnosis as just a state of awareness that involves a shift to right hemisphere dominance, possibly due to a decrease in left hemisphere involvement (e.g., Gruzelier, 1987; Gruzelier et al., 1984), we are beginning to conceptualize it also as a state that is an attentional amplifier of whatever task is at hand with possible shifts in cognitive strategies.

In conclusion, it is hoped that we have demonstrated how important the study of hypnosis and individual differences in hypnotic responsiveness can be to researchers in the field of cognitive psychophysiology. This paper has presented a series of studies that show exciting relationships between hypnotic responsiveness, traditionally thought to be be a personality trait, and individual differences in both cognitive and physiological flexibility. Future studies that examine the interactions between hypnotic responsiveness levels, cognitive functioning, and physiological functioning during conditions of waking and hypnosis should move us forward in our understanding of how cognitive and personality variables moderate cognitive and physiological functioning in various alternate states of awareness.

Acknowledgements. The preparation of this paper, as well as much of the research reported herein, was made possible through grants to Helen Crawford from The Spencer Foundation. We are greatly appreciative of their continuing support. The work with Mészáros was sponsored, in part, by the United States National Academy of Sciences Cooperative Scientific Exchange Program with the Hungarian Academy of Sciences. I am extremely appreciative of the opportunity this grant provided me to do research with Professor Mészáros, as well as to live in Hungary for an extended time. Special appreciation is given to the colleagues with whom I participated in collaborative research.

References

Allen, S.A. (1985). *Hypnotic responsiveness in children: Imaginative and creative correlates*. Unpublished doctoral disseration, University of Wyoming, USA.

Bányai, E.I., Mészáros, I., & Csokay, L. (1985). Interaction between hypnotist and subject: A social psychophysiological approach. In D. Waxman, P.C. Misra, M.A. Basker (Eds.), *Modern Trends in Hypnosis*. New York: Plenum.

Battig, W.F. (1979). Are the important "individual differences" between or within individuals? *Journal of Research in Personality, 13*, 546-558.

Bowers, P.G. (1978). Hypnotizability, creativity and the role of effortless experiencing. *International Journal of Clinical and Experimental Hypnosis, 26*, 184-202.

Chen, A.C.N., Dworkin, S.F., & Bloomquist, D.S. (1981). Cortical power spectrum analysis of hypnotic pain control in surgery. *International Journal of Neuroscience, 13*, 127-136.

Crawford, H.J. (1982). Hypnotizability, daydreaming styles, imagery vividness, and absorption: A multidimensional study. *Journal of Personality and Social Psychology, 42*, 915-926.

Crawford, H.J., & Allen, S.N. (1983). Enhanced visual memory during hypnosis as mediated by hypnotic responsiveness and cognitive strategies. *Journal of Experimental Psychology: General, 112*, 662-685.

Crawford, H.J., & Brown, A.N. (1987a). *Attentional processing performance remains the same during hypnosis and waking*. Manuscript in preparation.

Crawford, H.J., & Brown, A.N. (1987b). *Intensity of emotions: Differences between low and high hypnotizables*. Manuscript in preparation.

Crawford, H.J., Brown, A.N., & Heyman, S. (1987). *Hypnotic responsiveness and intense fears: Relationships in a normal college population*. Manuscript under editorial review.

Crawford, H.J., Brown, A.N., & Moon, C.E. (1987). *Sustained attentional abilities: Differences between low and high hypnotizables*. Manuscript under editorial review.

Crawford, H.J., & Grumbles, D. (1987). *Differential attentional processes inventory: Relationships between attentional styles and hypnotic responsiveness*. Manuscript in preparation.

Crawford, H.J., Gur, R., Skolnick, B., Gur, R., & Benson, D. (1986, July). *Regional cerebral blood flow and hypnosis: Differences between low and high hypnotizables*. Paper presented at the 3rd international conference of the International Organization of Psychophysiology, Vienna, Austria.

Crawford, H.J., Kitner-Triolo, M., Clarke, S., & Brown, A. (1988). *EEG activation patterns accompanying induced happy and sad moods: Moderating effects of hypnosis and hypnotic responsiveness level.* Paper presented at the annual scientific meeting of the Society for Clinical and Experimental Hypnosis, Asheville, North Carolina.

Crawford, H.J., Nomura, K., & Slater, H. (1983). Spatial memory processing: Enhancement during hypnosis. In J.E. Shorr, J. Conella, G. Sobel, & L. Robin (Eds.), *Imagery: Theoretical aspects and applications*. New York: Plenum.

Crawford, H.J., Skolnick, B.E., Benson, D.M., Gur, R.E., & Gur, R.C. (1985, August). *Regional cerebral blood flow in hypnosis and hypnotic analgesia*. Paper presented at the 10th international congress of Hypnosis and Psychosomatic Medicine, Toronto, Canada.

Crawford, H.J., Wallace, B., Nomura, K., & Slater, H. (1986). Eidetic-like imagery in hypnosis: Rare but there. *American Journal of Psychology, 99*, 527-546.

Cronbach, L.J. (1975). Beyond the two disciplines of scientific psychology. *American Psychologist, 30*, 116-127.

Diener, E., Larsen, R.J., Levine, S., & Emmons, R.A. (1985). Frequency and intensity: The underlying dimensions of affect. *Journal of Personality and Social Psychology, 48*, 1253-1265.

Evans, F.J. (1977). Hypnosis and sleep: The control of altered states of awareness. *Annals of the New York Academy of Sciences, 296*, 162-174.

Foenander, G., Burrows, G.D., Gerschman, J., & de L. Horne, D.J. (1980). Phobic behaviour and hypnotic susceptibility. *Australian Journal of Clinical and Experimental Hypnosis, 8*, 41-46.

Frankel, F.H. (1976). *Hypnosis: Trance as a coping mechanism*. New York: Plenum.

Frankel, F.H., & Orne, M.T. (1976). Hypnotizability and phobic behavior. *Archives of General Psychiatry, 33*, 1259-1261.

Graham, C., & Evans, F.J. (1977). Hypnotizability and the deployment of waking attention. *Journal of Abnormal Psychology, 86*, 631-638.

Gruzelier, J. (1987). The neuropsychology of hypnosis. In M. Heap (Ed.), *Hypnosis: Current clinical, experimental and forensic practices*. London: Croom Helm.

Gruzelier, J., Brow, T., Perry, A., Rhonder, J., & Thomas, M. (1984). Hypnotic susceptibility: A lateral predisposition and altered cerebral asymmetry under hypnosis. *International Journal of Psychophysiology, 2*, 131-139.

Hilgard, E.R. (1977). *Divided consciousness: Multiple controls in human thought and action*. New York: Wiley-Interscience.

Karlin, R.A. (1980). Hypnotizability and attention. *Journal of Abnormal Psychology, 88*, 92-95.

Karlin, R., Cohen, A., & Goldstein, L. (1981). *A shift to the right: EEG during hypnotic induction*. Paper presented at the annual scientific meeting of the Society for Clinical and Experimental Hypnosis, Portland, Oregon.

Karlin, R., Goldstein, L., Cohen, A., & Morgan, D. (1980). *Quantitated EEG, hypnosis, and hypnotizability*. Paper presented at the annual meeting of the American Psychological Association.

Larsen, R.J., & Diener, R. (1987). Emotional response intensity as an individual difference characteristic: A review. *Journal of Research in Personality, 21*, 1-39.

MacLeod-Morgan, C. (1979). Hypnotic susceptibility, EEG theta and alpha waves, and hemispheric specificity. In G.D. Burrows, D.R. Collison, & L. Dennerstein (Eds.), *Hypnosis 1979*. Amsterdam: Elsevier/North Holland.

MacLeod-Morgan, C. (1982). EEG lateralization in hypnosis: A preliminary report. *Australian Journal of Clinical and Experimental Hypnosis, 10*, 99-102.

MacLeod-Morgan, C., & Lack, L. (1982). Hemispheric specificity: A physiological concomitant of hypnotizability. *Psychophysiology, 19*, 687-690.

Mészáros, I., Bányai, E.I., & Greguss, A.C. (1982). Evoked potential, reflecting hypnotically altered state of consciousness. In G. Adam, I. Mészáros, & E.I. Bányai (Eds.), *Advances in Physiological Sciences: Vol. 17. Brain and behaviour*. Oxford: Pergamon.

Mészáros, I., Bányai, E.I., & Greguss, A.C. (1985). Evoked potential correlates of verbal versus imagery coding in hypnosis. In D. Waxman, P.C. Misra, & M.A. Basker (Eds.), *Modern trends in hypnosis*. New York: Plenum.

Mészáros, I., Bányai, E.I., & Greguss, A.C. (1986). *Enhanced right hemisphere activation during hypnosis: EEG and behavioral task performance evidence*. Paper presented at the third international conference of the International Organization of Psychophysiology, Vienna, Austria.

Pribram, K. (1977). The subdivisions of the frontal cortex revisited. In *The frontal lobes revisited*. New York: IRBN.

Sabourin, M.E., Cutcomb, S.D., & Pribram, K.H. (1987). *EEG correlates of hypnotic susceptbiility and hypnotic trance: I. Spectral Analysis*. Unpublished manuscript.

Shor, R.E. (1959). Hypnosis and the concept of the generalized reality-orientation. *American Journal of Psychotherapy, 13*, 582-602.

Spiegel, D., Cutcomb, S., Ren, C., & Pribram, K. (1985). Hypnotic hallucination alters evoked potentials. *Journal of Abnormal Psychology, 94*, 249-255.

Spiegel, H., & Spiegel, D. (1978). *Trance and treatment: Clinical uses of hypnosis*. New York: Basic Books.

Tellegen, A. (1981). Practicing the two disciplines for relaxation and enlightenment: Comment on "Role of the feedback signal in electromyograph biofeedback: The relevance of attention" by Qualls and Sheehan. *Journal of Experimental Psychology: General, 110*, 217-226.

Tellegen, A., & Atkinson, C. (1974). Openness to absorbing and self-altering experiences ("absorption"), a trait related to hypnotic susceptibility. *Journal of Abnormal Psychology, 83*, 268-277.

Walker, N.W., Garrett, J.B., & Wallace, B. (1976). Restoration of eidetic imagery via hypnotic age regression: A preliminary report. *Journal of Abnormal Psychology, 85*, 335-337.

Wallace, B. (1978). Restoration of eidetic imagery via hypnotic age regression: More evidence. *Journal of Abnormal Psychology, 87*, 673-675.

Wallace, B. (1986). *Modification of cognitive search strategies*. Paper presented at the annual meeting of the Psychonomics Society, New Orleans.

Wallace, R., Knight, T.A., & Garrett, J.B. (1976). Hypnotic susceptibility and frequency reports to illusory stimuli. *Journal of Abnormal Psychology, 85*, 558-563.

12. Interpretational Sets, Hypnotic Responding, and the Modification of Hypnotizability

N.P. Spanos

Introduction

College students are the typical subjects in most hypnosis experiments, and the majority of college students score in only the low to moderate range on standardized scales of hypnotizability (Spanos, Radtke, Hodgins, Stam, & Bertrand, 1983). Despite their relatively low hypnotizability scores, college students who volunteer for hypnosis experiments usually hold relatively positive attitudes toward hypnosis, are usually quite willing to cooperate with the hypnotist, and usually have the ability to imagine the scenes called for by the test suggestions (Spanos, Brett, Menary, & Cross, 1987). Moreover, when subjects are asked to predict their own level of hypnotic responsiveness, they tend to overestimate substantially the number of suggestions to which they will respond (Katsanis, Barnard, & Spanos, to be published).

When plotted, the relationship between hypnotizability and predictors such as attitudes, expectations, and absorption assumes a kind of fan shape. People with negative attitudes and expectations concerning hypnosis or with little imaginal ability almost always score low in hypnotizability. On the other hand, people with moderate to high scores on these predictors show wide variability in hypnotizability. These findings indicate that negative attitudes and expectations and the absence of imaginal ability serve to suppress hypnotic responding. However, when these characteristics are present to at least moderate degrees, hypnotizability scores vary from very high to very low. What, then, accounts for the wide range in hypnotizability scores seen among cooperative, imaginative subjects who hold positive expectations concerning hypnotic responding?

In this chapter I will review a number of studies which suggest that much of this variability can be understood in terms of the tacit interpretations that subjects hold about the test suggestions they are administered. According to this sociocognitive formulation, many subjects score low in hypnotizability because they interpret suggestions as requiring them *not* to make the behavioral responses called for. By teaching these subjects more appropriate interpretations, it should be possible to enhance substantially their levels of hypnotizability.

Interpretations of Test Suggestions

All hypnotizability scales involve administering a standardized series of test suggestions. Test suggestions are, however, ambiguous communications. They do not instruct subjects to carry out behavioral responses. Instead, they inform subjects that a response is occurring or will occur automatically (e.g., your arm is rising, feeling lighter and lighter). Subjects are frequently instructed to carry out imaginings that are consistent with the requisite behavioral response (e.g., imagine a balloon tied to your arm and lifting it in the air). Nevertheless, the behavioral response itself is defined as an event that must somehow occur automatically rather than as a self-initiated action (Spanos & Gorassini, 1984).

According to our sociocognitive account, hypnotic responding is goal-directed action and does not occur automatically (Spanos, 1986c). Many subjects, however, despite being cooperative and imaginative, are misled by the passive wording of suggestions. These subjects interpret suggestions literally, as requests simply to wait for suggested effects to happen by themselves. They place themselves in the role of being the passive observers of responses that they anticipate will occur automatically. Because hypnotic responses are not, in fact, automatic occurrences, these subjects tend to "fail" suggestions and to suffer disappointment when the hypnosis "didn't work."

Other subjects come tacitly to understand that suggestions are to be treated metaphorically rather than literally. These subjects carry out the behavioral responses called for, but at the same time, they become absorbed in imaginings that enable them to experience their goal-directed actions as involuntary happenings. It is subjects of this latter type that have been traditionally labeled as "highly hypnotizable." These subjects adopt an active interpretation of suggested demands, they enact the behavioral responses called for by suggestions, and they carry out the imaginings that allow them to experience and describe their responses as feeling involuntary.

We recently completed two interrelated studies that examined these ideas (Katsanis et al., to be published, studies 1 and 2). In the first study, 116 subjects predicted their responses to seven hypnotic test suggestions and immediately afterwards were tested for hypnotic responsiveness to these same suggestions. After responding to the suggestions, subjects completed a questionnaire which provided them with a set of four statements for each suggestion. Each statement described a different way of interpreting the suggestion, and subjects were asked to choose the interpretation that they had operated under during the suggestion period. The two most important alternatives in each set were a statement implying a passive interpretation (e.g., "I just waited to see if (my arm) rose by itself") and a statement implying an active interpretation (e.g., "I raised my arm and I imagined air being pumped into it so as to make it feel like it was light and rising by itself").

Overall, subjects "failed" substantially more suggestions than they "passed," and the most common interpretation chosen was to wait passively for suggested responses to happen. Subjects' expectations of "passing" suggestions correlated moderately with their actual responsiveness. Nevertheless, substantial variability in the degree of hypnotic responding remained even in subjects with uniformly high expectations. We divided the group of subjects with high expectancies into those who always chose a passive interpretation of suggestions and those who at least sometimes chose an active interpretation. Subjects who adopted an active interpretation obtained substantially higher scores on behavioral and subjective indices of hypnotizability than those who adopted a passive interpretation.

Our second study (Katsanis et al., to be published, study 2) was similar, but in this case we assessed subjects' interpretations before rather than after testing for hypnotizability. The results were the same as before. Subjects who intended to adopt a passive interpretation scored significantly lower on behavioral and subjective indices of hypnotizability than those who intended to adopt an active interpretation.

In study 2, we also assessed the vividness of subjects' imagery with a modification of the Betts questionnaire. Because test suggestions call for the construction of imaginary scenes, we reasoned that an active interpretational set would be most helpful to subjects who possessed the ability to generate vividly the imaginary experiences called for. Among subjects with very low imagery vividness scores, there was no significant correlation between the tendency to adopt an active interpretation and hypnotizability. However, among subjects with very high imagery vividness scores, the correlation between frequency of adopting an active interpretation and the behavioral index of hypnotizability was a whopping $r = .76$.

In summary, both of these studies indicate that hypnotic responsiveness is substantially influenced by the ways in which subjects interpret test suggestions. Subjects who adopt a passive interpretation of suggestions score lower in hypnotizability than those who adopt an active interpretation of the same suggestions. If this sociocognitive formulation is, in fact, accurate, then it should be possible to produce substantial enhancements in hypnotic responsiveness by teaching subjects low in hypnotizability to adopt an active interpretational set toward test suggestions. Moreover, the extent to which such teaching is effective is likely to be moderated by subjects' imaginal skills on the one hand, and by their attitudes toward hypnosis on the other.

Modifying Hypnotizability

Studies conducted in four independent laboratories (e.g., Diamond, 1972; Gfeller, Lynn, & Pribble, 1987; Sachs, 1971; Spanos, 1986a) now indicate that training procedures based on social learning principles can produce large gains in hypnotic susceptibility. For example, in our own laboratory we have developed a three-component skill training package that is aimed at teaching (a) positive attitudes toward hypnosis, (b) the use of imagery strategies for experiencing suggested effects, and (c) the adoption of an active interpretational set toward suggested demands. We have now completed eight experiments using our skill training package and in each experiment subjects low in hypnotizability who underwent skill training exhibited very large increases in hypnotizability (for a review, see Spanos, 1986a). Typically, half or more of the subjects with initially low hypnotizability who underwent skill training in these experiments scored in the high hypnotizability range on two different post-test scales administered several weeks apart. On the other hand, control subjects of low susceptibility never showed significant enhancements on these same hypnotizability post-tests.

In all of the studies that used our training package, skill-trained subjects exhibited large increments on both subjective and behavioral indices of hypnotizability. Moreover, in several studies (e.g., Gfeller et al., 1987; Spanos, Robertson, Menary, & Brett, 1986; Spanos, Lush, & Gwynn, 1987) training gains were shown to generalize to novel suggestions that were not included as practice items during training and even to particularly difficult or unusual items such as those for post-hypnotic responding, analgesia, selective amnesia, and "trance logic." One study (Spanos, Cross, Menary, & Smith, 1988) found that skill-trained subjects maintained enhanced hypnotizability more than a year after their training session.

Interpretation Set and Skill Training. In order to examine the role of interpretational set in the production of skill training gains, Spanos et al. (1986) gave a group of subjects low in hypnotizability our full three-component skill training package. A second group of low-hypnotizability subjects was administered a modified package that included positive information about hypnosis and encouraged the use of imagery strategies, but did *not* teach an active interpretation of suggestions. In other words, subjects in this modified group were not informed that suggested responses must be enacted. Instead, they were allowed to go on assuming that such responses happen automatically.

Subjects in both the complete and modified training groups showed large and equivalent increments in positive attitudes toward hypnosis. However, only those subjects who were administered the active interpretation component of skill training exhibited large gains on behavioral and subjective indices of hypnotizability.

In a more recent study (Spanos, Flynn, & Niles, 1988), we assessed the importance of interpretational set information while examining the relationship between subject-trainer rapport and hypnotizability gain. Subjects in one group were administered our skill training package, while those in the second group were exposed to a treatment that was designed to enhance rapport between subject and trainer while reinforcing a passive interpretation of suggestions. A third group of no treatment control subjects was post-tested without any intervening treatment. Subjects in the skill training and passive interpretation groups reported equal levels of rapport with and liking for the trainer. Nevertheless, the skill-trained subjects exhibited much higher post-test levels of hypnotizability than the controls, while the passive interpretation subjects failed to differ from the controls on post-tested hypnotizability.

Taken together, these two studies (Spanos, 1988; Spanos et al., 1986) indicate that learning *how* to interpret suggestions is a particularly important determinant of the enhancements in hypnotizability produced by skill training. In the absence of knowing how to interpret test suggestions, positive attitudes toward hypnosis and high levels of rapport with the trainer did not enhance hypnotizability.

Moderators of Hypnotizability Gain. The findings I have just reviewed do not imply that variables like attitudes toward hypnosis and rapport are irrelevant to the gains produced by skill training. Instead, these findings may simply mean that these variables are not, in themselves, sufficient for producing high levels of hypnotizability. In fact, two recent studies from our laboratory along with a study by Gfeller et al. (1987) indicate that variables like attitudes toward hypnosis, rapport, and imagery vividness play an important role in moderating the degree to which skill-trained subjects exhibit enhanced hypnotizability. Although subjects who undergo skill training show substantial enhancements in hypnotizability, they also show a good deal of variability in the magnitude of their hypnotizability enhancement. Spanos, Cross, Menary, Brett, and de Groh (1987) found that the degree of hypnotizability enhancement found among subjects of low hypnotizability who underwent skill training was predicted by both attitudinal and imaginal proclivity variables. Subjects who, despite skill training, maintained relatively negative attitudes toward hypnosis, showed lower post-training scores on behavioral and subjective indices of hypnotizability than did subjects whose attitudes toward hypnosis became highly positive following skill training. Moreover, subjects with relatively high scores on questionnaire measures of imagery vividness and absorption in imaginings benefitted more from skill training than did those with low scores on these imaginal propensity questionnaires.

Cross and Spanos (to be published) obtained similar results. In that study, subjects low in hypnotizability were selected on the basis on their having very high or very low scores on a questionnaire measure of imagery vividness. Half of the subjects in each group received a skill training, and the remainder served as controls. Both high- and low-imagery subjects showed significant enhancements on behavioral indices of hypnotizability following skill training. However, the high-imagery skill-trained subjects were significantly better than the low-imagery skill-trained subjects at interpreting their behavioral responses as occurring involuntarily. Hypnotizability gain in skill-trained subjects was also predicted by subjects' post-training attitudes toward hypnosis and by the trainer's ratings of subjects' receptivity toward the information presented during training. Related findings were presented by Gfeller et al. (1987). In that case, degree of rapport between trainer and subject was positively correlated with post-tested hypnotizability in skill-trained subjects.

Taken together, the findings reviewed thus far are consistent with the notion that hypnotic responding is goal-directed action. Subjects without any training who tacitly interpret suggestions as requests to bring about the behaviors and experiences called for are likely to "pass" suggestions. Those who adopt a passive interpretation toward these same suggestions tend to "fail" them. Training which is aimed at inculcating an active interpretational set toward suggestions produces substantial enhancements in hypnotizability. However, the extent to which skill trained subjects adopt and utilize an active interpretational set is dependent upon their receptivity to the communications transmitted during skill training. This receptivity is, in turn, influenced by their attitudes toward hypnosis and their rapport with and liking for the trainer. Subjects' utilization of an active interpretational set is also influenced by their imaginal propensities. Subjects who have difficulty generating and becoming absorbed in the imaginings called for by the suggestions have difficulty creating the subjective experiences called for. These subjects may be limited in the extent to which they can benefit from skill training packages that emphasise the importance of imaginal responding.

Skill Training and Compliance. The sociocognitive formulation that I have been outlining posits that skill trained subjects learn to subjectively experience the effects called for by test suggestions. Thus, when given an arm levitation suggestion these subjects do not simply raise their arms, they also develop (to different degrees) the experience of their arm rising by itself. There is, of course, an alternative explanation. Perhaps the results of skill training studies can be accounted for parsimoniousy in terms of social compliance. According to this hypothesis skill trained subjects do not learn to generate subjectively convincing displays of hypnotic behavior. Instead, they respond to the social pressures inherent in the skill training session by simply producing the requisite behavioral responses in the absence of the subjective experiences called for.

The compliance issue is complex and I do not wish to argue that skill trained subjects never comply or that compliance is not an important factor in hypnotic responding more generally. On the other hand, I doubt that compliance can serve as an adequate or primary account of the hypnotizability gains obtained in skill training studies.

It may be recalled that in the Spanos et al. (1986) and Spanos, Flynn, and Niles (1988, experiment 2) studies some subjects received skill training while others received training in which active interpretation information was omitted or training that emphasised a passive interpretation. Subjects in all of these treatments were told that their training was designed to enhance hypnotizability and that they were expected to show enhanced hypnotizability. Nevertheless, large hypnotizability gains were shown only by subjects who received skill training. It is difficult to account for these findings in terms of compliance. Instead, these findings indicate that skill trained subjects learned *how* to meet both the behavioral and subjective requirements of suggestions and then cooperated in fulfilling these requirements. However, subjects who received modified training or training that emphasised a passive interpretation, did not know how to meet the requirements of the suggestions. Despite the social pressures inherent in their training sessions, these subjects did not comply. Instead, they simply failed to respond to the suggestions.

A second source of evidence against the compliance hypothesis comes from studies that compared skill trained subjects to subjects who were explicitly instructed to fake behaving like excellent hypnotic subjects (i.e., simulators). If the enhancements produced by skill training were simply a matter of subjects "faking good," then one might expect skill trained subjects and simulators to perform similarly on behavioral and subjective indices of hypnotizability. However, the three studies that have compared skill trained subjects and simulators have found consistent differences in the performance of these groups (Spanos & Flynn, to be published; Spanos, Lush, & Gwynn, 1987; Spanos et al., 1986). For example, Spanos, Lush, and Gwynn compared the performance of skill trained subjects, simulators, and subjects who scored high in hypnotizability without training (natural highs). Subjects were tested on items which tap a pattern of responding which Orne (1959) has labeled a "tolerance for logical incongruity." These items assessed "incongruous writing" during age regression, "duality experiences" during age regression, and transparent visual hallucinations. In previous studies natural highs and simulators had performed differently on all of these items (for a review see Spanos, 1986b). Spanos, Lush, and Gwynn (1987) found that natural highs and skill trained subjects responded similarly on all of these tests and, in the case of each test, the subjects in these two groups showed significantly higher levels of "incongruous responding" than did simulators.

In summary, the interpretations of suggested demands that subjects adopt play an influencial role in determining their level of hypnotic responding. These interpretations are to a large extent fostered by the passive wording of typical test suggestions. Nevertheless, these interpretations are modifiable with skill training, and when subjects learn to adopt an active interpretation for suggestions they often exhibit substantial increments in hypnotizability. The extent to which skill training enhances hypnotizability is moderated by subjects' attitudes toward hypnosis as well as by their imaginal propensities. Skill training usually produced enhancements in subjective as well as behavioral responses, and these enhancements cannot be accounted for adequately in terms of compliance.

Acknowledgement. The research described in this paper was supported by a grant from the Social Sciences and Humanities Research Council of Canada.

References

Cross, W.P., & Spanos, N.P. (to be published). The effects of subjects' imagery vividness and receptivity on skill training induced gains in hypnotic susceptibility. *Imagination, Cognition and Personality.*

Diamond, M.J. (1972). The use of observationally presented information to modify hypnotic susceptibility. *Journal of Abnormal Psychology, 79,* 174-180.

Gfeller, J., Lynn, S., & Pribble, W. (1987). Enhancing hypnotic susceptibility: Interpersonal and rapport factors. *Journal of Personality and Social Psychology, 52,* 586-595.

Gorassini, D.R., & Spanos, N.P. (1986). A social-cognitive skills approach to the successful modification of hypnotic susceptibility. *Journal of Personality and Social Psychology, 50,* 1004-1012.

Katsanis, J., Barnard, J., & Spanos, N.P. (to be published). Self-predictions, interpretational set and imagery vividness as determinants of hypnotic responding. *Imagination, Cognition and Personality.*

Orne, M.T. (1959). The nature of hypnosis: Artifact and essence. *Journal of Abnormal and Social Psychology, 58,* 277-299.

Sachs, L.B. (1971). Construing hypnosis as modifiable behavior. In A. Jacobs & L.B. Sachs (Eds.), *Psychology of private events* (pp. 61-75). New York: Academic.

Spanos, N.P. (1986a). Hypnotic and the modification of hypnotic susceptibility : A social psychological perspective. In P. Naish (Ed.), *What is hypnosis?* (pp. 85-120). Philadelphia: Open University.

Spanos, N.P. (1986b). Hypnotic behaviour: A social psychological interpretation of amnesia, analgesia and trance logic. *Behavioral and Brain Sciences, 9,* 449-502.

Spanos, N.P. (1986c). Hypnosis, nonvolitional responding and multiple personality: A social psychological perspective. In B. Maher & W. Maher (Eds.), *Progress in experimental personality research, Vol. 14.* New York: Academic.

Spanos, N.P., Brett, P.J., Menary, E.P., & Cross, W.P. (1987). A measure of attitudes toward hypnosis: Relationships with absorption and hypnotic susceptibility. *American Journal of Clinical Hypnosis, 30,* 139-150.

Spanos, N.P., Cross, W.P., Menary, E.P., Brett, P.J., & de Groh, M. (1987). Attitudinal and imaginal ability predictors of social cognitive-skill training enhancements of hypnotic susceptibility. *Personality and Social Psychology Bulletin, 13,* 379-398.

Spanos, N.P., Cross, W.P., Menary, E.P., & Smith, J. (1988). Long term effects of cognitive skill training for the enhancement of hypnotic susceptibility. *British Journal of Experimental and Clinical Hypnosis, 5,* 73-78.

Spanos, N.P., & Gorassini, D.R. (1984). The structure of hypnotic test suggestions and attributions of responding involuntarily. *Journal of Personality and Social Psychology, 46,* 688-696.

Spanos, N.P., de Groh, M., & de Groot, H.P. (1987). Skill training for enhancing hypnotic susceptibility and word list amnesia. *British Journal of Experimental and Clinical Hypnosis, 4,* 15-23.

Spanos, N.P., & Flynn, D. (to be published). Simulation, Compliance, rapport and cognitive skill training in the enhancement of hypnotizability susceptibility. *British Journal of Experimental and Clinical Hypnosis.*

Spanos, N.P., Lush, N.I., & Gwynn, M.I. (1987) *Cognitive skill training enhancement of hypnotizability: Generalization effects and trance logic responding.* Unpublished manuscript, Carleton University.

Spanos, N.P., Radtke, H.L., Hodgins, D.C., Stam, H.J., & Bertrand, L.D. (1983). The Carleton University Responsiveness to Suggestion Scale: Normative data and psychometric properties. *Psychological Reports,* 523-535.

Spanos, N.P., Robertson, L.A., Menary, E.P., & Brett, P.J. (1986). Component analysis of cognitive skill training for the enhancement of hypnotic susceptibility. *Journal of Abnormal Psychology, 95,* 350-357.

Spanos, N.P., Flynn, D., & Niles, J. (1988). *Rapport and cognitive skill training in the enhancement of hypnotizability.* Unpublished manuscript, Carleton University.

13. Measurement and Individual Differences of Suggestibility: Some Comments

R.M. Lundy

Five papers are included in this section, each in its turn responding to Professor Eysenck's challenge to the Symposium to create a taxonomy that will facilitate the measurement and thus the scientific study of suggestion and suggestibility.

Netter's paper demonstrated that one facet of our topic, sensory suggestibility, can indeed be measured and that the relationship of this concept to other variables will help us to understand what we mean by suggestibility. Gudjonsson, by examining the closed interpersonal situation, the questioning procedure, and the relationship between interviewer and subject, has defined and explicated a response to leading questions he has come to call "interrogative suggestibility". Evans furthered our understanding by showing us, through factor analysis, the degree to which some things, particularly response to placebo and hypnotizability, are *not* suggestibility. Crawford and Spanos, both, directed their work toward the concept of hypnotic suggestibility, Crawford by attempting to explain individual differences in terms of a cognitive capacity and Spanos by emphasizing the modifiability of the response pattern of hypnotic suggestibility.

P. Netter: Sensory Suggestibility: Its Measurement, Individual Differences, and Relation to Placebo and Drug Effects. Among the several comments one might make about the Netter chapter, surely the first is on the care and perseverance with which the researchers in Gheorghiu's laboratory have developed instruments to measure sensory suggestibility. Although the end point may be only a single suggestibility score for the subject, that person will have sat before 12 highly advanced instruments, some electronic, that certainly appear to be measuring the subject's perception of sensory "changes," visual, auditory, and tactile.

A second comment bears on the reduction, if not the elimination, of interpersonal elements in the sensory suggestibility measurement process. It may be that the shadow that obfuscates our understanding of suggestibility, as well as the potential light for moderating it (see Spanos, this volume), are in the form of other persons in the situation. In the measurement of sensory suggestibility, we can be reasonably certain that the interpersonal elements are not of any great moment.

The relationships found between sensory suggestibility and physiological measures, such as blood pressure and heart rate, are intriguing, particularly when these relationships are curvilinear. Clearly, these findings call for more research on these complex relationships.

It is in the study of nicotine that a hypothesis for a biological basis of sensory suggestibility becomes formed. As the data from Netter's study suggest, the person who has high sensory suggestibility responds as though he or she is in a state of cortical underarousal - at least with respect to the cholinergic transmitter system. It will have to be explored whether this also relates to the observation of lower discriminative ability of highly suggestible persons suggested by Netter's data from the evaluation of headache scores by signal detection analysis in patients with headaches. Their incapacity to discriminate between an analgesic and a placebo when treated by the two drugs in alternating order in a long-term trial may reflect the same lowered capability of stimulus selection observed in acute trials after treatment with anticholinergic drugs like scopolamine.

Further studies might have to explore the nature of the relationship between cortical arousal of this type, which is mediated by cortical acetylcholine affecting the nicotine receptors, and the observation of increased peripheral indicators of autonomic arousal such as higher levels of heart rate and blood pressure in subjects of high sensory suggestibility, as reported by Neuhäuser et al.

Finally, the results reported by Netter should give us pause when we realize how many of our studies in pharmacology and physiology that involve a subject's perception of a stimulus or of stimulus change are conducted with the assumption that suggestibility is not involved! And what about important medical tests? (Our optometrists say, "Tell me when the lines are solid," just as Dr. Gheorghiu and his colleagues say, "Tell me when you se the light get brighter." For many of us [suggestible] persons, these lines probably become solid much sooner than they do for the rest of us [nonsuggestible] persons).

G.H. Gudjonsson: Theoretical and Empirical Aspects of Interrogative Suggestibility. Gudjonsson's work is very nearly unique, probably because few social scientists have started out, as Gudjonsson did, as a consultant in police interrogation. Thus we have interrogative suggestibility, with a distinctive definition, measuring instrument, theoretical model, and relationship to other characteristics of personality.

It is this relationship to personality characteristics that is more striking in Gudjonsson's paper. The relationships to intelligence, memory, self-esteem, assertiveness, and anxiety are straightforward and expected. The intriguing relationship is between interrogative suggestibility and the strategies of coping that subjects develop during interrogation. Those subjects who developed a strategy of "avoidance coping," of avoiding confrontation with the stressor during the test for suggestibility, were shown to be more suggestible. Those subjects whose coping strategies included critically examining the situation and its stress were less suggestible.

Both interrogative and sensory suggestibility are measured responses to suggestion, but a striking difference presents itself when one considers the interpersonal context in which they occur. In sensory suggestibility the interpersonal aspects are reduced to a minimum, while in interrogative suggestibility they are the essential elements in explaining the response.

F.J. Evans: The Independence of Suggestibility, Placebo Response, and Hypnotizability. Evans presents very solid statistical evidence that general suggestibility, the placebo response, and hypnotizability are distinct and separate constructs. After reviewing the factor analytic studies of measures of these three concepts, Evans concludes that hypnosis is allied with dissociation, that placebo response is allied with expectancy, and that suggestibility is allied with social pressure.

The singular contribution of Evans to this symposium is to alert us to the power of factor analysis, especially in our search for a taxonomy of suggestibility. What remains for factor analysis, however, is to help us isolate and define the general factor, or core, of suggestibility, if it exists, and to include in the factor analytic studies some of the newer measures, such as those of sensory suggestibility and interrogative suggestibility, that have been described at this symposium.

The work of Crawford and Spanos approaches suggestibility from hypnosis. Their emphasis has been to understand hypnotic suggestion for its own sake. If it then turns out to be representative of, or instructive for, the study of suggestibility in general, so much the better.

H.J. Crawford: Cognitive and Physiological Flexibility: Multiple Pathways to Hypnotic Reponsiveness. For Crawford the distinguishing characteristics of the highly hypnotizable subject are cognitive flexibility and the ability to control the focus of attention. Evidence appears to be mounting that subjects who are suggestible after undergoing a hypnotic induction, that is, who are hypnotizable, have the capacity to shift strategies to fit the task at hand.

An implication of these findings is that the ability to engage in hypnotic imagery and thus to experience hypnotic suggestions is part of a broader capacity to engage in cognitive shifts, in this case a shift from a reality orientation to an imaginal one. These shifts, though enhanced by another person in the case of hypnosis, are viewed as voluntary on the part of the subject. The subject can decide whether or not to make a shift.

As Crawford points out, however, this "capacity" to engage in cognitive shifts may reach detrimental levels for some persons who can no longer keep them under voluntary control.

N.P. Spanos: Interpretational Sets, Hypnotic Responding, and the Modification of Hypnotizability. Spanos, by taking to his experimental heart what some of the rest of us only verbalize - that hypnotizability is the measure of an ability or skill - has developed a procedure for increasing that skill. The procedure is neither difficult nor extensive but, most important, it works.

Subjects who are originally low in hypnotizability are taught to make an active, positive response to a suggestion at the same time that they develop a facilitating strategy of imagery for experiencing the suggested effect. According to Spanos, it is this active "interpretational set" toward the suggestion that leads to increased suggestibility for subjects who achieve low scores.

Although there remain some possible moderating factors in the current success of the procedure, for instance, the subject's general attitude toward the procedure and the subject's ability to visualize, these factors, themselves, may be modifiable by using Spanos's socio-cognitive formulation. If Spanos and his co-workers can succeed, we may find ourselves much closer to the point where all persons, regardless of their original level of hypnotizability, may be able to gain the benefits, such as moderation of pain, increased concentration, and control of habits, that mark the human potential of hypnotic suggestibility.

III

Psychophysiological Aspects of Suggestibility

14. Cortical Event-Related Evoked Potential Correlates of Hypnotic Hallucination

D. Spiegel

Introduction

Cortical event-related potentials (ERPs) have been productively employed in the study of attentional processes in humans. Since hypnosis involves an alteration in both attention (Spiegel & Spiegel, 1978; Tellegen & Atkinson, 1974) and perception (Orne, 1959), it makes sense to examine for any hypnotically induced effects of perceptual alteration on measures of ERP. The amplitude of the early exogenous components of the evoked response is related to stimulus intensity and selection of a perceptual channel (Ford, Roth, Dirk, & Kopell, 1978; Hillyard & Picton, 1979), while the later endogenous components are affected by changes in the strategy of information processing. For example, the amplitude of the P_{300} component of the evoked potential waveform is increased by the element of surprise and the relevance of the stimulus to a response task (Sutton, Braren, & Zubin, 1965; Naatanen, 1969; Hillyard, Picton, & Regan, 1978; Duncan-Johnson & Donchin, 1980; Johnson, 1980; Baribeau-Braun, Picton, & Gosselin, 1983).

This psychophysiological method of studying attention holds promise for more precise examination of hypnotic alterations in perception. The hypnotic state itself involves intense and focused concentration with a constriction of peripheral awareness (Hilgard, 1977; Spiegel & Spiegel, 1978; Van Nuys, 1973). Hypnotized individuals are in a state of resting alertness, and demonstrate an unusual ability to alter perception, for example by producing hallucinations, and to change motor function so that it seems relatively involuntary (Weitzenhoffer, 1980). Since these changes involve an apparent psychological influence on somatic function, one would expect to see some change in brain function during hypnotically induced hallucination. The underlying premise is not that the hypnotic state *per se* is characterized by some altered activity of the brain (Morgan, MacDonald, & Hilgard, 1974), but rather that highly hypnotizable individuals in a hypnotic state should show changes in ERPs which correspond to their subjective experience of perceptual alteration. If their hypnotically induced hallucination blocks perception of a stimulus, the amplitude of their ERP should be reduced.

Literature review

Previous findings in this area have conflicted. A number of studies have failed to demonstrate any differences of ERP during hypnotically induced hallucination (Amadeo & Yaŋovski, 1975; Andreassi, Balinsky, Gallichio, DeSimone, & Mellers, 1976; Beck & Barolin, 1965; Beck, Dustman, & Beier, 1966; Halliday & Mason, 1964; Serafetinides, 1968; Zakrzewski & Szelenberger, 1981). The sensory modalities that were studied included somatosensory, visual, and auditory. Possible explanations for this disagreement in findings include small sample sizes, the use of patients with severe neurological or psychiatric disorders, and semi-quantitative analysis of event-related potentials. Further, some studies employed hypnotic instructions to alter rather than eliminate perception of the stimulus, for example by making the stimulus less bright or loud. The process of carrying out such hypnotic instructions actually requires the subject to attend to a stimulus rather than ignore it. Thus, the process contradicts the content.

Some studies have shown reduction in the amplitude of the event-related response during a hypnotic instruction that the stimulus be perceived as attenuated (Clynes, Kohn, & Lifshitz, 1964; Galbraith, Cooper, & London, 1972; Guerrero-Figueroa & Heath, 1964; Hernandez-Peon & Donoso, 1959; Wilson, 1968). However, several were single-subject trials (Guerrero-Figueroa & Heath, 1964; Clynes et al., 1964). Galbraith et al. (1972) employed a more sophisticated design in that they compared the performance of subjects with high versus low hypnotizability on the Harvard Group Scale of Hypnotic Susceptibility (Shor & Orne, 1962) and used a crossover attention task comparing visual ERPs when subjects were counting clicks. Subjects with high hypnotizability reduced and those with low hypnotizability increased their EPRs to the visual stimuli. However, Galbraith et al. studied only a crudely averaged amplitude between 100 and 300 ms at C_Z, and the effect involved hypnotically concentrated attention rather than hallucination.

Two recent studies have provided results which apparently conflict more directly. Each examined the effect on the cortical ERP of a hypnotic hallucination intended to obstruct perception of a stimulus. One study showed an increase, and the other a decrease in P_{300} amplitude under seemingly similar circumstances. Barabasz and Lonsdale (1983) reported increases of amplitude in the olfactory EP of four highly hypnotizable subjects experiencing anosmia compared with five subjects low in hypnotizability attempting to simulate the response. Subjects were given the instruction for anosmia contained in item 9 of the Stanford Hypnotic Susceptibility Scale: Form C (SHSS:C; Weitzenhoffer & Hilgard, 1962), which is "You can no longer smell anything at all" (Hilgard, 1965). Subjects of high hypnotizability showed significantly increased P_{300} amplitudes to both weak and strong odors at the temporal leads T_3 and T_4, but not in a no-odor air puff control condition. In addition, highly hypnotizable subjects had significantly higher P_{300} amplitudes in hypnosis as compared with waking conditions for weak and strong odors. Subsequently, research on cerebral blood flow has also demonstrated hypnotically induced increases in temporal activity (Baer, Ackerman, Surman, Correia, Griffith, Alpert, & Hackett, 1985; Crawford, Skolnick, Benson, R.E. Gur, & R.C. Gur, 1985).

In a recent study, we (Spiegel, Cutcomb, Ren, & Pribram, 1985) demonstrated the opposite effect. We found a decrease in P_{300} amplitude among six highly hypnotizable subjects experiencing an obstructive hallucination, consisting of an imagined cardboard box blocking the view of the stimulus generator, a TV monitor flashing colored rectangular boxes. Highly hypnotizable subjects reported that they could not see the stimulus, and pressed a device in response to only 5 % of the target stimuli (Hansen & Hillyard, 1980), compared with 96 % for the controls of low hypnotizability. Recordings were made at F_Z, C_Z, P_Z, O_1 and O_2. There was significant decrease in the P_{300} component of the visual ERP throughout the scalp, and of N_{200} as well as P_{300} in the occipital region, the visual association area (see Figure 1). Further, the decrease was greater in the right as compared with the left occipital scalp electrode (O_2 versus O_1), suggesting greater involvement of the right hemisphere in generating the hallucinated image and reducing perception of the visual stimulus. Six controls low in hypnotizability attempting the same hallucination task showed no difference in the amplitude of their responses.

This observed reduction of amplitude was also significantly greater than differences observed among six other non-hypnotized controls instructed to attend actively (button press) and passively (no button pressing). Among these control subjects, differences in amplitude were strongest in the frontal and central leads as one would expect, reflecting the difference in motor activity. Unlike the experimental group, they showed virtually no differences between conditions in the occipital leads. Thus, the highly hypnotizables' subjective experience of attending to the hallucinated box rather than the stimulus generator was confirmed by the decrease in N_{200} and P_{300} amplitudes (see Figure 1).

This difference in findings was likely related to a surprise effect in the Barabasz and Lonsdale study. In it, subjects were told "You can no longer smell anything at all." When the obstructing

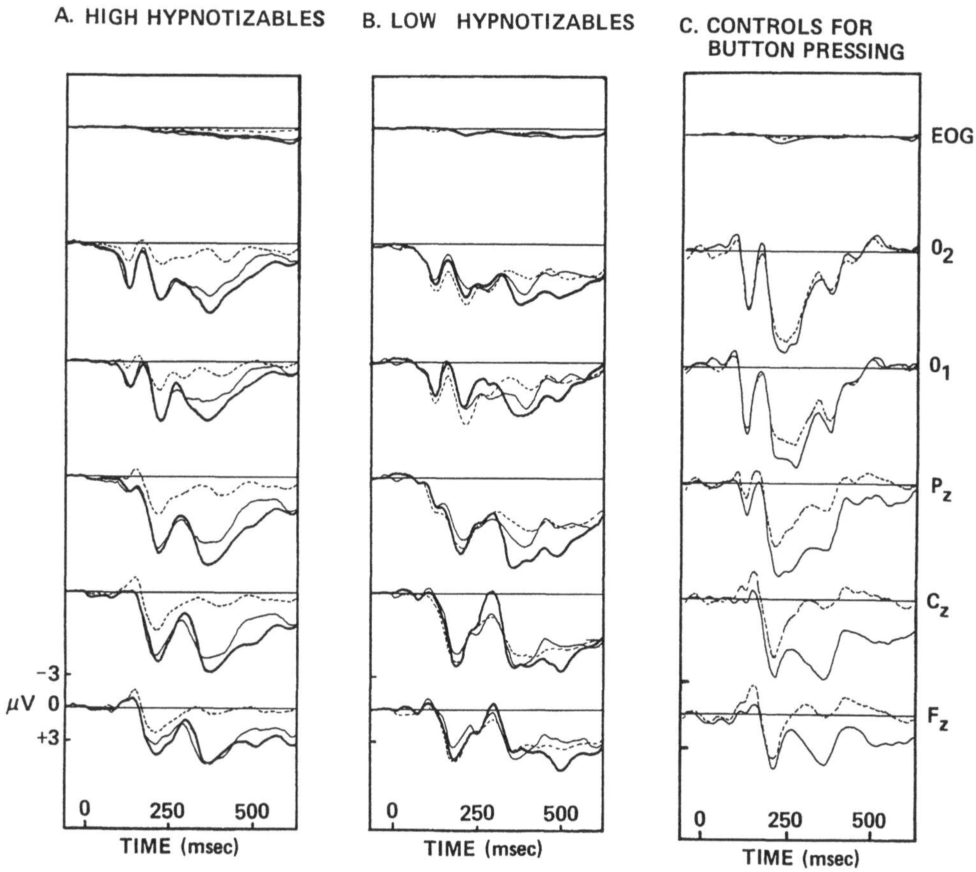

Figure 1. P_{300} amplitude is reduced throughout the scalp in the hypnotically induced obstructive hallucination condition (*dotted line*) as compared with hypnotically induced attention enhancement (*thick solid line*) and hypnotic stimulus diminution conditions (*thin solid line*), only among subjects of high hypnotizability. (Spiegel et al., 1985). (Copyright 1985 by the American Psychological Association. Reprinted by permission of the publisher)

hallucination was less than perfect, they were surprised by the smell, and novelty of a stimulus is usually associated with an icnrease in the P_{300} amplitude (Hillyard, Picton, & Regan, 1978; Baribeau-Braun, Picton, & Gosselin, 1983). The nature of the hypotic instruction meant that any smell at all was a clear contradiction, causing conflict about whether the paradigm or the subject's perception was primary. Given that the highly hypnotizable subjects concentrated intently and were desirous of pleasing, they may have been especially surprised that their anosmia was less than complete, hence the increase in P_{300} amplitude. The "surprise effect" explanation seems further supported by the increased P_{300} amplitudes among the subjects low in hypnotizability when presented with a puff of unexpectedly odorless air.

By contrast, in the Spiegel et al. (1985) study, subjects were instructed to concentrate on an image of a cardboard box which by implication would block view of the TV monitor generating the stimuli. The fact of obstructed view was therefore a secondary consequence of the hallucination, not a primary instruction, such as "You will no longer see anything at all on the screen." This means that in the 5 % of cases in which the highly hypnotizables did see something, they were not surprised or distracted from the primary task - they simply saw something "through " the hallucinated box, which is incongruous but not experienced as impossible. Their absorption in the hallucination experience was not disrupted by their perceptual experience.

More recently, we sought to replicate these findings in the visual system, using another perceptual channel. We chose somatosensory stimulation, in part because of its relevance to hypnotically produced analgesia (Spiegel, 1985). Preliminary findings from that study (Spiegel, Bierre, & Rootenberg, 1988) indicate a similar reduction in P_{300} amplitude when highly hypnotizable subjects experience an hallucination that their left hand is cold and numb. The hypnotically produced hallucination interferes with perception of the electrical stimulation being applied over the radial nerve. There was also a reduction in P_{100} amplitude in this condition, as well an increase in P_{100} when the highly hypnotizable subjects were asked to pay special attention to the stimuli. There were no such task-related differences among the subjects with low hypnotizability.

Conclusion

Major issues in the study of neurophysiological effects of hypnotically produced hallucination include the nature of the task, the subjects employed, and the measurement and analysis of ERPs. The literature indicates that hypnotic attention to a positive attentional task which distracts from another perception is more effective in reducing the ERP than is a simple instruction not to perceive a stimulus. A variety of attentional controls is crucial to establish a normal baseline and distinguish between hypnotically inducted hallucination and simple inattention. Further, to establish a hypnotic effect, it is necessary to compare the performances of subjects who score high with those who score low on one of the standard tests of hypnotizability. ERP measurements should include a standard montage of at least five and preferably more leads, and be analyzed using paradigms of peak selection with statistical analysis of amplitude and latency differences.

The physiological marker of the hypnotic state has been the holy grail of hypnotic psychophysiological research, and it has remained as elusive. However, reconceptualizing the hypnotic state as one that may not have a psychophysiological signature *per se*, but rather represents a heightened ability to exert psychological influence over physiological processes such as perception and autonomic and voluntary motor control, changes the nature of the search. Heightened hypnotic onctrol over somatic function has been observed with such parameters as skin temperature (Grabowska, 1971), blood flow (Dubin & Shapiro, 1974) and gastric acid secretion (Klein and Spiegel, 1988). One looks for an unusual ability to control task-related changes in perceptual and perhaps other neurophysiological functions among highly hypnotizable individuals carrying out tasks of perceptual alteration. A given measure need not be characteristically altered in the hypnotic state, but rather susceptible of directed change in either direction, depending on the nature of the task. Furthermore, this ERP measure can be used to discriminate between subjects high and low in hypnotizability solely on the basis of psychophysiologic measures of brain function during tasks involving perceptual alteration.

References

Amadeo, M., & Yanovski, A. (1975). Evoked potentials and selective attention in subjects capable of hypnotic analgesia. *International Journal of Clinical and Experimental Hypnosis, 23*, 200-210.

Andreassi, J.L., Balinsky, B., & Gallichio, J.A., De Simone, J.J., & Mellers, B.W. (1976). Hypnotic suggestion of stimulus change and visual cortical evoked potential. *Perceptual & Motor Skills, 42*, 371-378.

Baer, L., Ackerman, R., Surmon, O., Correia, J., Griffith, J., Alpert, N., & Hackett, T. (1985). PET studies during hypnosis and hypnotic suggestion. In P. Berner (Ed.) *Psychiatry: The State of the Art, Biological Psychiatry, Higher Nervous Activity* (pp. 293-298). New York: Plenum.

Barabasz, A.F., & Gregson, R. (1979). Antarctic wintering-over, suggestion and transient olfactory stimulation: EEG evoked potentials and electrodermal responses. *Biological Psychology, 9*, 285-295.

Barabasz, A.F., & Lonsdale, C. (1983). Effects of hypnosis on P_{300} olfactory-evoked potential amplitudes. *Journal of Abnormal Psychology, 92*, 520-523.

Baribeau-Braun, J., Picton, T.W., & Gosselin, J.U. (1983). A neurophysiological evaluation of abnormal information processing. *Science, 219*, 874-876.

Beck, E.C., Barolin, G.S. (1965). The effect of hypnotic suggestion on evoked potentials. *Journal of Nervous and Mental Disease, 140*, 154-161.

Beck, E.D., Dustman, R.D., Beier, E.G. (1966). Hpynotic suggestions and visually evoked potentials. *Electroencephalography & Clinical Neurophysiology, 20*, 397-400.

Clynes, M., Koh, M., & Lifshitz, K. (1964). Dynamics and spatial behavior of light-evoked potentials, their modification under hypnosis, and on-line correlation in relation to rhythmic components. *Annals of the New York Academy of Sciences, 112*, 468-509.

Crasilneck, H.B., Hall, J.A., (1985). *Clinial Hypnosis: Principles and Applications,* 2nd Ed. New York: Grune & Stratton.

Crawford, H., Skolnick, B., Benson, D., Gur, R.E., & Gur, R.C. (1985). Regional cerebral blood flow in hypnosis and hypnotic analgesia. Paper presented at the 10th International Congress of Hypnosis and Psychosomatic Medicine. Toronto, Canada, August.

Dubin, L.L., Shapiro, S.S. (1974). Use of hypnosis to facilitate dental extraction and hemostasis in a classic hemophiliac with a high antibody titer to factor VIII. *American Journal of Clinical Hypnosis, 17*, 79-83.

Duncan-Johnson, C.C., & Donchin, E. (1980). The relation of P_{300} latency to reaction time as a function of expectancy. *Progress in Brain Research, 54*, 717-722.
Ford, J.M., Roth, W.T., Dirk, S.J., & Kopell, B.S. (1978). Evoked potential correlates of signal recognition between and within modalities. *Science, 181*, 465-466.
Galbraith, G.C., Cooper, L.M., & London, P. (1972). Hypnotic susceptibility and the sensory evoked response. *Journal of Comparative & Physiological Psychology, 80*, 509-514.
Grabowska, M.J. (1971). The efect of hypnosis and hypnotic suggestion on the blood flow in the extremities. *Polish Medical Journal, 10*, 1044-1051.
Guerrero-Figueroa, R., & Heath, R.G. (1964). Evoked responses and changes during attentive factors in man. *Archives of Neurology, 10*, 74-84.
Halliday, A.M., & Mason, A.A. (1964). Cortical evoked potentials during hypnotic anaesthesia. *Electroencephalography & Clinical Neurophysiology, 16*, 312-314.
Hansen, J.C., & Hillyard, S.A. (1980). Endogenous brain potentials associated with selective auditory attention. *Electroencephalography & Clinical Neurophysiology, 49*, 277-290.
Hernandez-Peon, R., & Donoso, M. (1959). Influence of attention and suggestion upon subcortical evoked electric activity in the human brain. In L. Van Bogaert & J. Radermecker (Eds.), *First international congress of neurological sciences* (Vol. 3, pp. 385-396). London: Pergamon.
Hilgard, E.R. (1965). *Hypnotic susceptibility.* New York: Harcourt, Brace, & World.
Hilgard, E.R. (1977). *Divided consciousness: Multiple controls in human thought and action.* New York: Wiley.
Hillyard, S.A., Picton, T.W., & Regan, D. (1978). Sensation, perception, and attention: analysis using ERPs. In E. Callaway, P. Tueting, & S.H. Koslow (Eds.), *Event-related brain potentials in man.* New York: Academic.
Hillyard, S.A., Picton, T.W. (1979). Event-related brain potentials and selective information processing in man. In J.E. Desmedt (Ed.), *Progress in clinical neurophysiology* (Vol. 6, pp. 1-52). Basel: Karger.
Johnson, R. (1980). P_{300} amplitude and probabilistic judgements. *Progress in Brain Research, 54*, 723-729.
Klein, K., & Spiegel, D. (1988). Hypnotic alteration of gastric acid secretion. Submitted to *Journal of the American Medical Association.*
Morgan, A.H., MacDonald, H., & Hilgard, E.R. (1974). EEG alpha: Lateral asymmetry related to task and hypnotizability. *Psychophysiology, 11*, 275-282.
Naatanen, R. (1969). Anticipation of relevant stimuli and evoked potentials: A comment on Donchin's and Cohen's "averaged evoked potentials and intramodality selective attention." *Perceptual and Motor Skills, 28*, 639-646.
Orne, M.T. (1959). The nature of hypnosis: Artifact and essence. *Journal of Abnormal and Social Psychology, 58*, 277-299.
Serafetinides, E.A. (1968). Electrophysiological responses to sensory stimulation under hypnosis. *American Journal of Psychiatry, 125*, 112-113.
Shor, R.E., & Orne, E.C. (1962). *Harvard group scale of hypnotic susceptibility, form A.* Palo Alto: Consulting Psychologists.
Spiegel, D. (1980). Trance as metaphor: The symbolism of control. Chicago: Year Book Medical Publishers.
Spiegel, D. (1985). The use of hypnosis in controlling cancer pain. CA: *A Cancer Journal for Clinicians, 35*, 221-231.
Spiegel, D., Cutcomb, S., Ren, C., & Pribram, K. (1985). Hypnotic hallucination alters evoked potentials. *Journal of Abnormal Psychology, 94*, 249-255.
Spiegel, D., Bierre, P., & Rootenberg, J. (1988). Hypnotic alteration of somatosensory perception. Submitted to *American Journal of Psychiatry.*
Spiegel, H. (1970). Termination of smoking by a single treatment. *Archives of Environmental Health, 20*, 736-742.
Spiegel, H., & Spiegel, D. (1978). *Trance and treatment: Clinical uses of hypnosis.* New York: Basic. (Reissued by American Psychiatric Press, 1987).
Sutton, S., Braren, M., & Zubin, J. (1965). Evoked-potential correlates of stimulus uncertainty. *Science, 150*, 1187-88.

Tellegen, A., & Atkinson, G. (1974). Openness to absorbing and self-altering experiences ("absorption"), a trait related to hypnotic susceptibility. *Journal of Abnormal Psychology, 83*, 268-277.

Van Nuys, D. (1973). Meditation, attention, and hypnotic susceptibility: A correlation study. *International Journal of Clinical & Experimental Hypnosis, 21*, 59-69.

Weitzenhoffer, A.M. (1980). Hypnotic susceptibility revisited. *American Journal of Clinical Hypnosis, 22*, 130-146.

Weitzenhoffer, A.M., & Hilgard, E.R. (1962). *Stanford hypnotic susceptibility scale: form C.* Palo Alto: Consulting Psychologists.

Wilson, N.J. (1968). Neurophysiologic alterations with hypnosis. *Diseases of the Nervous System, 29*, 618-620.

Zakrzewski, K., & Szelenberger, W. (1981). Visual evoked potentials in hypnosis: A longitudinal approach. *International Journal of Clinical and Experimental Hypnosis, 29*, 77-86.

15. Hypnotic Susceptibility and Cerebral Hemisphere Preponderance: Verbal-Imaginal Discrimination Task

I. Mészáros, H.J. Crawford, C. Szabó, A. Nagy-Kovács and Z. Révész

Introduction

We all very well know the literature that shows that the left and right hemispheres are differentially involved in cognitive processing. The left hemisphere is often found to be more involved in analytical and sequential thought processes, and the right hemisphere is more involved in imaginal and holistic thought processes. Recent studies of behavioral task performance and EEG and electrodermal responses during hypnosis suggest that there is an enhancement of right hemisphere involvement. For example, the following have been demonstrated enhancements during hypnosis for hypnotically responsive individuals in imaginal and holistic thinking (e.g., Crawford & Allen, 1983; Gruzelier, 1987), EEG ratio shifts showing a greater right hemisphere involvement in relation to the left (e.g., Bányai, Mészáros, & Csokay, 1985; Chen, Dworkin, Bloomquist, 1981; MacLeod-Morgan, 1979, 1982; Mészáros, Crawford, Nagy-Kovács, & Szabó, 1987), shifts in evoked potential amplitude toward the right hemisphere (e.g., Mészáros, Bányai, & Greguss, 1982, 1985; Spiegel, Cutcomb, Ren, & Pribram, 1985), and decreases in left hemisphere involvement in studies of electrodermal responses (e.g., Gruzelier, 1987; Gruzelier, Brow, Perry, Rhonder, & Thomas, 1984). Some studies (e.g., Sabourin, Cutcomb, & Pribram, 1986) have reported no such EEG hemispheric shifts during hypnosis among high hypnotizables.

In our laboratories in Hungary a series of studies, reported at the Ninth and Tenth International Congresses of Hypnosis in Glasgow and Toronto, respectively (Bányai et al., 1985; Mészáros et al., 1985; Mészáros, Bányai, & Greguss, 1986), and to the International Organization of Psychophysiology in Vienna (Mészáros et al., 1986), have been done using a reaction time situation with a verbal-imaginal discrimination task in which the subject is given the opportunity to choose between imaginal and verbal stimuli. In comparison to low susceptibles, high susceptibles tend to choose imaginal more than verbal stimuli, particularly in hypnosis, and they have shorter reaction times to the imaginal stimuli than do lows. According to the interpretations of these studies, these results can be attributed to a more right hemispheric, imaginal and holistic, processing involvement of high susceptibles, particularly in hypnosis. In lows there was a prevalence of verbal choices, interpreted as a preference for analytical cognitive functioning, that was accompanied by greater left hemisphere EEG involvement. The predominance of imaginal choices in hypnosis was reflected in the EEG data of the high susceptibles: the power spectra of the right hemisphere were greater than those of the left hemisphere both in total power and in the alpha and beta bands.

These previous studies (e.g., Mészáros et al., 1986) have only examined fronto-occipital bipolar recording sites in the left and right hemispheres, which is a very gross, overall measure of hemispheric involvement. In the present study we were able to examine further the accompanying EEGs of low and high hypnotizables while performing the same imaginal-verbal discrimination task in a more refined manner, using recording sites at both the anterior, fronto-central regions of F3-C3, and F4-C4, and the posterior, parieto-occipital regions of P3-O1 and P4-O2. Based upon the literature, we felt it important to examine not only left-right hemisphere differences but also anterior-posterior differences between high and low susceptibles in waking and hypnosis. We anticipated finding hemispheric differences between lows and highs in hypnosis, similar to the previous work. As a post hoc analysis, we also explored whether response choice style (verbal vs. imaginal) was correlated with differential EEG hemispheric involvement.

Method

Subjects

Volunteer subjects were psychology or medical school students at Kossuth Lajos University who had been stringently screened on two measures of hypnotic responsiveness: Harvard Group Scale of Hypnotic Susceptibility, Form A (Shor & Orne, 1962) and an individual (Weitzenhoffer & Hilgard, 1962) or group version (Crawford & Allen, 1982) of the Stanford Hypnotic Susceptibility Scale, Form C (SHSS:C). In addition, subjects were strongly right-handed and reported no medical or physical problems. Thirteen low (0-3 SHSS:C) and 11 high (10-12 SHSS:C) hypnotizables participated in the EEG study. (Additional subjects were added to the same study that is reported by Crawford, this volume.)

Procedure

In one session subjects participated in counterbalanced conditions of waking (listen to a recording of a magazine article) and hypnosis (listen to a recording of a modified SHSS:C induction with all references of drowsiness/sleep removed). Subsequent to the article or induction, there was a baseline recording, and then subjects were exposed to counterbalanced forms of tasks to imagine a walk in the Hungarian countryside and a subtraction problem, followed by a reaction time task where subjects chose between imaginal and verbal stimuli. It is the latter task which is reported here.

Controlled by a Commodore 64 computer, stimuli were presented on a television screen in front of the subject in a darkened room separate from the experimenters, and subjects' choice for verbal or imaginal stimuli and reaction times were recorded. The stimuli of this task were composed of complex or simple imaginal and/or verbal visual materials, as shown in Figure 1. The stimuli were a triangle pointing either to the left or right side, and the Hungarian words *Bal* (left) or *Jobb* (right) written. In order to ensure that the subjects really read the words instead of processing them as an image on the basis of the first letter, the words were handwritten. The upper half of Figure 1 presents the complex stimuli. Row A shows two complex ambiguous stimuli, row B shows two complex unambiguous stimuli. The lower half of Figure 1 presents simple imaginal (row C) and simple verbal (row D) stimuli.

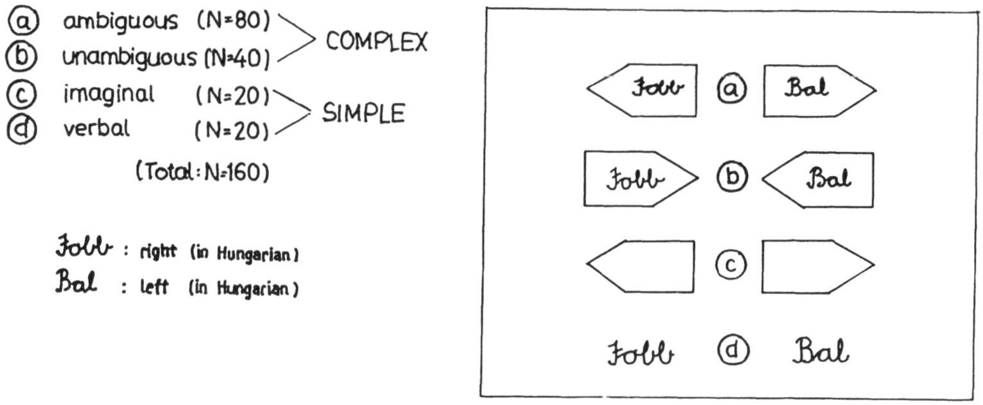

Figure 1. Experimental stimuli presented in verbal-imaginal discrimination task. *a*, complex: ambiguous (n = 80); *b*, complex: unambiguous (n = 40); *c*, simple: imaginal (n = 20); *d*, simple: verbal (n = 20); total n = 160. *Jobb*, right; *Bal*, left

Prior to the experiment proper, each subject had an opportunity to practice the task. Subjects had a push button in each hand, and they had to respond by pushing it. They were instructed to press either with their right or left hand in response to the perceived command of the stimuli, right or left. They were told, "Respond by pressing the button you feel necessary as soon and as correctly as you can." When presented with both a triangle and a word, they chose that which they preferred. During the two conditions of waking and hypnosis, subjects were instructed to open their eyes and attend to the television monitor according to previously given instructions which were repeated to them. The complex or simple ambiguous or unambiguous stimuli pairs were generated by a Commodore 64 for 10 ms. In each condition there were 160 stimuli presented in random order.

Response time and choice (left or right; verbal or imaginal material) were stored online on the Commodore 64 for subsequent analyses.

For the simultaneous recording of EEG, silver-silver chloride cup electrodes, fixed by collodium and grounded to both earlobes, were applied according to the International Ten-Twenty System. EEG activity was recorded bipolarly at anterior, fronto-central (F3-C3; F4-C4) and posterior, parieto-occipital (P3-O1; P4-O2) regions. The electrodes were tested just prior to the experiment to ensure impedances of less than 5 kΩ, as well balanced as possible across recording sites. The brain wave activity signals were passed through bioamplifiers in a Medicor EEG machine and amplified peak to peak 50 μV per centimeter with a filter rate of 0.3 time constant (TC) and a notch filter at 50 Hz and a sharp low-band pass filter at 70 Hz. Signals were then passed through an analogue to digital board and analyzed on a Commodore 64 computer every 10 s using a fast Fourier analysis between 1 and 64 Hz. The total amount of power for the delta, theta, alpha, and beta bands were calculated. Ratios between the left and right hemispheres at the anterior and posterior sites for alpha and beta hertz frequency bands were calculated online. (Theta and delta hertz bands were additionally evaluated, but will not be discussed here.) These ratio scores are referred to as Q scores (the mean difference between the mean powers of the left and right hemispheres divided by the average of the two powers).

Results and Discussion

Responses to Imaginal Component of Unambiguous and Ambiguous Stimuli

Recall that the subjects could respond to either the verbal or the imaginal part of the stimulus in the unambiguous situation. Of the 11 highs, six responded predominantly to the imaginal stimuli in waking and seven during hypnosis. Of the 13 lows, three responded to the imaginal stimuli in waking and only two during hypnosis. Thus, the highs preferred imaginal stimuli over verbal stimuli in both conditions to a greater extent than did the lows.

The percentage of responses that were to the imaginal component of the ambiguous stimuli during waking and hypnosis conditions indicated that high hypnotizables tended to respond more

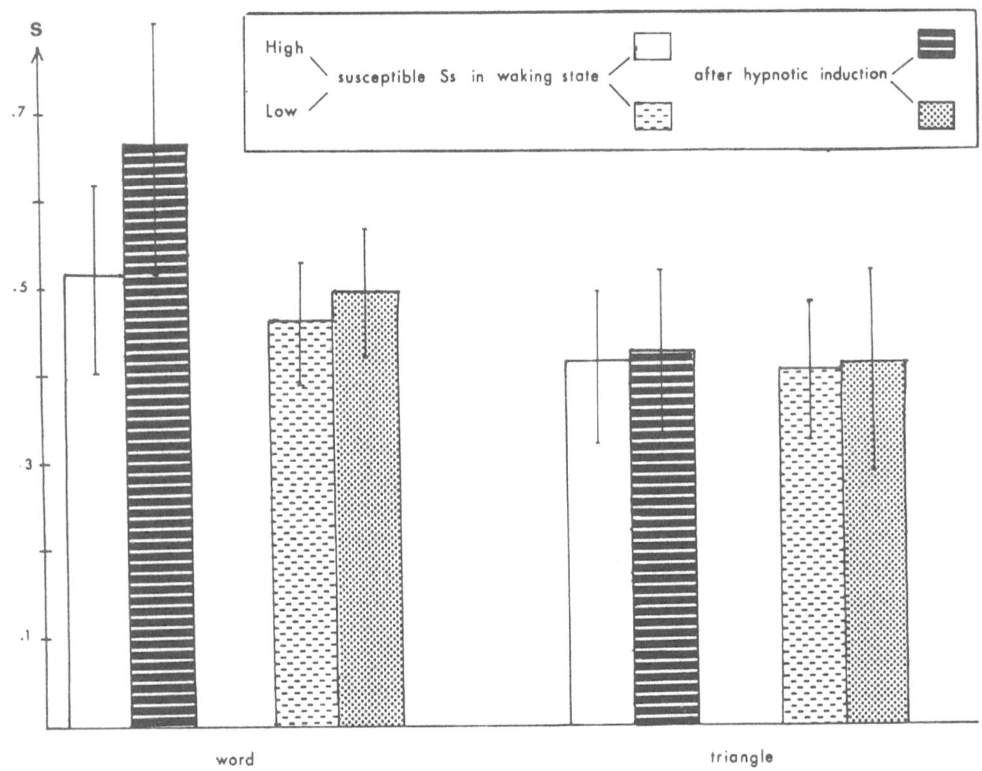

Figure 2. Averaged reaction time to complex ambiguous stimuli

to imaginal stimuli in hypnosis (96 %) than waking (86 %). In contrast, the lows responded substantially less to imaginal stimuli in both hypnosis (6 %) and waking (18 %).

Averaged Reaction Time to Simple and Complex Ambiguous Stimuli

As seen in Figure 2, high hypnotizables did not differ from lows in reaction times to either verbal (words) or imaginal (triangles) stimuli in waking conditions. The only significant interaction was when subjects responded to words: during hypnosis the highs had significantly longer reaction times than during waking ($P < 0.01$) while the lows did not differ.

Figure 3 gives the means of the averaged reaction times to simple stimuli (verbal or imaginal responses). The findings are similar to our earlier studies. For the high susceptibles in the waking state and in hypnosis, the responses to the triangle (imaginal) were significantly shorter than to the words ($P < 0.01$). In the low susceptible group there was a somewhat shorter latency to the words than to the triangle. There were no significant differences between conditions for lows.

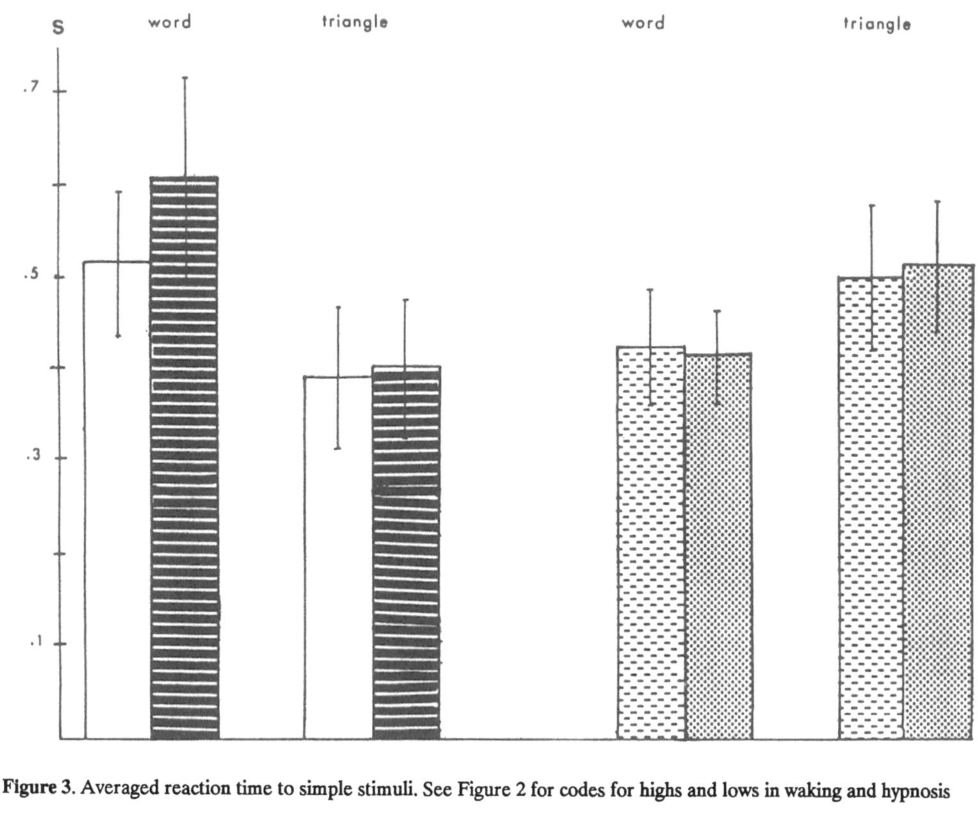

Figure 3. Averaged reaction time to simple stimuli. See Figure 2 for codes for highs and lows in waking and hypnosis

EEG activity during Verbal-Imaginal Discrimination Task

In this section we discuss the laterality quotients (Q ratios) between the left and right hemispheres in alpha and beta bands at the frontocentral (F3-C3; F4-C4) and parietocentral (P3-01; P4-02) sites.

According to our formula, the range of the Q ratios can go from +2 (left hemisphere dominant) to -2 (right hemisphere dominant). As can be seen in Figure 4 for beta, at both the frontocentral and parieto-occipital sites there were significant interactions between hypnotic level and condition. As would be expected from prior research, high hypnotizables showed greater hemispheric specificity than lows at the parieto-occipital sites. The highs tended to be more right hemisphere dominant during waking than the lows, which may reflect their accompanying preference for imaginal responses in the discrimination task. During hypnosis the highs showed a much greater right hemisphere dominance of beta. By contrast, at the frontocentral leads the lows tended to be somewhat more left hemisphere dominant than the highs during waking. During hypnosis the highs showed a much greater left hemisphere dominance of beta, while the lows showed a nonsignificant trend toward slightly less left hemisphere dominance.

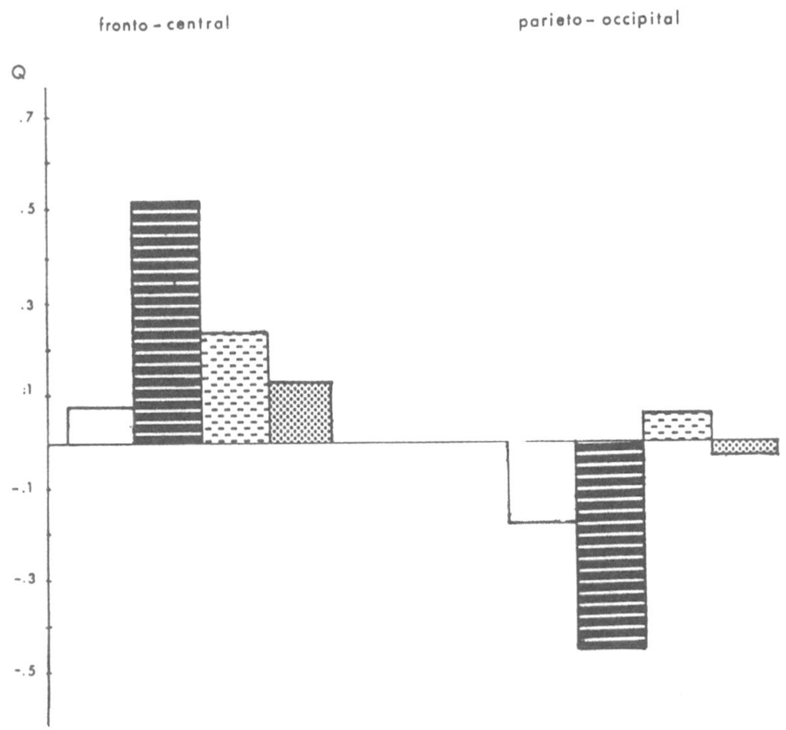

Figure 4. Prevalence of left (positive) or right (negative) hemispheric activity in the beta band. See Figure 2 for codes for highs and lows in waking and hypnosis

Additional EEG Analyses

When Crawford returned to the University of Wyoming after her research with us in Hungary, using another spectral analysis program, she analyzed the same EEG data which were stored online with a different computer system with fewer subjects (nine lows, eight highs) than previously reported here (see Crawford, this volume, for further details).

For the log transformed raw power data there were no theta differences. There was a significant interaction between site and hypnotic level for low alpha: in the right anterior region, the lows had greater power while the highs had greater power in the right posterior region. There was a significant interaction between hypnotic level and condition for high alpha: while the lows and highs did not differ during waking, during hypnosis the lows remained the same and the highs showed significant increases in integrated power. There were no significant power differences or interactions between lows and highs in the low, middle, and high beta bands. This is contrary to what might be expected given the common belief that alpha and beta covary negatively, something for which we did not find evidence in the present study or in our previous Hungarian studies.

While there were nonsignificant site main effects for low and high alpha, there were significant main effects for beta during the verbal-imaginal discrimination task. Consistently there was more beta activity in the posterior than anterior regions, as would be expected.

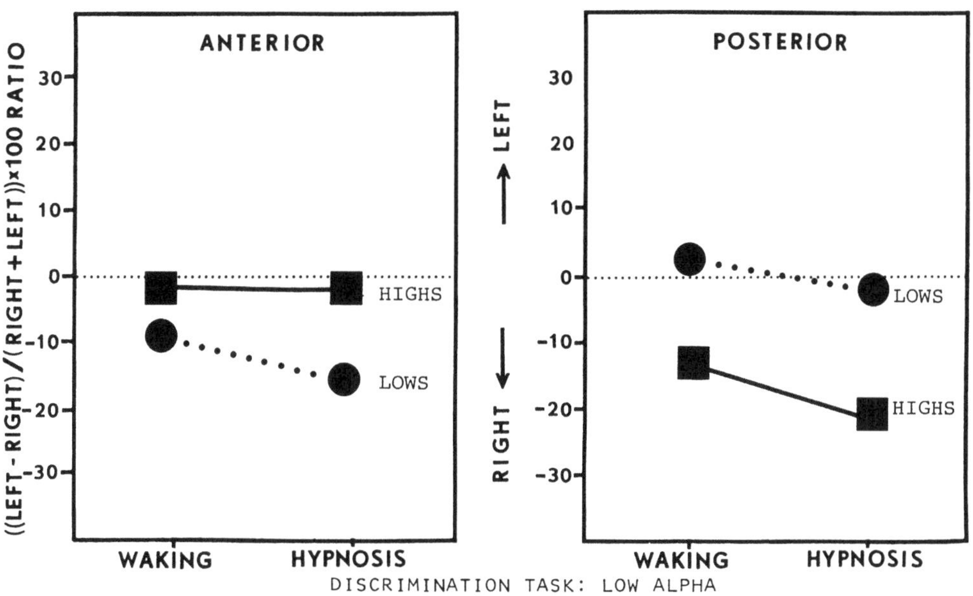

Figure 5. Anterior and posterior regions: low alpha band laterality ratio scores for low and high hypnotizables in waking and hypnosis. *Circles*, lows; *squares*, highs

When hemispheric laterality ratios, [(left - right) / (left + right)] x 100, were examined (range +1 to -1), a very interesting interaction between hypnotic level and site emerged consistently across the various tasks we studied. Crawford's paper in this volume briefly discusses our findings for the mathematics and imaginal tasks and baseline. As seen in Figure 5, there was a significant hypnotic level by anterior/posterior site interaction in low alpha. The highs are more right hemisphere dominant in the posterior, parieto-occipital region than the lows (-.18 and -.01 respectively) while the highs are significantly less right hemisphere dominant than the lows in the anterior frontocentral region (-.01 and -.11 respectively). We have speculated that the right hemisphere was more strongly activated in the posterior region because of the differential preference for imaginal responses among the highs, while at the same time the right hemisphere was less strongly activated in the anterior region because of possible accompanying global attentional processes which are associated with left frontal cortex involvement. The lows show a stronger right hemisphere anterior involvement suggesting possible localized, rather than global, attentional processing. Only with more refined EEG recordings at a number of sites can we determine whether the frontal cortex is differentially involved.

There was a trend ($P < .10$) for high alpha, which is shown in Figure 6, in the same direction. For the three beta bands, there were no significant interactions between hypnotic level and site. These are very exciting data as they suggest that the differential imaginal and verbal responses, accompanying possible attentional style differences, may correlate with differential EEG asymmetries between the anterior and posterior regions among the lows and highs.

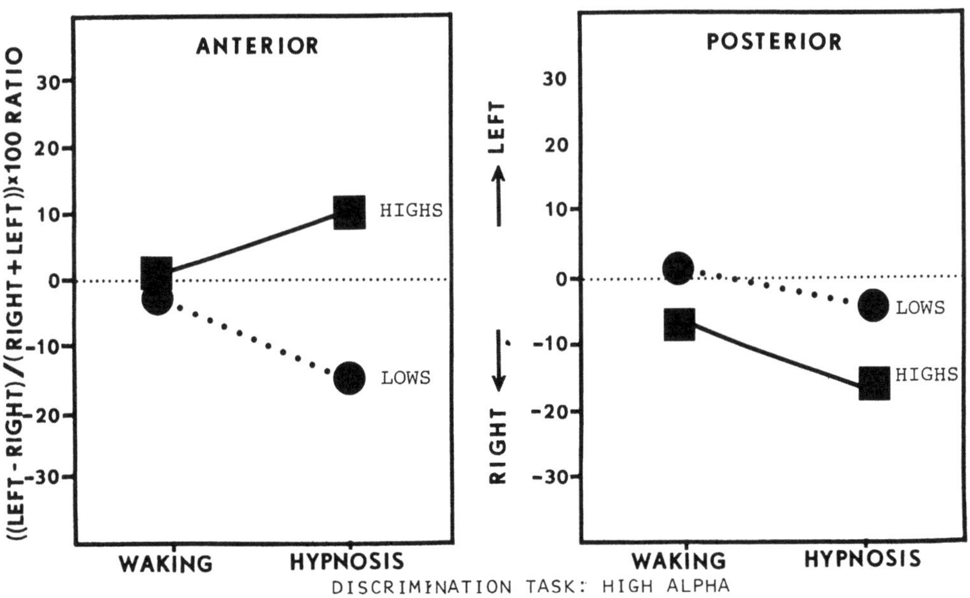

Figure 6. Anterior and posterior regions: high alpha band laterality ratio scores for low and high hypnotizables in waking and hypnosis. *Circles*, lows; *squares*, highs

Relationship of Strategy Choice to EEG Hemispheric Dominance

To explore the possibility that choice of strategy might correlate with differential beta hemispheric dominance, post hoc analyses were performed on those subjects who showed a stronger preference for imaginal (highs: n = 7; lows: n = 3) or verbal (highs: n = 4; lows: n = 11) responses across conditions. Figure 7 presents the Q scores which indicate right or left hemispheric dominant beta activity at the frontocentral and the parieto-occipital regions for those who showed a preference for imaginal responses or verbal responses. Regarding the first column, we see that the lows show a greater left hemisphere dominance during waking and hypnosis conditions in both the frontocentral and parieto-occipital regions. As would be expected, they did not differ across conditions. The highs who chose imaginal responses were somewhat left hemisphere dominant in both regions during waking, but tended to show differential EEG activation during hypnosis such that the frontocentral region was more left hemisphere dominant and the parieto-occipital region was more right hemisphere dominant.

When we examined the same subjects who had been chosen for differential verbal and imaginal responses on the verbal-imaginal discrimination task during the unrelated mathematical and imagining a walk tasks (that occurred prior to the discrimination task within each condition), we continued to see differences in EEG asymmetries in the two groups (Figure 8). In the frontocentral region there is a left-sided dominance for those highs who responded to the word, but only in hypnosis, and a very pronounced right-sided dominance in the same group, independently of hypnotic level, in the parieto-occipital region. Overall in those highs who responded to words, there is a very high left frontocentral dominance and a right parieto-occipital dominance.

While these are post hoc analyses, the data suggest that we should examine the interactions between waking/hypnosis conditions and hypnotic level *and* choice of response strategy. Only now are researchers beginning to examine the moderating effects of chosen strategy. The results presented here suggest that the strategy employed is an important moderator of EEG activity and can perhaps lead to a better understanding of individual differences in EEG activity.

Summary and Conclusion

Our earlier findings regarding response choices to imaginal and verbal stimuli were confirmed once again: regardless of condition, highs show a greater preference to respond to imaginal (triangle) than verbal (word) stimuli in the verbal-imaginal discrimination task, while lows show a preference for verbal responses. Additionally, highs showed significantly longer reaction times in the complex ambiguous condition to words during hypnosis than in the waking state, while lows did not differ. In the simple stimuli, highs were significantly faster in their responses to imaginal stimuli than lows, regardless of waking or hypnosis conditions.

Our EEG findings support prior research that there is differential EEG hemispheric involvement in waking and hypnosis that is moderated by hypnotic level. Two new findings contribute to the literature. First, we have presented evidence that highs show a substantially

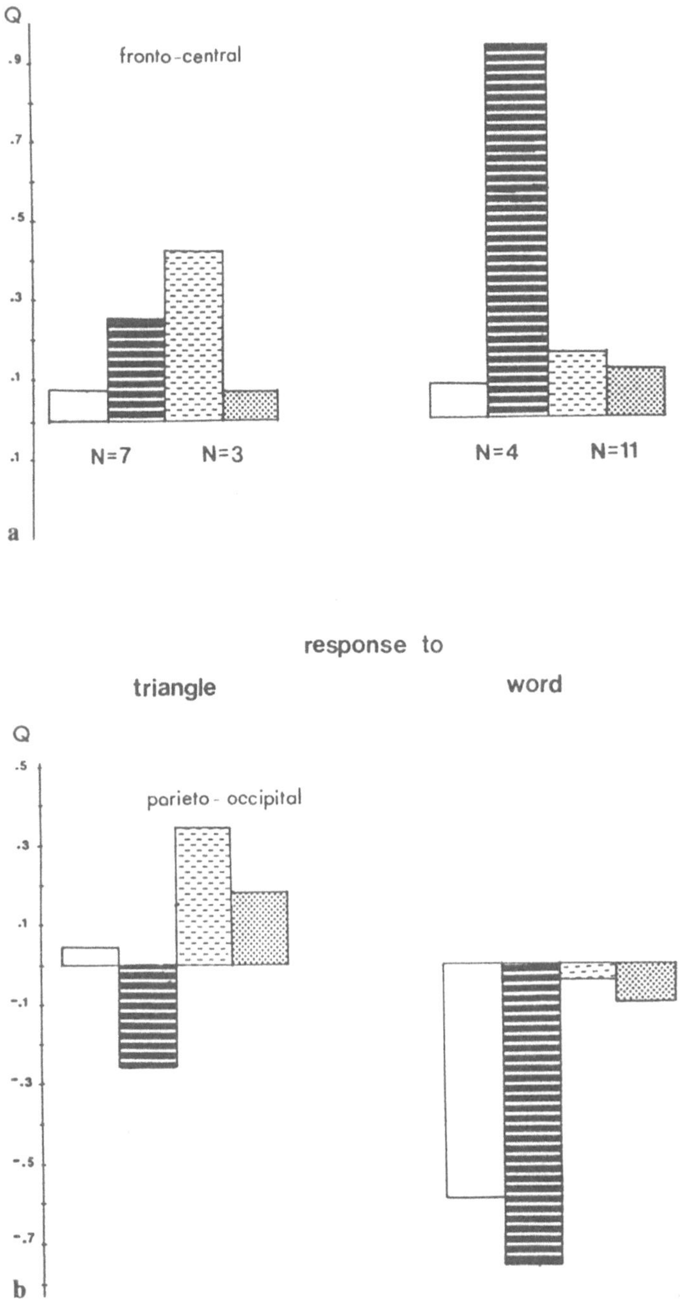

Figure 7a, b. Prevalence of lateralized hemispheric activity in verbal discrimination task: comparisons between those who preferred imaginal (triangle; *left column*) or verbal (word; *right column*) responses in the frontocentral (*a*) and parieto-occipital (*b*) regions. See Figure 2 for codes for highs and lows in waking and hypnosis

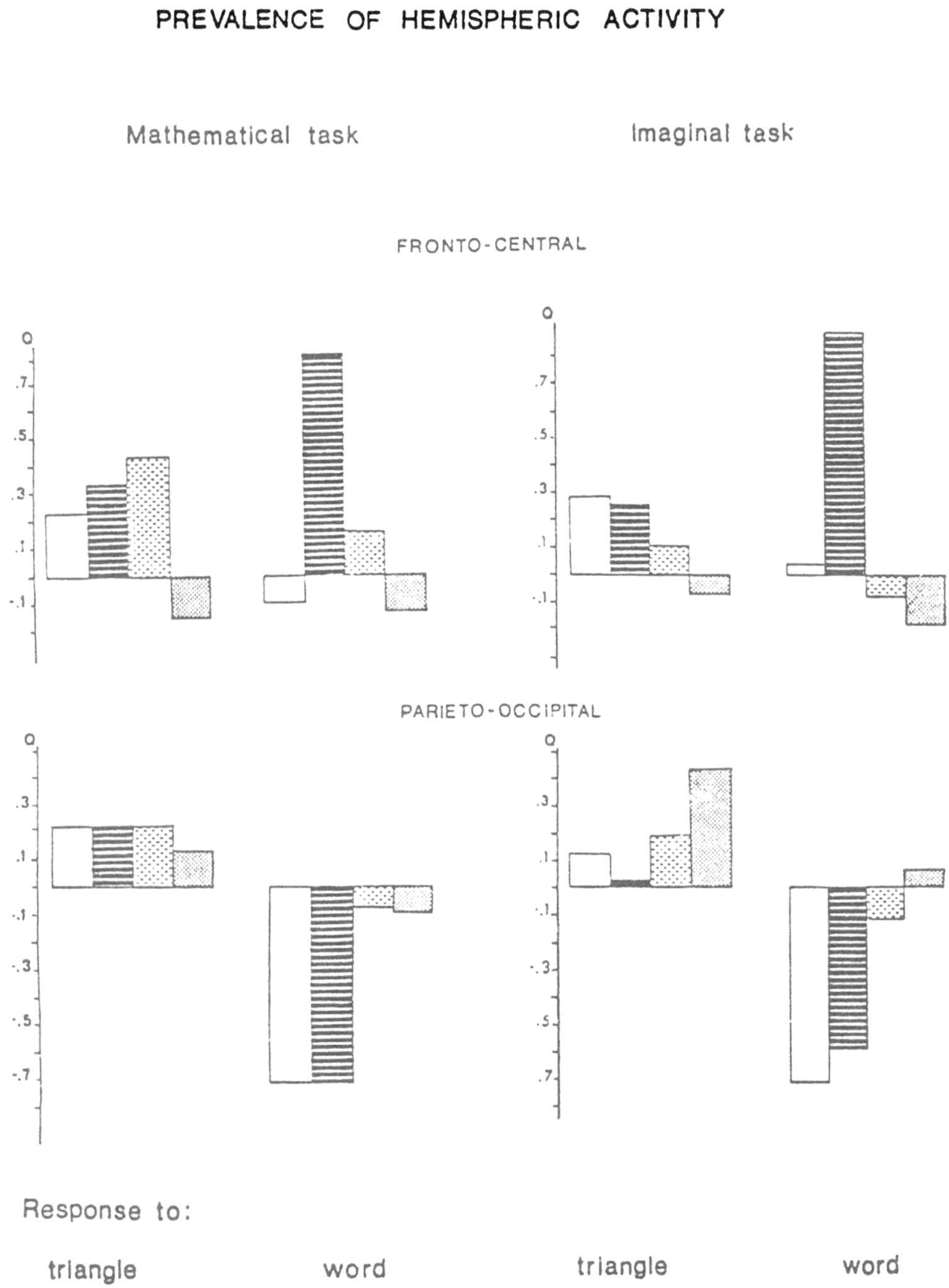

Figure 8a, b. Prevalence of lateralized hemispheric activity in mathematics and imagining a walk tasks: comparisons between those who preferred imaginal (triangle) or verbal (word) responses during the verbal-imaginal discrimination task. See Figure 2 for codes for highs and lows in waking and hypnosis different asymmetry between the anterior and posterior regions than do the low susceptibles. Secondly, the choice of response strategy in the verbal-imaginal discrimination task can moderate the EEG asymmetries differentially among low and high hypnotizables. Most interesting is the post hoc finding that these asymmetries also seem to appear in unrelated experimental tasks of mathematics and imagination of a walk with eyes closed.

In the past laterality ratios have been criticized because one cannot determine how the asymmetry effects are created: for instance, does the left hemisphere become less involved or the right hemisphere more involved? While we too report laterality ratios, we also present data that reports raw integrated power. It is our suggestion that researchers who use laterality ratios also examine their raw integrated amplitude means to help in the interpretation of the laterality ratios. As sophisticated computer systems become more available in the laboratory, this suggestion will become a reality.

Finally, it is important that more thorough studies of the frontocentral and parieto-occipital regions be conducted with monopolar, rather than bipolar, recordings and, if possible, with more electrode sites being evaluated.

Acknowledgement. The work reported herein was made possible by a grant to Crawford from the United States National Academy of Sciences and the Hungarian Academy of Sciences to participate in the Cooperative Scientific Exchange Program between scientists in these two countries. Subsequent EEG analyses in Wyoming were supported by a grant to HJC from The Spencer Foundation. We are extremely appreciative of this grant support.

References

Bányai, E.I., Mészáros, I., & Csokay, L. (1985). Interaction between hypnotist and subject: A social psychophysiological approach. In D. Waxman, P.C. Misra, M.A. Basker (Eds.), *Modern trends in hypnosis*. New York: Plenum.

Chen, A.C.N., Dworkin, S.F., & Bloomquist, D.S. (1981). Cortical power spectrum analysis of hypnotic pain control in surgery. *International Journal of Neuroscience, 13*, 127-136.

Crawford, H.J., & Allen, S.N. (1982). *Administration manual for the Stanford Group Hypnotic Susceptibility Scale, Form C.* Unpublished scale, University of Wyoming, Laboratory of Cognitive Processing, Department of Psychology, Laramie, WY, USA.

Crawford, H.J., & Allen, S.N. (1983). Enhanced visual memory during hypnosis as mediated by hypnotic responsiveness and cognitive strategies. *Journal of Experimental Psychology: General, 112*, 662- 685.

Gruzelier, J. (1987). The neuropsychology of hypnosis. In M. Heap (Ed.), *Hypnosis: Current clinical, experimental and forensic practices*. London: Croom Helm.

Gruzelier, J., Brow, T., Perry, A., Rhonder, J., & Thomas, M. (1984). Hypnotic susceptibility: A lateral predisposition and altered cerebral asymmetry under hypnosis. *International Journal of Psychophysiology, 2*, 131-139.

MacLeod-Morgan, C. (1979). Hypnotic susceptibility, EEG theta and alpha waves, and hemispheric specificity. In G.D. Burrows, D.R. Collison, & L. Dennerstein (Eds.), *Hypnosis 1979*. Amsterdam: Elsevier/North Holland Biomedical.

MacLeod-Morgan, C. (1982). EEG lateralization in hypnosis: A preliminary report. *Australian Journal of Clinical and Experimental Hypnosis, 10*, 99-102.

Mészáros, I., Bányai, E. I., & Greguss, A. C. (1982). Evoked potential, reflecting hypnotically altered state of consciousness. In G. Adam, I. Mészáros, & E.I. Bányai (Eds.), *Advances in physiological sciences. Vol. 17. Brain and behaviour*. Oxford: Pergamon.

Mészáros, I., Bányai, E.I., & Greguss, A.C. (1985). Evoked potential correlates of verbal versus imagery coding in hypnosis. In D. Waxman, P.C. Misra, & M.A. Basker (Eds.), *Modern trends in hypnosis*. New York: Plenum.

Mészáros, I., Bányai, E.I., & Greguss, A.C. (1986). *Enhanced right hemisphere activation during hypnosis: EEG and behavioural task performance evidence*. Paper presented at the proceedings of the 3rd international conference of the International Organization of Psychophysiology, Vienna, Austria.

Mészáros, I., Crawford, H.J., Nagy-Kovács, A., & Szabó, C. (1987). Asymmetry of EEG activity and verbal-imaginal discrimination as a consequence of hypnotic responsiveness and hypnotic state. *Neuroscience, 22*, [Suppl. 472].

Sabourin, M.E., Cutcomb, S.D., & Pribram, K.H. (1986). *EEG correlates of hypnotic susceptbility and hypnotic trance: Spectral Analysis*. Paper presented at the 3rd international conference of the International Organization of Psychophysiology, Vienna, Austria.

Shor, R.E., & Orne, E. (1962). *Harvard group scale of hypnotic susceptibillty, form A*. Palo Alto, CA: Consulting Psychologists.

Spiegel, D., Cutcomb, S., Ren, C., & Pribram, K.H. (1985). Hypnotic hallucination alters evoked potentials. *Journal of Abnormal Psychology, 94*, 249-255.

Weitzenhoffer A.M., & Hilgard, E.R. (1962). *Stanford hypnotic susceptibility scale, form C*. Palo Alto, CA: Consulting Psychologists.

16. 40-H_2 EEG and Hypnotizability During Mental Activity

F.S. Marucci, V. De Pascalis, M.P. Penna and E. Pessa

Introduction

In recent years, research into psychophysiological correlates of cognitive strategies and performance has examined the following relationships: (a) between EEG activity and hypnotic responsiveness; (b) between hypnotizability and cognitive processing in perception, mental imagery, and memory; and (c) between EEG rhythms, hemispheric dominance, and visual perception processes with respect to mental imagery and memory. In particular, EEG correlates of individual differences in cognitive abilities and hypnotic susceptibility have been examined.

As regards hypnotic susceptibility and cognitive activities, some research has examined hypnotizability with respect to speed of information processing in different experimental tasks, but this has produced contradictory results. Using a backward masking paradigm with bias-free and ceiling-free psychological tasks, Sturr and Church (1986) observed no significant relationship between hypnotic responsiveness and speed of visual information processing. On the other hand, Ingram, Saccuzzo, McNeill, and McDonald (1979), using the same paradigm, found that hypnotically susceptible subjects process information more quickly than unsusceptible ones. They interpreted the results as being due to the greater attentional and superior information processing abilities of high hypnotizables in comparison to lows.

Recently, Acosta and Crawford (1985) found differences between high and low hypnotizables in information transfer from iconic to short-term memory. They suggested that these differences depend on differences in subjective ability to shift from one strategy to another. Battig (1979) defined cognitive flexibility as the degree to which a person uses one of several available types of strategies during task performances and states of consciousness. Crawford (1985) suggested that flexibility is related to sustained attention, memory, problem solving, and other processes. The concept of cognitive flexibility, derived from Hilgard's (1977) theory of multiple cognitive control systems, has promoted interesting studies in which significant differences between high and low hypnotizables in a variety of attentional activities have been found. In MacLeod-Morgan's study (1979) the highly hypnotizable persons showed a greater EEG flexibility compared to the lows; the EEG findings were also confirmed with measures of regional cerebral blood flow (Crawford, Stolnick, Benson, Gur, & Gur, 1985). Individual differences in hypnotizability with respect to mental imagery and memory processes have shown the necessity of studying the nature of the processes involved in production and retention of mental images.

In recent years, the nature of mental images has characterized the debate on the structure and functions of imagery. The increase in scientific interest in cognitive representations of visual objects and mental image rotation was concomitant to the debate on the nature of mental imagery. Using the mental rotation paradigm, Shepard, Cooper and their colleagues (Cooper, 1975; Cooper & Shepard, 1973; Cooper & Podgorny, 1976; Shepard & Metzler, 1971) asked subjects to compare pairs of figures differing in angular rotation and orientation. The subjects' task was to decide as fast as possible whether the two figures were the same or different. A linear relationship between differences in orientation of two figures and response latencies was found. This fact was explained by hypothesizing an analogous rotation process. That is, the internal transformations, performed in mental images in a matching task, are the same as those transformations resulting from perception of external figures oriented differently.

With respect to imagery and memory relationships, Marks (1973) maintained that images have an important role in memory since they facilitate accurate recall, while Paivio (1971) suggested that imagery is based on stored information. Sheehan (1966, 1967) evaluated individual differences in imagery using an abridged version of Betts' Questionnaire on Mental Imagery and a rating scale of imagery vividness and found that there were differences related to accuracy of visual recall and memory. That is, differences in retention depend on differences in perception. As Sheehan maintained, high imagers perceive stimuli in a detailed way, while low imagers are less dependent on sensory input and use coding devices to process perceptual information. Actually, even though a positive relationship between mental imagery and hypnotizability is plausible, a significant correlation between these variables as measured by Betts' Questionnaire on Mental Imagery and tests of hypnotic responsiveness was not found. On the other hand, Hilgard (1981) suggested that high hypnotizables exhibit greater self-reported imagery.

Particular attention has been paid to evaluation of the relationship between mental imagery and cerebral activity. Galin and Ellis (1975) and Galin and Orstein (1972), assuming imagery to be a component of visual-spatial skills, found that these abilities involved right hemisphere activity. Also Robbins and McAdams (1974) suggested the existence of an association between right hemisphere activity and visual imagery. They, in fact, found an alpha suppression mainly in the right hemisphere during imagination of familiar visuo-spatial scenes; in contrast, this suppression was greater in the left hemisphere during imagination of verbal materials. However, as Zikmund (1972) noted, the EEG alpha blocking can hardly be used as a specific indicator of visual imagery since during spontaneous imagery it can depend on many factors, e.g., attentional level, orienting reaction. During evocation and retention of the images in the mind this suppression may be caused by effort.

Some studies have examined a fast-frequency, low-amplitude EEG signal centered at 40 Hz (36-44 bandwidth) within the beta spectrum. Sheer and his colleagues (Sheer, 1976; Spydell, Ford, & Sheer, 1979) suggested that this activity may reflect not only a state of focused arousal, but also a consequence of the interaction between cortical facilitation and the processing of specific sensory input. Task-dependent lateralizations of the 40-Hz EEG rhythm were found during a variety of cognitive performances; it was also found that 40-Hz EMG activity contributes slightly to 40-Hz EEG activity (Spydell et al., 1979; Loring & Sheer, 1984; Spydell & Sheer, 1982).

These studies were concerned with lateralization of 40-Hz EEG during spatial-verbal cognitive performances. Yet EEG activity during perception and mental manipulation of different spatial shapes remains unclear. The aim of the present study was to evaluate individual differences in hypnotizability in relation to 40-Hz EEG hemispheric involvement and EMG activity during visual perception, mental imagery rotation, and graphic reproduction conditions. Finally, taking into account the findings of MacLeod-Morgan (1979) and MacLeod-Morgan and Lack (1982), another aim of this work was to determine if high hypnotizables exhibit greater hemispheric specificity than low hypnotizables.

Method

Subjects and Their Hypnotizability

An original pool of 99 volunteers, all female students at the University of Rome, were invited to participate in an experiment "on perception" (no mention was made of hypnosis in the invitation). The subjects were all female because there is some evidence that females are significantly more susceptible than males (Bowers, 1971), and that sex is a moderating variable in the relation between hypnotic susceptibility and functional brain asymmetry (Gur & Gur, 1974). Moreover, there are also studies which indicate greater task-induced asymmetries in males than females (Ray, Morrell, Frediani, & Tucker, 1976; Trotman & Hamond, 1979; Glass, Butler, & Carter, 1984).

The subjects participated in a group (n = 30-40 persons) in three sessions on separate days to evaluate hypnotizability with the Harvard Group Scale of Hypnotic Susceptibility: Form A (HGSHS:A) (Shor & Orne, 1962). The scale was administered by tape recorder. A female experimenter established rapport with each group before the initial induction.

From the original pool 43 subjects who had participated in a previous experiment on psychophysiological correlates of emotions were selected on the basis of their hypnotizability level. Subjects were defined as being high hypnotizables (HI: n = 22, mean = 9.8, SD = 0.8) if their scores on the HGS were above 1 SD from the group mean (n = 99, mean = 6.5, SD = 2.4); an equivalent but opposite deviation defined the low hypnotizables (n = 21, mean = 2.9, SD = 1.3). All subjects (age 19-25 years) who participated in the electrophysiological recording had approximately normal or normal-corrected vision and were right-handed (they had a right-sided preference for writing, eating, kicking or hitting a ball, and right-handed close family members). Subjects were also tested on the State Anxiety Scale (before beginning the physiological recordings) and on separate days were exposed to the following tests: Trait Scale (X2) of the State-Trait Anxiety Inventory (STAI, Spielberger, Gorsuch, & Lushene, 1970), and the Tellegen Absorption Scale (TAS) (Tellegen & Atkinson, 1974).

Apparatus

Silver-silver chloride cup electrodes were fixed to left and right hemispheres approximately in the middle of the O1-P3-T5 triangle of the International 10-20 System on the left side of the scalp and in a corresponding location on the right side of the scalp. These electrode sites were chosen because they lie over the pariental-occipital-temporal junction, an area known to be involved in cognitive processes. Both electrodes were referenced to vertex (C_z). To detect the 40-Hz EEG from the EEG activity a two-channel 40-Hz EEG asymmetry system was built according to the method of Spydell et al. (1982). Since 40-Hz EEG activity may be contaminated by low-frequency muscle activity, EMG activity was recorded as a control. One EMG recording was obtained from bipolar leads, with both electrodes on the upper right and left trapezius of the neck, approximately 7 cm below the inion and 3 cm lateral to the midline. A ground electrode was placed on the forehead near the scalp. The EEG and EMG signals were amplified (gain = 200 000, bandwidth 0.16-200 Hz) using a low-noise differential amplifier (0.85 μV RMS of equivalent-input-noise voltage in the bandwidth 0.1-316 Hz, considering both inputs connected in common via 10 kΩ). High-pass filters were set at 10 Hz and low-pass filters at 90-Hz for both EEG and EMG amplifiers. A four-channel prolonged wave oscilloscope was used to permit visual inspection of high-frequency low-amplitude activity in the recording. To control muscle artifacts in the 40-Hz EEG, amplified EEG and EMG signals were sent to three control devices. Each control device amplified, filtered, rectified, and integrated 40-Hz (35-45-Hz bandwidth) and 70-Hz activity (64-76-Hz bandwidth) from the raw signal. Two control devices served for left and right EEG activity, one device served for analyses of EMG activity. The 40-Hz EEG detection device contained a circuit which allowed 40-Hz activity to trigger a monostable controlled digital clock which measured the production time in 0.01 s within a 2-s period. Periods were separated by 1.5-s intervals during which the time data displayed were tabulated. In the presence of 70-Hz activity in either an EEG or in the EMG channel, any 40-Hz activity in that channel (within 200 ms) was inhibited (see Sheer, 1976). A second control for muscle activity artifacts consisted of a detector which also inhibited (within 200 ms) the 40-Hz EEG activity in the EEG channel when this activity was concomitant with 40-Hz EMG. A time-constant and minimal amplitude criterion for detecting an occurrence of a burst of 40-Hz EEG and EMG response was set at 75 ms and 2.2 μV, respectively; the same criterion was used for the 70-Hz EMG signal. The amplitude criterion, however, was evaluated for each subject and set at the mean value for the amplitude variation within a 1-min baseline preceding each group of tasks (2.2-10 μV range). The time period in which the two EEG signals exceeded these criteria resulted in a digital time display. The mean amplitude of 40-Hz EMG in microvolts within the 2-s period was obtained. EEG was continuously monitored on the screen of a four-channel oscilloscope to record artifacts from bodily movements. A Schmitt trigger automatically eliminated 50-Hz artifact data by resetting to zero all the counters for that period.

Design

The experiment consisted of the combination of three factors: hypnotizability (high, low); condition (rest, visual perception, mental imagery rotation, or graphic reproduction activity); trial (curves, straight lines, geometrical shapes).

Stimuli

The stimuli used for the experiment were familiar figures like curves, straight lines, and geometrical shapes (triangles, rectangles, squares). Each stimulus consisted of a figure on which there was a black dot (the point of fixation). All figures were black, photographed and projected onto a screen situated at a distance of 150 cm in front of the observer. From this viewing position, each figure subtended a visual angle of 25°. A projection tachistoscope controlled the exposure duration of the figures.

Procedure

The subjects were not informed about specific experimental hypotheses, or their level of hypnotizability. They were informed about the psychophysiological problems of the research and phases of the experimental session. Each subject was seated in a comfortable chair in a dimly lit room and tested individually in a single session. These sessions lasted about 20 min and took place from 3 to 4 o'clock in the afternoon. Prior to the experimental trials, the electrodes were attached and subjects were familiarized with the tasks.

After completing some practice trials, each subject began the experimental trials. There were three blocks of four trials each: one for curves, one for straight lines, and one for geometrical shapes on the conditions of visual perception, mental imagery rotation, and reproduction of the rotated figure. The order of the blocks was counterbalanced across subjects.

Before each block a 2-min rest period, 1 min with eyes open and 1 min with eyes closed, was given in random order. During the visual perception of the presented stimuli, the subject kept her eyes fixed upon the projected figures. Each trial was announced to the subject by a warning tone lasting about 500 ms. The slides were presented 500 ms after the tone, and each lasted 250 ms.

In this experimental phase, only a 2-s period data sample of 40-Hz EEG density was collected. Following the stimulus presentation, the subject was required to perform a 6-s clockwise mental rotation around the fixation point with her eyes closed. Three 2-s period data samples of the density of 40-Hz EEG during rotation were recorded. The subject was then required to reproduce the rotated figure as it was represented to her in her mind at the moment at which a "click" stop signal prompted her to stop. She then had 6 s to reproduce the image on writing paper, during which three 2-s period acquisition data samples of 40-Hz activity were recorded.

An acquisition interval of 2 s was chosen during the visual perception condition for homogeneity with the other experimental conditions. Furthermore, the reduction of the interval to a period less than 2 s may have yielded a critical measure of the 40-Hz EEG occurrence. An interval of 2-s period could have produced only a slight reduction of the entity of the 40-Hz EEG responses to the slide stimuli.

Preparation of EEG and EMG Data

The time periods in which 40-Hz EE activity was present over 2-s periods were accumulated during 1-min eyes open and 1-min eyes closed rest periods. In the visual perception task a 2-s period of 40-Hz EEG was recorded during figure presentation. Three 2-s periods were collected during mental rotation and reproduction conditions. The 40-Hz EEG density was expressed in seconds per minute.

The mean amplitude of 40-Hz EMG was evaluated during the same experimental periods and expressed in μ V/min. These mean scores for each subject formed the basis for further data analyses (see Tables 1, 2). A two-tailed test with at least a value of $P < .05$ was selected and used throughout.

Results

Personality Differences Between Low and High Hypnotizables

Any personality differences in state and trait anxiety and absorption were assessed. State and trait anxiety (X1 and X2) mean scores did not differ between high and low hypnotizables (X1: 36.7 vs. 36.7, $df = 41$, $t = .01$, $P > .05$; X2: 39.0 vs. 42.6, $t = .75$; $P > .05$ for comparisons of high vs. lows, respectively). On the other hand, the Tellegen Absorption Scale mean score for high hypnotizables was significantly greater than that for lows (9.0 vs. 7.0, $t = 2.95$, $P < .01$).

Table 1. Means and standard deviations for right and left 40-Hz EEG densities (seconds per minute), for high ($n = 22$) and low ($n = 21$) hypnotizables

Conditions	High hypnotizables				Low hypnotizables			
	EEG left		EEG right		EEG left		EEG right	
	Mean	SD	Mean	SD	Mean	SD	Mean	SD
Rest (eyes open)	3.7	2.5	4.7	3.1	4.6	2.9	5.6	3.2
Rest (eyes closed)	4.1	2.6	4.9	3.2	4.6	2.5	5.4	2.3
Visual perception								
Curves	4.1	2.2	5.2	2.6	6.5	4.1	5.2	3.0
Straight lines	3.4	1.9	4.8	3.1	5.9	3.7	5.8	3.7
Geometrical shapes	4.0	2.5	5.1	3.5	7.3	4.9	6.1	3.7
Mental rotation								
Curves	5.0	3.6	3.9	2.4	6.4	3.3	5.9	3.8
Straight lines	4.4	3.0	3.6	2.1	6.0	3.5	5.9	3.9
Geometrical shapes	4.7	3.5	3.8	2.7	6.2	3.4	5.6	3.1
Graphic reproduction								
Curves	2.6	2.3	3.1	2.6	5.1	4.9	4.4	2.9
Straight lines	2.8	2.6	2.9	2.5	5.1	4.7	4.7	3.4
Geometrical shapes	2.7	2.2	3.4	2.8	4.6	4.6	4.2	3.0

The 40-Hz EEG in Left and Right Hemispheres and Relationship to 40-Hz EMG

The 40-Hz EEG density in the left and right hemispheres was assessed for each subject in the experimental conditions. Means computed for each condition and for groups divided according to hypnotizability are presented in Table 1 as a reference table. Table 2 shows respective means for 40 Hz EMG amplitudes. To evaluate the relationship between 40-Hz EEG density in left and right hemispheres and 40-Hz EMG amplitude, the Pearson correlation coefficients were computed. Table 3 shows the correlation coefficients for all trials and conditions. In all conditions the correlation coefficients were negative. In addition, the correlations in visual perception were significant for the left hemisphere; in mental rotation there were no significant coefficients except for the 40-Hz EEG density of the right hemisphere, which was significantly correlated with EMG amplitude during curve rotation. The 40-Hz EEG density of the left hemisphere was found significantly correlated with EMG activity during graphic reproduction.

The 40-Hz EMG Amplitude and Experimental Conditions

An analysis of variance with two levels of hypnotizability (high-low) as an independent factor x four levels of condition (rest, visual perception, mental rotation, graphic reproduction) x three levels of trial (curves, straight lines, geometrical shapes), the latter both as repeated

Table 2. Means and standard deviations for upper trapezius 40-Hz EMG amplitude (μV), for high (n = 22) and low (n = 21) hypnotizables

Conditions	High hypnotizables		Low hypnotizables	
	Mean	SD	Mean	SD
Rest (eyes open)	3.2	0.7	3.1	0.7
Rest (eyes closed)	3.2	0.8	3.1	0.7
Visual perception				
Curves	3.4	0.9	3.1	0.6
Straight lines	3.4	0.9	3.5	0.8
Geometrical shapes	3.3	0.8	3.4	0.7
Mental rotation				
Curves	3.4	0.8	3.2	0.7
Straight lines	3.4	1.0	3.3	0.7
Geometrical shapes	3.3	0.8	3.4	0.7
Graphic reproduction				
Curves	4.5	0.9	3.9	1.0
Straight lines	4.4	1.0	4.0	0.8
Geometrical shapes	4.6	1.1	4.0	0.8

Table 3. Correlation coefficients between 40-Hz EMG amplitude and left-right hemisphere 40-Hz EEG density across experimental conditions (n = 43 Ss)

	Visual Perception		Mental Rotation		Graphic Reproduction	
	Left	Right	Left	Right	Left	Right
Curves	-.29[a]	-.13	-.24	-.30[a]	-.38[b]	-.27[a]
Straight lines	-.28[a]	-.11	-.09	-.09	-.34[a]	-.14
Geometrical shapes	-.33[a]	-.23	-.15	-.16	-.45[c]	-.20

[a] $P < .05$
[b] $P < .01$
[c] $P < .001$

measurement factors, was carried out to evaluate the influence of experimental conditions on EMG activity. No significant main effect for hypnotizability was found [$F(1, 41) = .85$; mean standard error (MSE) = .18, $P > .05$], but the main effect in EMG data was significant for condition [$F(3, 123) = 67.79$, $MSE = .44$, $P < .001$], showing greater EMG levels in graphic reproduction, especially with respect to rest and also with respect to visual perception and mental imagery rotation conditions. Finally, the hypnotizability x condition interaction was also significant [$F(3, 123) = 3.47$, $MSE = .44$, $P < .02$].

Duncan's test showed that for low hypnotizables EMG amplitude in visual perception and mental imagery rotation was greater than EMG activity obtained during rest. On the other hand,

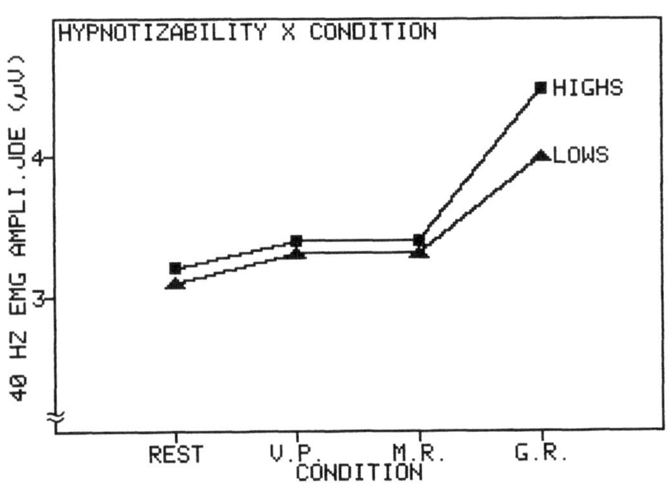

Figure 1. The 40-Hz EMG adjusted means during rest, visual perception (*V.P.*)., mental imagery rotation (*M.R.*), graphic reproduction (*G.R.*) conditions for high (*squares*) and low (*triangles*) hypnotizables

this difference was not observed for highly hypnotizable subjects under the same conditions. In summary, low hypnotizables, in contrast to highs, presented a significantly lower level (Duncan's test, $P < .05$) of EMG amplitude (4.0 vs. 4.5 for lows vs. highs, respectively). No other main or interaction effect was found. Finally, an analysis of variance across rest conditions did not show a main or interaction effect for hypnotizability. Nor was an effect for the eyes condition (closed/open) found (see Table 2, Figure 1).

The 40-Hz EEG, Hypnotizability, and Cognitive Activity

The effects of hypnotizability and cognitive activity on 40-Hz EEG density were examined based on the following nested factorial design: two levels of hypnotizability x two levels of hemisphere x four levels of condition (including the eyes-closed rest periods) x three levels of trial. Since significant correlations between 40-Hz EEG were evidenced in the visual perception and graphic reproduction activity conditions, an analysis of covariance was computed in which the EMG of the perception, rotation, and reproduction conditions was the covariate. The variance and covariance analyses were comparable and both exhibited the following main effects: (a) for hypnotizability [$F(1, 41) = 4.92$, $MSE = 120.12$, $P < .03$], a greater 40-Hz EEG density was shown for lows than for highs (5.5 vs. 4.0), (b) for condition [$F(1, 123) = 11.11$, $MSE = 15.70$, $P < .001$], a lower density in graphic reproduction and a higher density in the other conditions were evidenced.

Moreover, both the hypnotizability x hemisphere interaction [$F(1, 41) = 7.54$, $MSE = 4.36$, $P < .01$] and the hypnotizability x hemisphere x condition interaction [$F(3, 123) = 3.84$, $MSE = 6.92$, $P < .02$] were significant. Inspection of the means showed that there were

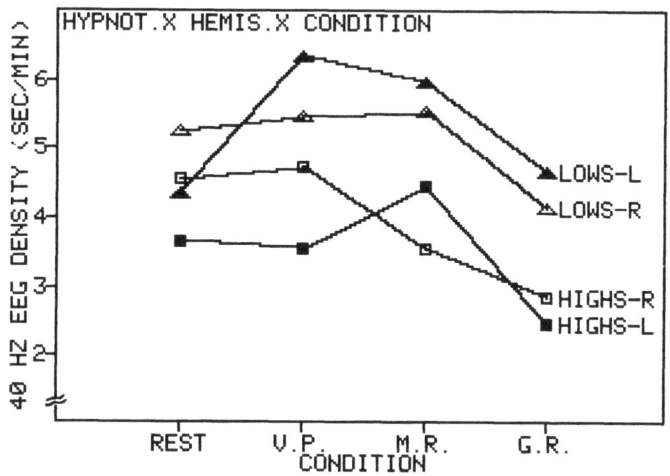

Figure 2. The 40-Hz EEG adjusted means during rest, visual perception (*V.P.*), mental imagery rotation (*M.R.*), graphic reproduction (*G.R.*) conditions, in left (*solid symbols*) and right (*open symbols*) hemispheres of high (*squares*) and low (*triangles*) hypnotizables

differential hemispheric trends between high and low hypnotizables. Low hypnotizables in the visual perception condition showed an increase of 40-Hz EEG density in the left hemisphere with respect to rest, while there was no change in the right hemisphere.

In contrast, high hypnotizables during visual perception did not show significant hemispheric changes with respect to rest. These subjects, on the other hand, exhibited an increase in the left and a decrease in the right 40-Hz hemisphere activity in the mental rotation condition with respect to the visual perception one (see Table 1, Figure 2).

Finally, an analysis of variance across rest condition (two levels of hypnotizability x two levels of hemisphere x two levels of eye-condition) displayed a main effect for hemisphere [$F(1, 41) = 9.84$, $MSE = 7.04$, $P < .003$]. This effect showed lower density in the left hemisphere with respect to the right. No other main or interactional effects were found.

The 40-Hz EEG Ratio, Hemispheric Specificity, and Hypnotizability

To evaluate the hypnotizability and hemisphere relationship, a 40-Hz EEG ratio score was computed using the formula: (right hemisphere 40-Hz density - left hemisphere 40-Hz density) / (right hemisphere 40-Hz density + left hemisphere 40-Hz density). A nested type analysis of variance with two levels of hypnotizability x four levels of condition x three levels of trials was performed. This analysis supplied identical results to those for 40-Hz EEG density scores. There was, in fact, a main effect for hypnotizability [$F(1, 41) = 4.01$, $MSE = .10$, $P < .05$], showing a greater positive ratio for high hypnotizables with respect to the lows (.05 vs. .005, respectively). There was also a main effect for condition [$F(3, 123) = 10.13$, $MSE = .11$, $P < .001$] and a

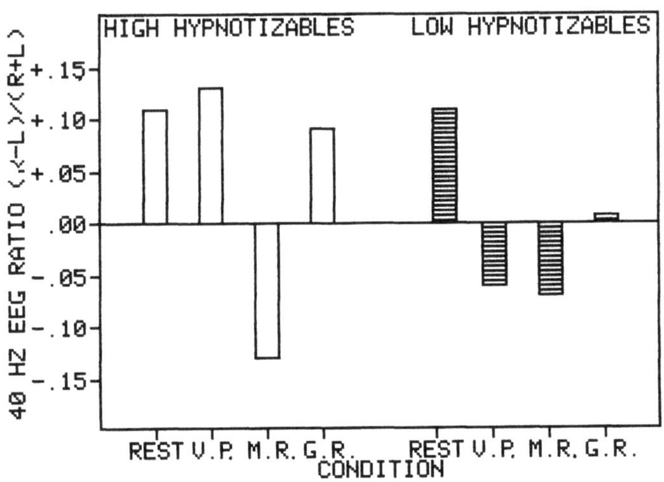

Figure 3. The 40-Hz EEG ratio during rest, visual perception (*V.P.*)., mental imagery rotation (*M.R.*), graphic reproduction (*G.R.*) conditions for high (*open columns*) and low (*shaded columns*) hypnotizables

Table 4. Means and standard deviations for 40-Hz EEG asymmetry ratios for high (n = 22) and Low (n = 21) hypnotizables

	High hypnotizables		Low hypnotizables	
	Mean	SD	Mean	SD
Rest	.11	.23	.11	.21
Visual perception	.13	.22	-.06	.20
Mental rotation	-.13	.31	-.07	.20
Graphic reproduction	.09	.18	.00	.31

hypnotizability x condition interaction effect [$F(3, 123) = 3.86$, $MSE = .11$, $P < .01$]. Duncan's test for multiple comparisons showed that highs, in mental imagery rotation, manifested a left hemisphere activation and a right hemisphere depression with respect to visual perception; in contrast, the lows did not exhibit any differences in hemisphere activation between perception and mental rotation conditions (see Table 4, Figure 3).

In order to evaluate the differences in hemispheric specificity, an index of hemispheric specificity (HS) was computed by subtracting the ratio for visual perception condition from the ratio for mental rotation condition. A negative HS index indicated a relatively greater left hemisphere activation during mental rotation and/or right hemisphere activation during visual perception.

If we assume that visual perception and mental rotation conditions activate the right hemisphere and the left hemisphere, respectively, then we may expect that highs would exhibit a greater negative HS index than lows. The differences in hemispheric specificity between groups were significant ($t = 3.57$, $df = 41$, $P < .01$). High hypnotizables, as expected, showed greater HS than lows (-.26 vs. -.01, respectively).

Discussion

This study has shown the following results: (a) individual differences in hypnotizability were reflected by the 40-Hz EEG activity; (b) high and low hypnotizables showed different hemispheric trends in visual perception and mental imagery rotation conditions in contrast to rest. With respect to the relationship between hypnotizability and 40-Hz EEG, the results revealed that in all task conditions, high hypnotizables showed lower 40-Hz EEG activity than lows. These findings are in accordance with the results obtained by De Pascalis et al. (1987) during recollection of affective experiences, but are the opposite of those obtained by Akpinar et al. (1971) in which the high hypnotizables showed a significantly greater level of 40-50-Hz activity during rest and reaction time task than the low hypnotizables. These contrasting results were probably due to the different methods used by these authors or to the fact that the authors did not control the anxiety levels across subjects. Thus it is not possible to establish if their results were the product of different hypnotizability levels or differences in anxiety levels. Our subjects did not show differences in state and trait anxiety; therefore we think that the results obtained did not depend on anxiety level.

However, we found a significant correlation between the Tellegen Absorption Scale and hypnotizability; that is, the high hypnotizables tended to show a greater absorptive capacity than the lows. Tellegen and Atkinson (1974) suggested that the absorptive capacity is related to the "total" attention characterizing the cognitive resources and the subject's performance, and that highs should exhibit a greater attentional level in task conditions than the lows. This assumption may be in contrast with our findings, in which the lows exhibited a 40-Hz EEG higher than the highs. In fact, if we assume that the high hypnotizables are more able to shut off external stimuli or to inhibit other responses that may be of a competitive nature, it is then feasible that highs require a lower arousability level than the lows. This means that in high hypnotizables the inhibition processes of competing stimuli are stronger than those in the lows.

The lowered level of attentive activity in high hypnotizables is in accordance with findings on alpha rhythm (e.g., De Pascalis et al., 1988; MacLeod-Morgan, 1979), on theta rhythm (e.g., Sabourin, Cutcomb, & Pribram, 1986), and on skin conductance (Gruzelier & Brow, 1985).

Moreover, hypnotizability moderated the relationship between hemispheric engagement and cognitive activity. Low hypnotizables exhibited in both hemispheres similar 40-Hz EEG density trends during visual perception, mental rotation, and reproduction tasks. These subjects showed no change in the right hemisphere in the visual perception condition in comparison to the rest condition, while they exhibited a notable increase in activity in the left. This means that the left hemisphere is more sensitive than the right to change in the cognitive activity connected with an enhanced arousal level. Moreover, in these subjects the activity did not increase in either hemisphere during the perception and mental imagery rotation tasks; in contrast, it decreased during the graphic reproduction condition. These last results were also found for the high hypnotizables and they could probably be attributed to the enhancement of muscular activity required by the reproduction condition. On the other hand, the highs exhibited different hemispheric patterns throughout different task conditions. In these subjects (compared to the lows) there was a greater right hemisphere activation during the rest and visual perception conditions. The highs showed hemispheric activity that differed in the visual perception and mental imagery rotation conditions. The decrease in right hemisphere activity was paralleled by an enhancement of the left hemisphere activity. These results are in accordance with the suggestions of MacLeod-Morgan (1979), MacLeod-Morgan and Lack (1982), and Karlin et al. (1983) who maintained that high hypnotizables make greater task-specific shifts in EEG alpha activity than lows.

According to Loring and Sheer (1984), if we assume that the mental rotation task requires a left hemisphere engagement, then we must suggest that the high hypnotizables complied better with the task requirement. In fact, these subjects exhibited right hemisphere inhibition and left hemisphere activation of 40-Hz EEG activity during the mental rotation task. The spatial characteristics of the figures presented could involve more right hemisphere engagement, but the task requirement of mental rotation could involve an analytical activity that could be characterized by a left hemisphere involvement. In fact, the rotation of the geometrical figures around the fixation point required the subjects to hold, during mental rotation, the same symmetry and the same angular inclination of constitutive elements of figures. We think that this task requires mental strategies characterized by sequential processing, focused attention, and an enhancement of the cognitive efforts and resources (see Kahneman, 1973) which might involve the left hemisphere.

Moreover, the reverse hemispheric trends of high hypnotizables during the mental rotation condition could be explained if we take into account the greater absorptive capacity of these subjects. Absorptive capacity, in fact, has been found positively related to hypnotizability (e.g., Finke & MacDonald, 1978; Sigman, Phillips, & Clifford, 1985), and our findings confirmed this relationship. Our results on 40-Hz EEG activity during the mental imagery rotation are similar to those of Loring and Sheer (1984), even though the tasks used in ours and in the other studies were different. In fact, our 40-Hz EEG ratio scores were -.13 vs. -.11, respectively. Loring and Sheer utilized the same experimental paradigm as that of Metzler and Shepard (1974). They utilized blocks of three-dimensional figure pairs that were presented to the subject in different spatial orientations. The subject was required to judge if figure pairs in a different spatial orientation were the same or different. Metzler and Shepard, like Loring and Sheer, inferred that this judgement involved a mental rotation. Mental activity was not formally required. Mental imagery rotation in our study was explicitly requested. The fact that our asymmetry ratios were similar to those obtained by these authors, suggests to us that their assumptions about the existence of mental imagery rotation are correct.

Moreover, these considerations are in accordance with theoretical and experimental evidence that attributes importance to the left hemisphere in mental imagery formation. As Farah, Gazzaniga, Holzman, and Kosslyn (1985) suggested, the generation of images requires a "componential information-processing" modality that predominantly involves left hemisphere activity. In particular, Farah (1984) reported that the loss of mental imagery is consequent to posterior left hemisphere damage.

The present study confirms the conclusions of Sheer and his colleagues (Spydell et al., 1979; Loring & Sheer, 1984; Spydell & Sheer, 1982) about the existence of an asymmetrical distribution of 40-Hz EEG in relation to task performances known to activate hemispheres differentially. However, our findings do not confirm a marked independence of 40-Hz EEG from EMG activity, as suggested by these authors. In fact, while 40-Hz EEG activity was independent of EMG in the mental rotation condition, both activities were found to be negatively related to the visual perception and graphic reproduction conditions.

Moreover, EMG activity of high hypnotizables during the shape reproduction condition was found to be significantly greater than that of the lows. These findings could be interpreted according to Stelmach and Kelso's (1977) suggestions, which refer to the greater involvement of highs than lows in the reproduction task.

Acknowledgement. Research was supported by a grant to F.S. Marucci from Consiglio Nazionale delle Richerche.

References

Acosta, E., Jr., & Crawford, E.J. (1985). Iconic memory and hypnotizability: processing speed, skill, or strategy differences. *International Journal of Clinical and Experimental Hypnosis, 33*, 3, 236-245.

Apkinar, S., Ulett, G.A., & Itil, T.M. (1971). Hypnotizability predicted by digital computer-analyzed EEG pattern. *Biological Psychiatry, 3*, 387-392.

Battig, W.F. (1979). Are the important "individual differences" between or within individuals? *Journal of Research in Personality, 13*, 546-558.

Bowers, K.S. (1971). Sex and susceptibility as moderator variables in the relationship of creativity and hypnotic susceptibility. *Journal of Abnormal Psychology, 78*, 93-100.

Cooper, L.A. (1975). Mental rotation of random two-dimensional forms. *Cognitive Psychology, 7*, 20-43.

Cooper, L.A., & Podgorny, P. (1976). Mental transformations and visual comparisons processing: Effects of complexity and similarity. *Journal of Experimental Psychology: Human Perception and Performance, 2*, 503-514.

Cooper, L.A., & Shepard, R.N. (1973). Chronometric studies of the rotation of mental images. In W.G. Chase (Ed.), *Visual information processing* (pp. 75-176). New York: Academic.

Crawford, H.J. (1985). *Cognitive flexibility dissociation, and hypnosis. Presidential address presented at the American Psychological Association,* Division 30 meeting, Los Angeles, California.

Crawford, H.J., Stolnick, B., Benson, D., Gur, R.E., & Gur, R.C. (1985). *Regional cerebral blood flow in hypnosis and hypnotic analgesia.* Paper presented at the 10th international congress of hypnosis and psychosomatic medicine, Toronto, Canada.

De Pascalis, V., Marucci, F.S., Penna, M.P., & Pessa, E. (1987). Hemispheric activity of 40 Hz EEG during recall of emotional events: differences between low and high hypnotizables. *International Journal of Psychophysiology, 5*, 167-180.

De Pascalis, V., Silveri, A., & Palumbo, G. (1988). EEG asymmetry during covert mental activity and its relationship with hypnotizability. *International Journal of Clinical and Experimental Hypnosis, 36* (1), 38.

Farah, M.J. (1984). The neurological basis of mental imagery: A componential analysis. *Cognition, 18*, 245-272.

Farah, M.J., Gazzaniga, M.S., Holtzman, J.D., & Kosslyn, S.M. (1985). A left hemisphere basis for visual mental imagery. *Neuropsychologia, 23* (1), 115-118.

Finke, A.R., & McDonald, H. (1978). Two personality measures relating hypnotic susceptibility to absorption. *International Journal of Clinical Hypnosis, 3*, 178-183.

Galin, D., & Ellis, R. (1975). Asymmetry in evoked potentials and an index of lateralized cognitive processes. *Neuropsychologia, 13*, 45-50.

Galin, D., & Orstein, R. (1972). Lateral specialization of cognitive mode: An EEG study. *Psychophysiology, 9*, 412-418.

Glass, A., Butler, S.R., & Carter, J.C. (1984). Hemispheric asymmetry of EEG alpha activation: Effects of gender and familiar handedness. *Biological Psychology, 19*, 169-187.

Gruzelier, J.H., & Brow, J.D. (1985). Psychophysiological evidence for a state theory of hypnosis and susceptibility. *Journal of Psychosomatic Research, 29*, 287-302.

Gur, R.C., & Gur, R.E. (1974). Handedness, sex and eyedness as moderating variables in the relation between hypnotic susceptibility and functional brain asymmetry. *Journal of Abnormal Psychology, 83*, 635-643.

Hilgard, E.R. (1977). *Divided Consciousness: Multiple control in human thought and action.* New York: Wiley.

Hilgard, E.R. (1981). Imagery and imagination in American psychology. *Journal of Mental Imagery, 5*, 5-66.

Ingram, R.E., Saccuzzo, D.P., McNeill, B.W., & McDonald, R. (1979). Speed of information processing in high and low susceptibility subjects: A preliminary study, *International Journal of Clinical and Experimental Hypnosis, 27* (1), 42-47.

Kahneman, D. (1973). *Attention and effort.* Englewood Cliffs, NJ: Prentice Hall.

Karlin, A.R., Cohen, A., & Goldstein, L. (1983). *A shift to the right: EEG-changes from rest to hypnotic induction.* Unpublished manuscript.

Loring, D.W., & Sheer, D.E. (1984). Laterality of 40 Hz EEG and EMG during cognitive performance. *Psychophysiology, 21,* 34-38.

MacLeod-Morgan, C. (1979). Hypnotic susceptibility, EEG theta and alpha waves, and hemispheric specificity. In G.D. Burrows, D.R. Collinsos, & L. Dennerstein (Eds.), *Hypnosis 1979.* Amsterdam: Elsevier.

MacLeod-Morgan, C., & Lack, L. (1982). Hemispheric specificity: A physiological concomitant of hypnotizability. *Psychophysiology, 19,* 687-690.

Marks, D.F. (1973). Visual imagery differences in the recall of pictures. *British Journal of Psychology, 64,* 17-24.

Metzler, J., & Shepard, R.N. (1974). Transformational studies of the internal representation of three-dimensional objects. In R.L. Solso (Ed.), *Theories in cognitive psychology: The Loyola Symposium* (pp. 147-201). New York: Lawrence Erlbaum.

Paivio, A. (1971). *Imagery and verbal processes.* New York: Holt, Rinehart and Winston.

Ray, W.J., Morrel, M., Frediani, A., & Tucker, D.M. (1976). Sex differences and lateral specialization of hemispheric functioning. *Neuropsychologia, 14,* 391-394.

Robbins, K., & McAdams, D. (1974). Interhemispheric alpha asymmetry and imagery mode. *Brain and Language, 1,* 189-193.

Sabourin, M.E., Cutcomb, S.D., & Pribram, K.H. (1986, July). *EEG correlates of hypnotic susceptibility and hypnotic trance: spectral analysis.* Paper presented at the meeting of the International Organization of Psychophysiology, Vienna.

Sheehan, P.W. (1966). Accuracy and vividness of visual images. *Perceptual and Motor Skills, 23,* 391-398.

Sheehan, P.W. (1967). A shortened form of Betts' questionnaire upon mental imagery. *Journal of Clinical Psychology, 23,* 386-389.

Sheer, D.E. (1976). Focused arousal and 40 Hz EEG. In R.M. Knight & D.J. Bakker (Eds.), *The neuropsychology of learning disorders.* (pp. 71-87). Baltimore: University Park.

Shepard, R.N., & Metzler, J. (1971). Mental rotation of three-dimensional objects. *Science, 171,* 701-703.

Shor, R.E., & Orne, E.C., (1962). *Harvard Group Scale of hypnotic susceptibility.* Palo Alto: Consulting Psychologists.

Sigman, A., Phillips, K.C., & Clifford, B. (1985). Attentional concomitants of hypnotic susceptibility. *British Journal of Experimental and Clinical Hypnosis, 2,* 69-75.

Spielberger, C.D., Gorsuch, R., & Lushene, R. (1970). *The State-Trait Anxiety Inventory (STAI) test manual.* Palo Alto: Consulting Psychologists.

Spydell, J.D., Ford, M.R., & Sheer, D.E. (1979). Task dependent cerebral lateralization of the 40 Hz EEG rhythm. *Psychophysiology, 16,* 347-350.

Spydell, J.D., & Sheer, D.E. (1982). Effect of problem solving on right and left hemisphere 40 Hertz EEG activity. *Psychophysiology, 19,* 420-425.

Stelmach, G.E., & Scott Kelso, J.A. (1977) Memory processes in motor control. In S. Dornic (Ed.), *Attention and performance: Vol. 6* (pp. 719-739). Hillsdale, NJ: Lawrence Erlbaum.

Sturr, J.F., & Church, K.L. (1986). Hypnotizability and speed of visual information processing. *International Journal of Clinical and Experimental Hypnosis, 34* (3), 234-241.

Tellegen, A., & Atkinson, G. (1974). Openness to absorbing and self-altering experiences ("absorption"), a trait related to hypnotic susceptibility. *Journal of Abnormal Psychology, 83,* 268-277.

Trotman, S.C.A., & Hammond, G.R. (1979). Sex differences in task-dependent EEG asymmetries. *Psychophysiology, 16,* 429-431.

Zikmund, V. (1972). Physiological correlates of visual imagery. In P.W. Sheehan (Ed.), *The function and nature of imagery* (pp. 355-387). New York: Academic.

17. Hypnotic Susceptibility, Alpha Waves and 40-H_2 EEG Rhythm, and Personality

V. De Pascalis

Introduction

One of the main problems of EEG studies on hypnosis is the attempt to distinguish the brain activity of a postulated hypnotic state from that known to characterize the waking and sleeping states. One question is the relationship of basic subject differences, i.e., "trait" differences, to the level of hypnotic susceptibility. In the late 1960s, the enhancement of EEG recording technique with quantification of filtered EEG bandwidths allowed better evaluation of the EEG and hypnotic susceptibility relationship. Most of the correlational studies of EEG and hypnotizability have measured alpha rhythm. Two major research trends have influenced the search for EEG correlates of hypnosis and hypnotic susceptibility: (a) attempts to evaluate the correlation between baseline alpha levels and hypnotic susceptibility; and (b) attempts to delineate differences between high and low hypnotizables in functional asymmetry of the two cerebral hemispheres. The former trend derived from the presumption of operant control of alpha rhythm (Kamiya, 1969) and its concurrence with an altered state of consciousness (Anand, Chhina, & Singh, 1961; Kasamatsu & Hirai, 1969; Tart, 1969): if alpha production had been related to hypnotic susceptibility, then an increase of alpha production by means of voluntary control procedures could have produced an enhancement of hypnotizability in low susceptible subjects. The latter trend arose from the first studies devoted to understanding functional hemispheric asymmetry (Sperry, 1968; Gazzaniga, 1970; Kinsbourne & Smith, 1974; Kimura, 1973). Despite technological and methodological advances, both lines of research have produced some equivocal results.

EEG Alpha and Hypnotic Susceptibility

The studies of London, Hart, and Leibovitz (1968), Nowlis and Rhead (1968), and Engstrom, London, and Hart (1970) reported that high susceptibles produced more waking alpha density than nonsusceptibles. Morgan, MacDonald, and Hilgard (1974) failed to find hemispheric differences in alpha activity, but they also observed a positive relationship of integrated amplitude alphas with hypnotic susceptibility. Although part of these studies corroborated the hypothesis of a relationship between alpha activity and hypnotic susceptibility, the main tendency was to attribute positive findings to the effect of uncontrolled situational and sampling variables. Evans (1972), in a review including an unpublished study of his own which failed to replicate the preceding results, pointed out that at rest alpha and initial assessment of hypnotizability may be affected by situational variables. In particular, he observed that in the cases in which positive findings were found, the subjects were acquainted with the object of the study and tried to comply with it. In another review, Dumas (1977) attributed the positive findings to sampling bias: i.e., when positive relationships were found, the subjects selected for the different studies were non-naive volunteers; in contrast, when subjects were "invited" to participate in the experiment, no significant correlations were found.

The Engstrom, London, and Hart (1970) study maintained that by increasing rest alpha levels in low susceptibles through biofeedback training, an increase of hypnotic susceptibility may also be produced. Evans (1972) criticized this study for incorrect data analysis. The revised versions (London, Cooper, & Engstrom, 1974; Engstrom, 1976) of the earlier study were also strongly criticized by Dumas (1977). Other experiments failed to find an alpha-hypnotizability relationship (Galbraith, London, Leibovitz, Cooper, & Hart, 1970; Travis, Kondo, & Knott, 1973; Edmonston & Grotevant, 1975; Evans, 1972; Sabourin, 1982; Sabourin, Cutcomb, & Pribram, 1986). Besides the situational and sampling factors, further methodological and procedural suggestions have been made to account for the discrepant results. Sabourin and his colleagues, emphasizing the limited attentional aspects of the alpha rhythm, proposed that a more detailed EEG analysis would provide more information. Finally, Paskewitz (1977) also maintained that alpha activity in the baseline condition is inappropriate for the study of the alpha-hypnotizability relationship. He has suggested that changes occurring in alpha rhythm in response to differing situations are a more appropriate variable to consider.

Hemispheric Asymmetry and Hypnotizability

This line of research attempts to delineate functional differences in hemispheric engagement between high and low hypnotizables. EEG alpha asymmetry has mainly been used as an index of task demands, wherein a decrease in alpha activity indicated which the activated hemisphere was (Doyle, Ornstein, & Galin, 1974; Dumas & Morgan, 1975; Davidson & Schwartz, 1977; Ehrlichman & Wiener, 1979; Osborne & Gale, 1976; Morgan, McDonald and MacDonald, 1971). According to the neodissociation interpretation of hypnosis (Hilgard, 1977), the capacity to become hypnotized is related to selective attention to monotonous stimulation and, therefore, inattention to irrelevant stimuli. Moreover, it has been suggested that the degree of brain lateralization during task processing may be associated with individual differences in selective attention or cognitive style. MacLeod-Morgan (1979) and MacLeod-Morgan and Lack (1982), as well as Karlin, Goldstein, Cohen, and Morgan (1980), measuring overall EEG or EEG alpha ratios, reported a significant relationship between hypnotic susceptibility and hemispheric specificity, indicating that high hypnotizables make greater task-specific shifts in hemisphere activation than lows. Few studies have explored the relationship between hemispheric specificity and responsiveness to hypnosis using EEG measures in the waking state or in a nonhypnotic condition. Bányai, Mészáros, and Greguss (1986) and Mészáros, Bányai, and Greguss (1986) reported greater hemispheric specificity for high hypnotizables than for lows, and an enhancement of right hemisphere involvement in hypnosis. Chen, Dworkin, and Bloomquist (1981) reported heightened theta and alpha activity in the nondominant right hemisphere during hypnosis in a single subject.

Using electrodermal and electrocortical responses, Gruzelier and his colleagues (Gruzelier & Brow, 1985; Gruzelier, Brow, Perry, Rhonder, & Thomas, 1984; Gruzelier, 1986) outlined two stages of a dynamic neuropsychological process in the induction of hypnosis. The first stage, prior to hypnosis, involves engagement of the focal attentional processes of the left hemisphere and the second selective inhibition of anterior and central left hemispheric processes with consequential release of right hemisphere activity. This activity appears to be associated with the suspension of planning and critical functions and the production of eidetic-like imagery, which commonly characterizes the hypnotic state. However, some studies have reported an increase of alpha production in hypnosis (Brady & Rosner, 1966; Melzack & Perry, 1975), others a significant decrease in alpha and a significant increase in beta activities (Marenina, 1959; Evans, 1972; Bauer & McCanne, 1980). Edmonston and Grotevant (1975) did not find changes in alpha activity during hypnosis, although a significant increase of alpha density was observed in the initial stage of the induction period (Edmonston, 1981).

Crawford, Skolnick, Benson, Gur and Gur (1985) presented a first study which examined the effect of hypnosis on regional cerebral blood flow (rCBF). No hemispheric differences of overall blood flow during rest were observed, and no main effects for waking vs. hypnosis or high vs. low hypnotizables were found. However, an interesting interaction between waking and hypnosis sessions with respect to hypnotizability was observed. During waking, the low and high hypnotizables had quite similar overall mean blood flows. Following a hypnotic induction, the high hypnotizables showed a dramatic increase in cerebral blood flow, whereas the low hypnotizables showed no differences. These findings provided support for the hypothesis that highs have not only a greater cognitive flexibility, but they also have greater physiological flexibility than the lows.

EEG Alpha and Hypnotizability: Our Findings

In order to evaluate differences in EEG alpha and hemispheric asymmetry between high and low hypnotizables, two studies were carried out in our laboratory. These studies addressed some of the questions regarding differences in alpha activity and task-specific shifts in hemispheric activation between high and low susceptibles. Since these studies were concerned only with the EEG-alpha correlates of hypnotizability, the subjects were not hypnotized during any aspect of the psychophysiological testing.

Experiment 1. The first study (De Pascalis, Silveri, & Palumbo, 1988) was devoted to evaluating the EEG alpha-hypnotizability and extending the MacLeod-Morgan and Lack (1982) findings of a significant relationship between hypnotizability and hemispheric specificity. Covert self-generated tasks, selected from the study of Ehrlichman and Wiener (1980), in which the range of cognitive activities resembled natural thinking were used. Two left hemisphere tasks (verbal long-term memory and multiplication task) and two right hemisphere tasks (visual long-term memory and fantasy task) were used. Our principal aims were to investigate in an eyes-closed waking condition whether: (a) the amount of alpha in the EEG is correlated with hypnotizability; (b) high hypnotizables would reveal higher hemispheric specificities during covert mental tasks compared to lows; and (c) verbal-numeric tasks involve more left hemisphere activation and imaginative-visual tasks more right hemisphere activation. Twenty high hypnotizables and twenty low hypnotizables (all women) were selected to serve as subjects. The subjects were selected firstly using the Harvard Group Scale of Hypnotic Susceptibility: Form A (HGSHS:A) (Shor & Orne, 1962) and later with the Stanford Scale of Hypnotic Susceptibility, Form C (SHSS:C) (Weitzenhoffer & Hilgard, 1962). The subjects were designated as being high and low in hypnotizability when their SHSS:C scores were 1 SD above and 1 SD below the group mean (highs: mean = 10.05, SD = 0.88; lows: mean = 2.75, SD = 1.49; overall group mean: mean = 6.51, SD = 2.33, n = 68). The subjects were volunteer students invited to participate in the experiment, and experiencing hypnosis for the first time. The integrated amplitude alpha, the alpha density, and the alpha ratio (right minus left) / (right plus left) [(R-L)/(R+L)] as a measure of hemispheric asymmetry were evaluated. After each task, subjects used a six-point scale to rate orally their degree of involvement in the task. The proportion of greater relative right hemisphere activation periods during right hemisphere tasks minus the analogous proportion during left hemisphere tasks was defined as "hemispheric specificity." A period exhibits a greater than ordinary right hemisphere activation if the right minus left amplitude for that period is lower than the individual mean difference evaluated for the entire experimental session. Greater relative left hemisphere activation is seen in the reverse case.

Analysis of variance was performed. The high hypnotizables generated significantly greater ($P < 0.05$) alpha amplitude in both hemispheres than the lows (see Figure 1) during an eyes-closed baseline condition and during a task condition. The alpha-hypnotizability relationship was also confirmed using the biserial coefficient of correlation. The biserial correlation coefficients between each right and left overall alpha amplitude in the baseline condition and the SHSS:C scores were 0.42 and 0.39, respectively ($P < 0.05$, n = 40). The alpha density was not correlated with hypnotizability (0.20 and 0.21 for left and right hemisphere, $P > 0.05$). However, alpha density has been shown to be an effective variable for distinguishing between high and low subjects in the sense that among subjects who presented high levels of alpha density there were significantly more highs than lows (13 high vs. 6 low hypnotizables), and vice versa for low levels of alpha density (14 low vs. 7 high hypnotizables).

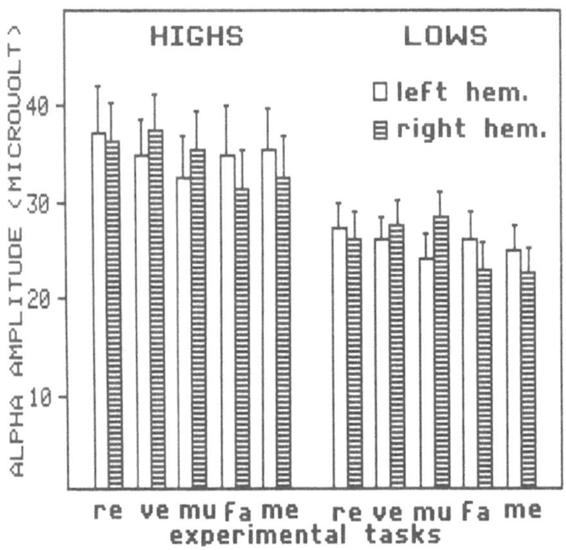

Figure 1. Left (*open columns*) and right (*shaded columns*) hemisphere alpha amplitude for high and low hypnotizables during rest (*re*) and verbal (*ve*), multiplication (*mu*), fantasy (*fa*), and visual long-term-memory (*me*) tasks

The pattern of task effect for alpha ratios between verbal/numeric and imaginative/visual memory tasks were in the expected direction (i.e., negative alpha ratios for right hemisphere tasks and positive alpha ratios for left hemisphere tasks). The high and low hypnotizables did not show different alpha ratios during the right and left hemisphere tasks, except for the multiplication task in which low subjects evidenced higher positive ratios compared to high groups (see Figure 2). Ratings of subjective task involvement were related to alpha ratio in verbal ($rho = 0.82, P < 0.01$) and multiplication ($rho = 0.31, P < 0.05$) tasks, while they were not so related in visual memory ($rho = -0.04$) and in fantasy ($rho = -0.18$). No relationship was found between hemispheric specificity and hypnotizability, and the highs did not show significantly greater hemisphere specificity compared to the lows (-0.024 vs. 0.13, $t = 0.98$, $df = 38$, $P > 0.05$). As far as EEG alpha asymmetry is concerned, our results confirmed those already described by Ehrlichman and Wiener (1980): verbal and multiplication ratings were related to alpha ratio, while visual memory and fantasy ratings were not. The differences in hemispheric asymmetry or hemispheric specificity between groups already described in the literature (e.g., MacLeod-Morgan, 1979; MacLeod-Morgan & Lack, 1982; Karlin et al., 1980; Mészáros et al., 1986) were not found in this study.

Experiment 2. Taking into account the fact that our study and others (e.g., Morgan et al., 1974) failed to find differences between high and low hypnotizables in task-related EEG-alpha asymmetry, a further experiment was carried out. It evaluated the possibility that task difficulty may affect hemispheric engagement and that such an influence may be reflected in the hypnotizability vs. EEG alpha asymmetry relationship (De Pascalis & Palumbo, 1986). This possibility was suggested by the observations of Galin, Johnston, and Herron (1978) in which task difficulty was found to affect EEG alpha asymmetry. These authors observed that alpha

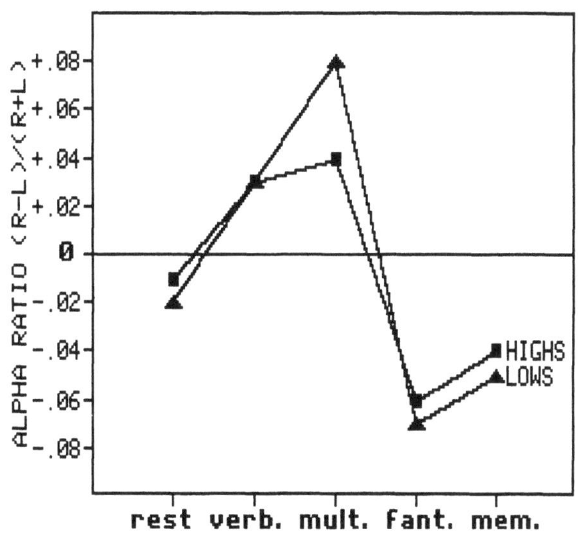

Figure 2. Alpha ratio for high (*squares*) and low (*triangles*) hypnotizables evaluated during rest, left hemisphere (verbal, multiplication) tasks and right hemisphere (fantasy, visual long-term memory) tasks

power increased in the harder tasks and that there were many individual differences in hemispheric envolvement with respect to task difficulty. Some subjects showed that alpha power increases more in the right, others more in the left, and others again in both hemispheres.

Parieto-occipital EEG alpha was recorded bilaterally while 20 high and 20 low hypnotizables (all women) performed one verbal and one tonal-memory task of low difficulty, and two other comparable tasks of high difficulty. Each subject in the verbal task of high difficulty was required to recognize which word in a list did not belong to the same category of the Italian grammar (i.e., noun, adverb, adjective). Each subject in the verbal task of low difficulty was required to respond by pressing a buzzer every time she heard a proper personal noun. In the tonal task of high difficulty, each subject was asked to decide which note in a four- or five-note tune had been changed when the tune was played a second time. each subject in the tonal task of low difficulty listened to a simple eight-bar melody played twice, she was required to signal, by pressing a buzzer, every time she detected a change during five consecutive performances of the melody in which several notes had been altered. After each trial, subjects used a six-point scale to rate the degree of difficulty experienced during the task fulfillment. Every task was performed twice, once with eyes open and once with eyes closed in a counterbalanced order. The integrated amplitude alpha and alpha ratio (R-L)/(R+L) were the dependent variables. Ratio scores were computed for each recording period separately and then averaged across conditions for each subjects.

High hypnotizables showed more alpha activity than low hypnotizables in the eyes-closed baseline condition (see Figure 3). This difference disappeared during all eyes-open and task conditions. This result confirmed the findings of McLeod-Morgan (1979) and of Morgan et al. (1974) where the highly hypnotizable subjects generated higher amplitude in the eyes-closed

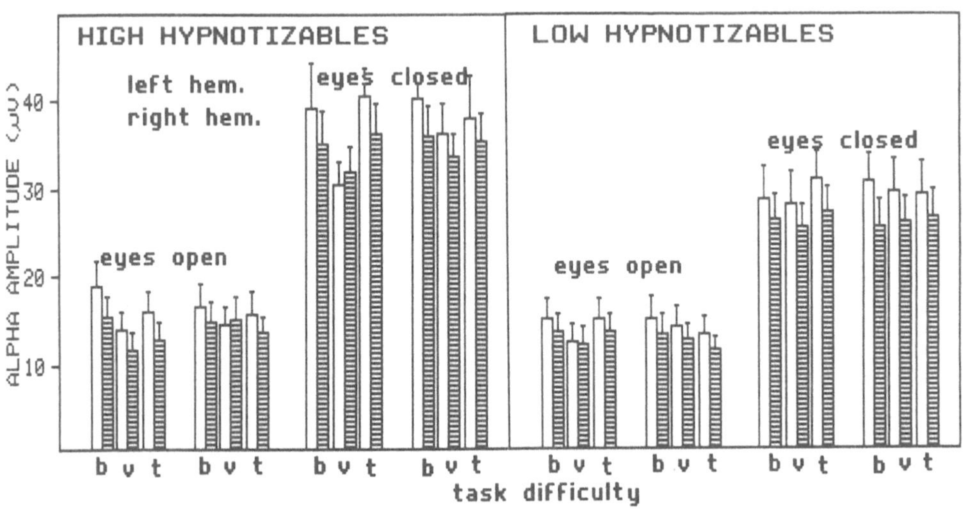

Figure 3. Left (*open columns*) and right (*shaded columns*) hemisphere alpha amplitude for high and low hypnotizables in high and low task difficulty. *b* = baseline; *v* = verbal; *t*, tonal

condition. It was suggested that in the eyes-closed rest condition the arousal level was minimal, less affected by task demands, therefore giving a truer comparison of the amount of alpha between groups.

With respect to the rest condition, verbal tasks showed a left hemisphere activation, while tonal-memory tasks did not show any hemispheric differences. No differences in hemispheric engagement were observed between groups during tasks. However, the alpha ratio of high and low hypnotizables showed opposite trends between low- and high-task difficulty. No differences between groups in the high-difficulty condition were observed (-0.055 vs. -0.055, for low and high hypnotizables, respectively), while in the less difficult condition low hypnotizables showed, compared to the highs, a greater negative alpha ratio score (-0.065 vs. -0.040 for low and high hypnotizables, respectively). Since in a posthoc comparison it was found that the high hypnotizables experienced less subjective difficulty in task performance than the lows, we suggested that these differences in hemispheric behavior between groups could have been influenced by differences in subjective task difficulty. Comparing the hemispheric asymmetry ratios in the rest condition between groups a lower negative alpha ratio (i.e., greater left hemisphere activation) for high subjects with respect to the lows was observed. This result is consistent with the Gruzelier et al.'s (1984) electrodermal findings in which hypnotically susceptible subjects, compared to the unsusceptibles, showed a pre-existing greater left hemisphere activation in the waking baseline condition.

Conclusion. With regard to the waking state EEG alpha vs. hypnotizability relationship, our studies suggested that eyes-closed alpha amplitude was greater for high hypnotizables than for lows. Results confirmed the MacLeod-Morgan (1979) findings regarding the fact that the eyes-closed condition emphasizes the discrimination of alpha amplitude between high and low subjects. Alpha amplitude, rather than alpha density, and the eyes-closed condition rather than eyes-open appear to be more appropriate for detecting differences between high and low hypnotizables. Dumas (1977), because of discrepant results between EEG alpha-hypnotizability studies, indicated the sampling variable as responsible for such relationships: in studies in which subjects were non-naive volunteers a significant correlation was found; in studies in which subjects were invited, or were unaware of the experimental focus when they volunteered, no correlation was found. Sampling variables do not explain our results; our subjects were naive women volunteers who were unaware of experimental hypotheses, but yet a significant positive correlation between alpha amplitude and hypnotizability was obtained. our examination of EEG alpha-hypnotizability studies revealed that beside the "situational" (Evans, 1972) and the "sampling" determinants (Dumas, 1977), other variables, such as the choice of alpha variable and the eyes-open/closed measurements during rest or task conditions, can affect the relationship. Some studies consider alpha density (e.g., Nowlis and Rhead, 1968; Engstrom et al., 1970; Coper and London, 1976), others alpha amplitude (e.g., Morgan et al., 1974; MacLeod-Morgan, 1979), and some both EEG variables (e.g., Evans, 1972). Furthermore, some studies presented correlations in a baseline eyes-open condition, others in a baseline eyes-closed condition, and others again during task performance. These different methodological procedures render any conclusion extremely difficult.

The hypothesis was suggested that the difference in alpha amplitude between groups might reflect basic differences in arousal level between the two groups: the high subjects are likely to be more relaxed than the lows. Nevertheless, this assumption is not a general one, Paskewitz and

Orne (1973) and Orne and Paskewitz (1974), in fact, observed that in dark adapted subjects, the relaxed condition does not produce increases of alpha activity, and that a reduction in alpha activity is not necessarily a consequence of heightened arousal. Taking into account these findings and the fact that in some studies correlations between alpha indices and hypnotizability are not found, we suggest that in the alpha-hypnotizability relationship there may be a series of intervening variables (e.g., personality, sampling, and situation-specific factors) which may moderate such a relationship.

Finally, our hemispheric asymmetry findings have confirmed the validity of alpha rhythm in detecting task-related asymmetries during covert mental tasks (experiment 1), as was found by Ehrlichman and Wiener (1980). They do not indicate, however, that there is a clear relationship between waking state EEG asymmetry and hypnotic susceptibility, as has been demonstrated by MacLeod-Morgan (1979) and by MacLeod-Morgan and Lack (1982). Experiment 2 has shown that hemispheric engagement may be affected by task difficulty, and that this effect may be reflected in a different way between groups: the highs showed greater relative left hemisphere engagement than the lows in the low-difficult condition (i.e., less negative alpha ratio, see Figure 3). In view of the influence of the task difficulty factor on hemispheric asymmetry (see Galin et al., 1978) and especially on the hypnotizability vs. EEG alpha-asymmetry relationship, we suggest that future studies should control this factor carefully.

Hypnotizability and 40-Hz EEG Activity: A Hypothesized Relationship.

Galbraith et al. (1970) reported that a 5-Hz value of the occipital autospectrum in the eyes-open condition was the most predictive variable of hypnotizability (evaluated with the Harvard Group Scale of Hypnotic Susceptibility, HGSHS). Another group of investigators (Akpinar, Ulett, & Itil, 1971; Ulett, Akpinar, & Itil, 1972) conducted a replication study in which hypnotizability (evaluated with the Barber Suggestibility Scale, BSS) correlated positively with slow wave (3-7-Hz) patterns and fast-frequency (40-50-Hz) activity.

Referring to the literature concerning the relevance of fast-frequency EEG activities, we find that a fast EEG activity centered on 40 Hz reflects a state of focused arousal, a component of attention, concentration, and problem solving (Sheer, 1970; Sheer, 1976). Focused arousal is a selective facilitatory process believed to result from activity in the rostral brain stem reticular formation which appears "to reflect an interaction between cortical facilitation and the processing of specific sensory input" (Spydell, Ford, & Sheer, 1979). Task-dependent lateralizations of the 40-Hz EEG rhythm have been found during a variety of cognitive performances, and 40-Hz EMG activity made little, if any, contribution to 40-Hz EEG (Spydell et al, 1979; Loring & Sheer, 1984; Spydell & Sheer, 1982). Biofeedback studies on voluntary control of 40-Hz EEG activity supported the findings that such an activity may be increased or decreased with biofeedback training, and that 40-Hz EEG may be independent of beta activity (Bird, Newton, Sheer, & Ford, 1978a; Bird et al., 1978b).

Assuming that hypnosis requires a state of narrowly focused attention and that 40-Hz EEG activity reflects cognitive mechanisms related to attentional components, it is possible to hypothesize that this fast EEG activity reflects differential attentional patterns between high and low hypnotizables. In particular, assuming a greater cognitive flexibility for high hypnotizables (i.e., the subjective ability to shift from one strategy to another, see Crawford, 1985), we hypothesized that such differences in cognitive flexibility may be paralleled by differences in 40-Hz EEG hemispheric specificity. That is, the high hypnotizables, compared to lows, might exhibit a more consistent task-related hemispheric shift of 40-Hz EEG activity. An experiment carried out in our laboratory (De Pascalis, Marucci, Penna, & Pessa, 1987) has confirmed this hypothesis using 40-Hz EEG recordings in the waking state. The study evaluated differences in hemispheric activity of 40-Hz EEG between low an high hypnotizables during recollection of life events which had positive and negative emotional contents. While it is generally accepted that highs have greater absorptive ability, as reflected by the Tellegen Absorption Scale (1974), negligible consideration has been given to the individual differences in hypnotizability. Bower, Gilligan, and Monteiro (1981) suggested that hypnosis facilitates the induction of sad and happy affects. Karlin, Weinapple, and Rochford (1979) reported three studies in which right hemisphere activation during negative affect was found in volunteer hypnotized students, while patients suffering from pain syndromes showed a decrease of right hemisphere activity following hypnotic analgesia.

Given the greater absorptive attentional abilities of highs, a further aim of our study was to see whether high hypnotizables experienced more intensive and vivid emotional states than lows and how these differences were reflected on 40-Hz EEG and EMG activities. Finally, the experiment also evaluated hemispheric engagement during positive and negative emotions; according to Davidson, Schwartz, Saron, Bennett, and Goleman (1979) and Tucker, Stenslie, Roth, and Shearer (1981), we expected to find a relative left hemisphere activation during positive emotions and a relative right hemisphere activation during negative emotions.

Subjects (22 high and 21 low hypnotizables, all women) were required to recollect six (three positive - gladness, happiness, satisfaction - and three negative - fear, sadness, anger) personal life events. The State-Trait Anxiety Inventory (Spielberger, Gorsuch, & Lushene, 1970), Maudsley Personality Inventory (Eysenck, 1959), the Tellegen Absorption Scale (Tellegen & Atkinson, 1974) and the Harvard Group Scale of Hypnotic Susceptibility: Form A (Shor & Orne, 1962) were administered. Self-report rating scores for vividness of visual imagery and emotional feeling of the material recalled were evaluated using a five-point scale; i.e., 1, "none (no emotion) at all", to 5, "perfectly clear vision (identical feeling) as in reality." Left and right 40-Hz EEG densities were obtained from the parietal-occipital-temporal junction, an area known to be involved in cognitive processes. A 40-Hz EEG ratio (R-L)/(R+L) as a measure of hemispheric asymmetry was obtained, and a hemispheric specificity (HS) index was calculated by subtracting the ratio for the positive emotion condition from the ratio for the negative one. A positive HS index should reflect a relatively greater right hemisphere activation in the negative emotion and/or a relatively greater left hemisphere activation in the positive emotional condition. In other words, the positive magnitude of the HS value reflects the extent to which a subject shows a shift between hemispheres in accordance with task demands.

The data analyses showed a lower 40-Hz EEG density for high hypnotizables than for lows in eyes-closed rest and task conditions (see Figure 4). This finding was confirmed in a later experiment carried out in our laboratory (see Marucci, De Pascalis, Penna, & Pessa, this volume). The upper trapezius EMG activity was found significantly and negatively related to the

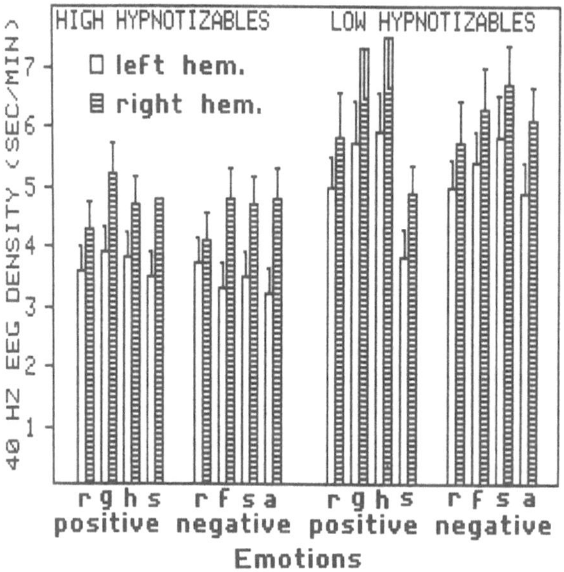

Figure 4. Forty-hertz EEG density of left (*open columns*) and right (*shaded columns*) hemisphere during recollection of positive and negative emotional events. Positive emotions: *r*, rest; *g*, gladness; *h*, happiness; *s*, satisfaction. Negative emotions: *r*, rest; *f*, fear; *s*, sadness; *a*, anger

40-Hz EEG in each positive emotional condition (r = -0.33, $P < 0.05$; r = -0.39, $P < 0.01$; r = -0.39, $P < 0.01$, for glad, happy and satisfying conditions, respectively); no significant correlations were found in the rest and negative emotional conditions ($P > 0.05$).

In view of the significant correlation between EMG and 40-Hz EEG, an analysis of covariance with EMG levels as a covariate was used for EEG data. The relationship between 40-Hz EEG asymmetry and emotional processing was moderated by hypnotizability. In high hypnotizables the rest condition (gladness minus rest: 0.4 on the left and 0.9 on the right hemisphere; happiness minus rest: 0.5 on the left and 0.6 on the right) showed an increase of density over both left and right hemispheres during gladness and happiness conditions, while they showed a depressed activity over the left and an increased activity over the right during negative emotional tasks (fear minus rest: -0.5 on the left and 0.7 on the right; sadness minus rest: -0.3 on the left and 0.8 on the right; anger minus rest: -0.6 on the left and 0.8 on the right). Low hypnotizables, however, did not exhibit differential hemispheric patterns that could be attributed to the different emotional valences. Similar findings were obtained using 40-Hz EEG ratios. Furthermore, high hypnotizables showed greater hemispheric specificity than the lows (0.06 vs. -0.02, respectively). No differences in vividness of visual material were found between high and low subjects, the high subjects reported greater emotional feeling ratings than the lows. In the positive emotion conditions, visual rating and emotion feeling were greater than those during negative ones. No relationship was found between personality variables and the HGSHS scale, except for absorption, where the mean score of highs was significantly greater than that of lows (9.0 vs. 7.0, t = 2.95, $P < 0.01$; df = 41).

Because there were no differences in state and trait anxiety between groups, the lower 40-Hz EEG density of highs with respect to lows was attributed to the greater absorptive attentional ability exhibited by the former. It is generally accepted that hypnosis is characterized by a state of narrowly focused attention in which a subject must inhibit other responses that may be of a competing nature. Thus, assuming that high hypnotizables are more able to obtain a state of narrowly focused attention, then it is possible to hypothesize that such an ability may also show up in the waking state; highs, compared to lows, employ less effort in complying with, or in shutting off distracting stimuli which are competitive with task requirements. Results suggest that emotional valence (positive or negative) is differentially represented in terms of 40-Hz EEG for high hypnotizables, while it is not so for lows. This last result was attributed to the fact that low hypnotizables showed less absorptive ability and lower emotional feeling ratings than the highs. High hypnotizables, in contrast, had greater access to affective events, and also showed greater hemispheric specificity than lows. The greater hemispheric specificity exhibited by the high subjects is in agreement with previous findings by MacLeod-Morgan (1979) and MacLeod-Morgan and Lack (1982), by Karlin et al. (1979, 1980), and also with findings of the Hungarian school (e.g., Mészáros et al., 1986). Moreover, the greater cognitive ability and the greater hemispheric specificity found for high subjects led us to maintain that the suggested differences in physiological flexibility between highs and lows (Crawford, 1985) also exist in the waking state.

Concerning hemispheric engagement in negative and positive emotions, our results are restricted to 40-Hz hemispheric patterns of high hypnotizables. They showed, however, that both hemispheres are involved during recall of positive emotional events, and depressed activity of the left and increased activity of the right accounted for recall of negative emotional events. Despite the existing differences in the EEG measures and recording sites between ours and previous studies, our results tend to support the findings of Tucker et al. (1981), Davidson et al. (1979), and Karlin et al. (1979). However, in our findings the left hemisphere activity, more than the right, was found to differentiate between positive and negative affective arousal, with relative left hemisphere inhibition and right hemisphere activation during the negative affective condition. Considering that we obtained a right hemisphere increase in 40-Hz EEG activity irrespective of task type, one possible explanation of our findings could be supplied by the attentional model of Dimond and Beaumont (1973), that is, the left hemisphere is better equipped to maintain selective or focal attention. These findings could also be explained by assuming that the recollection of a past event with positive emotional valence involved the focal attentional processes proper for an increase in left hemisphere activity, whereas the recollection of negative past events involved a reduction (inhibition) of the focal attentional left hemisphere processes. the right hemisphere, meanwhile, performs a monitoring and a synthesis function for the recollected positive and negative emotional materials. Finally, our findings also showed a relative dependence of EMG activity on emotion type: greater activity in the negative emotional condition than in the positive. EMG activity was also related to 40-Hz EEG in each positive emotional condition, while no relationship was found in the negative ones.

Suggestibility, Personality, and Hypnosis

General Considerations

The concept of suggestibility has been a central point in the development of a theory of hypnosis. Suggestibility was in some way connected with hypnosis, but the great majority of suggestibility tests which were used in the beginning of the twentieth century were later found to have no relationship with hypnotic susceptibility. One general element that was assumed to be related to hypnotic susceptibility was prestige suggestibility. Eysenck (1943) and Eysenck and Furneaux (1945) demonstrated that there is no unitary trait of suggestibility and that at least two factors were necessary to account for the intercorrelations amongst tests of suggestibility. The first factor, "primary suggestibility," is a reliable trait and involves the subject's execution of direct suggestions of motor movements without his conscious volitional participation. The second factor, "secondary suggestibility," involves the subject's experience of sensations or perceptions following the suggestions that such an experience will occur, without any objective basis. The primary suggestibility was related to hypnotic susceptibility, the secondary suggestibility was not. Concerning the relationship between ideomotor reactivity and hypnotic susceptibility, Eysenck postulated the distinction between "attitude" to hypnosis and "aptitude" for such behavior. The subject's attitude concerns the context in which certain behavior is suggested, while the subject's aptitude concerns an ability for hypnotic behavior and can be regarded as a fundamental personality trait. This dual point of view can explain many of the inconsistencies of hypnosis research. The social-interactional point of view (e.g., Barber, 1969; Sarbin & Coe, 1972; Spanos & Chaves, 1970) has focused on the role of attitude to explain hypnotic performance, but attitude does not rule out the question of individual differences in aptitude for hypnotic behavior. The state of consciousness theorists (e.g., Evans, 1968; Orne, 1959; Hilgard, 1969; Shor, 1959) recognize that many of the existing individual differences in hypnotizability are due to the aptitude of individuals to be hypnotized. Within the individual differences framework, the "state" viewpoint also allowed most useful research on hypnotic analgesia (Hilgard & Hilgard, 1975; Chertock, Michaux, & Droin, 1977) and led to the formulation of the neodissociation model of the hypnotic experience an pain reduction in hypnosis (Hilgard, 1973, 1977).

However, according to Spanos and Barber (1974) the state and nonstate viewpoint seem to be converging in their conceptualization of cognitive processes that characterize hypnotic behavior. The states of consciousness are regarded as categorial rather than causal phenomena. However, the difference between these two lines of hypnotic research (state and nonstate) is the difference in the kinds of research questions that the researcher tries to answer. The terms "trance" or "hypnotic state," although referring to hypnotic behavior as operationally defined by standard hypnotic tests, are also used to denote the existence of a state that differs from waking and sleep. This conceptualization has promoted the most useful studies aimed at establishing the psychophysiological correlates of the hypothesized altered state of consciousness.

Eysenck's concept of aptitude and attitude to hypnotic susceptibility was suggested before he had developed the neuroticism (N) and extraversion (E) scale. After the production of the Maudsley Personality Inventory (MPI; Eysenck & Eysenck, 1959), Furneaux and Gibson (1961) found that two groups could be defined as being susceptible to hypnosis: the stable extraverts (SE) and the neurotic introverts (NI). In a subsequent study, carried out at Stanford University, Hilgard and Bentler (1963) found that the N and E dimensions were significantly related to hypnotic susceptibility but in the opposite direction. These contrasting results were explained by cultural differences between American and British subjects, and between the criteria of selection and testing in the different studies. Lang and Lazovik (1962), considering E and N separately with respect to hypnotic susceptibility, found the susceptibility was positively related to the E and negatively to the N dimension of the MPI. Eysenck (1966) suggested that the relationship between personality variables and hypnotizability must take into account the interaction between the E and N dimensions, and he proposed the technique of analyzing bipolar co-ordinates to resolve this problem.

Personality, Suggestibility, and Hypnotic Susceptibility

Considering the fact that the personality and hypnotic susceptibility relationship remained unsolved, we designed a study to re-evaluate the possibilities of a link between the variables of the Eysenck Personality Questionnaire (EPQ; Eysenck, 1981) and hypnotic susceptibility. The purpose of this study was also to extend our preceding results regarding the relationship between absorptive ability as measured by Tellegen Absorption Scale (TAS; Tellegen and Atkinson, 1974) and hypnotic susceptibility. A further aim was to estimate the relationship between suggestibility, as measured by our version of the Suggestibility Scale (SS) of Gheorghiu and Reyher (1982) and hypnotic susceptibility. The Harvard Group Scale of Hypnotic Susceptibility, Form A (HGSHS:A, Shor & Orne, 1962), the EPQ and TAS scales were administered to 105 women students. A total of 97 of these subjects received the Stanford Hypnotic Susceptibility Scale, Form C (SHSS:C, Weitzenhoffer and Hilgard, 1962) and 81 of these participated in a session in which the SS was administered.

Hypnotic susceptibility was evaluated in two separate sessions in the following manner: first, the students participated in groups in a session (no more than 40 persons for session) to evaluate hypnotizability with th HGSHS:A. At a later individual session the SHSS:C was administered. The correlation between the subject's scores in the HGSHS:A and SHSS:C was .62 (n = 97). The subjects were all females, since there are suggestions indicating that sex may be a moderating variable in the relationship between personality variables and hypnotic susceptibility (Gibson & Corcoran, 1975). The basic data for the variables measured are reported in Table 1.

To evaluate the relationship between Lie Scale and neuroticism and extraversion scores (as measured by EPQ; Eysenck, 1981), the SHSS scores (n = 97 subjects) were taken as the measure of hypnotic susceptibility.

Gibson and Curran (1974), based on 43 subjects, supported the findings of Furneaux and Gibson (1961) showing stable extraverts (SE) and neurotic introverts (NI) tended to be the most susceptible, and neurotic extraverts (NE) and stable introverts (SI) the least susceptible. Gibson and Corcoran (1975), adding 45 subjects to the study of Gibson and Curran, obtained identical results for the pooled groups (n = 88 subjects), but they also found that the Lie scale (L) predicts hypnotic susceptibility among males ($r_t = -0.76$, $\chi^2 = 7.48$, $P < 0.01$), but not among females. The aim of our study was to evaluate if such differences also existed in our sample.

Lie Scale and Hypnotic Susceptibility

The Lie scale and SHSS were dichotomized at their medians and the cases pooled with respectively high and low levels of Lie and of susceptibility scores. No relationship between hypnotizability and the Lie scale was found. The four-fold table of pooled cases is shown on the left side of Table 2.

Extraversion, Neuroticism, and Susceptibility

The cases in the SE and NI quadrants were pooled and compared with the pooled NE and SI quadrants with respect to hypnotic susceptibility. The tetrachoric coefficient and χ^2 test showed

Table 1. Mean and standard deviation for personality, suggestibility, and hypnotic susceptibility variables.

Variable	(*n*)	Mean	SD
HGSHS: form A	105	6.76	3.09
SHSS: form C	97	6.79	2.58
TAS	105	7.86	2.57
SS[a]	81	7.91	3.15
EPQ:			
L	105	9.17	3.33
Extraversion		14.58	4.86
Neuroticism		13.62	4.57

[a] These data refer to 12 items in the suggestibility scale of Gheorghiu and Reyher (1982). A total score for each item was obtained by summing the scores obtained in the left- and right-sided administration of the test stimulus. The highest score obtainable from the two presentations was 24 (see De Pascalis & Caddia, 1985).

Table 2. Relationship between lie and extraversion/neuroticism variables, and hypnotic susceptibility

Hypnotic susceptibility (SHSS:C)	Lie - (*n*)	Lie + (*n*)	NE and SI (*n*)	SE and NI (*n*)
High	29	31	21	39
Low	13	24	23	14
	r_t = -0.21,	^{2} = 1.623, NS	r_t = 0.41,	^{2} = 6.813, $P < 0.01$

NS, not significant.

that E and N are positively related to hypnotic susceptibility (see right side of Table 2). However, observing the distribution of subjects reported in the four-fold table, it may be observed that SE and NI subjects tended to be the most susceptible while NE and SI were equally distributed with respect to hypnotic susceptibility.

Prediction of Hypnotic Susceptibility

To predict hypnotic susceptibility we carried out a step-wise multiple regression analysis using personality variables (i.e., TAS and E, N, L of the EPQ, and SS) as predictors and SHSS:C scores as the dependent variable. However, taking into account the fact that in our validation of the Gheorghiu and Reyher suggestibility scale (Gheorghiu & Reyher, 1982) three of the 12 items showed a low level of reliability (two auditory: A1 and A3, and one visual V2; see De Pascalis & Caddia, 1985), we considered as predictors two separate evaluations of suggestibility: one evaluation using all the 12 items (SS12) and one evaluation using nine items (SS9). The single predictor of hypnotizability was the TAS which was substantially related to hypnotic susceptibility and accounted for a 22 % of total variance. The SS and Eysenck's variables were not related to hypnotic susceptibility (SHSS:C) and accounted for a negligible percentage of total variance. The correlation matrix for all experimental variables was also calculated. While the SS12 was found to be related to HGSHS, the SS9 appeared to be relatively independent of hypnotic susceptibility. The value of correlation coefficients and their levels of significance are reported in Table 3.

Conclusion

No appreciable association between personality variables as measured by the EPQ and hypnotic susceptibility as measured by SHSS:C has been demonstrated in this study. The SE and NI subjects were found to be the most susceptible, but NE and SI were equally distributed with respect to hypnotic susceptibility. The independence of the Lie scale from SHSS:C, in female subjects, tends to support the existence of a "trait" valence to predict hypnotic susceptibility

Table 3. Multiple regression correlation on hypnotizability (SHSS:C) obtained for 81 subjects

Variable	Multiple regression	*r*	Change in *r*
TAS	0.469	0.220	0.220
SSS	0.611	0.374	0.154
N	0.637	0.406	0.032
L	0.642	0.412	0.006
E	0.643	0.413	0.001

rather than the existence of a unique situational factor. These findings indicate that the subjective capacity for absorbed and self-altering attention, as measured by TAS, is consistently associated with and represents an essential component of hypnotic susceptibility. Finally, the independence of sensory suggestibility, as measured by the suggestibility scale of Gheorghiu and Reyher (1982), from hypnotic susceptibility is in agreement with the suggestions of Evans (this volume) who claims that suggestibility and hypnosis are in part different processes.

References

Anand, B.K., Chhina, G.S., & Singh, B. (1961). Some aspects of electroencephalographic studies in yogis. *Electroencephalography and Clinical Neurophysiology, 13,* 452-456.

Akpinar, S., Ulett, G.A., & Itil, T.M. (1971). Hypnotizability predicted by digital computer-analyzed EEG pattern. *Biological Psychiatry, 3,* 387-392.

Bányai, E.I., Mészáros, I., & Greguss, A.C. (1986, July). *Psychophysiological correlates of the interaction between hypnotist and subject.* Paper presented at the Proceedings of the 3rd international conference of the International Organization of Psychophysiology, Vienna, Austria.

Barber, T.X. (1969). *Hypnosis a scientific approach.* New York: Van Nostrand Reinhold.

Bauer, K.E., & McCanne, T.R. (1980). Autonomic and central nervous system responding: During hypnosis and simulation of hypnosis. *International Journal of Clinical and Experimental hypnosis, 28,* 148-163.

Bird, B.L., Newton, F.A., Sheer, D.E., & Ford, M. (1978a). Behavioral and electroencephalographic correlates of 40 Hz EEG biofeedback training in humans. *Biofeedback and Self-Regulation, 3,* 13-28.

Bird, B.L., Newton, F.A., Sheer, D.E., & Ford, M. (1978b). Biofeedback training of 40 Hz EEG in humans. *Biofeedback and Self-Regulation, 3,* 1-11.

Brady, J.P., & Rosner, B.S. (1966). Rapid eye movements in hypnotically-induced dreams. *Journal of Nervous and Mental Disease, 143,* 28-35.

Bower, G.H., Gilligan, S.G., & Monteiro, K.P. (1981). Selectivity of learning caused by affective states. *Journal of Experimental Psychology: General (Washington), 110,* 451-473.

Bowers, K.S. (1971). Sex and susceptibility as moderator variables in the relationship of creativity and hypnotic susceptibility. *Journal of Abnormal Psychology, 78,* 93-100.

Chen, A.C.N., Dworkin, S.F., & Bloomquist, D.S. (1981). Cortical power spectrum analysis of hypnotic pain control in surgery. *International Journal of Neuroscience, 13,* 127-136.

Chertok, M.D., Michaux, D., & Droin, M.C. (1977). Dynamics of hypnotic analgesia. *Journal of Nervous and Mental Disease, 164,* 88-96.

Cooper, L.M., & London, P. (1976). Children's hypnotic susceptibility and EEG patterns. *International Journal of Clinical and Experimental Hypnosis, 24,* 140-148.

Crawford, H.J. (1985, August). *Cognitive flexibility dissociation, and hypnosis.* Presidential address presented at the American Psychological Association, Division 30, meeting, Los Angeles, California.

Crawford, H.J., Skolnick, B., Benson, D., Gur, R.E., & Gur, R.C. (1985, August). *Regional cerebral blood flow in hypnosis and hypnotic analgesia.* Paper presented at the 10th international congress of Hypnosis and Psychosomatic Medicine, Toronto, Canada.

Davidson, R., Schwartz, G.E., Saron, C., Bennett, J., & Goleman, D. (1979). Frontal versus parietal EEG asymmetry during positive and negative affect. *Psychophysiology, 16,* 202-203. (Abstract)

Davidson, R.J., & Schwartz, G.E. (1977). The influence of musical training on patterns of EEG asymmetry during musical and non-musical self-generation tasks. *Psychophysiology, 14,* 58-63.

De Pascalis, V., & Caddia, R. (1985). Effect of suggestion on perception: Replication of Gheorghiu and Reyher's study. *Perceptual and Motor Skills, 61,* 123-130.

De Pascalis, V., Marucci, F.S., Penna, M.P., & Pessa, E. (1987). Hemispheric activity of 40 Hz EEG during recall of emotional events: Differences between low and high hypnotizables. *International Journal of Psychophysiology, 5,* 167-180.

De Pascalis, V., & Palumbo, G. (1986). EEG alpha asymmetry: Task difficulty and hypnotizability. *Perceptual and Motor Skills, 62,* 139-150.

De Pascalis, V., Silveri, A., & Palumbo, G. (1988). EEG asymmetry during covert mental activity and its relationship with hypnotizability. *International Journal of Clinical and Experimental Hypnosis, 36,* 38.

Dimond, S.J., & Beaumont, J.G. (1973). Difference in the vigilance performance of the right and left hemispheres. *Cortex, 9,* 259-265.

Doyle, J.C., Ornstein, R., & Galin, D. (1974). Lateral specialization of cognitive mode II: EEG frequency analysis. *Psychophysiology, 11,* 567-578.

Dumas, R.A. (1977). EEG alpha-hypnotizability correlations: A review. *Psychophysiology, 14,* 431-438.

Dumas, R.A., & Morgan, A. (1975). EEG asymmetry as a function of occupation, task and task difficulty. *Neuropsychologia, 13,* 219-228.

Edmonston, W.E., Jr. (1981). *Hypnosis and relaxation. Modern verification of an old equation.* New York: Wiley.

Edmonston, W.E., Jr., & Grotevant, W.R. (1975). Hypnosis and alpha density. *American Journal of Clinical Hypnosis, 17,* 221-232.

Ehrlichman, H., & Wiener, M.S. (1979). Consistency of task-related EEG asymmetries. *Psychophysiology, 16,* 247-252.

Ehrlichman, H., & Wiener, M.S. (1980). EEG asymmetry during covert mental activity. *Psychophysiology, 17,* 228-235.

Engstrom, D.R. (1976). Hypnotic susceptibility, EG alpha, and self-regulation. In G.E. Schwartz & D. Shapiro (Eds.), *Advances in research: Vol. 1. Consciousness and self-regulation.* New York: Plenum.

Engstrom, D.R., London, P., & Hart, J.T. (1970). Hypnotic susceptibility increased by EEG alpha training. *Nature, 227,* 1261-1262.

Evans, F.J. (1968). Recent trends in experimental hypnosis. *Behavioral Science, 13,* 477-487.

Evans, F.J. (1972). Hypnosis and sleep: Techniques for exploring cognitive activity during sleep. In E. Fromm & R.E. Shor (Eds.), *Hypnosis: research developments and perspectives* (pp. 43-83). Chicago: Aldine Atherton.

Eysenck, H.J. (1943). Suggestibility and hysteria. *Journal of Neurology and Psychiatry, 6,* 22-31.

Eysenck, H.J. (1959). *Maudsley Personality Inventory.* London: University of London.

Eysenck, H.J. (1966). Personality and experimental psychology. *Bulletin of the British Psychological Society, 19,* 1-28.

Eysenck, H.J., & Furneaux, W. (1945). Primary and secondary suggestibility: An experimental and statistical study. *Journal of Experimental Psychology, 35,* 485-503.

Eysenck, S.B.G. (1981). National differences in personality: Sicily and England. *Italian Journal of Psychology, 8,* 87-93.

Furneaux, W.D., & Gibson, H.B. (1961). The Maudsley personality Inventory as a predictor of susceptibility to hypnosis. *International Journal of Clinical and Experimental Hypnosis, 9,* 167-177.

Galbraith, G.C., London, P., Leibovitz, M.P., Cooper, L.M., & Hart, J.T. (1970). EEG and hypnotic susceptibility. *Journal of Comparative and Physiological Psychology, 72,* 125-131.

Galin, D., Johnstone, J., & Herron, J. (1978). Effects of task difficulty on EEG measures of cerebral engagement. *Neuropsychologia, 16,* 461-472.

Gazzaniga, M.S. (1970). *The bisected brain.* New York: Appleton-Century-Crofts.

Gheorghiu, V.A., & Reyher, J. (1982). The effect of different types of influence on an "indirect-direct" form of a scale of sensory suggestibility. *American Journal of Clinical Hypnosis, 24,* 191-199.

Gibson, H.B., & Corcoran, M.E. (1975). Personality and differential susceptibility to hypnosis: Further replication and sex differences. *British Journal of Psychology, 66,* 513-520.

Gibson, H.B., & Curran, J.D. (1974). Hypnotic susceptibility and personality: a replication study. *British Journal of Psychology, 65,* 283-291.

Gruzelier, J. (1986, July). *Left and right hemisphere dynamics in the induction of hypnosis.* Paper presented at the proceedings of the 3rd international conference of the International Organization of Psychophysiology, Vienna, Austria.

Gruzelier, J., Brow, T., Perry, A., Rhonder, J., & Thomas, M. (1984). Hypnotic susceptibility: A lateral predisposition and altered cerebral asymmetry under hypnosis. *International Journal of Psychophysiology, 2,* 131-139.

Gruzelier, J.H., & Brow, J.D. (1985). Psychophysiological evidence for a state theory of hypnosis and susceptibility. *Journal of Psychosomatic Research, 29,* 287-302.

Hilgard, E.R. (1969). Altered states of awareness. *Journal of Nervous and Mental Disease, 149,* 68-79.

Hilgard, E.R. (1973). A neodissociation interpretation of pain reduction in hypnosis. *Psychological Review, 80,* 396-411.

Hilgard, E.R. (1977). *Divided consciousness.* New York: Wiley.

Hilgard, E.R., & Bentler, P.M. (1963). Predicting hypnotizability from the Maudsley Personality Inventory. *British Journal of Psychology, 54,* 63-69.

Hilgard, E.R., & Hilgard, J.R. (1975). *Hypnosis in the relief of pain.* Los Altos, CA: William Kaufmann,Inc. *184,* 190-201.

Kamiya, J. (1969). Operant control of the EEG alpha rhythm and some of its reported effects on consciousness. In C. Tart (Ed.), *Altered states of consciousness.* New York: Wiley.

Karlin, A.R., Goldstein, L., Cohen, A., & Morgan, D. (1980). *Hypnotizability, attention, and hemispheric EEG activity during verbal and nonverbal tasks.* Unpublished manuscript.

Karlin, R., Weinapple, M., Rochford, J., & Goldstein, L. (1979). Quantitated EEG features of negative affective states: Report of some hypnotic studies. *Research Communications in Psychiatry and Behavior, 4,* 397-413.

Kasamatsu, A., & Hirai, T. (1966). An electroencephalographic study on the Zen meditation (Zazen). *Folia Psychiatrica et Neurologica Japonica, 20,* 315-336.

Kimura, D. (1973). The asymmetry of the human brain. *Scientific American, 228,* 70-78.

Kinsbourne, M., & Smith, W.L. (1974). *Hemispheric disconnection and cerebral function.* Springfield, IL: C. Thomas.

Lang, P.J., & Lazovik, A.D. (1962). Personality and hypnotic susceptibility. *Journal of Consulting Psychology, 26,* 317-322.

London, P., Cooper, L.M., & Engstrom, D.R. (1974). Increasing hypnotic susceptibility by brain wave feedback. *Journal of Abnormal Psychology, 83,* 554-560.

London, P., Hart., J.T., & Leibovitz, M.P. (1968). EEG alpha rythms and susceptibility to hypnosis. *Nature, 219,* 71-72.

Loring, D.W., & Sheer, D.E. (1984). Laterality of 40 Hz EEG and EMG during cognitive performance. *Psychophysiology, 21,* 34-38.

MacLeod-Morgan, C. (1979). Hypnotic susceptibility, EEG theta and alpha waves, and hemispheric specificity. In G.D. Burrows, D.R. Collinsos, & L. Dennerstein (Eds.), *Hypnosis 1979.* Amsterdam: Elsevier, North-Holland.

MacLeod-Morgan, C., & Lack, L. (1982). Hemispheric specificity: A physiological concomitant of hypnotizability. *Psychophysiology, 19,* 687-690.

Marenina, A.I. (1959). Further investigations on the dynamics of cerebral potentials in the various phases of hypnosis in man. In *The central nervous system and human behavior,* pp. 645-649. *(translated from Russian).* Bethesda, MD: US Department of Health, Education and Welfare.

Melzack, R., & Perry, C. (1975). Self-regulation of pain: The use of alpha-feedback and hypnotic training for the control of chronic pain. *Experimental Neurology, 46,* 452-469.

Mészáros, I., Bányai, E., & Greguss, A.C. (1986, July). *Enhanced right hemisphere activation during hypnosis: EEG and behavioral task performance evidence.* Paper presented at the proceedings of the 3rd international conference of the International Organization of Psychophysiology, Vienna, Austria.

Morgan, A.H., McDonald, P.J., & MacDonald, H. (1971). Differences in bilateral alpha activity as a function of experimental task with a note on lateral eye movements and hypnotizability. *Neuropsychologia, 9,* 459-469.

Morgan, A.H., MacDonald, H., & Hilgard, E.R. (1974). EEG alpha: Lateral asymmetry related to task and hypnotizability. *Psychophysiology, 11,* 275-282.

Nowlis, D.P., & Rhead, J.C. (1968). Relation of eyes-closed resting EEG alpha activity to hypnotic susceptibility. *Perceptual and Motor Skills, 27,* 1047-1050.

Orne, M.T. (1959). The nature of hypnosis: Artifact and essence. *Journal of Abnormal and Social Psychology, 58,* 277-299.

Orne, M.T., & Paskewitz, D.A. (1974). Aversive situational effects on alpha feedback training. *Science, 186,* 458-460.

Osborne, K., & Gale, A. (1976). Bilateral EEG differentiation of stimuli. *Biological Psychology, 4,* 185-196.

Paskewitz, D.A. (1977). EEG alpha activity and its relationship to altered states of consciousness. *Annals of the New York Academy of Science, 296,* 154-161.

Paskewitz, D.A., & Orne, M.T. (1973). Visual effects on alpha feedback training. *Science, 181,* 360-363.

Sabourin, M.E. (1982). Hypnosis and brain function: EEG correlates of state/trait differences. *Research Communications in Psychology, Psychiatry, and Behavior, 7,* 149-168.

Sabourin, M.E., Cutcomb, S.D., & Pribram, K.H. (1986, July). *EEG correlates of hypnotic susceptibility and hypnotic trance: spectral analysis.* Paper presented at the meeting of the International Organization of Psychophysiology, Vienna, Austria.

Sarbin, T.R., & Coe, W.C. (1972). *Hypnosis: A social psychological analysis of influence communication.* New York: Holt, Rinehart and Winston.

Sheer, D.E. (1970). Electrophysiological correlates in memory consolidation. In G. Ungar (Ed.), *Molecular mechanisms in memory and learning* (pp. 177-211). New York: Plenum.

Sheer, D.E. (1976). Focused arousal and 40 Hz EEG. In R.M. Knight & D.J. Bakker (Eds.), *The neuropsychology of learning disorders* (pp. 71-87). Baltimore: University Park.

Shor, R.E. (1959). Hypnosis and the concept of the generalized reality orientation. *American Journal of Psychotherapy, 13,* 582-602.

Shor, E.R., & Orne, E.C. (1962). *Harvard Group Scale of hypnotic susceptibility.* Palo Alto: Consulting Psychologists.

Spanos, N.P., & Barber, T.X. (1974). Toward a convergence in hypnosis research. *American Psychologist, 29,* 500-511.

Spanos, N.P., & Chaves, J.F. (1970). Hypnosis research: A methodological critique of experiments generated by two alternative paradigms. *American Journal of Clinical Hypnosis, 13,* 108-127.

Sperry, R.W. (1968). Hemispheric deconnection and unity in conscious awareness. *American Psychologist, 23,* 723-733.

Spielberger, C.D., Gorsuch, R., & Lushene, R. (1970). *The State-Trait Anxiety Inventory (STAI) test manual.* Palo Alto: Consulting Psychologists.

Spydell, J.D., Ford, M.R., & Sheer, D.E. (1979). Task dependent cerebral lateralization of the 40 Hz EEG rhythm. *Psychophysiology, 16,* 347-350.

Spydell, J.D., & Sheer, D.E. (1982). Effect of problem solving on right and left hemisphere 40 Hertz EEG activity. *Psychophysiology, 19,* 420-425.

Tart, C. (1969). *Altered states of consciousness: A book of readings.* New York: Wiley.

Tellegen, A., & Atkinson, G. (1974). Openness to absorbing and self-altering experiences ("absorption"), a trait related to hypnotic susceptibility. *Journal of Abnormal Psychology, 83,* 268-277.

Travis, T.A., Kondo, C.Y., & Knott, J.R. (1973). Interaction of hypnotic suggestion and alpha enhancement. *Journal of Psychiatry, 130,* 1389-1391.

Tucker, D.M., Stenslie, C., Roth, R., & Shearer, S. (1981). Right frontal lobe activation and right hemisphere performance decrement during a depressed mood. *Archives of General Psychiatry, 38,* 169-174.

Ulett, G.A., Akpinar, S., & Itil, T.M. (1972). Hypnosis: physiological and pharmacological reality. *American Journal of Psychiatry, 128,* 799-805.

Weitzenhoffer, A.M., & Hilgard, E.R. (1962). *Stanford Hypnotic Susceptibility Scale, Form C.* Palo Alto: Consulting Psychologists.

18. Perceptual Styles in Chromatic Binocular Rivalry, Hypnotic Susceptibility, and Cerebral Dominance

V. RUGGIERI, R. CAPOZZI and G. CLAVENZANI

Introduction

In the present research we hypothesize that (a) there is a relation between hypnotic susceptibility and styles of cerebral dominance; (b) hetero-induced modifications of the functional relation of the two hemispheres (i.e., of the cerebral dominance) can also modify hypnotic susceptibility.

In previous research we described the process of cerebral dominance by following both the categorial and the dimensional approach; in the last study the responses are placed along a continuum (Ruggieri, Cei, Ceridono, & Bergerone, 1980). For this last concept the central hypothesis is that there is a functional, mobile equilibrium between the two hemispheres. Kinsbourne (1978) has demonstrated that there is a central inhibitory balance between the two hemispheres and that the organism shows behavior resulting from their interaction. Following this concept we have documented that for the sighting dominance (Ruggieri, Celli, & Crescenzi, 1982) subjects may be placed along a continuum that goes from a maximum of right dominance to a maximum of left dominance. The extreme positions indicate a maximum of activity in one hemisphere with a high inhibition of the contralateral one. In the intermediate portion of the continuum there are subjects whose dominance is small or absent. So we were able to classify subjects in four groups of dominance: right, left, intermediate, and fluctuating. Subjects of this last group showed evident changes in their dominance behavior. They could be, for example, right dominant in a measure at one time and left dominant on its repetition (Ruggieri et al., 1980, 1982).

We think that the problem of dominance presents other interesting aspects. On the basis of previous research on self-contact gesturing and eye contact in different stimulus situations (Ruggieri et al., 1982), we hypothesized that the left hemisphere was more involved in processes characterized by a strong relationship between the subject and the environment, while the right was more active in the so-called intrasubjective processes (for example, in the self-modulation of emotional states). In this framework we can consider the hypnotic condition as the result of a particular form of the hemispheric balance. In fact, in this case the attention of the subject is predominantly directed to him/herself while the contact with the environment is often sensorially restricted to the relation with the hypnotizer. But it is also true that during hypnosis it is possible to have a strong activity of the left hemisphere as in the case of high verbal activity. So we do not hypothesize an inhibition of the left hemisphere and an enhancement of the right but a balance of the two that can be both at high or low levels of activity. The next step of our construct is that hypnotic susceptibility presents a style of cerebral dominance similar to the hypnotic state, hypothesizing that highly susceptible subjects should usually be characterized by a balanced interhemispheric activity. Our hypothesis of an equilibrium relatively independent of the level of activity can explain the contradictory results of the literature about this topic (London, Hart, & Leibovitz, 1968; Nowlis & Rhead, 1968; Bakan & Svorad, 1969; Engstrom,

London, & Art, 1970; Morgan, MacDonald, & Hilgard, 1974; MacLeod-Morgan, 1979; Travis, Kondo, & Knott, 1973; Edmonston & Grotevant, 1975; Evans, 1972).

In order to verify our hypothesis we have examined the relation between hypnotic susceptibility and (a) the sighting eye dominance behavior (Porac & Coren, 1976) measured by our method (Ruggieri et al.; 1980); (b) the chromatic binocular rivalry. In order to study this last phenomenon we made subjects wear a pair of glasses with two lenses of different colors (red and green). In this situation they could see red, green, and red and green together (in different areas of the perceptual field), a new color derived by their fusion, an alternation of the two. If the subject mainly saw one color, it means that one eye (and one hemisphere) was completely dominant in organizing the visual perceptual experience. In this case we considered this phenomenon as an aspect of the sighting eye dominance in which the subject makes a "choice" between the two eyes: the activity of one eye is accompanied by a relative inhibition of the other. In natural vision there is an alternation in the activity of the two eyes as indicated by the first results in chromatic binocular rivalry research (Ruggieri & Capozzi, 1987). Differences among subjects exist in frequency of appearance and in duration of the colors.

We can now use the study of chromatic binocular rivalry (a) as an important index of the style of cerebral sighting dominance that we will examine in relation to hypnotic susceptibility; (b) as a psychophysiological behavior that can be manipulated in order to improve a condition of hemispheric balance.

In fact, we have suggested that an enhancement of the perceptual experience of fusion, indicating simultaneous activity of the two hemispheres, obtained by specific visual training would also enhance the response to a hetero-induced suggestion of heaviness. The experiment was composed of five phases: (a) measurement of ocular dominance; (b) spontaneous perceptual behavior in chromatic binocular rivalry; (c) first phase of suggestion of heaviness; (d) hetero-induced chromatic perceptual behavior in binocular rivalry (learning phase); (e) second phase of suggestion of heaviness.

Method

Subjects

The experimental sample included 30 undergraduate students (21 females and nine males) between 18 and 35 years of age. All subjects had 20/20 (10/10) visual acuity.

Apparatus and Procedure

Measurement of Ocular Dominance

The subject looked into a black box (112 x 38 x 33 cm) while his/her head was fixed on a headrest. The subject was exposed to two luminous rods, one fixed at 112 cm and the other mobile and placed at 45 cm. The subject could move the mobile rod to either side of a horizontal plane. The degree of shifting was read on a scale in millimeters.

The subject was given the following instructions: "Please sit comfortably and keep your head on the headrest. Look inside the box; you will see two rods. One is fixed to the background and the other is mobile and nearer to you. You have to operate the handle to move the mobile rod; you must align it so that its image overlaps the other at the back. You have to do the task according to my instructions."

The following sequence was presented twice: binocular vision, right monocular, left monocular. In the second measurement, right and left monocular visions were inverted. The score for sighting eye dominance was the difference between the scores for the left and right eyes, which were the algebraic difference in millimeters between binocular and monocular alignments obtained for each eye separately.

Spontaneous Chromatic Binocular Rivalry

Each subject was comfortably seated in an armchair 2 m from a fixed point on the wall. S/he was required to look through a pair of glasses with differently colored filters on each lens (Kodak Wratten Gelatin filter Nos. 8 and 47, corresponding to green 534 nm and red 602 nm). The filters were fixed with brackets which permitted easy application.

Each subject was given these instructions: "At my 'Start' you can open your eyes, look at the point on the wall and tell me the color or the colors you are seeing. The exercise will last for 1 min. Tell me if there are modifications in what you see. At the end of the minute I will tell you to close your eyes and I will change the filters. Please keep your eyes closed then. I will say 'Start' again, and you will begin the exercise for the second time".

First Phase of Suggested Heaviness

We used the arm immobilization point from the Stanford Hypnotic Susceptibility Scale, Form A, using it as a single index of hypnotic response, and not as a substitution for the whole scale. This was preceded by these instructions: "Well, you can close your eyes and try to relax now. Take a deep breath and continue to relax ... and while you relax you continue to perceive a feeling of heaviness in your body. And while you continue to relax, your body is more and more heavy and you can enjoy ... this feeling of heaviness and relaxation ... and you will feel this in your whole body." Then we began the arm immobilization (Weitzenhoffer & Hilgard, 1959, p. 20), excluding the first sentence ("You are very relaxed"). The item presents suggestions of heaviness and of difficulty of movement so that the subject may find it very hard to lift her/his right arm. After the last instruction we ended the item by saying to the subject: "Now your hand can come back to its normal weight; as soon as that happens, you can take one or two easy breaths and open your eyes feeling perfectly awake." Two different measures were taken: the first was the standard scoring for the items of the Stanford Scale (objective heaviness), and the second was by asking the subject how s/he could define her/his feeling of heaviness using one of these five sentences: "My hand had its normal weight / My hand was a bit heavier than usual / ... was heavier than usual / ... was very heavy / ... was very, very heavy." These sentences received scores from 0 to 4 (from normal to very heavy).

Learning Phase: Hetero-Induced Perceptual Behavior in Binocular Rivalry

This test consisted of one exposure with the same colored filters for a total of 2 min, with the following insructions: "I will present a new experience in which I will tell you what color (green - red - fusion) you should try to see. As soon as you perceive the suggested color, please answer 'Yes.' If it changes before I tell you a new color, please say 'Change'." Every 10 s a different suggestion of color was given so that each color was proposed four times.

Second Phase of Suggested Heaviness

The modality of this phase was the same as the first phase of suggested heaviness.

Scoring

Ocular Dominance

This score was the difference between the scores for the left and the right eyes which were the algebraic differences in millimeters between binocular and monocular alignment obtained for each eye separately. The final score was the mean between the first and the second measurements. We can consider four groups:
- Right dominant (scores from 2.5 to 4)
- Left dominant (scores from -4 to -2.5)
- Neither eye dominant (scores from -1.5 to 1.5)
- Fluctuating dominant (subjects changing the score between the first and the second measurement)

Perceptive Style

We noted three modalities of chromatic conflict resolution: a visual field entirely occupied by only one color ("Red" or "Green"), by a fusion of the two colors ("Fusion"), or divided into two fields of different colors ("Both"). We also considered the latency time (the time required to give the first answer: after the "Start" in spontaneous vision and after the color was proposed in the learning phase) and the alternation of color vision in the Learning period (one for "Latency" and one for "Change", respectively). The analysis of the chromatic binocular rivalry was applied to: (a) spontaneous perceptual behavior; (b) learning phase. We considered the frequency and the duration in seconds for each of the following categories: red, green, fusion, both, latency, change.

Results

Mean values and standard deviations of the variables examined in the five phases of the experiment appear in Table 1. In the same table the number of the objective responders in the

Table 1. Means and standard deviations of the variables of each phase; number of objective responders for each of the two suggestion phases

	First phase		Second phase										Third phase	
	Ocular dominance		Spontaneous behavior										Intensity of subjective evaluation of heaviness	Responders (n)
			Frequency					Duration						
	First measurement	Second measurement	Latency[a]	Red	Green	Both	Fusion	Latency[a]	Red	Green	Both	Fusion		
Mean	0.70	0.23	1.80	4.40	5.09	3.33	0.80	7.36	19.46	26.93	54.06	12.13	2.00	13
SD	3.17	3.31	0.41	5.17	5.71	2.85	1.49	4.83	19.40	26.62	38.39	24.54	2.05	

	Fourth phase										Fifth phase	
	Hetero-induced behavior (learning phase)										Intensity of subjective evaluation of heaviness	Responders (n)
	Frequency					Duration						
	Latency[a]	Change[b]	Red	Green	Fusion	Latency[a]	Change[b]	Red	Green	Fusion		
Mean	11.66	1.90	2.09	3.00	2.73	72.33	4.83	10.63	17.29	14.86	1.93	10
SD	1.02	2.32	1.56	1.46	1.25	16.86	6.84	10.01	10.59	8.87	1.20	

[a] Interval of time between onset of the stimulus and response.
[b] Perceptual deviation from the suggested vision.

first and in the second phases of heaviness suggestion are also indicated. The number of objective responders did not increase in the second phase of suggested heaviness. Also the scores of the subjective intensity of the perception of heaviness are not different between the two phases (t = 0.16, df = 28, P > 0. 05), but the scores of the two phases are positively correlated (rho = 0.49, df = 28, P < 0. 05).

The perception of red and green diminished consistently in the hetero-directed phase. The difference is statistically significant for red (t = 2.70, P < 0.05), for green the difference is near the level of significance (t = 1.80, P < 0.07). Green is stronger than red in the spontaneous phase (t = 2.72, P < 0.01). On the other hand, the experience of fusion shows a small, nonsignificant increase (t = 0.59, P > 0.05).

Concerning the relationship between ocular dominance and hypnotic susceptibility, our results indicate the following:

- A strong tendency toward a negative correlation between subjective perception of heaviness of the first and the second suggestion phase and first measurement of sighting eye dominance (rho = -0.314 and -0.312, respectively, P < 0.06). The correlation with the second measurement of sighting dominance is not statistically significant.
- Perception of heaviness (first phase only) is significantly correlated with spontaneous duration of fusion (rho = 0.34, P < 0.05).
- Considering the whole group of responders to the second phase of suggestion we found that there is an elevated number of "nondominant subjects" (i.e., fluctuating and intermediate subjects). These subjects are poorly represented in the nonresponder group. The opposite holds for the right-dominant subjects, who are prevalent in the nonresponder group. Left-dominant subjects are equally distributed in both groups. The difference is close to the level of significance (χ^2 = 5.87, df = 2, P = 0.06). These differences did not appear in the whole group of responders to the first phase of suggestion, where the "styles of dominance" were equally distributed between the two groups.

We find the following with respect to the relationship between hypnotic susceptibility and modifications in the perceptual responses provoked during the learning phase:

- The objective responders to the second phase of suggestion have a higher frequency of red during the learning phase (Kruskall & Wallis test, H = 5.97, P < 0.05) and higher duration (Mann-Whitney test, z = -2.08, P < 0.03) than the other subjects.
- The objective responders to the second phase of suggestion also presented a tendency to a higher frequency of perceptual "changes" than the other subjects (Kruskall & Wallis test, H = 3.18, P < 0.07). They also presented a higher score of duration of "change" (Mann-Whitney test, z = 1.85, P < 0.06).

Discussion

The literature on the relationship between hypnotic susceptibility and cerebral dominance has evidenced that highly susceptible subjects presented an enhancement of the alpha rhythmic activity in the left hemisphere during verbal tasks and in the right hemisphere during nonverbal tasks (MacLeod-Morgan, 1979; MacLeod-Morgan & Lack, 1982). These results emphasize the tendency to an elevated lateralization strictly related to specific tasks. But they do not say enough about the style of cerebral dominance at rest, nor do they clarify the basic characteristics of the hypnotic process before the task. Regarding the last problem, Mészáros, Bányai, and Greguss (1986) observed an enhancement of the alpha activity indicating a right hemisphere engagement during hypnosis. Other authors have not found any alpha-hypnotizability relation (Evans, 1972; Travis et al., 1973; Edmonston & Grotevant, 1975) and no differences in EEG asymmetry between high and low hypnotizables (Morgan et al., 1974; De Pascalis, Silveri, & Palumbo, 1987). Crawford (1985) underlined another aspect of the phenomenon, i.e., the cognitive flexibility of the highly hypnotizable subjects.

Our hypothesis followed Gruzelier's model (Gruzelier, Brow, Perry, Rhonder, & Thomas, 1984; Gruzelier and Brow, 1985) suggesting that the hypnotic condition results from a dynamic relation between the two hemispheres. It should be characterized by a relative inhibition of the left hemisphere and an enhancement of activity of the right. In this direction we underline the balance between the two hemispheres taking place during hypnosis. It should be more evident in highly hypnotizable subjects. Our data seem partially to confirm this hypothesis. In fact we found that the aptitude to perceive suggested heaviness had a significant correlation with the spontaneous duration of perceptual fusion of different colors (red and green). As indicated in the introduction, the fusion resulted from the balanced interaction of the two eyes; we consider it as a direct expression of balance between the two hemispheres.

Another interesting result indicated that subjects who responded to the second phase of suggestion are, with respect to cerebral sighting dominance (Porac & Coren, 1976) mainly nondominant. This group is composed of intermediate (i.e., with low cerebral asymmetry) and of fluctuating subjects (i.e., with changing hemispheric dominance; for example, their left hemisphere is dominant in the first measurement and the right is dominant in the second). The presence of fluctuating subjects in the group of responders recalls Crawford's hypothesis of cognitive flexibility (Crawford, 1985), while the presence of intermediate subjects emphasizes our model of hemispheric balance.

We hypothesized that a hetero-induced experience of fusion would also enhance the tendency to respond to a suggestion of heaviness. Our data did not confirm this hypothesis, but we think that the suggested fusion experience was too short to give any kind of result. Further research will have to confirm our results.

References

Bakan, P., & Svorad, D. (1969). Resting EEG alpha and asymmety of reflective lateral eye movement. *Nature (London), 223*, 975-976.

Crawford, H.J. (1985). *Cognitive flexibility, dissociation and hypnosis*. Presidential address presented at the American Psychological Association, Division 30, Los Angeles, USA.

De Pascalis, V., Silveri, A., & Palumbo, G. (in press). EEG asymmetry during covert mental activity and its relation with hypnotizability. *International Journal of Clinical and Experimental Hypnosis*.

Edmonston, W.E., Jr., & Grotevant, W.R. (1975). Hypnosis and alpha density. *American Journal of Clinical Hypnosis, 17*, 221-232.

Engstrom, D.R., London, P., & Art, J.T. (1970). Hypnotic susceptibility increased by EEG alpha training. *Nature (London), 227*, 1261-1262.

Evans, F.Y. (1972). Hypnosis and sleep: techniques for exploring cognitive activity during sleep. In E. Fromm & R.E. Shor (Eds.), *Hypnosis: Research, developments and perspectives* (pp. 43-83). Chicago: Aldine Atherton.

Gruzelier, J., & Brow, T. (1985). Psychological evidence for a state theory of hypnosis and susceptibility. *Journal of Psychosomatic Research, 29*, 287-302.

Gruzelier, J., Brow, T., Perry, A., Rhonder, J., & Thomas, M. (1984). Hypnotic susceptibility: a lateral predisposition and altered cerebral asymmetry under hypnosis. *International Journal of Psychophysiology, 2*, 131-139.

Kinsbourne, M. (1979). *Asymmetrical function of the brain*. Cambridge, MA: Cambridge University.

London, P., Hart, J.T., & Leibovitz, M.P. (1968). EEG alpha rhythms and susceptibility to hypnosis. *Nature (London), 219*, 71-72.

MacLeod-Morgan, C. (1979). Hypnotic susceptibility, EEG theta and alpha waves, and hemispheric specificity. In G.D. Burrows, D.R. Collinsos, & L. Dennerstein (Eds.), *Hypnosis* (pp. 181-188). Amsterdam: Elsevier.

MacLeod-Morgan, C., & Lack, L. (1982). Hemispheric specificity a physiological concomitant of hypnotizability. *Psychophysiology, 19*, 687-690.

Mészáros, I., Bányai, E., & Greguss, A.C. (1986). *Enhanced right hemisphere activation during hypnosis: EEG and behavioural task performance evidence*. Paper presented at the proceedings of the 3rd international conference of the International Organization of Psychophysiology, Vienna, Austria.

Morgan, A.H., MacDonald, H., & Hilgard, E.R. (1974). EEG alpha: lateral asymmetry related to task and hypnotizability. *Psychophysiology, 11*, 275-282.

Nowlis, D.P., & Rhead, J.C. (1968). Relation of eye-closed resting EEG alpha activity to hypnotic susceptibility. *Perceptual and Motor Skills, 27*, 1047-1050.

Porac, C., & Coren, S. (1976). The dominant eye. *Psychological Bulletin (Washington), 83*, 880-897.

Ruggieri, V., & Capozzi, R. (1987). *Chromatic binocular rivalry*. Unpublished manuscript.

Ruggieri, V., Cei, A., Ceridono, D., & Bergerone, C. (1980). Dimensional approach to the study of sighting dominance. *Perceptual and Motor Skills, 51*, 247-251.

Ruggieri, V., Celli, C., & Crescenzi, A. (1982). Self-contact and gesturing in different stimulus situations: relationship with cerebral dominance. *Perceptual and Motor Skills, 54*, 1003-1010.

Travis, T.A., Kondo, C.Y., & Knott, Y.R. (1973). Interaction of hypnotic suggestion and alpha enhancement. *Journal of Psychiatry, 130*, 1389-1391.

Weitzenhoffer, A.M., & Hilgard, E.R. (1959). *Stanford hypnotic susceptibility scale, form A*. Palo Alto: Consulting Psychologists.

19. Psychophysiological and Psychobiological Aspects of Suggestive Processes: A Commentary

W.E. EDMONSTON, JR.

The papers presented in this section all deal, rather directly, with the activity of the central nervous system. In many respects, the presentations appear to be a continuation of the search for a stable relationship between right hemisphere (RH) activity and either hypnotic susceptibility or hypnosis itself, but with a new perspective. From now on, we will not only explore left hemisphere (LH) and RH relationships, but anterior-posterior relationships as well; e.g., what cognitive changes as may occur in hypnosis may be more posteriorly located than we previously thought.

However, before I discuss two methodological considerations, let me comment on a general problem. Lundy has suggested that those individuals studying suggestibility have a great deal to offer other fields of investigation. Pharmacology was one field he mentioned, in that, few pharmacologists give more than passing consideration to the influence of simple - or complicated - suggestion on their studies of drug effectiveness. Certainly, alerting the pharmacologists to the possible influence of suggestion on their work would benefit both areas of study.

Lundy also suggested that "suggestologists" have an *obligation* to make their findings known to pharmacologists. I would like to suggest that we who work in hypnosis/suggestibility have an obligation to work more closely with neuroanatomists and neurophysiologists, so that their studies - as well as ours - can be better related to experiences of the human organism, so that the study of functional neuroanatomy has its focus in real life experiences.

It has been pointed out that people we label as highly susceptible to hypnosis show a slower central degradation of sensory impressions in stereographic studies. They demonstrate enhanced cerebral blood flow during hypnosis, implying an increase in cerebral metabolism. Further, data seem to show that the activity localizes in the right parietal-occipital region, rather than the anterior (frontal) regions. Ruggieri's work, highlighting the perceptual differences between the two eyes - right perceives figure, left perceives background - suggests a central distortion mechanism occurring in response to suggestion. After all, the images of the two eyes project to both superior colliculi, both lateral geniculates, and to both occipital lobes. These and other elements of Ruggieri's data present a major puzzle for the neuroanatomist, as do the data on the right and left hemispheres.

If, now, we were to go to a neuroanatomist with these findings and request some clarification, some functional explanation of what we have found, he or she would be at a loss, and could at best speculate that since the parietal areas seem associated with sensory input, auditory association, and linguistic abilities, there must be a functional connection between the words of the hypnotist, the suggester, and the condition of the cortex. But it would be that - speculation - for the detailed knowledge of functional relationships between electroencephalographic recordings, the experience of the individual, and the condition of the central nervous system are just not available in any detail. All the more reason to follow Lundy's suggestion and inform our colleagues in other disciplines of our puzzling findings in the hope that together we can better understand experience at all levels, be it a central distortion of sensory input or an alternate reality.

Now let me return to one of two methodological issues highlighted by the papers in this session. One of the major problems plaguing most of this work - and the efforts of Mészáros and Crawford, Marucci, and De Pascalis are no exception - is the reliance upon various ratios of hemispheric activity in evaluation; and worse yet is the problem of interpreting the relationship between hypnosis and cerebral dominance. Most of the results purport to find a relationship between RH activation and hypnosis, and thus we often read or hear that hypnosis is a RH phenomenon. But is it? Changes in the ratios used to arrive at that conclusion can be obtained by RH activation, by LH deactivation, or by some combination thereof. It is difficult to interpret ratio changes without knowing which elements are changing in which direction. "It is not possible to tell if a ratio has been modified by changing the numerator, the demoninator, or both when only the ratio figure [itself] is presented" (Donchin et al., 1977, p. 345). We will not know the correctness of interpretations based on ratios until comparison studies of the baseline range of variability in the two hemispheres are forthcoming.

A prime example of this dilemma is the study of a single subject by Chen, Dworkin, and Bloomquist (1981), which found that after an initial decrease in total cortical energy power output of both hemispheres with hypnotic induction, the LH continued to decrease as much as 80 % of baseline, while the RH stabilized. The authors concluded that since the RH "remained more active during hypnosis," hypnosis is a RH function. But, consider this idea for a moment. Suppose that the LH normally has a wider range of baseline output available to it than the RH, and that when the latter (the RH) reaches the floor of its range, the former (the LH) continues to deactivate. The investigator, then, is left with the impression that the RH has maintained a higher level of activation during hypnosis. While such an interpretation may be correct in absolute terms, baseline floor and ceiling effects must be taken into account when making an interpretation regarding function.

Gruzelier et al. (1984) found results similar to Chen et al., but their interpretation was slightly different. What they found was a slowing down of haptic processing in the right hand following hypnosis in highly susceptibility subjects. In addition, they found lateral asymmetries in baseline conditions in favor of the LH in their highly susceptible subjects. They concluded that: "left hemisphere dynamic processes were fundamental to the induction of hypnosis," in that, "susceptibility is associated both with a left bias prior to hypnosis and left hemisphere inhibition under hypnosis." In their view, that latter finding "permits the ascendancy of the right hemisphere through the attenuation of left hemisphere control. Thus inhibition of left hemisphere processes appears a prerequisite of successful hypnotic induction" (Gruzelier et al., 1984, p. 138).

Now, how does one interpret such data? Do we conclude that hypnosis is a RH process, because the RH is less inhibited than the left? Or do we conclude that hypnosis is a LH process, but an inhibitory rather than an excitatory one? Ratios of such data would clearly project a more active RH, but the manner by which such a ratio conclusion is reached is equally important. Might not such data argue for a difference between the two hemispheres in potential breadth of variability? Such baseline differences, as well as the LH bias of highly susceptible subjects, must and can be taken into account as we interpret our data on cerebral activity and hypnosis (See Edmonston & Moscovitz, to be published). Remember, our bodies pay little attention to the arbitrary divisions into "isolated" systems or left-right dichotomies we impose in our desperate attempts to simplify an enormously complicated functioning totality. The central nervous system is a compensatory system such that changes in one area are not ignored, but incorporated into a new alignment so that total performance continues albeit playing a slightly different concert.

Now for a few specific remarks. Spiegel's work on evoked responses and hallucinatory suggestion during hypnosis tells us that there is a greater suppression (inhibition) of the P_{300} component in the RH to a suggested visual image. His data certainly seem to substantiate William James's contention (1892/1984) that a central, rather than peripheral, distortion accounts for the effectiveness of suggestion. Or, put in Spiegel's words: "hypnotizable subjects are performing a different kind of mental work." I must say, though, that it would have been interesting to have had a control group that shifted its focus point between the intended stimuli and a pin-point located in front of the color stimuli. Then we might feel more comfortable that the phenomenon obtained was due to central rather than peripheral changes in the nervous system.

In fact, since Spiegel used color stimuli - blue and pink - we might speculate on what sort of results might have been obtained if we combined his earlier study with Ruggieri's earlier work. Did, for example, the eye dominance of the subjects affect Spiegel's results? Ruggieri's data seem to show that there is asymmetry in chromatic perception, which is different for eye dominance and for different wavelengths, as well as different depending upon whether the subjects are to make judgments based on brightness or saturation. Asymmetry for brightness is higher in the lower wavelengths - blue, for example. It may be that Spiegel's choice of chromatic stimulus enhanced perceptual asymmetry and might have affected the direction of his results with respect to RH and LH. At any rate, some combination of these two pieces of research might clarify even further our understanding of central mechanisms involved in hypnosis and suggestion.

Finally, it is encouraging to see someone working in EEG frequencies other than alpha and theta. Marucci, DePascalis, and Mészáros and Crawford have shown us that the beta range, too, has secrets to yield in our search for understanding. It is particularly refreshing to see cerebral dominance and left-right activity couched in terms of the beta range. Most studies of cerebral dominance speak of LH and RH activation, when they are really describing the absence of alpha rhythms. Measuring activity by assessing the actual activity range of the EEG is a welcome approach.

In their chapter, Marucci et al. use not only the beta range, but covariance data analysis as well. Baseline measures affect data interpretation and ratio evaluations do not necessarily lead to clear-cut interpretations (see above). One simple and relatively painless way of controlling for their influence is by statistical control. Marucci et al. are to be congratulated for being among the few investigators to recognize this simple expedient for removing EMG artifacts from EEG data. I do, however, have one methodological concern which could affect data interpretation. Ordinarily, tachistoscopic stimuli should be presented for no longer than 200 ms (preferably about 125 ms) to avoid the confounding of eye movement. These authors used a 250-ms exposure and, without some control for the subjects' moving their eyes and thus projecting the stimuli images on other than the right or left retinal field, the meaning of the obtained results may be different from that presented.

DePascalis's paper confirms a point made by Eysenck earlier in this volume, namely, that stable introverts and neurotic extraverts are the more suggestible of individuals. It is important to note that the physiological evaluation of suggestibility was done without the benefit of hypnotic induction, making the physiological concomitants of suggestibility, rather than those accompanying traditional hypnosis, the focus of his paper.

This observation leads me to a second methodological problem which I will note only briefly. Most of the papers collected in this volume deal with relationships between certain measures and "hypnotizability." "Hypnotizability" has, in every case, been determined by scores on the various hypnosis susceptibility scales such as the Stanford and the Harvard. I would like to suggest, however, that we have not, in reality, been discussing hypnotizability, but rather the focus of this volume - suggestibility. I would suggest that the authors of all of these papers substitute the word "suggestibility" for the word "hypnotizability" in their manuscripts, for that is what the scales may be measuring, rather than responsiveness to classically, historically defined hypnosis. Prof. Gheorghiu, in a stroke of decisive insight, included in the conference on which this volume is based colleagues investigating what they thought was hypnosis, when in reality they were researching the conference's central theme - suggestion and suggestibility.

References

Chen, A.C.N., Dworkin, S.F., & Bloomquist, D.S. (1981). Cortical power spectrum analysis of hypnotic pain in surgery. *International Journal of Neuroscience, 13*, 127-136.

Donchin, E., Kutas, M., & McCarthy, G. (1977). Electrocortical indices of hemisphere utilization. In S. Harnad et al. (Eds.), *Lateralization in the nervous system* (pp. 339-384). New York: Academic.

Edmonston, W.E., Jr., & Moscovitz, H. (to be published). Hypnosis and lateralized brain function. *International Journal of Clinical and Experimental Hypnosis.*

Gruzelier, J., Brow, T., Perry, A., Rhonder, J., & Thomas, M. (1984). Hypnotic susceptibility: A lateral predisposition and altered cerebral asymmetry under hypnosis. *International Journal of Psychophysiology, 2*, 131-139.

James, W. (1892/1984). *Psychology: Briefer course.* Cambridge, MA: Harvard University.

IV

Social and Cognitive Aspects of Suggestive Processes

20. Some Historical and Cultural Aspects of Suggestion

G. JAHODA

Introduction

There was a period, commencing in the 1880s, when hypnotism and suggestion enjoyed an enormous vogue. From the clinical field it spread to the social sciences, and the essentially social character of hypnotism and suggestibility was stressed by Gabriel Tarde (1884/1912): "Hypnotism is the experimental juncture of psychology and sociology; it shows us the most simplified sort of psychic life which can be conceived of under the form of the most elementary social relation."

The notion of "suggestion" became an all-purpose intellectual tool for explaining almost any social phenomenon - crime, religion, politics, war, and so on (Ellenberger, 1970). It was also believed to have considerable practical applications. For instance, one of Piaget's predecessors in Geneva advised his student teachers that children should be taught auto-suggestion in school; for this purpose he proposed that a Chevreul pendulum be transformed into a toy such as a bird pecking for a crumb (Baudouin, 1921). The single most important application, however, was concerned with crowd or mob behavior. His observations of riots during the Commune led LeBon to write in 1895 what Gordon Allport (1968) regarded as possibly the most influential book ever in social psychology, *La Psychologie des Foules*. Given the social upheavals in France at the time, it is not surprising that the nature of mobs should have fascinated contemporary thinkers. In 1882, Guy de Maupassant was moved to comment, rather unkindly, that a handful of strange and half-crazy psychologists were almost the only people who had penetrated the mystery of crowds (cited in Barrows, 1981).

During the first half of the present century interest in such topics waned, so that in the mid-1930s McDougall (1936, p. 2) complained that "Suggestion is a process which can be wholly ignored by psychologists so long as they are not concerned with social life". In fact, the most prevalent current formulations of the concept are of little help to social psychologists. If one looks at the definitions of "suggestion" provided in dictionaries of psychology, they remain essentially the same as that put forward by Freud in 1888: "... what distinguishes suggestion from other kinds of psychic influence, such as a command or the giving of a piece of information or instruction, is that in the case of a suggestion an idea is aroused in another person's brain which is not examined in regard to its origin but is accepted just as though it had arisen spontaneously in that brain." (Freud, 1888/1966, p.2).

The still prominent emphasis on the suspension of critical thought during suggestion appears to me a necessary but quite insufficient characterization. It is perhaps one end of a continuum which extends to altered states of consciousness accompanied by powerful emotional manifestations. LeBon (1881) was right when he proposed a gradient from simple suggestion to what he called "artificial somnambulism" induced, he believed, by charismatic leaders. On this last issue I believe that the formulation is unduly restrictive and that the influence of such leaders is merely a special case in a wider set of phenomena.

In order to explain what I meant here, I shall use a rather simple example. There has recently been a considerable amount of research on the role of suggestion in identification parades, or "lineups" as they are called in America. This followed a Supreme Court case cited in Malpass & Devine, 1984, p. 74) in which it was claimed that "the influence of improper suggestion upon identifying witnesses probably accounts for more miscarriages of justice than any other single factor". Research shows that suggestion takes two quite distinct forms. In one, which could be called a mild version of the "leadership" type, police provide cues for the witnesses leading them to pick a particular person. The other is a consequence of the fact that witnesses believe that the police have good reasons to be confident that the criminal is included in the parade, and it has been shown that in the absence of such an assumption their pattern of choice is rather different. Now what I want to emphasize is that in this second case the suggestion comes not directly from any person or persons, but is a function of a socially induced belief. Therefore, I should propose that what is called "suggestion" may also arise from the activation of relevant social belief systems in particular situations. In practice, these two elements are usually, though not invariably, confounded.

In addition to these purely social aspects, some other well-known factors that raise the level of susceptibility and alter the modes of psychological functioning should be mentioned briefly, because they are often either contrived or already established. They include rhythmical music, drugs, fatigue, hypoglycaemia, sleep deprivation, or some combination of these.

The remainder of this paper will be devoted to examples of contexts of various types for behavior that has in the past been attributed to "suggestion", "contagion", or "mass hysteria". The field is a wide one, and I have decided to confine my examples mainly to religious or quasi-religious settings where such phenomena can often be observed in more florid forms.

Cargo Cults and Other "Revitalization" Movements

The reason for beginning with an account of such phenomena, widespread in place and time, is their resemblance in certain important respects to the conditions of social upheaval prevalent when LeBon was writing. They also have something in common with the rise of modern dictatorships that promised a new earth and a new heaven and fomented fanatical enthusiasm in such suggestion-prone groups as were present at the Nuremberg rallies.

Historians have described "millenarian" movements in the Middle Ages and during the Reformation in Europe, and in mid-19th Century China. The first anthropological study was that of the *Ghost Dance* among Native Americans during the latter part of the 19th Century. propagated by a prophet, the Ghost Dance movement proclaimed that the Indian dead would return and bring back the old way of life, shattered by the whites, while the whites and their culture would themselves by destroyed. To bring this about, various rituals had to be performed, especially dances in the course of which people went into trance states during which they had the experience of speaking with dead relatives.

Since then, there have been numerous studies of such reactions to enforced culture change, oppression and poverty, among the most spectacular being the cargo cults of Melanesia. The name arises from the belief that a ship or, after World War II sometimes aircraft laden with European goods would arrive. The "Vailala madness" which arose in Papua around 1919 is an early example (Williams, 1934). Large numbers of people in the villages were affected by an epidemic of some kind of giddiness, reeling around without proper muscular control. The condition was reported to be accompanied by peculiar sensations in the stomach, and some of the leaders of the movement in such a state burst into unintelligible utterances said to be "Djaman" (German), though at other times their message was clear. Their main teaching was the prophecy of the coming of a steamship with the spirits of the dead ancestors on board. They would bring with them lots of trading goods to be distributed to the villages. The ancestors (who by a curious quirk were sometimes conceived as white) would restore all trade to its rightful managers, the Papuans, and get rid of the whites. It is also interesting to note that a decade later (i.e., a generation before the actual decolonization took place) it had turned into a living legend, with people believing that the vessel had actually called!

Trance and Possession

This is a very complex field, as both trance and possession are distinct and yet may be combined; or again, only the shaman or medium may fall into some altered state of consciousness, or most or all participants of a gathering may be affected.

Consider, first, Balinese trance as described by Geertz (1975, p. 36):

> The Balinese fall into extreme dissociated states in which they perform all sorts of spectacular activities - biting off the heads of living chickens, stabbing themselves with daggers, throwing themselves wildly about, speaking with tongues, performing miraculous feats of equilibration, mimicking sexual intercourse, eating feces, and so on, rather more easily and much more suddenly than most of us fall asleep. Trance states are a crucial part of every ceremony. In some, 50 or 60 people may fall, one after another ... emerging anywhere from 5 minutes to several hours later, totally unaware of what they have been doing and convinced, despite the amnesia, that they have had the most extraordinary and deeply satisfying experience a man can have.

This sequential pattern of falling - like a string of firecrackers going off, as one observer put it - indicative of contagion or suggestion as you prefer, is one that I have myself witnessed frequently, and I can also confirm the exhilaration following such an experience.

The notion of "possession" is an ancient one also in the Judeo-Christian tradition, and in the New Testament Jesus is said to have driven out devils. It is reflected today in such films as *The Exorcist.* Possession is not necessarily by evil spirits or devils - it can also be by the Holy Spirit. In the United States, the Pentecostal sects believe in such manifestations through speaking in tongues, snake-handling, dancing, rolling about the floor, screaming or similar emotional outbursts from which they evidently gain a great deal of satisfaction.

Possession trances are found in many parts of the world, and analyses of cases in Africa and Haiti in particular have led to the proposal that they tend to occur in rather rigidly stratified communities where possession by a figure of high status provides some outlets for dissatisfaction with ordinary everyday life. It might be noted that the Pentecostals have been drawn from mainly the poor and relatively uneducated in America.

Possession of an important kind is that in which a shaman, priest or medium becomes possessed by a god or spirit. In these cases, the possession is more controlled, commonly be prior training, and probably not infrequently faked. In any event, apparent possession lends special authority to the utterances of such an authority figure.

From this standpoint, an interesting marginal case is the *sar* cult of Somaliland and Ethiopia studies by Lewis (1986). The *sar* is a malevolent spirit whose victim is usually a married woman. Any ailment, physical or psychological, can be and often is interpreted as evidence of possession by a *sar* who makes demands for luxurious clothes, fine foods, perfume and so on. It is only after these demands have been met, and an expensive dance directed by a female shaman has been performed, that the *sar* can be expected to depart. In the cases collected by Lewis, the woman in question could almost invariably be shown to have had some grudge against her husband, perhaps because of his preparations to take a second wife. The nice question arises then concerning to what extent the women are just pretending in order to retaliate. Husbands almost invariably seem to take the view that their wives are malingering, but their general belief in *sar* remains strong and they are usually not prepared to take the risk of resisting the demands. It remains an open question how much is perhaps auto-suggestion on the part of the wives, or merely deliberate social influence!

Witchcraft

In 1692 in Salem a small group of young girls, following an attempt at fortune-telling that went wrong, began to exhibit bizarre symptoms not unlike those of the Vailala madness, which spread rapidly to other girls and young women. Pressed by senior adults in the community to identify their tormentors, they duly named three women as witches, one of whom confessed readily.

In parts of Africa witch-finders come into a village, parade the people and pick out the witches, who almost invariably confess to such things as extracting the internal organs of their victims to make medicine. it should be explained that witchcraft is often regarded as involuntary, a kind of affliction itself, whose removal is considered a benefit even by its practitioners. There follows a highly dramatic cleansing ritual in which I have seen, for instance, the supposed extraction from the witch's belly of the reptile causing the trouble. These previously afflicted persons are thereafter reintegrated into the community.

Underlying all this is an extremely widespread and intense belief that most if not all affliction and trouble come from witchcraft and sorcery (the line between them is not always clear). Of a sample of 280 West African university students, only 39 declared their absolute disbelief in witchcraft, while 98 stated that it certainly, and another 116 that it probably exists (Jahoda, 1970). In another inquiry conducted with some 500 literate and semi-literate adults in a variety of small towns and villages, the people were asked to describe any experience with witchcraft, sorcery or similar phenomena they themselves or a close relative or friend had experienced.

Roughly one third of them reported direct experience, another third occurrences within the extended family, and the remaining third included many who were vague or evasive about such experiences rather than clearly negative. These reports thus suggest very strong social support for such beliefs. One of the more common experiences described was that of seeing so-called witchcraft lights (curiously reminiscent of later UFO stories), with such sighting being followed usually by illness or other misfortune. The way to find out *who* was responsible is by consulting a diviner, another intriguing procedure that would take too long to describe here. Let me just say that the diviner, while seemingly giving information, usually subtly elicits information from the petitioner and brings suspicions out into the open. This pattern has also been noted by Thomas (1970) in English cases of witchcraft.

Physiological Effects

Under this heading phenomena of three types will be briefly described. Each is a function of deeply held beliefs, but only one can be viewed as the direct result of suggestion.

First, some African university students, usually among the most able and successful, develop symptoms such as headaches, extreme fatigue, and inability to concentrate. This is sufficiently common to have been given the label of "brain fag". It is associated with the belief that some people back home, envious of their success, have bewitched them.

Secondly, various florid symptoms are apt to occur in people guilty of either a transgression or the omission of an important ritual. I shall summarize one example among many cases studied by Field (1960), a medically qualified anthropologist. An illiterate farmer who was also an official at a shrine attended a funeral of someone "killed" by the god of the shrine, though such attendance is forbidden to servants of the shrine. He came home to his mother and told her that he had seen the ghost of the dead man, then fell down and lay stiff and mute for an hour. Then he became wildly agitated, though still mute, and was prevented only by several men from rushing into the bush. They carried him to the priest of the shrine who told him that his offence would be pardoned, whereupon he immediately returned to normality.

An example of the third type is known, in its extreme form as *voodoo death* (Cannon, 1942) or "death by suggestion" (Holt, 1969), though the case I observed was fortunately not fatal. On collecting my research assistant one morning, I found him exhibiting the symptoms of acute malaria, with which I was all too familiar. After I had insisted against his protests on taking him to a hospital, the physician there agreed with my diagnosis but, to our surprise, tests showed the absence of parasites in his blood. It turned out that after a quarrel he had been cursed and threatened with sorcery. Recourse to a traditional healer restored his health.

Conclusion

This presentation has concentrated on some rather esoteric and spectacular phenomena that used to be regarded as prime examples of the effects of "suggestion". Contemporary psychologists have not displayed much concern with such issues, which have been of interest to mainly historians and anthropologists. When these scholars discuss and seek to explain such behavioral patterns, they view them essentially as *social* events. On the occasions when they refer to the mental processes of the actors, they do so in terms of "common sense" psychology. Modestly they tend to leave more searching psychological interpretation to professional psychologists, although, as one of them said: "our initial advantages in perceiving a cultural and social system alien to us in space or time give us advantages in calling such data to the attention of psychologists." (Beidelman, 1970, p. 354).

One is led to ask whether psychological competence in general, and the concept of "suggestion" in particular, help us to understand and explain such phenomena better than other social scientists or historians? Regarding the first part of the question, it could be claimed that research on altered states of consciousness, including hypnotism and trance, may well provide in due course greater insights into the underlying processes. How far such insights would help our colleagues in neighboring disciplines to an enhanced understanding is debatable; it could be argued that the social context, too often ignored by psychologists, is of primary importance.

I am particularly sceptical about the ready and uncritical use of the label of "suggestion" as supposed explanation of a wide variety of phenomena of the type reviewed. It seems to me that the cognitive and affective factors involved are often emotionally charged systems of belief coupled either with negative elements such as fear, anxiety or discontent (nowadays often connected with rapid social change) or with the desire for positive gratification along established channels. These are probably more helpful in accounting for most of the behaviors described than is the notion of "suggestion" that is usually little more than a verbal label. There is no evidence that 17th century English or Americans or contemporary Africans or Papuans were or are more "suggestible" than modern Westerners. I am not even persuaded that an hypothesized general trait of "suggestibility" is of much value for understanding the phenomena discussed. An illustration based on my experience as an amateur conjurer will perhaps help indicate the reasons for this view. The background is, briefly, as follows: it involved a small group of African students in Africa, where I worked at the time. All these students had expressed their firm belief in the "magical powers" (their expression) of fetish priests. I declared that I could match some of their "supernatural" feats, and, as a fairly competent amateur conjurer, did so. Their response was one of surprise and admiration, which turned to dismay when I subsequently showed them how some of the tricks were done.

In Scotland even children tend to pester me with requests to be told how "the trick" is done; by contrast, these highly intelligent African students were content to accept what they witnessed as manifestations of "magic". It seems to me that it would be absurd to attribute this to differences in "suggestibility"; rather it is a function of culturally acquired conceptions of the world. European children soon learn scepticism with regard to the apparent violation of physical laws. Africans grow up in an atmosphere wherein belief in magic forms part of a coherent cosmology and, as such, apparent magic is not unduly surprising. Thus, it would probably make more sense to evaluate "suggestibility" of this kind not as a cause but rather as a domain-specific effect.

In conclusion, I venture to propose that within the field surveyed the notion of "suggestion" relevant to only a strictly limited set of phenomena. When used more broadly, the notion becomes little more than a pseudo-explanation and a substitute for careful analytical thought about the social and psychological processes involved.

References

Allport, G.W. (1968). The historical background of modern social psychology. In G. Lindzey & E. Aronson (Eds.), *The handbook of social psychology* (Vol. 1). Reading, MA: Addison-Wesley.

Barrows, S. (1981). *Distorting mirrors.* New Haven: Yale University. (Article by Guy de Maupassant in *Le Gaulois,* March 23, 1882).

Baudouin, C. (1921). *Suggestion et autosuggestion.* Neuchatel: Delachaux et Niestle.

Beidelman, T.O. (1970). Towards more open theoretical interpretations. In M. Douglas (Ed.), *Witchcraft confessions and accusations* (pp. 351-356). London: Tavistock.

Cannon, W.W. (1942). Voodoo death. *American Anthropologist, 44,* 169-181.

Ellenberger, H.F. (1970). *The discovery of the unconscious.* New York: Basic.

Field, M.J. (1960). *The search for security* (p. 247). London: Faber.

Freud, S. (1888/1966). Preface to the translation of Hippolyte Bernheim's *Suggestion* (Vol. 1). London. (Original edition published 1888).

Geertz, C. (1975). *The interpretation of cultures.* London: Hutchinson.

Holt, W.C. (1969). Death by suggestion. *Canadian Psychiatric Association Journal, 14,* 81-82.

Jahoda, G. (1970). Supernatural beliefs and cognitive structures among Ghanaian university students. *Journal of Cross-Cultural Psychology, 1,* 115-130.

LeBon, G. (1881). *L'Homme et les Sociétés* (Vol. 1, p. 396). Paris.

LeBon, G. (1895). *La psychologie des foules.* Paris: F. Olean.

Lewis, I.M. (1986). Religion in context, cults and charisma. Cambridge: Cambridge University.

Malpass, R.S., & Devine, P.G. (1984). Research on suggestion in lineups and photospreads. In G.L. Wells & E.F. Loftus (Eds.), *Eyewitness Testimony: Psychological perspectives.* Cambridge: Cambridge University.

McDougall, W. (1936). *Psychoanalysis and social psychology.* London: Methuen.

Tarde, G. (1884/1912). *Penal philosophy* (p. 192). Boston: Little, Brown. (English translation). [Originally from an article entitled Qu'est-ce qu'une société? *Revue Philosophique* (1884), *18,* 489-510].

Thomas, K. (1970). The relevance of social anthropology to the historical study of English witchcraft. In M. Douglas (Ed.), *Witchcraft confessions and accusations* (pp. 47-79). London: Tavistock.

Williams, F.E. (1934). The Vailala madness in retrospect. In E.E. Evans-Pritchard, R. Firth, B. Malinowski, & I. Schapera (Eds.), *Essays presented to C.G. Seligman.* London: Kegan Paul.

Suggested Reading

Boyer, P., & Nissenbaum, S. (1974). *Salem possessed.* Cambridge, Mass.: Harvard University.

Graumann, C.F., & Moscovici, S. (1986). *Changing conceptions of crowd mind and behaviour.* New York Berlin Heidelberg Tokyo: Springer.

Nye, R.A. (1975). *The origins of crowd psychology.* London: Sage.

21. Suggestion as Social Biasing of Meaning Tests: A Heiderian Extension of the Miller, Galanter, and Pribram Paradigm – Catalyzing McGuire's Theory of Attitude Change

E. SCHWANENBERG

Terminology and Phenomenology

Looking at the history of psychology, one may notice a definite parallel in the currents and countercurrents of scientific interest devoted, on the one hand, to the phenomena of emotion, and on the other, to those of suggestion. Both interests reached a climax at the beginning of the discipline; and both fell into disrepute because they were considered speculative and not amenable to methodologically sound and truly objective, operationally oriented scientific research. The name and fate, the rise and fall, of McDougall (1910, 1923) highlights that mainstream development of the discipline. Presently, however, emotion is having a strong comeback as a research topic in the field, with more and more journals and editorial boards being responsive to papers in this area. The present volume, which would have been unthinkable not so long ago, might testify that suggestion, too, is returning to the scientific scene. That coincidence is no happenstance: the early notion of suggestion had a strong connotative, if not denotative semantic link to the notion of emotional contagion (Gefühlsansteckung). As will be shown below, both phenomenologically and according to present theorizing, there is a decisively emotional component involved in the process of suggestion that can be seen on close analysis.

Returning to the historical antecedents of the present state of scientific affairs, we note that the general area of social influence (or social inducement) has never been eclipsed as a research topic. That area is, in fact, the center field of social psychology. When Asch (1951, 1956) objected to suggestion as a scientific explanation of social events because the term "suggestion" was considered to offer too descriptive and speculative an account of social behavior, he turned to the experimental study of conformity. Lewin's (1951) field theory and the action research connected with it were equally settled within the processes of social influence. The main involvement, however, of social psychological research addressing the phenomena of social influence was centered on attitude change; and the central notion in that regard was - and continues to be - not suggestion, but persuasion. Since the variables conducive to persuasion have been investigated rather extensively, and some of the brightest experts in social psychology have proceeded to bring theoretical order to the empirical relationships obtained (McGuire, 1968, 1972), the process model on persuasion which has resulted from this "systems" theorizing is (comparatively seen) a rock-bed foil on and against which conceptions of suggestion can be brought into profile (see following section of this paper).

McGuire himself legitimizes such perspective taking on and scrutinizing of this "theoretical housing" (McGuire, 1968, p. 127) - erected by him as an epistemic measure against the previous "confused state of affairs" in research on attitude change and integrating the "vast literature on the topic" that up to then consisted "largely of reports of isolated experiments" (p. 177) - when he summarizes:

> Attitude change, in its broader usage, refers to the general area of social influence processes, that is, how a person's feelings, beliefs, or behaviors are influenced by stimuli received from other people. This broad use includes a variety of social influence situations, such as suggestion and hypnosis, conformity, group discussion, mass media communication, and total institutions. (McGuire, 1972, p. 108)
>
> Hence, the theory applies to ... hypnotic or waking suggestibility [as in Hull's (1933) body sway inductions]; and to conformity to authority or group consensus [as in the Sherif (1935) or Asch (1956) conformity situations]; and to mass media persuasibility [as in Hovland's (1954) communication situations]. (McGuire, 1968, p. 175)

McGuire's own main application of his systems theory, however, is more narrowly focused on classical experimental research on "'attitude change' in the narrower sense of social influence exerted through verbal communication, usually in the form of written or spoken messages arguing for a point of view on some issue" (McGuire, 1972, p. 108). A paradigmatic study (by one of his students, Millman, 1965) which he reports "involved presenting 48 college students with a tape recorded discussion of a scholarly nature which argued that the population of China would soon reach a high figure (in excess of what most college students would spontaneously estimate without having been exposed to a persuasive recording)" (McGuire, 1968, p. 189). This is a rather typical example of the body of social influence processes that is addressed in standard attitude change research in general and by McGuire's theorizing in particular. This type of research was brought into prominence by Hovland at Yale and its theoretical undercurrents are still detectable in McGuire's systems theorizing. It is because of this origin that he calls his own information-processing theory of social influencing a "learning theory" approach (McGuire, 1968, p. 179).

Nevertheless, McGuire does address suggestion, too, though he mentions it rather in passing when he refers to a social influence situation *differing* from a persuasion situation:

> The typical suggestion situation entails a very repetitive message such as a three minute recital to the effect that "you are falling back, back ..." which seems so clearcut that any normal college sophomore presumably can grasp the gist of it. (McGuire, 1968, p. 185)

As opposed to the informational simplicity of suggestion in the clinical settings, the laboratory and field persuasion situations investigated in experimental attitude change psychology "involve argumentative messages of greater subtlety" (McGuire, 1968, p. 185). What McGuire is referring to here is a distinction between two basic types of "mediators" or mediating mechanisms. His information-processing theory of social influencing or social inducement, though, is conceived as "a six-step Markov chain" (McGuire, 1968, p. 179). It may, however, also be viewed as a two-process theory. There is the "receptivity" mediator (or process) comprised of the two (Markov chain) steps - attention and comprehension; and there is the "yielding" mediator (or process). According to McGuire, the (combined) receptivity is the prominent mediator in persuasion - in the sense of producing intra- and interpersonal variance - whereas the yielding mediator operates, for the main part, in suggestion:

> In suggestion situations the personality variable's relationship to the yielding mediator carries most of the weight in establishing its relationship to attitude change. (McGuire, 1968, p. 185)

That is, both types of mediators (or processes) are involved in both kinds of situations, persuasion as well as suggestion, but the relative weight or impact of the mediators is different for the two of them.

This provides us with a very important theoretical framework which brings both persuasion and suggestion phenomena into a common perspective of social influence processes. This will be taken up later in the present paper and elaborated upon; but, for the moment, we need to stress the fact that we know much more about persuasion in the social psychological laboratory and field settings than we do about suggestion. Interestingly, when promulgating his information-processing or learning theory approach emphasizing the receptivity mediator, McGuire (1968, p. 181) notes "that in most conventional thinking about personality-influencibility relationships, there is an overemphasis on the mediational role of yielding."

If that is so, the layman or -woman is evidently emphasizing suggestion, or at least focusing on that aspect of the persuasion phenomenon which comes close to it. In this case, one should ask the lay psychologist what he or she sees as suggestive about suggestion - or about the suggestion part in persuasion. If the author feels free to be a lay psychologist and asks himself this question - that is, if he draws upon a social phenomenological perspective - he would, as Heider (1958, pp. 12-13) did, turn to La Fontaine's fable of the fox and the crow:

> A fox once saw a crow fly off with a piece of cheese in its beak and settle on a branch of a tree. "That's for me, as I am a Fox," said Master Renard, and walked up to the foot of the tree. "Good-day, Mistress Crow," he cried. "How well you are looking today; how glossy your feathers; how bright your eye. I feel sure your voice must surpass that of other birds, just as your figure does; let me hear but one song from you that I may greet you as the Queen of Birds." The Crow lifted up her head and began to caw her best, but the moment she opened her mouth the piece of cheese fell to the ground, only to be snapped up by Master Fox. "That will do," said he. "That was all I wanted. In exchange for your cheese I will give you a piece of advice for the future - do not trust flatterers."

The knack of the story and the mediating mechanism which does the trick of dispossessing the crow of the cheese and enabling the fox to get hold of it is the fox's blatant success of suggesting to the crow that she really is, and can easily demonstrate that she is, the queen of birds. The fox does not argue with the crow in a way that might change her attitude about giving him the cheese, or even about opening her mouth. The fox's persuasion works by suggestion! And that is what gives the story its point.

Heider himself does not go into the analysis of persuasion versus suggestion; neither does he analyze "such concepts as flattery, trust, and showing off" (Heider, 1958, p. 13). If we try to collect what else a layman or laywoman would connect with suggestion, we come upon the notion of rationality versus irrationality. The fox acts in an extremely rational manner: in Heider's analysis, the fox cognitively elaborates and anticipatorily marshals a rather long causal sequence of events. At the end of it, both in theory and in practice, success (as intended) occurs and the fox possesses the cheese:

> The fox believes that flattery, which he *can cause*, will *cause* the bird to trust him and to *want* to show off, which in turn will *cause* the bird to *want* to sing. This will *cause* the crow to open his beak, which will *cause* the cheese to belong no longer to the crow. The fox *can* then *cause* the cheese to *belong* to him. (Heider, 1958, p. 13, Heider's italics)

The behavior of the crow, on the other hand, will probably be judged by the average person as rather stupid or irrational. This brings the notion of suggestion into rather close correspondence with the notion of abnormal behavior. Switching for the moment briefly from lay psychology to the science of social psychology, we may recall in pertinent fashion that in the aforementioned early beginnings of the study of suggestion this was indeed the conception which the French school of psychology (and psychiatry) harbored. This conception included further constitutive elements: crowd behavior was looked at as irrational and equated with abnormal behavior (remember Morton Prince's Journal of Abnormal and Social Psychology!), and females' and children's behavior (as compared with that of adult males) as well.

Apart from the ideological biases evident in this historical conception, there is one kernel of truth contained in it - pointing to a common denominator in those purportedly "irrational" phenomena. All exhibit an *emotional* or feeling component. The fox succeeds with his suggestion by imparting to the crow the (feeling of) pride of being the queen of birds. Also, we recall that McGuire in reporting on traditional persuasion research and applying the learning theory perspective to it,talks about "social influence exerted through verbal communication" (see above). This has in general implied rather argumentative and in that sense rational ways of social influence focusing on the receptivity mediator. By implication and in contrast, suggestion should make use more heavily of the nonverbal or paralinguistic channel. La Fontaine reports only on the fox's speech, but to get a full picture of why the fox succeeded with suggestion one would have to imagine the flattery contained in his voice and behavior as well. Nonverbal behavior may well have been the decisive factor in making the crow feel like the queen of birds. The same should be true of the so-called contagion effect in crowds, though for obvious reasons there are not very many hard experimental data to underline the point. The "milling" (Brown, 1965) which can be observed in crowds certainly disseminates (verbal) rumor but one should not overlook the decisive part played in information transfer by the expressive behaviors of the participants as can be easily induced from observations of revival meetings, aggressive mobs, and panics. In all these cases, what operates on attitudes is not so much persuasion but suggestion. In McGuire's terminology, the receptivity mediator carries far less weight than the yielding mediator does. If there is a cry "Fire!" the message is rather simple and easily comprehended; the impact on the yielding mediator, however, is enormous and instantaneous, even if there exists an attitude of not yielding to crowds.

This brings us to another distinctive aspect of suggestion versus persuasion. Though it may take a short time or a long time both to persuade and to apply suggestion, persuasion when it aims at attitude change and works *via* comprehension of arguments convinces by way of the newly discovered relatedness of events and the consequences that exist between one event and the other - the unit relations in the Heiderian sense. In that sense, persuasion, when it does lead to yielding, is as a result tied more into the cognitive structure of one's life space and is more trait-bound and less state-bound than suggestion, which may be a result of an inducement of a situational sentiment, a feeling, or even of an emotional contagion.

Nevertheless, the consequences of suggestion may not be fleeting, but may have longitudinal consequences in one's life space. A participant of a revival meeting may turn, for example, into an ardent believer and change his or her whole life style. There are also other biographical consequences which the person would have never been persuaded to accept by argument but in which he or she found himself/herself enmeshed as a result of an emotional situation operating heavily on the yielding mediator. There is the person who participated in an aggressive mob and got himself into jail. There is Othello who succumbed to Iago's suggestion that his wife Desdemona had committed adultery, making him fly into a (feeling of) rage with disastrous consequences. There is the notorious case of seduction. Having personally not done any empirical research in this area but having observed *post hoc* quite a few ensuing biographies, the reading of their message is that even in a postmodern society the consequences of seduction can be very substantial. Consider the case of Patty Hearst which would not have received such extended news coverage if her case had not been, biographically speaking, so amazing. Finally, consider the case of a nation, major parts of which succumbed to propaganda. In the Nazi era of German history, propaganda operated as persuasion with a heavy share of suggestion.

One may conclude from this list that suggestion, more so than persuasion, is something beyond the ordinary, and therefore, in keeping with information theory, elicits more attention from lay observers. There may also be a second reason why the layman or laywoman puts, in McGuire's terms (see above), "an overemphasis on the mediational role of yielding." The following section postulates that for the final attitude change - or for behavior in general (which it leads up to) - yielding is the step that counts most in the chain of information-processing leading up to attitude change. Therefore, in a functional perspective of social cognition, the yielding step is also more informative for a social observer, more so than the process of comprehension which is a step that is merely subsidiary to it.

Miller, Galanter, and Pribram Extended: Two Kinds of Tests Instead of One

The conceptual model or, in McGuire's terms, "theoretical housing" (McGuire, 1968, p. 172) which is below brought to bear upon the issues developed above from attitude change research and lay psychology is depicted in Figure 1. Because of present constraints of space we cannot go into the model's conceptual derivation and development which grew out of a theoretical critique of Schachter and Singer's (1962) notorious experiment (see Schwanenberg, 1981), the theorizing of Miller, Galanter, and Pribram (1960), and an extended purview of general notions in the field of psychology (see also Schwanenberg, 1984a). The model amounts to combining Miller, Galanter, and Pribram's basic cybernetic TOTE schema with the social phenomenology of Heider's (1958) to furnish one "theoretical housing" for both general and social (Schwanenberg, 1978) psychological phenomena. This marriage of viewpoints does not amount to an arbitrarily enforced conjugal bed in an inappropriate housing structure but rather to conviviality: Miller, Galanter, and Pribram's "subjective behaviorism" - looking at the plans and structure of behavior as they are made to fit the subjectively perceived environment - is quite congenial with Heider's lay epistemology.

The progeny of this conjunction is characterized by two distinctive features:

1. The organism or person is equipped with two different types of tests (discussed in this section).
2. Dyadic interpersonal relations as discussed by Heider in phenomenological terms can be modeled cybernetically by coupling two of the behavioral systems individually modeled in Figure 1 (discussed in the next section).

Heider (1958, p. 15) tells us what the person perceives and experiences as his or her subjective environment or life space:

> The most important characteristics of events that affect us are, first whether or not they are positive, pleasant, and satisfying, and second their causal sources. (Heider, 1958, p. 16)

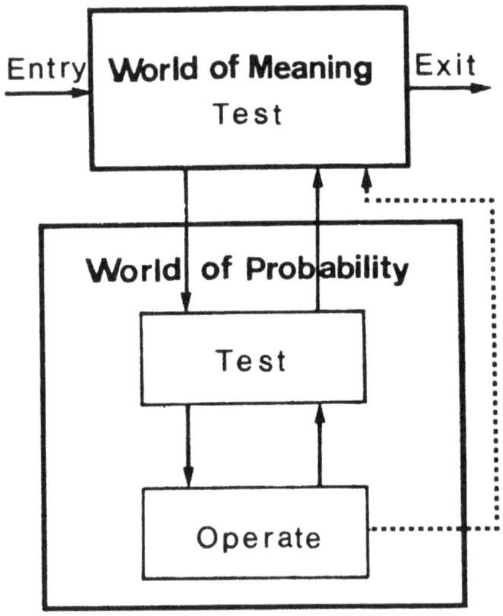

Figure 1. Cybernetic TOTE model comprising two different but interacting kinds of tests

In terms of the present connubial model - and in keeping with the subjective perspective of experiencing, perceiving, cognizing, or testing of the environment by the organism or person as evinced both in Heider's and in Miller, Galanter, and Pribram's theorizing - this amounts to checking upon two facets of the environment, or two conceptual worlds contained within the one phenomenal world: the world of meaning and the world of probability. Miller, Galanter, and Pribram's behavioral environment is only a probability world; Heider adds, so to speak, a meaning world. The world of meaning corresponds to Heider's notion of sentiment relations; the world of probability to Heider's unit relations. The meaning test is a feeling test and checks the environment as it relates to the needs, preferences, norms, values, ideals of the organism or person, extending from the sociobiological to the sociocultural domain. The probability test checks the causal, or more generally, relational structure of the environment, the constraints as well as the possibilities engendered by space and time and the laws of nature. The probability test is operative in instrumental behavior, the meaning test in consummatory behavior. The probability test is set for detecting the nonredundant events in the environment; the meaning test is set to secure redundancy, being equivalent to the mechanism of homeostasis. The test of probability is involved in McGuire's learning-theory mechanism or mediator labeled attention and comprehension (or receptivity) which decodes the relational structure of arguments; the meaning test is the one which is decisive for yielding (and specifically for the operation of suggestion).

Two additional features of the model are salient when considered in relation to McGuire's general theory of social influence processes. First, the meaning test is superordinate to the probability test, a conception which has independently also been developed and promulgated by Zajonc (1980) as the primacy of affect. [For a discussion of the controversy between Lazarus (1982, 1984) and Zajonc (1984), see Schwanenberg (1984a).] The primacy of affect (or feeling or sentiment) is also evident in Heider's (1958, pp. 121-123) thinking about and graphically

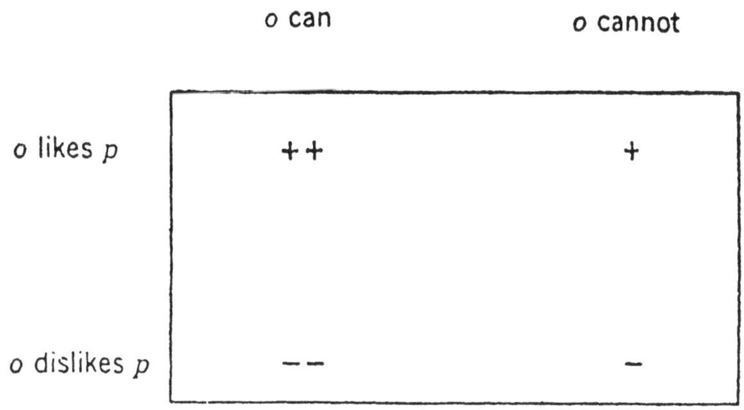

Figure 2. Different weight of the *can/cannot* and *like/dislike* dimensions when coping with the *can* and *want* of hostile others. "The square presents a field in which the vertical dimension means degrees of liking ranging from '*o* likes *p*' (the other person likes *p*) to '*o* dislikes *p*'; the horizontal dimension at the same time indicates the degrees of the power of *o* to cause benefit or harm ranging from '*o* can' to '*o* cannot.' The positive and negative signs within the square refer to the degree to which the situation conforms to *p*'s wishes" (Heider, 1958, p. 122)

representing of the "coping with the *can* and *want* of hostile others" (Figure 2). As can be taken from Heider's table the vertical or like/dislike dimension corresponding to the meaning test carries more weight than the horizontal or can/cannot dimension (corresponding to the probability test).

Secondly, there is a two-way connection or reciprocal interaction between the two mechanisms. These two features address the critique which McGuire (1972) himself has proposed regarding the hypothesized Markov-chain nature of social inducement processes. If the meaning test is primary, there may be an omission of earlier (i.e., comprehension) steps. We are also in a less awkward conceptual position when referring to potential or actual reversals in the order of steps: when theoretically conceiving of the phenomenon of selective attention we need not formulate "that yielding, in a sense, precedes attention" (McGuire, 1972, p. 133); we need only state that a biasing of the meaning test precedes the probability test. Similarly, the empirical paradox that proximal (i.e., comprehension) and distal (i.e., attitude change) dependent variables need not be correlated may be less of a theoretical stumbling block when viewed within this perspective: the way the interaction works between the two kinds of tests depends on (empirically yet to be determined) variables operative in the situation.

Equally, McGuire may be completely right when he presumes as a possible explanation for the lack of correlation between the dependent measures of the different mediators

> ... that our comprehension tests frequently do not measure the right thing. That is to say, it may be inappropriate to test the information-processing model by measuring the comprehension step in terms of recall of any testable material within the message. We have to ask more carefully not just how much is comprehended, but *what* is comprehended. For example, in the work on fear appeals, the comprehension test often measures how well the person remembers the threatening content and not just how well he remembers the urged

new attitude and behavior, although it is only the latter that the paradigm would say is related to attitude change. Perhaps if more care were taken in teasing out the pertinent aspects of the message for the comprehension test (rather than just measuring comprehension for such contents of the message as are easy to measure), the apparent paradox would at least partially dissolve. (McGuire, 1972, p.134, author's italics)

This amounts to saying that the information on which the meaning tests operate is of a different kind, and therefore needs other dependent measures, than the probability or structural relations tests.

McGuire (1968, pp. 182-184) makes another very pertinent theoretical proposal which should be taken into consideration when conceiving of the interaction of the two types of tests: based on attitude research data and on "considerations of efficiency" of organismic functioning he postulates that the interplay of the two mediators (or tests, as we may now call them) amounts to "a dynamic equilibrium situation," such that a person-environment constellation

... which has a positive relationship to reception, tends to be negatively related to yielding, and vice versa. ... It can be shown that when such a compensatory, dynamic equilibrium situation obtains as regards the mediators, the overall relationship will tend to be of (the) inverted-U shape under a wide range of parametric conditions.

Thus, McGüire's general thinking applies to a general cybernetic model of person-environment interactions by which social influence processes may be conceived to make inroads from one person to the other, operating on two differently functioning information tests. At the same time the cybernetic model integrates what McGuire (1972, p. 111) himself did not bring into the open (from his own theorizing). This integration encompasses on the one hand the notion of the two mediators' "receptivity" (or attention and comprehension) and "yielding"; and on the other, McGuire's use of the concept of "attitudes" in the broader sense as being constituted of both an evaluative (meaning test) and a belief (probability test) dimension.

Suggestion as Social Biasing of Meaning Tests

The tripartite cybernetic model depicted in Figure 1 conceptually and functionally orders the three constituents of attitudes, as classically enumerated in attitude change research:

Attitude change, in its broader usage, refers to the general area of social influence processes, that is, how a person's feeling, beliefs, or behaviors are influenced by stimuli received from other people. (McGuire, 1972, p. 108)

The model also allows us to go beyond the vacuous notion of "stimuli" by taking a closer and a more organized look of what those social influence processes are basically like as interpersonal processes. As Heider (1958, p. 1) delineates the subject matter of his lay psychology of interpersonal relations:

... the term "interpersonal relations" denotes relations between a few, usually two, people. How one person thinks and feels about another person, how he perceives him and what he does to him, what he expects him to do or think, how he reacts to the actions of the other -

> these are some of the phenomena that will be treated. ... the fact that the interrelation is with another person and not an object means that the psychological world of the other person as seen by the subject must enter into the analysis. Generally, a person reacts to what he thinks the other person is perceiving, feeling, and thinking, in addition to what the other person may be doing. In other words, the presumed events inside the other person's skin usually enter as essential features of the relation.

In terms of the present model, a person not only reacts (and proacts, to use Murray's, 1951, term) to the manifest behavioral operations of the other person, but also reacts to the latent probability and meaning tests behind them. This should be so since the outcomes of those tests determine what the other person is about to do. In fact, that is why there is some use in studying attitude change as a proximal dependent variable as against confining research endeavors to behavioral change as the more distal dependent variable. (The terms "proximal" and "distal" are, in this context of attitude research, McGuire's, 1972.) The lay person, too, observes the other person's operative behavior in order to intuitively or rationally infer the latent sources of the behavioral variance - the sentiments (meaning tests) and beliefs (probability tests) that engender manifest behaviors.

Applying this general theoretical perspective to the social phenomenon of suggestion, we note the following. First, there is intentional and unintentional behavior. Heider (1958, p. 245) himself, though not going specifically into the exploration of suggestion, uses prestige suggestion and behavioral contagion as examples of *unintentional* social influence. His main explorative interest, however, is in *intentional* social influence processes:

> We are concerned only with what Lippitt et al. (1952) call a direct influence attempt, which they define as "A social interaction in which one child consciously and deliberately tries to get another child to do something, in such a way that the research observer is aware of the intent."

Secondly, person *p*'s intent directed toward the other person *o* may be of two sorts as discussed by Heider (1958, p. 16) under the basic attributional concept of *causing*:

> ... personal causation not only effects changes in the physical environment, as when a man winds his watch; it also has social implications. Thus, "benefiting" means that a person has caused a change that is agreeable or positive to another person. Also, one person can cause another person to cause a change by asking him to do something, or commanding him, etc.

In other words, *p* may be intent just to benefit (or harm) *o* which in present cybernetic terms means that the ending of the intention resides in the effect *p*'s action has on *o*'s meaning test(s). The ending of the intention may, on the other hand, lie farther out and be more distal in that *p*'s action is intended to operate on *o*'s meaning and belief tests such that they cause the receiver *o* to operate or behave in a certain way as intended by the sender *p*: "One person can induce another to do something by producing conditions of action in the other person" (Heider, 1958, p. 244). This equally applies to producing conditions of nonaction or inaction: to omission as well as commission.

We are now conceptually ready to tackle the phenomenon of *intentional suggestion*. Since intentional behavior is also the main focus of interest in Miller, Galanter, and Pribram's (1960) paradigm, we might first take a look at their theorizing to find out what they might possibly have to say about suggestion. They have indeed a chapter entitled *Relinquishing the Plan*. Although this chapter deals mainly with the clinical phenomenon of hypnosis, their opening paragraph alludes to suggestion: "The problem of persuasion (or, in other contexts, seduction) has long fascinated some of our greatest psychologists" (Miller, Galanter, & Pribram, 1960, p. 103).

The notion of seduction brings us back to La Fontaine's and Heider's fable of the fox and the crow. Most laypersons will very probably see in this story less of a persuasion - the fox does not argue with the crow, nor the crow with the fox - than a suggestion, for the reasons which have been given above. Seduction stories - which fascinate the onlooker or listener - are suggestive of suggestion. The fox who wants to cause the crow to disengage herself from the cheese is in an even more instrumentally demanding position than a sexual seducer like Casanova or Don Juan because he and the crow are in competition for a scarce resource: delicious food. A sexual seducer, on the other hand, can play on cooperation and collective rationality: sex is a more mutual affair. Nevertheless, even sexual exploits like Casanova's and Don Juan's have from time immemorial entertained not only the seducers but also (third) parties other than the actors involved. From the perspective of social science and Lewinian field theory, the reason for this fascination is that the seducer has to operate against and circumvent or undercut the barriers of social norms: he (or she) needs to topple a taboo. The technique which he (or she) applies to achieve his (or her) aim is, as I would deduce, suggestion. The fox makes the crow yield in that he induces in her a feeling of glamor and pride: he biases her meaning test and, most importantly, one involving the (crow's) self or identity. This test is not a peripheral aspect but a central, global, or even existential facet of the whole process. In both Heider's and McGuire's works, we find independently the same theoretical clue how this comes about. Heider (1958, pp. 245-246) enumerates five different modes by which *p* may intentionally exert influence on *o*'s behavior. Numbers 2-5 have to do with:

2. persuasion - "*p* shows *o* the consequences of *x*";
3. outcome control (in the sense of Thibaut & Kelley, 1969) - "*p* can ... create consequences for *o* by promising reward or punishment";
4. request - "a request refers to a positive sentiment, and is based on the fact that *o* tends to benefit a *p* whom he likes"; and
5. command - "in this case the force in *o* toward doing *x* is created through the power relation between *p* and *o*."

Number 1 - in keeping with the opening fable of the fox and the crow - is suggestion, though Heider himself does not give it a name. If the reader capitalizes on his everyday knowledge or literacy and thinks of *p* as the seducer (the fox or Casanova) and of *x* as the consummatory object or as *o*'s act as intentionally and instrumentally envisaged by the seducer (glamor - covering up delicious food - on the one hand, sex on the other) he or she may flesh out for himself or herself Heider's (1958, p. 245) barren conceptual language:

> It is possible that *p* changes a proper valence for *o*. Something that was unattractive to *o* suddenly seems attractive because of *p*'s action; *o* wants to do it, and he is induced to think that *x* is good for him. It is possible for *p* to produce this change in the proper valence for *o* if he can manipulate the different conditions for the establishment of a positive valence by praising *x*, by persuading *o* that *x* is good, or by demonstratively enjoying *x*. In the mind of *o*, *p* only shows what is good; he is not the source of the valence but only the cause of *o*'s realizing the valence. The real source of the valence is in the properties of *x*; it is intrinsically good, and *p* helped *o* to become aware of it.

McGuire (1972, p. 115) refers to the same phenomenon or process when he describes the perceptual theory approaches to attitude change:

> The basic concept underlying the perceptual approaches to attitude change is that adjustment involves not only the person changing himself to conform to the demands of the environment, but also changing his perception of environmental demands to conform to his own needs. The altered perception may involve denial and pathological distortion, but more typically takes the form of selective attention and reinterpretation that lies within the normal range.

The valences (Heider) or environmental demands (McGuire) are, of course, Lewin's *Aufforderungscharaktere*; in present terms they are what the meaning tests signalize or signify. The seducer, or more generally, the one who exerts suggestion on another person, changes the bias or the tuning of the perceptual or cognitive input mechanisms at a strategic level. That level is imbued with feeling and it corresponds to the core regions of the self.

Since this biasing might be viewed as an attack on *o*'s autonomy, why should suggestion not in principle be prevented by reactance? Heider, in the quotation above, gives the clue in that *p* in exerting influence *via* suggestion recedes in the perceptual background; though he (or she) is the source of the influence on *o*, he (or she) is not a figure in *o*'s perceptual field. Although Heider does not stress this point, the other four modes of social influence make *p* stand out more saliently in *o*'s perception of forces operating on him (or her) and therefore should be more conducive to reactance. We might deduce from this that the cleverest way of exerting social influence is to apply suggestion! This is in the fact the way which the fox chose since he would have never been successful at persuading, forcing, begging, or commanding the crow to give him the cheese. It is also the way which Nazi propaganda chose. Nazi control did use persuasion, force, and command, but for a more total (and totalitarian) grip on the population it also used suggestion by propaganda. When effective, propaganda works by biasing a core meaning test and inducing - by means of a thundering symbolism - a personal feeling of grandeur derived from collective grandeur.

My clinical colleagues might object at this point that in applying hypnosis they are not by and of themselves Nazis, foxes, or Don Juans. This is obviously correct. There is a social contract involved in clinical practice by which the patient hands over parts of his (or her) autonomy to the practitioner. The case of clinical practice, however, conveniently demonstrates another functional prerequisite for successful suggestion: no exerting of suggestion by *p* on *o* without trust on *o*'s side! Whereas persuasion in the typical case has to work against scepticism and scrutiny, suggestion, if successfully achieved, keeps the scrutinizing of the credibility of the sender and of the truth value of the message at bay. In the fable of the fox and the crow there is no hint whatsoever that the crow was sceptical about the fox's message.

There would be less fascination about the workings of suggestion if it always took place within the context of a basically sympathetic relationship where trust would not need to be an issue, as in friendship, happy marriage, and clinical practice. It should, however, be viewed with certainty that no reader of or listener to La Fontaine's fable of the fox and the crow will imply or infer a loving or merely sympathetic attitude of the crow toward the fox (and vice versa) - otherwise the fable would take on an altogether different point, making the story rather dull. Similarly, it would have been beyond human capacity for Don Juan not only to have sex with but also to feel love for 1003 women, or for the less mythical Casanova (with regard to whatever number of women he put on his personal list). The fascinating thing about suggestion is that the feeling or meaning tests of *o* may resonate with the operations of a *p* who may apply suggestion mischievously, as a Machiavellian.

This leads in the end to a conceptual examination of the social dimensions of the meaning space in which the meaning tests of *o* operate (Schwanenberg, 1984b). Classical persuasion research as summarized by McGuire (1972, pp. 111-113; 1985, pp. 262-268) has explored credibility, attractiveness, and power variables as the main constituents of the source's (or *p*'s) impact on the receiver (or *o*). In Bales' and Cohen's (1979) SYMLOG space these three variables correspond to:

1. The forward-backward dimension referring to the normatively and rationally controlled versus uncontrolled nature of a person's behavior
2. The positive-negative or liking-disliking dimension
3. The upward-downward or dominance-submission dimension

We may hypothesize that the forward-backward or credibility dimension as well as the positive-negative or attractiveness dimension stand out as main contributors to persuasion variance. However, the amazing feature of suggestion is that the upward-downward dimension can be very influential here in that neither *p*'s norm-orientation, reality-controlled rationality, or trustworthiness in the eyes of *o* nor *o*'s liking for *p* is necessary for *p*'s suggestion to operate on *o*. The fox succeeds by putting himself in a downward position (since being positioned at the foot of the tree he cannot subjugate the crow to his will) and by elevating the crow upward to glamor.

More tragic and less comical are those cases where *p* is by chance or fate or personal effort in an upward position vis-à-vis a downward *o*. McGuire (1972, p. 129) refers to this state of affairs when he hypothesizes about the effect of anxiety on attitude change or, in present terms, on biasing the meaning test:

> While anxiety would have a detrimental effect on the other steps [especially comprehension], it is likely to have a facilitating effect on the yielding mediator. Among the characteristic responses attached to anxiety though previous drive-reducing reinforcement is a tendency to be subservient, to reduce one's self-esteem, self-confidence, etc. By evoking these response tendencies, the higher fear arousal should make the individual more compliant and yielding. (McGuire, 1972, p. 129, parentheses added)

In Bales' and Cohen's (1979) SYMLOG terms, a *p* who is UNB or upward, negative, and backward elicits in *o* such an anxiety state, making *o* pliable to *p*'s suggestion. Such a process should be assumed to have taken place when the anarchist captors operated on and biased Patty Hearst's meaning test (see discussion above). In cases where *o*'s downward position in the interpersonal meaning space is not linked to anxiety but more saliently with a feeling of personal unworthiness, *p* may induce this biasing of *o*'s personal meaning test by being himself UN, or upward and negative,towards *o*. This amounts to an aggressive unsympathetic debasing of *o*'s status, and also results in lowered self-esteem which again is conducive to increased suggestibility.

Concluding Remarks

The present conceptual analysis of the phenomena of suggestion and suggestibility is not the most routinized procedure of producing "findings" in behavioral science. Data can more easily be checked than concepts by colleagues, reviewers, and journal editors, thus making the mass production of data hardware to be preferred to the production of theoretical software. But for scientific progress we need both:

> ... if the workers in a field do not occasionally take time to sit back and consider the meaning of the concepts they use, the work in that field will lack the direction and the depth that it might have. ... This discussion must not be construed to mean that experimentation could be dispensed with. Our point is rather that each definite advance in science requires a theoretical analysis and conceptual clarification of the problem. (Heider, 1958, pp. V & 4)

Data would not be of any epistemic use if it were not for a theoretical grasp of reality, and theory would be useless if it could not make contact with reality through data. Typically, however, the epistemic process is shortcut in that the data-driven laboratory researcher turns it into a mere pragmatic process: "Is there any use of that conceptual analysis to make me produce data that can make their way (more) successfully into print?"

This is an easy question, but it is not to be answered easily: "In general, it seems to us that the adequate testing of a systems theory requires a more than usually elaborate empirical effort" (McGuire, 1968, p. 195). This effort stands in the way of making data have contact with advanced theory, but this is a demanding problem not only for those advancing conceptual frameworks but also for those residing on data. The empirical proof of the conceptual pudding is in the eating but the one who does not eat will never know the pudding.

The research problem is exacerbated for the phenomena of suggestion and suggestibility in that there are not very many hard data to start with. When McGuire developed his information-processing paradigm as a systems theory for attitude change based on persuasion, his conceptual approach was broader than usual. Still, he could rely on the universe of data produced in the Hovland tradition although, in broadening his approach, he went beyond a mere agglomeration of those data. He calls

> ... attention to the general necessity of [creating and] using any paradigm in conjunction with one's creative imagination, mastery of the empirical findings in the field, and personal grasp of the realities, if the paradigm is to be exploited adequately. (McGuire, 1972, p. 137, parentheses added)

Since empirical findings are lacking, the present author had, in order to get suggestion into view, mainly to rely on creative imagination and personal (i.e., phenomenological) grasp of the realities. But he also relied on theory, notably McGuire's, Miller, Galanter, and Pribram's, and Heider's. Since "a scientific theory is a packed-down synopsis of obained relationships" (McGuire, 1968, p. 171) - obtained, that is, both phenomenologically (as in Heider's case) and data-wise (as in McGuire's case) - the present conceptualizing does claim to have contact with the structure of reality. An easier way to talk about suggestion would certainly be to claim that it does not exist at all. This is the way which Duffy (1941, 1962) chose when confronting the issue of emotion. There is, however, not only the rise and fall of McDougall, there is also the name and fate of Duffy.

Acknowledgement. Peter Sheehan, from the University of Queensland, helpfully and efficiently standardized the English in the manuscript.

References

Asch, S.E. (1951). Effects of group pressure upon the modification and distortion of judgments. In H. Guetzkow (Ed.), *Groups, leadership, and men* (pp. 177-190). Pittsburgh, PA: Carnegie.

Asch, S.E. (1956). Studies of independence and conformity: A minority of one against an unanimous majority. *Psychological Monographs, 70*, No. 9 (Whole No. 416).

Bales, R.F., & Cohen, S.P. (1979). *Symlog: A manual for the case study of groups*. New York: Macmillan.

Brown, R. (1965). *Social psychology*. New York: Free.

Duffy, E. (1941). An explanation of "emotional" phenomena without the use of the concept "emotion". *Journal of General Psychology, 25*, 283-293.

Duffy, E. (1962). *Activation and behavior*. New York: Wiley.

Heider, F. (1958). *The psychology of interpersonal relations*. New York: Wiley.

Hovland, C.I. (1954). Effects of the mass media of communication. In G. Lindzey (Ed.), *Handbook of social psychology* (Vol. 2, pp. 1062-1103). Reading, MA: Addison-Wesley.

Hull, C.L. (1933). *Hypnosis and suggestibility*. New York: Appleton.

Lazarus, R.S. (1982). Thoughts on the relations between emotion and cognition. *American Psychologist, 37*, 1019-1024.

Lazarus, R.S. (1984). On the primacy of cognition. *American Psychologist, 39*, 124-129.

Lewin, K. (1951). *Field theory in social science*. New York: Harper and Row.

Lippitt, R., Polansky, F., Redl, F., & Rosen, S. (1952). The dynamics of power. *Human Relations, 5*, 37-64.

McDougall, W. (1910). *Introduction to social psychology*. Boston: Luce.

McDougall, W. (1923). *Outline of psychology*. New York: Scribner.

McGuire, W.J. (1968). Personality and attitude change: An information-processing theory. In A.G. Greenwald, T.C. Brock, & T.M. Ostrom (Eds.), *Psychological foundations of attitudes* (pp. 171-196). New York: Academic.

McGuire, W.J. (1972). Attitude change: The information-processing paradigm. In C.G. McClintock (Ed.), *Experimental social psychology* (pp. 108-141). New York: Holt, Rinehart, and Winston.

McGuire, W.J. (1985). Attitudes and attitude change. In G. Lindzey & E. Aronson (Eds.), *Handbook of social psychology* (3rd ed., Vol. 2, pp. 233-346). New York: Random House.

Miller, G.A., Galanter, E., & Pribram, K.H. (1960). *Plans and the structure of behavior*. New York: Holt, Rinehart, and Winston.

Millman, S. (1965). *The relationship between anxiety, learning, and opinion change*. Unpublished doctoral dissertation, Columbia University, New York.

Murray, H.A. (1951). Toward a classification of interaction. In T. Parsons & E.A. Shils (Eds.), *Toward a general theory of action* (pp. 434-464). Cambridge, MA: Harvard University.

Schwanenberg, E. (1978, March). *Notes on affectivity, general and social*. Paper presented at the 4th general meeting of the European Association of Experimental Social Psychology, Weimar, East Germany.

Schwanenberg, E. (1981). Sozialer Affekt: Konstruktüberprüfung des Schachter-Paradigmas (Social affect: Examining the constructs of the Schachter paradigm). In W. Michaelis (Ed.), *Bericht über den 32. Kongress der Deutschen Gesellschaft für Psychologie in Zürich 1980* (Vol. 1, pp. 317-324). Göttingen: Hogrefe.

Schwanenberg, E. (1984a, May). *World of probability and world of meaning: Vista on affect or Miller, Galanter, and Pribram revisited*. Paper presented at the 4th general meeting of the European Association of Experimental Social Psychology, Tilburg, The Netherlands.

Schwanenberg, E. (1984b, July). *Looking at the meaning world in groups*. Paper presented at the 2nd European workshop "SYMLOG and Interaction in Groups", Konstanz, FRG.
Sherif, M. (1935). A study of some social factors in perception. *Archives of Psychology,* No. 187, 60.
Thibaut, J.W., & Kelley, H.H. (1969). *The social psychology of groups*. New York: Wiley.
Zajonc, R.B. (1980). Feeling and thinking: Preferences need no inferences. *American Psychologist, 35*, 151-175.
Zajonc, R.B. (1984). On the primacy of affect. *American Psychologist, 39*, 117-123.

22. Memory Modification and the Role of the Media

E. LOFTUS and M.R. BANAJI

Introduction

Several years ago, two Filipino nurses, Filipina Narciso and Leonora Perez, were convicted of poisoning nine patients, two of whom died, at the Veterans Administration Hospital in Ann Arbor, Michigan (Jones, 1977). There was little doubt that a muscle-paralyzing drug called Pavulon had been injected into the victims causing instant suffocation, but the Federal Bureau of Investigation had difficulty finding evidence that would link anyone to crime. Surviving victims and staff members were hypnotized to "refresh" their memories. Early on, one witness under hypnosis remembered two different nurses as being in his room, but well before his attack. After the Filipino nurses became suspects and their pictures were in the newspapers and on television, two witnesses became certain that they had seen Filipino nurses in or near the rooms of their loved ones near the time that their breathing stopped. Did the media coverage refresh the witnesses' memories, or did it change their memories? Although we cannot be sure what happened in this case, it is of some interest that the trial judge, sufficiently troubled by the jury's guilty verdict, ordered a new trial for the nurses, and the prosecution decided not to retry the case.

The case of the Filipino nurses presents the opportunity to question the extent to which the media can influence the recollections of witnesses to past events. Such a notion should not seem anomalous at all. For example, the idea that memory is subject to deliberate and systematic distortion occurred to Martin Cruz Smith, author of the novel *Gorky Park*. In his book Smith asked, "What good is a witness? Their memories are indistinct after a day. After three months, frankly, I could get them to recognize anyone I wanted to." Before we explore this issue and place it in perspective, note that we are primarily discussing episodic memory, which "receives and stores information about temporally dated episodes or events, and temporal-spatial relations among these events" (Tulving, 1972, p. 385). We will, however, also discuss semantic memory, which receives and stores knowledge of general, factual knowledge.

In this paper, we raise issues related to the general topic of media influences on memory, a topic we refer to as the media/memory relationship. Next we discuss some ways in which memory for past events can become distorted by new inputs and report an experiment designed to treat this hypothesis. Finally, we consider the media itself as a potential vehicle for memory distortion.

Media and Memory

The media can potentially affect human memory in a number of significant ways. It has been amply demonstrated that portrayals in the media can influence people's knowledge and attitudes about such topics as crime (Gerbner & Gross, 1976), the elderly, and the role of women in our society (Gerbner, Gross, Elery, & Jackson-Beeck, 1977; Gerbner, Gross, Morgan, & Signorielli, 1980). Can the media influence episodic memory?

Some research has shown that people have fairly poor memories for episodic information received via the media (Bekerian & Baddeley, 1980; Wagenaar, 1978). A few years ago when a new international agreement among European radio stations required the British Broadcasting Corporation (BBC) to reassign some of the British radio wavelengths, the BBC embarked on a saturation advertising campaign to familiarize its radio audience with the changes. For 2 months, radio listeners found their favorite programs repeatedly interrupted by detailed information on the new wavelengths. Slogans and jingles were used to stamp the information into memory, and many listeners heard the campaign over a thousand times. However, when researchers studies its impact (Bekerian & Baddeley, 1980), they found that listeners' memories for the details of the new wavelengths were "appalling" (Baddeley, 1982, p. 31). Although they were well aware that a change was imminent, and many knew the date of that change, most listeners were unable to recall the numerical wavelength, and were much less easily able to locate their station on a radio dial when asked to. This study illustrates that mere repetition of information does not ensure that it is well remembered. What is important is how that information is processed.

Even though we can find instances where something that is experienced a thousand times has little effect on memory, a converse fact is also true: an event that we experience only once can have a profound effect on memory. Based upon a body of research on memory distortion, it seems plausible that some information presented by the media - even though experienced only once - could still have an impact on people's memories for their own past experiences. In the next section, we briefly review this memory distortion research and examine some of its implications regarding the media/memory relationship.

Memory for Past Experience

Memory Malleability

One characteristic of episodic memory suggested by Tulving (1972, 1983) is its greater relative vulnerability. The extraordinary malleability of memory has been recently demonstrated in our laboratory (Loftus, 1979, 1983). consider a typical experiment in which college students were presented with a film of an automobile accident and immediately afterward asked a series of questions about the accident. Some of the questions were designed to present misleading information (e.g., to suggest the existence of an object that did not in fact exist). Half the subjects were asked, "How fast was the white sports Datsun going when it passed the barn while traveling along the country road?" In fact, no barn existed. The remaining subjects were asked, "How fast was the white sports Datsun going while traveling along the country road?" Later all subjects were asked if they had seen a barn. When questioned again about the accident 1 week later, more then 17 % of those exposed to the false information said they had seen a barn. Apparently when subjects were led to assume the existence of a barn during their initial questioning, many of them incorporated the nonexistent barn into their recollections of the event. Moreover, a subsequent experiment showed that simply asking people whether they had or had not seen a barn - a question to which they usually answered "no" - was enough to increase the likelihood that they would later instate a barn into their memories of the accident. We argued that the false information had become integrated into the subjects' recollections of the event, supplementing their original memories of that event.

Yet, new information can do more than simply supplement a memory: it can apparently alter or transform the memory. In another study (Loftus, Miller, & Burns, 1978), subjects saw a series of slides depicting successive stages of an accident involving an automobile and a pedestrian. A red car was traveling along a side street toward an intersection at which there was a stop sign for half the subjects and a yield sign for the remaining subjects. For all students, the remaining slides showed the car turning right and knocking down a pedestrian crossing the street.

Immediately after viewing the slides, the subjects answered a number of questions, one of which presupposed the existence of either a stop sign or a yield sign. When the critical question asked earlier had presupposed a traffic sign consistent with what the subjects had actually seen, they chose the correct sign 75 % of the time; when the earlier question presupposed an inconsistent traffic sign, however, subjects chose the correct slide only 41 % of the time. This experiment suggests that presuppositions are capable of transforming memory as well as merely supplementing it.

Memory can, in fact, be moulded by so subtle an instrument as a strong verb. In another study, subjects were shown films of automobile accidents and then were asked questions about events in the films. Subjects estimated a higher speed when asked how fast the cars were going when they *smashed* into each other than they did when the verb "smashed" was replaced with the verbs "collided," "bumped," "contacted," or "hit". When tested a week later, those subjects who had been given the verb "smashed" (rather than "hit") were more likely to answer they had seen broken glass in the film, even though broken glass was not present. By using the word "smashed," the experimenter supplied a rather extreme description, and thus the subjects had a memory representation of an accident that was more severe than it was in fact. As a result, subjects were more likely to "remember" that broken glass existed because broken glass is associated with a severe accident.

These experiments, along with many others using similar procedures, suggest the elasticity of memory. False information can *supplement* the previously acquired memory (as in the experiment with the barn), or *transform* it (as in the experiments with the stop sign/yield sign and the broken glass.

Boundary Conditions for Memory Malleability

The alteration of recollection appears to be a fact of life. It is of theoretical and practical interest to know under what conditions people accept or resist suggestive information, and which of those conditions encourage or minimize distortion in the recollection of information. A number of separate lines of research help to delimit the boundary conditions for the *recollection change phenomenon,* a term meaning that memory is conducive to recollection change as memory fades (see Hall, Loftus, & Tousignant, 1984). One line of research concerns the delay intervals between viewing an initial event encountering subsequent misinformation, and engaging in a final test of recollection. People are more influenced by misinformation when longer intervals of time occur after events. Another line of research concerns the presence or absence of warnings. When warned about the possibility of receiving misinformation, people are better able to resist it. Apparently the warning motivates people to scrutinize the misinformation, which leads to the greater likelihood of their detecting and then resisting the misinformation. These different research pursuits on memory distortion are linked by a shared principle known as *discrepancy detection*, the detection of a conflict between the original memory and post-event information occurring when the post-event information is processed. A change in memory of an event is more likely to occur if discrepancies between the original event and the post-event misinformation are not immediately detected.

If we are correct about the important role that discrepancy detection plays in the acceptance of post-event information, we might predict that subjects who, on their own accord, read the post-event information slowly would be more resistant to that information than subjects who read it quickly.

Data bearing on this hypothesis can be found in Tousignant, Hall, and Loftus (1986). The first experiment in this series involved three major phases. First, subjects viewed a set of slides depicting a purse snatching. After viewing the slides, subjects were exposed to some post-event information and later tested for memory of the original event.

The post-event information was presented via a narrative that subjects read from a computer screen, containing misinformation for half the subjects. Misled subjects read that the victim walked under an overhanging restaurant sign although the actual sign was for a tavern. These subjects also read that the victim's friend had short, curly black hair although her hair was actually red. All subjects read the sentences in the narrative one at a time and pressed a button when they wished the next sentence to appear. Each of their reading times were recorded.

When subjects were tested, those who were exposed to misleading information made more errors, which was expected. Of major interest to the present discussion, however, is the analysis comparing the misinformed subjects who resisted the misinformation with the misinformed subjects who accepted the misinformation. Subjects who read the post-event narrative more slowly tended to be more resistant to the post-event misinformation. "Accurate" subjects took an average of 10.1 s per sentence to read the narrative, whereas "highly suggestible" subjects took an average of 7.6 s.

In similar experiments, half the subjects were instructed in how fast to read post-event information. Subjects who naturally read more slowly were more likely to detect a discrepancy between what they were reading and what they had stored in their memory. Likewise, subjects instructed to read slowly were more likely to detect a discrepancy than those instructed to read quickly. Results of our experiments suggest that longer reading times are associated with a greater scrutiny of post-event information. This leads to an increased likelihood that discrepancies will be detected and that the misinformation will be resisted.

Other boundary conditions for the misinformation effect have been empirically demonstrated. People have been shown to reject misinformation that is highly implausible and to reject misinformation - and correct information - presented by an apparently biased source. This evidence raises questions regarding whether people would be influenced by misinformation obtained from the media, and whether they would be differentially influenced depending on the degree of respect they have for the medium or for the journalist presenting the information.

The Fate of Memory

Our experiments have shown that a person's recollection can be altered by exposure to new information - there is still a question of why? Why is post-event information remembered instead of original, factual information? What happened to the actual information? Two hypotheses offering explanations are discussed below.

The *coexistence hypothesis* assumes that both original and post-event information exist in memory together. However, the introduction of post-event information is thought to cover up the original memories. Nevertheless, the original information is still potentially recoverable, only less accessible (Morton, Hammersley, & Bekerin, 1985). The *alteration hypothesis* suggests that original memory becomes altered as post-event information is processed. Consequently, the original information is irretrievable.

Determining which of the two hypotheses accurately describes what occurs in memory has enormous practical importance, since each bears heavily on attempts to correct a memory after it has been biased or fed misinformation. Under the coexistence view, retrieval techniques such as hypothesis or context reinstatement might access the original information. Under the alteration view, however, the only retrieval technique possible would be the realteration of memory.

The coexistence versus alteration distinction also has theoretical importance. The coexistence view is consistent with the idea that all information, once stored, remains in memory more or less permanently. The alteration view implies a true loss due to updating, substitution, or blending of new inputs.

Finally, it has been suggested that both of these positions are wrong: post-event information has no effect on memory at all (McCloskey & Zaragoza, 1985). According to this theoretical interpretation, post-event information influences only what people report, not their underlying memory traces. However, as has been shown, post-event information, under certain circumstances, can have a profound effect on what people say about their past, which is apparently incontrovertable, despite the theoretical dispute over the recoverability of original, underlying memory traces.

On the issue of the fate of memory, Loftus, Schooler, and Wagenaar (1985) have argued that it is probably fruitless to continue asking whether the pristine, original memory exists regarding specific events. Memories do not seem to be neat photographs containing only the original or only the new misleading information. Instead they may be more like montages containing original and new features blended holistically. Further research should answer the question of how the two sources of information - original and new - interact and evolve with one another.

Malleability and the Media

The Generalizability Issue

In psychological studies, post-event information is typically presented in the form of leading questions or a narrative ostensibly produced by another witness. However, it has been suggested (Loftus, 1979) that post-event information may come in a variety of forms - from conversations, newspaper stories, and so forth - all of which can have analogous influence. This suggestion is, of course, conjecture.

Simply because subjects in controlled psychological experiments are influenced by leading questions or the versions of others regarding an experimental event does not prove that real witnesses to live events have their memories transformed or distorted by post-event information more generally, or by media accounts more specifically. This is the generalizability issue.

A variety of studies conducted at the University of Washington for the past 10 years has demonstrated that real witnesses to live events can have their memories distorted. Students in undergraduate psychology courses have been trying to create memories for "live" witnesses for events that did not actually exist. These students have discovered how relatively easily creating memories can be accomplished. Indeed, a created memory can be as real as a memory resulting from ordinary perceptual sensations.

One group of students conducted their study in a train station. In this study, two female students entered the station, and one of them left her large bag on a bench. Afterward, both women walked away. While they were gone, a male student lurked over near the bag, reached in, and pretended to pull out an object and stuff it under his coat. He then walked away quickly. When the women returned, the woman who left the bag began to cry, "Oh my God, my tape recorder is missing!" She lamented that her boss had allowed her to take it home, that it was very expensive, and bemoaned the fact that she might lose her job. The two women then talked to nearby eyewitnesses. Most were extremely cooperative in offering sympathy and information. The "victim" asked for their phone numbers, and most witnesses complied.

One week later a student pretending to be an insurance agent called the witnesses as part of a "routine investigation of the theft." All were asked for details; and finally they were asked if they had seen the tape recorder. Although there was no tape recorder, about half of the witnesses "remembered" seeing it. When pressed for a description of what they saw, some said it was black, and others said gray. Some even said he tape recorder was in a case. Their descriptions indicated a rather vivid "memory" for a tape recorder that never was!

A Media Demonstration

In response to the classroom assignment, one student coincidentally conducted a "media" demonstration (Yagle, 1981). The memory he hoped to alter concerned a scene from a film released several years earlier, "The Man Who Fell to Earth" directed by Nicholas Roeg. In the scene, the star of the film, David Bowie, is driving a black limousine along a country road through some uninhabited backwoods. Suddenly, off to the side in a clearing, a group of early American settlers appear, who yell and point at the strange apparition of an automobile, and then vanish. The entire incident lasts approximately 10 s, and the scene is quite memorable.

Yagle, a reporter for the student newspaper, attempted to change the memories of persons who had seen this film. In his review of "Bad Timing," another film directed by Roeg, Yagle referred to the limousine scene in the "The Man Who Fell to Earth," and erroneously described the limousine as white.

In order to discover the effects of his misleading reference, Yagle hoped to interview two groups of subjects - those who had read his review and those who had not. To his dismay, Yagle found very few people who had seen the film, remembered the scene, and also read his review. Of the persons he interviewed, however, those who had not read the review remembered the limousine correctly as black. On the other hand, half of those who had read the review recalled that the limousine was white.

Media and Eyewitness Memory

It has long been suspected that the media can produce pretrial publicity, especially in sensational cases, that could bias potential jurors, and thereby deny the defendant the constitutional right to a fair trial by an impartial jury (Salas, 1984). There is yet another way in which the media may impact parties in litigation. For many events that the media portray, there are multiple witnesses (e.g., collapse of Hyatt Hotel, Kansas City; Bob's Big Boy massacre, Los Angeles; attempted assassination of President Ronald Reagan, Washington, D.C.; space shuttle explosion, Cape Canaveral). Often the media give details of an interview with one or more of these witnesses, and other witnesses or potential witnesses are thus exposed to these details. It seems reasonable to assume that later witnesses might have had their memories biased or contaminated by earlier accounts. These later witnesses may then testify in court about what they "remembered."

There are numerous reasons to suspect that post-event information provided by the mass media will influence memory to at least as great an extent as post-event information provided in experimental contexts. In experimental contexts, because post-event information has a greater impact if introduced after memory has faded, we have allowed memory to fade and, even after less than 1 hour, have seen significant contamination due to post-event information. After exposure to natural, highly newsworthy events, a person's memory may have many hours to fade before exposure to post-event information.

Vividness is another reason that media-presented post-event information might be especially potent. According to Nisbett and Ross (1980), a stimulus is vivid to the extent that it is "(a) emotionally interesting, (b) concrete and imagery-provoking, and (c) proximate in a sensory, temporal or spatial way" (p. 45). Vivid information is thought to be more persuasive than pallid information of equal or greater validity in part because it comes to mind more easily (Tversky & Kahneman, 1973). Although there is some question about the empirical evidence for special power of vivid stimuli (Taylor & Thompson, 1982), there seems to be agreement that individual case histories, often quite vivid, persuade more effectively than do group statistics, often dry and pallid (Fiske & Taylor, 1984). Thus, if a potential witness sees a witness on television talk about what he or she saw, this might be especially compelling in terms of the ability of the television account to distort the potential witness's memory.

The Media and Misinformation: An Experiment

We were interested in whether post-event information presented via media accounts can influence the memory of people who have actually witnessed an event. If media-presented information influences witness memory, we would expect that subjects exposed to a television report, for example, would remember the critical details of an original event less accurately than subjects who were not so exposed. Our preliminary work, designed to establish a paradigm to test the effects of misleading information presented by the mass media, was explored in a three-part experiment.

The Event. In this study, subjects viewed a 4 min videotape of a robbery and shooting incident used to train police officers (Geiselman, Fisher, MacKinnon, & Holland, 1985). The videotape depicts two police officers on rounds at night. One police officer talks to several people as he walks and often gives his partner information about the area. Suddenly, they hear shots and screams and see people rushing from a liquor store the officers had just passed. One suspect is immediately gunned down and is found by police officers who arrive later. Meanwhile, the two police officers chase the second robber and eventually find him in a trash container. The robber announces he is hit and asks the police officers not to shoot him, but the robber pulls out a gun and wounds one of them. His partner shoots the robber, wounding him.

The Misinformation. After a 10 min filler task following the viewing of the videotape, the second phase of the experiment occurred. Approximately half the subjects (the misled group) were exposed to misinformation presented as a 4 min television report of the incident. Subjects who watched this report were exposed to four items of misinformation (see Table 1). For example, they heard the reporter refer to the liquor store as Midtown Liquor Store when it was actually Pete's Liquor Store. They heard the reporter claim that the robber shouted from the container, "Don't shoot. I don't want to die." In the film, the robber had only said, "Don't shoot." In addition, misled subjects watched the television report under a pretext: they were led to believe

Table 1. Critical items: original event information versus misinformation

	Information presented in the original event	Information suggested in the television report
Item 1	Two robbers	Three robbers
Item 2	Car	Truck
Item 3	Pete's Liquor Store	Midtown Liquor Store
Item 4	"I'm hit. Don't shoot."	"Don't shoot. I don't want to die."

that they would have to decide whether the reporter was sufficiently talented to obtain a job in a major national news operation. The remaining subjects received no post-event information (control group). Instead of watching the television report, they continued to work on the filler task for an additional 4 min.

The Test. All subjects were asked to answer a series of questions based on their own personal memory of the robbery. Of the 17 questions on the test, four questions contained details based on the erroneous information given to the misled subjects; however, 13 of the questions were based solely on the film. Thus, subjects should perform comparably on these questions.

Results. The percentage of subjects in the misled and control conditions who gave the correct response, the suggested response, or some other response is shown in Table 2, and are collapsed across the four critical items. The pattern of data is in the predicted direction. Control subjects were more likely to pick the correct response than subjects who viewed the television report containing misinformation. On noncritical items (i.e., those items for which no misinformation was presented), there was no difference in accuracy for the experimental (93.2 %) and control (93.6 %) groups.

Collapsing across the four critical items, however, obscures the fact that there are significant item differences. Although misled subjects were less accurate than controls on all four critical items, misled subjects were strongly influenced by only two of the four pieces of misinformation. As seen in Table 3, which reports the percentage of correct responses, suggested responses, or other responses separately for each of the four critical items, the misled subjects remembered the name of the liquor store as Midtown Liquors, rather than Pete's. This resulted in poor performance in the misled condition compared to the controls (33 % versus 86 % correct).

Moreover, many misled subjects were influenced to believe they had heard the robber say, "I don't want to die" (37 % given suggested response versus none of control subjects). However, misled subjects were not influenced to believe there were three robbers instead o the actual two. Moreover, having been told in the television report that the vehicle behind which a robber had was a truck, not a car as in the film, did not seem to influence the misled subjects' memory.

We can only speculate about why certain items of misinformation had a strong impact whereas others did not. For all four critical items, the control group performed reasonably well

Table 2. Response to the critical items by the misled and control group

	Experimental group (n = 27) (%)	Control group (n = 22) (%)
Correct	62.03	87.49
Suggested answer	27.78	1.13
Other incorrect answer	10.18	11.35

Table 3. Response to each of the four critical items for misled and control subjects

	Experimental group (n = 27) (%)	Control group (n = 22) (%)
Correct		
Robbers	85.19	95.46
Vehicle	66.67	77.27
Liquor Store	3.33	86.36
Utterance	62.96	90.90
Suggested answer		
Robbers	11.11	00.00
Vehicle	3.70	00.00
Liquor Store	59.25	4.54
Utterance	37.04	00.00
Other errors		
Robbers	3.70	4.54
Vehicle	29.63	22.73
Liquor Store	7.42	9.10
Utterance	00.00	9.10

(77 %-95 % correct). It is unlikely that the performance of the control group determines whether misinformation will have a greater or lesser influence. For all four critical items, the suggested response was rarely given by control subjects (e.g., < 5 % of the time and for only one item). Therefore, the suggested response cannot influence memory except when it is so plausible that control subjects would have some tendency to also choose it.

The strongest misinformation effect occurred on the item referring to the name of the liquor store. Although the name was printed, somewhat obscurely, on the front of the store, one police officer also mentioned the name to his partner. This enabled control subjects to perform well. However, the television reporter mentioned the erroneous name twice, possibly ensuring that it was strongly encoded by viewers. This post-hoc analysis of why this single item worked so well is not particularly satisfying because post-event information can have a large impact, even when it is presented only once.

In addition to sorting out the item effects, there are a number of interesting issues which this type of research can address. Are people more readily influenced when the information comes from television or a newspaper? Because television presents information more vividly, a reasonable hypothesis predicts that a potential subject-witness would be more influenced by seeing a witness interviewed on television than by reading that interview in a newspaper. Vivid information has been shown to have a considerable impact on memory. Support for the superior power of vivid information comes from several sources, most notably Nisbett and Ross (1980), who have termed this power the *vividness criterion.*

Nisbett and Ross argue that vividly presented information has greater impact on judgments than "pallid and abstract propositions of substantially greater probative and evidentiary value" (1980, p. 44). At the time they made their argument, however, evidence for vividness was based mostly on anecdotes rather than on empirical research. To say with any confidence that television has more distorting power than print requires evidence from specific and focused research. Whether television print is more capable of distorting memory could depend on the nature of the post-event message. Indirectly related persuasion research has shown that a vivid presentation of a long or difficult message produced longer recall (Chaiken & Eagly, 1976; Wilson, 1974).

It would also be of interest to determine whether preexisting attitudes about the reliability of media reports affect the extent to which people's memories are contaminated by media-presented information. We could find that witnesses allow their memories to become contaminated only if they hold the media in high regard. According to a Newsweek poll (October 22, 1984, p. 68), 8 % of those polled believed that very little of what is read or heard in the news media can be believed, whereas 39 % claimed that most media-presented information can be believed. These two groups could be expected to be differentially influenced by media-presented misinformation.

Although no empirical research exists, it is reasonable to suppose that the various elements of the news media would be more or less able to distort memory. Elements that are held in high regard generally might be more influential. In the Newsweek poll cited earlier, over 80 % of respondents believed that television news is generally accurate, 77 % believed that radio news is generally accurate, 73 % believed that their local newspaper is generally accurate, and 29 % believed that the supermarket tabloids are generally accurate. A question for further research would be whether these beliefs translate into differential influence for television, radio, local newspapers, and tabloids.

Other Media Applications

Media and Flashbulb Memories

The memories of circumstances in which very surprising or consequential events are learned have been termed *flashbulb memories* (Brown & Kulik, 1977). The main ingredient for flashbulb memories seems to be a very high level of surprise, often accompanied by emotional arousal. The prototypical example of this is the memories created by the news on November 23, 1963: the day President Kennedy was assassinated. The Kennedy assassination created an extraordinarily powerful and widely shared flashbulb memory. In 1983, some 20 years after the assassination, empirical data were published suggesting that virtually every young adult who was 8 years of age and older in 1963 could recall something about his or her circumstances when they learned of Kennedy's assassination (Winograd & Killinger, 1983). Interestingly, people also recalled flashbulb memories 33 years after the assassination of Lincoln (Colegrove, 1982).

The Kennedy and Lincoln assassinations are not the only events that have created flashbulb memories. Other highly newsworthy events, as well as personally significant events, also create flashbulb memories. In 1986, memory researchers quietly talked about how the explosion of the space shuttle "Columbia" might become the new flashbulb memory, especially for Americans. One journalist echoed these feelings when he said, "We will all be able to say, all our days, where we were, what we were doing, what we thought and felt as we heard the radio or watched, again and again and again, that awesome and awful footage from 11:39 a.m. EST... Never had tragedy been so easy to see" (Champlin, 1986, p. 5G).

Because it suggests surprise and brevity, flashbulb memory is a reasonably good term for the phenomenon, but it is not perfect. A photograph taken with a flashbulb preserves everything within its scope; flashbulb memories do not. Their specialness has been seriously questioned (Rubin & Kozin, 1984), as well as their accuracy (Neisser, 1982). After all, even when people describe their flashbulb memories of highly newsworthy events, for example, are they remembering their actual experiences based on intact, original memories, or are they simply repeating memories *rehearsed* and embellished since the event?

The important role of rehearsal in producing flashbulb memories has been stressed by numerous researchers (e.g., Brown and Kulik, 1977; Neisser, 1982), although for different reasons. Some researchers (e.g., Brown & Kulik, 1977) believe that a flashbulb memory is established at the time an event occurs; rehearsal serves to maintain and elaborate the initially vivid memory. Other researchers believe that flashbulb memories are created after an event occurs; significance is attached to them later via rehearsal. Winograd and Killinger (1983) question whether a core memory persists through time or whether memory is continually updated and recorded. Both views of the process, however, predict a high correlation between reported rehearsals and the degree of elaboration found in the reports of flashbulb memories.

The mass media, then, may play a special role in creating flashbulb memories by presenting highly newsworthy events over and over again. Many people heard about the space shuttle explosion on the radio, watched it on television, read about it in local and national newspapers, and read about it yet again in weekly news magazines. What effect does this saturation of news have? The journalist quoted earlier also remarked about the power and responsibility of television (Champlin, 1986, p. 5G):

> Never had tragedy been so easy to see. The images of the launch, the widening plume a billowy white against the beautiful, cold, blue and cloudless sky, had never been so clear and perfect. Catastrophe - the firebrand pieces spraying into space - had never been so vivid, never seemed so much like cruel echoes of Hollywood special-effects detonations.

Our experiences with media may be a critical aspect of the establishment or maintenance of flashbulb memories of the space shuttle explosion or other vivid events. When experiences are widely shared through the mass media, the nature of the memories created by those experiences may actually be qualitatively affected. Our shared media environment has the potential for shaping our personal as well as our collective memories because what we remember is in large measure connected with what we rehearse, and the media can influence our memories by influencing what and how often we rehearse.

Media and Personal Experiences

There is another potential media influence on personal memories. This concerns the extent to which people might become confused, and "remember" events that were experienced via the mass media as though they happened to themselves. Could someone watch an explosion, a robbery, or an assassination on television and later come to believe he or she was actually present when the event occurred? This may sound far fetched - but not to some researchers. Media presentations influence semantic memory in general, and estimates of victimization and violent crime (Gerbner et al., 1977, 1980) more particularly. Doob and MacDonald (1979), however, question whether this causal relationship exists. If this is so, can television influence an individual's recollections of his or her own victimizations? Could people see a news report of a crime and much later think that that crime or a similar one happened to them? This is unlikely. There are reasons to be optimistic that news media reports do not influence personal recollections.

Some recent research shows that media impact occurs with societal level judgments about general problem importance or frequency but not with judgments about personal risk (Tyler & Cook, 1984). Based on this research, the news media does not influence personal recollections. On the other hand, media exposure to crime may influence those recollections in a number of ways. Recent theoretical research has shown that people occasionally confuse the memory of actually doing something with the memory of only imagining it (Johnson & Raye, 1981; Anderson, 1984), or the memory of actually seeing something with the memory of thinking about it. Given the pervasiveness of these types of errors, conceivably individuals could watch an event on television and recall it as something they really experienced.

The Media and One Man's Memory

The prospect that the media can affect memory sheds new light on one particular memory; namely, the memory of John Dean. Recall that Dean was former counsel to President Richard Nixon during the Watergate break-in. In June, 1973, Dean testified before a committee of the United States Senate, and he began his testimony with a 245-page statement describing dozens of meetings that he had attended with various other persons on Nixon's staff over the previous several years (Neisser, 1981, 1982). Because Dean's memory was so detailed, several Senators disbelieved Dean's testimony. One asked Dean, "Have you always had a facility for recalling the details of conversations which took place many months ago?" The Senator was especially impressed that Dean had done this without the benefit of notes or a daily diary.

Dean said he kept a newspaper clipping file from the date of the first Washington Post article until the time of the Senate hearings. He said he triggered his recollection by reading every single newspaper article, outlining what had happened, and then placing himself in the described scene.

Did the articles trigger his recollection, as Dean claimed, or did they partially supplement or distort his memory? Dean was unaware that all conversations in Nixon's Oval Office were secretly recorded. A psychologist, who made an extensive comparison of those tapes with Dean's senate testimonies, concluded that Dean was entirely wrong about the course of many conversations, but nevertheless recounted the facts of those conversations (Neisser, 1981, 1982). Yet, it is difficult to ascertain whether Dean truly remembered those facts or whether he reinstated those facts into his memory from his perusal of newspaper clippings.

A French writer, Maurice Halbwachs (1980), anticipated many of the ideas presented herein, and he may have not been surprised to find a blend of truth and fiction in John Dean's recollection. He talked about what happens when several people witness or participate in an episode and later one of them evokes the events for another. Very often, Halbwachs claimed, others can change the impression, or image, that we have kept of some distant fact.

> It might be that such images reproduce the past inaccurately, while that element or fragment of remembrance already in our mind is a more accurate expression: in this case a solid fund of fictitious remembrances is added to real remembrances. Conversely, it is possible that only the testimony of others is accurate and that they rectify and re-establish our remembrances in the process of being incorporated into it. In both cases these images blend into our remembrances and seemingly lend them their own substance... Just as we must introduce a small particle into a saturated medium to get crystallization, so must we introduce a "seed" of memory into that body of testimony external to us in order for it to turn into a solid mass of remembrances (p. 25).

References

Anderson, R.E. (1984). Did I do it, or did I only imagine doing it? *Journal of Experimental Psychology: General, 113,* 594-613.

Baddeley, A.D. (1982). *Your memory: A user's guide.* New York: MacMillan.

Bekerian, D.A., & Baddeley, A.D. (1980). Saturation advertising and the repetition effect. *Journal of Verbal Learning and Verbal Behavior, 19,* 17-25.

Bekerian, D.A., & Bowers, J.M. (1983). Eyewitness testimony: Were we misled? *Journal of Experimental Psychology: Learning, Memory, and Cognition, 9,* 139-145.

Brown, R., & Kuli, J. (1977). Flashbulb memories. *Cognition, 5,* 73-99.

Chaiken, S., & Eagly, A.H. (1976). Communication modality as a determinant of message persuasiveness and message comprehensibility. *Journal of Personality and Social Psychology, 34,* 605-614.

Champlin, C. (1986, February 2). Responsibility amid the horror. *The Denver Post,* p. 5G.

Colegrove, F.W. (1982). The day they heard about Lincoln. In U. Neisser (Ed.), *Memory observed* (pp. 41-42). San Francisco: Freeman.

Doob, A.N., & MacDonald, G.E. (1979). Television viewing and fear of victimization: Is the relationship causal? *Journal of Personality and Social Psychology, 37,* 170-179.

Fiske, S.T., & Taylor, S.E (1984). *Social cognition.* Reading, MA: Addison-Wesley.

Geiselman, R.E., Fisher, R.P., MacKinnon, D.P., & Holland, H.L. (1985). Eyewitness memory enhancement in the police interview: Cognitive Retrieval Mnemonics versus Hypnosis. *Journal of Applied Psychology, 70,* 401-412.

Gerbner, G., & Gross, L. (1976). The scary world of T.V.'s heavy viewer. *Psychology Today, 89,* 41-46.

Gerbner, G., Gross, L., Elery, M.F., & Jackson-Beeck, M. (1977). Violence profile No. 8: The highlights. *Journal of Communication, 27,* 171-180.

Gerbner, G., Gross, L., Morgan, M., & Signorielli, N. (1980). The mainstreaming of America: Violence profile No. 11. *Journal of Communication, 30*, 10-29.

Halbwachs, M. (1980). *The collective memory* (M. Douglas, Trans.). New York: Harper and Row. (Original work published 1950)

Hall, D.F., Loftus, E.F., & Tousignant, J.P. (1984). Post-event information and changes in recollection for a natural event. In G. Wells & E.F. Loftus (Eds.), *Eyewitness testimony: Psychological perspectives* (pp. 124-141). Cambridge University.

Johnson, M.K., & Raye, C.L. (1981). Reality monitoring. *Psychological Review, 88*, 67-85.

Jones, A. (1977). The Narciso-Perez case: Nurse hunting in Michigan. *Nation, 224*, 584-588.

Linton, M. (1979). I remember it well. *Psychology Today*, 81-86.

Loftus, E.F. (1979). *Eyewitness testimony.* Cambridge: Harvard University.

Loftus, E.F. (1983). Misfortune of memory. *Philosophical Transactions of the Royal Society, London, B302*, 413-421.

Loftus, E.F., Schooler, J.W., & Wagenaar, W.A. (1985). The fate of memory: Comment on McCloskey & Zaragoza. *Journal of Experimental Psychology: General, 114*, 375-380.

McCloskey, M., & Zaragoza, M. (1985). Misleading post-event information and memory for events: Arguments and evidence against memory impairment hypothesis. *Journal of Experimental Psychology. General, 114*, 3-18.

Morton, J., Hammersley, R.H., & Bekerian, D.A. (1985). Headed records: A model for memory and its failures. *Cognition, 20*, 1-23.

Neisser, U. (1981). John Dean's Memory: A case study. *Cognition, 9*, 1-22. Reprinted in Neisser, U. (1982). *Memory observed: Remembering in natural contexts.* San Francisco: Freeman.

Nisbett, R.E., & Ross, L. (1980). *Human inference: Strategies and shortcomings of social judgment.* Englewood Cliffs, NJ: Prentice Hall.

Pride, M. (1986, February 10). There had been a death in the family. *Newsweek*, p.

Rubin, D.C., & Kozin, M. (1984). Vivid memories. *Cognition, 16*, 1-9.

Salas, L. (1984). The press and the criminal justice system. In R. Surette (Ed.), *Justice and the media.* Springfield: Charles Thomas.

Taylor, S.E., & Thompson, S.C. (1982). Stalking the elusive "vividness" effect. *Psychological Review, 89*, 155-181.

Tousignant, J.P., Hall, D., & Loftus, E.F. (in press, 1986). Discrepancy detection and vulnerability to misleading post-event information. *Memory and Cognition, 14*, 329-338.

Tulving, E. (1972). Episodic and semantic memory. In E. Tulving & W. Donaldson (Eds.), *Organization of memory.* New York: Academic.

Tulving, E. (1983). *Elements of episodic memory.* Oxford, UK: Oxford University.

Tversky, A., & Kahneman, D. (1973). Availability: A heuristic for judging frequency and probability. *Cognitive Psychology, 5*, 207-232.

Tyler, T.R., & Cook, F.L. (1984). *Journal of Personality and Social Psychology, 47*, 693-708.

Wagenaar, W.A. (1978). Recalling messages broadcast to the general public. In M. Gruneberg, P. Morris, & R. Sykes (Eds.), *Practical aspects of memory.* London: Academic.

Wilson, C.E. (1974). The effect of medium or loss of information. *Journalism Quarterly, 51*, 111-116.

Winograd, E., & Killinger, W.A. (1983). Relating age at encoding in early childhood to adult recall: Development of flashbulb memories. *Journal of Experimental Psychology: General, 112*, 413-422.

Yagle, M. (1981). *The malleability of memory: The power of inaccurate newspaper accounts.* Unpublished manuscript. University of Washington, Department of Psychology, Seattle.

23. Response to Suggestions of Memory Distortion in Hypnosis: Sampling Cognitive and Social Factors

P.W. Sheehan

Introduction

The operation of memory processes in hypnosis is an important component of the study of suggestion and suggestibility. Not surprisingly, perhaps, the theoretical options are diverse. Sharp debate exists in the literature concerning whether hypnosis enhances memory accuracy or contributes actively toward distortion, and many theoretical processes are proposed as relevant to the arguments. Hypnosis, for example, is said by some to revive traces of the original perception, thereby facilitating vivid access to the original stimulus material; it may allow subjects to pay selective attention to the material to be remembered, thereby increasing the probability of accurate recall; or it may render the hypnotized subject more willing to guess, thereby increasing the probability of accurate recall; or it may render the hypnotized subject more willing to guess, thereby increasing response productivity and altering the criterion for response. Such issues are relevant to the current debate about the forensic utility of hypnosis. The major message of this paper is that our understanding of the processes at work must depend ultimately on a thorough and complete understanding of the parameters that shape and define the nature of the hypnotic response itself.

A variety of conditions has now been isolated which has produced data associated with the acceptance or incorporation of misleading information into memory. Relatively few attempts have been made, however, to integrate these findings and isolate patterns of coherence in the data. This paper looks across three different types of memory test situation in hypnosis and tries to isolate key parameters with a view to examining the hypothesis that memory error in hypnosis can be explained in terms of a general model, predicting uniform and consistent effects.

In the paper, "hypnosis" is accepted as a term which reflects the operation of a particular context of influence. This context heavily motivates a subject toward giving role-appropriate behavior, suggestion communications are typically used to alter or modify the subject's behavior, and person characteristics of the hypnotized subject interact with setting constraints to define the final, detailed form of the hypnotic response. It should also be recognized that there are optimal conditions for observing hypnotic responses that provide the "truest" conditions for assessing its meaning. Typically, these are provided by the administration of hypnotic induction instructions to subjects who have demonstrated previously that they are capable of responding positively to suggestions requiring them to distort reality in a radical way.

The three memory test situations examined in the paper are: (a) the subtle injection of false information about an event by suggestion after the event has taken place; (b) the application of explicit suggestion to establish a pseudomemory of an event that has occurred previously; and (c) the use of leading questions about a past event where the questions imply incorrect facts. All these communications of false information are postevent, each reflects the operation of suggestion (explicit, or otherwise) to communicate or imply specific information, and all of the communications cue distortion or memory error. With respect to the hypnotic literature, no sharp distinctions are usually drawn among these three situations, and one might reasonably expect that consistencies and regularities will occur in the data. Arguments extrapolating from the data to the real-life forensic setting certainly tend to assume that such regularities exist. One should not presuppose, however, that similar factors will characterize the explanation of effects associated with these different memory contexts.[1]

Postevent, Subtle Suggestion

This situation essentially adapted the procedures of Loftus, Miller, and Burns (1978) who found that subjects given misleading information prior to recall demonstrated less accurate memory performance than subjects who were given consistent or irrelevant information. Typically, the procedures used tested subjects initially for their memory of an incident shown in a slide series, and in so doing subtly introduced them to incorrect information about the events that subjects had perceived previously. After a period of time, subjects were retested by being presented with the incorrect information as an alternative for response. The measure of distortion that was of special interest was the acceptance or incorporation of the incorrect information into subjects' memory reports.

In a program of research that is reported more fully elsewhere (Sheehan, 1988), three false items of information were suggested subtly to subjects. The term "subtle" in this context is taken to indicate that the false information was given to subjects as an aside, preparatory to asking them later about other information in the event series. The method is such that even though suggestion has been delivered, the subject is very unlikely to realize that intent of the experimenter who cues the error.

Six independent studies were conducted in which these procedures were instituted, and in each study, misleading information was appreciably incorporated into subjects' memory reports. When the false information was introduced *before* hypnosis, the misinformation effect did not distinguish high or low suggestible subjects, hypnotizable or simulating subjects, or subjects given waking or hypnotic instruction. When the false information was introduced *after* hypnosis, however, effects that were distinctive to the hypnotic condition emerged.[2]

---

[1] Emphasis in this paper is placed on cognitive and social factors as they influence effects for subjects when encoding conditions are relatively comparable. Data appear elsewhere to indicate that when encoding conditions vary, the degree of acceptance of misleading information may well be affected. Subjects, for example, show greater acceptance of misleading information when they pay less (rather than more) attention to the thematic content of the stimuli at the time of encoding (Reid & Bruce, 1988). The focus of the present paper is on factors affecting distortion that are associated with post-encoding conditions or test procedures. The data presented do not determine whether memory is actually altered as a result of the acceptance of false information; it is possible, for instance, that priming effects or specific features of response options available at the time of retrieval operate to influence performance outcomes. However, the studies do address the issue of subjects' memory reports as they are influenced by the false information that is suggested to them.

[2] Study 6 was the exception, but here the time between presentation of the false information and test of memory was not comparable with the other studies.

Table 1 illustrates the pattern of findings in the series of studies as a whole and notes the presence of stimulus-specific effects. In each of the studies, this effect (defined in terms of the acceptance of the misleading information; see Sheehan, 1988, for details) was indicated by the misinformation effect being appreciably stronger for one stimulus rather than another. Consistently, through the program of work as a whole, the incorporation of false information occurred for some stimuli and not for others, and the strength of the incorporation effect was predictable from one study to the next in terms of which stimulus was used. The frequency with which this effect occurred was reliable. In the most theoretically significant of the studies (Study 4, Table 1; Sheehan, Grigg, & McCann, 1984) where hypnotic subjects were differentiated significantly from simulating subjects, results indicated that memory distortion could be a distinctive effect of hypnosis.

Table 1. Occurrence of misinformation effect for one or more stimuli across program of research

Study	Time of injection of false information	Presence/ absence	Related especially to hypnosis	Stim. specific effect
Study 1	Before hypnosis	Present[a]	No	Present
Study 2	Before hypnosis	Present[b,c]	No	Present
Study 3	Before hypnosis	Present[b,c]	No	Present
Study 4	After hypnosis	Present[a]	Yes, R/S[b]	Present
Study 5	After hypnosis	Present[b]	Yes, H/L[d]	Present
Study 6	After hypnosis	Present	No	Present

R/S indicates that effect is greater for real than for simulating subjects. H/L indicates that effect is greater for high than for low susceptible subjects. "Present" in the final column means that the effect favored the same stimulus in each study (the slogan "Nixon" on a jacket). It should be noted that subjects in study 6 incorporated misleading information into their memory reports, but no nonmisleading condition was used for the purposes of control (as in studies 1-5).

[a] $P < .01$

[b] $P < .001$

[c] Effect observed in free recall as well as recognition ($P < .05$ for study 2; and $P < .001$ for study 3).

[d] $P < .05$

Overall, one can conclude from the pattern of data for this effect that incorporation of misleading information into memory reports by these procedures of suggestion occurs frequently, the effect is readily quantifiable, some stimuli show the distortion effect more easily than others, and the effect is augmented in hypnosis when false information is given after, rather than before, hypnosis is introduced. Stimulus effects index the influence of nonhypnotic (social) factors that play a part in defining the degree of memory distortion that will be shown in hypnosis. The presence of a distinctive effect following hypnotic instruction points to factors of influence that are cognitive in character. In part, at least, explanation of the effect has been linked to the relative lack of attention to the false information that is presented, implicating distinctive attentional processing of the information suggested in hypnosis (see Sheehan et al., 1984).

Pseudomemory Suggestion

Relatively little direct experimental evidence is available on the use of explicit suggestion to create a well-defined pseudomemory. However, Orne (1979) first set out the procedures for the demonstration of pseudomemory in hypnotic subjects which were subsequently illustrated in a case application presented by Barnes (1982). Laurence and Perry (1983) provided the first experimental demonstration of the phenomenon in a procedure modeled on Orne's work. Labelle and Perry (1986) replicated the phenomenon, and Spanos and McLean (1986) and McCann and Sheehan (1987, 1988) conducted later studies that have extended the effect, using the same general paradigm of pseudomemory creation.

Essentially, this paradigm tests for experience of an event, introduces explicitly obvious suggestions for restructuring the event following hypnotic induction, and then routinely tests for the occurrence of false memory after hypnosis has been terminated and the subject has awakened.

In a series of studies utilizing a video tape of a simulated bank robbery (Yuille, 1982), McCann and Sheehan (1988) reported that the incidence of pseudomemory is stable and consistent when strict criteria of scoring are adopted, but the rate of occurrence is influenced particularly by social, contextual factors. Dependent upon particular hypnotist instructions, scoring criteria and stimulus features, incidence of pseudomemory ranged from 27 % to in excess of 75 % among susceptible subjects. The most interesting effect, however, was reflected in the capacity of the pseudomemory response to shift from one retrieval context to another. In a recent study (McCann & Sheehan, 1987), 32 highly susceptible subjects were tested subsequently for pseudomemory in recall. Half the sample was tested for recall followed by recognition, and the other half was tested for recognition prior to recall. The incidence of pseudomemory in recall was significantly lower when recognition came first in the testing sequence.

This research tells us that the phenomenon of pseudomemory is not a permanent response which prevents all access to other, conflicting memories, and the phenomenon is rather more contextually based, it would seem, than the data on the misinformation effect (reviewed in Table 1) would lead us to believe.

Table 2 sets out the incidence of the effect found by McCann and Sheehan (1987) for the two orders of conditions and reports the frequencies that were associated with the three false stimulus features of the video display that were suggested explicitly by the hypnotist: the robber wore a mask (which he did not), the robber entered from the right (when he entered from the left), and the robber swore heavily (which he did not). Overall, results showed very substantial differences in the impact of suggested events on the incidence of pseudomemory. Appreciable differences occurred in rate of frequency of the phenomenon, depending on the context in which it was tested. Incidence dropped markedly when the correct response was initially cued very strongly, compared with testing the response first in a context in which subjects were left free to report on events in their own way. Of possibly greatest theoretical interest, however, were two susceptible subjects who identified the target video correctly in recognition, but went on later to display pseudomemory in free recall immediately following. One might offer the provocative conclusion that for some persons at least, it seems that being right the first time means very little in remembering what is obvious in the next time round.

Table 2. Incidence of pseudomemory in recall across memory test conditions (for three suggested stimuli). (Data from McCann and Sheehan, 1987).

Order of conditions	Stimulus	Incidence of effect (*n*)	(%)
	Mask	5	71
Recall-recognition (n = 15)	Right	2	29
	Swearing	1	14
	Mask	2	100
Recognition-*recall* (n = 16)	Right	-	
	Swearing	-	

The incidence of any occurrence of pseudomemory was 46.7 % in recall-recognition order, and 12.5 % in recognition-recall order.

Leading Questions

In a number of studies in the program of work reported in Table 1, subjects were told by the hypnotist to close their eyes and imagine the scene where the robber was standing at the corner "about to cross the road." They were then asked to indicate, by raising the index finger of the right hand whether they could see "*the* traffic lights in this scene." This was a leading question in that the use of the definite article implied that the traffic lights were present (although they were not). The question tested for the occurrence of cued distortion where distortion was suggested relatively obviously and close to the time when memory was actually assessed. Table 3 sets out the incidence of effect in two studies when contrasting comparison groups were used. The table demonstrates that there were no differences in rate of performance between real and simulating subjects, and between high and low susceptible subjects, and that the rate of response to the suggestion that was communicated was only moderate in frequency. Findings suggest that previously reported interpretations of effects (e.g., hypnotized subjects are more likely to report the presence of nonpresent objects suggested by the use of the definite article than are subjects in a waking condition: see Putnam, 1979) are not entirely correct. There is no evidence from these data to imply that response to leading questions is reliably distinctive under conditions which optimally test hypnotic response.

When the explicitness of questions was modified in a later experiment, however, data showed effects which began to distinguish high susceptible from low susceptible subjects. In this independent study, high and low susceptible subjects were asked, "Do you remember that *a* set of traffic lights was there?". In this context, the communication of the suggestion was less apparent, and "obviousness" emerged as a possibly relevant factor. Here, high susceptible subjects reported

Table 3. Rate of response to leading question for three independent groups of subjects

Subject Group	Rate of response (n)	(%)
High susceptible, under hypnotic instruction	39	38.5
Faking insusceptible (simulating)	40	30.0
Motivated insusceptible, under hypnotic instruction	28[a]	21.4

[a] An additional 14 % of subjects in this group said that although they could not see the lights, they remembered they were there.

more frequently (20 %) than low susceptible subjects (0 %) that they saw a set of lights, and also reported more frequently that they remembered that the lights were there (27 %, n = 22, as compared with 9 %, n = 24, for low susceptible subjects). These data suggest that if hypnosis does play a distinctive part in determining memory distortion then this is most likely to be the case when the obviousness of suggestion is reduced, or the communication of suggestion is relatively subtle.

Discussion

Research that looks across different distortion test situations appears to highlight a lack of generality of effects. It seems more accurate to argue that results implicate a range of factors determining memory distortion effects in hypnosis that will differ in their impact from one situation to another. Data point collectively to the complex contribution of state instruction (hypnosis) to effects, as well as the need to define the nature of the interaction between state instruction and level of susceptibility as they relate to different memory test situations.

It is instructive to consider a little further the studies that have been highlighted in this paper. In the study by Sheehan et al. (1984; see study 4, Table 1) real subjects were differentiated from simulating subjects, with real subjects showing greater acceptance of incorrect information. This study did not determine, however, whether level of susceptibility (rather than hypnosis) was related to the effect, since the design used did not separate the influence of state instruction from the influence of degree of hypnotizability. the study is significant in that it took a very conservative index of memory distortion - one shown previously not to generally distinguish hypnosis from waking subjects (see Sheehan & Tilden, 1983) - and demonstrated that hypnosis was accompanied by *more* rather than less distortion. Such a finding (and the lack of evidence for any memory superiority effect) reinforces the view that memory in hypnosis does not revive traces of the original perception. Rather, hypnotic memory (as for waking memory) is conceptualized most adequately as a constructive product. The question remains, however, whether cognitive factors such as a "lowered level of critical scrutiny," or "reduced awareness of the false information" characterizes hypnotic subjects' reactions to memory suggestion in a distinctive way. It may well be that hypnosis has the greatest part to play in distorting memory when specific (and subtle) suggestions are not very recognizable as suggestions, because attention is diverted to other information contained in the hypnotic communication.

Turning to the second situation (pseudomemory), the analyses tell us something different. Here there were definite indications in the pseudomemory test situation that some subjects evidenced a conformity reaction, especially since rates of response were in excess of 75 % (as opposed to 27 %) for specific features of the event series (those that were highly compatible with the overall cue context of the stimulus sequence). If pseudomemory response is susceptible to social influence as much as these preliminary data indicate, then it is particularly important to determine the character of the phenomenon among subjects who vary in their susceptibility to suggestion. For those subjects who are likely to respond in a compliant or conforming way, it is possible that neither a high level of susceptibility nor hypnotic instruction are really necessary for gross distortion to occur. Just as further work is needed on Loftus' distortion index to unconfound the effects of state instruction and level of susceptibility, additional work is needed on pseudomemory to investigate the phenomenon among high, medium, and low hypnotizable subjects, operating under waking and hypnotic instruction.

Inquiring in a leading way represents the third main context for studying the generality of memory distortion effects in hypnosis. The major reference point for research on the impact of hypnosis on recall following the introduction of leading questions is the work by Putnam (1979) who studied state instruction conditions (hypnosis, waking) and temporal conditions (short, long delay) in recall. The major variable of interest to Putnam was the number of errors made on a questionnaire relating to a videotape enactment of a car-bicycle accident. After the relevant delay, subjects in the hypnosis group were asked questions that consisted of items phrased in a leading or a nonleading way, the leading questions suggesting false answers. Data showed that hypnotized subjects were appreciably more in error on the leading questions than subjects in a no hypnosis control group. Putnam, however, did not look systematically at the impact of level of susceptibility. Close reading of the published account indicates that subjects were for the most part moderate to high in hypnotic susceptibility. A follow-up study by Zelig and Beidleman (1981) investigated the impact of leading questions and found that subjects in the hypnosis (vs. waking) group responded more frequently in the direction implied by the leading questions. Subjects in this study, however, were also restricted to the moderate-high range of susceptibility. More recently, unpublished work by Rainer (1984) investigated comprehensively whether implanted false information and leading questions have a greater effect on high hypnotizable than low hypnotizable subjects during hypnosis. Her work showed that hypnosis per se, or as moderated by hypnotic susceptibility level, did not have a significant effect on accuracy or degree of response to leading questions. A number of her leading questions, however, contained blatantly contradictory information, and past research by Loftus (1979) has indicated that blatant misinformation is frequently rejected by subjects (stimulus features again seem to be important). When blatant contradictory material is not used, and subgroups of the total hypnotic population are canvassed, then state instruction might relate more reliably to the incorporation of incorrect information into memory via leading questions.

Conclusion

Many studies now bear upon the analysis of human memory performance in the hypnotic setting (for broad review see Relinger, 1984; Smith, 1983), but the methodologies associated with most of them are incomplete. A major conclusion I would draw on the evidence is that there is no general uniformity of effects. There are occasions on which memory appears relatively distorted in hypnosis, and occasions when it does not. Opportunities for transmitting inaccuracies differ greatly according to how exactly false information is suggested and a variety of parameters such as state instruction, stimulus attribute, level of awareness of the false information that is presented, and level of susceptibility most likely mediate performance effects differently in varying suggestion-communication settings that might at first appear "reasonably" similar.

It is my belief that if a general model does pertain to effects in the area of postevent suggested memory distortion, it is likely to be one in which different process dimensions are at times working together. There is evidence in the program of work that has been examined here, for example, that factors of compliance and genuine responsiveness operate jointly, with compliance perhaps operating most noticeably in cued distortion contexts (such as pseudomemory) in which subjects' awareness of the treatment manipulation is obvious.[3] Assessing the meaning of the relative contributions of these two factors (see also, Tellegen, 1978/1979) - as one moves from one area of cued distortion to another - poses for me perhaps the most interesting theoretical challenge in the field.

Acknowledgement. This paper was prepared with the support of the Australian Research Council through a grant made by that agency to the author for the analysis of hypnotic susceptibility and memory distortion in hypnosis.

References

Barnes, M.C. (1982). *Hypnosis on trial.* London: British Broadcasting Corporation Television Program.

Gudjonsson, G.H. (1984). A new scale of interrogative suggestibility. *Personality and Individual Differences, 5,* 303-314.

Labelle, L., & Perry, C.W. (1986). *Pseudomemory creation in hypnosis.* Paper presented at 94th Annual Convention of the American Psychological Association, Washington, D.C., August.

Laurence, J.R., & Perry, C.W. (1983). Hypnotically created memory among highly hypnotizable subjects. *Science, 222,* 523-524.

Loftus, E.F. (1979). *Eyewitness testimony.* Cambridge, MA: Harvard University.

Loftus, E.F., Miller, D.G., & Burns, H.J. (1978). Semantic integration of verbal information into a visual memory. *Journal of Experimental Psychology: Human Learning and Memory, 4,* 19-31.

[3] The distinction made here possibly relates to that offered by Gudjonsson (1984) between suggestive information that misleads and elements of a situation that convey interpersonal pressure. The two types of suggestibility implicated by these factors have been shown by Gudjonsson to be relatively independent, poorly correlated, and to load on separate factors.

McCann, T., & Sheehan, P.W. (1987). The breaching of pseudomemory under hypnotic instruction: Implications for original memory retrieval. *British Journal of Experimental and Clinical Hypnosis, 4,* 101-108.

McCann, T.E., & Sheehan, P.W. (1988). Hypnotically induced pseudomemories: Sampling their conditions among hypnotizable subjects. *Journal of Personality and Social Psychology, 54,* 339-346.

Orne, M.T. (1979). The use and misuse of hypnosis in court. *International Journal of Clinical and Experimental Hypnosis, 27,* 311-341.

Putnam, W.H. (1979). Hypnosis and distortions in eyewitness memory. *International Journal of Clinical and Experimental Hypnosis, 27,* 437-448.

Rainer, D.D. (1984). *Eyewitness testimony: Does hypnosis enhance accuracy, distortion, and confidence?* Unpublished doctoral dissertation, University of Wyoming, Laramie, Wyoming, USA.

Reid, J.D., & Bruce, D. (1988). On the external validity of questioning effects in eyewitness testimony. *International Review of Applied Psychology.* (in press)

Relinger, H. (1984). Hypnotic hypermnesia: A critical review. *American Journal of Clinical Hypnosis, 26,* 212-225.

Sheehan, P.W. (1988). Memory distortion in hypnosis. *International Journal of Clinical and Experimental Hypnosis.* (in press)

Sheehan, P.W., Grigg, L., & McCann, T. (1984). Memory distortion following exposure to false information in hypnosis. *Journal of Abnormal Psychology, 93,* 259-265.

Sheehan, P.W., & Tilden, J. (1983). Effects of suggestibility and hypnosis on accurate and distorted retrieval from memory. *Journal of Experimental Psychology: Learning, Memory and Cognition, 9,* 283-293.

Smith, M.C. (1983). Hypnotic memory enhancement of witnesses: Does it work? *Psychological Bulletin, 94,* 387-407.

Spanos, N.P., & McLean, J. (1986). Hypnotically created pseudomemories: Memory distortions or reporting biases. *British Journal of Experimental and Clinical Hypnosis, 3,* 155-159.

Tellegen, A. (1978/1979). On measures and conceptions of hypnosis. *American Journal of Clinical Hypnosis, 21,* 219-236.

Yuille, J. (1982). *Video as a medium for eyewitness research.* University of British Columbia, Canada.

Zelig, M., & Beidleman, W.B. (1981). The investigative use of hypnosis: A word of caution. *International Journal of Clinical and Experimental Hypnosis, 29,* 401-412.

24. A Mediational Theory of Susceptibility to Social Influence

W. J. McGuire

Psychology's two great discoveries, that everyone is basically the same and that everyone is fundamentally different, take turns in being the discipline's favorite insight. When a new topic becomes fashionable, its study usually opens with a "heroic age" in which researchers seek universal relationships; then, as multiplying studies bring complexities to light, there ensues a longer tidying-up era during which investigators look for interacting contextual variables which modify and even reverse the initially predicted relationship between the variables of interest. For example, when in the late nineteenth century the empirical study of memory began, Ebbinghaus and his early colleagues looked for general laws of learning; but interest gradually shifted from identifying *the* learning curve to investigating how its parameters are affected by characteristics of the task, the learner, and the situation.

Both personal and situational variables usually affect the output of interest, both as main effects and in interaction with the independent variables whose universal effects had first been sought. Either/or controversy often develops unnecessarily as regards the importance of situational versus personal factors, as if the operation of one rules out that of the other. This false controversy sometimes becomes aggravated by being associated with party labels, as when cognitive psychologists argue for task interactions, social psychologists for situational interactions, and personality psychologists for individual-differences interactions. The cyclical Establishment position in the unnecessary controversy regarding situational-versus-personal determination shows a quarter-century periodicity. In the 1920s, orthodoxy shifted toward situational specificity to the extreme of questioning the existence of general personality characteristics like honesty (Hartshorne & May, 1928), this shift being a reaction to the turn-of-the-century ascendancy of "faculty" psychology. By mid-century, there was a swing back to general trait theorizing (Allport, 1937; Murray, 1938) that emphasized cross-situational consistency of dynamic individual differences; then the situationalists gained ascendance again at the century's three-quarter mark (Endler & Hunt, 1968; Mischel, 1968); and now the pendulum is swinging back toward a renewed interest in personality variables (Buss & Craik, 1984; Epstein, 1983).

When empirical interest in personal variables first developed at the turn of the century, it focused primarily on abilities dimensions like sensory acuity and intelligence, but even at that early date some attention was paid to one dynamic personal characteristic, suggestibility. Disagreement between Charcot's Salpêtrière group and Liébeault's group at Nancy about the nature of hysterical suggestibility stimulated interest in the topic and Binet's (1900) book on the measurement of suggestibility was contemporaneous with his pioneering work on measuring intelligence. The first *Manual of Mental and Physical Tests* (Whipple, 1910) covered mostly tests of simple sensory and motor abilities, with suggestibility being one of the few personality traits for which there were already sufficient tests to warrant coverage. Thus, susceptibility to social influence may be the personality variable with the longest history as well as the longest past.

A Multi-Postulate Model of Susceptibility to Social Influence

Psychologists, like other scientists, are interested less in variables than in relationships between them. Once it was established that people differ measurably in their susceptibility to social influence, questions naturally arose as to how and why these individual differences in influenceability relate to other personal variables. In this chapter, we present a mediational theory to account for how different types of personal variables (demographics, abilities, personality characteristics, etc.) relate to the individual's susceptibility to various forms of social influence (modeling, suggestion, persuasion, etc.). A basic assumption in our theory is that between the social influence induction (e.g., presenting the person with a standard 3-min body-sway suggestion) and the measure of the person's compliance (e.g., his/her maximum sway in centimeters) there intervenes a chain of mediating processes including attending to the influence attempt, understanding its relevant content, agreeing with what is understood, acting on that agreement, etc.

To predict how some personal characteristic (e.g., intelligence) will be related to influenceability in a given situation one needs to analyze: (a) how that personal characteristic will affect each of the mediators (attention, comprehension, agreement, etc.) and (b) what proportion of the influenceability variance will in that situation be contributed by each of these mediators. It follows as a corollary that the relationship between the personal characteristic and susceptibility which is found in one influence situation may be generalized to other situations (e.g., the relationship of intelligence to susceptibility to persuasive propaganda may be generalized to its relationship to hypnotizability) by analyzing how the proportions of the net susceptibility variance contributed by the several mediators in the first situation corresponds to their contribution in the situation to which we wish to generalize. This plausible analytical model is powerful in yielding implications that correct common misperceptions and have a good track record of empirical verification.

Ours is an axiomatic theory in that it is composed of semi-independent postulates, each plausible and even obvious in itself, but yielding surprising theorems when pushed, especially in combination with the other postulates or when applied to new situations. We shall in this section describe five of our individual postulates and their general implications. Then in the following section, we shall bring these postulates together to account for how a diverse set of personal characteristics relate to susceptibility to social influence.

The Multiple-Mediator Postulate

We already mentioned above the gist of our first postulate, that multiple processes mediate between a person's being subjected to a social influence attempt and the amount of compliance with it that (s)he exhibits. Among the mediating processes are how much attention the person pays to the influence attempt, how much of the attended-to material is comprehended, how much of what is comprehended is agreed to, etc. It follows that how any personal variable affects net influenceability depends on how it affects each of the mediators. For example, how intelligence will relate to suggestibility depends on how intelligence affects each mediator -

attention, comprehension, agreement, etc. - and how important each mediator is for compliance with the suggestion.

This initial mediational postulate is plausible and even embarrassingly obvious, but failure to appreciate it leads to some common errors. For example, students of persuasion have an unfortunate tendency to infer how any variable will affect influenceability by analyzing that variable's effect on just one mediator, which usually is proneness to agree with influence inductions. This narrow perspective leads to inferring that influenceability is higher in children than adults, in people with low self-esteem than those with high, in the less intelligent than the highly intelligent, etc., because in each pair the second group is more resistant to agreeing when subjected to social influence. Our first postulate supplies the corrective of broadening the theorist's perspective beyond considering only the agreement mediator. When cognitive mediators like attention and comprehension are also taken into account, one's initial prediction that had been based narrowly on the agreement mediator alone is often reversed. For example, children tend to be more influenceable than adults because they agree more with the arguments that they absorb, but children tend to be less influenceable than adults because they absorb less owing to their lower attention and comprehension of the arguments presented. Our mediational analysis also shows how any personal variable's relationship to influenceability is likely to vary predictably across situations. In an influence situation where the attention and comprehension mediators contribute more to the ultimate compliance variance than does the agreement mediator, children are likely to be less susceptible than adults; but in situations where the agreement mediator contributes more to the variance, children are likely to be more susceptible.

The Combinational/Compensatory Postulate

Our second postulate has to do with how a personal variable's effects on each of these separate mediators combine to produce the net bottom-line relationship to compliance. Assuming for simplicity that all the mediating processes are measured on probabilistic scales (e.g.,the probability that each of the successive steps of attention, comprehension, agreement, etc., reaches a level that suffices to evoke the following step), then the personal variable's effect on net compliance will be the *product* of its effects on the set of mediating processes.

We add a controversial "compensatory" subassumption that personal variables typically affect the ultimate compliance outcome in opposite directions via different mediators. We already gave the example of the target persons' intelligence level as being negatively related to compliance via the agreement mediator (because intelligence reduces gullibility) and positively via the comprehension mediator (because intelligence facilitates understanding of what is being urged). This second postulate asserts that such compensatory combination is the rule rather than the exception. For example, anxiety tends to protect the person from being influenced by interfering with the attention and comprehension mediators, but anxiety tends to make the person more vulnerable to influence by augmenting the agreement mediator. It can be shown (McGuire, 1968, 1985) that such compensatory dynamics would, over a wide range of parameters, result in a nonmonotonic, inverted-U relationship between the personal variable and net compliance such

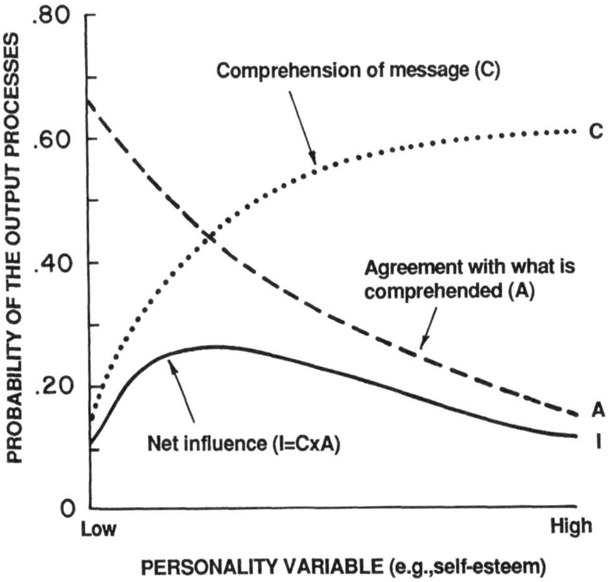

Figure 1. Depiction of the second (combinational/compensatory) postulate's corollary, that because personal variables tend to have opposite relations to influenceability via the cognitive (e.g., comprehension) and motivational (e.g., agreement) mediators, they will have a net nonmonotonic inverse-U relationship to influenceability

that persons in an intermediate range on the variable will be more influenceable than those very high or very low on it, as depicted in Figure 1.

There are both empirical and theoretical reasons for accepting the compensatory postulate. Empirical results show that numerous personal variables, when varied over a wide range, relate by this inverse-u function to influenceability (McGuire, 1968). For example, a study by Appley and Moeller (1963) found a nonmonotonic relationship between conformity and 33 of 38 personality variables. As regards the theoretical underpinnings of this compensatory principle, we make an Aristotelian argument that it is most adaptive to operate at a moderate range of influenceability: being excessively open to influence has the disadvantage of leaving the person pushed this way and that in a Brownian movement that would negate any effective course of action; and to be too impervious to influence would have the disadvantage of leaving the person unable to profit from the advice and experience of others and having to learn by his/her own errors. Where in the middle range it would be most adaptive for the person's influenceability to fall would differ depending on situational factors such as the source's credibility, the seriousness of consequences, etc. An optimal control system for keeping a response in the middle range, but able to shift readily from one to another set point within that range, is for it to be held there by two opposing forces that can vary independently with the circumstances. Further, as regards personality correlates of social influence, a person is likely to have learned how to deal with any characteristic that would make him/her hyperinfluenceable via one mediator by developing coping habits which would tend to protect him/her via other mediators from this excessive influenceability.

In general, the combinational/compensatory postulate assumes that any personal variable tends to be related to influenceability in opposite directions via alternative mediating processes. As a result, the personality variable tends to have, over its entire range, a nonmonotonic inverted-U relationship to net compliance; and the shape and maximum of this function tend to vary predictably with the amount of the variance in net compliance contributed by each mediator to which the personal variable has a compensatory positive or negative relationship.

The Situational-Weighting Postulate

The situational-weighting postulate implies that, because personal variables affect ultimate susceptibility via a series of independent mediators, one can predict the net relationship between the variable and susceptibility by considering the weighting of the mediators in the given situation, that is, the proportion of susceptibility variance contributed by each of the mediators. The theoretical structure of relationships is such that the parameters of the functions relating the personal variables to the mediators, and of the functions relating the mediators to the net compliance in any given situation, determine the resulting relationship between the personal variable and net compliance (McGuire, 1968). Hence, when these weighting parameters in the relationship between a personal variable and the mediating processes (comprehension, agreement, etc.) vary from situation to situation, then the relationship of the personal variable to net compliance will vary correspondingly in predictable ways (McGuire, 1968). For example, how intelligence, sex, self-esteem, or chronic anxiety of the target persons relate to their susceptibility to social influence will differ greatly between a hypnotizability situation and a complex-argument situation because these two situations differ sizably in how much variance in net influenceability is contributed by mediators such as comprehension.

The shape of the nonmonotonic relationship between a personal variable and influenceability, including the level on the variable at which maximum susceptibility occurs, will shift predictably among situations, depending on the parameters of the underlying relationships between the personal variable and each of the compensatory mediators in the given situation. Using intelligence as an illustrative personal variable, how these relationships will differ can be described for the two contrasting situations depicted in Figure 2. The first situation involves an influence communication so simple that virtually all participants will understand it fully, as might be the case when university students participate in a body-sway suggestibility experiment. In this typical suggestibility situation, the probability that the message will be fully comprehended is near the asymptote of 1.00 for all university students because the body-sway induction is so simple and repetitious. Hence, the comprehension mediator (which intelligence facilitates) will contribute little to the variance in compliance, and maximum susceptibility will occur at low levels of normal intelligence, beyond which suggestibility will fall as rising intelligence produces a decline in the agreement mediator. A contrasting second situation would be one involving complex persuasive arguments from a trusted source where agreement variance will be low but comprehension variance high, for example, in the case of an accountant's attempting to convince his/her client that a change of policy is necessary under a complex new tax law. How persuaded the client is to change his/her policy will depend mainly on how well (s)he can comprehend the trusted accountant's complicated arguments and recommendations, which comprehension should vary considerably as a function of the client's intelligence. But there will be relatively little variance via the agreement mediator in this tax-advice situation where the client has come to this trusted accountant with the intention of accepting his/her recommendations fully insofar as (s)he can comprehend them. Hence, in this tax situation there will be considerable variance due to the comprehension mediator (which intelligence facilitates) and little variance due to the agreement mediator (which intelligence inhibits), with the result that influenceability will increase as intelligence goes up through the normal range. The two contrasting situations, body-sway suggestion (in which intelligence will, through most of its range, be negatively related to influenceability) and the tax-advice situation (where intelligence through most of its range will be positively related to influenceability) are depicted in Figure 2.

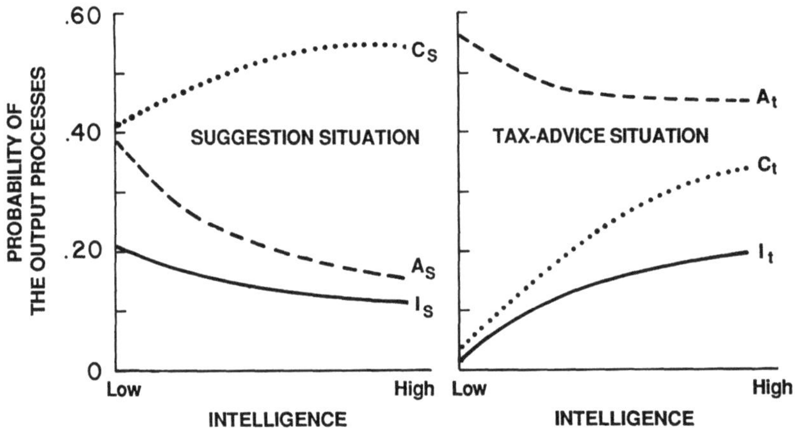

Figure 2. Depiction of the third (situational weighting) postulate's corollary that intelligence will have a negative relationship to simple suggestion influenceability (I_s) and a positive relationship to complex tax-advice influenceability (I_t) because of differences between the situations in the variance contributed by the comprehension mediator (C) and the agreement mediator (A)

The Confounded-Variable Postulate

The gist of our fourth postulate is that any personal characteristic typically exists, not as an isolated symptom, but within a syndrome of associated characteristics in which it has become embedded as a consequence of the person's long experience in coping with his/her chronic level on the personal characteristics. Appreciation that in the natural environment personal proclivities like self-esteem exist embedded in a syndrome of coping and exploiting tendencies serves as a useful corrective to the theorist's tendency to think about the characteristic abstractly, as if it existed in the pure state in which it is conceptualized, "with everything else equal." Recognition that everything else is not equal because of this syndrome embeddedness also reminds the researcher that when (s)he manipulates participants to differing momentary acute levels on a personal variable by laboratory inductions (e.g., manipulates participants' acute self-esteem levels by giving them success or failure experiences in the laboratory), this personal variable will function in the experiment as a pure symptom without its usual embeddedness in the confounding syndrome of variables which in the natural environment ordinarily moderates its relationships to influenceability or other dependent variables. These differences are discussed more fully in the next section on the chronic-versus-acute postulates. The point here is that to predict how some personal variable such as chronic self-esteem will relate to influenceability in the natural environment, the researcher should think of the variable within the confounding syndrome in which it would usually exist and not in the isolated purity in which it might enter our initial abstract thinking or to which we might manipulate it momentarily by acute laboratory inductions.

Around any important personal variable there tends to accrue a wide range of other associated variables including modes of coping with an undesirable level or modes of exploiting an advantageous level on the variable. Because of this embeddedness, persons with contrasting levels on a variable - for example, extraverts versus introverts, or those with high versus low intelligence - tend to live and act in different worlds, psychologically and sociologically. The terribly shy person tends to go through life, not writhing in painful embarrassment, but rather with a lifestyle that protects him/her from being in social situations where the shyness would be aversive.

The point of this fourth postulate is that in predicting how some personal characteristic (such as having a high level of neurotic anxiety) will be related to susceptibility to social influence, the researcher has to consider also the effects of its accrued syndrome of coping mechanisms (such as skill at avoiding fear-arousing situations). If a person's high anxiety would make him/her overly gullible owing to an excessive tendency to agree under pressure, then such a person is likely to protect him/herself from experiencing such pressures by developing a psychological style of low attention and comprehension in the face of influence attempts. This embeddedness, plus the third postulate, situational weighting, yield interaction predictions for personal characteristics like neurotic anxiety which make the person hypersusceptible to social influence by being too agreement prone and which protect the person from being influenced by reducing his/her attention to and comprehension of the influence attempt. From interaction prediction it follows that, as anxiety increases, influenceability will decline for a public health campaign using complex arguments urging adoption of some illness-avoiding behavior, but influenceability will rise for cognitively simple influence messages such as repetitious arm-levitation suggestion.

Several postulates assert that an intermediate level on the personal variable produces maximum influenceability (with the precise maxima shifting with circumstances), that personal variables tend to be related to influenceability in opposite ways via different mediators, and that any personality characteristic tends to get embedded in a syndrome of compensatory characteristics. Together these characteristics imply that people who differ widely in their level on an influence-relevant personal variable will tend to end up at similar intermediate levels of influenceability under a wide range of natural circumstances, so that main effects will tend to be small. On the other hand, the operation of the personal variable will show up in the form of predictable interactions. The lack of main effects could be due either to the mutual cancellations postulated or to generally weak relationships; the predicted interactions, if confirmed, will indicate that the lack of sizable main effects between personal characteristics and influenceability is due, not to lack of relationships, but to there being sizable relationships that are mutually cancelling in the manner postulated.

The Chronic-Versus-Acute Variable Postulate

The fifth postulate, the last of the assumptions in our general theory of influenceability that we shall consider here, pertains to readily manipulable personality variables more than to relatively fixed demographic or abilities variables. This postulate (derivable as a corollary from our second and fourth postulates) asserts that a personality variable like self-esteem is really two rather different variables depending on whether it is being considered as regards acutely manipulated levels or as regards chronic natural levels. For example, when the momentary level of acute self-esteem is manipulated by experimentally induced success and failure experiences, we are dealing with a pure self-esteem variable that is quite different from the confounded self-esteem variable obtained by selecting research participants who are at their different natural levels of chronic self-esteem.

Likewise, anxiety is a different variable depending on whether people are given a laboratory fear-arousing induction to manipulate anxiety as a pure symptom or whether people are selected at their varying levels of natural chronic anxiety which are likely to be embedded in a syndrome of coping mechanisms. The first, acute-variable case of manipulating the independent variable by treatments that place random subsets of participants on contrasting momentary levels of the personality variable varies the pure symptom as it is typically conceptualized in the researcher's abstract theorizing, but quite unlike the confounded syndrome in which the variable is likely to exist in the natural environment. In the second, chronic-variable case where the independent variable is allowed to fluctuate naturally by picking persons at their diverse natural levels of anxiety, the variable is being studied in its usual state of confounded embeddedness in a syndrome of coping variables in which chronic anxiety typically exists in the natural environment. How anxiety will relate to influenceability in this latter case depends, not only on its own effects on the several mediators, but also on how the other variables with which it is confounded affect those mediators.

Each of the two tactics for varying the characteristics has its uses. The acute manipulational tactic varies the (unnaturally) pure personal variable and so allows studying the theoretical "as-if" relationship to influenceability of the pure variable as it enters abstract conceptualization. The alternative correlational tactic of selecting people at their varying natural chronic levels on the personal variable allows studying its "as is" relationship to influenceability, which would allow valid generalization to natural situations. Each answer is meaningful and useful in its proper context, but the two answers are likely to be different. The researcher should use manipulated acute levels if (s)he is studying the relationships that would obtain within the abstract world of some theory of anxiety-in-itself; but (s)he should use the natural chronic levels if (s)he wants to generalize to natural situations and so should study the relationships of anxiety as it exists in its ordinary confounded state. As alternative methodological tactics, the two approaches have counterbalancing advantages. What this fifth postulate brings out is that these alternative tactics involve substantive as well as methodological differences to the extent that they actually investigate different personal variables, the acute manipulational tactic varying the pure, hypothetical symptom and the chronic, correlational approach varying the embedded natural syndrome.

A second clarifying corollary concerns joint use of acute and chronic variations of the personal variable. Its derivation requires the postulate's implication that most personal variables, over their entire range, are related to influenceability in an inverted-U function, with maximum influenceability occurring at intermediate levels of the personal variable. It follows that the acute manipulation of a personal variable could either increase or decrease the person's influenceability, depending on his/her chronic level on that variable. For example, because people at intermediate levels of self-esteem are most susceptible to influence, it follows that manipulating the person's acute self-esteem in the upward direction by giving him/her a laboratory success experience would raise the person's influenceability if (s)he is chronically very low in self-esteem, but lower influenceability for those whose chronic level of self-esteem is quite high. This set of relationships is depicted in Figure 3, using anxiety as the illustrative personal variable.

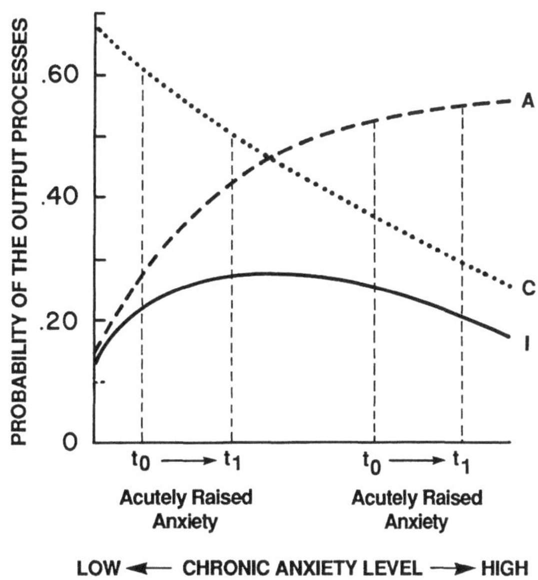

Figure 3. Depiction of the fifth postulate's corollary that an acute manipulation of a personality variable (e.g., anxiety) will have opposite positive versus negative effects on net influenceability, depending on whether the person is chronically low versus chronically high on that variable

These complexities, arising from the use of acute versus chronic variations of a personal variable, should be kept in mind when one is trying to predict the variable's relationship to influenceability. The distinction helps to untangle some of the knotty confusions reported in the empirical literature, as when one researcher reports a positive and another a negative relationship between the personal variable and susceptibility to influence. The analytical theory that we propose here shows these seeming contradictions are rich complexities predictable by this heuristically provocative theory whose complexity appropriately mirrors the complicated domain which it is supposed to reflect.

Relationships to Influenceability of Selected Personal Variables

In this section we shall illustrate the conjoint operation of the five postulates just reviewed by describing how a diverse set of personal variables relates to suggestibility and other types of influenceability. To widen the range of coverage, we shall select our examples from three widely different types of personal variables including a demographic variable (sex), an abilities variable (chronological age or years of education), and a personality variable (anxiety).

Sex Differences in Influenceability

Our earliest reviews of the research literature on sex differences and susceptibility to social influence (McGuire, 1968, 1969) concluded that there is a slight sex difference, statistically but not practically significant, in the direction that women are more susceptible to influence than are men, the size of the sex difference varying somewhat among types of influence situations. There followed a 1970s revisionism (e.g., Maccoby & Jacklin, 1974), when it was asserted that the empirical literature did not support this conclusion because most studies failed to find a significant sex difference. However, our conclusion was based on the evidence that when significant sex differences are found it is preponderantly in the direction of higher susceptibility in women, and that even in the studies not finding significant differences, the direction of the difference is preponderantly that of greater susceptibility in females (Block, 1976). More quantitative meta-analytical studies in the present decade (Cooper, 1979; Eagly & Carli, 1981) reconfirm the initial conclusions we based on qualitative review of the literature. Across the better studies there is a significantly greater influenceability in women than in men, (though the sex difference is of very modest magnitude, accounting for about 1 % of the variance in susceptibility) and with the difference being greatest in conformity situations where surveillance can be exercised over the degree of compliance.

Controversy on sex-difference topics is to be expected because ideology as well as political and economic interests interfere with objectivity, especially now when equal treatment of or outcomes between the sexes has become a salient social issue. Objectivity in interpreting the results may be facilitated if one keeps two considerations in mind. First, being resistant to social influence is not necessarily a Good Thing, like 1066; we have argued above that it is most adaptive to be at an intermediate level of influenceability. Secondly, it should be remembered that such sex differences as are found need not be due to genetics; they could as plausibly be a spillover into the laboratory of a cultural tendency for women to be socialized more than are men to play compliant roles (Buss, 1981; Eagly, 1983; Klein & Willerman, 1979; Weitzman,1979).

This slightly higher susceptibility in women than in men can be interpreted and elaborated in terms of our mediational theory. The first postulate, that there are multiple mediators, draws attention to the common error of predicting or explaining any relationship between a personal variable (such as sex) and influenceability too narrowly, solely in terms of the agreement mediator. In the narrow perspective of the agreement mediator, the apparent tendency for most cultures to socialize women more than men to be more agreement-prone could account for women's being the more influenceable. When we broaden our perspective to include cognitive mediators such as attention and comprehension, we note that females, especially in childhood and adolescent years, are superior to males in verbal skills; admittedly, it is again the case that many studies find no significant sex difference in verbal performance (Maccoby & Jacklin, 1974), but the differences which do occur are predominantly in the direction of superior verbal performance by girls over boys (Block, 1976; Hyde, 1981). Hence, girls' better comprehension also could account for their higher susceptibility to influence, especially in situations where the attention and comprehension mediators contribute substantially to the net compliance variance.

Because in the case of sex differences both the cognitive and motivational mediations would seem to make women more influenceable than men, the difficulty is not so much in accounting for why the slight sex difference is found as in accounting for why the difference is not greater, a question to which we shall return below. The finding that the sex difference in influenceability is greatest in simple conformity situations that allow surveillance of the target person's compliance (Eagly & Carli, 1981) suggests that the motivational, agreement mediator does contribute to the obtained sex difference in net influenceability. One could test whether the comprehension mediator also plays its predicted role by testing whether the sex difference in influenceability is greater for complex persuasive messages than for simple ones.

The inductions of hypnosis or body-sway typically used in suggestibility research tend to be so simple and repetitious that there would be very little variance in the normal adult population in attention and comprehension of the message, and so these cognitive mediators might seem to contribute little to any sex difference specifically in suggestibility. However, the cognitive mediators of suggestibility may be more subtle than simple verbal comprehension of the induction; they may involve imaginativeness more than passive information absorption (Bowers, 1982; Crawford, 1982; Hilgard, 1979; Sheehan, 1982; Sheehan & McConkey, 1982) and may involve attention of a right-hemisphere visual imagery type rather than of a left-hemisphere verbal type (Gur & Gur, 1974; MacLeod-Morgan & Lack, 1982). Perhaps there is a sex difference in the type of cognition associated with suggestibility such that women's greater verbal ability, far from making them more influenceable, interferes with a visual, imaginative style of cognition that enhances suggestibility; if so, women's verbal cognitive style may protect them against suggestibility and so counterbalance their greater vulnerability via the agreement mediator. This counterbalancing, which our second postulate asserts to be typical, would help explain why obtained main-effect sex differences are not as great as implied by the more simplistic analysis. More research is needed which would use direct measures and manipulations of the relevant cognitive and dynamic mediators in a variety of influence situations and would then partial out, by covariance or multiple regression analysis, the mediating role of each of the mutually cancelling intervening processes in accounting for sex differences in net compliance and for the contextual interactions.

Correctives to over-simplistic theorizing about how abilities variables such as mental or chronological age will relate to influenceability are offered by our first two postulates - that cognitive (attention and comprehension) as well as motivational (agreement) mediation are involved, and that the several mediators tend to have mutually compensatory effects, resulting in a net nonmonotonic relationship between any ability variable and influenceability. The layperson often conjectures simplistically that there will be a negative relationship between intelligence and susceptibility on the grounds that intelligence tends to increase resistance to agreeing (because the more intelligent person tends to have more backing for her/his initial stand, higher confidence, more daring to maintain a discrepant stand, etc.). However, the mediational postulate reminds us that cognitive processes like attention and comprehension also play mediating roles, via which intelligence will tend to make the person more susceptible to influence.

Overall, a nonmonotonic relationship would be predicted such that people of intermediate intelligence will be more influenceable than those of very high or very low intelligence; and that the intermediate band of intelligence that produces maximum influenceability will vary predictably among situations. Specifically, maximum influenceability will occur higher in the intermediate range of intelligence to the extent that cognitive mediators contribute appreciably to the influence variance; and maximum influenceability occurs lower in the intermediate range of intelligence to the extent that the agreement mediator accounts for more of the variance. The corrective value of this mediational analysis was shown in the World War II U.S. Army indoctrination studies of the persuasive impact of the *Why We Fight* films, which tended to increase with the viewers' years of education (Hovland, Lumsdaine, & Sheffield, 1949).

In suggestibility situations, the message is so simple and repetitious that the variance in influenceability contributed by the attention and comprehension mediators would be small and that contributed by the agreement mediator would be relatively large. Hence, maximum suggestibility should occur at relatively low levels of intelligence and suggestibility should go down as intelligence rises over the normal adult range. However, even inductions as simple as those used in suggestion studies impose enough demand on the attention and comprehension mediators so that at very low levels of cognitive functioning, such as would sometimes occur in schizophrenia or in the early childhood years, attention and comprehension may be so inadequate as to reduce hypnotizability and other types of suggestibility (Barber, Karacan & Calverly, 1964; Lavoie & Sabourin, 1980) unless schizophrenics in poor contact are excluded from the sample (Abrams, 1964).

Chronological age during the childhood years can be used as a rough measure of ability in studying ability's relationship to suggestibility. The compensatory postulate's prediction of a nonmonotonic inverse-u relationship between ability and suggestibility is borne out in a number of developmental studies (Barber & Calverly, 1963; London & Cooper, 1969; Messerschmidt, 1933; Morgan & Hilgard, 1973) which indicate that susceptibility to hypnosis and other forms of suggestion rises with age from the preschool years to a peak at about 9 or 10 years of age and then declines with age through adolescence until it levels out (presumably with ability) during the years of maturity. Admittedly, some good studies like Stukát's (1958) do not find the rise during the younger years, but this is plausibly attributable to the truncated age range used.

Personality Variables in Relationship to Influenceability

The complexities and confusions among the findings regarding how dynamic personality variables such as self-esteem and anxiety relate to influenceability can be untangled by our third, fourth, and fifth postulates. In the case of commonly studied personality variables like self-esteem, it is not difficult to find studies which among them include reports of positive, negative, U-shaped, and inverse-U relationships between self-esteem and influenceability (Cox & Bauer, 1964; Janis & Field, 1959; Lehmann, 1970; McGuire & Ryan, 1955; Silverman, 1964; Zellner, 1970). This variety of results is just what would be expected on the basis of our axiomatic theory and, more important, the theory accounts for which relationship will be found under which circumstances.

Anxiety will serve to illustrate how our theory accounts for, untangles, and predicts complex findings regarding the relationships between personality variables and susceptibility to social influence. In its pure form, anxiety, with its cue and drive components, would tend to enhance the person's vulnerability to influence by increasing proneness to agree but to protect against influenceability by interfering with attention and comprehension. This results in a nonmonotonic relationship such that maximum susceptibility would occur at moderate levels of anxiety where the person is anxious enough not to be apathetic but not so anxious as to be withdrawn from the situation (Lazarus, 1981; Leventhal & Nerenz, 1983).

Different relationships to influenceability would also occur depending on whether the anxiety is acutely induced by a fear-arousing induction or whether it is varied naturalistically by selecting a heterogeneous sample of persons who differ in levels of chronic anxiety that would have become embedded in different patterns of coping. Different levels of chronic anxiety would have distinctive effects due to the different syndromes of coping tendencies in which they would have become embedded; and so also would acute manipulations of anxiety have their peculiar effects, such as the tendency for fear-arousing inductions to evoke hostility and reactance as well as anxiety. Also, the chronic and acute variations will tend to interact with each other owing to the overall nonmonotonic relationship, in that using an acute fear induction to raise momentary anxiety level would increase the influenceability of someone chronically low in anxiety and decrease influenceability in someone chronically high in anxiety (Millman, 1968), as illustrated in Figure 3. The confounding of chronic level of anxiety with self-esteem and other personality variables which also affect the mediators further complicates chronic anxiety's relationship to influenceability in predictable ways (Lehmann, 1970).

Timing and type of the influence measure will also affect the obtained relationship. For example, anxiety tends to elicit coping by repression, and so a high fear-arousing message elicits more immediate intention to comply but less long-term actual compliance (Evans et al., 1970), a result that would be intensified in persons with a repressor style of coping. Thus, by taking into consideration these five postulates, it is possible to account for the complex pattern of obtained results, to derive new predictions about the relationships between personality variables and influenceability, and to design more effective social influence campaigns.

Recent Reconceptualizations

Two recent advances in social influence theory, the "cognitive responses" theorizing and the "central versus peripheral routes" theorizing, deserve special attention from students of susceptibility to suggestion and other forms of social influence, especially in conjunction with the mediational theory described here.

Our earliest formulation of this mediational theory (McGuire, 1968) discussed the cognitive mediating step of comprehension largely as it involves absorbing the information presented in the message from the outside source, as might be measured by a test of the amount of learning of arguments used in the social influence message. More recently, users of the "cognitive responses" approach (Greenwald, Brock, & Ostrom, 1968; McGuire, 1960; Petty, Ostrom, & Brock, 1981) have demonstrated that the cognitive mediating steps involve not only absorbing the information contained in the outside message, but also generating further cognitions not explicitly contained in the message but elicited by the message from material already in the receiver's cognitive arena. For example, the amount of attitude change induced by a persuasive message and the amount of action change to which it leads have been found to reflect not only the absorption of the arguments actually contained in the message, but also the amount of further arguments which exposure to the message provokes the receiver to generate for him/herself (Calder, Insko, & Yandell, 1974; Greenwald, 1968; McGuire, 1964; Watts, 1967).

The role of these self-generated cognitions, occasioned by the influence induction though not explicitly contained in it, is likely to be especially high in determining hypnotizability and other forms of suggestion. A number of studies have shown that hypnotizability is considerably affected by how actively the person's imagination is engaged (Hilgard, 1979), particularly in the form of elicited mental imagery (Sheehan, 1982). Hypnotizability research (Gur & Gur, 1974; MacLeod-Morgan & Lack, 1982) suggests that self-generated imagery cognitions are likely to play a more important mediational role than does the passive encoding of verbal material explicitly contained in the induction, although past social influence studies have focused more on the latter.

A second recent reorientation in social influence theorizing that bears on the relationships between personal variables and suggestibility is the notion of central vs. peripheral routes to persuasion (Krugman, 1977; Petty & Cacioppo, 1986; Ray, 1973). This distinction is particularly relevant to our situational-weighting postulate. When the influence situation is likely to evoke considerable cognitive elaboration (for example, because the importance of the issue or the ambiguity of the situation requires the person's careful analysis of the information) then influence is likely to occur via a central route involving the whole chain of postulated mediators. However, when the situation is such as to allow agreement to be decided on the basis of a simple peripheral cue (such as source credibility), without having to absorb and evaluate the information in the message, then the communication is likely to be processed via a short-cut peripheral route (Petty & Cacioppo, 1986). Hence, quite different relationships between personal variables and persuasive impact are likely to be found, depending on whether conditions result in the central or peripheral route's being used. The hypnotic situation tends to involve a very simple persuasive message whose incidental aspects such as hypnotist's status serve as crucial cues, and so would tend to involve the peripheral route. Hence, relationships between personal variables and hypnotizability would tend to be mediated by few intervening processes and to be determined by incidental cues of a striking emotional rather than an informational nature. There is the additional complication that hypnosis situations often elicit considerable apprehension in the target person (who may fear that being hypnotized will be a sign of weakness, or make one appear ridiculous, or produce long-term unpleasant side effects, etc.). Persons high in such worries would tend to process the information through the central route, carefully analyzing and evaluating the hypnotic induction. Insofar as the person falls into this hypnosis-apprehensive category, his/her personal variables would relate to suggestibility via more mediators, and more weight would be given to informational relative to emotional aspects of the induction. That apprehension level can divert the persuasion process into one or another of two quite different routes may explain why hypnotizability and its correlates are often affected by the person's attitude toward hypnosis (Melei & Hilgard, 1964; Sheehan & McConkey, 1982; Shor, Orne, & O'Connell, 1966).

In summary, the complexity and elusiveness of the relationships found between personal variables and suggestibility or other types of influence become more understandable when one uses an axiomatic theory such as the one we propose here, made up of plausible independent postulates. Such a theory accounts not only for the general complexity of the relationships generally obtained in the area, but also for the specific relationships that make up the complex picture. In addition to accounting for past complexities found, this approach suggests a wide range of new relationships for future investigation. In this light, the complexity and elusiveness of past findings become, not an embarrassment, but a promise of future riches.

Acknowledgment. The writing of this chapter was greatly facilitated by research grant MH 32588 received from the Interpersonal Processes and Problems Section, Behavioral Sciences Research Branch of the National Institute of Mental Health.

References

Abrams, S. (1964). The use of hypnotic techniques with psychotics. *American Journal of Psychotherapy, 18*, 79-94.

Allport, G.W. (1937). *Personality: A psychological interpretation*. New York: Holt.

Appley, M.H., & Moeller, G. (1963). Conforming behavior and personality variables in college women. *Journal of Personality and Social Psychology, 66*, 284-290.

Barber, T.X., & Calverley, D.S. (1963). "Hypnotic-like" suggestibility in children and adults. *Journal of Abnormal and Social Psychology, 66*, 589-597.

Barber, T.X., Karacan, I., & Calverley, D.S. (1964). Hypnotizability and suggestibility in chronic schizophrenics. *Archives of Genetic Psychiatry, 11*, 439-451.

Binet, A. (1900). *La Suggestibilité*. Paris: Scheicher Frères.

Block, J.H. (1976). Issues, problems & pitfalls in assessing sex differences: A critical review of "The psychology of sex differences." *Merrill-Palmer Quarterly, 22*, 283-308.

Bowers, P.G. (1982). The classic suggestion effect: Relationships with scales of hypnotizability, effortless experience, and imagery vividness. *International Journal of Clinical and Experimental Hypnosis, 30*, 270-279.

Buss, D.M. (1981). Sex differences in the evaluation and performance of dominant acts. *Journal of Personality and Social Psychology, 40*, 147-154.

Buss, D.M., & Craik, K.H. (1984). Acts, dispositions, and personality. *Progress in Experimental Personality Research, 13*, 241-301.

Calder, B.J., Insko, C.A., & Yandell, B. (1974). The relation of cognitive and memorial processes to persuasion in a simulated jury level. *Journal of Applied Social Psychology, 4*, 62-93.

Cooper, H.M. (1979). Statistically combining independent studies: A meta-analysis of sex differences in conformity research. *Journal of Personality and Social Psychology, 37*, 131-146.

Cox, D.F., & Bauer, R.A. (1964). Self-confidence and persuasibility in women. *Public Opinion Quarterly, 28*, 453-466.

Crawford, H.J. (1982). Hypnotizability, daydreaming style, imagery vividness, and absorption: A multidimensional study. *Journal of Personality and Social Psychology, 42*, 915-926.

Eagly, A.H. (1983). Gender and social influence: A social psychological analysis. *American Psychologist, 38*, 971-981.

Eagly, A.H., & Carli, L.L.(1981). Sex of researchers and sex-typed communications as determinants of sex differences in influenceability: A meta-analysis of social influence studies. *Psychological Bulletin, 90*, 1-20.

Endler, N.S. & Hunt, J.McV. (1968). S-R inventories of hostility and comparisons of the proportions of variance from persons, responses, and situations for hostility and anxiousness. *Journal of Personality and Social Psychology, 9*, 309-315.

Epstein, S. (1983). Aggregation and beyond: Some basic issues on the prediction of behavior. *Journal of Personality, 51*, 360-392.

Evans, R.I., Rozelle, R.M., Lasater, T.M., Dembroski, T.M., & Allen, B.P. (1970). Fear arousal, persuasion, and actual versus implied behavioral change: New perspective utilizing a real-life dental hygiene program. *Journal of Personality and Social Psychology, 16*, 220-227.

Greenwald, A.G. (1968) Cognitive learning, cognitive response to persuasion, and attitude change. In A.G. Greenwald, T.S. Brock, & T.M. Ostrom (Eds.), *Psychological foundations of attitudes* (pp. 147-170). New York: Academic.

Greenwald, A.G., Brock, T.S., & Ostrom, T.M. (Eds.). (1968). *Psychological foundations of attitudes*. New York: Academic.

Gur, R.C., & Gur, R.E. (1974). Handedness, sex, and eyedness as moderating variables in the relation between hypnotic susceptibility and functional brain asymmetry. *Journal of Abnormal Psychology, 83*, 635-643.

Hartshorne, H., & May, M.A. (1928). *Studies in the nature of character: V. Studies in deceit*. New York: Macmillan.

Hilgard, E.R. (1979). Divided consciousness in hypnosis: The implications of the hidden observer. In E. Fromm & R.E. Shor, *Hypnosis: Developments in research and new perspectives* (pp. 45-80). Chicago: Aldine.

Hovland, C.I., Lumsdaine, A.A. & Sheffield, F.D. (1949). *Studies in social psychology in World War II*. Vol. 3. *Experiments on mass communications*. Princeton, NJ: Princeton University.

Hyde, J.S. (1981). How large are cognitive gender differences? A meta-analysis using w^2 and *d*. *American Psychologist, 36*, 892-901.

Janis, I.L., & Field, P.B. (1959). Sex differences and personality factors related to persuasibility. In C.I. Hovland & I.L. Janis (Eds.), *Personality and persuasibility* (pp. 55-68). New Haven, CT: Yale University.

Klein, H.M., & Willerman, L. (1979). Psychological masculinity and femininity and typical and maximal dominance expression in women. *Journal of Personality and Social Psychology, 37*, 2059-2070.

Krugman, H. (1977). Memory without recall, exposure without perception. *Journal of Advertising Research, 17*(4), 7-12.

Lavoie, G., & Sabourin, M. (1980). Hypnosis and schizophrenia: A review of experimental and clinical studies. In G. Burrows & L. Dinnerstein (Eds.), *Handbook of hypnosis and psychosomatic medicine* (pp. 377-419). Amsterdam: Elsevier/North Holland.

Lazarus, R.S. (1981). The stress and coping paradigm. In C. Eisdorfer, D. Cohen, A. Kleinman & P. Maxim (Eds.), *Models for clinical psychopathology*. New York: Spectrum.

Lehmann, S. (1970). Personality and compliance: a study of anxiety and self-esteem in opinion and behavior change. *Journal of Personality and Social Psychology, 15*, 76-86.

Leventhal, H., & Nerenz, D. (1983). Representations of threat and the control of stress. In D. Meichenbaum & M. Jaremko (Eds.), *Stress reduction and prevention: A cognitive behavioral approach*. New York: Plenum.

London, P., & Cooper, L.M. (1969). Norms of hypnotic susceptibility in children. *Developmental Psychology, 1*, 113-124.

Maccoby, E.E., & Jacklin, C.N. (1974). *The psychology of sex differences*. Stanford, CA: Stanford University.

MacLeod-Morgan, C., & Lack, L. (1982). Hemispheric specificity: A physiological concomitant of hypnotizability. *Psychophysiology, 19*, 687-690.

McGuire, W.J. (1960). A syllogistic analysis of cognitive relationships. In M.J. Rosenberg and C.I. Hovland (Eds.), *Attitude organization and change* (pp. 65-111). New Haven: Yale University.

McGuire, W.J. (1964). Inducing resistance to persuasion. In L. Berkowitz (Ed.), *Advances in experimental social psychology* (Vol. 1, pp. 191-229). New York: Academic.

McGuire, W.J. (1968). Personality and susceptibility to social influence. In E.F. Borgatta & W.W. Lambert (Eds.), *Handbook of personality theory and research* (pp. 1130-1187). Chicago: Rand-McNally.

McGuire, W.J. (1969). Attitudes and attitude change. In G. Lindzey & E. Aronson (Eds.), *The handbook of social psychology* (2nd ed., Vol. 3, pp. 136-314). Reading, MA: Addison-Wesley.

McGuire, W.J. (1985). Attitudes and attitude change. In G. Lindzey & E. Aronson (Eds.), *The handbook of social psychology* (3rd ed., Vol. 2, pp. 233-346). New York: Random House.

McGuire, W.J. & Ryan, J. (1955). *Receptivity as a mediator of personality-persuasibility relationships*. University of Minnesota Laboratory for Research in Social Relations, 20 pp.

Melei, J., & Hilgard, E.R. (1964). Attitudes toward hypnosis, self-predictions and hypnotic susceptibility. *International Journal of Clinical and Experimental Hypnosis, 12*, 99-108.

Messerschmidt, R. (1933). Response of boys between the ages of 5 and 16 years to Hull's postural suggestion test. *Journal of Genetic Psychology, 43*, 405-421.

Millman, S. (1968). Anxiety, comprehension and susceptibility to social influence. *Journal of Personality and Social Psychology, 9*, 251-256.

Mischel, W. (1968). *Personality and assessment*. New York: Wiley.

Morgan, A.H. & Hilgard, E.R. (1973). Age differences in susceptibility to hypnosis. *International Journal of Clinical and Experimental Hypnosis, 21*, 78-85.

Murray, H.A. (1938). *Explorations in personality*. New York: Oxford.

Petty, R.E, & Cacioppo, J.T. (1986). *Communication and persuasion: Central and peripheral routes to attitude change*. New York: Springer.

Petty, R.E., Ostrom, T.M. & Brock, T.C. (Eds.). (1981). *Cognitive responses in persuasion*. Hillsdale, NJ: Erlbaum.

Ray, M.L. (1973). Marketing communication and the hierarchy of effects. In P. Clarke (Ed.), *New models for communications research*. Beverly Hills: Sage.

Sheehan, P.W. (1982). Imagery and hypnosis - Forging a link, at least in part. *Research in Community Psychology, Psychiatry, & Behavior, 7*, 257-272.

Sheehan, P.W., & McConkey, K.M. (1982). *Hypnosis and experience: The exploration of phenomena and process*. Hillsdale, NJ: Erlbaum.

Shor, R.E., Orne, M.T., & O'Connell, D.N. (1966). Psychological correlates of plateau hypnotizability in a special volunteer sample. *Journal of Personality and Social Psychology, 3*, 80-95.

Silverman, I. (1964). Differential effects of ego threat upon persuasibility for high and low self-esteem subjects. *Journal of Abnormal and Social Psychology, 69*, 567-572.

Stukát, K.-G. (1958). *Suggestibility: A factorial and experimental analysis*. Stockholm: Almqvist & Wiksell.

Watts, W.A. (1967). Relative persistence of opinion change induced by active compared to passive participation. *Journal of Personality and Social Psychology, 5*, 4-15.

Weitzman, L.J. (1979). *Sex role socialization: A focus on women*. Palo Alto, CA: Mayfield.
Whipple, G.M. (1910). *Manual of mental and physical tests*. Baltimore, MD: Warwick.
Zellner, M. (1970). Self-esteem, reception, and influenceability. *Journal of Personality and Social Psychology, 15*, 87-93.

25. Suggestion and Credibility: Lie Detection Based on Content-Related Cues

K. FIEDLER

The term "suggestive communication" refers to those pragmatic aspects of communication which are not stated explicitly by the sender but have to be "read between the lines" or inferred from contextual cues by the receiver. Suggestive processes come into play to the extent that communication goes beyond the mere coding and decoding of language signs or body signs (Austin, 1962; Higgins, 1981; Rommetveit, 1974). In fact, the directly stated contents of verbal messages often serve to distract the receiver from noticing subtle influences that reach the receiver via indirect paths (Loftus, 1975). One prominent variant of these phenomena, which the present chapter addresses, is the communication of *credibility* or, stated differently, the impression conveyed by the sender that he/she is telling the truth rather than lying. Accordingly, the problem of lie detection (DePaulo & Rosenthal, 1979; Ekman & Friesen, 1974) is conceived here as a paradigm for studying suggestive communication.

Indirect, or suggestive, communication is by no means confined to coping with taboo topics or highly embarrassing contents of speech (such as revealing intimate contents, or the way in which we try to transmit a signal to other people that we want to finish a conversation, or how we tell our guests that it is time now to go home). Rather, a *suggestive component is ubiquitous* in the sense that we cannot "not-communicate" or cease to express sympathy, mood, intelligence, how we define the situation, what the nature of the speech act is, and much more about the conversational context (Searle, 1976; Watzlawick, Beavin, & Jackson, 1967). This should be particularly evident for credibility which is ubiquitous and ever salient in everyday interaction, in politics, in the legal system, as well as in written documents (Bolinger, 1973). To tell the truth is tantamount to Grice's (1971) maxim of quality in cooperative communication.

Lying Among Other Types of Suggestive Influence

No doubt, appearing truthful and creating trust are important goals of communication in general, and it is obvious that management of credibility is relevant to social interaction. Before we look at some pertinent empirical findings, however, it is instructive to compare the concept of deception and lying, as a social phenomenon, with other concepts of social influence (Table 1) which traditionally appear in separate parts of the psychological literature and with reference to different research paradigms. The conceptual framework depicted in Table 1 may serve to clarify the relation of credibility management to other fields of suggestion research and at the same time sensitize the reader to the intrinsic similarity and fuzzy limits between seemingly independent research paradigms.

Although the classification of suggestive influences in Table 1 is arbitrary and does by no means represent the only possible distinctions, it reflects some differences in connotation or "surplus meaning" that might have contributed to the relative isolation of research paradigms. The

Table 1. Comparison of different approaches to suggestive influences

Mediating Process	Influence brought about by Intrinsic forces in the recipient	Extrinsic forces from the influence agent
Social or personal power	Modeling	Conformity
Verbally expressed information	Persuasion	Lying, deception
Nonvolitional processes	Constructive memory	Demand effects

classification is based on a twofold distinction corresponding to the rows and columns of Table 1. The three rows refer to different mediating processes, whereas the two columns reflect different pragmatic or dynamic relations between the agent of social influence (sender) and the object person (receiver).

In the case of both the *modeling* (Bandura, 1971) and the *conformity* approaches (Freedman & Doob, 1968), influence relies on social or personal, rather than informational, power (cf. first row). Although a social model may often be an "expert" and conformity pressures may reflect sound experience, the "surplus meaning" of the concepts serves to highlight social factors rather than message contents. The crucial feature which distinguishes the model's power from conformity pressure lies in the pragmatic relation between subject and object and roughly corresponds to the difference between voluntary and coercive forces. In "modeling," intrinsic forces within the object person are emphasized; in the "conformity" situation, the influence is silently attributed to the subject agent's external pressure.

In a similar vein, the distinction between *persuasion* (Petty, Ostrom, & Brock, 1981) and *lying or deception* (Zuckerman, DePaulo, & Rosenthal, 1981) in the middle row also reflects the difference between intrinsic conviction and external manipulation by invalid information. The influence attempt, however, is conceived as mediated by the power of information (or misinformation), rather than the appeal to social individuals. Again, the connotative difference should not be misunderstood as a sound theoretical distinction.

The remaining two variants also involve the transmission of information but in a much more subtle, nonvolitional, and often unconscious manner. The term *constructive memory* is meant to refer to those phenomena in which subtle linguistic presuppositions (Loftus, 1975) or priming influences (Neely, 1977) instigate the construction, in the object person, of scenarios or mental representations that cannot be separated in memory from the original external information. *Demand effects* (Orne, 1962), on the other hand, refer to similar influences elicited by subtle external forces. Again, the concepts place a different emphasis on either intrinsic or extrinsic factors, even though the distinction is unclear on the theoretical level (i.e., a "prime" can often be considered a "demand").

Within this conceptual context, the deception or lie detection approach can be characterized as follows. First, the psychology of the lie appears to be less associated, traditionally, with suggestion research than the other paradigms included in Table 1. Second, the various types of suggestive influences in social situations are more closely related than one would expect from the conceptual labels, the limits between paradigms being often blurred and far from exclusive. Thus, it is no coincidence that lying is especially likely in conformity or modeling situations. Persuasive rhetorics and lying are difficult to distinguish in reality; lying may not be intentional but reflect misleading memory constructions; or lying is often an attempt to cope with conflicting demand effects. And finally, the framework in Table 1 is intended to detach the psychology of the lie from an inappropriate moralist perspective and to treat lying as a normal communication construct (Knapp, Hart, & Dennis, 1974) applicable to everyone (Sacks, 1975).

A Brief Overview of Research on Human Lie Detection

Historically, empirical research on lie detection originated in two main traditions, the *physiological* polygraph approach and the *nonverbal communication* approach. The impact of linguistic (i.e., content-related) cues has been largely neglected at least in empirical research, although several authors have emphasized the potential importance of linguistic and pragmatic factors (cf. the reviews by Zuckerman et al., 1981; Kraut, 1980; and Knapp & Comadena, 1979). A sample of the most prominent physiological and nonverbal cues that have been shown to be useful in the two dominant research traditions is shown in Table 2. Although the list of cues is far from being exhaustive, it conveys a representative picture of the type of cues receiving most attention in previous research.

Table 2. Sample of physiological and nonverbal cues frequently cited in lie detection research

Physiological symptoms	Signs in nonverbal behavior
Galvanic skin resistance	Speech rate
Blood pressure	Speech hesitations
Respiration measures	Adaptors
Pupil dilation	Signs of nervousness
	Voice pitch

The physiological approach utilizing lie detectors (Lykken, 1974; Podlesny & Raskin, 1977) clearly originated in the context of interrogations by police and juridical examinations of witnesses and defendants. It should be noted that lying in this context is actually accompanied by a high degree of awareness of deception, and often "guilty knowledge" (Lykken, 1974) and anxiety. It is therefore no surprise that lying in such a setting may be identified by a polygraph recording fluctuations of arousal and autonomic activity.

Whether the validity of arousal-related physiological indicators can be generalized to lying in everyday contexts is a completely different question. Doubts will be raised to the extent that the following premises underlying the lie detector apparatus approach are not met in normal social interaction: (a) The liar has to be aware of the lie; (b) lying has to be an infrequent, unusual event so that habituation is low; (c) a minimal degree of fear or threat should be involved; (d) there must be an objective criterion which distinguishes the lie from truth; (e) and if these physiological cues are to play a role in everyday interaction, it is necessary for people to be equipped with appropriate receptors for detecting these cues. To the extent, however, that everyday lying is not characterized by awareness, is not an unusual deviation from the norm, no fear or threat is involved, and an objective truth criterion is unknown, there is less reason why lying should be manifested in physiological reactions.

A similar point can be made with respect to "body language" and the mediating role of nonverbal cues in lie detection. It is a well-established fact, to be sure, that nonverbal signs such as nervousness, adaptor movements, blushing, or disfluencies *can* reveal attempts to deceive. If, however, the liar can prepare his or her speech or control his or her affects and if the lie detector lacks the necessary receptors for detecting and understanding the nonverbal signals, the significance of this type of cue is also reduced. Furthermore, such nonverbal reflections of nervousness or bewilderment should disappear with practice, that is, when deviations from the norm of the "truth" become well-practiced routine behavior. Nonverbal communication is eliminated, by definition, whenever communication appears in written form or mediated by third persons.

In any case, there appears to be good reason to take a somewhat closer look at other potential cues, in particular, cues related to the text content itself. Cues of this kind may often be much more easily available in everyday communication than many physiological and nonverbal signs. The approach described below constitutes a small step in this direction.

Content-Related Cues to Credibility: An Empirical Approach

As an empirical starting point, a preliminary list of credibility-related cues was derived from an assessment of what might be called "lay epistemology" or "naive theories" of the lie. The rationale for such a common-sense approach lies in the assumption that the domain of content-based lie detection centers on everyday social interactions. Accordingly, common sense should reflect - in valid or biased form - at least part of the knowledge utilized in credibility judgments. The resulting cues are listed in Table 3 along with an indication of the corresponding lay theories of the lie.

It should be noted that the list not only includes primary candidates of content-related cues (such as intimacy, embellishment, base rate of reported event, verifiability, and desirability) but also two popular examples of extralinguistic cues, namely, body language and the notion of a "suspicious personality," whatever this may be. These two extraneous cues were not excluded from the analysis because they correspond to familiar lay theories as well. Furthermore, the body language cue provides us with an interesting baseline with which to compare the impact of content-related cues in lie detection.

Table 3. Credibility cues derived from naive theories of the lie

	Cue	Corresponding naive theory
1	Desirability	Lies serve the purpose of appearing socially desirable. Alternative: Negative self-descriptions raise suspicion.
2	Infrequency	Infrequent or unlikely episodes are unbelievable.
3	Intimacy	Liars avoid intimacy and trustful revealing of private reactions.
4	Embellishment	Vivid reports including many concrete details create the impression that the reported event was really experienced.
5	Suspicious personality	Some individuals possess certain physical, physiognomic, or behavioral characteristics that let them appear honest or dishonest.
6	Body language	Lying is reflected in nonverbal conspicuousness.
7	Verifiability	Definite and open statements which can be clearly verified or falsified render the concept of the lie more applicable.

A Lie Detection Game. In a preliminary study conducted as part of a seminar with 23 students as participants, a simple "lie detection game" was created in order to examine the usefulness of the diagnostic system depicted in Table 3. Each participant's task was to tell the rest of the audience an event that he or she had experienced either actually (truth condition) or allegedly (lie condition). While the allocation of students to the two experimental conditions was accomplished in a double-blind arrangement, the objective truth criterion could later be reconstructed from the serial position of the 23 contributions. Immediately after each report (usually about two or three sentences concerning a social or achievement-related episode), the audience ("lie detectors") had to indicate on a response sheet whether the report was veridical or not and what their subjective confidence was. After all the reports were presented and the reactions assessed, the messages were reconsidered in a second run and the audience had to analyze the contents of the communications with respect to the cues depicted in Table 3. This was accomplished by five-point numerical ratings of the degree to which the cues were perceived to be present in the communications. Subjective ratings (instead of more objective procedures) were used because the emphasis was on the subjective realization and interpretation of cues related to naive theories of the lie.

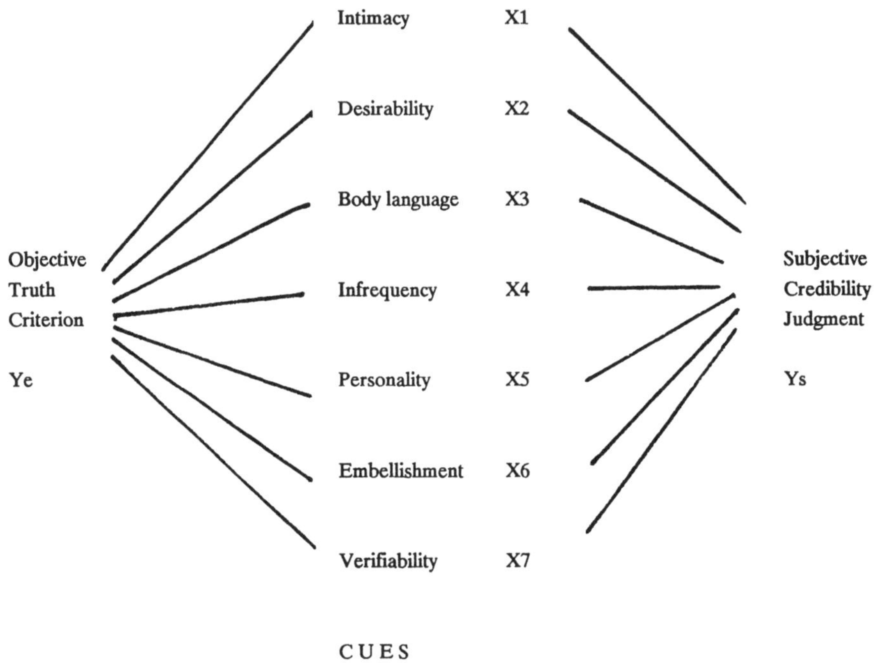

Figure 1. Lens model representation of experiment 1

The resulting data include (cf. Figure 1): The objective truth status of each message (Ye), its subjective assessment as true or false (Ys), plus its ratings regarding the content cues (X1 to Xn). These data were analyzed within the formalized framework of Brunswik's (1956) lens model (cf. Hursch, Hammond, & Hursch, 1964) as illustrated in Figure 1. Such an analysis amounts to a twofold multiple regression of the objective or ecological criterion Ye (left part of the diagram) and the subjective judgments Ys (right part) on the cues as predictors which mediate, as it were, the transmission of information between Ye and Ys. While the left-hand regression pertains to the *ecological validity* of the cue system, the right-hand regression refers to the subjects' *cue utilization.* The purpose of the analysis is not only to quantify performance or success in the lie detection task, but also to identify the mediating role of the cues (i.e., their beta coefficients) and to determine the similarity of the two patterns of beta coefficients measuring cue utilization and ecological validity.

The results of this preliminary study supported the assumption underlying the use of content-related cues derived from common-sense knowledge. Despite the small subject sample and imperfect methodology, the cue system was regularly related to the transmitted information. First of all, the multiple correlations of the cues with the objective truth criterion Ye (R = 0.59), as well as the subjective credibility judgments Ys (R = 0.61), were rather encouraging. The correlation between Ye and Ys as a direct measure of performance was r = 0.37 and only approached statistical significance. Weak and not always significant correlations are a typical outcome in research on human lie detection (Zuckerman et al., 1981), and they presumably reflect a necessary condition for the very phenomenon of the lie, namely, that detection has to be difficult.

Secondly, an analysis of the beta coefficients reveals the highest ecological validity for one particular cue, the frequency or base rate of the reported event. The common variance between Ye and Ys is largely due to the correct utilization of base rate information: Lies are actually characterized by infrequent and unusual episodes ($\beta = 0.56$), and this experience is correctly utilized in the credibility judgments ($\beta = 0.52$). The corresponding zero-order correlations of infrequency with Ye and Ys are $r = 0.45$ and $r = 0.52$, respectively. This finding is of some theoretical interest because it contradicts the common claim that human judges are insensitive to *base rate information* (Bar-Hillel, 1980; Borgida & Brekke, 1981; Kahneman & Tversky, 1972).

By contrast, the contribution of body language - the one cue which received most attention in previous research - was negligible and did not differ from chance. Obviously, under the present conditions, when communicators are engaged in informal conversation on everyday topics and can prepare for and carefully edit their communication, the experience of nonverbal conspicuousness does not seem to reveal the liar. This does not mean, of course, that nonverbal or paraverbal information was not utilized at all. In a very trivial sense, nonverbal (appearance) and paraverbal (voice) information constitute the medium in which the content-related cues such as desirability or suspicious personality are conveyed. However, the potential contribution of nonverbal information does not appear to be mediated by the subjective experience of body language but may be hidden in other dimensions which are more amenable to judgments and introspection. In other words, while lie detectors will surely process (molecular, unconscious) nonverbal information (which may be detectable by technical equipment), this information does not seem to be integrated into social perception of nonverbal conspicuousness.

Improving the Lie Detection Game. Encouraged by this preliminary study and the practicability of the lie detection game, a more systematic investigation was conducted using a larger sample of participants and an improved methodology. The intention was not only to replicate the preliminary results but also to extend and refine the empirical approach in several respects.

Sixty-four participants were asked to tell some episode or experience from their own life which had to be a true experience or a lie, depending on the experimental condition. They were completely free to report whatever event they wanted. The allocation of participants to the truth conditions was accomplished in a double-blind fashion. The resulting 64 reports were video-taped and presented to another group of judges whose task was to discriminate between lies and veridical reports. After they had classified the 64 communications and indicated their subjective confidence, the video-tape was shown for a second time to some of these judges who rated the communications for the relevant cue dimensions (i.e., desirability, base rates, body language, etc.). Two cues that had been excluded in the pilot study (i.e., intimacy and verifiability) were also taken into account in the content analysis.

In order to examine the judges' insight into their own cognitive process strategy of cue utilization, they were asked at the end of the experimental session to rank order the cues with respect to the weight they believed they had given a cue in the lie detection task. This new feature of the design allows us not only to compare *ecological validities* with measures of *cue utilization*, but also to examine the judges' *subjective insight* into their own strategies.

A first lens model analysis was computed on the group data; that is, the mean credibility judgments and cue ratings were averaged across all judges. As far as the replication aspect is concerned, the dominant role of the *base rates* (i.e., likelihood of reported contents) in subjective lie detection was confirmed (cf. Table 4). While the objective validity was considerably reduced (ß = 0.19 versus 0.56 in the first study), the base rate cue is given the greatest weight in the subjective credibility judgments (ß = 0.65). Infrequent events are regularly perceived as less credible and more often classified as lies than common events. Apparently, people rely on the base rate rule even when statistical frequency is a misleading source of information.

Table 4. Ecological validities, cue utilization, and awareness of cue utilization[a]

Cue	Beta coefficients referring to regression on: Ecological validity (64 items)	Cue utilization (64 items)	Ecological validity (37 easier items)	Cue utilization (37 easier items)	Awareness: Mean rank attributed to cue
Desirability	0.06	-0.17	-0.11	-0.19	3.71
Body Language	-0.18	0.02	-0.06	-0.08	3.43
Infrequency	0.19	0.65	0.51	0.51	2.43
Intimacy	-0.10	-0.45	-0.40	-0.39	3.86
Verifiability	0.13	0.14	0.21	0.20	3.43
Suspicious Personality	0.24	-0.02	0.22	0.20	3.57
Multiple *R*	0.33	0.69	0.71	0.72	

[a] Positive sign indicates positive relation of cue to high credibility.

Besides infrequency, however, *intimacy* affords another source of information which is utilized regularly to infer credibility. The more intimate or personally revealing a message is, the more credible it will appear (ß = -0.45), as if people have learned to associate private and intimate communications with trustful situations. As in the former experiment, the remaining cues play a subsidiary role in prediction of either the objective truth status or the subjective judgments.

The negative result concerning *body language* or nonverbal information is also replicated. Body language fails to contribute anything to the transmission of information between Ye and Ys. In fact, the sign of the validity coefficient for body language (ß = -0.18) is in the unexpected direction, indicating enhanced body language with veridical communication (cf. Table 4). Again, this finding should be interpreted with caution because it rests on a global judgmental measure of subjective nonverbal experience.

Perhaps the most regular aspect of the data obtained in many different analyses refers to the general *overutilization* of the cues stemming from common sense "theories." Thus, cue utilization (i.e., the right-hand multiple regression in Figure 1, yielding $R = 0.69$ as recorded in Table 4) is generally and consistently higher than the cues' objective validity (the left-hand regression in Figure 1, yielding $R = 0.33$ as shown in Table 4). In other words, subjective lie detection is subject to an illusionary belief in the cues representing popular lay theories of the lie. The weight given to the cues in credibility judgments is higher than justified by the actual diagnosticity of the cues, in line with the often noted overconfidence phenomenon (Oskamp, 1965). Such an analysis in terms of overconfidence is corroborated by the fact that success in the lie detection game is generally uncorrelated with subjective confidence judgments. Thus, human lie detectors appear to be ill-calibrated (Lichtenstein & Fischhoff, 1980) measurement devices; if they were properly calibrated, their confidence judgments ought to increase with successful detection.

Despite the rather low ecological validities in the group analysis, however, it is worth mentioning that the correlation between Ye and Ys is positive for all individual judges (range, 0.06-0.33; mean, $r = 0.19$), in line with the typical finding of low but above-chance performance in lie detection experiments. Considering the lens model solutions for individual judges, there is also a general consensus regarding the patterns of beta coefficients, in particular, the dominant role of the infrequency and intimacy cues, as well as the insignificance of body language as a diagnostic sign.

Meta-Cognitive Insight. There are marked differences between the actual utilization of cues of varying validity and the judges' subjective rank ordering of cues, indicating that lie detectors do not appear to have much insight into the cognitive process. There is no sizeable relation between the awareness ranks and the beta coefficients (ignoring the sign) in Table 4. To illustrate this point, the intimacy cue affords a nice example. Regardless of its low validity, intimacy was given a considerable weight in the credibility judgments, according to the actual assessment of the cue utilization strategies. When the judges were questioned about the weight they believed they had given to the different cues, however, they typically denied the importance of intimacy. Indeed, intimacy appears as the least relevant cue in the mean rank order (cf. Table 4).

Thus, although the strategies of lie detection are related to common-sense knowledge and shared by the majority of individual judges (infrequency receiving the highest beta coefficient value in six of eight individual analyses and intimacy receiving the highest or second-highest beta coefficient value in six of eight cases), their insight or introspection into this common "knowledge" seems to be rather restricted. Moreover, an analysis of the confidence ratings revealed that incorrect judgments were not accompanied by a decrease of confidence. This subsidiary finding is also in line with the lack of insight in the cognitive strategies used. If the cognitive process were more transparent and experienced more mindfully, the judges' confidence ratings should have been better calibrated.

Further Tests of the Cue System. Two supplementary analyses shall be mentioned briefly to illustrate the flexibility of the lens model approach and to preclude a possible criticism. The first of these analyses starts from the assumption that we may have to accept, as a matter of fact, that many communications perfectly disguise their truth status and that lie detection has a chance with only the remaining, imperfect communications. According to this argument, a more adequate picture of cue utilization and validities should emerge if the analysis is confined to that subset of communications which can be classified at all (i.e., which have an above-average chance of being classified correctly).

In such a selective analysis, of course, the beta coefficients increase markedly. This is not completely trivial because the artificial improvement might have been independent of the present set of content-related cues. However, the patterns of ecological validities and cue utilization increase and converge for the subset of easier communications. Thus, when lie detection is possible at all, features of message content appear to be highly revealing. Interestingly, however, the diagnostic value of body language remains as low as before and does not contribute anything even to the classification of easy communications (cf. Table 4).

The sharp increase in accounted variance also precludes an alternative interpretation of the prevailing overutilization effect. This might be interpreted as an artificial consequence of the low reliability with which the cues themselves are perceived or judged. If subjective judgments on cue dimensions were difficult and unreliable, then it would be no surprise to find low correlations with Ye and yet substantial correlations of the cue judgments with the judges' own credibility ratings. However, the drastic increase in cue validities for the "easier" communications shows that the cue system is in principle capable of "catching" a good deal of systematic variance. Unfortunately, the present data do not permit a direct estimate of the cues' reliability; correlations between different judges would confound reliability with differences in subjective perception.

Another analysis was conducted to compare the *subjective* cues considered here with a corresponding set of more *objective* cues that can be assessed by content analysis in a much more reliable manner. Thus, the objective word length of a statement was substituted for the embellishment rating, and ratings of verifiability were replaced by the linguistic distinction of actions versus feelings/opinions, etc. In short, the results were disappointing. The amount of accounted variance decreased, and the system of more objective cues, which do not involve subjective judgments, proved to be virtually worthless. While it is clear that the two cue systems may not be comparable for several reasons, the latter finding nevertheless illustrates that a lack of reliability may be (over)compensated by a gain in relevance or validity of subjective cues. At the same time, perfectly *reliable* objective cues may turn out to be worthless if they fail to catch the aspects to which lie detectors are really sensitive.

Thus far, several conclusions seem justified on the basis of the first two experiments. First, there can be no doubt that message content itself, as opposed to nonverbal and physiological cues, is readily utilized in everyday lie detection. Second, when these intralinguistic cues compete with the extralinguistic (i.e., nonverbal) cues within the same experimental task, the former may override the impact of the latter. And third, the introspective experience appears to be largely detached from the actual cognitive process of cue utilization. All of these conclusions are of theoretical as well as of practical concern.

Deconfounding Truth Status and Message Contents. In the two studies reported so far, the contents and cue values which characterize true and feigned messages are allowed to vary in an uncontrolled manner. Although this may enhance the representativeness of the design, an obvious disadvantage of this methodology is that message contents and truth status are confounded. Messages differing in their truth status may also differ in an unknown number of other attributes. The natural next step therefore is to hold the message contents constant and to manipulate the credibility of a message independently using deliberate changes in certain cue dimensions.

This was accomplished in a third experiment. One group of participants produced the original messages which consisted of adventurous or dangerous episodes in which they had allegedly been involved. Each participant in a second group received one of these original texts, in written from, and had to infer its veridicality. He or she was then asked to revise or edit the original text - making local additions, omissions, or replacements - so that the revision would appear more credible. Participants of this second group also content-analyzed the original texts on five cue dimensions (Desirability, Infrequency, Intimacy, Embellishment, and Verifiability) and described their revisions in terms of changes on the same cue dimensions.

Finally, a third group of judges were presented with lists of originals and revisions and asked to distinguish lies from veridical reports. Would the revisions be characterized by the same intuitive knowledge that was utilized in the first two experiments? And would the revisions be successful and increase the perceived degree of credibility?

The empirical answers to these questions are as follows. First, although the objective performance in the primary lie detection task is not above chance with these written communications, the subjective judgments are regularly related to the cue system. This repeated demonstration of overutilization is in accordance with the results already reported. Second, the changes which characterize the revisions can be described as changes along the same cue dimensions and in the direction suggested by the naive theories (cf. Table 4). Third, and most importantly, however, the revisions were perceived by an independent group of judges as significantly more credible, $t = 3.82$, $df = 19$, than the originals; that is, the revisions were successful.

This means that even though the knowledge shared by the participants of the second group concerning the role of the five cues may be stereotype and illusionary knowledge which is not justified by the cues' ecological validities, this knowledge can be used efficiently to increase credibility of communications. In this way, the use of partially erroneous cues is justified by its instrumental value, and illusionary beliefs become social reality.

Concluding Remark

In a civilized and democratic society where many important decisions are mediated or determined by language and discussion, the problem of lie detection provides a challenge for psychological research. Previous approaches to this problem have typically focussed on nonverbal and physiological cues in lie detection. The role of linguistic factors and message content itself has been acknowledged, to be sure, but was seldom considered in empirical research. In view of the fact that written and well-controlled communications are neutral with respect to the communicator's body signs, it seems worthwhile to consider the diagnostic impact of the message content as well. The research reported here is understood as a small contribution in this direction.

The present approach does not presuppose an ontological concept of truth. Communication often revolves around feelings, opinions, self-presentation, intentions, motives, and many other topics that lack an objective truth criterion. In all these cases, however, appearing credible and honest is an important goal of impression management, regardless of *what is* the truth. "Truth" is not only a fiction in many cases, it may also be a matter of degree. There is a steady continuum from the intentional, blatant lie to erroneous misinformation, with cases of self-justification, self-deception (Demos, 1960), and motivational biases in between. The ubiquitous question of credibility remains independent of these variations in verifiability.

Even though the lens model paradigm utilized in the empirical studies involves an ecological truth criterion (Ye), this does not constitute a necessary part of the design. Ye may as well refer to the communicators' intention rather than to an objective criterion. Ye may also refer to what the cultural community holds to be true or some other criterion which makes sense in the context of the theory being tested. Thus, the lens model approach is flexible enough to be adapted to lie detection in a broader sense.

Much additional evidence could be gained from applications of the present approach to applied fields such as advertisement, the credibility of public speech (e.g., politicians on television), or the problem of feigning or impression management in psychological tests in the context of the diagnostic process. Since emphasis is on content-related cues, looking at applied areas in specific social contexts seems to be a promising research strategy to uncover more content-related cues.

Applied studies of that kind should also help to disconfirm the claim that blatant lying, in its literal and moral sense, plays a central role for deceptive or suggestive communication. More subtle and culturally acceptable ways of deception should become apparent in those applied domains. A politician on television will hardly say what can be directly falsified because this would render him vulnerable. Rather, he will tend to avoid factual statements and prefer "soft" statements that cannot be clearly disconfirmed. The politician's way of "lying" (or deceiving, repressing, concealing, etc.) should thus be manifested in his indirect, noncommittal use of language. In advertisements, an effective way of "lying" should consist of letting consumers make wrong inferences about the product. In diagnostic settings, "lying" is accomplished in still another fashion (e.g., by repressing one's personal deficits and creating self-illusions).

At this point the circle is closed, and the similarity of lying to other kinds of suggestive communication, which was the starting point of this chapter, is apparent again. If the moralist view and the simplified ontological view of the lie is dismissed and a communication-theoretical perspective is adopted (Baskett & Freddle, 1974; Meerloo, 1978), the distinctions of Table 1 lose their absoluteness. At the same time, the phenomenon of the lie is recognized as a ubiquitous phenomenon rather than an exceptional deviation from an obligatory norm to tell the truth.

References

Austin, J.L. (1962). *How to do things with words*. Oxford: Oxford University.

Bandura, A. (1971). Vicarious and self-reinforcement processes. In R. Glaser (Ed.), *The nature of reinforcement*. New York: Academic.

Bar-Hillel, M. (1980). The base-rate fallacy in probability judgments. *Acta Psychologica, 44*, 211-233.

Baskett, G., & Freddle, R.O. (1974). Aspects of language pragmatics and the social perception of lying. *Journal of Psycholinguistic Research, 3*, 112-131.

Bolinger, D. (1973). Truth is a linguistic question. *Language, 49*, 539-550.
Borgida, E., & Brekke, N. (1981). The base rate fallacy in attribution and prediction. In J.H. Harvey, W. Ickes, & R.F. Kidd (Eds.), *New directions in attribution research*. Hillsdale, NJ: Erlbaum.
Brunswik, E. (1956). *Perception and the representative design of psychological experiments*. Berkeley: University of California.
Demos, R. (1960). Lying to oneself. *Journal of Philosophy, 57*, 588-594.
DePaulo, B.M., & Rosenthal, R. (1979). Telling lies. *Journal of Personality and Social Psychology, 37*, 1713-1722.
Ekman, P., & Friesen, W.V. (1974). Detecting deception from the body or face. *Journal of Personality and Social Psychology, 29*, 288-298.
Freedman, J.L., & Doob, A.N. (1968). *Deviancy*. New York: Academic.
Grice, H.P. (1971). Logic and conversation: The William James lectures, Harvard University, 1967-68. In P. Cole & J.L. Morgan (Eds.), *Syntax and semantics: Vol. 3. Speech acts*. New York: Academic.
Higgins, E.T. (1981). The "communication game": Implications for social cognition and persuasion. In E.T. Higgins, C.P. Herman, & M.P. Zanna (Eds.), *Social cognition: The Ontario Symposium*. Hillsdale, NJ: Erlbaum.
Hursch, C., Hammond, K.R., & Hursch, J. (1964). Some methodological considerations in multiple-cue probability studies. *Psychological Review, 71*, 42-60.
Kahneman, D., & Tversky, A. (1972). Subjective probability: A judgment of representativeness. *Cognitive Psychology, 3*, 430-554.
Knapp, M.L., & Comadena, M.E. (1979). Telling it like it isn't: A review of theory and research on deceptive communications. *Human Communication Research, 5*, 270-285.
Knapp, M.L., Hart, R.P., & Dennis, H.S. (1974). An exploration of deception as a communication construct. *Human Communication Research, 1*, 15-29.
Kraut, R.E. (1980). Humans as lie detectors: Some second thoughts. *Journal of Communication, 30*, 209-216.
Lichtenstein, S., & Fischhoff, B. (1980). Training for calibration. *Organizational Behavior and Human Performance, 26*, 149-171.
Loftus, E.F. (1975). Leading questions and the eyewitness report. *Cognitive Psychology, 7*, 560-572.
Lykken, D.T. (1974). Psychology and the lie detector industry. *American Psychologist, 29*, 725-739.
Meerloo, J.A. (1978). Camouflage versus communication: In the beginning was the lie. *Communication, 3*, 45.
Neely, J.H. (1977). Semantic priming and retrieval from lexical memory: Roles of inhibitionless spreading activation and limited-capacity attention. *Journal of Experimental Psychology: General, 106*, 226-254.
Orne, M.T. (1962). On the social psychology of the psychological experiment: With particular reference to demand characteristics and their implications. *American Psychologist, 17*, 776-783.
Oskamp, S. (1965). Overconfidence in case-study judgments. *Journal of Consulting Psychology, 29*, 261-265.
Petty, R., Ostrom, T.M., & Brock, T.C. (1981) (Eds.). *Cognitive responses in persuasion*. Hillsdale, NJ: Erlbaum.
Podlesny, J.A., & Raskin, D.C. (1977). Physiological measures and the detection of deception. *Psychological Bulletin, 84*, 782-799.
Rommetveit, R. (1974). *On message structure: A framework for the study of language and communication*. New York: Wiley.
Sacks, H. (1975). Everyone has to lie. In M. Sanches & B.G. Blount (Eds.), *Sociocultural dimensions of language use*. New York: Academic.
Searle, J.R. (1976). A classification of illocutionary acts. *Language and Society, 5*, 1-23.
Watzlawick, P., Beavin, J.H., & Jackson, D.D. (1967). *Pragmatics of human communication*. New York: Norton.
Zuckerman, M., DePaulo, B.M., & Rosenthal, R. (1981). Verbal and nonverbal communication of deception. In L. Berkowitz (Ed.), *Advances of experimental social psychology: Vol. 14*. New York: Academic.

26. Expectations, Confirmation Bias, and Suggestibility

H.W. BIERHOFF and R. KLEIN

This paper is intended to elucidate conceptual similarities between attitude change and suggestibility. In particular, we ask whether the tendency to retain an initial expectation is related to the tendency to comply with demands which suggest a biased sensory perception. We begin with a discussion of studies on the phenomenon of belief perseverance which is a paradigmatic example for the tendency to retain an initial expectation although contradictory evidence is available. In addition, we discuss briefly some studies on suggestibility with special emphasis on secondary or sensory suggestibility. In the empirical part we describe an experiment which was intended to answer some of the questions which are raised in the first part.

Conceptual Similarities Between Relief Perseverance and Suggestibility

When an expectation has been formed, the question is raised as to how disconfirming informations are taken into account in an overall judgment. Anderson, Lepper, and Ross (1980) reported experimental results which point to a perseverance of expectations. They used fictitious assumptions with regard to the relationship between risk taking and fire-fighting ability. On the basis of two case studies (of a successful and an unsuccessful fire-fighter), the hypothesis was suggested to the subjects that either high risk taking or low risk taking was associated with fire-fighting ability.

After reading the evidence about the positive or negative relationship in the correlational theory, subjects were informed that the evidence was contrived ("debriefing"). Subjects learned that they were randomly assigned to a positive or negative correlational theory. Different dependent measures (e.g., assessment of the true relationship between risk taking and fire-fighting ability) showed that the initial expectations tended to persevere although the experimenter explicitly mentioned that he had provided fictitious information.

One feature of this study is that concrete case studies were used for the manipulation of initial theories. From a theoretical viewpoint, case studies are not very informative for general conclusions with regard to a relationship between two variables. But because concrete information is lively and easy to understand this convinces most people (Hamill, Wilson, & Nisbett, 1980).

Anderson (1983) showed that abstract information, which is in the form of a statistical summary of 20 cases, elicits less belief perseverance than two concrete case studies. Therefore, the conclusion is justified that concrete information elicits stronger expectations than abstract information.

Most comparisons which are indicative of belief perseverance include a positive-relationship condition and a negative-relationship condition (e.g., positive correlation between risk taking and success as a fire-fighter). These comparisons show whether divergent expectations result in different beliefs. In addition, it is informative to compare the positive condition and the negative condition with their respective control conditions in which only the expectation is elicited and no contradictory information is added (expectation only condition).

In the study by Anderson et al. (1980) these control conditions were included in the design. The results indicated that the disconfirming evidence weakened the initial expectations (Figure 1).

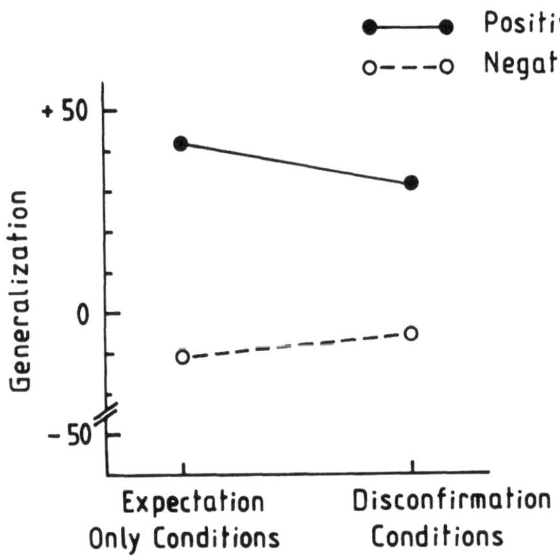

Figure 1. Belief perseverance of correlational theories (from Anderson et al., 1980). Subjects read five vignettes in which the target person had the choice between a risky and a cautious response. The dependent variable is the difference between the estimate of percentage of risk responses which superior fire-fighters give minus the percentage of risk responses by inferior fire-fighters. This dependent measure varied between +100 (only superior fire-fighters prefer risk responses) and -100 (only inferior fire-fighters prefer risk responses) *Solid circles*, positive relationship; *open circles*, negative relationship

But the difference between the positive and the negative conditions remained highly significant after the disconfirming information was presented during the debriefing.

In general, belief perseverance refers to the tendency to retain an initial hypothesis about a social event although contradictory information challenges the original expectation. For example, a listener might hear that a target person acts reliably and is dependable. Additional information might reveal that the same target person acted unpredictably and erratically. If the listener sticks to the initial impression of high reliableness, the initial hypothesis about the target person will prevail.

This phenomenon of belief perseverance is reminiscent of the phenomenon of suggestibility. We can ignore for the moment the fact that suggestibility researchers were primarily interested in individual differences, while perseverance researchers focused on general tendencies in person perception. What are the characteristics of suggestibility which closely resemble the features of belief perseverance?

Suggestibility is related to influenceability of feelings, beliefs, perceptions, and actions by direct or indirect communications. Suggestions are transmitted by cues which slip in unconsciously. Therefore, control and monitoring systems of the individual are - at least in part - circumvented by the suggestion (Gheorghiu, Chap. 6, this volume).

In many cases distorting cues elicit expectations. This is especially valid for so-called secondary suggestibility (Eysenck, 1947, this volume) which refers to sensory influenceability. Secondary suggestibility is defined as "the experience on the part of the subject of a sensation or perception consequent upon the direct or implied suggestion that such an experience will take place, in the absence of any objective basis for the sensation or perception" (Eysenck, 1947, p. 167).

By indirectly suggesting a hypothesis, subjects are prompted to see ambiguous stimuli in a distorted way. This process was described by Postman (1953) in his hypothesis-information theory of cognition (see also Bruner, 1957; Bruner & Postman, 1949). Postman assumed that organisms expect a specific range of events on the basis of a range of hypotheses. In addition, the strength of a hypothesis has important consequences for the process of checking and revising a perceptual hypothesis: "... a very strong hypothesis will tend to be confirmed even when most of the available information is inappropriate ..." (Postman, 1953, p. 252).

A number of tests are available which allow measurement of secondary suggestibility. For example, the test "line pair" is based on the initial expectation that the two lines in a pair will be equal in length. But subsequent trials consist exclusively of lines which are unequal in length. The measure of suggestibility is derived from the number of times a subject responds with "equal" in these critical trials (Stukat, 1958).

Secondary suggestibility is closely related to expectations. In the same vein, belief perseverance is a result of the development of strong initial hypotheses. The experimenter offers a specific frame of reference. If the subject accepts this anchor for judgment, an initial expectation is formed which might later influence the interpretation of disconfirming evidence.

Expectations which bias cognitive processes in suggestibility tests are derived from information which gives a specific meaning to the test situation. These expectations can be understood as cognitive schemata (Bierhoff, 1989). In the same vein, belief perseverance is based on initial hypotheses about social events.

The main difference between belief perseverance and secondary suggestibility seems to be that secondary suggestibility refers to sensory distortions while perseverance refers to distorted beliefs and attitudes. This difference does not exclude the possibility that the basic processes underlying both phenomena are fairly similar and correspond to Postman's (1953) hypothesis-information theory of cognition (see also Wyer & Srull, 1986).

It is this correspondence between belief perseverance and secondary suggestibility which motivated the study reported in the second part of this chapter. In particular, we assumed that subjects who show a strong perseverance tendency will prove to be more suggestible in a test of secondary suggestibility, because belief perseverance and secondary suggestibility are based on the tendency to emphasize the initial expectation relative to subsequent contradictory evidence.

Experimental Research

Description of the Study

In our empirical study confirmation bias and suggestibility were measured. For the assessment of confirmation bias we prepared written scenarios (see also Bierhoff, Buck, Klein, & Blanz, 1986). The first message subjects received indicated that the target person was an unreliable person. Several concrete examples were used to describe the low reliableness of the target person. The second message described a social episode which identified the target person as reliable. In a third message the target person was again portrayed as reliable. In summary, the initial expectation was disconfirmed by two social episodes. All information was presented in a concrete information mode (see also Nisbett & Ross, 1980).

For each individual subject we constructed two measures of belief perseverance by taking the difference between perception of reliableness of the target person after reading the initial evidence and perceptions of the target person after reading the second and third message, respectively. These perceptions were assessed by a questionnaire measuring perceived reliableness and perceived trustworthiness of a target person (Buck & Bierhoff, 1986; Johnson-George & Swap, 1982). Because utilization of difference scores creates a problem for their reliability, reliability of the difference scores was assessed by computing Cronbach's *alpha*.

In addition, subjects participated in a suggestibility test. Because we were interested in the after effects of initial expectations, we selected a test of secondary suggestibility. From the work of Stukat (1958) we concluded that the test of line pairs would be appropriate for our purposes.

This test begins with a series of instruction and suggestion of five pairs of lines. Subjects are instructed to respond with "equal" if a pair of lines is of equal length. If the lines in a pair are judged to be unequal, no verbal response is required. Practice trials consist of three equal pairs of equal length and two pairs of unequal length. This suggestion phase is followed by 30 trials in which only pairs of unequal length are shown. The differences in length vary between just noticeable (1 cm) to quite obvious (2.5 cm). Each line was shown for 1 s on a screen with a 1 s interval between the lines of a pair. After a response interval in which no lines were shown the procedure was continued automatically.

We constructed four measures of suggestibility. First, an overall score was formed by adding all "equal" responses. In addition, three subtest scores were computed by adding the responses to the 12 pairs with small differences (1-1.5 cm), the ten pairs with medium differences (2 cm), and the eight pairs with large differences (2.5 cm), respectively.

Results

The results are based on 91 subjects. First, we will discuss the results for the perseverance test and the suggestibility test separately. With respect to the perseverance test, the first message created, as expected, a rather negative impression of the target person which was improved after the presentation of the disconfirming social episodes. Respective means for the reliableness scale and the trustworthiness scale are shown in Figure 2 ($n = 87$ for this analysis due to missing data).

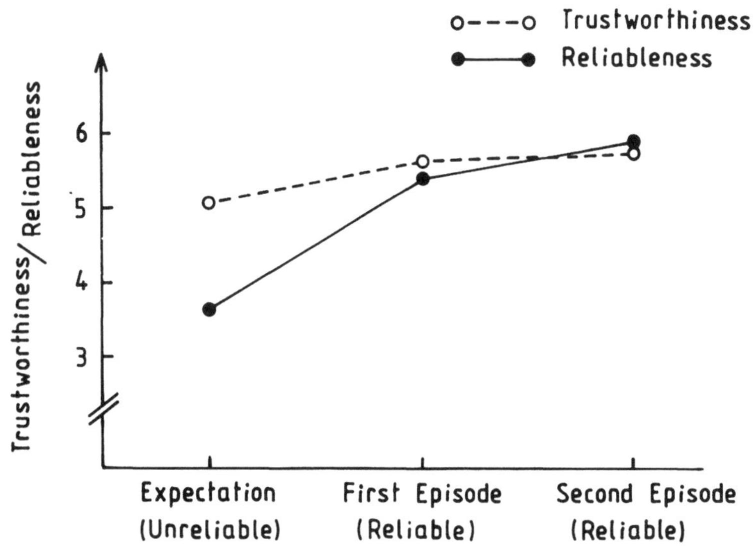

Figure 2. Perceived reliableness (*solid circles*) and perceived trustworthiness (*open circles*) of the target person as a function of expectations and social episodes

Repeated measurements analysis of variance performed on these data yielded significant main and interaction effects. $F(1, 86) = 12.54$, $P < .001$ for reliableness vs. trustworthiness, $F(2, 172) = 128.75$, $P < .001$ for measurements, and $F(2, 172) = 68.59$, $P < .001$ for the interaction. These effects indicate that the general level of perceived trustworthiness was higher than the general level of perceived reliableness. In addition, perceived trust increased across measurements in correspondence with the manipulation. (The linear contrast with weights -1, 0, +1 was highly significant, $t(172) = 10.797, P < .001$).

These effects were modified by a significant interaction which indicates that the increase in reliableness was more pronounced than the increase in trustworthiness. This is reasonable because the manipulation of trust was intended to influence the perceived reliableness of the target person. Since perceived reliableness and trustworthiness are moderately correlated (Buck & Bierhoff, 1986), manipulation of reliableness had an attenuated effect on perceived trustworthiness. The respective contrast in the interaction (Rosenthal & Rosnow, 1985) is highly significant, $t(172) = 11.206, P < .001$.

From the data summarized in Figure 2 we computed change scores for each subject on both scales:

1. The absolute difference between first and second measurements.
2. The absolute difference between first and third measurements.
3. The absolute difference between second and third measurements.[1]

While the third score served as a control measure, the first and second scores were intended to tap belief perseverance. On these measures *smaller* differences indicate stronger perseverance of initial expectations.

While the internal consistencies of the scales were high, the question arises as to how reliable the change scores are because change scores tend to be unreliable (Bereiter, 1963; Stelzl, 1982). The change scores between first and second measurements (1.) proved to be sufficiently consistent, *alpha* = .795 and .746 for reliableness and trustworthiness, respectively. The change scores between first and third measurements (2.) also proved to be sufficiently reliable, *alpha* = .866 and .707, respectively. The control change scores (3.) were only marginally reliable, *alpha* = .618 and .527, respectively. In these analyses, the item-based change scores were used. The relatively high internal consistencies may be explained by only moderately high correlations between measurements.

The test of line pairs proved to be one of those showing the highest loadings on a second order factor of suggestibility derived in a second order factor analysis of suggestibility tests by Stukat (1958, p. 91). In the earlier study with a Swedish adult sample a mean overall suggestibility score of 7.09 was reported which is quite close to the mean score of 9.18 in our sample. Most of our subjects' responses ranged between scores of 6 and 12 (SD = 3.70). The score distribution was approximately normal.

McGuire (1968) mentioned the disappointingly low reliability of suggestibility tests. We computed internal consistency coefficients of the suggestibility scores. Only the subtest of small differences proved to be sufficiently consistent, *alpha* = .63. In contrast, the internal consistencies of the subtests based on medium and large differences were insufficient, *alpha* = .43 and .36, respectively. The total 30-item test reached an internal consistency of .62. Therefore, we selected the most consistent subscale as our main measure of suggestibility. The mean on this subscale of small differences was 4.65 (SD = 2.45).

The hypothesis was that subjects who show more suggestibility according to the lines test would manifest more confirmation bias than less suggestible subjects. Therefore, high suggestibility should be associated with smaller change scores on measures 1. and 2. as defined above.

---

[1] An analysis of the direction of change indicated that - in line with the manipulation - nearly all changes in 1. and 2. were due to an increased estimate of the trust of the target person at the second and third measurements. The results are essentially the same if algebraic differences are used. Absolute differences were preferred because we were interested in detecting the individual tendency to maintain the first position.

A median split on the distribution of suggestibility scores was performed. The resulting factor (low suggestibility vs. high suggestibility) constituted the main independent variable in an analysis of variance of the change scores. Dependent measures were the difference variables 1., 2., and 3. described above. While the difference variables 1. and 2. reflect the tendency to maintain the original hypothesis in the perseverance test, the difference variable 3. is a control measure. It controls for spontaneous fluctuations between measurement points. Because the change scores on the reliableness scale and on the trustworthiness scale were taken into consideration, the resulting design was a 2 (suggestibility groups) x 2 (trust scales) x 3 (difference variables) factorial design with repeated measurements on the second and third factors.

The relevant means are depicted in Figure 3. The hypothesis predicts that the low suggestibility

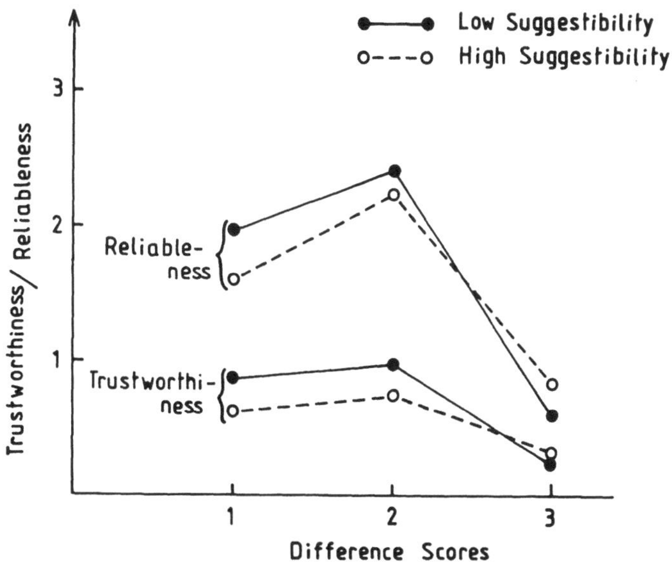

Figure 3. Change in perceived reliableness and trustworthiness of the target person as a function of suggestibility, $n = 87$. The difference scores tap the change in perceived trust between base rate and first episode (*1*), base rate and second episode (*2*), and first and second episodes (*3*), respectively (see text). Higher differences indicate more change. The low (*solid circles*) and high (*open circles*) suggestibility groups were derived from a median split [n(low) = 44; n(high) = 43] performed on the subtest of small differences in the test of line pairs

group should score higher than the high suggestibility group on difference variables 1. and 2., while no difference is predicted for difference variable 3. This pattern of results should emerge both for the reliableness scale and the trustworthiness scale.

The hypothesis is tested by the two-way interaction between suggestibility (low, high) and change (difference variables 1., 2., 3.). In addition, a planned comparison was performed with one degree of freedom to test the hypothesis directly (Rosenthal & Rosnow, 1985). An inspection of

Figure 3 shows that the highly suggestible group exhibited lower change scores on difference variables 1. and 2. while this pattern was slightly reversed for difference variable 3. The corresponding interaction effect was significant, $F(2,170) = 4.03$, $P < .02$. The effect remains significant after a Greenhouse-Geisser correction ($P < .05$). The planned comparison was also significant, $t(170) = 1.962$, $P < .05$. These results support the basic hypothesis of the study.

In summary, these results indicate that highly suggestible subjects retained their initial judgment on the target person more than low suggestibles although low suggestibles tended to change their judgments more in the control comparison (3.). Therefore, highly suggestible subjects tended to manifest more belief perseverance.

A classification of subjects into three groups of high, medium, and low suggestibility led to similar results. This analysis showed that especially the high group exhibited the pattern of belief perseverance. Further analyses indicated that the confirmation bias is somewhat stronger for males than for females although no significant sex effects emerged.

Concluding Comments

The theoretical analysis advanced in the first part of this chapter revealed certain conceptual similarities between belief perseverance and suggestibility. Both phenomena refer to processes of hypothesis confirmation. An initial hypothesis is suggested by early information, while later information contradicts the initial impression.

This theoretical view leads to the intriguing speculation that highly suggestible persons are less inclined to yield to attempts at social influence under certain conditions than low suggestibles. In particular, after establishment of a strong initial expectation suggestible persons should be inclined to retain the initial position when contradictory information is added. Therefore, under these circumstances suggestible subjects should exhibit less attitude change because they should be inclined to yield strongly to the subtle pressure which fosters a stable frame of reference. This strong initial hypothesis should resist contradictory messages to a certain degree because later information is assimilated to the frame of reference (Bierhoff et al., 1986; Jones & Goethals, 1972). Therefore, suggestible persons should be influenced less by expectation-discrepant messages. The tendency to assimilate new evidence to current schemata and prototypes was observed in a number of studies (e.g., Cantor & Mischel, 1979; Zadney & Gerard, 1974).

The empirical test of the hypothesis is complicated by the possibility that suggestible persons might manifest a general tendency to yield to social influence (McGuire, 1968). Our hypothesis implies that this general tendency to yield is reversed by the formation of a stable frame of reference. Therefore, the tendency to stick to biased beliefs should surpass any tendency to yield to subsequent attempts of social influence. As a consequence, suggestible persons might exhibit high influenceability only when no firm belief system is established in the first place. They might be susceptible to social influence which transmits anchors of judgment (i.e., a frame of reference). But after establishment of these judgment anchors, suggestible persons should be those who tend to stick to the existing frame of reference.

Our results, which support this hypothesis, must be interpreted with caution. Although the expected effects were observed, they tended to be fairly small. For example, suggestibility and difference variable 1. for reliableness are correlated by $r = -.18$ ($P < .05$). In addition, generalizability of the results is limited. For example, suggestible persons might show more attitude change in the typical attitude change experiment which does not build up firm judgment anchors before counterattitudinal messages are presented. In addition, the hypothesis seems to be supported more for younger than for older subjects (as further data indicate) and for males more than for females.

Whether or not a suggestible person manifests large attitude change may depend on the focus of attention. When the focus of attention is on initial expectations, suggestible persons should tend to be resistant to attempts of influence (Scheier, Carver, & Gibbons, 1979). The typical procedure of tests of secondary suggestibility focuses subjects' attention on initial expectations. Secondary suggestibility refers to the establishment of a strong frame of reference which biases later perceptions of disconfirming events.

In the same vein, the perseverance of expectations in studies on confirmation bias rests on the tendency of initial expectations to color the judgments of subsequent events which deviate from the expected state. In another study (Bierhoff et al., 1986) we found that belief perseverance is likely to occur when expectations are transmitted by concrete examples. In contrast, abstract summaries of evidence seem to be a less effective procedure for the establishment of a strong judgment anchor. It is interesting to note that the procedures which are used in tests of secondary suggestibility exploit concrete examples for the evocation of distorted perceptions of certain stimuli.

McGuire (1968) was one of the first authors who systematically explored the possibility that suggestibility and influenceability are related concepts. His summary of the available evidence suggests that little correlation between suggestibility and influenceability has been found. The evidence is inconclusive. Our approach offers a conceptual clarification which might explain this state of affairs. It seems to be important to make a distinction between forming judgment anchors and yielding to social influence. It is conceivable that it is easy to convince suggestible persons that a specific judgment anchor should be adopted. As a consequence, they might be inclined to assimilate subsequent evidence to their dominant structure of knowledge.

On the other hand, after establishment of a frame of reference, suggestible persons might be relatively invulnerable when discrepant information must be processed. Only when no judgment anchor has been established might suggestible persons respond compliantly to social pressure. This analysis implies that suggestible persons are more susceptible to social influence when no established frame of reference is available and less susceptible when they assimilate new evidence into a stable frame of reference. Future studies should explore this possibility further.

Acknowledgement. We are grateful to Mathias Blanz who assisted in the planning phase of this study, and Klaus Fiedler and Robert Rosenthal for their helpful comments on the manuscript. The preparation of the manuscript was supported by the helpful comments of the participants during the international symposium on suggestion and suggestibility. We are also grateful to Pieter Bienert, Markus Haberkorn, Birgit Kreipe, Elisabeth Montag, and Mechthild Schenk for their help in collecting the data.

References

Anderson, C.A. (1983). Abstract and concrete data in the perseverance of social theories: When weak data lead to unshakeable beliefs. *Journal of Experimental Social Psychology, 19,* 93-108.

Anderson, C.A., Lepper, M.R., & Ross, L. (1980). Perseverance of social theories: The role of explanation in the persistence of discredited information. *Journal of Personality and Social Psychology, 39,* 1037-1049.

Bereiter, C. (1963). Some persisting dilemmas in the measuring of change. In C.W. Harris (Ed.), *Problems in measuring change* (pp. 3-20). Madison, WI: University of Wisconsin.

Bierhoff, H.W. (1989, in press). *The perception of persons.* New York Berlin Heidelberg: Springer.

Bierhoff, H.W., Buck, E., Klein, R., & Blanz, M. (1986). *Bestätigung und Widerlegung von Erwartungen über die Verläßlichkeit einer Person: Beharrungstendenzen bei konkreten und abstrakten Personeninformationen.* [Confirmation and refutation of expectations about a person's reliability: Perseverance with concrete and abstract person information]. Marburg: Philipps University, Department of Psychology.

Bruner, J.S. (1957). On perceptual readiness. *Psychological Review, 64,* 123-152.

Bruner, J.S., & Postman, L. (1949). Perception, cognition, and behavior. *Journal of Personality, 18,* 14-31.

Buck, E., & Bierhoff, H.W. (1986). Verläßlichkeit und Vertrauenswürdigkeit: Skalen zur Erfassung des Vertrauens in eine konkrete Person. [Reliability and trustworthiness: scales for measuring trust in a concrete person]. *Zeitschrift für Differentielle und Diagnostische Psychologie, 7,* 205-223.

Cantor, N., & Mischel, W. (1979). Prototypicality and personality: Effects on free recall and personality impressions. *Journal of Research in Personality, 13,* 187-205.

Eysenck, H.J. (1947). *Dimensions of personality.* London: Routledge.

Hamill, R., Wilson, T.D., & Nisbett, R.E. (1980). Insensitivity to sample bias: Generalizing from atypical cases. *Journal of Personality and Social Psychology, 39,* 578-589.

Johnson-George, C., & Swap, W.C. (1982). Measurement of specific interpersonal trust: Construction and validation of a scale to assess trust in a specific other. *Journal of Personality and Social Psychology, 43,* 1306-1317.

Jones, E.E., & Goethals, G.R. (1972). Order effects in impression formation: Attribution context and the nature of the entity. In E.E. Jones, D.E. Kanouse, H.H. Kelley, R.E. Nisbett, S. Valins & B. Weiner (Eds.), *Attribution: Perceiving the causes of behavior* (pp. 27-46). Morristown, NJ: General Learning.

McGuire, W.J. (1968). Personality and susceptibility to social influence. In E.F. Borgatta & W.W. Lambert (Eds.), *Handbook of personality theory and research* (pp. 1130-1187). Chicago, IL: Rand McNally.

Nisbett, R.E., & Ross, L. (1980). *Human inference: Strategies and shortcomings of social judgment.* Englewood Cliffs, NJ: Prentice-Hall.

Postman, L. (1953). Toward a general theory of cognition. In J.H. Rohrer & M. Sherif (Eds.), *Social psychology at the crossroads* (pp. 242-272). New York: Harper.

Rosenthal, R., & Rosnow, R.L. (1985). *Contrast analysis. Focused comparison in the analysis of variance.* Cambridge: Cambridge University.

Scheier, M.F., Carver, C.S., & Gibbons, F.X. (1979). Self-directed attention, awareness of bodily states, and suggestibility. *Journal of Personality and Social Psychology, 37,* 1576-1588.

Stelzl, I. (1982). *Fehler und Fallen der Statistik* [Mistakes and traps in statistics]. Bern: Huber.

Stukat, K.G. (1958). *Suggestibility: A factorial and experimental analysis.* Stockholm: Almquist and Wiksell.

Wyer, R.S., & Srull, T.K. (1986). Human cognition in its social context. *Psychological Review, 93,* 322-359.

Zadney, J., & Gerard, H.B. (1974). Attributed intentions and informational selectivity. *Journal of Experimental Social Psychology, 10,* 34-52.

27. Indirect Suggestion as a Research Tool

H. LACHNIT

Rationale and Method

This paper proposes that methods of indirect suggestion can serve as tools in conducting research in various areas of psychology. These methods will be exemplified by an experiment in which we studied the effects of anticipation on behavior in an achievement-oriented situation. By having adopted ideas from the field of classical conditioning, we were able to induce and manipulate expectations about the difficulty of tasks in an indirect nonverbal manner.

Asratyan (1965) showed that classical conditioning can be brought under contextual control. Identical conditioned stimuli elicit different conditioned responses depending on different contextual stimuli. For instance, after a subject has received some training in an experimental chamber that is illuminated by a blue light, a 1000-Hz tone paired with shock will elicit a conditioned response. The same conditioned stimulus presented unpaired (without unconditioned stimulus), if a yellow light is on, will not elicit a conditioned response. In this example the reflex activity is clearly under contextual control.

In accordance with this approach, we presented series of tasks from a test measuring power of concentration (Abels, 1965) in differently colored frames. For each subject there was a contingency between two colors of frames and two difficulties of tasks. For instance, the subjects had 3.5 s to solve a task presented within the yellow frame; the subjects had 6.5 s to solve a task presented within the blue frame. In this example the tasks in the blue frame were "easy" and those in the yellow frame were "difficult." The subjects were not told anything about these contingencies, the colored frames were not even mentioned in the instructions. The subjects were only told that they were undergoing a test of power of concentration consisting of nine series of 30 tasks each. And they were told that between every two series there would be a period of rest.

Each series started with a presentation of a yellow or blue colored frame which was then presented throughout the series. After 20 s, the tasks were presented within this frame. Within each series the maximum duration of exposure of each task was constant. In "easy" series each task was presented for 6.5 s; in the "difficult" series each task was presented for 3.5 s. If the subject was able to solve the task (pressing one of four buttons according to the presence or absence of certain "target" stimuli) within this time, that particular presentation was ended. Following an incorrect response, there was a signal consisting of a 1000-Hz pure tone of 70 dB (A). If the subject did not respond within the duration of presentation (omission) this too was an incorrect response. Each of our 52 subjects was presented with four "easy" and four "difficult" series in random order. The contingency of color and task difficulty was made equivalent across subjects. In the ninth series all subjects received the 30 tasks with an average duration of presentation of 5 s. However, by random selection half of the subjects received these tasks in the "difficult" frame, whereas the other half received identical tasks in the "easy" frame.

To summarize, we intended to elicit different expectations about the difficulty of the tasks at the beginning of the test series, whereas the objective difficulty was held constant for all subjects.

After the experiment there was an interview serving as an experimental check: 20 out of 52 subjects were able to verbalize the correct contingency. In each group ten of the 26 subjects were able to verbalize the correct contingency, whereas 16 subjects failed in each group. The ten subjects in the group with "easy" frames constituted the condition "expectation easy." The ten subjects in the group with "difficult" frames constituted the condition "expectation difficult." The remaining 32 subjects (16 subjects in each group) constituted the condition "no expectation." These three groups are not equivalent to experimentally formed groups; the constituent members are self-selected on the basis of statements made in postexperimental interviews. In principle, these statements could have been influenced by the subject's reaction time, accuracy, and omissions. However, there are no strong reasons for attributing the following results to those unknown influences. Why, for instance, should high *and* low reaction times and accuracy enable the verbalization of the correct contingency, but not intermediate behavior?

Results

Three dependent variables (reaction time, percentage of correct responses, percentage of omissions) were analyzed. The 30 tasks of the ninth series were blocked (ten trials per block). The 3 x 3 (groups x blocks) analyses of variance showed the following results.

Subjects expecting "difficult" tasks worked significantly faster than those expecting "easy" tasks, whereas the group with no expectation fell in between [main effect group $F(2, 49) = 5.93$, $P < .005$; Scheffé's critical differences: 161 and 216.25]. All groups showed a significant increase across blocks [$F(2, 98) = 15.3$, $P < .001$; Scheffé's critical difference: 20.03]; the interaction was not significant [$F(4, 98) = 0.72$]. For further details, see left-hand panel of Figure 1.

Subjects expecting "difficult" tasks made significantly more correct responses than those expecting "easy" tasks, again the group with no expectation fell in between [$F(2, 49) = 5.84$, $P < .006$; Scheffé's critical differences: 1.478 and 1.984]. The block effect [$F(2, 98) = 1.28$], and the interaction ($F = 1.34$) failed to reach significance (see also lower part of Figure 1).

Subjects expecting "difficult" tasks had significantly fewer omissions than those expecting "easy" tasks [$F(2, 49) = 7.27$, $P < .002$; Scheffé's critical differences: 1.253 and 1.683]. While the interaction was not significant [$F(4, 98) = 1.53$], the percentage of omissions increased significantly across blocks [$F(2, 98) = 4.17$, $P < .02$; Scheffé's critical difference: 0.68]. For further details see right-hand panel of Figure 1.

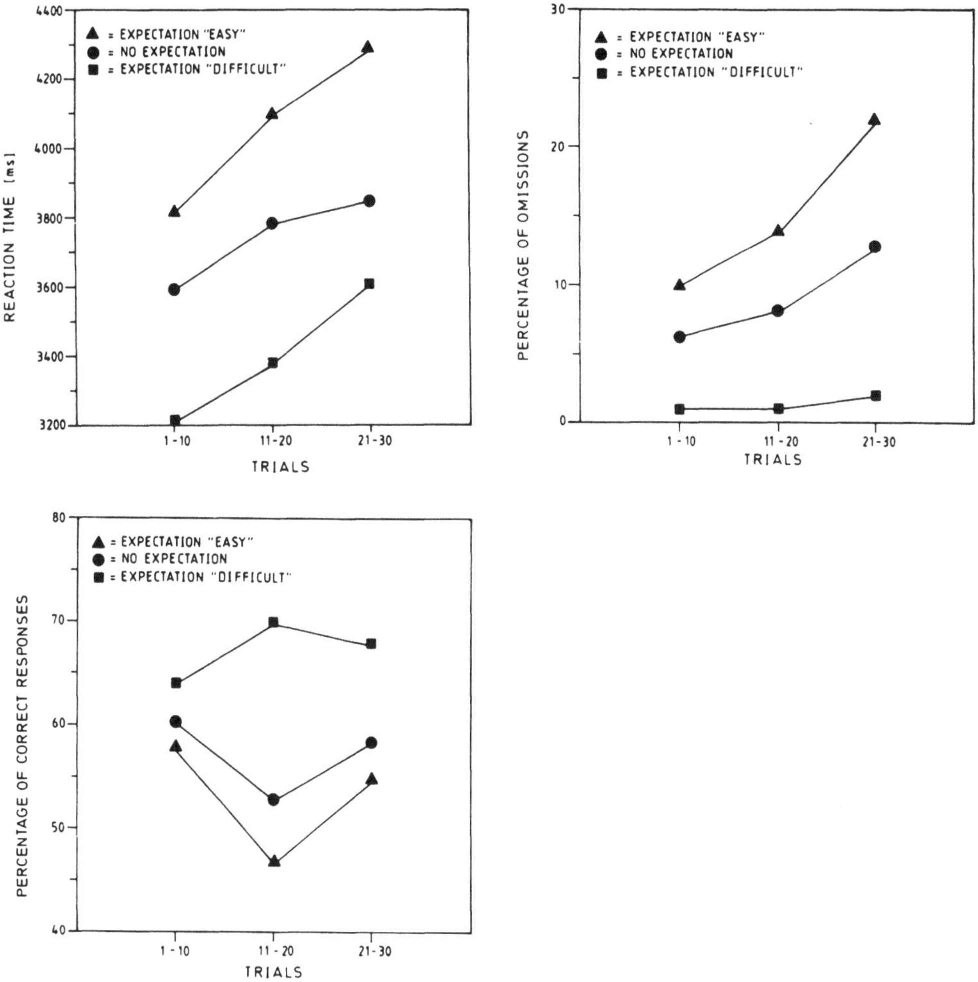

Figure 1. Reaction times, percentage of correct responses, and percentage of omissions for three groups plotted across blocks

Discussion

This pattern of results demonstrates an influence of anticipation of the difficulty of a task on behavior. Expecting "difficult" tasks clearly led to greater achievement. The subjects with such expectations had more correct responses and fewer omissions, and they worked faster than subjects who had expected "easy" tasks. This effect of anticipation was stable across blocks. In other words, the experience with the objective difficulty of 30 tasks did not compensate for the inadequate (in relation to objective difficulty) subjective estimation of the difficulty of tasks.

Most of the literature on self-expectations as well as more traditional research on the effects of suggestion reported the opposite result, that expecting difficult tasks leads to worse performance. However, research based on attribution theory showed findings with "apparent contradiction of the body of thought and research dealing with the concept of suggestion effect" (Storms & Nisbett, 1970, p. 326). Perhaps the current outcome falls within the scope of Wortman's and Brehm's (1975) integration of reactance theory (Brehm, 1972) and the model of learned helplessness (Seligman, 1975).

Although not all the subjects became conscious of the rule suggested indirectly by our treatment, this indirect method appears to be an alternative to direct verbal induction of expectancy. First, in examining the effect of a special expectation, in our study the expectation of the difficulty of a task, it is necessary to control for other effects of set. By using indirect nonverbal instructions, we overcame some of the problems being discussed as "social psychology of the experiment." Second, the indirect method used seemed to have more environmental validity. In real life, we often infer our sets or attitudes in a similarly indirect manner.

References

Abels, D. (1965). *Konzentrations-Verlaufs-Test K-V-T.* Göttingen: Hogrefe.

Asratyan, A.E. (1965). *Compensatory adaption, reflex activity, and the brain* (S.A. Corsen, Trans.). New York: Oxford University.

Brehm, J.W. (1972). *Responses to loss of freedom. A theory of psychological reactance.* Morristown, N.J.: General Learning.

Seligman, M.E.P. (1975). *Helplessness: On depression, development, and death.* San Francisco: Freeman.

Storms, M.D., & Nisbett, R.E. (1970). Insomnia and the attribution process. *Journal of Personality and Social Psychology, 16*, 319-328.

Wortman, C.B., & Brehm, J.W. (1975). Responses to uncontrollable outcomes: An integration of reactance theory and the learned helplessness model. In L. Berkowitz (Ed.), *Advances in Experimental Social Psychology: Vol. 8.* New York: Academic.

28. Slight Manipulations with Great Effects: On the Suggestive Impact of Vocal Parameter Change

T. GEHM, J. APPEL and D. APSEL

Introduction

The extraordinary impact of voice quality on the message transferred is a phenomenon of everyday life. Sayings like "It is the tone that makes the music," or idioms like "To find the right tone" or "To set the tone" point out that messages with the same content have a different influence on an audience if they are uttered in a different way. This phenomenon has already been underlined in early descriptions of rhetorical hints. Authors like Cicero (1976) or Quintillian (1972, 1975) have supplied detailed descriptions on the impact of different ways of speaking. The effect of voice quality on perception of a message transferred and on the willingness to perform this message has also been taken up in many areas of psychological research. Since Trager's (1958) first attempts to systematize different features of voice quality, numerous investigations, especially in the area of social psychology, have been undertaken to unravel the function of voice quality on processes of person perception and social influence. Thus, vocal parameters have been regarded as decisive for processes of attitude change, especially inducing conformity (Scherer, 1972), mediating experimenter effects (Orne, 1962) and have thus been looked upon as a decisive determinant for bringing about complex phenomena such as self-fulfilling prophecy (Rosenthal, 1966).

With closer reference to processes concerning suggestivity and suggestibility, the pioneering works of Weitzenhoffer (for a recent summary see Weitzenhoffer, 1985) and Barber, Spanos, and Chaves (1974) point out the extreme importance of voice quality. Referring to practical experience they have given elaborate descriptions on the importance of vocal characteristics such as intonation, inflection, and volume. Strong emphasis is placed on techniques in the proper use of vocal expressions such as alternations in the volume of the voice, changes in the inflection and modulation of the voice, changes in the rate of delivery, stressing of particular words, and the insertion of suitable pauses between ideas suggested. The effect of these techniques is certainly well known to everyone working in the field.

In contrast to the outstanding importance of voice quality, an overview on experimental investigations on this topic (Scherer, 1982) reveals that we have to admit that we know very little about the mechanisms of these processes, nor can we describe the crucial parameters of the suggestive effect of voice quality. So far it is unclear which qualities of the voice are really substantial for inducing a suggestive effect.

There are several reasons for this. First, this is a methodological problem. One has to keep in mind that while verbal signs are coded arbitrarily, discretely, and invariantly, nonverbal signs are usually coded iconically, continuously, and probabilistically (Giles, Scherer, & Taylor, 1979). Therefore, unequivocal characteristics are not easily determined. Secondly, voice quality is not at all a one-dimensional phenomenon. Concerning the audible signal, various features can be distinguished. Thus, Scherer (1978) has demonstrated that resonance, breathiness, darkness, thinness, loudness, sharpness, warmth, coarseness, and pitch of the voice have differential influence on processes of personality inference. However, up to now we have no empirical findings which show to what extent these qualities of the voice are performed consistently or can be measured reliably, whether they are dimensional, or whether all of them are suitable to describe any voice. Everyday experience seems to support the thesis that some of them are ideographic descriptions of certain voices rather than general categories. Trying to ascertain clear definitions for these by describing respective physical qualities of the intonation contour is only partially helpful as clear relations between audible voice qualities and patterns in the intonation contour are rare.

To account for this one only has to keep in mind that in order to examine the suggestive effect of voice quality several interrelated processes have to be considered. Therefore, one first has to consider how voice qualities are produced by speakers. First, paralinguistic phenomena are induced by certain patterns of nervous impulses and muscle innervations. These processes may be described in terms of physiology. Secondly, these physiological processes lead to certain positions and movement samples of the structures of phonation and articulation which may be described on the so-called phonatory-articulatory level. Only as a result of these constellations on a physical level of description do we consider sound waves. (For an explicit description of these three levels, see Scherer, 1982, pp. 89ff.)

Furthermore, as usually systematized by a lens model of communication (Brunswik, 1956), processes of the percipient also contribute to the final impression on an auditor. In this process it is the combined appearance of different voice qualities that leads to special attributions. Thus, taking the example of extraversion and trying to eliminate the decisive qualities of the extraverted voice, Scherer (1978) has shown that usually a rather complex pattern of voice qualities influences the final impression of personality traits inferred.

However, for the investigation of the practical effects of voice quality on suggestive processes, it is not sufficient to investigate its inner structure. One also has to take into account that the pointed inset of voice quality is usually combined with other cues within the communication channel and to conceptualize communicating subjects as "multi-channel senders" (Birdwhistell, 1970). Characterizing the effect of messages, Mehrabian (1972) has proposed to distinguish between the verbal content, the vocal, and the visual channel of information transfer. In this context, vocal cues are usually applied in combination with mimic behavior and gestures. These additional aspects again are hard to quantify. Besides, as empirical investigations on the attribution processes (based on multi-channel presentation of verbal and nonverbal cues) highlight, the significance of each of these channels seems to be different depending on the nature of personality traits to be inferred and the criteria used as an indicator of personality attributions (Scherer, Scherer, Hall, & Rosenthal, 1977). Empirical investigations on this point up to now have not only had to face tremendous methodological problems, but have also been rather irregular. Mehrabian's (1972) optimism in presenting percentage values of the importance of each channel has already been modified by Scherer's finding (Scherer et al., 1977) that specific personality inferences seem to be transferred by specific channels.

In contrast to the methodological problems concerning a comprehensive model, empirical findings on single parameters are quite impressive. Barber and Calverley (1964), Duncan and

Rosenthal (1968), and Scherer, Rosenthal and Koivumaki (1972) have shown that already the variation of only a limited number of parameters of voice quality may bring about considerable differences in the suggestive effect of a message. Mostly because of the very simple and controllable form of technical application and the unequivocalness of its physical correlate (namely the amplitude of the intonation contour), the effect of modulations of loudness of particular words in a text on the impression formation and arousing conformity has been systematically examined. The extremely great importance of this parameter is perhaps most obviously demonstrated in the investigation by Scherer et al. (1972).

In this experiment differential vocal emphasis in a tape-recorded instruction for a person perception task was manipulated by mechanically raising or lowering the volume of key words describing the success or failure of response alternatives on a rating scale. In a series of three experiments, subjects exposed to success emphasis in the instruction rated the stimulus persons as more successful than did subjects exposed to failure emphasis. The investigation provided support for the extraordinary importance of modulation of the voice as a decisive parameter of nonverbal communication. However, there are still some problems concerning the internal validity of these findings. In this design the text read was meant as the instruction for an experiment with the reader being present as the experimenter. Therefore (according to McGuire's, 1969, classification of situations containing social influence), one may regard the situation as a typically suggestive situation with the impact that change of opinion is a result of the immediate and personal reward caused by the reader's presence (for further detail of such an argumentation, see Lazarsfeld & Menzel, 1964). Thus, in this constellation the effect of a change of opinion is supposed to be mediated by demand characteristics of the experimental situation.

To prove the impact of voice modulation by itself, we want to briefly report a paradigm in which only voice quality is decisive. The purpose of an investigation of this kind is not only to quantify the effect of voice modulation, but also to present some insight into the mechanisms that finally lead to the suggestive effect.

Method

In this empirical investigation the mere effect of voice modulation and the experimenter effect were separated. Therefore, subjects (n = 60) were exposed to texts taken from a radio report. This was clearly one-directional communication, typical of a mass media situation. As the experimenters were different from the reader - in contrast to Scherer's (Scherer et al., 1982) investigation - demand characteristics did not have to be considered. The texts had a duration of about 3 min. In these texts the volume of the words "only slight" and "quite great," both appearing twice, was modified. (This was performed by means of a file-oriented software editor for digitized speech processing. For further details of the procedure applied, see Standke, 1980). For different experimental groups this modulation was performed in two directions and with two degrees of intensity. Thus, the loudness of the accentuated words, as the first independent variable, was increased for half of the experimental group to such an extent that this change was clearly audible (an assumption tested in a separate pretest). For the other subjects, the volume was increased so that it was just in a subliminally audible range. (In another pretest varying loudness in a step-wise manner, a diminution to one half of the amplitude of the audible condition could be demonstrated as just subliminal.) Independently of this variation, as the second independent variable, the direction of loudness alteration was varied. For half of the subjects the loudness of the words pointing out a positive attitude toward the topic was increased and for those revealing a negative attitude it was decreased. For the other group of subjects this change was realized in the opposite direction. Both variables were varied in a complete design, and for each treatment 12 subjects (half of them female and half male) were tested. The text was also presented to a control group of another 12 subjects without alterations. All subjects were exposed to both texts, and the sequence of the texts was balanced. As investigations on the mechanisms of attitude change in the area of social psychology have shown that willingness to change attitudes is dependent on the relevance of the topics (see Fiske & Taylor, 1984; Petty, Cacioppo, & Goldman, 1981), we also varied the average ego-involvement in the texts. Therefore, all subjects listened to a text with a low and one with a high degree of ego-involvement. According to the results of a pretest eliminating the average degree of ego-involvement of political and social events at this time, a text concerning the political changes on the Philippine Islands after ex-President Marcos had left the country represented the low and a text concerning the consequences to health emerging from the accident in the nuclear plant of Chernobyl represented the high involvement condition. For ease of understanding, the experimental design is summarized in Table 1.

Table 1. Experimental design of the experiment presented (further details in the text)

Range of loudness alteration	Direction of loudness alteration		
	None	Antagonistic to context variables	Supporting context variables
None	6 females, 6 males Topic 1, topic 2		
Subliminal		6 females, 6 males Topic 1, topic 2	6 females, 6 males Topic 1, topic 2
Audible		6 females, 6 males Topic 1, topic 2	6 females, 6 males Topic 1, topic 2

After presentation of the tape-recorded stimulus texts, the attitude toward these topics was ascertained by indirect measurement. In this procedure subjects for each of the texts were asked to rate the likelihood of six statements as headlines of newspaper articles in the near future. Obviously, in this strategy the effect of the experimental variation is measured only as an extra influence added to the verbal content that is induced by the mere exposure to the information in the text. This should be regarded as a conservative effect concerning the influence of vocal parameter change. Finally, in order to examine the effect of the experimental variation, subjects were asked whether they had noticed anything strange in the texts they had heard.

The data available were evaluated mainly by means of analyses of variance (using the BMDP2V program, Dixon, 1985). In the procedure applied, basically the effect of each of the different treatments was estimated by a comparison to the effect elicited by exposure of the text without voice modulation. A detailed description of the findings (as well as a much more sophisticated discussion) may be found in the original report of the data (Appel, 1988).

Results and Discussion

The basic results of this experiment are shown in Table 2. In the table a coefficient for the subjects' opinion concerning the text, and the ratio of subjects who did and who did not realize the experimental variation are indicated for both the experimental and the control group.

An overview reveals that although an increase of modulation generally led to a (nonsignificant) enhancement of opinion change, there is one condition in which the experimental variation of loudness of voice brought about a rather significant effect. This was the case when the modulation of the voice was *very strong* (variable extension of change of loudness), *supporting positive items* of the text presented (variable direction of change of loudness), and when the *ego-*

Table 2. Survey of the effects of voice modulation on changes of opinion

Range of loudness alteration	Direction of loudness alteration					
	None		Antagonistic to context variables		Supporting context variables	
None	51.9	36.6				
	(12 / 0)					
Subliminal			59.5	33.4	58.1	37.7
			(12 / 0)		(12 / 0)	
Audible			54.5	33.3	63.6*	32.8
			(3 / 9)		(11 / 1)	

In the first line of each cell for each of the topics a coefficient determining the average opinion of the subjects is listed (first the low ego-involvement case). The ratio of subjects who did not and who did realize the experimental variation is added in parentheses in the second line (further details in the text).

*, significant effect

involvement of the text was *low*. (The respective F value was 9.251 indicating significance at a level of $P = 0.006$.) As in most studies on persuasion, gender specificities could not be found.

The significance of the central finding can be interpreted in two ways. The constellation of a very severe manipulation coherent with the content of the message, both significant only for a relatively irrelevant topic on the one hand, points out the limitations of the effect of nonverbal cues. On the other hand, one should keep in mind how restricted the situation of communication was. (a) it was only one-directional communication, thus more a mass media than a suggestive situation; (b) there was no visual information available which - as mentioned above - is very often necessary to support the suggestive message underlying vocal cues; (c) only one parameter of voice quality was changed and this for only four words of a 3-min text; (d) the effect of loudness alteration was not measured separately from the effect of the verbal content information. (It should be noted that both aspects cannot be separated completely anyhow. The manipulation of the voice - as in the experimental design presented here - always influences certain words and therefore certain semantic aspects of the text.) With respect to these conservative circumstances, the finding may be interpreted as outstanding proof for the suggestive qualities of vocal cues.

A closer analysis of the conditions of the effect elicited is necessary to integrate both interpretations. Therefore, another interesting finding should be mentioned. Although the modulation of the voice was - as examined in the pretest - clearly audible, in the experimental group with a significant attitude change only one of the 12 listeners realized that there was any artificial change of the speaker's voice during the presentation of the text. In the experimental constellation with the same extent of modulation but in the other semantic direction (which did not bring about a significant attitude change), the modulation was noted by nine of the 12 raters. Although our design cannot unravel the impact of both variables (direction and realization of voice modulation), there is theoretical evidence that it was necessary for the subjects not to realize the manipulation of the voice quality in order to elicit a significant attitude change.

First, this assumption is in line with an interesting side effect of the experiment by Scherer et al. (1972). In this empirical constellation the effect of voice manipulation vanished when the modified text was presented to the auditorium twice. This may also have augmented the effect that the manipulation has become too obvious and has therefore prevented an extension of the suggestive effect. It is also in line with a general model of persuasion proposed by Petty and Cacioppo (1981). The authors maintain the assumption that in addition to logical deliberations (on the so-called central route of information processing) especially less involved people operate automatically with either little conscious thought, or (as McGuire, 1969 has suggested) as "lazy organisms." On this (so-called peripheral) route of information processing the situational characteristics are important. This theoretical framework is suitable to explain why in the low-involvement condition voice quality (as a noncontent component of the message) becomes a decisive component. Furthermore, it accounts for the apparent necessity of not realizing the manipulation. The realization of the manipulation may lead to a switch to the central route of information processing and therefore reduce the importance of vocal parameters in general. It seems legitimate to conclude that this may have been the case for the antagonistic accentuation condition in which the contrast between the accentuation and the verbal content may have led to the switch to the central route and therefore to a diminution of the impact of voice modulation.

(A finding of Miller, Maruyama, Beaber, & Valone, 1976, concerning the impact of speed of speech on persuasion is in striking resemblance with the argumentation presented here.)

Taking these additional points into account, the following hypothesis concerning the mechanism of suggestion by means of vocal parameter change can be maintained. First, the empirical findings provide evidence that already very limited (in amount) modulations bring about a significant effect. Secondly, the effect is only obtained if the range of loudness alteration is distinct. Nonetheless, it should not detract too much attention from the verbal message of the text. Therefore, the direction of loudness alteration in particular should not be antagonistic to the contents of the message. Finally, it should be noted that an effect of slight manipulations - like the ones used in the experiment presented here - cannot necessarily be assumed if the verbal content of the message is of great importance for the respective receiver.

Conclusions

These conclusions - although taken from an experimental constellation with a very limited resemblance to the typical suggestive situation - are in accordance with recommendations made on the basis of practical experience. Voice modulations should be applied economically, but still pointedly, and they should not be obvious. Parenthetically, these recommendations are in line with Gheorghiu's (see Chap. 6, this volume) approach to a phenomenology of suggestions as something underlying cognitive processes. Although at the current state of the art a detailed analysis of the underlying microprocesses can only be speculative, the effect demonstrated may thus be interpreted as an argument for considering these mechanisms as important amplifiers of a transferred message. It is to be expected that further investigations on these mechanisms may not only be fruitful for the understanding of suggestive effects (in the restricted meaning proposed by McGuire's, 1969, classification) but for the suggestion that takes place in every communicational process.

The rather limited extent of cues necessary for this purpose was a central topic of the investigation presented here. However, in order to describe how far their impact can extend, one should keep in mind the differences between the special constellation of an experiment and the suggestive situations considered in applied psychology, as for instance in a therapy under hypnosis. In this context the combined application of cues on different channels usually leads to the desired effect of suggestibility. Therefore, in spite of the methodological problems outlined, for the understanding of these processes it seems necessary to investigate how and to what extent the effect presented here may be magnified by additional changes induced on other parameters of the voice as well as the combined effect of cues on different channels.

With regard to this topic, we finally want to present some theoretical considerations and a few preliminary results that may possibly help us to find a way out of the dilemma of complexity in practical situations and the need for a refinement of parameters in empirical research. They are based on considerations that highlight the phylo- and ontogenetic development of nonverbal cues. As pointed out for instance by Leyhausen (1967), many cues of human nonverbal communication have precursors in primate communication and are of great transcultural stability or have developed as the result of long-term stimulus classification processes in early childhood. From this developmental and functional point of view there is some validity for the assumption that the nonverbal characteristics of suggestive situations are also the same or at least similar to the ones relevant in prototypical situations. Therefore, the kind of situation which is functionally equivalent to a suggestive situation should first be identified. Everyday considerations would make it plausible to focus attention on the processes which make a child feel secure and confident. Then, the constellation of vocal or situational parameters which are relevant for these prototypical situations should be systematized. Furthermore, the question of whether functionally equivalent patterns can be found in suggestive situations should be investigated. The joint consideration of various aspects proposed in such an approach originates from an attempt to do justice to the multi-channel data aggregation in everyday communication.

There is already some evidence for the feasibility of an integrative approach of this sort. According to empirical findings and to theoretical considerations, Scherer has argued that different emotional states may be characterized as a typical outcome constellation of a (phylogenetically pre-established) series of information processing steps (see e.g., Scherer, 1986; Gehm & Scherer, 1988). It is assumed that the structures of phonation and articulation are influenced by each of these steps (see e.g., Gehm & Scherer, 1986). Therefore, emotion-specific changes of vocal parameters can be systematized by investigating regularities of the underlying processes of situation-specific information processing. From this point of view, the determination of typical information-processing steps may also prevail as a plausible framework to determine patterns of vocal or situational parameters that are effective in suggestive situations.

The investigation of these microprocesses, of course, especially when taking into account person-specific patterns of information processing, will have to face a lot of methodological problems. However, the extraordinary impact of even slight nonverbal changes seems to make taking the risk unavoidable.

References

Appel, J. (1988). *Auditive Textwahrnehmung und Einstellung.* [Auditory text perception and attitude]. Unpublished diploma thesis, Justus-Liebig-University, Giessen, FRG.

Barber, T.X., & Calverley, D.S. (1964). Effects of E's tone of voice on "hypnotic-like" suggestibility. *Psychological Reports, 15*, 139-144.

Barber, T.X., Spanos, N.P., & Chaves, J.F. (1974). *Hypnotism, imagination and human potentialities.* New York: Pergamon.

Birdwhistell, R.L. (1970). *Kinesics and context.* Philadelphia.

Brunswik, E. (1956). *Perception and the representative design of psychological experiments.* Berkeley: University of California.

Cicero, M.T. (1976). *De oratore.* Stuttgart: Reclam.

Dixon, W.J. (Ed.). (1985). *BMDP. Statistical software.* Berkeley: University of California.

Duncan, S., & Rosenthal, R. (1968). Vocal emphasis in experimenters' instruction reading as unintended determinant of subjects' responses. *Language and Speech, II*, I, 20-26.

Fiske, S.T., & Taylor, S.E. (1984). *Social cognition.* Reading, MA: Addison-Wesley.

Gehm, T., & Scherer, K.R. (1986, March). *Der Einfluß emotionsantezedenter Faktoren auf Parameter der vokalen Kommunikation*. [The influence of emotion-antecedent factors on parameters of vocal communication]. Paper presented at the 28th meeting of experimentally working psychologists, Saarbrücken, FRG.

Gehm, T., & Scherer, K.R. (1988). Relating situation evaluation to emotion differentiation. In K.R. Scherer (Ed.), *Facets of emotion. Recent research*. Hillsdale, NJ: Lawrence Erlbaum.

Giles, H., Scherer, K.R., & Taylor, P.M. (1979). Speech markers in social interaction. In K.R. Scherer & H. Giles (Eds.), *Social markers in speech*. Cambridge: Cambridge University.

Lazarsfeld, P.F., & Menzel, H. (1964). Massenmedien und personaler Einfluß. [Mass media and social influence]. In W. Schramm (Ed.), *Grundlagen der Kommunikationsforschung*. München: Juventa.

Leyhausen, P. (1967). Biologie von Ausdruck und Eindruck. [Biology of expression and impression]. *Psychologische Forschung, 31*, 113-176.

McGuire, W.J. (1969). The nature of attitudes and attitude change. In E.F. Borgatta & W.W. Lambert (Eds.), *Handbook of personality theory and research*. Chicago: Rand McNally.

Mehrabian, A. (1972). *Nonverbal communication*. Chicago: Aldine-Atherton.

Miller, N., Maruyama, G., Beaber, R., & Valone, K. (1976). Speed of speech and persuasion. *Journal of Personality and Social Psychology, 34*, 615-624.

Orne, M. (1962). On the social psychology of the psychological experiment. *American Psychologist, 17*, 776-783.

Petty, R.E., & Cacioppo, J.T. (1981). *Attitudes and persuasion: Classic and contemporary approaches*. Dubuque, IA: Brown.

Petty, R.E., Cacioppo, J.T., & Goldmann, R. (1981). Personal involvement as a determinant of argument-based persuasion. *Journal of Personality and Social Psychology, 41*, 847-855.

Quintilian, M.F. (1972, 1975). *Institutiones Oratoriae Libri XI*. Darmstadt: Wissenschaftliche Buchgesellschaft.

Rosenthal, R. (1966). *Experimenter effects in behavioral research*. New York: Appleton-Century Crofts.

Scherer, K.R. (1978). Personality inference from voice quality: The loud voice of extraversion. *European Journal of Social Psychology, 8*, 467-487.

Scherer, K.R. (Ed.). (1982). *Vokale Kommunikation: Nonverbale Aspekte des Sprachverhaltens*. [*Vocal communication: Nonverbal aspects of speech*]. Weinheim: Beltz.

Scherer, K.R. (1986). Vocal affect expression. A review and a model for future research. *Psychological Bulletin, 99*, 143-165.

Scherer, K.R., Rosenthal, R., & Koivumaki, J. (1972). Mediating interpersonal expectancies via vocal cues: Differential speech intensity as a means of social influence. *European Journal of Social Psychology, 2*(2), 163-176.

Scherer, K.R., Scherer, U., Hall, J.A., & Rosenthal, R. (1977). Differential attribution of personality based on multichannel presentation of verbal and nonverbal cues. *Psychological Research, 39*, 221-247.

Standke, R. (1980). GISYS. Ein Software-Editor zur fileorientierten digitalen Sprachverarbeitung im Zeitbereich. [A software editor for file related digital speach producing]. In W. Michaelis (Ed.), *Bericht über den 32. Kongreß der Deutschen Gesellschaft für Psychologie in Zürich 1980* (Vol. 1). Göttingen: Hogrefe.

Trager, G.L. (1958). Paralanguage: A first approximation. *Studies in Linguistics, 13*, 1-12.

Weitzenhoffer, A.M. (1985). Hypnotism and altered states of consciousness. In A. Sugarman & R.E. Tarter (Eds.), *Expanding dimensions of consciousness*. New York: Springer.

29. Suggestion, Self-Attribution, and Behavior

J. Haisch

Introduction

Within self-attribution research, it frequently proves difficult to experimentally induce the desired self-attribution. In most research paradigms, subjects are either instructed to self-attribute actions and occurrences, or they are given information to experience systematically a self-causation of *single* actions and occurrences. It is often doubted whether such experimental procedures fulfill the prerequisites for valid self-attributions (Krahé, 1984). Such doubts should be taken seriously for the following reasons:

1. Subjects have their own history of self-causation outside the laboratory setting.
2. The effectiveness of attribution manipulation depends on the subjects' perceptions of the artificiality of the experimental task.
3. Many experimental manipulations of subjective inferences fail to influence subjects.

As a consequence, in such experimental procedures subjects may indicate self-attributions without being aware of the relevant details of the experimental task or of their own behaviors (Stiensmeier, 1986). In such cases, little significance can be given to subjects' self-attributions.

How can we improve our methods of suggesting self-attributions in an experimental setting? A review of the literature on self-attribution (e.g., Lepper, Ross, & Lau, 1986; Liu & Steele, 1986; Webb, Worchel & Brown, 1986; Russel, McAuley, & Tarico, 1987) suggests that we should pay attention to the following points:

1. The extent to which the subjects regard the experimental task as being novel, interesting, and important.
2. That the subject's relevant experiences in the experiment are of sufficient duration.
3. That the relevant data of the experiment are witnessed by other persons.
4. That the experimental task attracts the subject's attention.
5. The importance of the subject's knowledge about self-causation in everyday situations.

If, in an experimental setting, these prerequisites are met, the subject's attributions can be expected to be more accurate than the attributions of an observer. As recent work suggests (Gavanski & Hoffmann, 1987), the accuracy of subjects' self-attributions depends on their access to relevant *covariation information*. On the other hand, suggestions of such covariation information offer the possibility of inducing self-attributions which correspond to experimental manipulations but which, in fact, are inaccurate. This should be the case especially when the above-mentioned experimental prerequisites are adhered to.

Interestingly, whereas access to covariation information implies that persons draw inferences on "rational" grounds, the suggestion of information which is relevant for assessing covariation implies that such persons can be led to make inferences on an "irrational" basis.

Suggestion and Consequences of Self-Attribution

An experiment by Stevens and Jones (1976) exemplifies the explanatory power of attribution theory with regard to the informational prerequisites of suggestions of self-attributions. In this experiment, subjects participating in a recognition test received false feedback which systematically suggested high or low consistency of achievement in the test, high or low distinctiveness, and high or low consensus of these achievements According to Kelley's (1967, 1971, 1973) attribution theory, subjects should self-attribute their performance in the recognition test if they integrate information applying the covariation method and if their performance is of low distinctiveness, low consensus, and high consistency. The basis of suggesting information within this experimental paradigm consists of varying the feedback on consistency, consensus, and distinctiveness. In general, suggestion of self- (or other) attribution should be successful when feedback corresponds to Kelley's attribution theory, and when the five above-mentioned experimental requirements are taken into consideration while constructing the experimental task.

Regarding the consequences of suggested self-attributions, the distinction between short-term and long-term causal chains (see Kelley, 1983) seems appropriate. *Short-term causal chains* refer to sequences of information, attribution, and behavior which are experienced only once by the subject; *long-term causal chains* refer to such sequences which are experienced consistently and repetitively. If a self-attribution is suggested within a short-term causal chain, its influence on the subject's subsequent behavior should be minimal. On the other hand, if a self-attribution is suggested within a long-term causal chain, subjects infer to "ability" or "lack of ability". If "ability" is inferred, ability-related behaviors will be repeated in the future (e.g., achievement rates will continue to be high); if "lack of ability" is inferred, behavior related to this lacking ability will be suppressed (e.g., high achievement rates will diminish).

According to the five desiderata mentioned at the outset, in the experiments to be described self-attributions were suggested by applying the following general measures:

1. The experiments were presented as being in the field of recognition memory; the student subjects were promised a detailed report on their individual recognition memory at the end of the experiment.
2. The realization and the consequences of self-attribution suggestions were tested within short-term as well as long-term causal chains.
3. Suggestions of self-attributions were made in the presence of other subjects.
4. Subjects' attention was directed toward the experimental task.
5. Within the experiments on long-term causal chains, it was hoped that subjects' prior knowledge of self-causation would be counterbalanced.

Experimental Studies

The experiments consisted of a recognition test with a number of subtests. The experimental stimulus was a square or round grid with 12 fields, each of which contained three or four randomly distributed black dots; in pretests, the stimuli were recognized correctly 51 % of the trials.

The experiment on short-term causal chains consisted of three experimental sessions and six recognition subtests; the experiment on long-term causal chains consisted of six experimental sessions and 12 recognition subtests. In other words, in each experimental session, subjects worked on two recognition subtests. In the experiment on short-term causal chains, two subjects participated in the two initial experiments and one subject was tested in the third session; in the experiment on long-term causal chains, subjects were tested in pairs in the experimental sessions

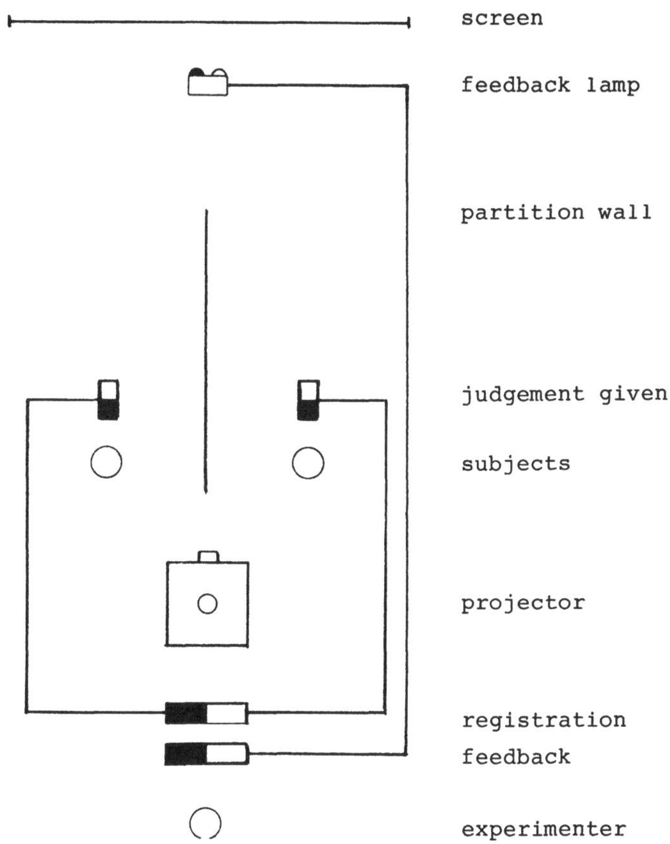

Figure 1. The experimental situation created to test the behavioral consequences of short-term as well as long-term causal chains

two to five. In other words, whereas experimental manipulations were essentially administered to dyads, single subjects were examined in the final test phase. Figure 1 shows details of the experimental situation.

The most important aspect of the experimental situation is that subjects cannot perceive the judgments of their experimental partners, but they can perceive the judgment feedback received by themselves and their partners. An additional important factor is that the difficulty of recognizing the experimental stimuli used in each subtest was such (just slightly above the chance recognition performance of the pretests) that the experimenter's feedback - which followed a prearranged plan - appeared credible to the subjects. The following procedure was carried out to lend additional credibility to the experiment: Each recognition subtest contained three stimuli which had proved easy to recognize in the pretest. The subjects' judgments of these stimuli received the feedback "correct recognition."

In the recognition phase, the feedback to the subject's judgment was also visible to the test partner (to avoid series effects the subjects' judgments were systematically alternated). Within the prescribed plan of judgment feedback for each subject, feedback information was presented so as to fulfill the criteria of attribution theory for self-attribution (low consensus, low distinctiveness, high consistency, good/poor performance by the relevant subjects with all experimental stimuli and in all experimental sessions). As is indicated by Table 1, low consensus is established within a recognition subtest (21 stimuli within each recognition phase) by giving one subject a high achievement feedback (17 hits) and the other one a low achievement feedback (10 hits); low distinctiveness information is established by giving identical (high or low) achievement feedback across various experimental stimuli; high consistency is finally suggested to the subjects by giving identical (high or low) achievement feedback across experimental sessions.

Two recognition subtests were solved by each subject within an experimental session. The time lapse between the two experimental sessions ranged from 1 day to 1 week. In the manipulation phases, subjects received feedback in the manner just described; in the final testing phases they did not receive any feedback.

Table 1. Suggestion of self-attribution within short-term and long-term causal chains

Self-attribution	Feedback during the experimental sessions
Short-term causal chains (experiment 1)	Independently of experimental sessions 1 and 2 Independently of experimental stimuli Subject 1 is more efficient than subject 2
Long-term causal chains (experiment 2)	Independently of experimental sessions 1, 2, 3, 4, 5, and 6 Independently of experimental stimuli Subject 1 is more efficient than subject 2 High achievement is typical only for subject 1

Table 1 summarizes the suggestion of self-attributions within short-term and long-term causal chains, that is, within two complex experiments, both of which were carried out with 64 student subjects. The table shows the information received by the "success" and "failure" subjects as a result of the feedback to the judgments in the recognition subtests. The information was constructed to correspond to the informational requirements of self-attributions (Kelley, 1973).

With regard to the behavioral consequences of suggested self-attributions, the final experimental sessions are devoted to testing achievement effects within recognition tasks. However, the first result reported is a check of the suggestion of self-attribution manipulation within one experiment. A post experimental questionnaire shoed that self-attributions were suggested to all subjects. All of the subjects working under the experimental condition of "self-caused successes" inferred having caused their successes themselves, whereas all of the subjects working under the experimental condition of "self-caused failure" inferred having caused their failures in the experimental tasks themselves. Moreover, all "successful" subjects inferred having good recognition abilities, and all of the "failure" subjects inferred having bad abilities. If the massive failure experiences of some subjects are considered, it could be expected that these subjects would terminate the experiment. In fact, none of th subjects - neither the "successful" nor the "non-successful" - terminated the experiment in either of the test conditions (short-term or long-term causal chains).

Table 2 documents an improvement in achievement after a self-caused failure. The analysis of variance of the short-term causal chains shows a significant effect of the performance increase after failure ($F = 4.12$; $df = 1.56$; $P < 0.05$). The analysis of variance of long-term causal chains also shows a significant effect of the performance improvement caused by failure ($F = 4.72$; $df = 1.42$; $P < 0.05$). Interestingly, the performance increase after both short-term and long-term failure occurs in the ensuing test phase, that is, after feedback manipulations have been terminated and the tasks are undertaken by the subject in the absence of a partner. From a theoretical point of view, the increase in performance in the test phase is surprising - especially after long-term failure, that is, after six sessions and various recognition subtests in which failure is experienced in direct contrast to the "successes" of the subjects' partners. This finding cannot be explained by Weiner's (1986) general theory of achievement, as Weiner generally

Table 2. Average achievement rates (minimum 0, maximum 21) in the testing phase and average change of performance based on the performance in the manipulation and the testing phase

Self-attribution	Success	Failure
Experiment 1: short-term causal chains		
Achievements	13.0	14.3
Achievement changes	+ 1.12	+ 3.87
Experiment 2: long-term causal chains		
Achievements	11.1	14.5
Achievement changes	- 0.44	+ 2.09

hypothesizes subjects' hopelessness as well as decreasing achievement rates if failure is attributed to any stable cause as, for example, one's own lack of ability.

To further analyze the unexpected results, another experiment was conducted consisting of six experimental sessions and 12 experimental tasks. In contrast to the experiments just described, the student subjects (n = 64) in this experiment received feedback for all recognition tasks; that is, subjects also received feedback for the final recognition tests in which achievement effects were assessed. Subjects were assigned at random to one of the four experimental feedback conditions. Table 3 summarizes the corresponding achievement effects. Interestingly, continued failures after long-term self-caused failures resulted in the highest average rates of correct recognitions, whereas success after long-term self-caused success resulted in the lowest average rates of correct recognitions.

Table 3. Average achievement rates (minimum 0, maximum 21) after consistent and inconsistent feedback (experiment 3)

Manipulation phase (tasks 1-9)	Testing phase (tasks 10-11)	
	Success	Failure
Success	9.6	11.0
Failure	11.6	14.0

Discussion

How can these results be explained? First of all, the data clearly show that a *suggestion of self-attribution* can be accomplished within the experimental paradigm described above. All subjects' self-attributions corresponded to the experimental manipulations, that is, possible previous experiences concerning self-causation were successfully neutralized. An examination of the *sequences* of correct recognitions across *all* experimental tasks (see Table 4) leads me to propose the following explanation of the behavioral consequences of these suggestions (Haisch, 1987): after experiencing the consequences of his or her actions in a new task, the actor will critically test whether these consequences covary with time or other modalities. In other words, the actor tests whether his or her actions lead to the same or different consequences when applied to different tasks or to different situations. In cases of undesirable action effects, the person will make an effort when testing the covariation; the actor increases his or her effort in order to apply the covariation test under subjectively optimal conditions. If the covariation test does *not* result in a covariation of action consequences over time or modalities (i.e., if the self-attributions of the consequences of one's actions remain unchallenged), no further covariation test is carried out and no further increase in effort will be applied. However, as soon as a change in the conditions for taking action appears, the actor repeats the covariation test and examines the consistency of failure. This implies that a considerable period of time elapses before the actor gives up the idea of possessing at least some "ability" to solve the tasks successfully. He or she assumes that he or she just does not know the exact conditions under which his or her ability can be optimally applied.

In short, in this attributional explanation of achievement strivings, it is assumed that self-attributions, once accomplished, are tested repeatedly to examine the recurrence of the attribution to the self. By repeating covariation tests and examining the recurrence of self-attributions, the actor subjectively holds a "*true*" as well as an *immediate* view of his or her own person with respect to subjectively important tasks and situations. This attributional explanation of achievement strivings is at variance with Weiner's attributional theory of achievement and emotion (1986), as he would expect a decrease in performance as a consequence of the attribution of failure to a stable cause.

Table 4 summarizes rates of correct recognitions over four experimental sessions with identically constructed recognition tasks. No systematic and clearly superior achievements are found within the conditions of this table. This table clearly demonstrates that achievement differences reported in Table 3 do not emerge only after a change in construction of the recognition tasks; this change, which permits the application of a new covariation test, occurs after withdrawal of the subjects' partners in the recognition tests.

Table 4. Average achievement rates (minimum 0, maximum 21) during manipulation phase (experiment 3)[a]

	Session 1		Session 2		Session 3		Session 4	
	Task 2	Task 3	Task 4	Task 5	Task 6	Task 7	Task 8	Task 9
Success	9.3	11.6	9.7	10.6	11.4	11.4	10.3	10.3
Failure	11.0	10.9	10.9	11.0	10.9	10.1	10.3	10.9

[a] Results of the first experimental session are not reported, as in this session subjects received only the global feedback "extraordinarily good/bad recognizer" at the end of the experimental task.

The reader may be of the opinion that I am overstating my case and may add that there was a lack of experimental controls. However, the following controls were included in the experiments:

1. The suggestion of *external* attributions, so that the suggestion of self-attributions can be compared with suggestions of attributions to causes outside the subject.
2. The *observer's* attributions, so that self-attributions which can be expected to underly various subjectively motivated deformations (e.g., Stevens & Jones, 1976) can be compared with attributions of (neutral) evaluators of the information given.

In accordance with the informational requirements of attribution theory, subjects were suggested to attribute their behavioral consequences to the *stimuli* of the experimental tasks, to other *subjects*, or to *time and modalities*. Interestingly, manipulation of these suggestions was not as successful as the suggestion of self-attributions. Only 63 % to 75 % of the subjects attributed their behaviors according to the experimental manipulations. As to the *consequences* of these attributions, the results show that achievement rates differ to a much *lesser* degree than in the case of self-attributions.

The actors' experiences with the recognition tasks were also attributed by observers. About 70 % of the observers correctly attributed the self-caused successes in accordance with the experimental manipulations; self-attributions of failures were correctly attributed by observers in about 91 % of the cases. Observers of long-term causal chains correctly attributed actors' behaviors in 50 %-69 % of the cases (in interpreting these results it should be kept in mind that 25 % of correct attributions would be expected by chance). The results show that *self*-attributions as well as *external* attributions by actors and observers may be suggested by manipulating feedback as described in these experiments.

What then is the implication of these results? If a person solves a task and thereby processes distinctiveness, consistency, and consensus information, a self-concept of high or low ability (Meyer, 1984) - concerning this and similar tasks - may be suggested to this person. This suggested self-concept need not correspond to reality in any way. In the experiments reported here, those subjects who had a self-concept of low ability were in fact highly successful, whereas those subjects who had a self-concept of high ability were unsuccessful (Table 3).

At present, the suggestion of self-caused failures seems to correlate with a self-concept of low abilities and with the possibility of subsequent improvements of achievement. The application of this finding to the field of education promises to be fruitful (Kennedy & Willcutt, 1964; Hasselhorn, 1987), and some further experiments will be conducted within this applied setting.

Acknowledgements. The research reported in this chapter was supported by grants Ha 1159/2-1 and Ha 1159/2-2 of the *Deutsche Forschungsgemeinschaft*. Thanks are due William Gilmour and Klaus Fiedler for their invaluable comments on an earlier version of this chapter.

References

Gavanski, I., & Hoffman, C. (1987). Awareness of influences on one's own judgments: The roles of covariation detection and attention to the judgment process. *Journal of Personality and Social Psychology*, *52*, 453-463.

Haisch, J. (1987). *Selbstattribution und Verhalten*. Weinheim: Deutscher Studien Verlag.

Hasselhorn, M. (1987). Lern- und Gedächtnisförderung bei Kindern. Ein systematischer Überblick über die experimentelle Trainingsforschung. *Zeitschrift für Entwicklungspsychologie und Pädagogische Psychologie, 19*, 116-142.

Kelley, H.H. (1967). Attribution theory in social psychology. In D. Levine (Ed.), *Nebraska symposium on motivation* (Vol. 15, pp. 192-238). Lincoln: University of Nebraska.

Kelley, H.H. (1971). *Attribution in social interaction*. Morristown, N.J.: General Learning.

Kelley, H.H. (1973). The process of causal attributions. *American Psychologist, 28,* 107-128.

Kelley, H.H. (1983). Perceived causal structures. In J. Jaspars, F.D. Fincham, & M. Hewstone (Eds.), *Attribution theory and research: Conceptual, developmental and social dimensions* (pp. 343-369). London: Academic.

Kennedy, W.A., & Willcutt, H.C. (1964). Praise and blame as incentives. *Psychological Bulletin, 62,* 323-332.

Krahé, B. (1984). Der "self-serving bias" in der Attributionsforschung: Theoretische Grundlagen und empirische Befunde. *Psychologische Rundschau, 35,* 79-97.

Lepper, M.R., Ross, L., & Lau, R.R. (1986). Persistence of inaccurate beliefs about the self: Perseverance effects in the classroom. *Journal of Personality and Social Psychology, 50,* 482-491.

Liu, T.J., & Steele, C.M. (1986). Attribution analysis of self-affirmation. *Journal of Personality and Social Psychology, 51,* 531-540.

Meyer, W.U. (1984). *Das Konzept von der eigenen Begabung.* Bern: Huber.

Russell, D.W., Mc Auley, E., & Tarico, V. (1987). Measuring causal attributions for success and failure: A comparison of methodologies for assessing causal dimensions. *Journal of Personality and Social Psychology, 52,* 1248-1257.

Stevens, L., & Jones, E. (1976). Defensive attribution and the Kelley Cube. *Journal of Personality and Social Psychology, 34,* 809-820.

Stiensmeier, J. (1986). Wichtigkeit und Kontrollerleben als Bedingungen von Lageorientierung. *Archiv für Psychologie, 138,* 127-138.

Webb, W.M., Worchel, S., & Brown, E.H. (1986). The influence of control on self-attributions. *Social Psychology Quarterly, 49,* 260-267.

Weiner, B. (1986). *An attributional theory of motivation and emotion.* New York Berlin Heidelberg: Springer.

30. The Manifold Facets of Social Influence: A Comment on the Social Psychological Contributions

K. Fiedler

Note. The present text largely follows an improvised comment that was given spontaneously and without prior knowledge of the papers presented at the Rauischholzhausen conference. This may have influenced the style and referentiality of the text. Although it might have been possible to write a new comment based on the written contributions to this book, it was decided to retain the original ideas generated in the conference.

No doubt, the social psychological contributions included in this section testify to the creativity and originality of methods utilized in the study of suggestion and suggestibility. A variety of experimental tools - from conditioning to hypnosis - have served in the investigation of such diverse phenomena as memory distortions (Loftus and Banaji; Sheehan), belief perseverance (Bierhoff and Klein), self-attribution (Haisch), communication (Gehm, Appel, and Apsel), lie detection (Fiedler), and aspiration level in achievement situations (Lachnit). This empirical research has been accompanied by valuable expositions of the cultural and historical background (Jahoda) and the adaptive context (Schwanenberg) of suggestive influence, and the outlines of an intriguing and heuristically useful theory of the mediation of such influences have been formulated (McGuire).

In spite of this diversity in method and contents, the ten chapters are related to each other at the conceptual level. They share as a common denominator the reference to a general topic, namely, the plasticity of stimulus-response connections. To the extent that reactions to stimuli are not strictly determined but leave some adaptive range for mediational processes, suggestive influences come into play as an ever present complementary force that modifies or shapes the impact of external stimuli.

From this perspective, it is no surprise that all empirically oriented chapters are somehow concerned with *moderator* variables. Again, it is the diversity of moderator variables that has to be emphasized. The moderators considered by McGuire are the characteristics of tasks and attributes of personality which may influence the "locus" of suggestibility. For instance, intelligent people seem to be more susceptible to the quality of arguments during the stage of message comprehension, while less intelligent people are more likely to *yield* to social influences (see Schwanenberg) regardless of the quality of arguments. Thus, *personality characteristics* such as intelligence may determine the stage or influence situation in which people are most vulnerable. Alternatively, Sheehan, in his discussion of the effects of misinformation on memory, stresses the *point in time* at which misinformation is provided as well as the subjects' *awareness* of being misinformed as important moderators. And Loftus and Banaji are concerned with the *medium* of information transmission as a moderator of suggestive memory distortions.

Bierhoff and Klein identify the perseverance of belief or the strength of *initial expectations* as a factor that may, or may not, prevent highly susceptible people from being influenced. In a similar vein, Fiedler is concerned with *stereotype expectations* as moderating variables in the cognitive process of lie detection. And Gehm, Appel, and Apsel have drawn our attention to *intonation* and *vocal parameters*.

The contributions by Lachnit and Haisch differ from the others in that they do not examine suggestive influences on some cognitive representation (memory, beliefs) but rely on measures of performance as the dependent variables. Both authors share an emphasis on the *level of comparison*, induced by suggestive techniques as a moderator of subsequent performance.

The diversity and originality of methods proposed to investigate these variables and to bring about suggestive influences are no less impressive. They range from conditioning (Lachnit) to misinformation (Sheehan), acoustic manipulations (Gehm, Appel, and Apsel), and the use of leading questions (Loftus and Banaji). Space does not allow the discussion of the virtues and heuristic potential of all these experimental techniques.

Figure 1 may help to elucidate some essential differences between these various approaches, on the one hand, as well as their relatedness, on the other hand. This diagram stresses the *temporal-pragmatic* conditions of suggestive influences as a central organizer. While all the papers were, as already noted, somehow concerned with moderators, an important theoretical difference stems from the timing of three relevant constituents: (1) the presentation of stimulus information, (2) the suggestion, and (3) some subsequent test or response measure.

The three paradigms reviewed by Sheehan, "post-event, subtle suggestion," "pseudomemory," and "leading questions" all refer to misleading information induced after the initial stimulus encoding but prior to a final recall test, either during the period of retention (Figure 1a) or immediately at the time of retrieval as part of a recall test (Figure 1b). Loftus' work apparently falls in the same category. The manipulation of vocal emphasis by Gehm et al. is simultaneous with the presentation or reception of stimuli (Figure 1c). The induction of a level of aspiration in the studies of Lachnit and Haisch is accomplished in a preceding phase which is prior to both stimulus and response or test (Figure 1d). Likewise, the prior expectations examined by Bierhoff and Klein can be classified as belonging to the latter class. Such a temporal-pragmatic framework may not only help to account for reported differences in the effectiveness of suggestive influences (cf., for instance, Sheehan, McGuire) but may also be useful in understanding some of the more radical deviations or paradoxical results to be discussed below.

Here I come to the ironical point that I want to emphasize in my comment. In spite of the multitude of suggestive phenomena resulting from the combination of methods, time pragmatics, and materials, the emerging picture is still too restricted in one important respect. In all empirical studies and theoretical accounts, it is tacitly presupposed that suggestions will have a congruent effect in the intended direction, or, in other words, an "assimilation" effect (Upshaw, 1968). Even McGuire seems to exclude from consideration the possibility that suggestions may cause a "boomerang" or "contrast" effect. It almost went unnoticed that instances of such seemingly paradoxical findings were actually reported here, hardly acknowledged as a challenge to general theories of suggestive influence. Thus, the induction of a failure experience was shown by Lachnit as well as Haisch to *increase*, rather than decrease, success on a subsequent performance task. Similarly, the results of Bierhoff and Klein imply that susceptibility to contradictory information may serve to increase, rather than decrease, initially held beliefs. Could it be a coincidence that each of these three cases belongs to the same temporal-pragmatic

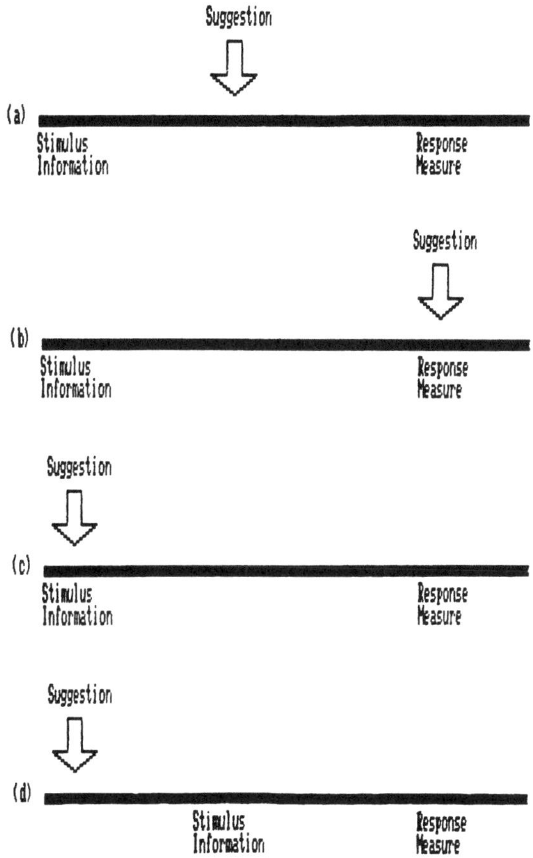

Figure 1. Temporal-pragmatic conditions of social influence

condition, namely, to the condition in which an anchor or comparison level is induced prior to taking in the relevant information (Figure 1d)?

A glance at the psychological literature and the phenomenal world reveals that the allegedly paradoxical results may reflect a more general rule of when to expect assimilation (i.e., congruent influence effects) and when to expect contrast (i.e., incongruent effects). Strack, Schwarz, and Gschneidinger (1985), in an ingenious study of mood influences on judgments of well-being, noted that a present mood state will usually create assimilation (i.e., positive mood will increase subjective well-being), whereas references to past mood states may elicit a contrast effect (i.e., compared with a past positive mood, present well-being is judged to be inferior). Apparently, the influence of a mood state depends on whether it blends with current events (to produce assimilation) or is dissociated from current stimuli as an anchor or as a normative standard (producing contrast). Consistent with this interpretation, Martin (1986) as well as Herr, Sherman, and Fazio (1983) provide evidence that assimilation is more likely to occur when using moderate anchors, whereas too extreme anchors that are dissociated and classified in a different category will often produce contrast effects. This is, after all, consistent with the early perspective of Sherif and Hovland (1961) on assimilation and contrast.

In which direction will people bias their judgments of someone they love? Will they judge the loved one more leniently (assimilation) or more critically (contrast) than do other people? Certainly, common sense shows evidence for both opposite tendencies. Again, the present analysis would suggest that the outcome depends on whether love blends with the perception of the loved person's behavior or functions as a presumptive standard with which the loved one's behavior is compared. In other words, it depends on whether love is a current state or an ideal.

The very fact that tasks of the type represented in Figure 1d yielded contrast or incongruent suggestion effects may reflect the same principle. Strong expectations induced before a focal experimental task begins may be dissociated as an external anchor or a normative standard rather than being associated or blended with the stimulus information.

This is, of course, but one post hoc account of some unexpected reversals in suggestion experiments that seem to lie beyond the scope of theoretical conceptions of suggestibility. However, regardless of whether the importance of the temporal conditions highlighted in Figure 1 receives support by future research, the inclusion and clarification of the assimilation-contrast issue seem to provide a promising aim of research on suggestibility.

To me, this remains an open-ended question arising from this original and varied section of social psychological contributions. Focussing theoretical attention on those reversal phenomena, rather than treating them merely as noteworthy exceptions, may not only be a fruitful empirical endeavor but should also lead to theoretical progress. The answer to the open-ended question, in my view, would require the rediscovery of an additional concept in suggestion research: the respondent's *frame of reference* (cf. Uznadze, 1939). Does the suggestive manipulation influence the subject's standard of reference (leading to contrast) or his/her own position relative to such a standard (leading to assimilation)? In my opinion, this distinction seems to be at the core of any comprehensive theory of suggestion.

References

Herr, P.M., Sherman, S.J., & Fazio, R.H. (1983). On the consequences of priming: Assimilation and contrast effects. *Journal of Experimental Social Psychology, 19*, 323-340.

Martin, L.L. (1986). Set/reset: Use and disuse of concepts in impression formation. *Journal of Personality and Social Psychology, 51*, 493-504.

Sherif, M., & Hovland, C.I. (1961). *Social judgment: Assimilation and contrast effects in communication and attitude change*. New Haven: Yale University.

Strack, F., Schwarz, N., & Gschneidinger, E. (1985). Happiness and reminiscing: The role of time perspective, mood, and mode of thinking. *Journal of Personality and Social Psychology, 49*, 1460-1469.

Upshaw, H.S. (1968). Cognitive consistency in the psychology of judgment. In R.P. Abelson, E. Aronson, W.J. McGuire, T.M. Newcomb, M.J. Rosenberg, & P.H. Tannenbaum (Eds.), *Theories of cognitive consistency: A sourcebook*. Chicago: Rand McNally.

Uznadze, D.N. (1939). Untersuchungen zur Psychologie der Einstellung. *Acta Psychologica, 4*, 323-360.

Subject Index

Altered state of
  consciousness 85, 221, 232, 257, 260
Anticipation 349
Arousal 227 f., 231, 325 f.
Assimilation 372
Attention 157, 164 f., 185 f.
Attitude 289
  change 263 f., 270, 273, 318, 344 f., 354-356
Attribution 41, 361 f., 366-368
Autokinetic phenomenon 19, 27
Autosuggestion 70
Belief 81 f., 87, 116, 118, 256, 260, 271
  perseverance 337-340
Communication, analyses 105
  credibility 326, 330, 332-334
  everyday 357
  lens model of 330 f., 352
  lie detection 82 f.
  nonverbal 266, 325 f., 329 f., 353, 357
  verbal and nonverbal
    cues 352
  voice modulation 356 f.
Conditioning 60, 101, 347
Constructivism 40
  autopoiesis 93
  radical 94
  reality criteria 94-96
  reality testing 95
  self-referentiality 93
Control systems 36, 104, 156, 338 f.
Coping 38, 40 f., 108, 139, 142, 310-312, 317
Deception 23, 27, 323 f.
EEG, alpha, beta, and
  theta 196 f.
  cortical event-related
    potential 183 f.
  40 Hz 206-217, 228 f.
  hemisphere shift 158
  hemispheric laterality
    ratio 164, 198
  left and right hemisphere 159, 160 f., 191 f., 196 f., 211, 214 f.
  method 161, 193 f.
  P_{100}, P_{200}, and P_{300} 183-186
EMG 208, 212 f., 217, 229 f.
Emotion 84, 158
Expectation 8
Experimenter effect 353
Feedback 139, 362-366
Field theory 263, 272
  valence 100, 102, 272 f.
Frame of reference 37, 339, 344 f., 372
Goal directed behavior 40
Hypnosis, amnesia 7 f., 75 f.
  analgesia 151 f.
  animal magnetism 72
  attitude 169, 172
  ceiling effect 10
  cortical inhibition 16, 75 f.
  EEG correlates 221
  goal directed 9, 173
  hallucination 183 f.
  hemispheric specifity 155
  history 69, 87 f.
  hypersuggestibility 75 f.
  hypnotic induction 95
  inner processes 8
  involvement 9
  left and right hemisphere 247
  memory error 295
  rapport 172
  simulator 174
  spontaneous manifestations 6
  transition to normal state 7 f.
Hypnosis and suggestion,
  connections 10, 148
  epistemology 91
  history 3, 255
  hypnosis without suggestion 6
  methodological problems 9
  relationship 4 f.
Hypnotic susceptibility,
  anxiety 311
  cognitive flexibility 155, 179, 205, 229, 247
  compliance 173 f.
  EEG alpha and beta
    activity 223 f.
  EEG correlates 223
  Harvard Group Scale 158, 184, 192, 207, 223
  hemisphere activity 216
    asymmetry 227
    dominance 198 f.
    equilibrium between
      hemispheres 241
    specifity 231
  low and high 157, 160-164, 170 f., 184, 186 f., 191, 194 f., 207, 224-227, 299-301
  mediating processes 306
  moderator variables 172
  net compliance 307-309
  ocular dominance 244, 246
  personality variables 233-235
  physiological flexibility 155, 159, 179
  Stanford Scale 148, 158, 192, 223
  training 171 f.
  trait 155
Identification 36
Imagination 17 f., 69
  ideomotor processes 17, 24, 28, 65 f.
  mental imagery rotation 209
  vividness 17, 156, 171, 173, 206
Information processing,
  covariation information 361
  mediating mechanisms 264 f.
  post event information 282, 285-287
  strategy 157, 199, 202, 217
  unconscious 40
Involvement 4, 26, 158
Memory 28, 279
  constructive 324
  discrepancy detection 282
  distortion 280, 297, 300
  episodic 280
  flashbulb 289 f.
  malleability 280-283
  media effects 285-292
  misinformation 286-288, 296 f.
  pseudomemory 298, 301
  reality monitoring 96, 116, 291
  recognition 362
  semantic 291

short-term and long-term 205, 362-366
tests 295
witness 286
Neodissociation theory 36
Perception 27
binocular rivalry 242 f.
and imagination 95
modalities 124
multistable 92
subliminal stimulation 88
Personal constructs, construct changes 80
dichotomous nature 82
internal confirmation 79, 81, 83, 86
repertory test 79
Personality, features 13, 26
tests 14
Persuasion 83, 101, 318 f.
Phenomenal world 268
Placebo 32, 57, 128, 150 f., 178
Possession trance 257
Propaganda 273
rCBF (regional cerebral blood flow) 159, 223
Reaction time 195, 348
Relaxation 73-75, 119
REM (rapid eye moving) 149
Risk taking 337
Ritual 256, 259
Role playing 85
Self-fulfilling prophecy 34
Self-organization 92 f.
Suggestibility, age 15, 125, 316 f.
anxiety 140 f., 317
attitude and aptitude 59 f., 232
body sway 58 f., 61 f., 150, 309 f.
conditioning 16
drug effects 60, 130-132, 178
extravert and introvert 62, 65
factors 13, 18
heat illusion test 17
high, medium, and low 16, 60, 130, 342-344
history 29
intelligence 14, 85, 125, 306, 316
interrogative 14 f., 135, 140, 178
leading question 136
locus of control 16
mediator variables 371
mental health 13 f.
motor 148
multi-dimensionality 12
neuroticism 14, 61 f.
normal and abnormal 71
persistence 59
prestige 147
primary, secondary, and tertiary VI, 21, 25, 32, 58, 70, 72 f., 113, 145-147, 232, 339, 342
right and left hemisphere 315
satiation 16
self-esteem 85, 312 f.
sensory 23, 123, 177
sensory suggestibility scale 17, 124
sex 125, 314 f.
tests 10, 18, 20, 25, 29, 72 f., 146, 150, 339, 342
trait 57, 61 f., 84, 115, 125, 232, 260, 305
uncertainty 138 f.
voice qualities 351 f.
witness 136
Suggestion, allergic reactions 57
as if 42, 103
association 34
basic concepts 33
classification 105
conceptual features 103, 114
conditioning 35
content, form, and mode 21-23, 106-109
cues 30, 107
definition 33, 99 f., 105, 255
direct and indirect 7, 11, 20-22, 70, 72, 124, 350
doctrine of suggestion 3 f.
expectation 138 f.
functional connection to cortex 249
history V, 29, 99
intentionality 271 f.
involvement 108
leading question 284, 299
model 107
moderating variables 34
monoideism 33 f.
motor behavior 24
physiological effects 259
placebo effect 13
prestige 70, 104
rationality and irrationality 33, 102 f., 265
sleep 149
substitution 42
theories 30 f.
therapy 39, 357
uncertainty 19
verbal and nonverbal 22, 35, 38
witness 284
TOTE schema 267
Witchcraft 258

MIX
Papier aus verantwortungsvollen Quellen
Paper from responsible sources
FSC® C105338

If you have any concerns about our products,
you can contact us on
ProductSafety@springernature.com

In case Publisher is established outside the EU,
the EU authorized representative is:
Springer Nature Customer Service Center GmbH
Europaplatz 3, 69115 Heidelberg, Germany

Printed by Libri Plureos GmbH
in Hamburg, Germany